Foundations of
Financial Management

SEVENTEENTH EDITION

Stanley B. Block
Texas Christian University

Geoffrey A. Hirt
DePaul University

Bartley R. Danielsen
North Carolina State University

FOUNDATIONS OF FINANCIAL MANAGEMENT, SEVENTEENTH EDITION

Published by McGraw-Hill Education, 2 Penn Plaza, New York, NY 10121. Copyright © 2019 by McGraw-Hill Education. All rights reserved. Printed in the United States of America. Previous editions © 2017, 2014, and 2011. No part of this publication may be reproduced or distributed in any form or by any means, or stored in a database or retrieval system, without the prior written consent of McGraw-Hill Education, including, but not limited to, in any network or other electronic storage or transmission, or broadcast for distance learning.

Some ancillaries, including electronic and print components, may not be available to customers outside the United States.

This book is printed on acid-free paper.

4 5 6 7 8 9 BKM 21 20 19 18

ISBN 978-1-260-01391-7
MHID 1-260-01391-X

Portfolio Manager: *Charles Synovec*
Product Developers: *Allison McCabe*
Marketing Manager: *Trina Maurer*
Content Project Managers: *Fran Simon/Angela Norris*
Buyer: *Sandy Ludovissy*
Design: *Jessica Cuevas*
Content Licensing Specialists: *Melissa Homer*
Cover Image: *©fototrav/Getty Images*
Compositor: *SPi Global*

All credits appearing on page or at the end of the book are considered to be an extension of the copyright page.

Library of Congress Cataloging-in-Publication Data
Names: Block, Stanley B., author. | Hirt, Geoffrey A., author. | Danielsen,
    Bartley R., author.
Title: Foundations of financial management / Stanley B. Block, Texas
    Christian University, Geoffrey A. Hirt, DePaul University, Bartley R.
    Danielsen, North Carolina State University.
Description: Seventeenth Edition. | Dubuque : McGraw-Hill Education, [2018] |
    Revised edition of the authors' Foundations of financial management, [2017]
Identifiers: LCCN 2018023101 | ISBN 9781260013917 (alk. paper)
Subjects: LCSH: Corporations—Finance.
Classification: LCC HG4026 .B589 2018 | DDC 658.15—dc23 LC record available at
https://lccn.loc.gov/2018023101

The Internet addresses listed in the text were accurate at the time of publication. The inclusion of a website does not indicate an endorsement by the authors or McGraw-Hill Education, and McGraw-Hill Education does not guarantee the accuracy of the information presented at these sites.

mheducation.com/highered

About the Authors

Stanley B. Block
Texas Christian University

Geoffrey A. Hirt
DePaul University

Bartley R. Danielsen
North Carolina State University

Preface

Forty-two years have passed since we began writing the first edition of this text, and many things have changed during that time including the author team.

First of all, the field of finance has become much more analytical, with the emphasis on decision-oriented approaches to problems rather than the old, descriptive approach. We have increased the use of analytical approaches to financial problems in virtually every chapter of the book. But we also have stayed with our basic mission of making sure students are able to follow us in our discussions throughout the text. While the 17th edition is considerably more sophisticated than the initial edition, it is still extremely "reader friendly." As the analytical skills demanded of students have increased, so has the authors' care in presenting the material.

Using computers and calculators has become considerably more important over the last quarter century, and this is also reflected in the 17th edition where we have added Excel tables and calculator keystroke solutions within key chapters. We offer Web Exercises at the end of every chapter, URL citations throughout the text, a library of course materials for students and faculty, computerized testing software and PowerPoint® for the faculty, *Connect*, an online assignment and assessment solution, and LearnSmart with SmartBook, a truly innovative adaptive study tool and eBook.

Throughout the past 42 years, this text has been a leader in bringing the real world into the classroom, and this has never been more apparent than in the 17th edition. Each chapter opens with a real-world vignette, and the Finance in Action boxes (found in virtually every chapter) describe real-world activities and decisions made by actual businesses. We are also up-to-date on the latest tax and financial reporting legislation including the 2017 Tax Cuts and Jobs Act.

The international world of finance has become much more important and the text has expanded its international coverage tenfold since the first edition. Where there is an international application for a financial issue, you are very likely to find it in this text.

Furthermore, the 17th edition continues to give modest coverage to the recession and liquidity crisis that has engulfed the U.S. and world economies in the latter part of the 2000–2009 decade (and into the current decade). Special attention is given to the banking sector and the critical need for funding that almost all businesses face. The issue of changing regulations is also covered.

However, there is one thing that has not changed over the last 42 years— we still write the entire book and all of the problems ourselves! We believe our devotion of time, energy, and commitment over these years is the reason for our reputation for having produced a high-quality and successful text—edition after edition.

Employers of business graduates report that the most successful analysts, planners, and executives are both effective and confident in their financial skills. We concur. One of the best ways to increase your facility in finance is to integrate your knowledge from prerequisite courses. Therefore, the text is designed to build on your basic knowledge from courses in accounting and economics. By applying tools learned in these courses, you can develop a conceptual and analytical understanding of financial management.

We realize, however, that for some students time has passed since you have completed your accounting courses. Therefore, we have included Chapter 2, a thorough review of accounting principles, finance terminology, and financial statements. With a working knowledge of Chapter 2, you will have a more complete understanding of the impact of business decisions on financial statements. Furthermore, as you are about to begin your career you will be much better prepared when called upon to apply financial concepts.

In general, tables and figures with real-world numbers have been updated or replaced, and the discussions concerning those tables and figures have been rewritten accordingly.

Chapter-by-Chapter Changes

Chapter 1 Coverage of behavioral finance has been enhanced with the inclusion of Richard Thaler's Nobel Prize in Economic Sciences as well as Eugene Fama's Nobel Prize for his work on the efficient market hypothesis. The section "Forms of Organization" includes the impact of the 2017 Tax Cuts and Jobs Act on all types of organizations, including C corporations, S corporations, and all forms of pass-through structures such as sole proprietorships, partnerships, and limited liability companies. Both the Finance in Action box on endangered public companies and the FIA box on 3M were revised. The Web Exercise was also revised to make it consistent with the current website.

Chapter 2 All of the tables have been updated or revised. The discussion of how depreciation, taxes, and cash flows are linked has been clarified. The Finance in Action box describing corporate "tax inversions" has been significantly revised with reference to the 2017 Tax Cuts and Jobs Act and includes a graphic of worldwide corporate tax rates from the OECD. The section "Income Tax Considerations" includes an updated discussion of the 2017 Tax Cuts and Jobs Act, including its impact on the cost of a tax-deductible expense, depreciation as a tax shield, and the resultant cash flow. The PepsiCo Web Exercise has been updated.

Chapter 3 The introduction comparing Colgate-Palmolive with Procter & Gamble has been revised and updated. Tables 3-4, 3-5, 3-6, and 3-8 have been revised to be more consistent with the new corporate tax rates. Abercrombie & Fitch has been replaced with Target in the Du Pont model and in the comparison to Walmart Stores Inc. The discussion of liquidity ratios has been revised. The Apple and IBM ratio comparisons have been updated with new numbers. The discussion on deflation has been revised to bring it up to date with the current economic environment. The IBM Web Exercise has been revised.

Chapter 4 The introduction has been updated as well as the Finance in Action box describing the interaction of Tesla's marketing and financial forecasting activities. The section "Percentage-of-Sales Method" has been slightly revised to bring more clarity to the discussion. The Web Exercise on Barnes & Noble has been updated and revised.

Chapter 5 The introduction discussing the airline industry and the cost of oil has been updated with new data. The discussion of the degree of operating leverage replaces Dow Chemical with American Airlines. A new Finance in Action box using Apple to demonstrate leverage replaces the old FIA box on the Intel Corporation. The Web Exercise on United Airlines has been updated and revised.

Chapter 6 The FIA box on RFID technology has been updated. Figure 6-2 featuring Briggs & Stratton has been revised with new data and the discussion describing the cyclicality has been modified. Figure 6-3 comparing seasonal sales and earnings per share of Macy's and Target has been updated with new data and the analysis is revised to be consistent with the new figure. Figures 6-9, 6-10, and 6-11 and all of the data and discussion about yield curves, interest rates, working capital, and current ratios have been updated, including the Web Exercise at the end of the problem set.

Chapter 7 The FIA box on working capital has been updated. The section discussing a lockbox system has been expanded. Figure 7-4 and the discussion of SWIFT have been revised. Table 7-1 has been updated with 2018 data. For a change of pace and a little fun, a new FIA box features the inventory control system in the International Space Station. The Web Exercise has been revised to work with the new website at the B2B company Perfect Commerce.

Chapter 8 The chapter introduction featuring Yum! Brands credit agreements has been updated to reflect new agreements. Figures 8-1 and 8-2 as well as Table 8-1 have been revised with new data and discussion of interest rates and commercial paper. The Finance in Action box on the LIBOR price-fixing scandal has been revised, as has the FIA box on LendingClub's initial public offering. The Web Exercise on General Electric Capital has been significantly revised, given GE's exit from many of its previous activities.

Chapter 9 The calculator appendix previously found at the end of Chapter 10 has been moved to Chapter 9 and is Appendix 9C. The FIA box has been rewritten to include the August 2017 Powerball jackpot winner of $758 million.

Chapter 10 The introduction to the chapter featuring Coca-Cola has been revised. Table 10-4 has been updated and the discussion describing the table has been revised. The Web Exercise featuring ExxonMobil has been revised to coincide with changes to the website.

Chapter 11 Table 11-2 and the corresponding financial calculator example on yield to maturity has been revised with new numbers using the Goal Seek function in Excel's RATE function. The information in Table 11-3 has been replaced with new data. And the cost of debt capital example has been changed to be more consistent with a lower tax rate. Table 11-4 on long-term debt has been updated. The numbers in the cost of common equity have changed. The practice problems and most of the homework problems have been revised to reflect 25 percent and 21 percent tax rates. The Web Exercise has been changed to be consistent with changes in Intel's website.

Chapter 12 The section on accounting versus cash flows has been updated to reflect the impact of lower tax rates. The section on the rules of depreciation is new with a discussion of how the 2017 Tax Cuts and Jobs Act modified the rules. The section "The Tax Rate" is new and includes the impact of the 2017 Tax Cuts and Jobs Act and how state tax rates can affect the average tax rate. Table 12-14 on cash flow related to the purchase of machinery has been revised as well as Table 12-15 on net present value. The whole section on the replacement decision now reflects lower tax rates and has been comprehensively revised, including all tables. The section on elective expensing has been rewritten to reflect the new 2018 tax code. The practice problem sets and many of the homework problems have been updated with lower tax rates. The Web Exercise featuring Texas Instruments has been updated.

Chapter 13 The introduction on Apache Corp. has been updated. Table 13-2 has been updated with new information and the Web Exercise is changed to be consistent with Alcoa's website.

Chapter 14 The entire section on international capital markets has been rewritten and updated with Figure 14-1 being new and Table 14-1 updated. Figure 14-2 now has two panels analyzing internally generated funds and the relationship between earnings, dividends, retained earnings, and depreciation. Modest updates were made on the U.S. markets and Table 14-2 covering foreign stock exchanges now examines markets by geographical regions.The Web Exercise has been revised to coincide with changes to the NYSE website.

Chapter 15 The introduction has been rewritten and Table 15-1 is populated with new IPO data from 2014 through January 2018. Table 15-1 includes IPOs from Saudi Arabia, Italy, Hong Kong, India, Brazil, and the United States. The global ranking of investment bankers has been updated to include 2016 versus 2017. Table 15-3 now focuses on the leading investment banker by fees generated rather than revenue generated and is current through 2017. It also ranks the leaders by category, by regions, and by industries. Table 15-4 has been added and focuses on fees and number of deals by the four areas of M&A, equity offerings, bond offerings, and loans for the four quarters in 2017. Table 15-7 updates the information of debt and equity capital markets book-runner rankings. The Web Exercise has been updated.

Chapter 16 All tables and real-world examples have been updated. Material linking the time series of Walmart's leverage levels and times-interest-earned ratios to changes in long-term interest rates over the last two decades has been updated.

Figure 16-3 has been updated to include the last three years of data. A new Finance in Action box featuring bonds issued by Inter Milan has replaced the old box on Alibaba bonds. Perhaps the most significant change to the chapter is an entirely new section, "Leasing as a Form of Debt," that was driven by the 2017 Tax Cuts and Jobs Act. Appendix 16B on lease-versus-purchase has been deleted. As in the other chapters, the Web Exercise has been updated.

Chapter 17 The introductory example of TowerJazz has been updated and modified and the name changed to Tower Semiconductor. All the information in Table 17-1 has been updated. The Finance in Action box on Hewlett-Packard has been replaced with a new FIA box on Facebook with a focus on corporate governance and a comparison of Facebook with Apple and 3M on stewardship, environment, social, and governance. Table 17-2 on rights offerings has been updated with new data. Table 17-3 has been replaced with new data and expanded to include deposit receipts by major world markets. Finally, the impact of the 2017 Tax Cuts and Jobs Act on preferred stock has been included, as it significantly changes the tax treatment by corporations owning preferred stock of other companies. The Web Exercise on 3M has been revised.

Chapter 18 The introduction has been amended to include the purchase of SAB-Miller by Anheuser-Busch. Table 18-1 has been updated with new numbers, as has the Finance in Action box on dividend aristocrats. Figure 18-2 now features the Standard & Poors 500 Index for dividends, retained earnings, and total profit, and the text describing Figure 18-2 has been significantly revised. The new tax rates for the Tax Cuts and Jobs Act of 2017 are now presented in Table 18-3. The impact of the new tax law on capital gains and dividends is discussed. Because the 2017 Tax Cuts and Jobs Act will allow companies to repatriate over $1 trillion of cash held overseas, Table 18-8 features companies announcing stock repurchases in December of 2017 after the tax act was passed. The amount totals over $100 billion. An entirely new Facebook Web Exercise is presented.

Chapter 19 The introduction replaces AAR Corp. with BioMarin Pharmaceutical. Tables 19-1, 19-2, 19-3, and 19-5 have all been revised with new companies and data. The discussions pertaining to each table have been modified to focus on the impact of the new data. The Web Exercise has been revised to coincide with the CBOE website.

Chapter 20 The introduction includes an update on Berkshire Hathaway's purchase of Pilot Flying J. Table 20-1 has been updated to present the largest mergers from 2010 to 2018. Figure 20-1 presents mergers and acquisitions in North America from 1985 to 2017. Information on tax inversions has been changed to recognize that the 2017 Tax Cuts and Jobs Act makes tax inversions unnecessary. The example of a tax loss carry-forward has been modified to reflect a lower corporate tax rate. The section on hostile merger takeover activities uses the Broadcom attack on Qualcomm as an example and Figure 20-3 shows the decline in hostile merger and acquisition activity between 1985 and 2017. The Web Exercise on Berkshire Hathaway has been modified.

Chapter 21 International financial management tables and figures of exchange rates and currency cross rates have been updated with current data. The hedging examples using forward and futures contracts have been updated with the text reflecting the new data found in the currency cross rates Table 21-2. The Finance in Action box on how Coca-Cola manages currency risk has been updated. The impact of the 2017 tax law on the deferral of taxes on foreign earnings is discussed. The Finance in Action box on political risk in Argentina has been updated.

Successful improvements from the previous editions that we have built on in the 17th edition include:

Functional Integration We have taken care to include examples that are not just applicable to finance students but also to marketing, management, and accounting majors.

Small Business Since over two-thirds of the jobs created in the U.S. economy are from small businesses, we have continued to note when specific financial techniques are performed differently by large and small businesses.

Comprehensive International Coverage We have updated and expanded coverage of international companies, markets, and events throughout the text.

Contemporary Coverage The 17th edition continues to provide updated real-world examples, using companies easily recognized by students to illustrate financial concepts presented in the text.

Chapter Features

Integration of Learning Objectives to Discussion Questions and Problems

The Learning Objectives (LOs) presented at the beginning of each chapter serve as a quick introduction to the material students will learn and should understand fully before moving to the next chapter. Every discussion question and problem at the end of each chapter refers back to the learning objective to which it applies. This allows instructors to easily emphasize the Learning Objective(s) as they choose.

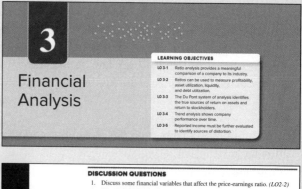

3

Financial Analysis

LEARNING OBJECTIVES

LO 3-1 Ratio analysis provides a meaningful comparison of a company to its industry.

LO 3-2 Ratios can be used to measure profitability, asset utilization, liquidity, and debt utilization.

LO 3-3 The Du Pont system of analysis identifies the true sources of return on assets and return to stockholders.

LO 3-4 Trend analysis shows company performance over time.

LO 3-5 Reported income must be further evaluated to identify sources of distortion.

DISCUSSION QUESTIONS

1. Discuss some financial variables that affect the price-earnings ratio. *(LO2-2)*
2. What is the difference between book value per share of common stock and market value per share? Why does this disparity occur? *(LO2-3)*
3. Explain how depreciation generates actual cash flows for the company. *(LO2-5)*
4. What is the difference between accumulated depreciation and depreciation expense? How are they related? *(LO2-5)*
5. How is the income statement related to the balance sheet? *(LO2-1 & 2-3)*
6. Comment on why inflation may restrict the usefulness of the balance sheet as normally presented. *(LO2-3)*

Chapter Opening Vignettes

We bring in current events (such as business-to-business online ventures and competition among air carriers) as chapter openers to illustrate the material to be learned in the upcoming chapter.

f you're in the market for dental products, look no further than Colgate-Palmolive. The firm has it all: every type of toothpaste you can imagine (tartar control, cavity protection, whitening enhancement), as well as every shape and size of toothbrush. While you're getting ready for the day, also consider its soaps, shampoos, and deodorants (Tom's of Maine, Speed Stick, Lady Speed Stick, etc.). If you decide to clean your apartment or dorm room, Colgate-Palmolive will provide you with Ajax, Palmolive dish soap, and a long list of other cleaning products.

All this is somewhat interesting, but why mention these subjects in a finance text? Well, Colgate-Palmolive has had some interesting profit numbers recently. Its profit margin in 2017 was 15 percent, and its return on assets was 19.4 percent. While these numbers are higher than those of the average company, the 2017 number that blows analysts away is its return on stockholders' equity of over 900 percent (the norm is 15–20 percent). In fact, this

Expanded! Finance in Action Boxes

These boxed readings highlight specific topics of interest that relate to four main areas: managerial decisions, global situations, technology issues, and ethics. The inclusion of ethics is relevant given the many recent corporate scandals and the resulting governance issues. Web addresses are included in applicable boxes for easy access to more information on that topic or company.

Tesla's Sales Forecasts: Where Marketing and Finance Come Together

Finance in **ACTION**

Managerial

All the financial analysis in the world can prove useless if a firm does not have a meaningful sales projection. To the extent that the firm has an incorrect sales projection, an inappropriate amount of inventory will be accumulated, projections of accounts receivable and accounts payable will be wrong, and profits and cash flow will be off target. Although a corporate treasurer may understand all the variables influencing income statements, balance sheets, cash budgets, and so on, she is out of luck if the sales projection is wrong.

For example, Tesla Motors produces and

A Morgan Stanley auto analyst estimated that Tesla would sell 40 percent fewer cars than had previously been forecast. Although sales projections had previously been for 500,000 cars by 2020, new projections were for only 300,000. With plummeting oil prices, Tesla's stock fell over 30 percent. Another problem for Tesla is that the forecasts made by Elon Musk, the CEO, have always proved to be way too optimistic, with the actual results falling short of projections.

Over the last two decades, the marketing profession has developed many sophisticated

Excel, Calculator Solutions, and Formulas

$$FV_A = \$1,000 \left[\frac{(1+0.10)^4 - 1}{0.10} \right] = \$4,641$$

Because this problem involves an annuity rather than a single payment, when solving with a financial calculator, the value that we enter for the $\boxed{\text{PMT}}$ key is −$1,000. Now we enter a zero for the $\boxed{\text{PV}}$ key. As we computed earlier using the future value of an annuity equation, we find that when the interest rate is 10%, the future value of a 4-year, $1,000 annuity is $4,641.

Excel's **FV** function can also produce the future value of an annuity stream. The **FV** function assumes that each payment is at the end of a period as shown in the previous timeline. The annuity amount is entered as the **pmt** argument. The function in cell D1 uses cell references for the arguments in cells B1 to B4. The function in cell D5 uses hardcoded values. The values produced by the **FV** function are identical to the calculator solution, but hardcoded solutions should be avoided in preference to cell referenced solutions.

FINANCIAL CALCULATOR

FV of Annuity

Enter	Function
4	N
10	I/Y
−1000	PMT
0	PV
Function	Solution
CPT	
FV	4,641.00

	A	B	C	D	E	F
1	rate	10.00%		=FV(B1,B2,B3,B4)		
2	nper	4.00		**FV**(rate, nper, pmt, [pv], [type])		
3	pmt	−1000		$4,641.00		
4	pv	0				
5				=+FV(0.1,4,−1000,0)		
6				**FV**(rate, nper, pmt, [pv], [type])		
7				$4,641.00		

In Chapters 9, 10, and 12, the authors have included discussions on how the examples are solved using Excel, financial calculators, and formulas. Newly formatted spreadsheet tables and screen captures detail the step-by-step method to solve the examples. The financial calculator keystrokes in the margins give instructors and students additional flexibility. The material can be presented using traditional methods without loss of clarity because the margin content supplements the prior content, which has been retained. The book and solutions manual provide Excel, calculator, and formula explanations for these very important calculations.

Table 5-3 Volume-cost-profit analysis: Conservative firm

Units Sold	Total Variable Costs	Fixed Costs	Total Costs	Total Revenue	Operating Income (Loss)
0	$ 0	$12,000	$ 12,000	$ 0	$(12,000)
20,000	32,000	12,000	44,000	40,000	(4,000)
30,000	48,000	12,000	60,000	60,000	0
40,000	64,000	12,000	76,000	80,000	4,000
60,000	96,000	12,000	108,000	120,000	12,000
80,000	128,000	12,000	140,000	160,000	20,000
100,000	160,000	12,000	172,000	200,000	28,000

Pulling It Together with Color

Throughout the 17th edition, the authors make color an integral part of the presentation of finance concepts. Color is applied consistently across illustrations, text, and examples in order to enhance the learning experience. We hope that the color in this edition assists your understanding and retention of the concepts discussed.

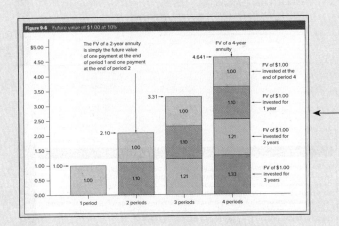

Figure 9-6 Future value of $1.00 at 10%

Digital Illustrations of Time Value of Money (Chapter 9)

The concept of the "time value of money" is one of the most difficult topics in any financial management course for professors to communicate to students. We think we have created a visual method for teaching future value and present value of money that will help you understand the concept simply and quickly. The 17th edition includes new interactive digital illustrations of four key figures in the text that visually relate future values and present values. We hope you agree that this visual presentation helps those students who are less comfortable with the math.

End-of-Chapter Features

Review of Formulas

At the end of every chapter that includes formulas, we provide a list for easy reviewing purposes.

REVIEW OF FORMULAS

1. K_d (cost of debt) $= Y(1 - T)$ (11-1)
    Y is yield
    T is corporate tax rate

2. K_p (cost of preferred stock) $= \dfrac{D_p}{P_p - F}$ (11-2)

    D_p is the annual dividend on preferred stock
    P_p is the price of preferred stock
    F is flotation, or selling, cost

Practice Problems and Solutions

Two practice problems are featured at the end of each chapter. They review concepts illustrated within the chapter and enable the student to determine whether the material has been understood prior to completion of the problem sets. Detailed solutions to the practice problems are found immediately following each problem.

PRACTICE PROBLEMS AND SOLUTIONS

1. *a.* You invest $12,000 today at 9 percent per year. How much will you have   *Future value*
         after 15 years?   *Present value*
    b. What is the current value of $100,000 after 10 years if the discount rate is   *(LO9-2 & 9-3)*
         12 percent?
    c. You invest $2,000 a year for 20 years at 11 percent. How much will you have
         after 20 years?

Labeled Discussion Questions and Problems

The material in the text is supported by over 250 questions and 475 problems in this edition, to reinforce and test your understanding of each chapter. Care has been taken to make the questions and problems consistent with the chapter material, and each problem is labeled with its topic, learning objective, and level of difficulty to facilitate that link. Every problem and solution has been written by the authors, and all of the quantitative problems are assignable in *Connect*.

PROBLEMS
 Selected problems are available with Connect. Please see the preface for more information.

Basic Problems

1. Shock Electronics sells portable heaters for $35 per unit, and the variable cost to   *Break-even analysis*
    produce them is $22. Mr. Amps estimates that the fixed costs are $97,500.   *(LO5-2)*
    a. Compute the break-even point in units.
    b. Fill in the table (in dollars) to illustrate the break-even point has been
         achieved.

    Sales ....   _____
    − Fixed costs ....   _____
    − Total variable costs ....   _____

Comprehensive Problems

Several chapters have comprehensive problems that integrate and require the application of several financial concepts into one problem. Additional comprehensive problems are included in the Instructor's Manual for select chapters.

COMPREHENSIVE PROBLEM

Medical Research Corporation is expanding its research and production capacity to   *Medical Research*
introduce a new line of products. Current plans call for the expenditure of $100 million   *Corporation*
on four projects of equal size ($25 million each), but different returns. Project A is in   *(Marginal cost*
blood clotting proteins and has an expected return of 18 percent. Project B relates to a   *of capital and*
hepatitis vaccine and carries a potential return of 14 percent. Project C, dealing with a   *investment returns)*
cardiovascular compound, is expected to earn 11.8 percent, and Project D, an invest-   *(LO11-5)*
ment in orthopedic implants, is expected to show a 10.9 percent return.
    The firm has $15 million in retained earnings. After a capital structure with
$15 million in retained earnings is reached (in which retained earnings represent
60 percent of the financing), all additional equity financing must come in the form of
new common stock.

Web Exercises

Each chapter includes at least one Web exercise to help pull more relevant real-world material into the classroom. The exercises ask students to go to a specific website of a company and make a complete analysis similar to that demonstrated in the chapter. These exercises provide a strong link between learning chapter concepts and applying them to the actual decision-making process.

Less Managing. More Teaching. Greater Learning.

McGraw-Hill Connect

 McGraw-Hill *Connect* is an online assignment and assessment solution aid that connects students with the tools and resources they'll need to achieve success.

McGraw-Hill *Connect* helps prepare students for their future by enabling faster learning, more efficient studying, and higher retention of knowledge.

McGraw-Hill *Connect* Features

Connect offers a number of powerful tools and features to make managing assignments easier, so faculty can spend more time teaching. With *Connect,* students can engage with their coursework anytime and anywhere, making the learning process more accessible and efficient. *Connect* offers you the features described next.

Simple Assignment Management

With *Connect,* creating assignments is easier than ever, so you can spend more time teaching and less time managing. The assignment management function enables you to:

- Create and deliver assignments easily with selectable end-of-chapter questions and test bank items.
- Streamline lesson planning, student progress reporting, and assignment grading to make classroom management more efficient than ever.
- Go paperless with the SmartBook eBook and online submission and grading of student assignments.

Smart Grading

When it comes to studying, time is precious. *Connect* helps students learn more efficiently by providing feedback and practice material when they need it, where they need it. When it comes to teaching, your time also is precious. The grading function enables you to:

- Have assignments scored automatically, giving students immediate feedback on their work and side-by-side comparisons with correct answers.
- Access and review each response; manually change grades or leave comments for students to review.
- Reinforce classroom concepts with practice tests and instant quizzes.

Instructor Library

The *Connect* Instructor Library is your repository for additional resources to improve student engagement in and out of class. You can select and use any asset that enhances your lecture. This library contains information about the book and the authors, as well as all of the instructor supplements for this text, including:

- **Instructor's Manual** Revised by author Geoff Hirt, the manual helps instructors integrate the graphs, tables, perspectives, and problems into a lecture format. Each chapter opens with a brief overview and a review of key chapter concepts. The chapter is then outlined in an annotated format to be used as an in-class reference guide by the instructor.
- **Solutions Manual** Updated by author Bart Danielsen, the manual includes detailed solutions to all of the questions and problems, set in a larger type font to facilitate their reproduction in the classroom. Calculator, Excel, and formula solutions are included for all relevant problems.
- **Test Bank** This question bank includes over 1,500 multiple-choice and true/false questions, with revisions and updates made by Katie Landgraf, University of Hawaii. Updates to the questions correspond to the revisions in the 17th edition. Also included are short answer questions and matching quizzes. The test bank is assignable in *Connect* and EZ Test Online and available as Word files.
- **PowerPoint Presentations** These slides, updated by Leslie Rush, University of Hawaii, contain lecture outlines and selected exhibits from the book in a four-color, electronic format that you can customize for your own lectures.

Student Study Materials

The *Connect* Student Study Center is the place for students to access additional resources. The Student Study Center:

- Offers students quick access to lectures, course materials, eBooks, and more.
- Provides instant practice material and study questions, easily accessible on the go.

Diagnostic and Adaptive Learning of Concepts: LearnSmart and SmartBook

LEARNSMART® Students want to make the best use of their study time. The LearnSmart adaptive self-study technology within *Connect* provides students with a seamless combination of practice, assessment, and remediation for every concept in the textbook. LearnSmart's intelligent software adapts to every student response and automatically delivers concepts that advance students' understanding while reducing time devoted to the concepts already mastered. The result for every student is the fastest path to mastery of the chapter concepts. LearnSmart:

- Applies an intelligent concept engine to identify the relationships between concepts and to serve new concepts to each student only when he or she is ready.
- Adapts automatically to each student, so students spend less time on the topics they understand and practice more those they have yet to master.
- Provides continual reinforcement and remediation but gives only as much guidance as students need.

- Integrates diagnostics as part of the learning experience.
- Enables instructors to assess which concepts students have efficiently learned on their own, thus freeing class time for more applications and discussion.

 SMARTBOOK® SmartBook®, powered by LearnSmart, is the first and only adaptive reading experience designed to change the way students read and learn. It creates a personalized reading experience by highlighting the most impactful concepts a student needs to learn at that moment in time. As a student engages with SmartBook, the reading experience continuously adapts by highlighting content based on what the student knows and doesn't know. This ensures that the focus is on the content he or she needs to learn, while simultaneously promoting long-term retention of material. Use SmartBook's real-time reports to quickly identify the concepts that require more attention from individual students—or the entire class. The end result? Students are more engaged with course content, can better prioritize their time, and come to class ready to participate.

Student Progress Tracking

Connect keeps instructors informed about how each student, section, and class is performing, allowing for more productive use of lecture and office hours. The progress-tracking function enables you to:

- View scored work immediately and track individual or group performance with assignment and grade reports.
- Access an instant view of student or class performance relative to learning objectives.
- Collect data and generate reports required by many accreditation organizations, such as AACSB.

For more information about *Connect*, go to connect.mheducation.com or contact your local McGraw-Hill sales representative.

Acknowledgments

We are extremely grateful to the following instructors for their valuable reviews on previous editions:

Alan Adams	Joseph Bentley	Rosemary Carlson
Ahmed Al Asfour	William J. Bertin	Alan J. Carper
Dwight C. Anderson	Debela Birru	Cheryl Chamblin
Eric Anderson	Robert Boatler	Leo Chan
Andreas Andrikopoulos	Walter Boyle	Rolf Christensen
Antonio Apap	Wendell Bragg	Steven Christian
Kavous Ardalan	Alka Bramhandkar	Andreas Christofi
John Backman	Jeb Briley	E. Tylor Claggett
Charles Barngrover	Dallas Brozik	Margaret Clark
Larry Barraza	Georgia Buckles	Henry Co
Brian T. Belt	Richard Burton	Nanette Cobb
James Benedum	Richard Butler	Allan Conway
Omar Benkato	Ezra Byler	Tom Copeland
Michael Bentil	Kevin Cabe	Walter R. Dale

Jeffrey S. Dean
Andrea DeMaskey
James Demello
Bob Diberio
Clifford A. Diebold
Darla Donaldson
Jeff Donaldson
Tom Downs
David Durst
Fred Ebeid
Scott Ehrhorn
Jeff Eicher
Marumbok Etta
Michael Evans
Gregory Fallon
Barry Farber
George Fickenworth
O. L. Fortier
Mike Fioccoprile
Gary Florence
Mohamed Gaber
Robert Gaertner
Jim Gahlon
Ashley Geisewite
James Gentry
Elizabeth Goins
Bernie J. Grablowsky
Bill Greer
Debbie Griest
Kidane Habteselassie
John R. Hall
Thomas R. Hamilton
Walt Hammond
Frank Harber
Carole Harris
Eric Haye
Charles Higgins
Eric Hoogstra
Stanley Jacobs
Bharat Jain
Jerry James
Joel Jankowski
Victoria Javine
Gerald S. Justin
Fredric S. Kamin
Moonsoo Kang

Peter R. Kensicki
Tom Kewley
Jim Keys
Robert Kleiman
Ken Knauf
Raj Kohli
Charles Kronche
Ronald Kudla
Morris Lamberson
Linda Lange
Joe Lavely
Sharon Lee
Joseph Levitsky
John H. Lewis
Terry Lindenberg
Joe Lipscomb
John P. Listro
Wilson Liu
Jim Lock
Doug Lonnstrom
Leslie Lukasik
Claude Lusk
Kelly Manley
Ken Mannino
Paul Marciano
John D. Markese
Peter Marks
Thomas Maroney
Kooros Maskooki
Bill Mason
Joe Massa
John Masserwick
Patricia Matthews
Michael Matukonis
K. Gary McClure
Grant McQueen
Wayne E. McWee
Stuart Michelson
Vassil Mihov
Jerry D. Miller
David Minars
Mike Moritz
Heber Moulton
Matt Muller
Vivian Nazar
Srinivas Nippani

Kenneth O'Brien
Bryan O'Neil
Dimitrios Pachis
Coleen C. Pantalone
Robert Pavlik
Rosemary C. Peavler
Mario Picconi
Beverly Piper
Harlan Platt
Ralph A. Pope
Roger Potter
Franklin Potts
Dev Prasad
Cynthia Preston
Chris Prestopino
Frances A. Quinn
James Racic
David Rankin
Dan Raver
Robert Rittenhouse
Mauricio Rodriguez
Frederick Rommel
Marjorie Rubash
Gary Rupp
Philip Russel
Gayle Russell
Robert Saemann
Olgun Fuat Sahin
Ajay Samant
Atul Saxena
Timothy Scheppa
Sandra Schickele
James Scott
Abu Selimuddin
Gowri Shankar
Joanne Sheridan
Fred Shipley
Larry Simpson
Larry Smith
William Smith
Jan R. Squires
Sundaram Srinivasan
Cliff Stalter
Jack Stone
Thad Stupi
Diane Suhler

Mark Sunderman	Mark Vaughan	Annie Wong
Robert Swanson	Donald E. Vaughan	Don Wort
Tom Szczurek	Andrew Waisburd	Ergun Yener
Glenn Tanner	Ken Washer	Lowell Young
Richard Taylor	William Welch	Emily Zeitz
Robert Taylor	Gary Wells	Terry Zivney
Mike Toyne	Larry White	Linda Wiechowski
Mike Tuberose	Howard R. Whitney	Matt Wirgau
Cathyann Tully	Philip L. Wiggle	Charles Zellerbach
Lana Tuss	Lawrence Wolken	Miranda Zhang

We would like to give special thanks to John Plamondon for his excellent data gathering using DePaul's Bloomberg terminals and his construction of figures and tables in many of the chapters. Marisa Evans, David Golder, Henry Stilley, Chelsea Tate, Katherine Boliek, Chase Crone, Cameron Monahan, Munroe Danielsen, and Ashley Smith have been invaluable in assisting with text, solutions, and *Connect* content. We would also like to thank Allison McCabe, product developer; Chuck Synovec, portfolio manager; Fran Simon, content project manager; Trina Maurer, marketing manager; Xin Lin, digital product analyst; Angela Norris, assessment content project manager; Jessica Cuevas, designer; and the entire team at McGraw-Hill for its feedback, support, and enduring commitment to excellence.

Stanley B. Block
Geoffrey A. Hirt
Bartley R. Danielsen

Brief Contents

Contents

PART 4 | THE CAPITAL BUDGETING PROCESS

List of Selected Managerial Examples and Boxes

List of Selected Global Examples and Boxes

Introduction

CHAPTER 1
The Goals and Activities of Financial Management

>>> **RELATED WEBSITES**

www.3m.com
www.jnj.com

1

The Goals and Activities of Financial Management

LEARNING OBJECTIVES

LO 1-1 The field of finance integrates concepts from economics, accounting, and a number of other areas.

LO 1-2 A firm can have many different forms of organization.

LO 1-3 The relationship of risk to return is a central focus of finance.

LO 1-4 The primary goal of financial managers is to maximize the wealth of the shareholders.

LO 1-5 Financial managers attempt to achieve wealth maximization through daily activities such as credit and inventory management and through longer-term decisions related to raising funds.

LO 1-6 The financial turmoil that roiled the markets between 2001 and 2012 resulted in more regulatory oversight of the financial markets.

3M is one of those companies that is more adept than others at creating products, marketing those products, and being financially astute. 3M is the world leader in optical films, industrial and office tapes, and nonwoven fabrics. Consumers may recognize 3M as the maker of Post-it notes, Scotch tape, and sponges, in addition to thousands of other diverse products such as overhead projectors and roofing granules. The company has always been known for its ability to create new products and markets, and, at times, as much as 35 percent of its sales have been generated from products developed in the previous five years. To accomplish these goals, 3M's research and development has to be financed, the design and production functions funded, and the products marketed and sold worldwide. This process involves all the functions of business.

Did you ever stop to think about the importance of the finance function for a $32 billion multinational company like 3M where 60 percent of sales are international? Someone has to manage the international cash flow, bank relationships, payroll, purchases of plant and equipment, and acquisition of capital. Financial decisions must be made concerning the feasibility and profitability of the continuous stream of new products developed through 3M's very creative research and development efforts. The financial manager needs to keep his or her pulse on interest rates, exchange rates, and the tone of the money and capital markets.

To have a competitive multinational company, the financial manager must manage 3M's global affairs and react quickly to changes in financial markets and exchange rate fluctuations. The board of directors and chief executive officer rely on the financial division to provide a precious resource—capital—and to manage it efficiently and profitably. If you would like to do some research on 3M, you can access its home page at www.3m.com. If you would like to understand more about how companies make financial decisions, keep reading.

The Field of Finance

The field of finance is closely related to economics and accounting, and financial managers need to understand the relationships between these fields. Economics provides a structure for decision making in such areas as risk analysis, pricing theory through supply and demand relationships, comparative return analysis, and many other important areas. Economics also provides the broad picture of the economic environment in which corporations must continually make decisions. A financial manager must understand the institutional structure of the Federal Reserve System, the commercial banking system, and the interrelationships between the various sectors of the economy. Economic variables, such as gross domestic product, industrial production, disposable income, unemployment, inflation, interest rates, and taxes (to name a few), must fit into the financial manager's decision model and be applied correctly. These terms will be presented throughout the text and integrated into the financial process.

Accounting is sometimes said to be the language of finance because it provides financial data through income statements, balance sheets, and the statement of cash flows. The financial manager must know how to interpret and use these statements in allocating the firm's financial resources to generate the best return possible in the long run. Finance links economic theory with the numbers of accounting, and all corporate managers—whether in production, sales, research, marketing, management, or long-run strategic planning—must know what it means to assess the financial performance of the firm.

Many students approaching the field of finance for the first time might wonder what career opportunities exist. For those who develop the necessary skills and training, jobs include corporate financial officer, banker, stockbroker, financial analyst, portfolio manager, investment banker, financial consultant, or personal financial planner. As we progress through the text, you will become increasingly familiar with the important role of the various participants in the financial decision-making process. A financial manager addresses such varied issues as decisions on plant location, the raising of capital, or simply how to get the highest return on x million dollars between five o'clock this afternoon and eight o'clock tomorrow morning.

Evolution of the Field of Finance

Like any discipline, the field of finance has developed and changed over time. At the turn of the 20th century, finance emerged as a field separate from economics when large industrial corporations in oil, steel, chemicals, and railroads were created by early industrialists such as Rockefeller, Carnegie, Du Pont, and Vanderbilt. In these early days, a student of finance would spend time learning about the financial instruments that were essential to mergers and acquisitions. By the 1930s, the country was in its worst depression ever, and financial practice revolved around such topics as the preservation of capital, maintenance of liquidity, reorganization of financially troubled corporations, and bankruptcy process. By the mid-1950s, finance moved away from its descriptive and definitional nature and became more analytical. One of the major advances was the decision-oriented process of allocating **financial capital** (money) for the purchase of **real capital** (long-term plant and equipment). The enthusiasm for more detailed analysis spread to other decision-making areas of the firm—such as cash and inventory management, capital structure theory, and dividend policy. The emphasis also shifted from that of the outsider looking in at the firm to that of the financial manager making tough day-to-day decisions that would affect the firm's performance.

Modern Issues in Finance

Modern financial management has focused on risk-return relationships and the maximization of return for a given level of risk. The award of the 1990 Nobel Prize in Economics to Professors Harry Markowitz and William Sharpe for their contributions to the financial theories of risk-return and portfolio management demonstrates the importance of these concepts. In addition, Professor Merton Miller received the Nobel Prize in Economics for his work in the area of **capital structure theory** (the study of the relative importance of debt and equity). These three scholars were the first professors of finance to win Nobel Prizes in Economics, and their work has been very influential in the field of finance over the last 50 years. Since then, others have followed. In 2013 Eugene Fama won the Nobel Prize in Economics for his work in the area of the efficient market hypothesis (EMH).

Finance continues to become more analytical and mathematical. New financial products with a focus on hedging are being widely used by financial managers to reduce some of the risk caused by changing interest rates and foreign currency exchange rates. As a counterbalance to more quantitative analysis, the psychology of financial decision making, called behavioral finance, has become more widely taught in the classroom. Amos Tversky and Daniel Kahneman were pioneers in the psychology of cognitive bias in the handling of risk. The risk-return trade-off decision is an important concept in finance and economics. Tversky died in 1996, but Kahneman received the Nobel Prize in Economics in 2002 for his work with Tversky. The 2017 Nobel Prize was won by Richard Thaler, who, like Tversky and Kahneman, was a pioneer in behavioral finance. His research is focused on human irrationality and conflicts with the normal economic theory that people make rational decisions, especially when it comes to risk-return trade-offs.

While increasing prices, or **inflation**, have always been a key variable in financial decisions, it was not very important from the 1930s to about 1965 when it averaged about 1 percent per year. However, after 1965 the annual rate of price increases began to accelerate and became quite significant in the 1970s when inflation reached double-digit levels during several years. Inflation remained relatively high until 1982 when the U.S. economy entered a phase of **disinflation** (a slowing down of price increases). The effects of inflation and disinflation on financial forecasting, the required rates of return for capital budgeting decisions, and the cost of capital are quite significant to financial managers and have become more important in their decision making.

Risk Management and a Review of the Financial Crisis

The impact of the financial crisis that started in 2008 lingered into 2013 and early 2014, but by the end of 2017 the U.S. economy was growing at close to 2.5 percent real GDP, and many expected 2018 to grow over 3 percent because of tax reform enacted by Congress at the end of 2017. This crisis resulted in government intervention to save the banking system, followed by legislation (and new regulations) to reduce banks' willingness to take on too much risk. In this brief introduction, we want to emphasize risk management issues. Risk management will continue to have a strong focus in the future until people forget the financial crisis that began with the housing bubble in the early part of the new millennium. The unwillingness to enforce risk management controls at most financial institutions allowed the extension of credit to borrowers who had high-risk profiles and, in too many cases, no chance of paying back their loans. In addition to the poor credit screening of borrowers, quantitative financial engineers created portfolios of mortgage-backed securities that included many of these risky loans. The rating agencies gave these products high credit ratings (AAA), so investors, including sophisticated institutional investors, thought the assets were safe. As the economy went into a recession and borrowers stopped making their loan payments, these mortgage-backed securities fell dramatically in value, and many financial institutions had huge losses on their balance sheets, which they were forced to write off with mark-to-market accounting standards. In some cases, the write-offs reduced bank capital to precarious levels or even below the minimum required level, forcing the banks to raise more capital.

To make matters more complicated, new unregulated products called **credit default swaps (CDS)** were created as insurance against borrowers defaulting on their loans. These credit default swaps were backed by some of the same financial institutions that lacked enough capital to support the insurance that they guaranteed. Liquidity dried up, markets stopped working, and eventually the government stepped into the breach by forcing mergers and infusing capital into the financial institutions.

By fall 2008, Bear Stearns, the fifth-largest investment bank, was forced to merge with JPMorgan Chase, a strong bank. By September 15, 2009, Lehman Brothers, the fourth-largest investment bank, declared bankruptcy, and even Merrill Lynch had to be saved by merging with Bank of America. The Federal Deposit Insurance Corporation seized Washington Mutual on September 25, and again JPMorgan Chase was called on to take over the operations of the biggest bank failure in U.S. history. As the markets continued to disintegrate, the Federal Reserve provided $540 billion to help money market funds meet their redemptions. The crisis continued into 2009, and by February Congress agreed on a $789 billion stimulus package to help keep the economy afloat. Both Chrysler (in April) and General Motors (in June) filed for bankruptcy, and by September 2009, with the help of the Federal Reserve, money and capital markets became more stable and began to function properly.

This crisis created the longest recession since the Great Depression and forced financial institutions to pay more attention to their risk controls. Money became tight and hard to find unless a borrower had a very high credit rating. Chief executives who had previously ignored the warnings of their risk management teams now gave risk managers more control over financial transactions that might cause a repeat of the calamity.

The Dodd–Frank Act

In response to the financial crisis, Congress passed the **Dodd–Frank Act**, officially known as the Wall Street Reform and Consumer Protection Act of 2010. The act purports to promote financial stability by improving accountability and transparency in the overall financial system, protecting taxpayers by improving the stability of large, diversified financial institutions, and protecting consumers from abusive practices in the financial services industry. Dodd–Frank is the first major financial regulatory change in the United State since the Great Depression.

Dodd–Frank has many different sections, and rather than listing each section by title, we provide an overview of the law and its areas of impact. The act created the Financial Stability Oversight Council and the Office of Financial Research within the Treasury Department. These offices are intended to identify systematic risks, reduce moral hazard, and maintain the stability of the U.S. financial system. The law provides for the orderly liquidation or bankruptcy of nonbank financial companies, including broker-dealers and insurance companies. It also consolidates different regulators into fewer federal entities so that it is more difficult for financial firms to pick the least burdensome regulator. Hedge funds and other investment advisors are now required to register with the Securities and Exchange Commission (SEC).

Dodd–Frank also established the Federal Insurance Office within the Treasury Department to oversee the insurance industry and streamline state-based insurance regulation. The act contains the controversial Volcker Rule, which limits the amount of speculative investing a regulated and federally insured depository institution can engage in. This limits large financial institutions from having proprietary, in-house hedge funds and private equity investments. Because much of the financial crisis was blamed on derivative securities, especially credit default swaps, the law requires that over-the-counter derivatives such as credit default swaps be cleared through formal exchanges and regulated either by the SEC or the CFTC (Commodity Futures Trading Commission).

A large part of Dodd–Frank deals with consumer protection and the powers of the Bureau of Consumer Financial Protection. The oversight given to the bureau allows it to dictate the fees that banks charge and the types of products they offer. This power in the hands of a regulator has been widely criticized in the banking community as an attack on free markets.

Several issues have arisen since the act was signed into law. While Dodd–Frank outlines several broad goals and assigns regulatory responsibility, the actual rule-making and implementation have been largely left to the different agencies charged with enforcement. The actual agency-level rulemaking has been delayed as the different regulators attempt to design regulations that conform to the letter of the law. Further, there is a large gray area in the actual activities that are treated as distinct by Dodd–Frank. For instance, the limits on proprietary trading by federally insured financial institutions, also known as the Volcker Rule, assumes that there is a clear distinction between market-making activities and proprietary trading when this is not always the case. New laws often have unintended consequences and are amended or fine-tuned many years later. Many banks and financial institutions have complained that the Volcker Rule has reduced market liquidity to the point that some securities (especially bonds) don't have enough buyers and sellers to create prices. The Republican Congress and President Trump have promised to fix some of the unintended consequences, and they continue to revise and eliminate some of the regulations.

The Impact of Information Technology

The Internet has been around for a long time, but only in the 1990s did it start to be applied to commercial ventures as companies tried to get a return on their previous technology investments.

The rapid development of computer technology, both software and hardware, turned the Internet into a dynamic force in the economy and has affected the way business is conducted. The rapid expansion of the Internet has allowed the creation of many new business models and companies such as Amazon.com, eBay, Facebook, Netflix, Twitter, and Google. It has also enabled the acceleration of e-commerce solutions for "old economy" companies. These e-commerce solutions include different ways to reach customers—the business to consumer model (B2C)—and more efficient ways to interact with suppliers—the business to business model (B2B).

Ralph S. Larsen, former chairman and CEO of Johnson & Johnson, said in 1999, "The Internet is going to turn the way we do business upside down—and for the better. From the most straightforward administrative functions, to operations, to marketing and sales, to supply chain relationships, to finance, to research and development, to customer relationships—no part of our business will remain untouched by this technological revolution."[1] Twenty years later his predictions have been on the spot.

For a financial manager, e-commerce impacts financial management because it affects the pattern and speed with which cash flows through the firm. In the Internet's business to business model (B2B), orders can be placed, inventory can be managed, and bids to supply product can be accepted, all online. The B2B model can help companies lower the cost of managing inventory, accounts receivable, and cash. Where applicable we have included examples throughout the book to highlight the impact of e-commerce and the Internet on the finance function.

Activities of Financial Management

Having examined the field of finance and some of its more recent developments, let us turn our attention to the activities financial managers must perform. It is the responsibility of financial management to allocate funds to current and fixed assets, to obtain the best mix of financing alternatives, and to develop an appropriate dividend policy within the context of the firm's objectives. These functions are performed on a day-to-day basis as well as through infrequent use of the capital markets to acquire new funds. The daily activities of financial management include credit management, inventory control, and the receipt and disbursement of funds. Less routine functions encompass the sale of stocks and bonds and the establishment of capital budgeting and dividend plans.

As indicated in Figure 1-1, all these functions are carried out while balancing the profitability and risk components of the firm.

The appropriate risk-return trade-off must be determined to maximize the market value of the firm for its shareholders. The risk-return decision will influence

---

[1]Johnson & Johnson *1999 Annual Report*, p. 4.

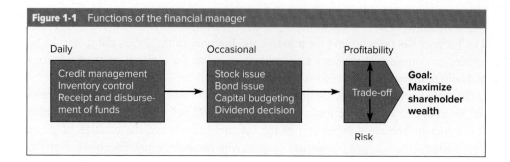

Figure 1-1 Functions of the financial manager

not only the operational side of the business (capital versus labor or Product A versus Product B) but also the financing mix (stocks versus bonds versus retained earnings).

Forms of Organization

The finance function may be carried out within a number of different forms of organizations. Of primary interest are the sole proprietorship, the partnership, and the corporation. There are many reasons to choose one of these forms of organizations. The number of people in the organization is one factor. The liability of the owners is another. Other reasons are the complexity involved with state and federal regulations and how these organizations are taxed. This is borne out by the 2017 Tax Cuts and Jobs Act, which significantly modified taxation for all these forms of organizations.

Impact of 2017 Tax Cuts and Jobs Act on Organizations   Since all forms of organizations are impacted by the Tax Cuts and Jobs Act, we present a brief summary of the issues involved. The most significant change is that the corporate tax rate goes from 35 percent to 21 percent, which puts U.S. companies on competitive footing with other countries.

Sole proprietorships, partnerships, and limited liability partnerships are considered pass-through forms of organizations because the income passes through to the owners and is taxed at the owner's individual rate. To reduce the burden on small firms, the government established a 20 percent deduction of qualified business income from pass-through businesses. The 20 percent deduction reduces taxable income, and combining this with lower individual tax rates will allow businesses meeting the requirements to pay less in taxes than under the tax law that prevailed in 2017.

Sole Proprietorship   The **sole proprietorship** form of organization represents single-person ownership and offers the advantages of simplicity of decision making and low organizational and operating costs. Most small businesses with 1 to 10 employees are sole proprietorships. The major drawback of the sole proprietorship is that there is unlimited liability to the owner. In settlement of the firm's debts, the owner can lose not only the capital that has been invested in the business but also personal assets. This drawback can be serious, and you should realize that few lenders are willing to advance funds to a small business without a personal liability commitment.

The profits or losses of a sole proprietorship are taxed as though they belong to the individual owner. Thus if a sole proprietorship makes $50,000, the owner will claim the profits on his or her tax return. (In the corporate form of organization, the

The Endangered Public Company

An article in *The Economist* describes the decline of the public company in the United States. It states that the number of public companies in the United States has fallen 38 percent since 1997 and 48 percent in Britain. In addition, the number of initial public offerings (IPOs) in America declined from an average of 311 per year in the 1980–2000 period to 99 per year in the 2001–2011 period, with only 81 in 2011.

However, recent statistics show that IPOs have rebounded. IPO data are lumpy and dependent on the economy and the tone of the stock market. In 2013, 157 companies went public and another 206 in 2014. During the 2017 bull market there were 108 IPOs and the average from 2012 to 2017 was 126. So perhaps the public company is not dead yet. *The Economist* points out that Mark Zuckerberg of Facebook didn't really want to take his firm public, but because of U.S. law, his hand was forced in a sense. If a U.S. company has more than 500 shareholders, it is required to publish quarterly financial reports just as if it were a publicly listed company. So while Zuckerberg took Facebook public, he structured the company so that he kept most of the voting rights. This is not unusual with family-owned companies. The Ford family has managed to maintain control of Ford Motor Company with a 40 percent controlling vote.

The burdens of regulation have grown heavier for public companies. Corporate executives complain that it is impossible to focus on the long term when institutional investors and shareholders seem to value short-term results. The result is that privately held companies are increasing in number. Companies like McGraw-Hill Education, the publisher of this text, are privately held.

Other types of business organizations have arisen. For example, one-third of America's tax reporting businesses now classify themselves as partnerships. These partnerships can come in various forms such as limited liability limited partnerships (LLLPs), publicly traded partnerships (PTPs), real estate investment trusts (REITs), and private partnerships such as those of most private equity partnerships that own whole companies that are not publicly traded. The authors attribute the rise of private companies during this time period to the Sarbanes–Oxley Act of 2002, which put a heavy financial burden on smaller companies.

In emerging market foreign countries, state-owned enterprises (SOEs) are quite common as these countries emerge from controlled economies to more open economies. For example, SOEs make up 80 percent of China's companies, 62 percent of Russia's companies, and 38 percent of Brazil's companies. State-owned enterprises are politically protected and often are central to a country's economy. One such example is Gazprom in Russia, the biggest natural gas company.

The question for the future is will these new forms of businesses continue to multiply while publicly held companies continue to decline, or is this just a reaction to the financial crisis and the slow growth period of 2000 to 2012.

Sources: "The Endangered Public Company: The Big Engine That Couldn't," *The Economist*, May 19, 2012, pp. 27–30; Initial Public Offerings: Updated Statistics Jay R. Ritter, Cordell Professor of Finance, University of Florida, January 3, 2018.

corporation pays a tax on profits, and then the owners of the corporation pay a tax on any distributed profits.) Approximately 72 percent of the 30 million business firms in this country are organized as sole proprietorships.

Partnership   The second form of organization is the **partnership**, which is similar to a sole proprietorship except there are two or more owners. Multiple ownership makes it possible to raise more capital and to share ownership responsibilities. Most partnerships are formed through an agreement between the participants, known as the

articles of partnership, which specify the ownership interest, the methods for distributing profits, and the means for withdrawing from the partnership. For taxing purposes, partnership profits or losses are allocated directly to the partners, and there is no double taxation as there is in the corporate form.

Like the sole proprietorship, the partnership arrangement carries unlimited liability for the owners. While the partnership offers the advantage of *sharing* possible losses, it presents the problem of owners with unequal wealth having to absorb losses. If three people form a partnership with a $10,000 contribution each and the business loses $100,000, one wealthy partner may have to bear a disproportionate share of the losses if the other two partners do not have sufficient personal assets.

To circumvent this shared unlimited liability feature, a special form of partnership, called a **limited liability partnership**, can be utilized. Under this arrangement, one or more partners are designated general partners and have unlimited liability for the debts of the firm; other partners are designated limited partners and are liable only for their initial contribution. The limited partners are normally prohibited from being active in the management of the firm. You may have heard of limited partnerships in real estate syndications in which a number of limited partners are doctors, lawyers, and CPAs and there is one general partner who is a real estate professional. Not all financial institutions will extend funds to a limited partnership.

Corporation   In terms of revenue and profits produced, the corporation is by far the most important type of economic unit. While only about 20 percent of U.S. business firms are corporations, they are dominated by large corporations like Apple, Microsoft, Amazon, Exxon, and Walmart. Approximately 80 percent of sales and 70 percent of profits can be attributed to the corporate form of organization. The **corporation** is unique—it is a legal entity unto itself. Thus the corporation may sue or be sued, engage in contracts, and acquire property. A corporation is formed through **articles of incorporation**, which specify the rights and limitations of the entity.

A corporation is owned by shareholders who enjoy the privilege of limited liability, meaning their liability exposure is generally no greater than their initial investment.[2] A corporation also has a continual life and is not dependent on any one shareholder for maintaining its legal existence.

A key feature of the corporation is the easy divisibility of the ownership interest by issuing shares of stock. While it would be nearly impossible to have more than 10,000 or 20,000 partners in most businesses, a corporation may have several hundred thousand shareholders. For example, General Electric has 8.7 billion shares of common stock outstanding with 57.3 percent institutional ownership (pension funds, mutual funds, etc.), while Microsoft with 7.7 billion shares outstanding has 75.5 percent institutional ownership.

The shareholders' interests are ultimately managed by the corporation's board of directors. The directors may include key management personnel of the firm as well as directors from outside the firm. Directors serve in a fiduciary capacity for the shareholders and may be liable for the mismanagement of the firm. After the collapse of

---

[2]An exception to this rule is made if shareholders buy their stock at less than par value. Then they would be liable for up to the par value.

corporations such as Enron and WorldCom due to fraud, the role of outside directors became much more important, and corporations were motivated to comply with more stringent corporate governance laws mandated by Congress. Outside directors may make from $5,000 per year for serving on the board of small companies, but directors serving on the boards of S&P 500 companies earn fees of more than $250,000 per year, on average. Directors serving on the audit and compensation committees are frequently paid additional fees.

Because the corporation is a separate legal entity, it reports and pays taxes on its *own* income. As previously mentioned, any remaining income that is paid to the shareholders in the form of dividends will require the payment of a second tax by the shareholders. One of the key disadvantages to the corporate form of organization is this potential double taxation of earnings. The company pays taxes on its income and, when stockholders receive their dividends, they pay a second tax. This tax on dividends ranges from 0 percent for low-income individuals to 15 percent and finally 23.8 percent for people in the highest tax bracket.

There is, however, one way to completely circumvent the double taxation of a normal corporation, and that is through formation of an S corporation. With an **S corporation**, the income is taxed as direct income to the stockholders and thus is taxed only once as normal income, similar to a partnership. Nevertheless, the shareholders receive all the organizational benefits of a corporation, including limited liability. The S corporation designation can apply to domestic corporations that have up to 100 stockholders and have only one class of stock with allowable shareholders being individuals, estates, and certain trusts.

The **limited liability company (LLC)** has become a popular vehicle for conducting business because of its highly flexible structure. An LLC is not technically a corporation, but like a corporation it provides limited liability for the owners. LLCs can be taxed as sole proprietorships, partnerships, corporations, or S corporations, depending upon elections made by the owners.

While the proprietorship, traditional partnership, and various forms of limited partnerships are all important, the corporation is given primary emphasis in this text. Because of the all-pervasive impact of the corporation on our economy, and because most growing businesses eventually become corporations, the effects of most decisions in this text are often considered from the corporate viewpoint.

Corporate Governance

As we learned in the previous section, the corporation is governed by the board of directors, led by the chairman of the board. In many companies, the chairman of the board is also the CEO, or chief executive officer. During the stock market collapse of 2000–2002, many companies went bankrupt due to mismanagement or, in some cases, financial statements that did not accurately reflect the financial condition of the firm because of deception as well as outright fraud. Companies such as WorldCom reported over $9 billion of incorrect or fraudulent financial entries on their income statements.

Enron also declared bankruptcy after it became known that its accountants kept many financing transactions "off the books." The company had more debt than most of its investors and lenders knew about. Many of these accounting manipulations were too sophisticated for the average analyst, banker, or board member to understand. In the Enron case, the U.S. government indicted its auditor, Arthur Andersen, and because of the indictment, the Andersen firm was dissolved. Because of these accounting scandals, there was a public outcry for corporate accountability, ethics reform, and an explanation of why the corporate governance system had failed.

Again, in the financial crisis in 2007–2009 it appeared that boards of directors didn't understand the risk that their management had taken in extending mortgages to high credit risks. Even senior management didn't understand the risk embodied in some of the mortgage-backed securities that their organizations had bought for investments. This total lack of risk management oversight continued to put a focus on corporate governance issues. With these two events coming so close together, many questioned the ability of large companies and financial institutions to regulate themselves. Why didn't the boards of directors know what was going on and stop it? Why didn't they fire members of management and clean house? Why did they allow such huge bonuses and executive compensation when companies were performing so poorly? One result was the passing of the Wall Street Reform and Consumer Protection Act of 2010 (Dodd–Frank), as discussed earlier in the chapter.

The issues of corporate governance are really agency problems. **Agency theory** examines the relationship between the owners and the managers of the firm. In privately owned firms, management and owners are usually the same people. Management operates the firm to satisfy its own goals, needs, financial requirements, and the like. However, as a company moves from private to public ownership, management now represents all the owners. This places management in the agency position of making decisions that will be in the best interests of all shareholders. Because of diversified ownership interests, conflicts between managers and shareholders can arise that impact the financial decisions of the firm. When the chairman of the board is also the chief executive of the firm, stockholders recognize that the executive may act in his or her own best interests rather than those of the stockholders of the firm. In the prior bankruptcy examples, that is exactly what happened. Management filled their own pockets and left the stockholders with little or no value in the company's stock. In the WorldCom case, a share of common stock fell from the $60 range to eventually being worthless, and Bernie Ebbers, the CEO and chairman of the board, ended up in jail. Because of these potential conflicts of interest, many hold the view that the chairman of the board of directors should be from outside a company rather than an executive of the firm.

Because **institutional investors** such as pension funds and mutual funds own a large percentage of stock in major U.S. companies, these investors are having more to say about the way publicly owned corporations are managed. As a group they have the ability to vote large blocks of shares for the election of a board of directors. The threat of their being able to replace poorly performing boards of directors makes institutional investors quite influential. Since pension funds and mutual funds represent individual workers and investors, they have a responsibility to see that firms are managed in an efficient and ethical way.

The Sarbanes–Oxley Act

Because corporate fraud during the Internet bubble had taken place at some very large and high-profile companies, Congress decided that it needed to do something to control corrupt corporate behavior. The major accounting firms had failed to detect fraud in their accounting audits, and outside directors were often not provided with the kind of information that would allow them to detect fraud and mismanagement. Because many outside directors were friends of management and had been nominated by management, there was a question about their willingness to act independently in carrying out their fiduciary responsibility to shareholders.

The **Sarbanes–Oxley Act** of 2002 set up a five-member Public Company Accounting Oversight Board with the responsibility for establishing auditing standards within companies, controlling the quality of audits, and setting rules and standards for the independence of the auditors. It also puts great responsibility on the internal audit committee of each publicly traded company to enforce compliance with the act. The major focus of the act is to make sure that publicly traded corporations accurately present their assets, liabilities, and equity and income on their financial statements. Originally, there were complaints about the cost of implementing the act and concerns about its effectiveness. After getting systems in place to monitor activity, many companies found the results to be more positive than negative.

Goals of Financial Management

Let us look at several alternative goals for the financial manager as well as the other managers of the firm. One may suggest that the most important goal for financial management is to "earn the highest possible profit for the firm." Under this criterion, each decision would be evaluated on the basis of its overall contribution to the firm's earnings. While this seems to be a desirable approach, there are some serious drawbacks to profit maximization as the primary goal of the firm.

First, a change in profit may also represent a change in risk. A conservative firm that earned $1.25 per share may be a less desirable investment if its earnings per share increase to $1.50, but the risk inherent in the operation increases even more.

A second possible drawback to the goal of maximizing profit is that it fails to consider the timing of the benefits. For example, if we could choose between the following two alternatives, we might be indifferent if our emphasis were solely on maximizing earnings.

	Earnings per Share		
	Period One	Period Two	Total
Alternative A	$1.50	$2.00	$3.50
Alternative B	2.00	1.50	3.50

Both investments would provide $3.50 in total earnings, but Alternative B is clearly superior because the larger benefits occur earlier. We could reinvest the difference in earnings for Alternative B one period sooner.

Finally, the goal of maximizing profit suffers from the almost impossible task of accurately measuring the key variable in this case: profit. As you will observe throughout the text, there are many different economic and accounting definitions of profit, each open to its own set of interpretations. Furthermore, problems related to inflation and international currency transactions complicate the issue. Constantly improving methods of financial reporting offer some hope in this regard, but many problems remain.

A Valuation Approach

While there is no question that profits are important, the key issue is how to use them in setting a goal for the firm. The ultimate measure of performance is not what the firm earns but how the earnings are *valued* by the investor. In analyzing the firm, the investor will also consider the risk inherent in the firm's operation, the time pattern over which the firm's earnings increase or decrease, the quality and reliability of reported earnings, and many other factors. The financial manager, in turn, must be sensitive to all of these considerations. He or she must question the impact of each decision on the firm's overall valuation. If a decision maintains or increases the firm's overall value, it is acceptable from a financial viewpoint; otherwise, it should be rejected. This principle is demonstrated throughout the text.

Maximizing Shareholder Wealth

The broad goal of the firm can be brought into focus if we say the financial manager should attempt to *maximize the wealth of the firm's shareholders* through achieving the highest possible value for the firm. **Shareholder wealth maximization** is not a simple task because the financial manager cannot directly control the firm's stock price but can only act in a way that is consistent with the desires of the shareholders. Since stock prices are affected by expectations of the future as well as by the current economic environment, much of what affects stock prices is beyond management's direct control. Even firms with good earnings and favorable financial trends do not always perform well in a declining stock market over the short term.

The concern is not so much with daily fluctuations in stock value as with long-term wealth maximization. This can be difficult in light of changing investor expectations. In the 1950s and 1960s, the investor emphasis was on maintaining rapid rates of earnings growth. In the 1970s and 1980s, investors became more conservative, putting a premium on lower risk and, at times, high current dividend payments.

In the early and mid-1990s, investors emphasized lean, efficient, well-capitalized companies able to compete effectively in the global environment. But by the late 1990s, there were hundreds of high-tech Internet companies raising capital through initial public offerings of their common stock. Many of these companies had dreams but little revenue and no earnings, yet their stock sold at extremely high prices. Some in the financial community said that the old valuation models were dead, didn't work, and were out of date; earnings and cash flow didn't matter anymore. Alan Greenspan, then chairman of the Federal Reserve Board, made the now famous remark that the high-priced stock market was suffering from "irrational exuberance." By late 2000, many of these companies turned out to be short-term wonders. A few years later, hundreds were out of business. The same scenario played out with the housing bubble of 2001–2006, which collapsed in 2007. The financial problems that followed carried on into 2012, and while stock prices recovered from their bottom in 2009, valuations stayed depressed and did not hit new all-time highs until April 2015. New highs continued to be set monthly into 2018. This is the result of global economic growth and the optimism that the Tax Cuts and Jobs Act of 2017 was expected to have on companies' earnings.

Management and Stockholder Wealth

Does modern corporate management always follow the goal of maximizing shareholder wealth? Under certain circumstances, management may be more interested in maintaining its own tenure and protecting "private spheres of influence" than in maximizing stockholder wealth. For example, suppose the management of a corporation receives a tender offer to merge the corporation into a second firm; while this offer might be attractive to shareholders, it might be quite unpleasant to present management. Historically, management may have been willing to maintain the status quo rather than to maximize stockholder wealth.

As mentioned earlier, this is now changing. First, in most cases "enlightened management" is aware that the only way to maintain its position over the long run is to be sensitive to shareholder concerns. Poor stock price performance relative to other companies often leads to undesirable takeovers and proxy fights for control. Second, management often has sufficient stock option incentives that will motivate it to achieve market value maximization for its own benefit. Third, powerful institutional investors are making management more responsive to shareholders.

Social Responsibility and Ethical Behavior

Is our goal of shareholder wealth maximization consistent with a concern for social responsibility for the firm? In most instances the answer is yes. By adopting policies that maximize values in the market, the firm can attract capital, provide employment, and offer benefits to its community. This is the basic strength of the private enterprise system.

Nevertheless, certain socially desirable actions such as pollution control, equitable hiring practices, and fair pricing standards may at times be inconsistent with earning the highest possible profit or achieving maximum valuation in the market. For example, pollution control projects frequently offer a negative return. Does this mean firms should not exercise social responsibility in regard to pollution control? The answer is no—but certain cost-increasing activities may have to be mandatory rather than voluntary, at least initially, to ensure that the burden falls equally over all business firms. However, there is evidence that socially responsible behavior can be profitable. For example, 3M estimates that its Pollution Prevention Pays (3P) program has had financial benefits as well as social benefits. This program has been in place for over 34 years and during this time has prevented the release of more than 3.8 billion pounds

Managerial

Given that stock market investors emphasize financial results and the maximization of shareholder value, does it makes sense for a company to be socially responsible? Can companies be socially responsible and oriented toward shareholder wealth at the same time? We think so, and while the results of social responsibility are hard to measure, the results of creating goodwill and high employee morale can often create cost savings and a motivated and highly productive workforce.

3M is a manufacturing company and therefore uses large quantities of raw material and has tons of waste from its production processes. How it deals with these issues says a lot about the company's social responsibility. The company has the following programs in place to deal with sustainability issues: Eco-Efficiency Management, Climate Change & Energy Management, Pollution Prevention, Water Management, and Reducing Waste. For 17 years 3M has been a leading company in the Dow Jones Sustainability Index and in May 2007 was awarded the first annual Clean Air Excellence Gregg Cooke Visionary Program Award by the U.S. Environmental Protection Agency.

The company has focused on the environment and social responsibility since 1960. 3M has pursued a series of five-year plans, and between 2000 and 2010, it either met or exceeded its goals. For example, one goal was to reduce volatile air emissions indexed to net sales by 25 percent, and it achieved a reduction of 58 percent. A goal to reduce waste to net sales by 25 percent was also exceeded. 3M has further reduced worldwide greenhouse gas emissions between 1990 and 2011 by 95 percent.

3M continues to win awards for its social behavior. In 2017 it was on the list of the "World's Most Ethical Companies" for the fourth year in a row. Forbes included 3M on its 2017 list of the "World's Most Reputable Companies" and it was listed in first place among companies that millennials want to work for, edging out Apple, Google, and Amazon. We can only speculate that the reason it is on top is its social reputation for work life excellence and diversity.

While sustainability and environmental issues are important issues for social responsibility, other activities are also important. 3M promotes community involvement and has traditionally given more than 2 percent of its pretax profits to well-defined programs related to the environment, education, arts and culture, and health and human services.

The management of 3M has many sustainability goals and programs in place to measure the progress in meeting those goals. Its goals for 2025 are all indexed to sales. Here is a list of goals:

1. Improve energy efficiency by 30 percent.
2. Reduce global water use by 10 percent.
3. Reduce greenhouse gas emissions by 50 percent below 2002 benchmark.
4. Help customers reduce greenhouse gas emissions by 250 million tons by use of 3M products.
5. Reduce global manufacturing waste by 10 percent.

You can view 3M's goals in detail for 2025 at www.3m.com/3M/en_US/sustainability-us/goals-progress/.

www.3m.com

of pollutants and saved over $1.7 billion. See the nearby box for more about how 3M is a socially responsible citizen.

Unethical and illegal financial practices on Wall Street by corporate financial "dealmakers" have made news headlines from the late 1980s until the present, and insider trading is a good example of both. **Insider trading** occurs when someone uses information that is not available to the public to profit from trading in a company's publicly traded securities. This practice is illegal and is protected against by the Securities and Exchange Commission (SEC). Sometimes the insider is a company manager; other times it is the company's lawyer, its investment banker, or even the printer of the company's financial statements. Anyone who has knowledge before public dissemination of that information stands to benefit from either good news or bad news. Trading on private information serves no beneficial economic or financial purpose to the public. It could be argued that insider trading hurts the average shareholder's interests because it destroys confidence in the securities markets by making the playing field uneven for investors. If participants feel the markets are unfair, it could destroy firms' ability to raise capital or maximize shareholder value. The penalties for insider trading can be severe—there is a long history of insider traders who have gone to prison.

Since 2010, hedge funds have been under attack by the U.S. government. Several funds have been indicted for insider trading. An article in *The Wall Street Journal* stated, "Some legal specialists say authorities appear to be seeking to criminalize typical market behavior, such as hedge funds vying to gain an edge by gathering intelligence on a company from a wide range of sources. The issue is blurry because insider trading isn't defined by statute. The dividing line between criminal and legitimate behavior has evolved in cases stretching back decades, as courts interpreted the antifraud provisions of securities law enacted after the 1929 stock market crash."[3]

Ethics and social responsibility can take many different forms. Ethical behavior for a person or company should be important to everyone because it creates an invaluable reputation. However, once that reputation is lost because of unethical behavior, it is very difficult to get back. Proof of this comes from insider trading cases against hedge funds that proved not to stand up in court, but nevertheless, the hedge funds went out of business because just the whiff of bad behavior forced them to close their doors. Some companies are more visible than others in their pursuit of these ethical goals, and most companies that do a good job in this area are profitable, save money, and are good citizens in the communities where they operate.

The Role of the Financial Markets

You may wonder how a financial manager knows whether he or she is maximizing shareholder value and how ethical (or unethical) behavior may affect the value of the company. This information is provided daily to financial managers through price changes determined in the financial markets. But what are the financial markets? **Financial markets** are the meeting place for people, corporations, and institutions that either need money or have money to lend or invest. In a broad context, the financial markets exist as a vast global network of individuals and financial institutions that may be lenders, borrowers, or owners of public companies worldwide. Participants in the financial markets also include national, state, and local governments that are primarily borrowers of funds for highways, education, welfare, and other public activities; their markets are referred to as **public financial markets**. Corporations such as Coca-Cola, Nike, and Ford, on the other hand, raise funds in the **corporate financial markets**.

---

[3]*Source:* Pulliam, S., Rothfield, M., and Strasburg, J. "The Hedge Funds Raided in Probe," *The Wall Street Journal*, November 22, 2010.

Structure and Functions of the Financial Markets

Financial markets can be broken into many distinct parts. Some divisions such as domestic and international markets, or corporate and government markets, are self-explanatory. Others such as money and capital markets need some explanation. **Money markets** are markets dealing with short-term securities that have a life of one year or less. Securities in these markets include commercial paper sold by corporations to finance their daily operations and certificates of deposit with maturities of less than one year sold by banks. Examples of money market securities are presented more fully in Chapter 7.

Capital markets are generally defined as markets where securities have a life of more than one year. Although capital markets are long-term markets, as opposed to short-term money markets, it is common to break down the capital markets into intermediate markets (1 to 10 years) and long-term markets (greater than 10 years). The capital markets include securities such as common stock, preferred stock, and corporate and government bonds. Capital markets are fully presented in Chapter 14. Now that you have a basic understanding of the makeup of the financial markets, you need to understand how these markets affect corporate managers.

Allocation of Capital

A corporation relies on financial markets to provide funds for short-term operations and for new plant and equipment. A firm may go to the markets and raise financial capital either by borrowing money through a debt offering of corporate bonds or short-term notes, or by selling ownership in the company through an issue of common stock. When a corporation uses financial markets to raise new funds, called an initial public offering, or IPO, the sale of securities is said to be made in the **primary market** by way of a new issue. After the securities are sold to the public (institutions and individuals), they are traded in the **secondary market** between investors. It is in the secondary market that prices are continually changing as investors buy and sell securities based on their expectations of a corporation's prospects. It is also in the secondary market that financial managers are given feedback about their firms' performance.

How does the market allocate capital to the thousands of firms that are continually in need of money? Let us assume that you graduate from college as a finance major and are hired to manage money for a wealthy family like the Rockefellers. You are given $250 million to manage and you can choose to invest the money anywhere in the world. For example, you could buy common stock in Microsoft, the American software company, or in Nestlé, the Swiss food company, or in Cemex, the Mexican cement company; you could choose to lend money to the U.S. or Japanese government by purchasing its bonds; or you could lend money to ExxonMobil or BP. Of course, these are only some of the endless choices you would have.

How do you decide to allocate the $250 million so that you will maximize your return and minimize your risk? Some investors will choose a risk level that meets their objective and maximize return for that given level of risk. By seeking this risk-return objective, you will bid up the prices of securities that seem underpriced and have potential for high returns and you will avoid securities of equal risk that, in your judgment, seem overpriced. Since all market participants play the same risk-return game, the financial markets become the playing field, and price movements become the winning or losing score. Let us look at only the corporate sector of the market and 100 companies of equal risk. Companies with expectations for high return will have higher relative common stock prices than companies with poor expectations. Since the securities' prices in the market reflect the combined judgment of all the players, price movements provide feedback to corporate managers and let them know whether the market thinks they are winning or losing against the competition.

Those companies that perform well and are rewarded by the market with high-priced securities have an easier time raising new funds in the money and capital markets than their competitors. They are also able to raise funds at a lower cost. Go back to that $250 million you are managing. If ExxonMobil wants to borrow money from you at 5 percent and Chevron is also willing to pay 5 percent but is riskier, to which company will you lend money? If you chose ExxonMobil, you are on your way to understanding finance. The competition between the two firms for your funds will eventually cause Chevron to offer higher returns than ExxonMobil, or it will have to go without funds. In this way, the money and capital markets allocate funds to the highest-quality companies at the lowest cost and to the lowest-quality companies at the highest cost. In other words, firms pay a penalty for failing to perform competitively.

Institutional Pressure on Public Companies to Restructure

Sometimes an additional penalty for poor performance is a forced restructuring by institutional investors seeking to maximize a firm's shareholder value. As mentioned earlier, institutional investors have begun to flex their combined power, and their influence with corporate boards of directors has become very visible. Nowhere has this power been more evident than in the area of corporate restructuring. **Restructuring** can result in changes in the capital structure (liabilities and equity on the balance sheet). It can also result in the selling of low-profit-margin divisions with the proceeds of the sale reinvested in better investment opportunities. Sometimes restructuring results in the removal of the current management team or large reductions in the workforce. Restructuring also has included mergers and acquisitions of gigantic proportions unheard of in earlier decades. Rather than seeking risk reduction through diversification, firms are now acquiring greater market shares, brand name products, hidden assets values, or technology—or they are simply looking for size to help them compete in an international arena.

The restructuring and management changes at Hewlett-Packard, McGraw-Hill, and Tribune Corporation during the last decade were a direct result of institutional investors affecting change by influencing the boards of directors to exercise control over all facets of the companies' activities. Without their attempt to maximize the value of their investments, many of the above-mentioned restructuring deals would not have taken place. And without the financial markets placing a value on publicly held companies, the restructuring would have been much more difficult to achieve. Some companies, like Starbucks, restructured because the founder and large stockholder came back and refocused the company after a dramatic drop in the stock price. Others, like American Airlines, were forced to restructure because of bankruptcy.

Internationalization of the Financial Markets

International trade is a growing trend that is likely to continue. Global companies are becoming more common, and international brand names like Sony, Coca-Cola, Nestlé, and Mercedes-Benz are known the world over. McDonald's hamburgers are eaten throughout the world, and McDonald's raises funds on most major international money and capital markets. The growth of the global company has led to the growth of global fund raising as companies search for low-priced sources of funds.

In a recent annual report, Coca-Cola stated that it conducted business in 200 countries and 73 different currencies and borrowed money in yen, euros, and other international currencies.

This discussion demonstrates that the allocation of capital and the search for low-cost sources of financing are now an international game for multinational companies. As an exclamation point, consider all the non-U.S. companies who want to raise money in the United States. More and more foreign companies have listed their shares on the New York Stock Exchange, and hundreds of foreign companies have stock traded in the United States through American Depository Receipts (ADRs).

We live in a world where international events affect economies of all industrial countries and where capital moves from country to country faster than was ever thought possible. Computers interact in a vast international financial network, and markets are more vulnerable to the emotions of investors than they have been in the past. The corporate financial manager has an increasing number of external impacts to consider. Future financial managers will need sophistication to understand international capital flows, computerized electronic funds transfer systems, foreign currency hedging strategies, and many other functions.

Information Technology and Changes in the Capital Markets

Technology has significantly impacted capital markets. In particular, trading costs for securities have been driven down. Firms and exchanges at the front of the technology curve have created tremendous competitive pressures on organizations that initially resisted change. As a result, many stock markets and brokerage firms have merged, often across international borders, in an attempt to remain viable.

In the late 1990s and early 2000s, advances in computer technology stimulated the creation of electronic communications networks (ECNs). These electronic markets had speed and cost advantages over traditional markets and took market share away from the New York Stock Exchange. If you can't beat them, join them, so the New York Stock Exchange merged with Archipelago, the second-largest ECN. The NASDAQ stock market, which was already an electronic market, bought Instinet, the largest ECN, from Reuters and merged their technology platforms.

Additionally, the cost pressures and the need for capital caused the major markets to become for-profit, publicly traded companies. The first to go public was the Chicago Mercantile Exchange, followed by NASDAQ, the NYSE, and the Chicago Board of Trade. Once these exchanges became publicly traded, they were able to use their shares for mergers and acquisitions. In 2007, the New York Stock Exchange merged with EuroNext, a large European exchange, and became a global market. In 2012 the NYSE/EuroNext was bought by ICE, the Intercontinental Exchange. ICE was a young but very successful electronic exchange specializing in derivative products and commodities. NASDAQ merged with the OMX, a Nordic stock exchange. Because the OMX is considered a leader in trading technology, it has over 35 stock exchanges worldwide using its technology. In 2007, the Chicago Board of Trade and the Chicago Mercantile Exchange merged, and so the trend to bigger and more global markets with low-cost structures continues. The future will likely bring an increased emphasis on globalization of markets through technology.

Another area where the Internet has played its role is in the area of retail stock trading. Firms like Charles Schwab, E*TRADE, TD Ameritrade, and other discount brokerage firms allow customers to trade using the Internet and have created a competitive problem for full-service brokers such as Merrill Lynch and Morgan Stanley. These discount firms have forced the full-service retail brokers to offer Internet trading to their customers, even though Internet trading is not as profitable for them as trading through their brokers.

Algorithmic trading that relies on mathematical programs designed to take advantage of price trends, volatility, or technical indicators has gained in popularity. This would not be possible without current computer power. These issues and others will be developed more fully in the capital market section of the text.

Format of the Text

The material in this text is covered under six major headings. We will progress from the development of basic analytical skills in accounting and finance to the utilization of decision-making techniques in working capital management, capital budgeting, long-term financing, and other related areas. A total length of 21 chapters should make the text appropriate for one-semester coverage.

We aim to present a thorough grounding in financial theory in a highly palatable and comprehensive fashion—with careful attention to definitions, symbols, and formulas. The intent is to enable students to develop a thorough understanding of the basic concepts in finance.

Parts

1. Introduction   This section examines the goals and objectives of financial management. The emphasis on decision making, and risk management is stressed, with an update of significant events influencing the study of finance.

2. Financial Analysis and Planning   First, we have the opportunity to review the basic principles of accounting as they relate to finance (financial statements and funds flow are emphasized). Understanding the material in Chapter 2 is a requirement for understanding the topics of working capital management, capital structure, cost of capital, and capital budgeting.

Additional material in this part includes a thorough study of ratio analysis, budget construction techniques, and development of comprehensive pro forma statements. The effect of heavy fixed commitments, in the form of either debt or plant and equipment, is examined in a discussion of leverage.

3. Working Capital Management   The techniques for managing the short-term assets of the firm and the associated liabilities are examined. The material is introduced in the context of risk-return analysis. The financial manager must constantly choose between liquid, low-return assets (perhaps marketable securities) and more profitable, less liquid assets (such as inventory). Sources of short-term financing are also considered.

4. The Capital Budgeting Process   The decision on capital outlays is among the most significant a firm will have to make. In terms of study procedure, we attempt to carefully lock down "time value of money" calculations, then proceed to the valuation of bonds and stocks, emphasizing present value techniques. The valuation chapter develops the traditional dividend valuation model and examines bond price sensitivity in response to discount rates and inflation. An appendix presents the supernormal dividend growth model, or what is sometimes called the "two-stage" dividend model. After careful grounding in valuation practice and theory, we examine the cost of capital and capital structure. The text then moves to the actual capital budgeting decision, making generous use of previously learned material and employing the concept of marginal analysis. The concluding chapter in this part covers risk-return analysis in capital budgeting, with a brief exposure to portfolio theory and a consideration of market value maximization.

5. Long-Term Financing   Here we introduce you to U.S. financial markets as they relate to corporate financial management. We consider the sources and uses of funds in the capital markets—with warrants and convertibles covered, as well as the more conventional methods of financing. The guiding role of the investment banker in the distribution of securities is also analyzed. Furthermore, we encourage you to think of leasing as a form of debt.

6. Expanding the Perspective of Corporate Finance   A chapter on corporate mergers considers external growth strategy and serves as an integrative tool to bring together such topics as profit management, capital budgeting, portfolio considerations, and valuation concepts. A second chapter on international financial management describes the growth of the international financial markets, the rise of multinational business, and the related effects on corporate financial management. The issues discussed in these two chapters highlight corporate diversification and risk reduction.

LIST OF TERMS

financial capital   3
real capital   3
capital structure theory   4
inflation   4
disinflation   4
credit default swaps (CDS)   5
Dodd–Frank Act   5
sole proprietorship   8
partnership   9
articles of partnership   10
limited liability partnership   10
corporation   10
articles of incorporation   10
S corporation   11

limited liability company (LLC)   11
agency theory   12
institutional investors   12
Sarbanes–Oxley Act   13
shareholder wealth maximization   14
insider trading   16
financial markets   17
public financial markets   17
corporate financial markets   17
money markets   18
capital markets   18
primary market   18
secondary market   18
restructuring   19

DISCUSSION QUESTIONS

1. How did the recession of 2007–2009 compare with other recessions since the Great Depression in terms of length? *(LO1-3)*

2. What effect did the recession of 2007–2009 have on government regulation? *(LO1-3)*

3. What advantages does a sole proprietorship offer? What is a major drawback of this type of organization? *(LO1-2)*

4. What form of partnership allows some of the investors to limit their liability? Explain briefly. *(LO1-2)*

5. In a corporation, what group has the ultimate responsibility for protecting and managing the stockholders' interests? *(LO1-2)*

6. What document is necessary to form a corporation? *(LO1-2)*

7. What issue does agency theory examine? Why is it important in a public corporation rather than in a private corporation? *(LO1-4)*

8. Why are institutional investors important in today's business world? *(LO1-4)*

9. Why is profit maximization, by itself, an inappropriate goal? What is meant by the goal of maximization of shareholder wealth? *(LO1-4)*

10. When does insider trading occur? What government agency is responsible for protecting against the unethical practice of insider trading? *(LO1-1)*

11. In terms of the life of the securities offered, what is the difference between money and capital markets? *(LO1-5)*

12. What is the difference between a primary and a secondary market? *(LO1-5)*

13. Assume you are looking at many companies with equal risk. Which ones will have the highest stock prices? *(LO1-3)*

14. What changes can take place under restructuring? In recent times, what group of investors has often forced restructuring to take place? *(LO1-5)*

15. How did the Sarbanes–Oxley Act impact corporations' financial reports? *(LO1-6)*

16. Name the departments, offices, or agencies that were created by the Dodd–Frank legislation. *(LO1-6)*

WEB EXERCISE

1. Ralph Larsen, former chairman and CEO of Johnson & Johnson, was quoted in this chapter concerning the use of the Internet. Johnson & Johnson has been one of America's premier companies for decades and has exhibited a high level of social responsibility around the world. Go to the Johnson & Johnson website at www.jnj.com.

2. Click on "Our Social Impact." Scroll down and click on "Our Credo." Now scroll to the left of the page and click on the "Our Credo" link. Read the first two paragraphs and write a brief summary of the credo. Return to the home page and click on "Investors." Then scroll down and click on "SEC Filings." To view the most recent annual report, go to the heading "View," choose "Annual," and then click "Update" to the right. The first report will be the most recent annual report. Click on "Annual Report."

3. Scroll down the annual report until you see "Consolidated Statement of Earnings" for the last few years.

4. Compute the percentage change between the last two years for the following (numbers are in millions of dollars):

   a. Sales to customers

   b. Net earnings

   c. Earnings per share

5. Generally speaking, is Johnson & Johnson growing by more or less than 10 percent per year?

Note: Occasionally a topic we have listed may have been deleted, updated, or moved into a different location on a website. If you click on the site map or site index, you will be introduced to a table of contents that should aid you in finding the topic you are looking for.

Financial Analysis and Planning

>>> RELATED WEB SITES

www.goldmansachs.com
www.ml.com
www.morganstanley.com
www.ratefinancials.com

www.ibm.com
www.radioshack.com
www.sony.com
www.honda.com

www.fujitsu.com
www.hitachi.com
www.mitsubishi.com
finance.yahoo.com

Review of Accounting

LEARNING OBJECTIVES

LO 2-1 The income statement measures profitability.

LO 2-2 The price-earnings ratio indicates the relative valuation of earnings.

LO 2-3 The balance sheet shows assets and the financing of those assets with debt and equity.

LO 2-4 The statement of cash flows indicates changes in the cash position of the firm.

LO 2-5 Depreciation provides a tax reduction benefit that increases cash flow.

McDonald's does not show up on the "best restaurant" lists in many cities, but if you are looking for an inexpensive meal in a hurry, there is a good chance that you might pick Combo #1 at one of McDonald's 35,000 locations. No restaurant chain has been more successful. The company serves almost 70 million meals around the world each day.

McDonald's is sometimes portrayed as a villain by social activists. However, if you are an investor, you probably see the company in a kind light. McDonald's has raised its dividend from $0.40 per share in 2003 to $4.04 in 2018. This long-term growth has been powered by a dependable earnings stream of approximately $5 billion per year. Its recent return on assets is almost 16 percent. Many businesses would like to copy the McDonald's formula for success. Chipotle Mexican Grill is one firm that thought it had copied the formula pretty well. That should not be a surprise, since Chipotle was a McDonald's subsidiary until 2006. Chipotle reported net income of over $475 million in 2015, a return on assets of over 18 percent. But food safety scares in 2016 drove Chipotle's stock down by more than 50 percent. Net income declined so much that Chipotle's return on assets fell to less than 1 percent.

Net income is just one piece of accounting data that financial managers, investors, and bankers track. Without accounting data, these financial professionals would be flying blind. The same can be said for the data of IBM, Procter & Gamble, Microsoft, or any other major U.S. corporation.

The language of finance flows logically from accounting. To ensure that you are adequately prepared to study significant financial concepts, we must lock in the preparatory material from the accounting area. Much of the early frustration suffered by students who have difficulty with finance can be overcome if such concepts as retained earnings, shareholders' equity, depreciation, and historical/replacement cost accounting are brought into focus.

In this chapter, we examine the three basic types of financial statements—the income statement, the balance sheet, and the statement of cash flows—with particular attention paid to the interrelationships among these three measurement devices. As special preparation for finance students, we briefly examine income tax considerations affecting financial decisions.

Income Statement

The **income statement** is the major device for measuring the profitability of a firm over a period of time. An example of the income statement for the Kramer Corporation is presented in Table 2-1.

Table 2-1   Kramer Corporation income statement

KRAMER CORPORATION
Income Statement
For the Year Ended December 31, 2018

1. Sales	$2,000,000
2. Cost of goods sold	1,500,000
3. Gross profit	$ 500,000
4. Selling and administrative expense	279,500
5. Depreciation expense	50,000
6. Operating profit (EBIT)*	$ 170,500
7. Interest expense	20,000
8. Earnings before taxes (EBT)	$ 150,500
9. Taxes	40,000
10. Earnings after taxes (EAT)	$ 110,500
11. Preferred stock dividends	10,500
12. Earnings available to common stockholders	$ 100,000
13. Common shares outstanding	100,000
14. Earnings per share	$ 1.00

*Earnings before interest and taxes.

First, note that the income statement covers a defined period of time, whether it is one month, three months, or a year. The statement is presented in a stair-step, or progressive, fashion so we can examine the profit or loss after each type of expense item is deducted.

We start with sales and deduct cost of goods sold to arrive at gross profit. The $500,000 thus represents the difference between the cost of purchased or manu-factured goods and the sales price. We then subtract selling and administrative expense and depreciation from gross profit to determine our profit (or loss) purely from operations of $170,500. It is possible for a company to enjoy a high gross profit margin (25–50 percent) but a relatively low operating profit because of heavy expenses incurred in marketing the product and managing the company.[1]

Having obtained operating profit (essentially a measure of how efficient manage-ment is in generating revenues and controlling expenses), we now adjust for revenues and expenses not related to operational matters. In this case, we pay $20,000 in interest and arrive at earnings before taxes of $150,500. The tax payments are $40,000, leaving aftertax income of $110,500.

---

[1]Depreciation was not treated as part of goods sold in this instance, but rather as a separate expense. All or part of depreciation may be treated as part of cost of goods sold, depending on the circumstances.

Return to Capital

Before proceeding further, we should note that there are three primary sources of capital—the bondholders, who received $20,000 in interest (item 7); the preferred stockholders, who receive $10,500 in dividends (item 11); and the common stockholders. After the $10,500 dividend has been paid to the preferred stockholders, there will be $100,000 in earnings available to the common stockholders (item 12). In computing **earnings per share**, we must interpret this in terms of the number of shares outstanding. As indicated in item 13, there are 100,000 shares of common stock outstanding, so the $100,000 of earnings available to the common stockholders may be translated into earnings per share of $1. Common stockholders are sensitive to the number of shares outstanding—the more shares, the lower the earnings per share. Before any new shares are issued, the financial manager must be sure the cash received from the sale will eventually generate sufficient earnings to avoid reducing earnings per share.

The $100,000 of profit ($1 earnings per share) may be paid out to the common stockholders in the form of dividends or retained in the company for subsequent reinvestment. The reinvested funds theoretically belong to the common stockholders, who hope they will provide future earnings and dividends. In the case of the Kramer Corporation, we assume $50,000 in dividends will be paid out to the common stockholders, with the balance retained in the corporation for their benefit. A short supplement to the income statement, a statement of retained earnings (Table 2-2), usually indicates the disposition of earnings.[2]

Table 2-2   Kramer Corporation statement of retained earnings

STATEMENT OF RETAINED EARNINGS For the Year Ended December 31, 2018	
Retained earnings, balance, January 1, 2018	$250,000
Add: Earnings available to common stockholders, 2018	100,000
Deduct: Cash dividends declared in 2018	50,000
Retained earnings, balance, December 31, 2018	$300,000

We see that a net value of $50,000 has been added to previously accumulated earnings of $250,000 to arrive at $300,000.

Price-Earnings Ratio Applied to Earnings per Share

A concept utilized throughout the text is the **price-earnings ratio**. This refers to the multiplier applied to earnings per share to determine current value of the common stock. In the case of the Kramer Corporation, earnings per share were $1. If the firm had a price-earnings ratio of 20, the market value of each share would be $20 ($1 × 20). The price-earnings ratio (or P/E ratio, as it is commonly called) is influenced by the earnings and the sales growth of the firm, the risk (or volatility in performance), the debt-equity structure of the firm, the dividend payment policy, the quality of

---

[2]The statement may also indicate any adjustments to previously reported income as well as any restrictions on cash dividends.

management, and a number of other factors. Since companies have various levels of earnings per share, price-earnings ratios allow us to compare the relative market value of many companies based on $1 of earnings per share.

The P/E ratio indicates expectations about the future of a company. Firms expected to provide returns greater than those for the market in general with equal or less risk often have P/E ratios higher than the market P/E ratio. Expectations of returns and P/E ratios do change over time, as Table 2-3 illustrates. Looking at the bottom line for the Standard & Poor's 500 Index, it is clear that the P/E of the overall market has varied considerably over the last 25 years. Notice, however, that individual companies' P/E ratios are even more volatile.

Price-earnings ratios can be confusing. When a firm's earnings are dropping rapidly or perhaps even approaching zero, its stock price, though also declining, may not match the magnitude of the falloff in earnings. This process can give the appearance of an increasing P/E ratio under adversity. This happens from time to time in cyclical industries. For example, in 2001 Cisco Systems (as shown in Table 2-3) was trading at a P/E ratio of 58 because of cyclically low earnings. You can find other examples of this phenomenon with Southwest Air in 2010 and Bank of America in 2015.

Table 2-3   Price-earnings ratios for selected U.S. companies

	January 3, 1994	January 2, 1996	January 2, 2001	January 3, 2006	January 4, 2010	January 2, 2013	January 2, 2015	January 2, 2018
Bank of America	*dd	16	10	11	35	10	45	17
Cisco Systems	41	28	58	19	23	8	19	20
Ford Motor Co.	14	9	5	7	*dd	8	10	12
Intel Corp.	12	19	19	18	17	11	16	16
Johnson & Johnson	17	27	31	18	14	13	16	24
McDonald's Corp.	19	21	23	17	16	15	19	25
Southwest Air	36	17	28	38	62	10	26	25
Textron Inc.	14	27	10	17	49	11	22	25
Walmart Stores	26	27	38	18	15	14	18	26
S&P 500 Index	23	25	23	17	18	14	19	26

*dd means the company is operating at a deficit and has no P/E ratio at the time because there are no positive earnings per share.

Note: January price-earnings ratios are based on the previous 12 months' earnings per share and could change in later editions after annual earnings are announced.

Limitations of the Income Statement

The economist defines income as the change in real worth that occurs between the beginning and the end of a specified time period. To the economist, an increase in the value of a firm's land as a result of a new shopping mall being built on adjacent property is an increase in the real worth of the firm and therefore represents income. Similarly, the elimination of a competitor might also increase the firm's real worth and therefore result in income in an economic sense. The accountant does not ordinarily employ such broad definitions. Accounting values are established primarily by actual transactions, and income that is gained or lost during a given period is a function of verifiable transactions. While the potential sales price of a firm's property may go from $100,000 to $200,000 as a result of new developments in the area, stockholders may perceive only a much smaller gain or loss from actual day-to-day operations.

Also, as will be pointed out in Chapter 3, "Financial Analysis," there is some flexibility in the reporting of transactions, so similar events may result in differing measurements of income at the end of a time period. The intent of this section is not to criticize the accounting profession, for it is among the best organized, trained, and paid professions, but to alert you to imperfections already recognized within the profession.

Balance Sheet

The **balance sheet** indicates what the firm owns and how these assets are financed in the form of liabilities or ownership interest. While the income statement purports to show the profitability of the firm, the balance sheet delineates the firm's holdings and obligations. Together, these statements are intended to answer two questions: How much did the firm make or lose, and what is a measure of its worth? A balance sheet for the Kramer Corporation is presented in Table 2-4.

Note that the balance sheet is a picture of the firm at a point in time—in this case, December 31, 2018. It does not purport to represent the result of transactions for a specific month, quarter, or year, but rather is a cumulative chronicle of all transactions that have affected the corporation since its inception. In contrast, the income statement measures results only over a short, quantifiable period. Generally, balance sheet items are stated on an original cost basis rather than at current market value.

Interpretation of Balance Sheet Items

Asset accounts are listed in order of **liquidity** (convertibility to cash). The first category of *current assets* covers items that may be converted to cash within one year (or within the normal operating cycle of the firm). A few items are worthy of mention. *Marketable securities* are temporary investments of excess cash. The value shown in the account is the fair market value. *Accounts receivable* include an allowance for bad debts (based on historical evidence) to determine their anticipated collection value. *Inventory* may be in the form of raw material, goods in process, or finished goods, while *prepaid expenses* represent future expense items that have already been paid, such as insurance premiums or rent.

Investments, unlike marketable securities, represent a longer-term commitment of funds (at least one year). They may include stocks, bonds, or investments in other corporations. Frequently, the account will contain stock in companies that the firm is acquiring.

Plant and equipment is carried at original cost minus accumulated depreciation. Accumulated depreciation is not to be confused with the depreciation expense item indicated in the income statement in Table 2-1. Accumulated depreciation is the sum of all past and present depreciation charges on currently owned assets, while depreciation expense is the current year's charge. If we subtract accumulated depreciation from the original value, the balance ($500,000) tells us how much of the original cost has not been expensed in the form of depreciation.

Table 2-4   Kramer Corporation balance sheet

KRAMER CORPORATION Statement of Financial Position (Balance Sheet) December 31, 2018		
Assets		
Current assets:		
Cash		$ 40,000
Marketable securities		10,000
Accounts receivable	$ 220,000	
Less: Allowance for bad debts	20,000	200,000
Inventory		180,000
Prepaid expenses		20,000
Total current assets		$ 450,000
Other assets:		
Investments		50,000
Fixed assets:		
Plant and equipment, original cost	$1,100,000	
Less: Accumulated depreciation	600,000	
Net plant and equipment		500,000
Total assets		$1,000,000
Liabilities and Stockholders' Equity		
Current liabilities:		
Accounts payable		$ 80,000
Notes payable		100,000
Accrued expenses		30,000
Total current liabilities		$ 210,000
Long-term liabilities:		
Bonds payable		90,000
Total liabilities		$ 300,000
Stockholders' equity:		
Preferred stock, $100 par value, 500 shares		$ 50,000
Common stock, $1 par value, 100,000 shares		100,000
Capital paid in excess of par (common stock)		250,000
Retained earnings		300,000
Total stockholders' equity		$ 700,000
Total liabilities and stockholders' equity		$1,000,000

Total assets are financed through either liabilities or stockholders' equity. Liabilities represent financial obligations of the firm and move from current liabilities (due within one year) to longer-term obligations, such as bonds payable in 2025.

Among the short-term obligations, *accounts payable* represent amounts owed on open account to suppliers, while *notes payable* are generally short-term signed obligations to the banker or other creditors. An *accrued expense* is generated when a service has been provided or an obligation incurred and payment has not yet taken place. The firm may owe workers additional wages for services provided or the government taxes on earned income.

In the balance sheet, we see the $1,000,000 in total assets of the Kramer Corporation was financed by $300,000 in debt and $700,000 in the form of stockholders' equity. Stockholders' equity represents the total contribution and ownership interest of preferred and common stockholders.

The *preferred stock* investment position is $50,000, based on 500 shares at $100 par. In the case of *common stock,* 100,000 shares have been issued at a total par value of $100,000, plus an extra $250,000 in *capital paid in excess of par* for a sum of $350,000. We can assume that the 100,000 shares were originally sold at $3.50 each, as shown below.

100,000 shares	$1.00	Par value	$100,000
	2.50	Capital paid in excess of par	250,000
	$3.50	Price per share	$350,000

Finally, there is $300,000 in *retained earnings* in Table 2-4. This value, previously determined in the statement of retained earnings (Table 2-2), represents the firm's cumulative earnings since inception minus dividends and any other adjustments.

Concept of Net Worth

Stockholders' equity minus the preferred stock component represents the **net worth,** or **book value,** of the firm. There is some logic to the approach. If you take everything that the firm owns and subtract the debt and preferred stock obligation,[3] the remainder belongs to the common stockholder and represents net worth. In the case of the Kramer Corporation, using data from Table 2-4, we show the following:

Total assets	$1,000,000
Total liabilities	− 300,000
Stockholders' equity	$ 700,000
Preferred stock obligation	− 50,000
Net worth assigned to common	$ 650,000
Common shares outstanding	100,000
Net worth, or book value, per share	$ 6.50

The original cost per share was $3.50; the net worth, or book value, per share is $6.50; and the market value (based on an assumed P/E ratio of 15 and earnings per share of $1) is $15. This last value is of primary concern to the financial manager, security analyst, and stockholders.

Limitations of the Balance Sheet

Lest we attribute too much significance to the balance sheet, we need to examine some of the underlying concepts supporting its construction. Most of the values on the balance sheet are stated on a historical or original cost basis. This may be particularly

---

[3]An additional discussion of preferred stock is presented in Chapter 17, "Common and Preferred Stock Financing." Preferred stock represents neither a debt claim nor an ownership interest in the firm. It is a hybrid, or intermediate, type of security.

troublesome in the case of plant and equipment and inventory, which may now be worth two or three times the original cost or—from a negative viewpoint—may require many times the original cost for replacement. While the U.S. accounting community is moving toward International Financial Reporting Standards (IFRS), which tend to recognize current value, the pace has been slow.

The accounting profession has been grappling with this problem for decades, and the discussion becomes particularly intense each time inflation rears its ugly head. In October 1979, the Financial Accounting Standards Board (FASB) issued a ruling that required large companies to disclose inflation-adjusted accounting data in their annual reports. This information was to be disclosed in addition to the traditional historical cost data and could show up in footnotes or in a separate, full-fledged financial section with detailed explanations. However, with the decline in the inflation rate to historically low levels, the standard is no longer in force, and inflation-adjusted data are no longer required in any form. If a company wishes to adjust its balance sheet or income statement data for inflation, it is purely a voluntary act.

Table 2-5 looks at large disparities between market value (stock price) per share and historical book value per share for a number of publicly traded companies in January 2018. Besides asset valuation, a number of other factors may explain the wide differences between per share values, such as industry outlook, growth prospects, quality of management, and risk-return expectations. Generally, companies with high growth prospects sell at higher price-to-book values than companies with low growth prospects. Stock repurchase programs are an area sometimes overlooked by analysts. This phenomenon shows up in the UPS, IBM, Kellogg, PepsiCo and Apple examples. These companies have repurchased millions of their own shares,

Table 2-5 Comparison of market value to book value per share in January 2018

Corporation	Market Price per Share	Book Value per Share	Ratio of Market Price to Book Value
UPS*	123.67	1.75	70.67
Verizon	53.53	6.58	8.14
IBM*	154.25	21.20	7.28
Kellogg*	67.97	5.59	12.16
PepsiCo*	118.06	9.45	12.49
Apple*	172.26	26.15	6.59
Adobe	177.70	17.19	10.34
Microsoft	85.95	11.61	7.40
Oracle	46.63	13.53	3.45
Google	1,065.00	226.11	4.71
eBay	38.06	10.76	3.54
Southern Co.	47.17	24.00	1.97
Kohl's	56.35	29.93	1.88
Comstock Resources	9.01	−21.29	N/A

*Companies with large stock repurchases over time.

thus reducing their equity (book value) and raising the price-to-book-value ratio. Also notice that Comstock Resources has a negative book value. Comstock is a Texas-based oil and gas company. During the last half of 2014, the price of crude oil fell by 50 percent, and the price of Comstock fell by 98 percent over two years. Write-downs of company assets created a negative book value.

Statement of Cash Flows

The accounting profession designates the statement of cash flows as the third required financial statement, along with the balance sheet and income statement. Referred to as *Statement of Financial Accounting Standards (SFAS) No. 95,* it replaces the old statement of changes in financial position.

The purpose of the **statement of cash flows** is to emphasize the critical nature of cash flow to the operations of the firm. According to accountants, cash flow represents cash or cash equivalent items that can easily be converted into cash within 90 days (such as a money market fund).

The income statement and balance sheet that we have studied thus far are normally based on the accrual method of accounting, in which revenues and expenses are recognized as they occur, rather than when cash actually changes hands. For example, a $100,000 credit sale may be made in December 2018 and shown as revenue for that year—despite the fact the cash payment will not be received until March 2019. When the actual payment is finally received under accrual accounting, no revenue is recognized (it has already been accounted for). The primary advantage of accrual accounting is that it allows us to match revenues and expenses in the period in which they occur in order to appropriately measure profit; but a disadvantage is that adequate attention is not directed to the actual cash flow position of the firm.

Say a firm made a $1 million profit on a transaction but will not receive the actual cash payment for two years. Or perhaps the $1 million profit is in cash but the firm increased its asset purchases by $3 million (a new building). If you merely read the income statement, you might assume the firm is in a strong $1 million cash position; but if you go beyond the income statement to cash flow considerations, you would observe the firm is $2 million short of funds for the period.

As a last example, a firm might show a $100,000 loss on the income statement, but if there were a depreciation expense write-off of $150,000, the firm would actually have $50,000 in cash. Since depreciation is a noncash deduction, the $150,000 deduction in the income statement for depreciation can be added back to net income to determine cash flow.

The statement of cash flows addresses these issues by translating income statement and balance sheet data into cash flow information. A corporation that has $1 million in cash flow can determine whether it can afford to pay a cash dividend to stockholders, buy new equipment, or undertake new projects.

Developing an Actual Statement

We shall use the information previously provided for the Kramer Corporation in this chapter to illustrate how the statement of cash flows is developed.

But first, let's identify the three primary sections of the statement of cash flows:

1. Cash flows from operating activities.
2. Cash flows from investing activities.
3. Cash flows from financing activities.

After each of these sections is completed, the results are added together to compute the net increase or decrease in cash flow for the corporation. An example of the process is shown in Figure 2-1. Let's begin with cash flows from operating activities.

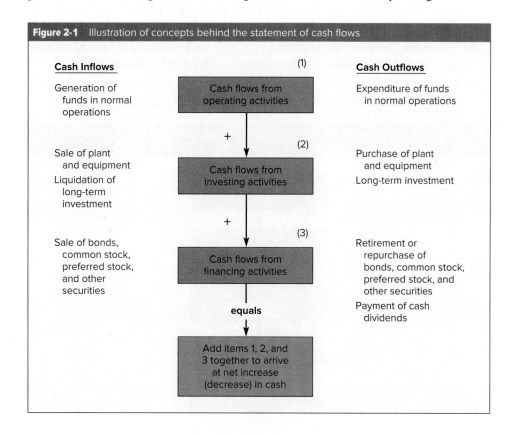

Figure 2-1   Illustration of concepts behind the statement of cash flows

Determining Cash Flows from Operating Activities

Basically, we are going to translate *income from operations* from an accrual to a cash basis. According to *SFAS No. 95,* there are two ways to accomplish this objective. First, the firm may use a *direct method,* in which every item on the income statement is adjusted from accrual accounting to cash accounting. This is a tedious process, in which all sales must be adjusted to cash sales, all purchases must be adjusted to cash purchases, and so on. A more popular method is the *indirect method,* in which net income represents the starting point and then adjustments are made to convert net income to cash flows from operations.[4] This is the method we will use. Regardless of whether the direct or indirect method is used, the same final answer will be derived.

---

[4]The indirect method is similar to procedures used to construct the old sources and uses of funds statement.

We follow these procedures in computing **cash flows from operating activities** using the indirect method.[5] These steps are illustrated in Figure 2-2 and described here:

- Start with net income.
- Recognize that depreciation is a noncash deduction in computing net income and should be added back to net income to increase the cash balance.
- Recognize that increases in current assets are a use of funds and *reduce* the cash balance (indirectly)—as an example, the firm spends more funds on inventory.
- Recognize that decreases in current assets are a source of funds and *increase* the cash balance (indirectly)—that is, the firm reduces funds tied up in inventory.
- Recognize that increases in current liabilities are a source of funds and increase the cash balance (indirectly)—the firm gets more funds from creditors.
- Recognize that decreases in current liabilities are a use of funds and *decrease* the cash balance (indirectly)—that is, the firm pays off creditors.

Figure 2-2   Steps in computing net cash flows from operating activities using the indirect method

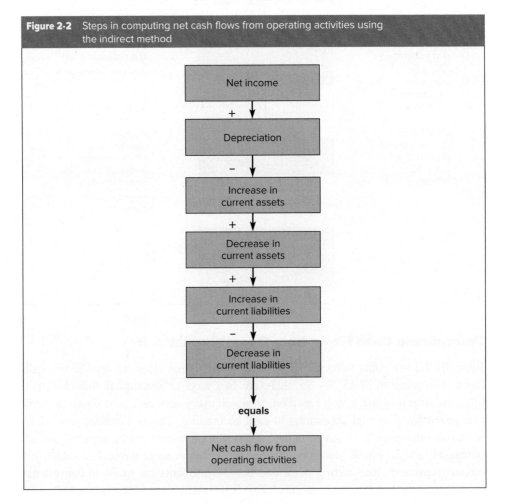

---

[5]In addition to the items mentioned, we may need to recognize the gains or losses on the sale of operating and nonoperating assets. We exclude these for ease of analysis.

We will follow these procedures for the Kramer Corporation, drawing primarily on material from Table 2-1 (the previously presented income statement) and from Table 2-6 (which shows balance sheet data for the most recent two years).

The analysis is presented in Table 2-7. We begin with net income (earnings after taxes) of $110,500 and add back depreciation of $50,000. We then show that increases in current assets (accounts receivable and inventory) reduce funds and decreases in current assets (prepaid expenses) increase funds. Also, we show increases in current liabilities (accounts payable) as an addition to funds and decreases in current liabilities (accrued expenses) as a reduction of funds.

Table 2-6 Kramer Corporation comparative balance sheets

KRAMER CORPORATION
Comparative Balance Sheets

	Year-End 2017		Year-End 2018	
Assets				
Current assets:				
Cash		$ 30,000		$ 40,000
Marketable securities		10,000		10,000
Accounts receivable (net)		170,000		200,000
Inventory		160,000		180,000
Prepaid expenses		30,000		20,000
Total current assets		$400,000		$ 450,000
Investments (long-term)		20,000		50,000
Plant and equipment	$1,000,000		$1,100,000	
Less: Accumulated depreciation	550,000		600,000	
Net plant and equipment		450,000		500,000
Total assets		$870,000		$1,000,000
Liabilities and Stockholders' Equity				
Current liabilities:				
Accounts payable		$ 45,000		$ 80,000
Notes payable		100,000		100,000
Accrued expenses		35,000		30,000
Total current liabilities		$180,000		$ 210,000
Long-term liabilities:				
Bonds, payable 2025		40,000		90,000
Total liabilities		$220,000		$ 300,000
Stockholders' equity:				
Preferred stock, $100 par value		$ 50,000		$ 50,000
Common stock, $1 par value		100,000		100,000
Capital paid in excess of par		250,000		250,000
Retained earnings		250,000		300,000
Total stockholders' equity		$650,000		$ 700,000
Total liabilities and stockholders' equity		$870,000		$1,000,000

Table 2-7 Kramer Corporation cash flows from operating activities

Net income (earnings after taxes) (Table 2-1)...		$110,500
Adjustments to determine cash flow from operating activities:		
Add back depreciation (Table 2-1)...	$50,000	
Increase in accounts receivable (Table 2-6)...	(30,000)	
Increase in inventory (Table 2-6)	(20,000)	
Decrease in prepaid expenses (Table 2-6)..	10,000	
Increase in accounts payable (Table 2-6)...	35,000	
Decrease in accrued expenses (Table 2-6)	(5,000)	
Total adjustments		40,000
Net cash flows from operating activities...		$150,500

We see in Table 2-7 that the firm generated $150,500 in cash flows from operating activities. Of some significance is that this figure is $40,000 larger than the net income figure shown on the first line of the table ($110,500). A firm with little depreciation and a massive buildup of inventory might show lower cash flow than reported net income. Once cash flows from operating activities are determined, management has a better feel for what can be allocated to investing or financing needs (such as paying cash dividends).

Determining Cash Flows from Investing Activities

Cash flows from investing activities represent the second section in the statement of cash flows. The section relates to long-term investment activities in other issuers' securities or, more importantly, in plant and equipment. Increasing investments represent a *use* of funds, and decreasing investments represent a *source* of funds.

Examining Table 2-6 for the Kramer Corporation, we show the information in Table 2-8.

Table 2-8 Kramer Corporation cash flows from investing activities

Increase in investments (long-term securities) (Table 2-6)..	($30,000)
Increase in plant and equipment (Table 2-6)...	(100,000)
Net cash flows from investing activities...	($130,000)

Determining Cash Flows from Financing Activities

In the third section of the statement of cash flows, **cash flows from financing activities**, we show the effects of financing activities on the corporation in Table 2-9. Financing activities apply to the sale or retirement of bonds, common stock, preferred stock, and other corporate securities. Also, the payment of cash dividends is considered a financing activity. The sale of the firm's securities represents a *source* of funds, and the retirement or repurchase of such securities represents a *use* of funds. The payment of dividends also represents a *use* of funds.

Table 2-9   Kramer Corporation cash flows from financing activities

Increase in bonds payable (Table 2-6)..	$ 50,000
Preferred stock dividends paid (Table 2-1)	(10,500)
Common stock dividends paid (Table 2-2)..	(50,000)
Net cash flows from financing activities	($10,500)

In Table 2-9, the financing activities of the Kramer Corporation are shown using data from Tables 2-1, 2-2, and 2-6.

Combining the Three Sections of the Statement

We now combine the three sections of the statement of cash flows to arrive at the one overall statement that the corporation provides to security analysts and stockholders. The information is shown in Table 2-10.

Table 2-10   Kramer Corporation statement of cash flows

KRAMER CORPORATION
Statement of Cash Flows
For the Year Ended December 31, 2018

Cash flows from operating activities:		
Net income (earnings after taxes)...		$110,500
Adjustments to determine cash flow from operating activities:		
Add back depreciation..	$ 50,000	
Increase in accounts receivable	(30,000)	
Increase in inventory..	(20,000)	
Decrease in prepaid expenses	10,000	
Increase in accounts payable..	35,000	
Decrease in accrued expenses	(5,000)	
Total adjustments		40,000
Net cash flows from operating activities................................		$150,500
Cash flows from investing activities:		
Increase in investments (long-term securities).............................	$(30,000)	
Increase in plant and equipment	(100,000)	
Net cash flows from investing activities..		(130,000)
Cash flows from financing activities:		
Increase in bonds payable	$ 50,000	
Preferred stock dividends paid	(10,500)	
Common stock dividends paid...	(50,000)	
Net cash flows from financing activities		(10,500)
Net increase (decrease) in cash flows		$ 10,000

Accounting systems are products of the economic climates in which they function. In the past, each major country had its own unique financial statement reporting standards that had grown out of the needs and desires of the investing public in that country. As economies and capital markets have become global, market participants have expressed a desire for a uniform reporting standard. This has culminated in the creation of International Financial Reporting Standards (IFRS) by the International Accounting Standards Board (IASB). These standards were first developed in Europe and have been adopted by many other countries, with the exception of the United States. In the United States, the Financial Accounting Standards Board (FASB) has developed its own set of reporting standards known as generally accepted accounting principles, or U.S. GAAP. Many international companies and investors have expressed the desire to have one global standard to ease the preparation and interpretability of financial statements across borders. A multiyear project was begun in 2004 between the IASB and FASB to work toward convergence of the different frameworks for financial reporting. While many standards have been aligned, significant differences remain between the IFRS and U.S. GAAP standards. A summary of these differences follows.

At the macro level, the two accounting systems contain similar principles and objectives. However, a key difference is that for many years U.S. GAAP was a rules-based accounting system, meaning that compliance with individual rules concerning preparation and representation were valued above satisfying an overall accounting principle. This changed with the passing of Sarbanes–Oxley after numerous accounting scandals in the United States. U.S. preparers of financial statements must now focus on compliance with the broad accounting principles instead of the specific rules governing presentation. IFRS has always been a principles-based accounting system.

On the balance sheet and income statement, the valuation of inventories under IFRS requires that product costs should correspond to the order in which they are placed into inventory. Under IFRS, specific identification is preferable, but when not practical, FIFO (first-in-first-out inventory cost method) should

be used. LIFO (last-in-first-out inventory cost method) is explicitly forbidden under IFRS. Under U.S. GAAP, a firm is not mandated to match product costs with inventory purchasing flows and may choose from FIFO, LIFO, or specific identification methods. If LIFO is used, the LIFO reserve must be reported in the footnotes so that an analyst can reconcile between a firm using LIFO and another using FIFO. These differences can have an effect on many commonly used financial ratios. For instance, if we compare a company that uses LIFO to one that uses FIFO, the company applying LIFO will have a lower profit margin and current ratio and a higher degree of financial leverage and inventory turnover.

Under both U.S. GAAP and IFRS, inventories can be revalued if the current market value falls below the cost of the products (this is referred to as the "lower of cost or net realizable value" rule). Under IFRS, inventory write-downs can be reversed if the value of the inventory rises. Inventory write-down reversals are explicitly forbidden under U.S. GAAP.

Also, property, plant, and equipment (PP&E) are reported at cost less accumulated depreciation on the balance sheet under both IFRS and U.S. GAAP. However, under IFRS, PP&E can be revalued (similar to the treatment of inventories). If the valuation is downward, the loss is reported in net income for the period unless the downward revaluation offsets a previous upward revaluation. Upward revaluations are reported in equity unless the revaluation is reversing a previous downward revaluation. PP&E upward revaluations are not allowed under U.S. GAAP. Similar treatment can also be applied to intangible assets such as patents and trademarks. An analyst should remove the upward revaluations of both inventories and long-term assets for companies reporting under IFRS so they are comparable to companies reporting under U.S. GAAP. Failure to do so may distort asset-based activity ratios such as return on assets and asset turnover.

On the income statement, IFRS requires that the depreciation method applied must actually reflect the pattern by which the long-term asset is consumed or depleted. Under IFRS, cost allocation methods for long-term assets must be reviewed annually to ensure that they reflect the true depreciation. The firm must change the depreciation method if the current method does not reflect the true cost allocation. U.S. GAAP does not have such a requirement, and the depreciation methods are at the discretion of company management. While this difference may not cause the need for an adjustment (other than an adjustment made to reconcile different depreciation methods), an analyst may find that the company reporting under IFRS uses a method that more accurately reflects the true cost allocation.

The structure of the statement of cash flows is consistent between the two accounting systems in that operating, investing, and financing cash flows are segregated. The key difference is the classification of different cash flows between the two systems. In general, U.S. GAAP is more stringent as to how the activities should be classified. For example, under U.S. GAAP, interest received, dividends received, and interest paid must be categorized as operating activities, but under IFRS, interest received and dividends received can be classified under the operating or investing sections, while interest paid can be classified under either the operating or financing section. Under IFRS, dividends paid can also be categorized as either operating or financing cash flows. Under U.S. GAAP, dividends paid must be classified under the financing section of the cash flow statement. When comparing the cash flow statements of one company reporting under U.S. GAAP and another reporting under IFRS, an analyst should make adjustments to the statements to reconcile the treatment of the different cash flow items. Not doing so would affect all of the cash flow–based ratios such as operating cash flow to revenue or cash flow return on assets.

We see in Table 2-10 that the firm created excess funds from operating activities that were utilized heavily in investing activities and somewhat in financing activities. As a result, there is a $10,000 increase in the cash balance, and this can also be reconciled with the increase in the cash balance of $10,000 from $30,000 to $40,000, as previously indicated in Table 2-6.

One might also do further analysis on how the buildups in various accounts were financed. For example, if there is a substantial increase in inventory or accounts receivable, is there an associated buildup in accounts payable and short-term bank loans? If not, the firm may have to use long-term financing to carry part of the short-term needs. An even more important question might be this: How are increases in long-term assets being financed? Most desirably, there should be adequate long-term financing and profits to carry these needs. If not, short-term funds (trade credit and bank loans) may be utilized to carry long-term needs. This is a potentially high-risk situation, in that short-term sources of funds may dry up while long-term needs continue to demand funding. In the problems at the back of the chapter, you will have an opportunity to further consider these points.

Depreciation and Funds Flow

One of the most confusing items to finance students is whether depreciation is a source of funds to the corporation. In Table 2-7, we listed depreciation as a source of funds (cash flow). This item deserves further clarification. The reason we added back depreciation was not that depreciation was a new source of funds, but rather that we had subtracted this noncash expense in arriving at net income and now have to add it back to determine the amount of actual funds on hand.

Depreciation represents an attempt to allocate the initial cost of an asset over its useful life. In essence, we attempt to match the annual expense of plant and equipment ownership against the revenues being produced. Nevertheless, the charging of depreciation is purely an accounting entry and does not directly involve the movement of funds. To go from accounting flows to cash flows in Table 2-7, we restored the noncash deduction of $50,000 for depreciation that was subtracted in Table 2-1, the income statement.

Let us examine a simple case involving depreciation in Table 2-11. Assume we purchase a machine for $500 with a five-year life and we pay for it in cash. Our depreciation schedule calls for equal annual depreciation charges of $100 per year for five years. Assume further that our firm has $1,000 in earnings before depreciation and taxes, and the tax obligation is $300. Note the difference between accounting flows and cash flows for the first two years in Table 2-11.

Since we took $500 out of cash flow originally in year 1 (in column B) to purchase equipment, we do not wish to take it out again. Thus we add back $100 in depreciation (in column B) each year to "wash out" the subtraction in the income statement.

While depreciation does not have a direct effect on cash flows, it does affect cash flows indirectly through taxable income. Since depreciation acts as a tax shield, it can alter the amount of taxes that a business is required to pay. If taxable income is lower, then taxes will be lower, and therefore cash outflow is increased.

Table 2-11   Comparison of accounting and cash flows

	Year 1	
	(A) **Accounting Flows**	**(B)** **Cash Flows**
Earnings before depreciation and taxes (EBDT)............	$1,000	$1,000
Depreciation...	100	100
Earnings before taxes (EBT)...	$ 900	$ 900
Taxes..	300	300
Earnings after taxes (EAT)...	$ 600	$ 600
Purchase of equipment...		(500)
Depreciation charged without cash outlay.....................		100
Cash flow...		$ 200

	Year 2	
	(A) **Accounting Flows**	**(B)** **Cash Flows**
Earnings before depreciation and taxes (EBDT)............	$1,000	$1,000
Depreciation...	100	100
Earnings before taxes...	$ 900	$ 900
Taxes..	300	300
Earnings after taxes (EAT)...	$ 600	$ 600
Depreciation charged without cash outlay.....................		100
Cash flow...		$ 700

Switzerland, a Beautiful Place to Pay Your Taxes

Corporations, like individuals, pay income taxes to the federal government, and in most states they must also pay state income taxes. When companies do business overseas, they must also pay taxes in foreign countries. However, over the last 25 years most countries have reduced their corporate tax rates, in part to attract new investment. Lower corporate tax rates can have an enormous impact on companies' aftertax income and on their market value.

Zug, Switzerland, a small city approximately 15 miles from Zurich, is a low-tax region that has become the headquarters for numerous multinational companies. To understand the attraction of Zug, consider a U.S.-headquartered company that makes $100 million per year pretax and pays a 39 percent federal and state tax rate. (This was a normal circumstance prior to 2018.) This leaves $61 million that can be paid to the shareholders. Now consider the effect on shareholders if this company had been headquartered in Zug. The average company in Zug pays only a 15.5 percent rate. As a result, this company's shareholders would have kept $84.5 million. That is almost 40 percent more!

a foreign company in a low-tax country, but even small start-ups have been tempted by the lower taxes, as well as higher valuations that headquartering in Zug could bring. Rather than starting a business in the United States, some entrepreneurs moved abroad specifically to raise money used to acquire U.S.-based businesses.

Faced with a continuing exodus of corporate taxpayers, Congress lowered the federal corporate tax rate from 35 percent to 21 percent, beginning in 2018, substantially reducing incentives to relocate overseas.

However, as seen in the accompanying chart, this tax rate cut does not really make the United States a low-tax jurisdiction. As you can see in the graph, before the rate reduction the United States had the highest corporate tax rate. Now the U.S. rate is nearer to the median for OECD countries. This may not be true for very long because foreign governments can be expected to further cut their rates, including several cantons like Zug in Switzerland.

	United States	Zug, Switzerland
Pretax income	$100 million	$100 million
(Corporate income tax rate)	39%	15.5%
Tax lost	$39 million	$15.5 million
Income available to shareholders	$61 million	$84.5 million

In recent years, several multinational companies have avoided U.S. taxes through a technique known as tax inversion. A tax inversion involves relocating a corporation's headquarters to a low-tax country while keeping operations in the United States. As we have seen, headquartering overseas can provide more profits for shareholders and, therefore, increase the value of the company. If a tax inversion is properly planned, it is still possible to conduct most normal operations in the United States.

Large tax inversions have been accomplished by merging a U.S. corporation with

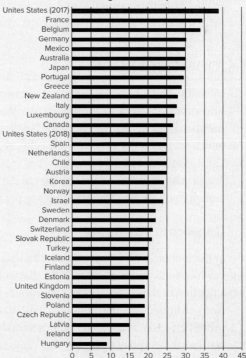

Average Overall Corporate Tax Rate

Data source: OECD, January 2018.

Free Cash Flow

A term that has received increasingly greater attention lately is **free cash flow (FCF)**. This is actually a by-product of the previously discussed statement of cash flows. The calculation of free cash flow is shown below.

	Year 2
Cash flow from operating activities	$700
Minus: Capital expenditures (required to maintain the productive capacity of the firm)	500
Minus: Dividends (needed to maintain the necessary payout on common stock and to cover any preferred stock obligation)	100
Free cash flow	$100

The concept of free cash flow forces the stock analyst or banker not only to consider how much cash is generated from operating activities but also to subtract out the necessary capital expenditures on plant and equipment to maintain normal activities. Similarly, dividend payments to shareholders must be subtracted out because these dividends must generally be paid to keep shareholders satisfied.

The balance, free cash flow, is then available for *special financing activities.* In the last decade, special financing activities have often been synonymous with leveraged buyouts, in which a firm borrows money to buy its stock and take itself private, with the hope of restructuring its balance sheet and perhaps going public again in a few years at a higher price than it paid. Leveraged buyouts are discussed more fully in Chapter 15. The analyst or banker normally looks at *free cash flow* to determine whether there will be sufficient excess funds to pay back the loans taken out to finance the leveraged buyout.

Income Tax Considerations

Virtually every business financial decision is influenced by federal income tax considerations. Primary examples are the lease versus purchase decision, the issuance of common stock versus debt decision, and the decision to replace an asset. While the intent of this section is not to review the rules, regulations, and nuances of the Federal Income Tax Code, we will examine how tax matters influence corporate financial decisions. The primary orientation will be toward the principles governing corporate tax decisions, though many of the same principles apply to a sole proprietorship or a partnership.

Corporate Tax Rates

In December 2017, Congress passed a major tax bill that provides the largest overhaul to the corporate tax rules since 1986. Beginning in 2018, one of the major changes is the reduction of the corporate tax rate from as high as 35 percent to a flat rate of 21 percent. Keep in mind that corporations may also pay some state and foreign taxes, so the overall effective rate can be higher than 21 percent. Prior to the enactment of the new tax law, the corporate tax rate was progressive, meaning lower levels of income (such as $50,000 or $100,000) were taxed at lower rates than the highest levels of income, which were taxed at 35 percent. The reduction in the corporate tax rate to a flat rate of

The Tax Cuts and Jobs Act of 2017 was the most significant corporate tax overhaul since 1986. The headline corporate tax change is that the corporate tax rate has been reduced to a flat rate of 21 percent. Prior to 2018, the corporate tax rate was 35 percent. The 21 percent rate is the lowest tax rate since 1939. The rate reduction is an effort to make the US tax system more competitive with other countries. Even with the rate reduction, the US is not considered a low tax country, but the rate is more in line with other countries.

The Act made numerous other important corporate tax revisions:

- The corporate alternative minimum tax (AMT) was repealed.

- A territorial system of taxation was implemented. Previous law taxed US corporations on worldwide income, a method which was at odds with tax systems in other countries around the world.

- Multinational corporations in the US are subjected to a one-time repatriation tax on deferred foreign profits (8 percent) and 15.5 percent on foreign-based cash. It was estimated that US multinationals had accumulated more than $3 trillion dollars overseas. The new regime encourages businesses to bring money back to the US to invest in businesses and job creation.

- Companies with net operating losses (NOLs) will no longer be able to carry back losses to previous tax years and receive a refund for prior taxes paid. NOL carryforwards are still allowed, but they are limited to 80 percent of taxable income. Previously, carryforwards could completely eliminate a subsequent year's tax.

- Corporate interest expense deductions are also limited by the law. For the years 2018 – 2021, companies can only deduct interest expense of up to 30 percent of EBITDA (earnings before interest, taxes, depreciation, and amortization). In 2022, the limitation tightens further. Interest expense will be capped at 30 percent of EBIT (earnings before interest and taxes) but *after* depreciation and amortization expenses. For many companies, EBIT is a much smaller number than EBITDA. The impact of this change makes borrowing money more expensive for highly leveraged companies.

- The corporate "dividends received" deduction was reduced. Previously, in order to reduce the double-taxation of corporate earnings, when a corporation owned 20 percent or more of the stock of another company and received dividends, the receiving corporation was entitled to exclude 80 percent of the dividends from taxable income. Dividends received from less-than-20-percent-owned companies received a 70 percent deduction. The new law reduces these deductions to 65 percent and 50 percent.

- The Section 179 deduction which allows a corporation to expense qualified assets was increased from $500,000 to $1,000,000 per year.

- Bonus depreciation, which is additional first-year depreciation, was temporarily increased from 50% to 100% until 2023. Then the first-year bonus depreciation is phased down.

Another tax change is important for people who are considering whether to organize their business as a taxable corporation or use some other business form. Pass through businesses such as S Corps, LLCs, sole proprietorships, and partnerships now enjoy a 20% deduction on qualified business income. In other words, when a pass-through entity earns $100, the shareholder/partner is only subject to tax on $80 of the income. However, many shareholders will have tax rates higher than the 21 percent corporate tax rate. This provision expires December 31, 2025.

21 percent was done to make the U.S. corporate tax rate more competitive with rates imposed by other countries and to encourage economic activity in the United States. See the OECD chart on page 43 for a comparison of tax rates across the world.

Cost of a Tax-Deductible Expense

The businessperson often states that a tax-deductible item, such as interest on business loans, travel expenditures, or salaries, costs substantially less than the amount expended, on an aftertax basis. We shall investigate how this process works. Let us examine the tax statements of two corporations—the first pays $100,000 in interest, and the second has no interest expense. An average tax rate of 25 percent (21 percent federal and 4 percent state) is used for ease of computation.

	Corporation A	Corporation B
Earnings before interest and taxes	$400,000	$400,000
Interest	100,000	0
Earnings before taxes (taxable income)	$300,000	$400,000
Taxes (25%)	75,000	100,000
Earnings after taxes	$225,000	$300,000
Difference in earnings after taxes		$75,000

Although Corporation A paid out $100,000 more in interest than Corporation B, its earnings after taxes are only $75,000 less than those of Corporation B. Thus we say the $100,000 in interest costs the firm only $75,000 in aftertax earnings. The aftertax cost of a tax-deductible expense can be computed as the actual expense times one minus the tax rate. In this case, we show $100,000 (1 − tax rate), or $100,000 × 0.75 = $75,000. The reasoning in this instance is that the $100,000 is deducted from earnings before determining taxable income, thus saving $25,000 in taxes and costing only $75,000 on a net basis.

Because a dividend on common stock is not tax-deductible, we say it cost 100 percent of the amount paid. From a purely corporate cash flow viewpoint, the firm would be indifferent between paying $100,000 in interest and $75,000 in dividends.

Depreciation as a Tax Shield

Although depreciation is not a new source of funds, it provides the important function of shielding part of our income from taxes. Let us examine Corporations A and B again, this time with an eye toward depreciation rather than interest. Corporation A charges off $100,000 in depreciation, while Corporation B charges off none.

	Corporation A	Corporation B
Earnings before depreciation and taxes	$400,000	$400,000
Depreciation	100,000	0
Earnings before taxes	$300,000	$400,000
Taxes (25%)	75,000	100,000
Earnings after taxes	$225,000	$300,000
+ Depreciation charged without cash outlay	100,000	0
Cash flow	$325,000	$300,000
Difference		$25,000

We compute earnings after taxes and then add back depreciation to get cash flow. The difference between $325,000 and $300,000 indicates that Corporation A enjoys $25,000 more in cash flow. The reason is that depreciation shielded $100,000 from taxation in Corporation A and saved $25,000 in taxes, which eventually showed up in cash flow. Though depreciation is not a new source of funds, it does provide tax shield benefits that can be measured as depreciation times the tax rate, or in this case $100,000 \times 0.25 = $25,000. A more comprehensive discussion of depreciation's effect on cash flow is presented in Chapter 12, as part of the long-term capital budgeting decision.

SUMMARY

The financial manager must be thoroughly familiar with the language of accounting to administer the financial affairs of the firm. The income statement provides a measure of the firm's profitability over a specified period. Earnings per share represent residual income to the common stockholder that may be paid out in the form of dividends or reinvested to generate future profits and dividends. A limitation of the income statement is that it reports income and expense primarily on a transaction basis and thus may not recognize certain major economic events as they occur.

A concept utilized throughout the text is the price-earnings ratio. This refers to the multiplier applied to earnings per share to determine current value of the common stock. The P/E ratio indicates expectations about the future of a company. Firms expected to provide returns greater than those for the market in general with equal or less risk often have P/E ratios higher than the market P/E ratio. Of course, the opposite effect would also be true.

The balance sheet is like a snapshot of the financial position of the firm at a point in time, with the stockholders' equity section purporting to represent ownership interest. Because the balance sheet is presented on a historical cost basis, it may not always reflect the true value of the firm.

The statement of cash flows, the third major statement the corporation presents to stockholders and security analysts, emphasizes the importance of cash flow data to the operations of the firm. It translates the information on the income statement and balance sheet that was prepared on an accrual accounting basis to a cash basis. From these data, the firm can better assess its ability to pay cash dividends, invest in new equipment, and so on.

Depreciation represents an attempt to allocate the initial cost of an asset over its useful life. In essence, we attempt to match the annual expenses of plant and equipment ownership against the revenues being produced. Nevertheless, the charging of depreciation is purely an accounting entry and does not directly involve the movement of funds. To go from accounting flows to cash flows, we restore the noncash deduction for depreciation that was subtracted in the income statement.

LIST OF TERMS

income statement	27	balance sheet	30
earnings per share	28	liquidity	30
price-earnings ratio	28	net worth (book value)	32

statement of cash flows 34		cash flows from financing activities 38	
cash flows from operating activities 36		depreciation 42	
cash flows from investing activities 38		free cash flow (FCF) 44	

DISCUSSION QUESTIONS

1. Discuss some financial variables that affect the price-earnings ratio. *(LO2-2)*

2. What is the difference between book value per share of common stock and market value per share? Why does this disparity occur? *(LO2-3)*

3. Explain how depreciation generates actual cash flows for the company. *(LO2-5)*

4. What is the difference between accumulated depreciation and depreciation expense? How are they related? *(LO2-5)*

5. How is the income statement related to the balance sheet? *(LO2-1 & 2-3)*

6. Comment on why inflation may restrict the usefulness of the balance sheet as normally presented. *(LO2-3)*

7. Explain why the statement of cash flows provides useful information that goes beyond income statement and balance sheet data. *(LO2-4)*

8. What are the three primary sections of the statement of cash flows? In what section would the payment of a cash dividend be shown? *(LO2-4)*

9. What is free cash flow? Why is it important to leveraged buyouts? *(LO2-4)*

10. Why is interest expense said to cost the firm substantially less than the actual expense, while dividends cost it 100 percent of the outlay? *(LO2-1)*

PRACTICE PROBLEMS AND SOLUTIONS

Determination of
profitability
(LO2-1)

1. LeBron Furniture Company has the following financial data. Prepare an income statement and compute earnings per share. See Table 2-1 as an example.

Sales	$1,300,000
Depreciation expense	70,000
Cost of goods sold	800,000
Interest expense	30,000
Selling and administrative expense	140,000
Common shares outstanding	60,000
Taxes	75,000
Preferred stock dividends	5,000

Determination of
profitability
(LO2-2)

2. Northern Energy Company has assets of $7,000,000, liabilities of $4,000,000, and $500,000 in preferred stock outstanding. Four hundred thousand common stock shares have been issued.

    a. Compute book value per share.

    b. If the firm has earnings per share of $1.10 and a P/E ratio of 15, what is the stock price per share?

    c. What is the ratio of market value per share to book value per share?

Solutions

1.

Sales	$1,300,000
Cost of goods sold	800,000
Gross profit	$ 500,000
Selling and administrative expense	140,000
Depreciation expense	70,000
Operating profit	$ 290,000
Interest expense	30,000
Earnings before taxes	$ 260,000
Taxes	75,000
Earnings after taxes	$ 185,000
Preferred stock dividends	5,000
Earnings available to common stockholders	$ 180,000
Common shares outstanding	60,000
Earnings per share	$ 3.00

2. *a.* Use the example material on page 32 to compute book value per share.

Total assets	$7,000,000
Total liabilities	4,000,000
Stockholders' equity	$3,000,000
Preferred stock obligation	500,000
Net worth assigned to common stockholders	$2,500,000
Common shares outstanding	400,000
Book value per share	$ 6.25

b. EPS × P/E ratio = Stock price per share

$$\$1.10 \times 15 = \$16.50$$

c. $\dfrac{\text{Market value}}{\text{Book value}} = \dfrac{\$16.50}{6.25} = 2.64\text{x}$

PROBLEMS

≡connect Selected problems are available with Connect. Please see the preface for more information.

Basic Problems

1. Frantic Fast Foods had earnings after taxes of $420,000 in 20X1 with 309,000 shares outstanding. On January 1, 20X2, the firm issued 20,000 new shares. Because of the proceeds from these new shares and other operating improvements, earnings after taxes increased by 30 percent.

   Income statement (LO2-1)

   a. Compute earnings per share for the year 20X1.
   b. Compute earnings per share for the year 20X2.

Income statement
(LO2-1)

2. Sosa Diet Supplements had earnings after taxes of $800,000 in 20X1 with 200,000 shares of stock outstanding. On January 1, 20X2, the firm issued 50,000 new shares. Because of the proceeds from these new shares and other operating improvements, earnings after taxes increased by 30 percent.

    a. Compute earnings per share for the year 20X1.

    b. Compute earnings per share for the year 20X2.

Gross profit
(LO2-1)

3. *a.* Swank Clothiers had sales of $383,000 and cost of goods sold of $260,000. What is the gross profit margin (ratio of gross profit to sales)?

    b. If the average firm in the clothing industry had a gross profit of 25 percent, how is the firm doing?

Operating profit
(LO2-1)

4. A-Rod Fishing Supplies had sales of $2,500,000 and cost of goods sold of $1,710,000. Selling and administrative expenses represented 10 percent of sales. Depreciation was 6 percent of the total assets of $4,680,000. What was the firm's operating profit?

Income statement
(LO2-1)

5. Arrange the following income statement items so they are in the proper order of an income statement:

Taxes	Earnings per share
Shares outstanding	Earnings before taxes
Interest expense	Cost of goods sold
Depreciation expense	Earnings after taxes
Preferred stock dividends	Earnings available to common
Operating profit	stockholders
Sales	Selling and administrative expense
Gross profit	

Income statement
(LO2-1)

𝄪

6. Given the following information, prepare an income statement for the Dental Drilling Company.

Selling and administrative expense...	$112,000
Depreciation expense..	73,000
Sales	489,000
Interest expense..	45,000
Cost of goods sold..	156,000
Taxes..	47,000

Income statement
(LO2-1)

7. Given the following information, prepare an income statement for Jonas Brothers Cough Drops.

Selling and administrative expense...	$ 328,000
Depreciation expense..	195,000
Sales	1,660,000
Interest expense..	129,000
Cost of goods sold..	560,000
Taxes..	171,000

8. Prepare an income statement for Franklin Kite Co. Take your calculations all the way to computing earnings per share.

Determination of profitability (LO2-1)

Sales	$900,000
Shares outstanding	50,000
Cost of goods sold	400,000
Interest expense	40,000
Selling and administrative expense	60,000
Depreciation expense	20,000
Preferred stock dividends	80,000
Taxes	50,000

9. Prepare an income statement for Virginia Slim Wear. Take your calculations all the way to computing earnings per share.

Determination of profitability (LO2-1)

Sales	$1,360,000
Shares outstanding	104,000
Cost of goods sold	700,000
Interest expense	34,000
Selling and administrative expense	49,000
Depreciation expense	23,000
Preferred stock dividends	86,000
Taxes	100,000

10. Precision Systems had sales of $820,000, cost of goods of $510,000, selling and administrative expense of $60,000, and operating profit of $103,000. What was the value of depreciation expense? Set up this problem as a partial income statement and determine depreciation expense as the "plug" figure required to obtain the operating profit.

Income statement (LO2-1)

11. Stein Books Inc. sold 1,900 finance textbooks for $250 each to High Tuition University in 20X1. These books cost $210 to produce. Stein Books spent $12,200 (selling expense) to convince the university to buy its books.

Depreciation and earnings (LO2-1)

   Depreciation expense for the year was $15,200. In addition, Stein Books borrowed $104,000 on January 1, 20X1, on which the company paid 12 percent interest. Both the interest and principal of the loan were paid on December 31, 20X1. The publishing firm's tax rate is 30 percent.
   Did Stein Books make a profit in 20X1? Please verify with an income statement.

Intermediate Problems

12. Lemon Auto Wholesalers had sales of $1,000,000 last year, and cost of goods sold represented 78 percent of sales. Selling and administrative expenses were 12 percent of sales. Depreciation expense was $11,000 and interest expense for the year was $8,000. The firm's tax rate is 30 percent.

Determination of profitability (LO2-1)

   a. Compute earnings after taxes.
   b. Assume the firm hires Ms. Carr, an efficiency expert, as a consultant. She suggests that by increasing selling and administrative expenses to 14 percent of sales, sales can be increased to $1,050,900. The extra sales

effort will also reduce cost of goods sold to 74 percent of sales. (There will be a larger markup in prices as a result of more aggressive selling.) Depreciation expense will remain at $11,000. However, more automobiles will have to be carried in inventory to satisfy customers, and interest expense will go up to $15,800. The firm's tax rate will remain at 30 percent. Compute revised earnings after taxes based on Ms. Carr's suggestions for Lemon Auto Wholesalers. Will her ideas increase or decrease profitability?

Balance sheet
(LO2-3)

13. Classify the following balance sheet items as current or noncurrent:

Retained earnings	Bonds payable
Accounts payable	Accrued wages payable
Prepaid expenses	Accounts receivable
Plant and equipment	Capital in excess of par
Inventory	Preferred stock
Common stock	Marketable securities

Balance sheet and
income statement
classification
(LO2-1 & 2-3)

14. Fill in the blank spaces with categories 1 through 7:
1.   Balance sheet (BS)
2.   Income statement (IS)
3.   Current assets (CA)
4.   Fixed assets (FA)
5.   Current liabilities (CL)
6.   Long-term liabilities (LL)
7.   Stockholders' equity (SE)

Indicate Whether Item Is on Balance Sheet (BS) or Income Statement (IS)	If on Balance Sheet, Designate Which Category	Item
_____	_____	Accounts receivable
_____	_____	Retained earnings
_____	_____	Income tax expense
_____	_____	Accrued expenses
_____	_____	Cash
_____	_____	Selling and administrative expenses
_____	_____	Plant and equipment
_____	_____	Operating expenses
_____	_____	Marketable securities
_____	_____	Interest expense
_____	_____	Sales
_____	_____	Notes payable (6 months)
_____	_____	Bonds payable, maturity 2019
_____	_____	Common stock
_____	_____	Depreciation expense
_____	_____	Inventories
_____	_____	Capital in excess of par value
_____	_____	Net income (earnings after taxes)
_____	_____	Income tax payable

15. Arrange the following items in proper balance sheet presentation:

Development of
balance sheet
(LO2-3)

Accumulated depreciation	$309,000
Retained earnings	187,000
Cash	14,000
Bonds payable	136,000
Accounts receivable	54,000
Plant and equipment—original cost	775,000
Accounts payable	35,000
Allowance for bad debts	9,000
Common stock, $1 par, 100,000 shares outstanding	100,000
Inventory	70,000
Preferred stock, $59 par, 1,000 shares outstanding	59,000
Marketable securities	24,000
Investments	20,000
Notes payable	34,000
Capital paid in excess of par (common stock)	88,000

16. Elite Trailer Parks has an operating profit of $200,000. Interest expense for the year was $10,000; preferred dividends paid were $18,750; and common dividends paid were $30,000. The tax was $61,250. The firm has 20,000 shares of common stock outstanding.

Earnings per share
and retained earnings
(LO2-1 & 2-3)

    a. Calculate the earnings per share and the common dividends per share for Elite Trailer Parks.

    b. What was the increase in retained earnings for the year?

17. Quantum Technology had $669,000 of retained earnings on December 31, 20X2. The company paid common dividends of $35,500 in 20X2 and had retained earnings of $576,000 on December 31, 20X1. How much did Quantum Technology earn during 20X2, and what would earnings per share be if 47,400 shares of common stock were outstanding?

Earnings per share
and retained earnings
(LO2-1 & 2-3)

18. Botox Facial Care had earnings after taxes of $370,000 in 20X1 with 200,000 shares of stock outstanding. The stock price was $31.50. In 20X2, earnings after taxes increased to $436,000 with the same 200,000 shares outstanding. The stock price was $42.00.

Price-earnings ratio
(LO2-2)

    a. Compute earnings per share and the P/E ratio for 20X1. The P/E ratio equals the stock price divided by earnings per share.

    b. Compute earnings per share and the P/E ratio for 20X2.

    c. Give a general explanation of why the P/E ratio changed.

19. Stilley Corporation had earnings after taxes of $436,000 in 20X2 with 200,000 shares outstanding. The stock price was $42.00. In 20X3, earnings after taxes declined to $206,000 with the same 200,000 shares outstanding. The stock price declined to $27.80.

Price-earnings ratio
(LO2-2)

    a. Compute earnings per share and the P/E ratio for 20X2.

    b. Compute earnings per share and the P/E ratio for 20X3.

    c. Give a general explanation of why the P/E changed. You might want to consult the text to explain this surprising result.

Cash flow
(LO2-4)

20. Identify whether each of the following items increases or decreases cash flow:

Increase in accounts receivable	Decrease in prepaid expenses
Increase in notes payable	Increase in inventory
Depreciation expense	Dividend payment
Increase in investments	Increase in accrued expenses
Decrease in accounts payable	

Depreciation and cash flow
(LO2-5)

21. The Rogers Corporation has a gross profit of $880,000 and $360,000 in depreciation expense. The Evans Corporation also has $880,000 in gross profit, with $60,000 in depreciation expense. Selling and administrative expense is $120,000 for each company.

Given that the tax rate is 40 percent, compute the cash flow for both companies. Explain the difference in cash flow between the two firms.

Free cash flow
(LO2-4)

22. Nova Electrics anticipates cash flow from operating activities of $6 million in 20X1. It will need to spend $1.2 million on capital investments to remain competitive within the industry. Common stock dividends are projected at $0.4 million and preferred stock dividends at $0.55 million.

a. What is the firm's projected free cash flow for the year 20X1?

b. What does the concept of free cash flow represent?

Book value
(LO2-3)

23. Landers Nursery and Garden Stores has current assets of $220,000 and fixed assets of $170,000. Current liabilities are $80,000 and long-term liabilities are $140,000. There is $40,000 in preferred stock outstanding and the firm has issued 25,000 shares of common stock. Compute book value (net worth) per share.

Book value and market value
(LO2-2 & 2-3)

24. The Holtzman Corporation has assets of $400,000, current liabilities of $50,000, and long-term liabilities of $100,000. There is $40,000 in preferred stock outstanding; 20,000 shares of common stock have been issued.

a. Compute book value (net worth) per share.

b. If there is $22,000 in earnings available to common stockholders and Holtzman's stock has a P/E of 18 times earnings per share, what is the current price of the stock?

c. What is the ratio of market value per share to book value per share?

Book value and market value
(LO2-2 & 2-3)

25. Amigo Software Inc. has total assets of $889,000, current liabilities of $192,000, and long-term liabilities of $154,000. There is $87,000 in preferred stock outstanding. Thirty thousand shares of common stock have been issued.

a. Compute book value (net worth) per share.

b. If there is $56,300 in earnings available to common stockholders and the firm's stock has a P/E of 23 times earnings per share, what is the current price of the stock?

c. What is the ratio of market value per share to book value per share? (Round to two places to the right of the decimal point.)

Book value and P/E ratio
(LO2-2 & 2-3)

26. Vriend Software Inc.'s book value per share is $15.20. If earnings per share is $1.88 and the firm's stock trades in the stock market at 3.5 times book value per share, what will the P/E ratio be? (Round to the nearest whole number.)

Advanced Problems

27. For December 31, 20X1, the balance sheet of Baxter Corporation was as follows:

Construction of income statement and balance sheet (LO2-1 & 2-3)

Current Assets		Liabilities	
Cash	$ 15,000	Accounts payable	$ 17,000
Accounts receivable	20,000	Notes payable	25,000
Inventory	30,000	Bonds payable	55,000
Prepaid expenses	12,500		
Fixed Assets		**Stockholders' Equity**	
Plant and equipment (gross)	$255,000	Preferred stock	$ 25,000
Less: Accumulated		Common stock	60,000
depreciation	51,000	Paid-in capital	30,000
Net plant and equipment	$204,000	Retained earnings	69,500
		Total liabilities and	
Total assets	$281,500	stockholders' equity	$281,500

Sales for 20X2 were $245,000, and the cost of goods sold was 60 percent of sales. Selling and administrative expense was $24,500. Depreciation expense was 8 percent of plant and equipment (gross) at the beginning of the year. Interest expense for the notes payable was 10 percent, while the interest rate on the bonds payable was 12 percent. This interest expense is based on December 31, 20X1 balances. The tax rate averaged 20 percent.

$2,500 in preferred stock dividends were paid, and $5,500 in dividends were paid to common stockholders. There were 10,000 shares of common stock outstanding.

During 20X2, the cash balance and prepaid expenses balances were unchanged. Accounts receivable and inventory increased by 10 percent. A new machine was purchased on December 31, 20X2, at a cost of $40,000.

Accounts payable increased by 20 percent. Notes payable increased by $6,500 and bonds payable decreased by $12,500, both at the end of the year. The preferred stock, common stock, and paid-in capital in excess of par accounts did not change.

a. Prepare an income statement for 20X2.

b. Prepare a statement of retained earnings for 20X2.

c. Prepare a balance sheet as of December 31, 20X2.

28. Refer to the following financial statements for Crosby Corporation:

Statement of cash flows (LO2-4)

a. Prepare a statement of cash flows for the Crosby Corporation using the general procedures indicated in Table 2-10.

b. Describe the general relationship between net income and net cash flows from operating activities for the firm.

c. Has the buildup in plant and equipment been financed in a satisfactory manner? Briefly discuss.

d. Compute the book value per common share for both 20X1 and 20X2 for the Crosby Corporation.

e. If the market value of a share of common stock is 3.3 times book value for 20X1, what is the firm's P/E ratio for 20X2?

CROSBY CORPORATION Income Statement For the Year Ended December 31, 20X2	
Sales	$ 2,200,000
Cost of goods sold	1,300,000
Gross profit	$ 900,000
Selling and administrative expense	420,000
Depreciation expense	150,000
Operating income	$ 330,000
Interest expense	90,000
Earnings before taxes	$ 240,000
Taxes	80,000
Earnings after taxes	$ 160,000
Preferred stock dividends	10,000
Earnings available to common stockholders	$ 150,000
Shares outstanding	120,000
Earnings per share	$ 1.25

Statement of Retained Earnings For the Year Ended December 31, 20X2	
Retained earnings, balance, January 1, 20X2	$500,000
Add: Earnings available to common stockholders, 20X2	150,000
Deduct: Cash dividends declared and paid in 20X2	50,000
Retained earnings, balance, December 31, 20X2	$600,000

Comparative Balance Sheets For 20X1 and 20X2		
	Year-End 20X1	Year-End 20X2
Assets		
Current assets:		
Cash	$ 70,000	$ 100,000
Accounts receivable (net)	300,000	350,000
Inventory	410,000	430,000
Prepaid expenses	50,000	30,000
Total current assets	$ 830,000	$ 910,000
Investments (long-term securities)	80,000	70,000
Plant and equipment	2,000,000	2,400,000
Less: Accumulated depreciation	1,000,000	1,150,000
Net plant and equipment	$ 1,000,000	$ 1,250,000
Total assets	$ 1,910,000	$ 2,230,000

(*continued*)

Liabilities and Stockholders' Equity

Current liabilities:

Accounts payable	$ 250,000	$ 440,000
Notes payable..	400,000	400,000
Accrued expenses..	70,000	50,000
Total current liabilities..	$ 720,000	$ 890,000
Long-term liabilities:		
Bonds payable, 20X2	70,000	120,000
Total liabilities	$ 790,000	$1,010,000
Stockholders' equity:		
Preferred stock, $100 par value...	$ 90,000	$ 90,000
Common stock, $1 par value..	120,000	120,000
Capital paid in excess of par..	410,000	410,000
Retained earnings..	500,000	600,000
Total stockholders' equity..	$1,120,000	$1,220,000
Total liabilities and stockholders' equity.............................	$1,910,000	$2,230,000

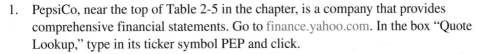

W E B   E X E R C I S E

1. PepsiCo, near the top of Table 2-5 in the chapter, is a company that provides comprehensive financial statements. Go to finance.yahoo.com. In the box "Quote Lookup," type in its ticker symbol PEP and click.

2. Scroll across from "Summary" to "Financials" and click. This will take you to the "Income Statement." Compute the annual percentage change between the three years for the following:

    a.   Total revenue.

    b.   Net income applicable to common shares.

3. Now click on "Balance Sheet" and compute the annual percentage change between the three years for the following:

    a.   Total assets

    b.   Total liabilities

4. Write a one-paragraph summary of how the company is doing.

Note: Occasionally a topic we have listed may have been deleted, updated, or moved into a different location on a website. If you click on the site map or site index, you will be introduced to a table of contents that should aid you in finding the topic you are looking for.

3

Financial Analysis

I f you're in the market for dental products, look no further than Colgate-Palmolive. The firm has it all: every type of toothpaste you can imagine (tartar control, cavity protection, whitening enhancement), as well as every shape and size of toothbrush. While you're getting ready for the day, also consider its soaps, shampoos, and deodorants (Tom's of Maine, Speed Stick, Lady Speed Stick, etc.). If you decide to clean your apartment or dorm room, Colgate-Palmolive will provide you with Ajax, Palmolive dish soap, and a long list of other cleaning products.

All this is somewhat interesting, but why mention these subjects in a finance text? Well, Colgate-Palmolive has had some interesting profit numbers recently. Its profit margin in 2017 was 15 percent, and its return on assets was 19.4 percent. While these numbers are higher than those of the average company, the 2017 number that blows analysts away is its return on stockholders' equity of over 900 percent (the norm is 15–20 percent). In fact, this ROE is so high and unrealistic that some financial services list the number as not meaningful (NMF). The major reason for this abnormally high return is its high debt-to-total-assets ratio of over 95 percent. This means that the firm's debt represents more than 95 percent of total assets and stockholders' equity less than 5 percent. Almost any amount of profit will appear high in regard to the low value of stockholders' equity.

In contrast, its largest competitor, Procter & Gamble, has a different capital structure. Procter & Gamble is financed with 45.8 percent debt and 54.2 percent equity. Because of this more conservative capital structure, the company reports only a 17.8 percent return on stockholders' equity. One capital structure is not necessarily better than the other, but this kind of financial analysis will be examined in this chapter.

In Chapter 2, we examined the basic assumptions of accounting and the various components that make up the financial statements of the firm. We now use this fundamental material as a springboard into financial analysis—to evaluate the financial performance of the firm.

The format for the chapter is twofold. In the first part, we use financial ratios to evaluate the relative success of the firm. Various measures such as net income to sales and current assets to current liabilities will be computed for a hypothetical company and examined in light of industry norms and past trends.

In the second part of the chapter, we explore the impact of inflation and disinflation on financial operations. You will begin to appreciate the impact of rising prices (or at times, declining prices) on the various financial ratios. The chapter concludes with a discussion of how other factors—in addition to price changes—may distort the financial statements of the firm. Terms such as *net income to sales, return on investment,* and *inventory turnover* take on much greater meaning when they are evaluated through the eyes of a financial manager who does more than merely pick out the top or bottom line of an income statement. The examples in the chapter are designed from the viewpoint of a financial manager (with only minor attention to accounting theory).

Ratio Analysis

Ratios are used in much of our daily life. We buy cars based on miles per gallon; we evaluate baseball players by earned run and batting averages, basketball players by field goal and foul-shooting percentages, and so on. These are all ratios constructed to judge comparative performance. Financial ratios serve a similar purpose, but you must know what is being measured to construct a ratio and to understand the significance of the resultant number.

Financial ratios are used to weigh and evaluate the operating performance of the firm. While an absolute value such as earnings of $50,000 or accounts receivable of $100,000 may appear satisfactory, its acceptability can be measured only in relation to other values. For this reason, financial managers emphasize ratio analysis.

For example, are earnings of $50,000 actually good? If we earned $50,000 on $500,000 of sales (10 percent "profit margin" ratio), that might be quite satisfactory— whereas earnings of $50,000 on $5,000,000 could be disappointing (a meager 1 percent return). After we have computed the appropriate ratio, we must compare our results to those achieved by similar firms in our industry, as well as to our own performance record. Even then, this "number-crunching" process is not fully adequate, and we are forced to supplement our financial findings with an evaluation of company management, physical facilities, corporate governance, sustainability, and numerous other factors.

Many libraries and universities subscribe to financial services such as Bloomberg, Standard & Poor's Industry Surveys and Corporate Reports, the Value Line Investment Survey FactSet, and Moody's Corporation. Standard & Poor's also leases a computer database called S&P IQ to banks, corporations, investment organizations, and universities. Compustat contains financial statement data on over 99,000 global securities for a 20-year period. Ratios can also be found on such websites as finance.yahoo.com. These data can be used for countless ratios to measure corporate performance. The ratios used in this text are a sample of the major ratio categories used in business, but other classification systems can also be constructed.

Classification System

We will separate 13 significant ratios into four primary categories:

A. Profitability ratios
  1. Profit margin
  2. Return on assets (investment)
  3. Return on equity

B. Asset utilization ratios
    4. Receivables turnover
    5. Average collection period
    6. Inventory turnover
    7. Fixed asset turnover
    8. Total asset turnover
C. Liquidity ratios
    9. Current ratio
    10. Quick ratio
D. Debt utilization ratios
    11. Debt to total assets
    12. Times interest earned
    13. Fixed charge coverage

The first grouping, the **profitability ratios**, allows us to measure the ability of the firm to earn an adequate return on sales, total assets, and invested capital. Many of the problems related to profitability can be explained, in whole or in part, by the firm's ability to effectively employ its resources. Thus the next category is **asset utilization ratios**. Under this heading, we measure the speed at which the firm is turning over accounts receivable, inventory, and longer-term assets. In other words, asset utilization ratios measure how many times per year a company sells its inventory or collects all of its accounts receivable. For long-term assets, the utilization ratio tells us how productive the fixed assets are in terms of generating sales.

In category C, the **liquidity ratios**, the primary emphasis moves to the firm's ability to pay off short-term obligations as they come due. In category D, **debt utilization ratios**, the overall debt position of the firm is evaluated in light of its asset base and earning power.

The users of financial statements will attach different degrees of importance to the four categories of ratios. To the potential investor or security analyst, the critical consideration is profitability, with secondary consideration given to such matters as liquidity and debt utilization. For the banker or trade creditor, the emphasis shifts to the firm's current ability to meet debt obligations. The bondholder, in turn, may be primarily influenced by debt to total assets—while also eyeing the profitability of the firm in terms of its ability to cover debt obligations. Of course, the experienced analyst looks at all the ratios, but with different degrees of attention.

Ratios are also important to people in the various functional areas of a business. The marketing manager, the head of production, the human resource manager, and many of their colleagues must all be familiar with ratio analysis. For example, the marketing manager must keep a close eye on inventory turnover; the production manager must evaluate the return on assets; and the human resource manager must look at the effect of "fringe benefits" expenditures on the return on sales.

The Analysis

Definitions alone carry little meaning in analyzing or dissecting the financial performance of a company. For this reason, we shall apply our four categories of ratios to a hypothetical firm, the Saxton Company, as presented in Table 3-1. The use of ratio analysis is rather like solving a mystery in which each clue leads to a new area of inquiry.

Table 3-1   Financial statement for ratio analysis

SAXTON COMPANY
Income Statement
For the Year Ended December 31, 2018

Sales (all on credit)	$4,000,000
Cost of goods sold	3,000,000
Gross profit	$1,000,000
Selling and administrative expense*	450,000
Operating profit	$ 550,000
Interest expense	50,000
Other income (expense), net	(225,000)
Net income before taxes	$ 275,000
Taxes	75,000
Net income	$ 200,000

*Includes $50,000 in lease payments.

Balance Sheet
As of December 31, 2018

Assets

Cash	$ 30,000
Marketable securities	50,000
Accounts receivable	350,000
Inventory	370,000
Total current assets	$ 800,000
Net plant and equipment	800,000
Net assets	$1,600,000

Liabilities and Stockholders' Equity

Accounts payable	$ 50,000
Notes payable	250,000
Total current liabilities	$ 300,000
Long-term liabilities	300,000
Total liabilities	$ 600,000
Common stock	400,000
Retained earnings	600,000
Total liabilities and stockholders' equity	$1,600,000

A. Profitability Ratios   We first look at profitability ratios. The appropriate ratio is computed for the Saxton Company and is then compared to representative industry data.

	Saxton Company	Industry Average
1. **Profit margin** $= \dfrac{\text{Net income}}{\text{Sales}}$	$\dfrac{\$200,000}{\$4,000,000} = 5\%$	6.7%
2. **Return on assets** (investment) =		
a. $\dfrac{\text{Net income}}{\text{Total assets}}$	$\dfrac{\$200,000}{\$1,600,000} = 12.5\%$	10%
b. $\dfrac{\text{Net income}}{\text{Sales}} \times \dfrac{\text{Sales}}{\text{Total assets}}$	$5\% \times 2.5 = 12.5\%$	$6.7\% \times 1.5 = 10\%$
3. **Return on equity** =		
a. $\dfrac{\text{Net income}}{\text{Stockholders' equity}}$	$\dfrac{\$200,000}{\$1,000,000} = 20\%$	15%
b. $\dfrac{\text{Return on assets (investment)}}{(1 - \text{Debt/Assets})}$	$\dfrac{0.125}{1 - 0.375} = 20\%$	$\dfrac{0.10}{1 - 0.33} = 15\%$

In analyzing the profitability ratios, we see the Saxton Company shows a lower return on the sales dollar (5 percent) than the industry average of 6.7 percent. However, its return on assets (investment) of 12.5 percent exceeds the industry norm of 10 percent. There is only one possible explanation for this occurrence—a more rapid turnover of assets than that generally found within the industry. This is verified in Ratio 2*b,* in which sales to total assets is 2.5 for the Saxton Company and only 1.5 for the industry. Thus Saxton earns less on each sales dollar, but it compensates by turning over its assets more rapidly (generating more sales per dollar of assets).

Return on total assets as described through the two components of profit margin and asset turnover is part of the **Du Pont system of analysis**.

$$\text{Return on assets (investment)} = \text{Profit margin} \times \text{Asset turnover}$$

The Du Pont company was a forerunner in stressing that satisfactory return on assets may be achieved through high profit margins or rapid turnover of assets, or a combination of both. We shall also soon observe that under the Du Pont system of analysis, the use of debt may be important. The Du Pont system causes the analyst to examine the sources of a company's profitability. Since the profit margin is an income statement ratio, a high profit margin indicates good cost control, whereas a high asset turnover ratio demonstrates efficient use of the assets on the balance sheet. Different industries have different operating and financial structures. For example, in the heavy capital goods industry the emphasis is on a high profit margin with a low asset turnover—whereas in food processing, the profit margin is low and the key to satisfactory returns on total assets is a rapid turnover of assets.

Equally important to a firm is its return on equity or ownership capital. For the Saxton Company, return on equity is 20 percent, versus an industry norm of 15 percent. Thus the owners of Saxton Company are more amply rewarded than are other shareholders in the industry. This may be the result of one or two factors: a high return on total assets or a generous utilization of debt or a combination thereof. This can be seen through Ratio 3*b,* which represents a modified or second version of the Du Pont formula.

Note that the numerator, return on assets, is taken from Ratio 2*b,* which represents the initial version of the Du Pont formula (Return on assets = Net income/Sales

× Sales/Total assets). Return on assets is then divided by [1 − (Debt/Assets)] to account for the amount of debt in the capital structure. In the case of the Saxton Company, the modified version of the Du Pont formula shows

$$\text{Return on equity} = \frac{\text{Return on assets (investment)}}{(1 - \text{Debt/Assets})}$$

$$= \frac{12.5\%}{1 - 0.375} = 20\%$$

Actually, the return on assets of 12.5 percent in the numerator is higher than the industry average of 10 percent, and the ratio of debt to assets in the denominator of 37.5 percent is higher than the industry norm of 33 percent. Please see the denominators in Ratio 3*b* to confirm these facts. Both the numerator and denominator contribute to a higher return on equity than the industry average (20 percent versus 15 percent). Note that if the firm had a 50 percent debt-to-assets ratio, return on equity would go up to 25 percent.[1]

$$\text{Return on equity} = \frac{\text{Return on assets (investment)}}{(1 - \text{Debt/Assets})}$$

$$= \frac{12.5\%}{1 - 0.50} = 25\%$$

This does not necessarily mean debt is a positive influence, only that it can be used to boost return on equity. The ultimate goal for the firm is to achieve maximum valuation for its securities in the marketplace, and this goal may or may not be advanced by using debt to increase return on equity. Because debt represents increased risk, a lower valuation of higher earnings is possible.[2] Every situation must be evaluated individually.

You may wish to review Figure 3-1, which illustrates the key points in the Du Pont system of analysis.

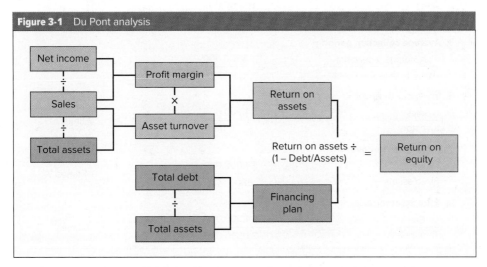

Figure 3-1   Du Pont analysis

---

[1]The return could be slightly different than 25 percent because of changing financial costs with higher debt.
[2]Further discussions of this point are presented in Chapter 5, "Operating and Financial Leverage," and Chapter 10, "Valuation and Rates of Return."

As an example of the Du Pont analysis, Table 3-2 compares two well-known retail store chains, Walmart and Target. In 2017, Target was more profitable in terms of profit margins (3.9 percent versus 2.8 percent). However, Walmart turned over its assets 2.4 times a year versus a slower 1.9 times for Target. Walmart's long-held philosophy was set by its late founder, Sam Walton: Give the customer a bargain in terms of low prices (and low profit margins) but move the merchandise quickly (higher turnover).

Multiplying each company's profit margin by the asset turnover, we see that Walmart and Target have similar returns on assets. However, notice that Walmart is more conservatively financed than Target. Walmart's capital structure is 60.9 percent debt. Target uses 70.7 percent debt. As a result, Target's return on equity was significantly higher. Keep in mind that a higher debt ratio also creates a more volatile ROE. While Target's ROE was higher than Walmart's, economic growth was high in 2017. If the economy falters, Target's ROE will probably fall more than Walmart's.

Finally, as a general statement in computing all the profitability ratios, the analyst must be sensitive to the age of the assets. Plant and equipment purchased 15 years ago may be carried on the books far below its replacement value in an inflationary economy. A 20 percent return on assets purchased in the early 1990s may be inferior to a 15 percent return on newly purchased assets.

B. Asset Utilization Ratios   The second category of ratios relates to asset utilization, and the ratios in this category may explain why one firm can turn over its assets more rapidly than another. Notice that all of these ratios relate the balance sheet (assets) to the income statement (sales). The Saxton Company's rapid turnover of assets is primarily explained in Ratios 4, 5, and 6.

	Saxton Company	Industry Average
4. **Receivables turnover =** Sales (credit) / Receivables	$\dfrac{\$4,000,000}{\$350,000} = 11.4$	10 times
5. **Average collection period =** Accounts receivable / Average daily credit sales	$\dfrac{\$350,000}{\$11,111} = 32$	36 days
6. **Inventory turnover =** Sales / Inventory	$\dfrac{\$4,000,000}{\$370,000} = 10.8$	7 times
7. **Fixed asset turnover =** Sales / Fixed assets	$\dfrac{\$4,000,000}{\$800,000} = 5$	5.4 times
8. **Total asset turnover =** Sales / Total assets	$\dfrac{\$4,000,000}{\$1,600,000} = 2.5$	1.5 times

Saxton collects its receivables faster than does the industry. This is shown by the receivables turnover of 11.4 times versus 10 times for the industry, and in daily terms by the average collection period of 32 days, which is 4 days faster than the industry norm.

Table 3-2 Return on equity: Walmart vs. Target using the Du Pont method of analysis, 2017

Name	A Profit Margin	B Asset Turnover	A × B Return on Assets	C Debt/ Assets	D = (1 – C) 1 – Debt/ Assets	(A × B)/D Return on Equity
Walmart Stores Inc.	2.81%	2.44	6.86%	60.87%	39.13%	17.54%
Target	3.94%	1.86	7.31%	70.74%	29.26%	24.99%

Data: January 1, 2018

The average collection period suggests how long, on average, customers' accounts stay on the books. The Saxton Company has $350,000 in accounts receivable and $4,000,000 in credit sales, which when divided by 360 days yields average daily credit sales of $11,111. We divide accounts receivable of $350,000 by average daily credit sales of $11,111 to determine how many days credit sales are on the books (32 days).

In addition, the firm turns over its inventory 10.8 times per year, as contrasted with an industry average of 7 times.[3] This tells us that Saxton generates more sales per dollar of inventory than the average company in the industry, and we can assume the firm uses very efficient inventory-ordering and cost-control methods.

The firm maintains a slightly lower ratio of sales to fixed assets (plant and equipment) than does the industry (5 versus 5.4), as shown above. This is a relatively minor consideration in view of the rapid movement of inventory and accounts receivable. Finally, the rapid turnover of total assets is again indicated (2.5 versus 1.5).

C. Liquidity Ratios   After considering profitability and asset utilization, the analyst needs to examine the liquidity of the firm. The Saxton Company's liquidity ratios fare well in comparison with the industry. Notice that Saxton's current ratio is higher than the industry average because it has more current assets, relative to its current liabilities. This suggests that Saxton should be in a relatively good position to pay its current debts as they come due. Likewise, Saxton's quick ratio is higher than its average competitor's. Further analysis might involve building a cash budget to determine if the firm can meet each maturing obligation as it comes due.

	Saxton Company	**Industry Average**
9. **Current ratio =**		
$\dfrac{\text{Current assets}}{\text{Current liabilities}}$	$\dfrac{\$800,000}{\$300,000} = 2.67$	2.1 times
10. **Quick ratio =**		
$\dfrac{\text{Current assets} - \text{Inventory}}{\text{Current liabilities}}$	$\dfrac{\$430,000}{\$300,000} = 1.43$	1.0 times

D. Debt Utilization Ratios   The last grouping of ratios, debt utilization, allows the analyst to measure the prudence of the debt management policies of the firm.

---

[3]This ratio may also be computed by using "Cost of goods sold" in the numerator. While this offers some theoretical advantages in terms of using cost figures in both the numerator and denominator, Dun & Bradstreet and other credit reporting agencies generally show turnover using sales in the numerator.

Debt to total assets of 37.5 percent as shown in Ratio 11 is slightly above the industry average of 33 percent, but well within the prudent range of 50 percent or less.[4]

	Saxton Company	Industry Average
11. **Debt to total assets** = $\dfrac{\text{Total debt}}{\text{Total assets}}$	$\dfrac{\$600,000}{\$1,600,000} = 37.5\%$	33%
12. **Times interest earned** = $\dfrac{\text{Income before interest and taxes}}{\text{Interest}}$	$\dfrac{\$550,000}{\$50,000} = 11$	7 times
13. **Fixed charge coverage** = $\dfrac{\text{Income before fixed charges and taxes}}{\text{Fixed charges}}$	$\dfrac{\$600,000}{\$100,000} = 6$	5.5 times

Ratios for times interest earned and fixed charge coverage show that the Saxton Company debt is being well managed compared to the debt management of other firms in the industry. Times interest earned indicates the number of times that income before interest and taxes covers the interest obligation (11 times). The higher the ratio, the stronger is the interest-paying ability of the firm. The figure for income before interest and taxes ($550,000) in the ratio is the equivalent of the operating profit figure presented in the upper part of Table 3-1.

Fixed charge coverage measures the firm's ability to meet all fixed obligations rather than interest payments alone, on the assumption that failure to meet any financial obligation will endanger the position of the firm. In the present case, the Saxton Company has lease obligations of $50,000 as well as the $50,000 in interest expenses. Thus the total fixed charge financial obligation is $100,000. We also need to know the income before all fixed charge obligations. In this case, we take income before interest and taxes (operating profit) and add back the $50,000 in lease payments.

Income before interest and taxes	$550,000
Lease payments	50,000
Income before fixed charges and taxes	$600,000

The fixed charges are safely covered 6 times, exceeding the industry norm of 5.5 times. The various ratios are summarized in Table 3-3. The conclusions reached in comparing the Saxton Company to industry averages are generally valid, though exceptions may exist. For example, a high inventory turnover is considered "good" unless it is achieved by maintaining unusually low inventory levels, which may hurt future sales and profitability.

---

[4]From the Du Pont system of analysis discussed earlier in the chapter, we used total debt to total assets. There are also other important debt measures used for different purposes, such as long-term debt to equity.

Table 3-3   Ratio analysis

	Saxton Company	Industry Average	Conclusion
A. Profitability			
1. Profit margin	5.0%	6.7%	Below average
2. Return on assets	12.5%	10.0%	Above average due to high turnover
3. Return on equity	20.0%	15.0%	Good, due to Ratios 2 and 11
B. Asset Utilization			
4. Receivables turnover	11.4	10.0	Good
5. Average collection period	32.0	36.0	Good
6. Inventory turnover	10.8	7.0	Good
7. Fixed asset turnover	5.0	5.4	Below average
8. Total asset turnover	2.5	1.5	Good
C. Liquidity			
9. Current ratio	2.67	2.1	Good
10. Quick ratio	1.43	1.0	Good
D. Debt Utilization			
11. Debt to total assets	37.5%	33.0%	Slightly more debt
12. Times interest earned	11.0	7.0	Good
13. Fixed charge coverage	6.0	5.5	Good

In summary, the Saxton Company more than compensates for a lower return on the sales dollar by a rapid turnover of assets, principally inventory and receivables, and a wise use of debt. You should be able to use these 13 measures to evaluate the financial performance of any firm.

Trend Analysis

Over the course of the business cycle, sales and profitability may expand and contract, and ratio analysis for any one year may not present an accurate picture of the firm. Therefore, we look at the **trend analysis** of performance over a number of years. However, without industry comparisons even trend analysis may not present a complete picture.

For example, in Figure 3-2 we see that the profit margin for the Saxton Company has improved, while asset turnover has declined. This by itself may look good for the profit margin and bad for asset turnover. However, when compared to industry trends, we see the firm's profit margin is still below the industry average. With asset turnover, Saxton has improved in relation to the industry, even though it is in a downward trend. Similar data could be generated for the other ratios.

By comparing companies in the same industry, the analyst can examine and compare trends over time. In looking at the computer industry data in Table 3-4, it is apparent that profit margins and returns on equity have changed over time for IBM and Apple. This is primarily due to intensified competition within the industry. IBM began to feel the squeeze on profits first, beginning in 1991, and actually lost money in 1993. By 1994, Lou Gerstner had taken over as chairman and chief executive officer at IBM and had begun turning the company around; by 1997, IBM was back to its old levels of profitability and hitting all-time highs for return on stockholders' equity. This continued

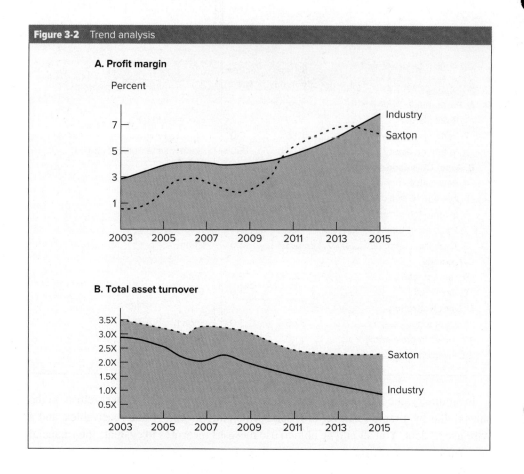

Figure 3-2   Trend analysis

A. Profit margin

Percent

B. Total asset turnover

until the recession of 2001–2002. During the next decade, IBM engaged in financial engineering. It kept repurchasing shares of stock in the market, reducing its share count from 29.7 billion shares in 2004 to 17.2 billion shares in 2014. During the same years, its revenues decreased from $96.3 billion to $94.5 billion.

In 2003, Apple Computer began its amazing 10-year run, creating the iPod, annual versions of the iPhone, the iPad, the iPad mini, and new versions of its MacBook and iMac computers. Note that even though Apple's profit margin far exceeds that of IBM, IBM still has a higher return on equity. This takes us back to the Du Pont model. IBM has a debt-to-assets ratio of 84.5 percent in its capital structure, while Apple has a 64.3 percent debt-to-assets ratio.

Apple was almost debt free until 2013 when, under pressure from institutional stockholders, the company agreed to sell a total of $35.3 billion of debt and use the proceeds to buy back stock and raise its dividends. From 2015 to 2017, Apple spent almost $100 billion buying back stock and substantially increasing its debt-to-assets ratio. In contrasting the two companies, we should point out that while IBM's revenues were stagnant from 2004 to 2017, Apple grew its revenues from $8.2 billion in 2004 to $229.234 billion, almost tripling IBM's 2017 revenues of $78.4 billion.

What will be the trends for these two companies for the rest of the decade? Technology is changing so quickly that no one can say. Both are likely to remain lean in operating expenses but highly innovative in new product development.

Table 3-4   Trend analysis in the computer industry

	IBM		Apple	
	Profit Margin	**Return on Equity**	**Profit Margin**	**Return on Equity**
1988	9.7	14.9	9.8	43.5
1989	6.0	9.6	8.6	36.5
1990	8.7	14.8	8.5	32.4
1991	−4.4	−7.2	4.9	19.3
1992	−7.7	−15.4	7.5	26.8
1993	−12.9	−35.2	1.1	4.1
1994	4.7	14.3	3.4	14.1
1995	5.8	18.5	3.8	16.0
1996	7.1	24.8	−8.3	−32.9
1997	7.8	29.7	−14.8	−67.2
1998	7.7	32.6	5.2	24.3
1999	8.8	39.0	9.8	27.0
2000	9.2	39.7	9.8	22.5
2001	9.3	35.2	−0.5	−0.6
2002	4.4	15.5	1.1	1.6
2003	8.5	29.9	1.1	1.7
2004	7.8	25.1	3.3	5.9
2005	8.7	24.5	9.5	21.2
2006	10.4	30.8	10.3	22.8
2007	10.5	36.6	14.2	28.5
2008	11.9	58.8	16.3	33.2
2009	14.0	74.4	19.2	30.5
2010	14.9	64.9	21.5	35.3
2011	14.8	73.4	23.9	41.7
2012	15.9	88.0	26.7	35.3
2013	16.5	72.3	21.7	30.0
2014	16.0	87.0	21.6	35.4
2015	16.1	93.8	22.9	44.8
2016	14.9	65.2	21.2	35.6
2017	7.3	32.5	21.1	36.1

Impact of Inflation on Financial Analysis

Before, coincident with, or following the computation of financial ratios, we should explore the impact of **inflation** and other sources of distortion on the financial reporting of the firm. As illustrated in this section, inflation causes phantom sources of profit that may mislead even the most alert analyst. Disinflation also causes certain problems, and we shall consider these as well.

The major problem during inflationary times is that revenue is almost always stated in current dollars, whereas plant and equipment or inventory may have been purchased at lower price levels. Thus profit may be more a function of increasing prices than of satisfactory performance. Although inflation has been moderate since the early 1990s, it tends to reappear, so you should be aware of its consequences.

Finance in
ACTION

**Are Financial Analysts Friends or Foes to Investors?
Reader Beware!**

Managerial

Financial analysis is done not only by managers of the firm but by outside analysts as well. These outside analysts normally supply data to stock market investors.

One of the problems that was detected after the great bull market of the 1990s was that analysts were not always as objective as they should have been. This unfortunate discovery helped intensify the bear market of the early 2000s.

The reason that many analysts lack objectivity is that they work for investment banking–brokerage firms that not only provide financial analysis for investors but also underwrite the securities of the firms they are covering. Underwriting activity involves the distribution of new securities in the public markets and is highly profitable to the investment banker. For example, Goldman Sachs, a major Wall Street investment banking firm, may not only be doing research and financial analysis on General Electric or Eastman Kodak but also profiting from investment banking business with these firms.

Since the fees from investment banking activities contribute heavily to the overall operations of the investment banker, many analysts for investment banking firms "relaxed their standards" in doing financial analysis on their clients in the 1990s.

As an example, Goldman Sachs, Merrill Lynch, and other Wall Street firms often failed to divulge potential weaknesses in the firms they were investigating for fear of losing the clients' investment banking business. Corporations that were being reported upon were equally guilty. Many a corporate chief officer told an investment banker that "if you come out with a negative report, you will never see another dollar's worth of our investment banking business." Morgan Stanley, a major investment banker, actually had a written internal

policy for analysts never to make negative comments about firms providing investment banking fees. Pity the poor investor who naively followed the advice of Morgan Stanley during the mid-1990s.

After the market crash of the early 2000s, the SEC and federal legislators began requiring investment bankers to either fully separate their financial analysis and underwriting business or, at a minimum, fully divulge any such relationships. For example, Merrill Lynch now states in its research reports, *"Investors should assume that Merrill Lynch is seeking or will seek investing banking or other business relationships with the companies in this report."*

The government is also requiring investment bankers to provide independent reports to accompany their own in-house reports. These independent reports are done by fee-based research firms that do not engage in underwriting activities. Independent firms include Standard & Poor's, Value Line, Morningstar, and other smaller firms. They tend to be totally objective and hard-hitting when necessary.

Some independent research firms know more about a company than it knows about itself. Take the example of Sanford C. Bernstein & Co. and Cisco Systems in late 2000. Bernstein analyst Paul Sagawa downgraded Cisco for investment purposes, even though Cisco Chief Executive Officer John T. Chambers respectfully disagreed. The astute independent analyst anticipated the end of the telecom boom and knew the disastrous effect it would have on Cisco because the company would lose key telecom customers. When the disaster finally occurred, CEO Chambers told investors that "no one could have predicted it. It was like a 100-year flood." Apparently, he forgot about the Sagawa report he had read and dismissed only a few months before.

An Illustration

The Stein Corporation shows the income statement for 2018 in Table 3-5. At year-end the firm also has 100 units still in inventory at $1 per unit.

Assume that in the year 2019 the number of units sold remains constant at 100. However, inflation causes a 10 percent increase in price, from $2 to $2.20. Total sales will go up to $220, as shown in Table 3-6, but with no actual increase in physical volume. Further, assume the firm uses FIFO inventory pricing, so that inventory first

| Table 3-5 | Stein Corporation income statement for 2018 |

STEIN CORPORATION Net Income for 2018		
Sales	$200	(100 units at $2)
Cost of goods sold	100	(100 units at $1)
Gross profit	$100	
Selling and administrative expense	20	(10% of sales)
Depreciation	10	
Operating profit	$ 70	
Taxes (24%)	17	
Aftertax income	$ 53	

| Table 3-6 | Stein Corporation income statement for 2019 |

STEIN CORPORATION Net Income for 2019		
Sales	$220	(100 units at 2000 price of $2.20)
Cost of goods sold	100	(100 units at $1.00)
Gross profit	$120	
Selling and administrative expense	22	(10% of sales)
Depreciation	10	
Operating profit	$ 88	
Taxes (24%)	21	
Aftertax income	$ 67	

purchased will be written off against current sales. In this case, 2018 inventory will be written off against year 2019 sales revenue.

In Table 3-6, the company appears to have increased profit by $14 compared to that shown in Table 3-5 (from $53 to $67) simply as a result of inflation. But not reflected is the increased cost of replacing inventory and plant and equipment. Presumably, **replacement costs** have increased in an inflationary environment.

As mentioned in Chapter 2, inflation-related information was formerly required by the FASB for large companies, but this is no longer the case. It is now purely voluntary. What are the implications of this type of inflation-adjusted data? From a study of 10 chemical firms and 8 drug companies, using current cost (replacement cost) data found in the financial 10K statements these companies filed with the Securities and Exchange Commission, it was found that the changes shown in Table 3-7 occurred in their assets, income, and selected ratios.[5]

The comparison of replacement cost and historical cost accounting methods in the table shows that replacement cost reduces income but at the same time increases assets. This increase in assets lowers the debt-to-assets ratio, since debt is a monetary asset that is not revalued because it is paid back in current dollars. The decreased debt-to-assets ratio would indicate the financial leverage of the firm is decreased, but a look at the

[5]Jeff Garnett and Geoffrey A. Hirt, "Replacement Cost Data: A Study of the Chemical and Drug Industry for Years 1976 through 1978." Replacement cost is but one form of current cost. Nevertheless, it is often used as a measure of current cost.

	10 Chemical Companies		8 Drug Companies	
	Replacement Cost	**Historical Cost**	**Replacement Cost**	**Historical Cost**
Increase in assets	28.4%	—	15.4%	—
Decrease in net income before taxes	45.8%	—	19.3%	—
Return on assets	2.8%	6.2%	8.3%	11.4%
Return on equity	4.9%	13.5%	12.8%	19.6%
Debt-to-assets ratio	34.3%	43.8%	30.3%	35.2%
Interest coverage ratio (times interest earned)	7.1 times	8.4 times	15.4 times	16.7 times

Table 3-7   Comparison of replacement cost accounting and historical cost accounting

interest coverage ratio tells a different story. Because the interest coverage ratio measures the operating income available to cover interest expense, the declining income penalizes this ratio, and the firm has decreased its ability to cover its interest cost.

Disinflation Effect

As long as prices continue to rise in an inflationary environment, profits appear to feed on themselves. The main problem is that when price increases moderate (**disinflation**), there will be a rude awakening for management and unsuspecting stockholders as expensive inventory is charged against softening retail prices. A 15 or 20 percent growth rate in earnings may be little more than an "inflationary illusion." Industries most sensitive to inflation-induced profits are those with cyclical products, such as lumber, copper, rubber, and food products, as well as those in which inventory is a significant percentage of sales and profits.

A leveling off of prices is not necessarily bad. Even though inflation-induced corporate profits may be going down, investors may be more willing to place their funds in financial assets such as stocks and bonds. The reason for the shift may be a belief that declining inflationary pressures will no longer seriously impair the purchasing power of the dollar. Lessening inflation means the required return that investors demand on financial assets will be going down, and with this lower demanded return, future earnings or interest should receive a higher current valuation.

None of this happens with a high degree of certainty. To the extent that investors question the permanence of disinflation (leveling off of price increases), they may not act according to the script. That is, lower rates of inflation will not necessarily produce high stock and bond prices unless reduced inflation is sustainable over a reasonable period.

Whereas financial assets such as stocks and bonds have the potential (whether realized or not) to do well during disinflation, such is not the case for tangible (real) assets. Precious metals, such as gold and silver, gems, and collectibles, which boomed in the highly inflationary environment of the late 1970s, fell off sharply a decade later, as softening prices reduced the perceived need to hold real assets as a hedge against inflation. The shifting back and forth by investors between financial and real assets may occur many times over a business cycle.

Deflation   There is also the danger of **deflation**, actual declining prices in which everyone gets hurt from bankruptcies and declining profits. Deflation was a major contributor to the length and severity of the worldwide Great Depression of the 1930s. Deflation occurred again in Russia, Japan, and other foreign countries in 1998, and it became a concern in the United States during the "Great Recession" from 2007 to 2012. The Federal Reserve and other national banks would rather have a low-inflation economy (1 or 2 percent per year) than a deflationary economy.

Other Elements of Distortion in Reported Income

The effect of changing prices is but one of a number of problems the analyst must cope with in evaluating a company. Other issues, such as the reporting of revenue, the treatment of nonrecurring items, and the tax write-off policy, cause dilemmas for the financial manager or analyst. We can illustrate this point by considering the income statements for two hypothetical companies in the same industry, as shown in Table 3-8. Both firms had identical operating performances for 2018—but Company A is very conservative in reporting its results, while Company B has attempted to maximize its reported income.

If both companies had reported income of $280,000 in the prior year of 2017, Company B would be thought to be showing substantial growth in 2018 with net income of $700,000, while Company A would be reporting a "flat," or no-growth, year in 2018. However, we have already established that the companies have equal operating performances.

Explanation of Discrepancies

Let us examine how the inconsistencies in Table 3-8 can occur. Emphasis is given to a number of key elements on the income statement. The items being discussed here are not illegal but reflect flexibility in financial reporting.

Sales   Company B reported $200,000 more in sales, although actual volume was the same. This may be the result of different concepts of revenue recognition.

For example, certain assets may be sold on an installment basis over a long period. A conservative firm may defer recognition of the sales or revenue until each payment is received, while other firms may attempt to recognize a fully effected sale at

Table 3-8 Income Statements		
INCOME STATEMENTS **For the Year 2018**		
	Conservative Firm A	**High Reported Income Firm B**
Sales	$4,000,000	$4,200,000
Cost of goods sold	3,000,000	2,700,000
Gross profit	$1,000,000	$1,500,000
Selling and administrative expense	450,000	450,000
Operating profit	$ 550,000	$1,050,000
Interest expense	50,000	50,000
Net income before taxes	$ 500,000	$1,000,000
Taxes (30%)	150,000	300,000
Net income transferred to retained earnings	$ 350,000	$ 700,000

Ethics

Perhaps "sustainability" isn't the first word that comes to mind when someone thinks about the garbage business. However, today's waste industry leaders not only develop sanitary landfills with synthetic liners and ground water monitoring wells but are often at the forefront of community recycling and renewable energy efforts.

When Lonnie Poole started Waste Industries in 1970, he didn't know that the company would grow to be one of the country's largest waste companies, but like most entrepreneurs, he did believe that he could build a business for the long haul. Focused on a commitment to service, Poole knew that his company had to find ways to offer service options that were both economically viable and environmentally sustainable. Sometimes projects provided an adequate near-term return on assets (ROA) and they made sense from a sustainability perspective. Other times, doing the right thing from a long-term sustainability perspective meant Waste Industries needed to find a way to overcome short-term financial considerations.

Take the company's recycling effort as an example. Waste Industries has been engaged in recycling since the 1970s. From an ROA perspective, it was hard to justify the firm's recycling efforts. At first, there was no market for the recyclables. Instead of selling recycled paper, the firm had to *pay* paper companies to haul recycled paper away. Over time, Waste Industries' investments in sustainability began to pay off. Due to its early investments, today

an infrastructure has developed to recycle more waste at lower costs.

Based purely on a short-run ROA, the firm's long-term commitment was not justified, but Poole's commitment to recycling and other sustainable practices were part of a wider corporate culture focused on treating customers, employees, and the broader community with respect.

Now business researchers are finding that Poole may have simply been ahead of his time. When Harvard researchers examined the impact of corporate sustainability initiatives on long-term firm performance, they discovered both higher ROA and higher ROE (return on equity) for firms whose executives promoted sustainability within their firms.

Philosophers and religious leaders have long touted the "Golden Rule" as a basic ethical code, which states people should do to others what they would wish done to themselves. Like many successful businesspeople, Poole believed sustainability meant making a positive difference in the communities his company served, enriching the lives of employees, and forging meaningful relationships with vendors and suppliers. In the long run, these values paid off. Perhaps this is why a basic rule for ethical behavior is called "golden."

Source: Eccles, R.G., Ioannou, I., and Serafelm, G. "The Impact of a Corporate Culture of Sustainability on Corporate Behavior and Performance," *NBER Working Paper No. 17950*, 2012.

---

the earliest possible date. Similarly, firms that lease assets may attempt to consider a long-term lease as the equivalent of a sale, while more conservative firms recognize as revenue each lease payment only when it comes due. Although the accounting profession attempts to establish appropriate methods of financial reporting through generally accepted accounting principles, reporting varies among firms and industries.

Cost of Goods Sold   The conservative firm (Company A) may well be using **LIFO** accounting in an inflationary environment, thus charging the last-purchased, more expensive items against sales, while Company B uses **FIFO** accounting—charging off less expensive inventory against sales. The $300,000 difference in cost of goods sold may also be explained by varying treatment of research and development costs and other items.

Net Income

Firm A has reported net income of $350,000, while Firm B claims $700,000. The $350,000 difference is attributed to different methods of financial reporting, and it should be recognized as such by the analyst. No superior performance has actually taken place. The analyst must remain ever alert in examining each item in the financial statements, rather than accepting bottom-line figures.

SUMMARY

Ratio analysis allows the analyst to compare a company's performance to that of others in its industry. Ratios that initially appear good or bad may not retain that characteristic when measured against industry peers.

There are four main groupings of ratios. Profitability ratios measure the firm's ability to earn an adequate return on sales, assets, and stockholders' equity. The asset utilization ratios tell the analyst how quickly the firm is turning over its accounts receivable, inventory, and longer-term assets. Liquidity ratios measure the firm's ability to pay off short-term obligations as they come due, and debt utilization ratios indicate the overall debt position of the firm in light of its asset base and earning power.

The Du Pont system of analysis first breaks down return on assets between the profit margin and asset turnover. The second step shows how this return on assets is translated into return on equity through the amount of debt the firm has. Throughout the analysis, the analyst can better understand how return on assets and return on equity are derived.

Over the course of the business cycle, sales and profitability may expand and contract, and ratio analysis for any one year may not present an accurate picture of the firm. Therefore, we look at the trend analysis of performance over a period of years.

A number of factors may distort the numbers accountants actually report. These include the effect of inflation or disinflation, the timing of the recognition of sales as revenue, the treatment of inventory write-offs, and so on. The well-trained financial analyst must be alert to all of these factors.

LIST OF TERMS

profitability ratios 59	**debt utilization ratios** 60
profit margin	**debt to total assets**
return on assets	**times interest earned**
return on equity	**fixed charge coverage**
asset utilization ratios 60	**Du Pont system of analysis** 62
receivables turnover	**trend analysis** 67
average collection period	**inflation** 69
inventory turnover	**replacement costs** 71
fixed asset turnover	**disinflation** 72
total asset turnover	**deflation** 72
liquidity ratios 60	**LIFO** 74
current ratio	**FIFO** 74
quick ratio	

DISCUSSION QUESTIONS

1. If we divide users of ratios into short-term lenders, long-term lenders, and stockholders, which ratios would each group be *most* interested in, and for what reasons? *(LO3-2)*

2. Explain how the Du Pont system of analysis breaks down return on assets. Also explain how it breaks down return on stockholders' equity. *(LO3-3)*

3. If the accounts receivable turnover ratio is decreasing, what will be happening to the average collection period? *(LO3-2)*

4. What advantage does the fixed charge coverage ratio offer over simply using times interest earned? *(LO3-2)*

5. Is there any validity in rule-of-thumb ratios for all corporations, such as a current ratio of 2 to 1 or debt to assets of 50 percent? *(LO3-2)*

6. Why is trend analysis helpful in analyzing ratios? *(LO3-4)*

7. Inflation can have significant effects on income statements and balance sheets, and therefore on the calculation of ratios. Discuss the possible impact of inflation on the following ratios, and explain the direction of the impact based on your assumptions. *(LO3-5)*

    a. Return on investment

    b. Inventory turnover

    c. Fixed asset turnover

    d. Debt-to-assets ratio

8. What effect will disinflation following a highly inflationary period have on the reported income of the firm? *(LO3-5)*

9. Why might disinflation prove favorable to financial assets? *(LO3-5)*

10. Comparisons of income can be very difficult for two companies, even though they sell the same products in equal volume. Why? *(LO3-2)*

PRACTICE PROBLEMS AND SOLUTIONS

Profitability ratios
(LO3-2)

1. Barnes Appliances has sales of $10,000,000, net income of $450,000, total assets of $4,000,000, and stockholders' equity of $2,000,000.

    a. What is the profit margin?

    b. What is the return on assets?

    c. What is the return on equity?

    d. The debt-to-assets ratio is currently 50 percent. If it were 60 percent, what would the return on equity be? To answer this question, use Ratio 3*b* in the text.

All 13 ratios
(LO3-2)

2. The Gilliam Corp. has the following balance sheet and income statement. Compute the profitability, asset utilization, liquidity, and debt utilization ratios.

GILLIAM CORPORATION		
Balance Sheet		
December 31, 20X1		

Assets

Current assets:

Cash	$	70,000
Marketable securities		40,000
Accounts receivable (net)		250,000
Inventory		200,000
Total current assets	$	560,000

(continued)

(*continued*)

GILLIAM CORPORATION	
Balance Sheet	
December 31, 20X1	

Investments	100,000
Net plant and equipment	440,000
Total assets	$1,100,000
Liabilities and Stockholders' Equity	
Current liabilities:	
Accounts payable	$ 130,000
Notes payable	120,000
Accrued taxes	30,000
Total current liabilities	$ 280,000
Long-term liabilities:	
Bonds payable	$ 200,000
Total liabilities	$ 480,000
Stockholders' equity	
Preferred stock, $100 par value	$ 150,000
Common stock, $5 par value	50,000
Capital paid in excess of par	200,000
Retained earnings	220,000
Total stockholders' equity	$ 620,000
Total liabilities and stockholders' equity	$1,100,000

GILLIAM CORPORATION	
Income Statement	
For the Year Ending December 31, 20X1	

Sales (on credit)	$2,400,000
Less: Cost of goods sold	1,600,000
Gross profit	$ 800,000
Less: Selling and administrative expenses	560,000*
Operating profit (EBIT)	$ 240,000
Less: Interest expense	30,000
Earnings before taxes (EBT)	$ 210,000
Less: Taxes	75,000
Earnings after taxes (EAT)	$ 135,000

*Includes $40,000 in lease payments.

Solutions

1. *a.* $\text{Profit margin} = \dfrac{\text{Net income}}{\text{Sales}} = \dfrac{\$450,000}{\$10,000,000} = 4.5\%$

   b. $\text{Return on assets} = \dfrac{\text{Net income}}{\text{Total assets}} = \dfrac{\$450,000}{\$4,000,000} = 11.25\%$

   c. $\text{Return on equity} = \dfrac{\text{Net income}}{\text{Stockholders' equity}} = \dfrac{\$450,000}{\$2,000,000} = 22.5\%$

   d.   Return on equity $= \dfrac{\text{Return on assets (investment)}}{(1 - \text{Debt/Assets})} = \dfrac{11.25\%}{(1 - 0.6)}$

$$= \dfrac{11.25\%}{0.4} = 28.13\%$$

2. **Profitability ratios**

   1. Profit margin $= \dfrac{\text{Net income}}{\text{Sales}} = \dfrac{\$135,000}{2,400,000} = 5.63\%$

   2. Return on assets $= \dfrac{\text{Net income}}{\text{Total assets}} = \dfrac{\$135,000}{1,100,000} = 12.27\%$

   3. Return on equity $= \dfrac{\text{Net income}}{\text{Stockholders' equity}} = \dfrac{\$135,000}{620,000} = 21.77\%$

Asset utilization ratios

   4. Receivables turnover $= \dfrac{\text{Sales (credits)}}{\text{Accounts receivable}} = \dfrac{\$2,400,000}{250,000} = 9.6 \text{ times}$

   5. Average collection period $= \dfrac{\text{Accounts receivable}}{\text{Avg. daily credit sales}} = \dfrac{\$250,000}{6,667} = 37.5 \text{ days}$

   6. Inventory turnover $= \dfrac{\text{Sales}}{\text{Inventory}} = \dfrac{\$2,400,000}{200,000} = 12 \text{ times}$

   7. Fixed asset turnover $= \dfrac{\text{Sales}}{\text{Fixed assets}} = \dfrac{\$2,400,000}{440,000} = 5.45 \text{ times}$

   8. Total asset turnover $= \dfrac{\text{Sales}}{\text{Total assets}} = \dfrac{\$2,400,000}{1,100,000} = 2.18 \text{ times}$

Liquidity ratios

   9. Current ratio $= \dfrac{\text{Current assets}}{\text{Current liabilities}} = \dfrac{\$560,000}{280,000} = 2 \text{ times}$

  10. Quick ratio $= \dfrac{\text{Current assets} - \text{Inventory}}{\text{Current liabilities}} = \dfrac{\$560,000 - 200,000}{280,000}$

$$= \dfrac{360,000}{280,000} = 1.29 \text{ times}$$

Debt utilization ratios

  11. Debt to total assets $= \dfrac{\text{Total debt}}{\text{Total assets}} = \dfrac{\$480,000}{1,100,000} = 43.64\%$

  12. Times interest earned $= \dfrac{\text{Income before interest and taxes}}{\text{Interest}}$

       Note: Income before interest and taxes equals operating profit, \$240,000.

       Times interest earned $= \dfrac{240,000}{30,000} = 8 \text{ times}$

13. $\text{Fixed charge coverage} = \dfrac{\text{Income before fixed charges and taxes}}{\text{Fixed charges}}$

Income before fixed charges and taxes = Operating profit + Lease payments*

$$\$240{,}000 + \$40{,}000 = \$280{,}000$$

Fixed charges = Lease payments = Interest

$$\$40{,}000 + \$30{,}000 = \$70{,}000$$

$$\text{Fixed charge coverage} = \dfrac{\$280{,}000}{70{,}000} = 4 \text{ times}$$

PROBLEMS

connect Selected problems are available with Connect. Please see the preface for more information.

Basic Problems

1. Low Carb Diet Supplement Inc. has two divisions. Division A has a profit of $156,000 on sales of $2,010,000. Division B is able to make only $28,800 on sales of $329,000. Based on the profit margins (returns on sales), which division is superior?

   Profitability ratios (LO3-2)

2. Database Systems is considering expansion into a new product line. Assets to support expansion will cost $380,000. It is estimated that Database can generate $1,410,000 in annual sales, with an 8 percent profit margin. What would net income and return on assets (investment) be for the year?

   Profitability ratios (LO3-2)

3. Polly Esther Dress Shops Inc. can open a new store that will do an annual sales volume of $837,900. It will turn over its assets 1.9 times per year. The profit margin on sales will be 8 percent. What would net income and return on assets (investment) be for the year?

   Profitability ratios (LO3-2)

4. Billy's Crystal Stores Inc. has assets of $5,960,000 and turns over its assets 1.9 times per year. Return on assets is 8 percent. What is the firm's profit margin (return on sales)?

   Profitability ratios (LO3-2)

5. Elizabeth Tailors Inc. has assets of $8,940,000 and turns over its assets 1.9 times per year. Return on assets is 13.5 percent. What is the firm's profit margin (returns on sales)?

   Profitability ratios (LO3-2)

6. Dr. Zhivàgo Diagnostics Corp.'s income statement for 20X1 is as follows:

   Profitability ratios (LO3-2)

Sales	$2,790,000
Cost of goods sold	1,790,000
Gross profit	$1,000,000
Selling and administrative expense	302,000
Operating profit	$ 698,000
Interest expense	54,800
Income before taxes	$ 643,200
Taxes (30%)	192,960
Income after taxes	$ 450,240

   a. Compute the profit margin for 20X1.

   b. Assume that in 20X2, sales increase by 10 percent and cost of goods sold increases by 20 percent. The firm is able to keep all other expenses the

*Lease payments are in a footnote on the income statement (middle of page 66).

same. Assume a tax rate of 30 percent on income before taxes. What is income after taxes and the profit margin for 20X2?

Profitability ratios
(LO3-2)

7. The Haines Corp. shows the following financial data for 20X1 and 20X2:

	20X1	20X2
Sales	$3,230,000	$3,370,000
Cost of goods sold	2,130,000	2,850,000
Gross profit	$1,100,000	$ 520,000
Selling & administrative expense	298,000	227,000
Operating profit	$ 802,000	$ 293,000
Interest expense	47,200	51,600
Income before taxes	$ 754,800	$ 241,400
Taxes (35%)	264,180	84,490
Income after taxes	$ 490,620	$ 156,910

For each year, compute the following and indicate whether it is increasing or decreasing profitability in 20X2 as indicated by the ratio:

a.   Cost of goods sold to sales.

b.   Selling and administrative expense to sales.

c.   Interest expenses to sales.

Profitability ratios
(LO3-2)

8. Easter Egg and Poultry Company has $2,000,000 in assets and $1,400,000 of debt. It reports net income of $200,000.

a.   What is the firm's return on assets?

b.   What is its return on stockholders' equity?

c.   If the firm has an asset turnover ratio of 2.5 times, what is the profit margin (return on sales)?

Profitability ratios
(LO3-2)

9. Network Communications has total assets of $1,500,000 and current assets of $612,000. It turns over its fixed assets three times a year. It has $319,000 of debt. Its return on sales is 8 percent. What is its return on stockholders' equity?

Profitability ratios
(LO3-2)

10. Fondren Machine Tools has total assets of $3,310,000 and current assets of $879,000. It turns over its fixed assets 3.6 times per year. Its return on sales is 4.8 percent. It has $1,750,000 of debt. What is its return on stockholders' equity?

Profitability ratios
(LO3-2)

11. Baker Oats had an asset turnover of 1.6 times per year.

a.   If the return on total assets (investment) was 11.2 percent, what was Baker's profit margin?

b.   The following year, on the same level of assets, Baker's asset turnover declined to 1.4 times and its profit margin was 8 percent. How did the return on total assets change from that of the previous year?

Du Pont system of analysis
(LO3-3)

12. AllState Trucking Co. has the following ratios compared to its industry for last year:

	AllState Trucking	Industry
Return on sales	3%	8%
Return on assets	15%	10%

Explain why the return-on-assets ratio is so much more favorable than the return-on-sales ratio compared to the industry. No numbers are necessary; a one-sentence answer is all that is required.

13. Front Beam Lighting Company has the following ratios compared to its industry for last year:

Du Pont system of analysis (LO3-3)

	Front Beam Lighting	Industry
Return on assets	12%	5%
Return on equity	16%	20%

Explain why the return-on-equity ratio is so much less favorable than the return-on-assets ratio compared to the industry. No numbers are necessary; a one-sentence answer is all that is required.

14. Gates Appliances has a return-on-assets (investment) ratio of 8 percent.

Du Pont system of analysis (LO3-3)

   a. If the debt-to-total-assets ratio is 40 percent, what is the return on equity?

   b. If the firm had no debt, what would the return-on-equity ratio be?

Intermediate Problems

15. Using the Du Pont method, evaluate the effects of the following relationships for the Butters Corporation:

Du Pont system of analysis (LO3-3)

   a. Butters Corporation has a profit margin of 7 percent and its return on assets (investment) is 25.2 percent. What is its assets turnover?

   b. If the Butters Corporation has a debt-to-total-assets ratio of 50 percent, what would the firm's return on equity be?

   c. What would happen to return on equity if the debt-to-total-assets ratio decreased to 35 percent?

16. Jerry Rice and Grain Stores has $4,780,000 in yearly sales. The firm earns 4.5 percent on each dollar of sales and turns over its assets 2.7 times per year. It has $123,000 in current liabilities and $349,000 in long-term liabilities.

Du Pont system of analysis (LO3-3)

   a. What is its return on stockholders' equity?

   b. If the asset base remains the same as computed in part *a,* but total asset turnover goes up to 3, what will be the new return on stockholders' equity? Assume that the profit margin stays the same, as do current and long-term liabilities.

17. Assume the following data for Cable Corporation and Multi-Media Inc.:

Interpreting results from the Du Pont system of analysis (LO3-3)

	Cable Corporation	Multi-Media Inc.
Net income	$ 31,200	$ 140,000
Sales	317,000	2,700,000
Total assets	402,000	965,000
Total debt	163,000	542,000
Stockholders' equity	239,000	423,000

   a. Compute the return on stockholders' equity for both firms using Ratio 3*a.*
Which firm has the higher return?

   b. Compute the following additional ratios for both firms:

      Net income/Sales

      Net income/Total assets

      Sales/Total assets

      Debt/Total assets

   c. Discuss the factors from part *b* that added or detracted from one firm
having a higher return on stockholders' equity than the other firm, as
computed in part *a.*

Average collection period
(LO3-2)

18. A firm has sales of $3 million, and 10 percent of the sales are for cash.
The year-end accounts receivable balance is $285,000. What is the average
collection period? (Use a 360-day year.)

Average daily sales
(LO3-2)

19. Martin Electronics has an accounts receivable turnover equal to 15 times.
If accounts receivable are equal to $80,000, what is the value for average
daily credit sales?

Inventory turnover
(LO3-2)

20. Perez Corporation has the following financial data for the years 20X1 and 20X2:

	20X1	20X2
Sales	$8,000,000	$10,000,000
Cost of goods sold	6,000,000	9,000,000
Inventory	800,000	1,000,000

   a. Compute inventory turnover based on Ratio 6, Sales/Inventory, for each year.

   b. Compute inventory turnover based on an alternative calculation that is used
by many financial analysts, Cost of goods sold/Inventory, for each year.

   c. What conclusions can you draw from part *a* and part *b*?

Turnover ratios
(LO3-2)

21. Jim Short's Company makes clothing for schools. Sales in 20X1 were
$4,820,000. Assets were as follows:

Cash	$ 163,000
Accounts receivable	889,000
Inventory	411,000
Net plant and equipment	520,000
Total assets	$1,983,000

   a. Compute the following:

     1. Accounts receivable turnover

     2. Inventory turnover

     3. Fixed asset turnover

     4. Total asset turnover

b.   In 20X2, sales increased to $5,740,000 and the assets for that year were as follows:

Cash	$ 163,000
Accounts receivable	924,000
Inventory	1,063,000
Net plant and equipment	520,000
Total assets	$2,670,000

Once again, compute the four ratios.

c.   Indicate if there is an improvement or a decline in total asset turnover, and based on the other ratios, indicate why this development has taken place.

22.   The balance sheet for Stud Clothiers is shown below. Sales for the year were $2,400,000, with 90 percent of sales sold on credit.

Overall ratio analysis
(LO3-2)

STUD CLOTHIERS			
Balance Sheet 20X1			
Assets		**Liabilities and Equity**	
Cash	$ 60,000	Accounts payable	$ 220,000
Accounts receivable	240,000	Accrued taxes	30,000
Inventory	350,000	Bonds payable (long-term)	150,000
Plant and equipment	410,000	Common stock	80,000
		Paid-in capital	200,000
		Retained earnings	380,000
Total assets	$1,060,000	Total liabilities and equity	$1,060,000

Compute the following ratios:

a.   Current ratio

b.   Quick ratio

c.   Debt-to-total-assets ratio

d.   Asset turnover

e.   Average collection period

23.   The Lancaster Corporation's income statement is given below.

a.   What is the times-interest-earned ratio?

b.   What would be the fixed-charge-coverage ratio?

Debt utilization ratios
(LO3-2)

LANCASTER CORPORATION	
Sales	$246,000
Cost of goods sold	122,000
Gross profit	$124,000
Fixed charges (other than interest)	27,500
Income before interest and taxes	$ 96,500
Interest	21,800
Income before taxes	$ 74,700
Taxes (35%)	26,145
Income after taxes	$ 48,555

Debt utilization
and Du Pont
system of analysis
(LO3-3)

24. Using the income statement for Times Mirror and Glass Co., compute the following ratios:

    a. The interest coverage

    b. The fixed charge coverage

    The total assets for this company equal $80,000. Set up the equation for the Du Pont system of ratio analysis, and compute *c*, *d*, and *e*.

    c. Profit margin

    d. Total asset turnover

    e. Return on assets (investment)

TIMES MIRROR AND GLASS COMPANY	
Sales	$126,000
Less: Cost of goods sold	93,000
Gross profit	$ 33,000
Less: Selling and administrative expense	11,000
Less: Lease expense	4,000
Operating profit*	$ 18,000
Less: Interest expense	3,000
Earnings before taxes	$ 15,000
Less: Taxes (30%)	4,500
Earnings after taxes	$ 10,500

*Equals income before interest and taxes.

Debt utilization
(LO3-2)

25. A firm has net income before interest and taxes of $193,000 and interest expense of $28,100.

    a. What is the times-interest-earned ratio?

    b. If the firm's lease payments are $48,500, what is the fixed charge coverage?

Advanced Problems

Return on assets
analysis *(LO3-2)*

26. In January 2007, the Status Quo Company was formed. Total assets were $544,000, of which $306,000 consisted of depreciable fixed assets. Status Quo uses straight-line depreciation of $30,600 per year, and in 2007 it estimated its fixed assets to have useful lives of 10 years. Aftertax income has been $29,000 per year each of the last 10 years. Other assets have not changed since 2007.

    a. Compute return on assets at year-end for 2007, 2009, 2012, 2014, and 2016. (Use $29,000 in the numerator for each year.)

    b. To what do you attribute the phenomenon shown in part *a*?

    c. Now assume income increased by 10 percent each year. What effect would this have on your preceding answers? (A comment is all that is necessary.)

27. Jolie Foster Care Homes Inc. shows the following data:

Trend analysis
(LO3-4)

Year	Net Income	Total Assets	Stockholders' Equity	Total Debt
20X1	$155,000	$2,390,000	$ 761,000	$1,629,000
20X2	191,000	2,700,000	966,000	1,734,000
20X3	208,000	2,730,000	1,770,000	960,000
20X4	192,000	2,470,000	2,220,000	250,000

a.   Compute the ratio of net income to total assets for each year, and comment on the trend.

b.   Compute the ratio of net income to stockholders' equity, and comment on the trend. Explain why there may be a difference in the trends between parts a and b.

28. Quantum Moving Company has the following data. Industry information also is shown.

Trend analysis
(LO3-4)

	Company Data		Industry Data on Net Income/Total Assets
Year	Net Income	Total Assets	
20X1	$424,000	$2,843,000	14.0%
20X2	428,000	3,267,000	9.8
20X3	412,000	3,834,000	3.9
Year	Debt	Total Assets	Industry Data on Debt/Total Assets
20X1	$1,722,000	$2,843,000	56.6%
20X2	1,732,000	3,267,000	42.0
20X3	1,950,000	3,834,000	38.0

As an industry analyst comparing the firm to the industry, are you likely to praise or criticize the firm in terms of the following?

a.   Net income/Total assets

b.   Debt/Total assets

29. The Global Products Corporation has three subsidiaries.

Analysis by divisions
(LO3-2)

	Medical Supplies	Heavy Machinery	Electronics
Sales	$20,040,000	$5,980,000	$4,730,000
Net income (after taxes)	1,700,000	592,000	402,000
Assets	8,340,000	8,760,000	3,570,000

a.   Which division has the lowest return on sales?

b.   Which division has the highest return on assets?

c.   Compute the return on assets for the entire corporation.

d.   If the $8,760,000 investment in the heavy machinery division is sold off and redeployed in the medical supplies subsidiary at the same rate of return on assets currently achieved in the medical supplies division, what will be the new return on assets for the entire corporation?

30. Omni Technology Holding Company has the following three affiliates:

	Software	Personal Computers	Foreign Operations
Sales	$40,200,000	$60,080,000	$100,680,000
Net income (after taxes)	2,086,000	2,880,000	8,510,000
Assets	5,820,000	25,790,000	60,630,000
Stockholders' equity	4,090,000	10,170,000	50,950,000

  a. Which affiliate has the highest return on sales?

  b. Which affiliate has the lowest return on assets?

  c. Which affiliate has the highest total asset turnover?

  d. Which affiliate has the highest return on stockholders' equity?

  e. Which affiliate has the highest debt ratio? (Assets minus stockholders' equity equals debt.)

  f. Returning to part *b,* explain why the software affiliate has the highest return on total assets.

  g. Returning to part *d,* explain why the personal computer affiliate has a higher return on stockholders' equity than the foreign operations affiliate, even though it has a lower return on total assets.

31. The Canton Corporation shows the following income statement. The firm uses FIFO inventory accounting.

CANTON CORPORATION	
Income Statement for 20X1	
Sales	$272,800 (17,600 units at $15.50)
Cost of goods sold	123,200 (17,600 units at $7.00)
Gross profit	$149,600
Selling and administrative expense	13,640
Depreciation	15,900
Operating profit	$120,060
Taxes (30%)	36,018
Aftertax income	$ 84,042

  a. Assume in 20X2 the same 17,600-unit volume is maintained but that the sales price increases by 10 percent. Because of FIFO inventory policy, old inventory will still be charged off at $7 per unit. Also assume selling and administrative expense will be 5 percent of sales and depreciation will be unchanged. The tax rate is 30 percent. Compute aftertax income for 20X2.

  b. In part *a,* by what percentage did aftertax income increase as a result of a 10 percent increase in the sales price? Explain why this impact took place.

  c. Now assume that in 20X3 the volume remains constant at 17,600 units, but the sales price decreases by 15 percent from its year 20X2 level. Also, because of FIFO inventory policy, cost of goods sold reflects the inflationary conditions of the prior year and is $7.50 per unit. Further, assume selling and administrative expense will be 5 percent of sales and depreciation will be unchanged. The tax rate is 30 percent. Compute the aftertax income.

32. Construct the current assets section of the balance sheet from the following data. (Use cash as a plug figure after computing the other values.)

Using ratios to construct financial statements *(LO3-2)*

Yearly sales (credit)	$420,000
Inventory turnover	7 times
Current liabilities	$80,000
Current ratio	2
Average collection period	36 days

Current assets: $

   Cash .... _____

   Accounts receivable .... _____

   Inventory .... _____

     Total current assets .... _____

33. The Griggs Corporation has credit sales of $1,200,000. Given these ratios, fill in the following balance sheet.

Using ratios to construct financial statements *(LO3-2)*

Total assets turnover	2.4 times
Cash to total assets	2.0%
Accounts receivable turnover	8.0 times
Inventory turnover	10.0 times
Current ratio	2.0 times
Debt to total assets	61.0%

GRIGGS CORPORATION
Balance Sheet

Assets		**Liabilities and Stockholders' Equity**	
Cash .... _____		Current debt .... _____	
Accounts receivable .... _____		Long-term debt .... _____	
Inventory .... _____		Total debt .... _____	
Total current assets .... _____		Equity .... _____	
Fixed assets .... _____		Total debt and	
Total assets .... _____		stockholders' equity .... _____	

34. We are given the following information for the Pettit Corporation:

Using ratios to determine account balances *(LO3-2)*

Sales (credit)	$3,549,000
Cash	179,000
Inventory	911,000
Current liabilities	788,000
Asset turnover	1.40 times
Current ratio	2.95 times
Debt-to-assets ratio	40%
Receivables turnover	7 times

Current assets are composed of cash, marketable securities, accounts receivable, and inventory. Calculate the following balance sheet items:

a.   Accounts receivable

b.   Marketable securities

c. Fixed assets

d. Long-term debt

35. The following information is from Harrelson Inc.'s financial statements. Sales (all credit) were $28.50 million for last year.

Sales to total assets	1.90 times
Total debt to total assets	35%
Current ratio	2.50 times
Inventory turnover	10.00 times
Average collection period	20 days
Fixed asset turnover	5.00 times

Fill in the balance sheet:

Cash	_____	Current debt	_____
Accounts receivable	_____	Long-term debt	_____
Inventory	_____	Total debt	_____
Total current assets	_____	Equity	_____
Fixed assets	_____	Total debt and equity	_____
Total assets	_____		

36. Using the financial statements for the Snider Corporation, calculate the 13 basic ratios found in the chapter.

SNIDER CORPORATION
Balance Sheet
December 31, 20X1

Assets

Current assets:

Cash	$ 52,200
Marketable securities	24,400
Accounts receivable (net)	222,000
Inventory	238,000
Total current assets	$536,600
Investments	65,900
Plant and equipment	$615,000
Less: Accumulated depreciation	(271,000)
Net plant and equipment	$344,000
Total assets	$946,500

Liabilities and Stockholders' Equity

Current liabilities:

Accounts payable	$ 93,400
Notes payable	70,600
Accrued taxes	17,000
Total current liabilities	$181,000

(continued)

(*continued*)

SNIDER CORPORATION
Balance Sheet
December 31, 20X1

Long-term liabilities:	
Bonds payable	$153,200
Total liabilities	$334,200
Stockholders' equity:	
Preferred stock, $50 per value	$100,000
Common stock, $1 par value	80,000
Capital paid in excess of par	190,000
Retained earnings	242,300
Total stockholders' equity	$612,300
Total liabilities and stockholders' equity	$946,500

SNIDER CORPORATION
Income statement
For the Year Ending December 31, 20X1

Sales (on credit)	$2,064,000
Less: Cost of goods sold	1,313,000
Gross profit	$ 751,000
Less: Selling and administrative expenses	496,000*
Operating profit (EBIT)	$ 255,000
Less: Interest expense	26,900
Earnings before taxes (EBT)	$ 228,100
Less: Taxes	83,300
Earnings after taxes (EAT)	$ 144,800

*Includes $36,100 in lease payments.

37. Given the financial statements for Jones Corporation and Smith Corporation shown here,

    a.   To which one would you, as credit manager for a supplier, approve the extension of (short-term) trade credit? Why? Compute all ratios before answering.

    b.   In which one would you buy stock? Why?

✖

Ratio computation
and analysis
(*LO3-2*)

JONES CORPORATION			
Current Assets		**Liabilities**	
Cash	$ 20,000	Accounts payable	$100,000
Accounts receivable	80,000	Bonds payable (long-term)	80,000
Inventory	50,000		
Long-Term Assets		**Stockholders' Equity**	
Fixed assets	$500,000	Common stock	$150,000
Less: Accumulated depreciation	(150,000)	Paid-in capital	70,000
Net fixed assets*	350,000	Retained earnings	100,000
Total assets	$500,000	Total liab. and equity	$500,000

(*continued*)

(*continued*)

JONES CORPORATION	
Sales (on credit)	$1,250,000
Cost of goods sold	750,000
Gross profit	$ 500,000
Selling and administrative expense[†]	257,000
Less: Depreciation expense	50,000
Operating profit	$ 193,000
Interest expense	8,000
Earnings before taxes	$ 185,000
Tax expense	92,500
Net income	$ 92,500

*Use net fixed assets in computing fixed asset turnover.
[†]Includes $7,000 in lease payments.

SMITH CORPORATION			
Current Assets		**Liabilities**	
Cash	$ 35,000	Accounts payable	$ 75,000
Marketable securities	7,500	Bonds payable (long-term)	210,000
Accounts receivable	70,000		
Inventory	75,000		
Long-Term Assets		**Stockholders' Equity**	
Fixed assets	$500,000	Common stock	$ 75,000
Less: Accum. dep.	(250,000)	Paid-in capital	30,000
Net fixed assets*	250,000	Retained earnings	47,500
Total assets	$437,500	Total liab. and equity	$437,500

*Use net fixed assets in computing fixed asset turnover.

SMITH CORPORATION	
Sales (on credit)	$1,000,000
Cost of goods sold	600,000
Gross profit	$ 400,000
Selling and administrative expense[†]	224,000
Depreciation expense	50,000
Operating profit	$ 126,000
Interest expense	21,000
Earnings before taxes	$ 105,000
Tax expense	52,500
Net income	$ 52,500

[†]Includes $7,000 in lease payments.

COMPREHENSIVE PROBLEM

Lamar Swimwear

(Trend analysis and industry comparisons)

(*LO3-4*)

Bob Adkins has recently been approached by his first cousin, Ed Lamar, with a proposal to buy a 15 percent interest in Lamar Swimwear. The firm manufactures stylish bathing suits and sunscreen products.

Mr. Lamar is quick to point out the increase in sales that has taken place over the last three years, as indicated in the income statement, Exhibit 1. The annual growth rate is 25 percent. A balance sheet for a similar time period is shown in Exhibit 2, and selected industry ratios are presented in Exhibit 3. Note the industry growth rate in sales is only 10 to 12 percent per year.

There was a steady real growth of 3 to 4 percent in gross domestic product during the period under study.

Exhibit 1

LAMAR SWIMWEAR Income Sheet			
	20X1	**20X2**	**20X3**
Sales (all on credit)	$1,200,000	$1,500,000	$1,875,000
Cost of goods sold	800,000	1,040,000	1,310,000
Gross profit	$ 400,000	$ 460,000	$ 565,000
Selling and administrative expense*	239,900	274,000	304,700
Operating profit (EBIT)	$ 160,100	$ 186,000	$ 260,300
Interest expense	35,000	45,000	85,000
Net income before taxes	$ 125,100	$ 141,000	$ 175,300
Taxes	36,900	49,200	55,600
Net income	$ 88,200	$ 91,800	$ 119,700
Shares	30,000	30,000	38,000
Earnings per share	$2.94	$3.06	$3.15

*Includes $15,000 in lease payments for each year.

Exhibit 2

LAMAR SWIMWEAR Balance Sheet			
Assets	**20X1**	**20X2**	**20X3**
Cash	$ 30,000	$ 40,000	$ 30,000
Marketable securities	20,000	25,000	30,000
Accounts receivable	170,000	259,000	360,000
Inventory	230,000	261,000	290,000
Total current assets	$ 450,000	$ 585,000	$ 710,000
Net plant and equipment	650,000	765,000	1,390,000
Total assets	$1,100,000	$1,350,000	$2,100,000
Liabilities and Stockholders' Equity			
Accounts payable	$ 200,000	$ 310,000	$ 505,000
Accrued expenses	20,400	30,000	35,000
Total current liabilities	$ 220,400	$ 340,000	$ 540,000
Long-term liabilities	325,000	363,600	703,900
Total liabilities	$ 545,400	$ 703,600	$1,243,900
Common stock ($2 par)	60,000	60,000	76,000
Capital paid in excess of par	190,000	190,000	264,000
Retained earnings	304,600	396,400	516,100
Total stockholders' equity	$ 554,600	$ 646,400	$ 856,100
Total liabilities and stockholders' equity	$1,100,000	$1,350,000	$2,100,000

Exhibit 3

Selected Industry Ratios			
	20X1	**20X2**	**20X3**
Growth in sales	—	10.00%	12.00%
Profit margin	7.71%	7.82%	7.96%
Return on assets (investment)	7.94%	8.86%	8.95%
Return on equity	14.31%	15.26%	16.01%
Receivables turnover	9.02X	8.86X	9.31X
Average collection period	39.9 days	40.6 days	38.7 days
Inventory turnover	4.24X	5.10X	5.11X
Fixed asset turnover	1.60X	1.64X	1.75X
Total asset turnover	1.05X	1.10X	1.12X
Current ratio	1.96X	2.25X	2.40X
Quick ratio	1.37X	1.41X	1.38X
Debt to total assets	43.47%	43.11%	44.10%
Times interest earned	6.50X	5.99X	6.61X
Fixed charge coverage	4.70X	4.69X	4.73X
Growth in EPS	—	10.10%	13.30%

The stock in the corporation has become available due to the ill health of a current stockholder, who is in need of cash. The issue here is not to determine the exact price for the stock, but rather whether Lamar Swimwear represents an attractive investment situation. Although Mr. Adkins has a primary interest in the profitability ratios, he will take a close look at all the ratios. He has no fast-and-firm rules about required return on investment, but rather wishes to analyze the overall condition of the firm. The firm does not currently pay a cash dividend, and return to the investor must come from selling the stock in the future. After doing a thorough analysis (including ratios for each year and comparisons to the industry), what comments and recommendations do you offer to Mr. Adkins?

COMPREHENSIVE PROBLEM

Sun Microsystems

(Trends, ratios, stock performance)

(LO3-1, LO3-2, LO3-3, LO3-4)

Sun Microsystems is a leading supplier of computer-related products, including servers, workstations, storage devices, and network switches. In 2009, Sun Microsystems was acquired by Oracle Corporation.

In the letter to stockholders as part of the 2001 annual report, President and CEO Scott G. McNealy offered the following remarks:

> Fiscal 2001 was clearly a mixed bag for Sun, the industry, and the economy as a whole. Still, we finished with revenue growth of 16 percent—and that's significant. We believe it's a good indication that Sun continued to pull away from the pack and gain market share. For that, we owe a debt of gratitude to our employees worldwide, who aggressively brought costs down—even as they continued to *bring exciting new products to market.*

The statement would not appear to be telling you enough. For example, McNealy says the year was a mixed bag with revenue growth of 16 percent. But what about earnings?

You can delve further by examining the income statement in Exhibit 4. Also, for additional analysis of other factors, consolidated balance sheet(s) are presented in Exhibit 5.

1. Referring to Exhibit 4, compute the annual percentage change in net income per common share-diluted (second numerical line from the bottom) for 1998–1999, 1999–2000, and 2000–2001.

2. Also in Exhibit 4, compute net income/net revenue (sales) for each of the four years. Begin with 1998.

3. What is the major reason for the change in the answer for Question 2 between 2000 and 2001? To answer this question for each of the two years, take the ratio of the major income statement accounts to net revenues (sales).

    Cost of sales

    Research and development

    Selling, general and administrative expense

    Provision for income tax

4. Compute return on stockholders' equity for 2000 and 2001 using data from Exhibits 4 and 5.

Exhibit 4

SUN MICROSYSTEMS INC.
Summary Consolidated Statement of Income (in millions)

	2001 Dollars	2000 Dollars	1999 Dollars	1998 Dollars
Net revenues	$18,250	$15,721	$11,806	$9,862
Costs and expenses:				
Cost of sales	$10,041	$ 7,549	$ 5,670	$4,713
Research and development	2,016	1,630	1,280	1,029
Selling, general and administrative	4,544	4,072	3,196	2,826
Goodwill amortization	261	65	19	4
In-process research and development	77	12	121	176
Total costs and expenses	$16,939	$13,328	$10,286	$8,748
Operating income	1,311	2,393	1,520	1,114
Gain (loss) on strategic investments	(90)	208	—	—
Interest income, net	363	170	85	48
Litigation settlement	—	—	—	—
Income before taxes	$ 1,584	$ 2,771	$ 1,605	$1,162
Provision for income taxes	603	917	575	407
Cumulative effect of change in accounting principle, net	(54)	—	—	—
Net income	$ 927	$ 1,854	$ 1,030	$ 755
Net income per common share-diluted	$ 0.27	$ 0.55	$ 0.31	$ 0.24
Shares used in the calculation of net income per common share-diluted	3,417	3,379	3,282	3,180

Exhibit 5

SUN MICROSYSTEMS INC.
Consolidated Balance Sheets (in millions)

	2001	2000
Assets		
Current assets:		
Cash and cash equivalents	$ 1,472	$ 1,849
Short-term investments	387	626
Accounts receivable, net of allowances of $410 in 2001 and $534 in 2000	2,955	2,690
Inventories	1,049	557
Deferred tax assets	1,102	673
Prepaids and other current assets	969	482
Total current assets	$ 7,934	$ 6,877
Property, plant and equipment, net	2,697	2,095
Long-term investments	4,677	4,496
Goodwill, net of accumulated amortization of $349 in 2001 and $88 in 2000	2,041	163
Other assets, net	832	521
	$18,181	$14,152
Liabilities and Stockholders' Equity		
Current liabilities:		
Short-term borrowings	$ 3	$ 7
Accounts payable	1,050	924
Accrued payroll-related liabilities	488	751
Accrued liabilities and other	1,374	1,155
Deferred revenues and customer deposits	1,827	1,289
Warranty reserve	314	211
Income taxes payable	90	209
Total current liabilities	$ 5,146	$ 4,546
Deferred income taxes	744	577
Long-term debt and other obligations	1,705	1,720
Total debt	$ 7,595	$ 6,843
Commitments and contingencies		
Stockholders' equity:		
Preferred stock, $0.001 par value, 10 shares authorized (1 share which has been designated as Series A Preferred participating stock); no shares issued and outstanding	—	—
Common stock and additional paid-in-capital, $0.00067 par value, 7,200 shares authorized; issued: 3,536 shares in 2001 and 3,495 shares in 2000	6,238	2,728
Treasury stock, at cost: 288 shares in 2001 and 301 shares in 2000	(2,435)	(1,438)
Deferred equity compensation	(73)	(15)
Retained earnings	6,885	5,959
Accumulated other comprehensive income (loss)	(29)	75
Total stockholders' equity	$10,586	$ 7,309
	$18,181	$14,152

5. Analyze your results in Question 4 more completely by computing Ratios 1, 2*a*, 2*b*, and 3*b* (all from this chapter) for 2000 and 2001. Actually the answer to Ratio 1 can be found as part of the answer to Question 2, but it is helpful to look at it initially.

    What do you think was the main contributing factor to the change in return on stockholders' equity between 2000 and 2001? Think in terms of the Du Pont system of analysis.

6. The average stock prices for each of the four years shown in Exhibit 4 were as follows:

1998	11¼
1999	16¾
2000	28½
2001	9½

    a. Compute the price-earnings (P/E) ratio for each year. That is, take the stock price shown above and divide by net income per common stock-dilution from Exhibit 4.

    b. Why do you think the P/E changed from its 2000 level to its 2001 level? A brief review of P/E ratios can be found under the heading "Price-Earnings Ratio Applied to Earnings per Share" in Chapter 2.

7. The book values per share for the same four years discussed in the preceding question were

1998	$1.18
1999	$1.55
2000	$2.29
2001	$3.26

    a. Compute the ratio of price to book value for each year.

    b. Is there any dramatic shift in the ratios worthy of note?

WEB EXERCISE

1. IBM was mentioned in the chapter as having an uneven performance. Let's check this out. Go to its website, www.ibm.com, and follow the steps listed here. Under "About IBM" at the bottom of the page, select "Investor Relations." Select "Financial info" (next to "Overview").

2. Scroll down one line and select "Stock Charts." How has IBM's stock been doing recently?

3. Click on "Financial Snapshot." Assuming IBM's historical price-earnings ratio is 18, how does it currently stand?

4. Assuming its annual dividend yield is 2.5 percent, how does it currently stand?

5. Assuming IBM's historical "LT" (long-term) debt/equity is 100 percent, how does it currently stand? Generally speaking, is that good or bad?

6. Assuming its historical return on assets is 10 percent, how does it currently stand? Generally speaking, is that good or bad?

Note: Occasionally a topic we have listed may have been deleted, updated, or moved into a different location on a website. If you click on the site map or site index, you will be introduced to a table of contents that should aid you in finding the topic you are looking for.

4

Financial Forecasting

Forecasting for the future has never been easy, but in recent years it has become increasingly difficult for those in the retail industry. Let's consider Dollar General Corp. How does it intend to meet its goals in the future? While many retail stores have suffered in recent years, dollar stores such as Dollar General have been one of the few retail stores to buck the trend. In fact, between 2008 and 2017, Dollar General's store count and square footage grew by 6 and 8 percent, respectively, per year.

Now Dollar General operates more than 14,000 stores in 44 states, and it sells more than $22 billion annually. Of course, even at that size, Walmart is much larger, with 22 times as much revenue. Dollar General differentiates itself from Walmart by locating in shopping plazas or strip malls of smaller communities. Seventy percent of its stores are in cities with populations of 22,000 or less.

The company's motto of "Save Time. Save Money. Every Day!" emphasizes its goal of offering consumers the lowest prices. For example, a 2014 study by Kantar Retail concluded that in Massachusetts, Dollar General had lower prices than any other retailer on a basket of commonly purchased goods. This pricing strategy can be risky because it results in very slim profit margins. When profit margins are tight, good financial forecasting becomes critical.

If there is one skill that is essential for a financial manager to develop, it is the ability to plan ahead and to make necessary adjustments before events actually occur. We likely could construct the same set of external events for two corporations (inflation, recession, severe new competition, and so on), and one firm would survive, while the other would not. The outcome might be a function not only of their risk-taking desires but also of their ability to hedge against risk with careful planning.

While we may assume that no growth or a decline in volume is the primary cause for a shortage of funds, this is not necessarily the case. A rapidly growing firm may witness a significant increase in accounts receivable, inventory, and plant and equipment that cannot be financed in the normal course of business. Assume sales go from $100,000 to $200,000 in one year for a firm that has a 5 percent profit margin on sales. At the same time, assume assets represent 50 percent of sales and go from $50,000 to $100,000 as sales double. The $10,000 of profit (5 percent × $200,000) will hardly be adequate to finance the $50,000 asset growth. The remaining $40,000 must come from suppliers, the bank, and perhaps stockholders. You should recognize that profit alone is generally inadequate to finance significant growth and a comprehensive financing plan must be developed. Too often, the small businessperson (and sometimes the big one as well) is mystified by an increase in sales and profits but less cash in the till.

Constructing Pro Forma Statements

The most comprehensive means of financial forecasting is to develop a series of pro forma, or projected, financial statements. We will give particular attention to the **pro forma income statement**, the **cash budget**, and the **pro forma balance sheet**. Based on the projected statements, the firm is able to estimate its future level of receivables, inventory, payables, and other corporate accounts as well as its anticipated profits and borrowing requirements. The financial officer can then carefully track actual events against the plan and make necessary adjustments. Furthermore, these statements are often required by bankers and other lenders as a guide for the future.

A systems approach is necessary to develop pro forma statements. We first construct a pro forma income statement based on sales projections and the production plan, then translate this material into a cash budget, and finally assimilate all previously developed material into a pro forma balance sheet. The process of developing pro forma financial statements is depicted in Figure 4-1. We will use a six-month time frame to facilitate the analysis, though the same procedures could be extended to one year or longer.

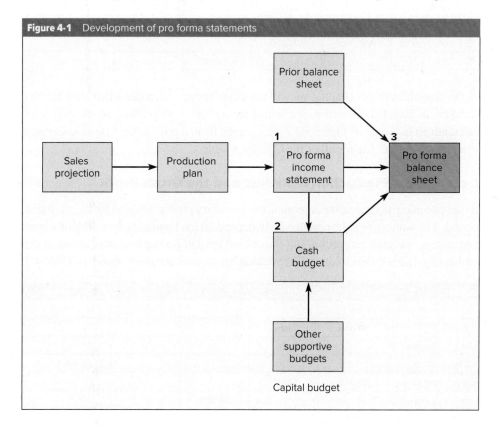

Figure 4-1   Development of pro forma statements

Pro Forma Income Statement

Assume the Goldman Corporation has been asked by its bank to provide pro forma financial statements for midyear 2019. The pro forma income statement will project how much profit the firm anticipates making over the ensuing time period. In developing the pro forma income statement, we will follow four important steps:

1. Establish a sales projection.
2. Determine a production schedule and the associated use of new material, direct labor, and overhead to arrive at gross profit.
3. Compute other expenses.
4. Determine profit by completing the actual pro forma statement.

Establish a Sales Projection

For analysis, we shall assume the Goldman Corporation has two primary products: wheels and casters. Our sales projection calls for the sale of 1,000 wheels and 2,000 casters at prices of $30 and $35, respectively. As indicated in Table 4-1, we anticipate total sales of $100,000.

Table 4-1	Projected wheel and caster sales (first six months, 2019)					
	A	B	C	D	E	F
2		**Wheels**	**Casters**			
3	Quantity	1,000	2,000			
4	Sales price	$30	$35			
5	Sales revenue	$30,000	$70,000			
6	Total			$100,000		

For the tables in this chapter, we will use color-coded conventions that have become standard in Excel. Blue values are initial inputs (or assumptions). Black values are calculations in the table. Green values are pulled from a prior table. Log in to Connect to access the Excel file for all of the Chapter 4 tables.

Determine a Production Schedule and the Gross Profit

Based on anticipated sales, we determine the necessary production plan for the six-month period. The number of units produced will depend on the beginning inventory of wheels and casters, our sales projection, and the desired level of ending inventory. Assume that on January 1, 2019, the Goldman Corporation has in stock the items shown in Table 4-2.

Table 4-2	Stock of beginning inventory					
	A	B	C	D	E	F
9		**Wheels**	**Casters**			
10	Quantity	85	180			
11	Cost	$16	$20			
12	Total value	$1,360	$3,600			
13	Total			$4,960		

Tesla's Sales Forecasts: Where Marketing and Finance Come Together

All the financial analysis in the world can prove useless if a firm does not have a meaningful sales projection. To the extent that the firm has an incorrect sales projection, an inappropriate amount of inventory will be accumulated, projections of accounts receivable and accounts payable will be wrong, and profits and cash flow will be off target. Although a corporate treasurer may understand all the variables influencing income statements, balance sheets, cash budgets, and so on, she is out of luck if the sales projection is wrong.

For example, Tesla Motors produces and sells electric cars, and it may have the potential to become the Apple computer of the car industry. However, Tesla's success partially depends upon gasoline prices. While expensive gas is harmful to the overall economy, it is a sales elixir for Tesla. When oil prices dropped more than 40 percent in 2014, gas prices plunged, and projections produced by Tesla's marketing group began to look too rosy.

A Morgan Stanley auto analyst estimated that Tesla would sell 40 percent fewer cars than had previously been forecast. Although sales projections had previously been for 500,000 cars by 2020, new projections were for only 300,000. With plummeting oil prices, Tesla's stock fell over 30 percent. Another problem for Tesla is that the forecasts made by Elon Musk, the CEO, have always proved to be way too optimistic, with the actual results falling short of projections.

Over the last two decades, the marketing profession has developed many sophisticated techniques for analyzing and projecting future sales, but it is important for financial managers to realize that projections are often inherently risky. The financial manager must look to the marketing staff to help project sales, but a good financial analyst will also seek to determine how risky these sales projections may prove to be. Worst-case scenarios must be recognized so that surprises do not become financial disasters.

We will add the projected quantity of unit sales for the next six months to our desired ending inventory and subtract our stock of beginning inventory (in units) to determine our production requirements. This process is illustrated below.

Units
+ Projected sales
+ Desired ending inventory
− Beginning inventory
= Production requirements

Following this process, in Table 4-3 we see a required production level of 1,015 wheels and 2,020 casters.

Table 4-3	Production requirements for six months			
	A	B	C	D
16		**Wheels**	**Casters**	
17	Projected unit sales (Table 4-1)	+1,000	+2,000	
18	Desired ending inventory (assumed to represent 10% of unit sales for the time period)	+100	+200	
19	Beginning inventory (Table 4-2)	−85	−180	
20	Units to be produced	1,015	2,020	

We must now determine the cost to produce these units. In Table 4-2 we see that the cost of units in stock was $16 for wheels and $20 for casters. However, we shall assume the price of materials, labor, and overhead going into the new products is now $18 for wheels and $22 for casters, as indicated in Table 4-4.

Table 4-4	Unit costs					
	A	B	C	D	E	F
23		**Wheels**	**Casters**			
24	Materials	$10	$12			
25	Labor	5	6			
26	Overhead	3	4			
27	Total	$18	$22			

The *total* cost to produce the required new items for the next six months is shown in Table 4-5.

Table 4-5	Total production costs				
	A	B	C	D	E
30		**Wheels**	**Casters**		
31	Units to be produced (Table 4-3)	1,015	2,020		
32	Cost per unit (Table 4-4)	$18	$22		
33	Total cost	$18,270	$44,440	$62,710	

Cost of Goods Sold   The main consideration in constructing a pro forma income statement is the costs specifically associated with units sold during the time period (the **cost of goods sold**). Note that in the case of wheels we anticipate sales of 1,000 units, as indicated in Table 4-1, but we are producing 1,015, as indicated in Table 4-3, to increase our inventory level by 15 units. For profit measurement purposes, we will *not* charge these extra 15 units against current sales.[1] Furthermore, in determining the cost of the 1,000 units sold during the current time period, we will *not* assume that all of the items sold represent inventory manufactured in this period. We shall assume the Goldman Corporation uses FIFO (first-in, first-out) accounting and it will first allocate the cost of current sales to beginning inventory and then to goods manufactured during the period.

In Table 4-6, we look at the revenue, associated cost of goods sold, and gross profit for both products. For example, 1,000 units of wheels are to be sold at a total revenue of $30,000. Of the 1,000 units, 85 units are from beginning inventory at a $16 cost, and the balance of 915 units is from current production at an $18 cost. The total cost of goods sold for wheels is $17,830, yielding a gross profit of $12,170. The pattern is the same for casters, with sales of $70,000, cost of goods sold of $43,640, and gross profit of $26,360. The combined sales for the two products are $100,000, with cost of goods sold of $61,470 and gross profit of $38,530.

---

[1]Later in the analysis we will show the effect these extra units have on the cash budget and the balance sheet.

Table 4-6	Allocation of manufacturing cost and determination of gross profits					
	A	B	C	D	E	F
36			**Wheels**		**Casters**	**Combined**
37	Quantity sold (Table 4-1)		1,000		2,000	3,000
38	Sales price		$30		$35	
39	Sales revenue		$30,000		$70,000	$100,000
40	Cost of goods sold:					
41	Old inventory (Table 4-2)					
42	Quantity (units)	85		180		
43	Cost per unit	$16		$20		
44	Total		$1,360		$3,600	
45	New inventory (the remainder)					
46	Quantity (units)	915		1,820		
47	Cost per unit (Table 4-4)	$18		$22		
48	Total		16,470		40,040	
49	Total cost of goods sold		$17,830		$43,640	$ 61,470
50	Gross profit		$12,170		$26,360	$ 38,530

At this point, we also compute the value of ending inventory for later use in constructing financial statements. As indicated in Table 4-7, the value of ending inventory will be $6,200.

Table 4-7	Value of ending inventory				
	A	B	C	D	E
53	+ Beginning inventory (Table 4-2)	$4,960			
54	+ Total production costs (Table 4-5)	62,710			
55	Total inventory available for sales	$67,670			
56	− Cost of goods sold (Table 4-6)	61,470			
57	Ending inventory	**$6,200**			

Other Expense Items

Having computed total revenue, cost of goods sold, and gross profits, we must now subtract other expense items to arrive at a net profit figure. We deduct general and administrative expenses as well as interest expenses from gross profit to arrive at earnings before taxes, then subtract taxes to determine aftertax income, and finally deduct dividends to ascertain the contribution to retained earnings. For the Goldman Corporation, we shall assume general and administrative expenses are $12,000, interest expense is $1,500, and dividends are $1,500.

Actual Pro Forma Income Statement

Combining the gross profit in Table 4-6 with our assumptions on other expense items, we arrive at the pro forma income statement presented in Table 4-8. As shown toward the bottom of the table, we anticipate earnings after taxes of $20,024, dividends of $1,500, and an increase in retained earnings of $18,524.

Table 4-8   Income statement

	A	B	C	D	E
61	Pro Forma Income Statement June 30, 2019				
62	Sales revenue (Table 4-1)		$100,000		
63	Cost of goods sold (Table 4-6)		61,470		
64	Gross profit		$38,530		
65	General and administrative expense		12,000		
66	Operating profit (EBIT)		$26,530		
67	Interest expense		1,500		
68	Earnings before taxes (EBT)		$25,030		
69	Taxes (20%)*		5,006		
70	Earnings after taxes (EAT)		$20,024		
71	Common stock dividends		1,500		
72	Increase in retained earnings		**$18,524**		

*A 20 percent tax rate is used for simplicity.

Cash Budget

As previously indicated, the generation of sales and profits does not necessarily ensure there will be adequate cash on hand to meet financial obligations as they come due. This was especially true in the credit crisis period of 2007–2009 as many firms had to go into temporary bankruptcy. Macy's and Chrysler are two examples.

A profitable sale may generate accounts receivable in the short run but no immediate cash to meet maturing obligations. For this reason, we must translate the pro forma income statement into cash flows. In this process, we divide the longer-term pro forma income statement into smaller and more precise time frames to anticipate the seasonal and monthly patterns of cash inflows and outflows. Some months may represent particularly high or low sales volume or may require dividends, taxes, or capital expenditures.

Cash Receipts

In the case of the Goldman Corporation, we break down the pro forma income statement for the first half of the year 2019 into a series of monthly cash budgets. In Table 4-1, we showed anticipated sales of $100,000 over this time period; we shall now assume these sales can be divided into monthly projections, as indicated in Table 4-9.

Table 4-9   Monthly sales pattern

	C	D	E	F	G	H
2	**January**	**February**	**March**	**April**	**May**	**June**
3	$15,000	$10,000	$15,000	$25,000	$15,000	$20,000

A careful analysis of past sales and collection records indicates 20 percent of sales is collected in the month of sales and 80 percent in the following month. The cash receipt pattern related to monthly sales is shown in Table 4-10. It is assumed that sales for December 2018 were $12,000.

Table 4-10   Monthly cash receipts

	A	B	C	D	E	F	G	H	I	J
6		**December**	**January**	**February**	**March**	**April**	**May**	**June**		
7	Sales	$12,000	$15,000	$10,000	$15,000	$25,000	$15,000	$20,000		
8	Collections:									
9	(20% of current sales)		$3,000	$2,000	$3,000	$5,000	$3,000	$4,000	$16,000	Ending A/R
10	Collections:									
11	(80% of previous month's sales)		9,600	12,000	8,000	12,000	20,000	12,000		
12	Total cash receipts		$12,600	$14,000	$11,000	$17,000	$23,000	$16,000		

Ending accounts receivable:
$20,000   June sales
−4,000   Collected
$16,000

The cash inflows will vary between $11,000 and $23,000, with the high point in receipts coming in May.

We now examine the monthly outflows.

Cash Payments

The primary considerations for cash payments are monthly costs associated with inventory manufactured during the period (material, labor, and overhead) and disbursements for general and administrative expenses, interest payments, taxes, and dividends. We must also consider cash payments for any new plant and equipment, an item that does not show up on our pro forma income statement. Costs associated with units manufactured during the period may be taken from the data provided in Table 4-5. In Table 4-11, we simply recast these data in terms of material, labor, and overhead.

Table 4-11   Component costs of manufactured goods

	A	B	C	D	E	F	G	H
15		**Wheels**				**Casters**		
16		**Units Produced**	**Cost per Unit**	**Total Cost**	**Units Produced**	**Cost per Unit**	**Total Cost**	**Combined Cost**
17	Materials	1,015	$10	$10,150	2,020	$12	$24,240	$34,390
18	Labor	1,015	5	5,075	2,020	6	12,120	17,195
19	Overhead	1,015	3	3,045	2,020	4	8,080	11,125
20								$62,710

We see that the total costs for components in the two products in Table 4-11 are materials, $34,390; labor, $17,195; and overhead, $11,125. We shall assume all these costs are incurred on an equal monthly basis over the six-month period. Even though the sales volume varies from month to month, we assume we are employing level monthly production to ensure maximum efficiency in the use of various productive resources. Average monthly costs for materials, labor, and overhead are shown in Table 4-12.

Table 4-12	Average monthly manufacturing costs		
	A	B	C	D
23		**Total Costs**	**Time Frame**	**Average Monthly Cost**
24	Materials	$34,390	6 months	$5,732
25	Labor	17,195	6 months	2,866
26	Overhead	11,125	6 months	1,854

We shall pay for materials one month after the purchase has been made. Labor and overhead represent direct monthly cash outlays, as is true of interest, taxes, dividends, and the purchases of $8,000 in new equipment in February and $10,000 in June. We summarize all of our cash payments in Table 4-13. Past records indicate that $4,500 in materials was purchased in December.

Table 4-13	Summary of all monthly cash payments							
	A	B	C	D	E	F	G	H	I
29		**December**	**January**	**February**	**March**	**April**	**May**	**June**	
30	From Table 4-12:								
31	Monthly material purchase	$4,500	$5,732	$5,732	$5,732	$5,732	$5,732	$5,732	Ending A/P
32	Payment for material (prior month's purchase)		$4,500	$5,732	$5,732	$5,732	$5,732	$5,732	
33	Monthly labor cost		2,866	2,866	2,866	2,866	2,866	2,866	
34	Monthly overhead		1,854	1,854	1,854	1,854	1,854	1,854	
35	From Table 4-8:								
36	General and administrative expense ($12,000 over 6 months)		2,000	2,000	2,000	2,000	2,000	2,000	
37	Interest expense							1,500	
38	Taxes (two equal payments)				2,503			2,503	
39	Cash dividend							1,500	
40	Also:								
41	New equipment purchases			8,000				10,000	
42	Total payments		$11,220	$20,452	$14,955	$12,452	$12,452	$27,955	

Actual Budget

We are now in a position to bring together our monthly cash receipts and payments into a cash flow statement, illustrated in Table 4-14. The difference between monthly receipts and payments is net cash flow for the month.

Table 4-14	Monthly cash flow					
	A	B	C	D	E	F	G
45		**January**	**February**	**March**	**April**	**May**	**June**
46	Total receipts (Table 4-10)	$12,600	$14,000	$11,000	$17,000	$23,000	$ 16,000
47	Total payments (Table 4-13)	(11,220)	(20,452)	(14,955)	(12,452)	(12,452)	(27,955)
48	Net cash flow	$1,380	($6,452)	($3,955)	$ 4,548	$10,548	($11,955)

The primary purpose of the cash budget is to allow the firm to anticipate the need for outside funding at the end of each month. In the present case, we shall assume the Goldman Corporation wishes to have a minimum cash balance of $5,000 at all times. If it goes below this amount, the firm will borrow funds from the bank. If it goes above $5,000 and the firm has a loan outstanding, it will use the excess funds to reduce the loan. This pattern of financing is demonstrated in Table 4-15; this table illustrates a fully developed cash budget with borrowing and repayment provisions.

Table 4-15	Cash budget with borrowing and repayment provisions					
	A	B	C	D	E	F	G
51		January	February	March	April	May	June
52	Net cash flow	$ 1,380	($6,452)	($3,955)	$4,548	$10,548	($11,955)
53	Beginning cash balance	5,000*	6,380	5,000	5,000	5,000	11,069
54	Cumulative cash balance	$ 6,380	($72)	$1,045	$9,548	$15,548	($886)
55	Monthly loan (or repayment)	—	5,072	3,955	(4,548)	(4,479)	5,886
56	Cumulative loan balance	—	5,072	9,027	4,479	—	**5,886**
57	Ending cash balance	$ 6,380	$5,000	$5,000	$5,000	$11,069	**$5,000**

*We assume the Goldman Corporation has a beginning cash balance of $5,000 on January 1, 2019, and it desires a minimum monthly ending cash balance of $5,000.

The first line in Table 4-15 shows net cash flow (from Table 4-14), which is added to the beginning cash balance to arrive at the cumulative cash balance. The fourth entry is the additional monthly loan or loan repayment, if any, required to maintain a minimum cash balance of $5,000. To keep track of our loan balance, the fifth entry represents cumulative loans outstanding for all months. Finally, we show the cash balance at the end of the month, which becomes the beginning cash balance for the next month.

At the end of January the firm has $6,380 in cash, but by the end of February the cumulative cash position of the firm is negative, necessitating a loan of $5,072 to maintain a $5,000 cash balance. The firm has a loan on the books until May, at which time there is an ending cash balance of $11,069. During April and May the cumulative cash balance is greater than the required minimum cash balance of $5,000, so loan repayments of $4,548 and $4,479 are made to retire the loans completely in May. In June the firm is once again required to borrow $5,886 to maintain a $5,000 cash balance.

Pro Forma Balance Sheet

Now that we have developed a pro forma income statement and a cash budget, it is relatively simple to integrate all of these items into a pro forma balance sheet. Because the balance sheet represents cumulative changes in the corporation over time, we first examine the *prior* period's balance sheet and then translate these items through time to represent June 30, 2019. The last balance sheet, dated December 31, 2018, is shown in Table 4-16.

Table 4-16	Balance sheet December 31, 2018				
	A	B	C	D	E
3	Balance Sheet December 31, 2018				
4	**Assets**				
5	Current assets:				
6	Cash		$5,000		
7	Marketable securities		3,200		
8	Accounts receivable		9,600		
9	Inventory		4,960		
10	Total current assets		$22,760		
11	Plant and equipment		27,740		
12	Total assets		$50,500		
13	**Liabilities and Stockholders' Equity**				
14	Accounts payable		$4,500		
15	Notes payable		0		
16	Long-term debt		15,000		
17	Common stock		10,500		
18	Retained earnings		20,500		
19	Total liabilities and stockholders' equity		$50,500		

In constructing our pro forma balance sheet for June 30, 2019, some of the accounts from the old balance sheet will remain unchanged, while others will take on new values, as indicated by the pro forma income statement and cash budget. The process is depicted in Figure 4-2.

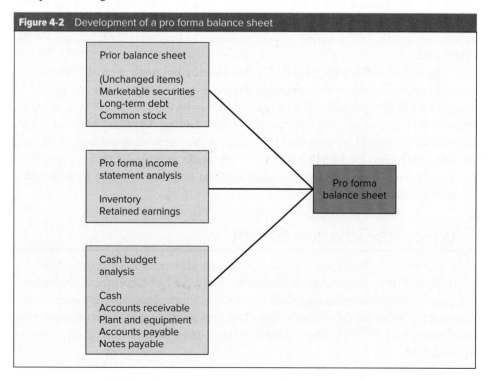

Figure 4-2 Development of a pro forma balance sheet

Explanation of Pro Forma Balance Sheet

We now present the new pro forma balance sheet as of June 30, 2019, in Table 4-17. Each item in Table 4-17 can be explained on the basis of a prior calculation or assumption. The explanations begin below the table.

Table 4-17	Pro forma balance sheet June 30, 2019			
	E	F	G	H	I
3			Pro Forma Balance Sheet June 30, 2019		
4	**Assets**				
5	Current assets:				
6	1. Cash		$5,000	Table 4-15	
7	2. Marketable securities		3,200	Table 4-16	
8	3. Accounts receivable		16,000	Table 4-10	
9	4. Inventory		6,200	Table 4-7	
10	Total current assets		$30,400		
11	5. Plant and equipment		45,740	Table 4-16 plus 4-13	
12	Total assets		$76,140		
13	**Liabilities and Stockholders' Equity**				
14	6. Accounts payable		$5,732	Table 4-13	
15	7. Notes payable		5,886	Table 4-15	
16	8. Long-term debt		15,000	Table 4-16	
17	9. Common stock		10,500	Table 4-16	
18	10. Retained earnings		39,024	Table 4-16 plus Table 4-8	
19	Total liabilities and stockholders' equity		$76,142		

1. Cash ($5,000)—minimum cash balance, as shown in Table 4-15.
2. Marketable securities ($3,200)—remains unchanged from prior period's value in Table 4-16.
3. Accounts receivable ($16,000)—based on June sales of $20,000 in Table 4-10. Twenty percent will be collected that month, while 80 percent will become accounts receivable at the end of the month.

$$
\begin{array}{ll}
\$20,000 & \text{Sales} \\
\underline{\times 80\%} & \\
\$16,000 & \text{Receivables}
\end{array}
$$

4. Inventory ($6,200)—ending inventory, as shown in Table 4-7.
5. Plant and equipment ($45,740).

Initial value (Table 4-16)	$27,740
Purchases* (Table 4-13)	18,000
Plant and equipment	$45,740

*For simplicity, depreciation is not explicitly considered.

6. Accounts payable ($5,732)—based on June purchases in Table 4-13. They will not be paid until July and thus are accounts payable.

7. Notes payable ($5,886)—the amount that must be borrowed to maintain the cash balance of $5,000, as shown in Table 4-15.

8. Long-term debt ($15,000)—remains unchanged from prior period's value in Table 4-16.

9. Common stock ($10,500)—remains unchanged from prior period's value in Table 4-16.

10. Retained earnings ($39,024)—initial value plus pro forma income.

Initial value (Table 4-16)	$20,500
Transfer of pro forma income to retained earnings (Table 4-8)	18,524
Retained earnings	$39,024

Analysis of Pro Forma Statement

In comparing the pro forma balance sheet (Table 4-17) to the prior balance sheet (Table 4-16), we note that assets are up by $25,642.

Total assets (June 30, 2019)	$76,142
Total assets (Dec. 31, 2018)	50,500
Increase	$25,642

The growth was financed by accounts payable, notes payable, and profit (as reflected by the increase in retained earnings). Though the company will enjoy a high degree of profitability, it must still look to bank financing of $5,886 (shown as notes payable in Table 4-17) to support the increase in assets. This represents the difference between the $25,642 buildup in assets and the $1,232 increase in accounts payable, as well as the $18,524 buildup in retained earnings.

Percent-of-Sales Method

An alternative to tracing cash and accounting flows to determine financial needs is to assume that accounts on the balance sheet will maintain a given percentage relationship to sales. We then indicate a change in the sales level and ascertain our related financing needs. This is known as the **percent-of-sales method**. For example, for the Howard Corporation, introduced in Table 4-18, we show the following balance sheet accounts in dollars and their percentage of sales, based on a sales volume of $200,000.

Cash of $5,000 represents 2.5 percent of sales of $200,000; receivables of $40,000 are 20 percent of sales; and so on. No percentages are computed for notes payable, common stock, and retained earnings because they are not assumed to maintain a direct relationship with sales volume.

Table 4-18   Balance sheet and percentage-of-sales table for Howard Corporation

	A	B	C	D
3	HOWARD CORPORATION Balance Sheet and Percent-of-Sales Table			
4	**Assets**		**Liabilities and Stockholders' Equity**	
5	Cash	$5,000	Accounts payable	$40,000
6	Accounts receivables	40,000	Accrued expenses	10,000
7	Inventory	25,000	Notes payable	15,000
8	Total current assets	$70,000	Common stock	10,000
9	Plant and equipment	50,000	Retained earnings	45,000
10	Total assets	$120,000	Total liabilities and stockholders' equity	$120,000
11	**$200,000 Sales Percent of Sales**			
12	Cash	2.5%	Accounts payable	20.0%
13	Accounts receivable	20.0	Accrued expenses	5.0
14	Inventory	12.5		25.0%
15	Total current assets	35.0%		
16	Plant and equipment	25.0		
17		60.0%		

Once we know how much money we need to finance our growth, we will then decide whether to finance the sales growth with an increase in notes payable or the sale of common stock or long-term debt. There are two possible scenarios for our calculations. First, if the company is operating at full capacity, it will need to buy new plant and equipment to produce more goods to sell. Second, if the company is operating at less than full capacity, it can increase sales with its current plant and equipment, so it will only need to add more current assets to increase its sales.

In the case of full capacity, any dollar increase in sales will necessitate a 35 percent increase in current assets, as well as a 25 percent increase in plant and equipment. These percentages are found in the bottom half of Table 4-18. Of this 60 percent, 25 percent will be spontaneously or automatically financed through accounts payable and accrued expenses, leaving 35 percent to be financed by profit or additional outside sources of financing. We will assume the Howard Corporation has an aftertax return of 6 percent on the sales dollar, and 50 percent of profits are paid out as dividends.[2]

If sales increase from $200,000 to $300,000, the $100,000 increase in sales will necessitate $35,000 (35 percent) in additional financing. Since we will earn 6 percent on total sales of $300,000, we will show a profit of $18,000. With a 50 percent dividend payout, $9,000 will remain for internal financing. This means $26,000 out of the $35,000 must be financed from outside sources. Our formula to determine the need for new funds follows.

---

[2]Some may wish to add back depreciation under the percent-of-sales method. Most, however, choose the assumption that funds generated through depreciation (in the sources and uses of funds sense) must be used to replace the fixed assets to which depreciation is applied.

Creating forecasts and producing detailed pro forma financial statements rarely start out as anyone's idea of a good time. The level of detail required, the complexity of the decisions necessary, and the research required to make any of those decisions can be daunting, especially to a first-time entrepreneur. So why is it so important for entrepreneurs to thoughtfully develop their financial forecasts? The answer is twofold. First and foremost, as Bobby Bahram of Excelerate Health Ventures, an early-stage venture fund in the Research Triangle Park region of North Carolina, says, "The number one job for a startup CEO is not to run out of money." Thinking through how much cash you have, how much cash you need, and the different scenarios you may face is the ultimate responsibility for an entrepreneur, and your financial statements are your toolbox.

The second reason that pro formas are so important is that potential investors want to be able to evaluate the financial outlook for the firm. Many entrepreneurs will seek investment either from "angel" investors or venture capital funds, and what these investors are looking for are:

1. To clearly understand the short-term (12- to 18-month) cash forecasts.

2. To comprehend key operational factors such as the firm's

    a. Burn rate (how fast it is spending money).

    b. Runway (how long it will have enough cash funds to operate)

    c. Value-changing milestones (key points at which the company's value changes because of a significant accomplishment).

In the end, the difference between well-crafted and poorly done financial forecasts comes down not only to the accuracy and the depth of the analysis but also to the entrepreneur's ability to simply articulate and discuss the numbers. Venture capitalists like Bahram look for aspiring entrepreneurs who focus first on detailed monthly cash-based financials, especially for seed and early-stage ventures. Too often, entrepreneurs use templates that introduce complexity that is not needed in the start-up phase. Simple metrics are frequently the most important, and entrepreneurs who add unneeded complexity to pro formas are often better off spending their time on operating and improving their new business.

Required new funds—

$$(\text{RNF}) = \frac{A}{S}(\Delta S) - \frac{L}{S}(\Delta S) - PS_2(1 - D) \qquad (4\text{-}1)$$

where

$\frac{A}{S}$ = Relationship of variable assets to sales [60%]

ΔS = Change in sales [$100,000]

$\frac{L}{S}$ = Relationship of variable liabilities to sales [25%]

P = Profit margin [6%]

S_2 = New sales level [$300,000]

D = Dividend payout ratio [0.50]

Plugging in the values, we show

$$\text{RNF} = 60\% \ (\$100,000) - 25\% \ (\$100,000) - 6\% \ (\$300,000) \ (1 - 0.50)$$
$$= \$60,000 - \$25,000 - \$18,000 \ (0.50)$$
$$= \$35,000 - \$9,000$$
$$= \$26,000 \text{ required sources of new funds (at full capacity)}$$

Presumably, the $26,000 can be financed at the bank or through some other appropriate source.

What if the company is operating at less than full capacity and doesn't need to buy new plant and equipment? This often happens when the economy is coming out of a recession. In this case, we will need to increase our assets by the 35 percent of spontaneous current assets. Repeating the equation gives us this:

$$RNF = 35\% \ (\$100,000) - 25\% \ (\$100,000) - 6\% \ (\$300,000) \ (1 - 0.50)$$
$$= \$35,000 - \$25,000 - \$18,000 \ (0.50)$$
$$= \$35,000 - \$25,000 - \$9,000$$
$$= \$1,000 \text{ required sources of new funds (at less than full capacity)}$$

Notice that when we don't need to buy new equipment, the required new funds amount drops significantly. In this case, we need an extra $1,000 of financing.

Using the percent-of-sales method is much easier than tracing through the various cash flows to arrive at the pro forma statements. Nevertheless, the output is much less meaningful, and we do not get a month-to-month breakdown of the data. The percent-of-sales method is a broad-brush approach, while the development of pro forma statements is more exacting. Of course, whatever method we use, the results are only as meaningful or reliable as the assumptions about sales and production that went into the numbers.

SUMMARY

Financial forecasting allows the financial manager to anticipate events before they occur, particularly the need for raising funds externally. An important consideration is that growth may call for additional sources of financing because profit is often inadequate to cover the net buildup in receivables, inventory, and other asset accounts.

A systems approach is necessary to develop pro forma statements. We first construct a pro forma income statement based on sales projections and the production plan, then translate this material into a cash budget, and finally assimilate all previously developed material into a pro forma balance sheet.

An alternative to tracing cash and accounting flows to determine financial needs is to assume that accounts on the balance sheet will maintain a given percentage relationship to sales. We can then indicate a change in the sales level and ascertain our related financing needs. This is known as the percent-of-sales method.

Regardless of what method is used to forecast the future financial needs of the firm (whether it is pro forma financial statements or the percent-of-sales method), the end product is the determination of the amount of new funds needed to finance the activities of the firm.

For firms that are in highly seasonal businesses, it is particularly important to identify peaks and slowdowns in the activities of the firm and the associated financial requirements.

LIST OF TERMS

DISCUSSION QUESTIONS

1. What are the basic benefits and purposes of developing pro forma statements and a cash budget? *(LO4-1)*

2. Explain how the collections and purchases schedules are related to the borrowing needs of the corporation. *(LO4-4)*

3. With inflation, what are the implications of using LIFO and FIFO inventory methods? How do they affect the cost of goods sold? *(LO4-2)*

4. Explain the relationship between inventory turnover and purchasing needs. *(LO4-2)*

5. Rapid corporate growth in sales and profits can cause financing problems. Elaborate on this statement. *(LO4-1)*

6. Discuss the advantage and disadvantage of level production schedules in firms with cyclical sales. *(LO4-5)*

7. What conditions would help make a percent-of-sales forecast almost as accurate as pro forma financial statements and cash budgets? *(LO4-3)*

PRACTICE PROBLEMS AND SOLUTIONS

Cost of goods sold—FIFO and LIFO *(LO4-2)*

1. At the end of January, Medical Products Corp. had 625 units in inventory, which cost $15 to produce. During February, the firm produced 550 units at a cost of $20 per unit. If the firm sold 800 units in February, what was the cost of goods sold?

    a. Assume FIFO inventory accounting.

    b. Assume LIFO inventory accounting.

Schedule of cash receipts *(LO4-2)*

2. Eaton Stores has forecast credit sales for the fourth quarter of the year:

September (actual)	$100,000
Fourth Quarter	
October	$ 70,000
November	50,000
December	80,000

Experience has shown that 30 percent of sales receipts are collected in the month of sale and 60 percent in the following month, and 10 percent are never collected. Prepare a schedule of cash receipts for Eaton Stores covering the fourth quarter (October through December).

Solutions

1. *a.* FIFO accounting

    Cost of goods sold on 800 units

Old inventory:		
Quantity (units)	625	
Cost per unit	$15	
Total		$ 9,375
New inventory:		
Quantity (units)	175	
Cost per unit	$20	
Total		3,500
Total cost of goods sold		$12,875

b. LIFO accounting

Cost of goods sold on 800 units

New inventory:		
Quantity (units)	550	
Cost per unit	$20	
Total		$11,000
Old inventory:		
Quantity (units)	250	
Cost per unit	$15	
Total		3,750
Total cost of goods sold		$14,750

2.

	September	October	November	December
Sales	$100,000	$70,000	$50,000	$80,000
Collections:				
(30% of current sales)		21,000	15,000	24,000
Collections:				
(60% of previous month's sales)		60,000	42,000	30,000
Total cash receipts		$81,000	$57,000	$54,000

The 10 percent that is never collected does not go into the schedule of cash receipts.

PROBLEMS

■ connect Selected problems are available with Connect. Please see the preface for more information.

Basic Problems

1. Eli Lilly is very excited because sales for his nursery and plant company are expected to double from $600,000 to $1,200,000 next year. Eli notes that net assets (Assets − Liabilities) will remain at 50 percent of sales. His firm will enjoy an 8 percent return on total sales. He will start the year with $120,000 in the bank and is bragging about the Jaguar and luxury townhouse he will buy. Does his optimistic outlook for his cash position appear to be correct? Compute his likely cash balance or deficit for the end of the year. Start with beginning cash and subtract the asset buildup (equal to 50 percent of the sales increase) and add in profit.

Growth and financing (LO4-4)

Growth and
financing
(LO4-4)

2. Philip Morris expects the sales for his clothing company to be $550,000 next year. Philip notes that net assets (Assets − Liabilities) will remain unchanged. His clothing firm will enjoy a 12 percent return on total sales. He will start the year with $150,000 in the bank. What will Philip's ending cash balance be?

Growth and
financing
(LO4-4)

3. Galehouse Gas Stations Inc. expects sales to increase from $1,550,000 to $1,750,000 next year. Galehouse believes that net assets (Assets − Liabilities) will represent 50 percent of sales. His firm has an 8 percent return on sales and pays 45 percent of profits out as dividends.

    a. What effect will this growth have on funds?

    b. If the dividend payout is only 25 percent, what effect will this growth have on funds?

Sales projections
(LO4-2)

4. The Alliance Corp. expects to sell the following number of units of copper cables at the prices indicated, under three different scenarios in the economy. The probability of each outcome is indicated. What is the expected value of the total sales projection?

Outcome	Probability	Units	Price
A	0.70	225	$20
B	0.10	370	35
C	0.20	510	45

Sales projections
(LO4-2)

5. Bronco Truck Parts expects to sell the following number of units at the prices indicated under three different scenarios in the economy. The probability of each outcome is indicated. What is the expected value of the total sales projection?

Outcome	Probability	Units	Price
A	0.40	350	$21
B	0.10	600	30
C	0.50	1,050	35

Sales projections
(LO4-2)

6. Cyber Security Systems had sales of 3,500 units at $75 per unit last year. The marketing manager projects a 30 percent increase in unit volume sales this year with a 40 percent price increase. Returned merchandise will represent 8 percent of total sales. What is your net dollar sales projection for this year?

Sales projections
(LO4-2)

7. Dodge Ball Bearings had sales of 15,000 units at $45 per unit last year. The marketing manager projects a 30 percent increase in unit volume sales this year with a 20 percent price decrease (due to a price reduction by a competitor). Returned merchandise will represent 8 percent of total sales. What is your net dollar sales projection for this year?

Production
requirements
(LO4-2)

8. Sales for Ross Pro's Sports Equipment are expected to be 4,800 units for the coming month. The company likes to maintain 10 percent of unit sales for each month in ending inventory. Beginning inventory is 300 units. How many units should the firm produce for the coming month?

9. Vitale Hair Spray had sales of 13,000 units in March. A 70 percent increase is expected in April. The company will maintain 30 percent of expected unit sales for April in ending inventory. Beginning inventory for April was 650 units. How many units should the company produce in April?

Production
requirements
(LO4-2)

10. Delsing Plumbing Company has beginning inventory of 16,500 units, will sell 55,000 units for the month, and desires to reduce ending inventory to 25 percent of beginning inventory. How many units should Delsing produce?

Production
requirements
(LO4-2)

11. On December 31 of last year, Wolfson Corporation had in inventory 450 units of its product, which cost $22 per unit to produce. During January, the company produced 850 units at a cost of $25 per unit. Assuming that Wolfson Corporation sold 800 units in January, what was the cost of goods sold (assume FIFO inventory accounting)?

Cost of goods
sold—FIFO
(LO4-2)

12. At the end of January, Higgins Data Systems had an inventory of 650 units, which cost $16 per unit to produce. During February the company produced 950 units at a cost of $19 per unit. If the firm sold 1,150 units in February, what was its cost of goods sold (assume LIFO inventory accounting)?

Cost of goods
sold—FIFO
(LO4-2)

13. At the end of January, Mineral Labs had an inventory of 775 units, which cost $12 per unit to produce. During February the company produced 900 units at a cost of $16 per unit. If the firm sold 1,500 units in February, what was the cost of goods sold?

    a. Assume LIFO inventory accounting.

    b. Assume FIFO inventory accounting.

Cost of goods
sold—LIFO and
FIFO
(LO4-2)

Intermediate Problems

14. Convex Mechanical Supplies produces a product with the following costs as of July 1, 20X1:

Gross profit and
ending inventory
(LO4-2)

Material	$ 6
Labor	4
Overhead	2
	$12

    Beginning inventory at these costs on July 1 was 5,000 units. From July 1 to December 1, Convex produced 15,000 units. These units had a material cost of $10 per unit. The costs for labor and overhead were the same. Convex uses FIFO inventory accounting.

    Assuming that Convex sold 17,000 units during the last six months of the year at $20 each, what would gross profit be? What is the value of ending inventory?

15. The Bradley Corporation produces a product with the following costs as of July 1, 20X1:

Gross profit and
ending inventory
(LO4-2)

Material	$4 per unit
Labor	4 per unit
Overhead	2 per unit

Beginning inventory at these costs on July 1 was 3,250 units. From July 1 to December 1, 20X1, Bradley Corporation produced 12,500 units. These units had a material cost of $5, labor of $4, and overhead of $5 per unit. Bradley uses LIFO inventory accounting.

Assuming that Bradley Corporation sold 14,000 units during the last six months of the year at $19 each, what is its gross profit? What is the value of ending inventory?

Gross profit and ending inventory (LO4-2)

16. Sprint Shoes Inc. had a beginning inventory of 9,250 units on January 1, 20X1. Here were the costs associated with the inventory:

Material	$15.00 per unit
Labor	8.00 per unit
Overhead	7.10 per unit

During 20X1, the firm produced 43,000 units with the following costs:

Material	$17.50 per unit
Labor	8.80 per unit
Overhead	10.30 per unit

Sales for the year were 47,350 units at $44.60 each. Sprint Shoes uses LIFO accounting. What was the gross profit? What was the value of ending inventory?

Schedule of cash receipts (LO4-2)

17. J. Lo's Clothiers has forecast credit sales for the fourth quarter of the year:

September (actual)	$70,000
Fourth Quarter	
October	$60,000
November	55,000
December	80,000

Experience has shown that 30 percent of sales are collected in the month of sale, 60 percent are collected in the following month, and 10 percent are never collected.

Prepare a schedule of cash receipts for J. Lo's Clothiers covering the fourth quarter (October through December).

Schedule of cash receipts (LO4-2)

18. Simpson Glove Company has made the following sales projections for the next six months. All sales are credit sales.

March	$41,000
April	50,000
May	32,000
June	47,000
July	58,000
August	62,000

Sales in January and February were $41,000 and $39,000, respectively. Experience has shown that of total sales receipts 10 percent are uncollectible, 40 percent are collected in the month of sale, 30 percent are collected in the following month, and 20 percent are collected two months after sale.

Prepare a monthly cash receipts schedule for the firm for March through August.

19. Watt's Lighting Stores made the following sales projection for the next six months. All sales are credit sales.

Schedule of cash receipts (LO4-2)

March	$35,000
April	41,000
May	30,000
June	39,000
July	47,000
August	49,000

Sales in January and February were $38,000 and $37,000, respectively.

Experience has shown that of total sales, 10 percent are uncollectible, 30 percent are collected in the month of sale, 40 percent are collected in the following month, and 20 percent are collected two months after sale.

Prepare a monthly cash receipts schedule for the firm for March through August.

Of the sales expected to be made during the six months from March through August, how much will still be uncollected at the end of August? How much of this is expected to be collected later?

20. Ultravision Inc. anticipates sales of $290,000 from January through April. Materials will represent 50 percent of sales, and because of level production, material purchases will be equal for each month during the four months of January, February, March, and April.

Schedule of cash payments (LO4-2)

Materials are paid for one month after the month purchased. Materials purchased in December of last year were $25,000 (half of $50,000 in sales). Labor costs for each of the four months are slightly different due to a provision in the labor contract in which bonuses are paid in February and April. Here are the labor figures:

January	$15,000
February	18,000
March	15,000
April	20,000

Fixed overhead is $11,000 per month. Prepare a schedule of cash payments for January through April.

21. The Denver Corporation has forecast the following sales for the first seven months of the year:

Schedule of cash payments (LO4-2)

January	$15,000	May	$15,000
February	17,000	June	21,000
March	19,000	July	23,000
April	25,000		

Monthly material purchases are set equal to 40 percent of forecast sales for the next month. Of the total material costs, 50 percent are paid in the month of purchase and 50 percent in the following month. Labor costs will run $4,500 per month, and fixed overhead is $4,500 per month. Interest payments on the debt will be $3,500 for both March and June. Finally, the Denver salesforce will receive a 3.00 percent commission on total sales for the first six months of the year, to be paid on June 30.

Prepare a monthly summary of cash payments for the six-month period from January through June. (Note: Compute prior December purchases to help get total material payments for January.)

Schedule of cash payments
(LO4-2)

22. Wright Lighting Fixtures forecasts its sales in units for the next four months as follows:

March	4,000
April	10,000
May	8,000
June	6,000

Wright maintains an ending inventory for each month in the amount of one and one-half times the expected sales in the following month. The ending inventory for February (March's beginning inventory) reflects this policy. Materials cost $7 per unit and are paid for in the month after production. Labor cost is $3 per unit and is paid for in the month incurred. Fixed overhead is $10,000 per month. Dividends of $14,000 are to be paid in May. Eight thousand units were produced in February.

Complete a production schedule and a summary of cash payments for March, April, and May. Remember that production in any one month is equal to sales plus desired ending inventory minus beginning inventory.

Schedule of cash payments
(LO4-2)

23. The Volt Battery Company has forecast its sales in units as follows:

January	1,300	May	1,850
February	1,150	June	2,000
March	1,100	July	1,700
April	1,600		

Volt Battery always keeps an ending inventory equal to 110 percent of the next month's expected sales. The ending inventory for December (January's beginning inventory) is 1,460 units, which is consistent with this policy.

Materials cost $14 per unit and are paid for in the month after purchase. Labor cost is $7 per unit and is paid in the month the cost is incurred. Overhead costs are $8,500 per month. Interest of $8,500 is scheduled to be paid in March, and employee bonuses of $13,700 will be paid in June.

Prepare a monthly production schedule and a monthly summary of cash payments for January through June. Volt Battery produced 1,100 units in December.

Cash budget
(LO4-2)

24. Graham Potato Company has projected sales of $6,000 in September, $10,000 in October, $16,000 in November, and $12,000 in December. Of the company's sales, 20 percent are paid for by cash and 80 percent are sold on

credit. Experience shows that 40 percent of accounts receivable are paid in the month after the sale, while the remaining 60 percent are paid two months after. Determine collections for November and December.

Also assume Graham's cash payments for November and December are $13,000 and $6,000, respectively. The beginning cash balance in November is $5,000, which is the desired minimum balance.

Prepare a cash budget with borrowing needed or repayments for November and December. (You will need to prepare a cash receipts schedule first.)

Advanced Problems

25. Harry's Carryout Stores has eight locations. The firm wishes to expand by two more stores and needs a bank loan to do this. Mr. Wilson, the banker, will finance construction if the firm can present an acceptable three-month financial plan for January through March. The following are actual and forecast sales figures:

Complete cash budget (LO4-2)

Actual		Forecast		Additional Information	
November	$260,000	January	$400,000	April forecast	$400,000
December	340,000	February	440,000		
		March	410,000		

Of the firm's sales, 60 percent are for cash and the remaining 40 percent are on credit. Of credit sales, 20 percent are paid in the month after sale and 80 percent are paid in the second month after the sale. Materials cost 20 percent of sales and are purchased and received each month in an amount sufficient to cover the following month's expected sales. Materials are paid for in the month after they are received. Labor expense is 50 percent of sales and is paid for in the month of sales. Selling and administrative expense is 15 percent of sales and is paid in the month of sales. Overhead expense is $31,000 in cash per month.

Depreciation expense is $10,600 per month. Taxes of $8,600 will be paid in January, and dividends of $5,000 will be paid in March. Cash at the beginning of January is $92,000, and the minimum desired cash balance is $87,000.

For January, February, and March, prepare a schedule of monthly cash receipts, monthly cash payments, and a complete monthly cash budget with borrowings and repayments.

26. Archer Electronics Company's actual sales and purchases for April and May are shown here along with forecast sales and purchases for June through September:

𝙕

Complete cash budget (LO4-2)

	Sales	Purchases
April (actual)	$370,000	$155,000
May (actual)	350,000	145,000
June (forecast)	325,000	145,000
July (forecast)	325,000	205,000
August (forecast)	340,000	225,000
September (forecast)	380,000	220,000

The company makes 20 percent of its sales for cash and 80 percent on credit. Of the credit sales, 50 percent are collected in the month after the sale and 50 percent are collected two months later. Archer pays for 20 percent of its purchases in the month after purchase and 80 percent two months after.

Labor expense equals 15 percent of the current month's sales. Overhead expense equals $12,500 per month. Interest payments of $32,500 are due in June and September. A cash dividend of $52,500 is scheduled to be paid in June. Tax payments of $25,500 are due in June and September. There is a scheduled capital outlay of $350,000 in September.

Archer Electronics' ending cash balance in May is $22,500. The minimum desired cash balance is $10,500. Prepare a schedule of monthly cash receipts, monthly cash payments, and a complete monthly cash budget with borrowing and repayments for June through September. The maximum desired cash balance is $50,500. Excess cash (above $50,500) is used to buy marketable securities. Marketable securities are sold before borrowing funds in case of a cash shortfall (less than $10,500).

Percent-of-sales method
(LO4-3)

27. Owen's Electronics has nine operating plants in seven southwestern states. Sales for last year were $100 million, and the balance sheet at year-end is similar in percentage of sales to that of previous years (and this will continue in the future). All assets (including fixed assets) and current liabilities will vary directly with sales. The firm is working at full capacity.

Balance Sheet (in $ millions)			
Assets		**Liabilities and Stockholders' Equity**	
Cash	$ 7	Accounts payable	$ 20
Accounts receivable	25	Accrued wages	7
Inventory	28	Accrued taxes	13
Current assets	$ 60	Current liabilities	$ 40
Fixed assets	45	Notes payable	15
		Common stock	20
		Retained earnings	30
		Total liabilities and	
Total assets	$105	stockholders' equity	$105

Owen's Electronics has an aftertax profit margin of 10 percent and a dividend payout ratio of 45 percent.

If sales grow by 20 percent next year, determine how many dollars of new funds are needed to finance the growth.

Percent-of-sales method
(LO4-3)

28. The Manning Company has financial statements as shown next, which are representative of the company's historical average. The firm is expecting a 35 percent increase in sales next year, and management is concerned about the company's need for external funds. The increase in sales is expected to be carried out without any expansion of fixed assets, but rather through more efficient asset utilization in the existing store. Among liabilities, only current liabilities vary directly with sales.

Using the percent-of-sales method, determine whether the company has external financing needs, or a surplus of funds. (Hint: A profit margin and payout ratio must be found from the income statement.)

Income Statement	
Sales	$250,000
Expenses	192,000
Earnings before interest and taxes	$ 58,000
Interest	7,500
Earnings before taxes	$ 50,500
Taxes	15,500
Earnings after taxes	$ 35,000
Dividends	$ 7,000

Balance Sheet			
Assets		**Liabilities and Stockholders' Equity**	
Cash	$ 8,500	Accounts payable	$ 26,400
Accounts receivable	63,000	Accrued wages	2,350
Inventory	91,000	Accrued taxes	3,750
Current assets	$162,500	Current liabilities	$ 32,500
Fixed assets	85,000	Notes payable	7,500
		Long-term debt	17,500
		Common stock	125,000
		Retained earnings	65,000
		Total liabilities and	
Total assets	$247,500	stockholders' equity	$247,500

29. Conn Man's Shops, a national clothing chain, had sales of $350 million last year. The business has a steady net profit margin of 9 percent and a dividend payout ratio of 25 percent. The balance sheet for the end of last year is shown.

Percent-of-sales method *(LO4-3)*

The firm's marketing staff has told the president that in the coming year there will be a large increase in the demand for overcoats and wool slacks. A sales increase of 20 percent is forecast for the company.

Balance Sheet End of Year (in $ millions)			
Assets		**Liabilities and Stockholders' Equity**	
Cash	$ 25	Accounts payable	$ 64
Accounts receivable	40	Accrued expenses	31
Inventory	82	Other payables	45
Plant and equipment	133	Common stock	50
		Retained earnings	90
		Total liabilities and	
Total assets	$280	stockholders' equity	$280

All balance sheet items are expected to maintain the same percent-of-sales relationships as last year,* except for common stock and retained earnings. No change is scheduled in the number of common stock shares outstanding, and retained earnings will change as dictated by the profits and dividend policy of the firm. (Remember, the net profit margin is 9 percent.)

a.   Will external financing be required for the company during the coming year?

b.   What would be the need for external financing if the net profit margin went up to 10.5 percent and the dividend payout ratio was increased to 60 percent? Explain.

---

*This included fixed assets, as the firm is at full capacity.

COMPREHENSIVE PROBLEM

Mansfield Corporation

(External funds requirement)

(LO4-4)

Mansfield Corporation had 20X1 sales of $100 million. The balance sheet items that vary directly with sales and the profit margin are as follows:

	Percent
Cash	5%
Accounts receivable	15
Inventory	20
Net fixed assets	40
Accounts payable	15
Accruals	10
Profit margin after taxes	10%

The dividend payout rate is 50 percent of earnings, and the balance in retained earnings at the end of 20X1 was $33 million. Notes payable are currently $7 million. Long-term bonds and common stock are constant at $5 million and $10 million, respectively.

a.   How much additional external capital will be required for next year if sales increase 15 percent? (Assume that the company is already operating at full capacity.)

b.   What will happen to external fund requirements if Mansfield Corporation reduces the payout ratio, grows at a slower rate, or suffers a decline in its profit margin? Discuss each of these separately.

c.   Prepare a pro forma balance sheet for 20X2, assuming that any external funds being acquired will be in the form of notes payable. Disregard the information in part *b* in answering this question (that is, use the original information and part *a* in constructing your pro forma balance sheet).

COMPREHENSIVE PROBLEM

The difficult part of solving a problem of this nature is to know what to do with the information contained within a story problem. Therefore, this problem will be easier to complete if you rely on Chapter 4 for the format of all required schedules.

Marsh Corporation
(Financial forecasting with seasonal production)
(LO4-5)

The Marsh Corporation makes standard-size 2-inch fasteners, which it sells for $155 per thousand. Mr. Marsh is the majority owner and manages the inventory and finances of the company. He estimates sales for the following months to be

January	$263,500 (1,700,000 fasteners)
February	$186,000 (1,200,000 fasteners)
March	$217,000 (1,400,000 fasteners)
April	$310,000 (2,000,000 fasteners)
May	$387,500 (2,500,000 fasteners)

Last year Marsh Corporation's sales were $175,000 in November and $232,500 in December (1,500,000 fasteners).

Mr. Marsh is preparing for a meeting with his banker to arrange the financing for the first quarter. Based on his sales forecast and the following information, which he has provided, your job as his new financial analyst is to prepare a monthly cash budget, monthly and quarterly pro forma income statements, a pro forma quarterly balance sheet, and all necessary supporting schedules for the first quarter.

History shows that Marsh Corporation collects 50 percent of its accounts receivable in the normal 30-day credit period (the month after the sale) and the other 50 percent in 60 days (two months after the sale). It pays for its materials 30 days after receipt. In general, Mr. Marsh likes to keep a two-month supply of inventory in anticipation of sales. Inventory at the beginning of December was 2,600,000 units. (This was not equal to his desired two-month supply.)

The major cost of production is the purchase of raw materials in the form of steel rods, which are cut, threaded, and finished. Last year, raw material costs were $52 per 1,000 fasteners, but Mr. Marsh has just been notified that material costs have risen, effective January 1, to $60 per 1,000 fasteners. The Marsh Corporation uses FIFO inventory accounting. Labor costs are relatively constant at $20 per thousand fasteners, since workers are paid on a piecework basis. Overhead is allocated at $10 per thousand units, and selling and administrative expense is 20 percent of sales. Labor expense and overhead are direct cash outflows paid in the month incurred, while interest and taxes are paid quarterly.

The corporation usually maintains a minimum cash balance of $25,000, and it puts its excess cash into marketable securities. The average tax rate is 40 percent, and Mr. Marsh usually pays out 50 percent of net income in dividends to stockholders. Marketable securities are sold before funds are borrowed when a cash shortage is faced. Ignore the interest on any short-term borrowings. Interest of $8,000 on the long-term debt is paid in March, but it is allocated over each month for accounting purposes. Taxes and dividends are paid in March.

As of year-end, the Marsh Corporation balance sheet was as follows:

	A	B	C	D
1	**MARSH CORPORATION** **Balance Sheet** **December 31, 20X1**			
2	**Assets**			
3	Current assets:			
4	Cash	$ 30,000		
5	Accounts receivable	320,000		
6	Inventory	237,800		
7	Total current assets		$ 587,800	
8	Fixed assets:			
9	Plant and equipment	$1,000,000		
10	Less: Accumulated depreciation	200,000	800,000	
11	Total assets		$1,387,800	
12	**Liabilities and Stockholders' Equity**			
13	Accounts payable	$ 93,600		
14	Notes payable	0		
15	Long-term debt, 8 percent	400,000		
16	Common stock	504,200		
17	Retained earnings	390,000		
18	Total liabilities and stockholders' equity	$1,387,800		

WEB EXERCISE

1. Barnes & Noble is a company in transition in terms of financial performance. Go to www.barnesandnoble.com.
2. Scroll to the bottom of the page and click on "Investor Relations." What is the current stock price?
3. Return to the main "Investor Relations" tab and click on "Financial News." Write a brief paragraph summary of any two press releases appearing in this box (two paragraphs in total).
4. Go back to "Investor Relations" and click the link titled "Annual Reports." Open the most recent annual report.
5. Scroll down on the left-hand bookmarks until you get to "Consolidated Statements of Operations." Has Barnes & Noble been profitable in the last three years?
6. Click on "Consolidated Balance Sheet." What is the ratio of "Total Current and Non-Current Liabilities to Total Assets" for the past two periods? Anything over 70 percent is considered too high. How does Barnes & Noble look?

Note: Occasionally a topic we have listed may have been deleted, updated, or moved into a different location at a website. If you click on the site map or site index, you will be introduced to a table of contents that should aid you in finding the topic you are looking for.

LEARNING OBJECTIVES

LO 5-1 Leverage represents the use of fixed cost items to magnify the firm's results.

LO 5-2 Break-even analysis allows the firm to determine the magnitude of operations necessary to avoid loss.

LO 5-3 Operating leverage indicates the extent to which fixed assets (plant and equipment) are utilized by the firm.

LO 5-4 Financial leverage shows how much debt the firm employs in its capital structure.

LO 5-5 Combined leverage takes into account both the use of fixed assets and debt.

LO 5-6 By increasing leverage, the firm increases its profit potential, but also its risk of failure.

Operating and Financial Leverage

In the physical sciences as well as in politics, the term **leverage** has been popularized to mean the use of special force and effects to produce more than normal results from a given course of action. In business the same concept is applied, with the emphasis on the employment of fixed cost items in anticipation of magnifying returns at high levels of operation. You should recognize that leverage is a two-edged sword—producing highly favorable results when things go well and quite the opposite under negative conditions.

Just ask the airline industry. Firms such as American Airlines, Delta, Southwest, and United Airlines were all flying high before the turn of the century because of favorable economic conditions, high capacity utilization, and relatively low interest rates on debt. Such was not the case in the next decade when high leverage in the form of high-cost fixed assets (airplanes) and high-cost debt was causing severe consequences in a weak economy. A series of bankruptcies followed as high fixed costs could not be overcome. TWA filed for bankruptcy in 2001, United Airlines and U.S. Airways in 2002, Northwest and Delta in 2005, Frontier in 2008, and finally American Airlines in 2011.

Between 2000 and 2005, Delta saw its EPS go from $6.87 to a negative $12.80. In 2007, American Airlines had a profit of $504 million but lost close to $6 billion over the next four years. As we noted, the company finally bit the bullet and declared bankruptcy in 2011. In all cases (TWA was bought by American), the airlines continued to operate; they restructured under the supervision of the bankruptcy court and eventually emerged as publicly traded companies again. By early 2015, the airlines were flying high again. Their planes were full, profits soared, and they were taking delivery of new fuel-efficient planes. Between 2014 and 2016, oil prices collapsed from over $100 per barrel to as low as $30 per barrel. Because fuel makes up over 30 percent of an airline's cost, American Airlines' stock price soared. As good times continued into 2018, it became easy to forget that leverage can work both ways. American Airlines chairman and CEO Doug Parker told analysts, "I don't think we're ever going to lose money again. We have an industry that's going to be profitable in good and bad times."

Only time will tell if this prediction will hold up, but in this chapter we will discuss how the effects of financial leverage and operating leverage suggest that Mr. Parker's prediction is, at the least, a very bold one.

Leverage in a Business

Assume you are approached with an opportunity to start your own business. You are to manufacture and market industrial parts, such as ball bearings, wheels, and casters. You face two primary decisions.

First, you must determine the amount of fixed cost plant and equipment you wish to use in the production process. By installing modern, sophisticated equipment, you can virtually eliminate labor in the production of inventory. At high volume, you will do quite well, as most of your costs are fixed. At low volume, however, you could face difficulty in making your fixed payments for plant and equipment. If you decide to use expensive labor rather than machinery, you will lessen your opportunity for profit, but at the same time you will lower your exposure to risk (you can lay off part of the workforce).

Second, you must determine how you will finance the business. If you rely on debt financing and the business is successful, you will generate substantial profits as an owner, paying only the fixed interest costs of debt. Of course, if the business starts off poorly, the contractual obligations related to debt could mean bankruptcy. As an alternative, you might decide to sell equity rather than borrow, a step that will lower your own profit potential (you must share with others) but minimize your risk exposure.

In both decisions, you are making explicit decisions about the use of leverage. To the extent that you go with a heavy commitment to fixed costs in the manufacturing process, you are employing operating leverage. To the extent that you use debt in financing the firm, you are engaging in financial leverage. We shall carefully examine each type of leverage and then show the combined effect of both.

Operating Leverage

Operating leverage reflects the extent to which fixed assets and associated fixed costs are utilized in the business. As indicated in Table 5-1, a firm's operational costs may be classified as fixed, variable, or semivariable.

Table 5-1 Classification of costs		
Fixed	**Variable**	**Semivariable**
Lease	Raw material	Utilities
Depreciation	Factory labor	Repairs and maintenance
Executive salaries	Sales commissions	
Property taxes		

For purposes of analysis, variable and semivariable costs will be combined. To evaluate the implications of heavy fixed asset use, we employ the technique of break-even analysis.

Break-Even Analysis

How much will changes in volume affect cost and profit? At what point does the firm break even? What is the most efficient level of fixed assets to employ in the firm?

A break-even chart is presented in Figure 5-1 to answer some of these questions. The number of units produced and sold is shown along the horizontal axis, and revenue and costs are shown along the vertical axis.

Figure 5-1   Break-even chart: Leveraged firm

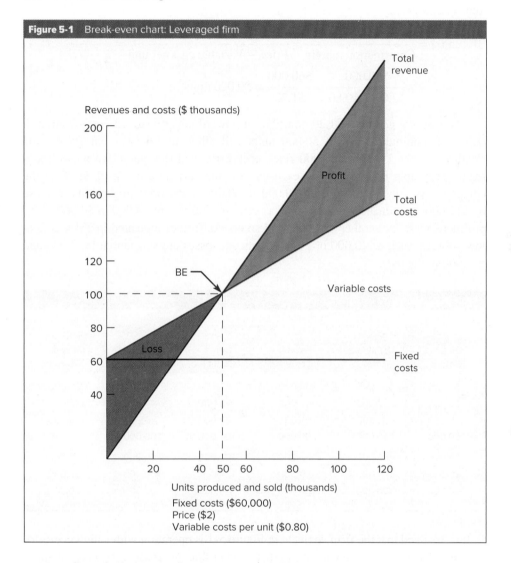

Note, first of all, that our fixed costs are $60,000, regardless of volume, and that our variable costs (at $0.80 per unit) are added to fixed costs to determine total costs at any point. The total revenue line is determined by multiplying price ($2) times volume.

Of particular interest is the break-even (BE) point at 50,000 units, where the total costs and total revenue lines intersect. The numbers are as follows:

Units = 50,000				
Total Variable Costs (TVC)	Fixed Costs (FC)	Total Costs (TC)	Total Revenue (TR)	Operating Income (loss)
(50,000 × $0.80) $40,000	$60,000	$100,000	(50,000 × $2) $100,000	0

The break-even point for the company may also be determined by use of a simple formula—in which we divide fixed costs by the contribution margin on each unit sold, with the **contribution margin** defined as price minus variable cost per unit. The formula is as follows:

$$\text{BE (units)} = \frac{\text{Fixed costs}}{\text{Contribution margin}} = \frac{\text{Fixed costs}}{\text{Price} - \text{Variable cost per unit}} = \frac{FC}{P - VC} \quad (5\text{-}1)$$

$$\frac{\$60,000}{\$2.00 - \$0.80} = \frac{\$60,000}{\$1.20} = 50,000 \text{ units}$$

Since we are getting a $1.20 contribution toward covering fixed costs-from each unit sold, minimum sales of 50,000 units will allow us to cover our fixed costs (50,000 units × $1.20 = $60,000 fixed costs). Beyond this point, we move into a highly profitable range in which each unit of sales brings a profit of $1.20 to the company. As sales increase from 50,000 to 60,000 units, operating profits increase by $12,000, as indicated in Table 5-2; as sales increase from 60,000 to 80,000 units, profits increase by another $24,000; and so on. As further indicated in Table 5-2, at low volumes such as 40,000 or 20,000 units our losses are substantial ($12,000 and $36,000 in the red).

Table 5-2 Volume-cost-profit analysis: Leveraged firm					
Units Sold	Total Variable Costs	Fixed Costs	Total Costs	Total Revenue	Operating Income (Loss)
0	$ 0	$60,000	$ 60,000	$ 0	$(60,000)
20,000	16,000	60,000	76,000	40,000	(36,000)
40,000	32,000	60,000	92,000	80,000	(12,000)
50,000	40,000	60,000	100,000	100,000	0
60,000	48,000	60,000	108,000	120,000	12,000
80,000	64,000	60,000	124,000	160,000	36,000
100,000	80,000	60,000	140,000	200,000	60,000

It is assumed that the firm depicted in Figure 5-1 is operating with a high degree of leverage. The situation is analogous to that of an airline that must carry a certain number of people to break even but beyond that point is in a very profitable range. This has certainly been the case with Southwest Airlines, which has its home office in Dallas, Texas, but also flies to many other states. The airline systematically offers lower fares than American, Delta, and other airlines to ensure maximum capacity utilization.

A More Conservative Approach

Not all firms would choose to operate at the high degree of operating leverage exhibited in Figure 5-1. Fear of not reaching the 50,000-unit break-even level might discourage some companies from heavy utilization of fixed assets. More expensive variable costs might be substituted for automated plant and equipment. Assume fixed costs for a more conservative firm can be reduced to $12,000—but variable costs will go from

$0.80 to $1.60. If the same price assumption of $2 per unit is employed, the break-even level is 30,000 units, as shown here:

$$\text{BE (units)} = \frac{\text{Fixed costs}}{\text{Price} - \text{Variable cost per unit}} = \frac{\text{FC}}{P - \text{VC}} = \frac{\$12,000}{\$2 - \$1.60}$$

$$= \frac{\$12,000}{\$0.40}$$

$$= 30,000 \text{ units}$$

With fixed costs reduced from $60,000 to $12,000, the loss potential is small. Furthermore, the break-even level of operations is a comparatively low 30,000 units. Nevertheless, the use of a virtually unleveraged approach has cut into the potential profitability of the more conservative firm, as indicated in Figure 5-2.

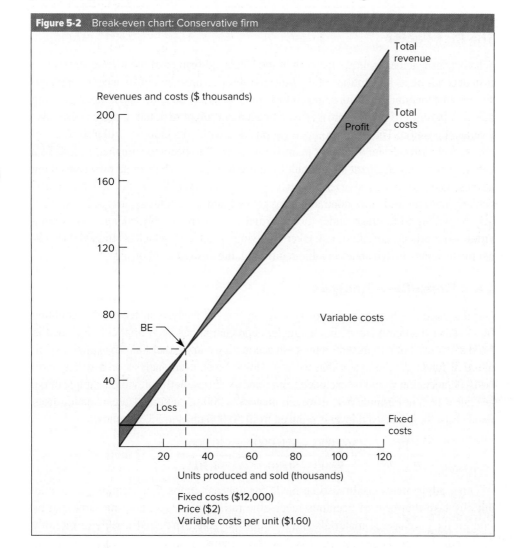

Figure 5-2 Break-even chart: Conservative firm

Even at high levels of operation, the potential profit in Figure 5-2 is small. As indicated in Table 5-3, at a 100,000-unit volume, operating income is only $28,000—some $32,000 less than that for the "leveraged" firm previously analyzed in Table 5-2.

Table 5-3 Volume-cost-profit analysis: Conservative firm					
Units Sold	Total Variable Costs	Fixed Costs	Total Costs	Total Revenue	Operating Income (Loss)
0	$ 0	$12,000	$ 12,000	$ 0	$(12,000)
20,000	32,000	12,000	44,000	40,000	(4,000)
30,000	48,000	12,000	60,000	60,000	0
40,000	64,000	12,000	76,000	80,000	4,000
60,000	96,000	12,000	108,000	120,000	12,000
80,000	128,000	12,000	140,000	160,000	20,000
100,000	160,000	12,000	172,000	200,000	28,000

The Risk Factor

Whether management follows the path of the leveraged firm or of the more conservative firm depends on its perceptions of the future. If the vice president of finance is apprehensive about economic conditions, the conservative plan may be undertaken. For a growing business in times of relative prosperity, management might maintain a more aggressive, leveraged position. The firm's competitive position within its industry will also be a factor. Does the firm desire to merely maintain stability or to become a market leader? To a certain extent, management should tailor the use of leverage to meet its own risk-taking desires. Those who are risk-averse (prefer less risk to more risk) should anticipate a particularly high return before contracting for heavy fixed costs. Others, less averse to risk, may be willing to leverage under more normal conditions. Simply taking risks is not a virtue—our prisons are full of risk takers. The important idea, which is stressed throughout the text, is to match an acceptable return with the desired level of risk.

Cash Break-Even Analysis

Our discussion to this point has dealt with break-even analysis in terms of accounting flows rather than cash flows. For example, depreciation has been implicitly included in fixed expenses, but it represents a noncash accounting entry rather than an explicit expenditure of funds. To the extent that we were doing break-even analysis on a strictly cash basis, depreciation would be excluded from fixed expenses. In the previous example of the leveraged firm in Formula 5-1, if we eliminate $20,000 of "assumed" depreciation from fixed costs, the break-even level is reduced from 50,000 units to 33,333 units.

$$\frac{FC}{P - VC} = \frac{(\$60,000 - \$20,000)}{\$2.00 - \$0.80} = \frac{\$40,000}{\$1.20} = 33,333 \text{ units}$$

Other adjustments could also be made for noncash items. For example, sales may initially take the form of accounts receivable rather than cash, and the same can be said for the purchase of materials and accounts payable. An actual weekly or monthly cash budget would be necessary to isolate these items.

While cash break-even analysis is helpful in analyzing the short-term outlook of the firm, particularly when it may be in trouble, break-even analysis is normally conducted on the basis of accounting flows rather than strictly cash flows. Most of the assumptions throughout this chapter are based on concepts broader than pure cash flows.

Degree of Operating Leverage

Degree of operating leverage (DOL) may be defined as the percent change in operating income that occurs as a result of a percent change in units sold.

$$DOL = \frac{\text{Percent change in operating income}}{\text{Percent change in unit volume}} \qquad (5\text{-}2)$$

Highly leveraged firms, such as Ford Motor Company or American Airlines, are likely to enjoy a substantial increase in income as volume expands, while less leveraged firms will participate in an increase to a lesser extent. Degree of operating leverage should be computed only over a profitable range of operations. However, the closer DOL is computed to the company break-even point, the higher the number will be due to a large percentage increase in operating income.[1]

Let us apply the formula to the leveraged and conservative firms previously discussed. Their income or losses at various levels of operation are summarized in Table 5-4.

Table 5-4 Operating income or loss		
Units	**Leveraged Firm (Table 5-2)**	**Conservative Firm (Table 5-3)**
0	$(60,000)	$(12,000)
20,000	(36,000)	(4,000)
40,000	(12,000)	4,000
60,000	12,000	12,000
80,000	36,000	20,000
100,000	60,000	28,000

We will now consider what happens to operating income as volume moves from 80,000 to 100,000 units for each firm. We will compute the degree of operating leverage (DOL) using Formula 5-2.

Leveraged Firm

$$DOL = \frac{\text{Percent change in operating income}}{\text{Percent change in unit volume}} = \frac{\dfrac{\$24,000}{\$36,000} \times 100}{\dfrac{20,000}{80,000} \times 100}$$

$$= \frac{67\%}{25\%} = 2.7$$

---

[1]While the value of DOL varies at each level of output, the beginning level of volume determines the DOL regardless of the location of the endpoint.

Conservative Firm

$$\text{DOL} = \frac{\text{Percent change in operating income}}{\text{Percent change in unit volume}} = \frac{\dfrac{\$8,000}{\$20,000} \times 100}{\dfrac{20,000}{80,000} \times 100}$$

$$= \frac{40\%}{25\%} = 1.6$$

We see that the DOL is much greater for the leveraged firm, indicating at 80,000 units a 1 percent increase in volume will produce a 2.7 percent change in operating income, versus a 1.6 percent increase for the conservative firm.

The formula for degree of operating leverage may be algebraically manipulated to read

$$\text{DOL} = \frac{Q(P - \text{VC})}{Q(P - \text{VC}) - \text{FC}} \tag{5-3}$$

where

Q = Quantity at which DOL is computed.

P = Price per unit.

VC = Variable costs per unit.

FC = Fixed costs.

Using the newly stated formula for the first firm at $Q = 80,000$, with $P = \$2$, $\text{VC} = \$0.80$, and $\text{FC} = \$60,000$,

$$\text{DOL} = \frac{80,000(\$2.00 - \$0.80)}{80,000(\$2.00 - \$0.80) - \$60,000}$$

$$= \frac{80,000(\$1.20)}{80,000(\$1.20) - \$60,000} = \frac{\$96,000}{\$96,000 - \$60,000}$$

$$\text{DOL} = 2.7$$

we once again derive an answer of 2.7.[2] The same type of calculation could also be performed for the conservative firm.

---

[2]The formula for DOL may also be rewritten as

$$\text{DOL} = \frac{Q(P - \text{VC})}{Q(P - \text{VC}) - \text{FC}} = \frac{Q(P) - Q(\text{VC})}{Q(P) - Q(\text{VC}) - \text{FC}}$$

We can rewrite the second terms as

$QP = S$, or Sales (Quantity × Price)

$Q(\text{VC}) = \text{TVC}$, or Total variable costs (Quantity × Variable costs per unit)

FC = Total fixed costs (remains the same term)

We then have

$$\text{DOL} = \frac{S - \text{TVC}}{S - \text{TVC} - \text{FC}}, \text{ or } \frac{\$160,000 - \$64,000}{\$160,000 - \$64,000 - \$60,000} = \frac{\$96,000}{\$36,000} = 2.7$$

Limitations of Analysis

Throughout our analysis of operating leverage, we have assumed that a constant or linear function exists for revenues and costs as volume changes. For example, we have used $2 as the hypothetical sales price at all levels of operation. In the "real world," however, we may face price weakness as we attempt to capture an increasing market for our product, or we may face cost overruns as we move beyond an optimum-size operation. Relationships are not so fixed as we have assumed.

Nevertheless, the basic patterns we have studied are reasonably valid for most firms over an extended operating range (in our example, that might be between 20,000 and 100,000 units). It is only at the extreme levels that linear assumptions fully break down, as indicated in Figure 5-3.

Figure 5-3   Nonlinear break-even analysis

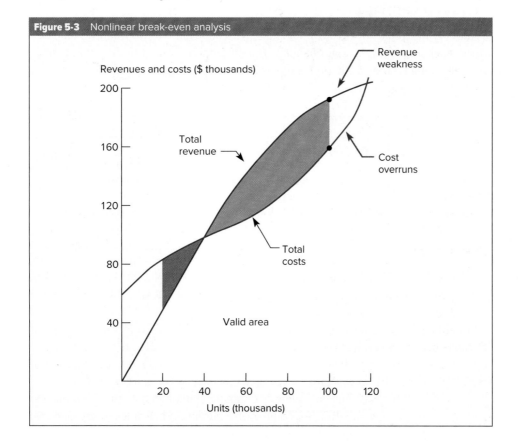

Financial Leverage

Having discussed the effect of fixed costs on the operations of the firm (operating leverage), we now turn to the second form of leverage. **Financial leverage** reflects the amount of debt used in the capital structure of the firm. Because debt carries a fixed obligation of interest payments, we have the opportunity to greatly magnify our results at various levels of operations. You may have heard of the real estate developer who borrows 100 percent of the costs of his project and will enjoy an infinite return on his zero investment if all goes well. If it doesn't, then he is in serious trouble or bankruptcy.

It is helpful to think of *operating leverage* as primarily affecting the left-hand side of the balance sheet and *financial leverage* as affecting the right-hand side.

Assets	Liabilities and Net Worth
Operating leverage	Financial leverage

Whereas operating leverage influences the mix of plant and equipment, financial leverage determines how the operation is to be financed. It is possible for two firms to have equal operating capabilities and yet show widely different results because of the use of financial leverage.

Impact on Earnings

In studying the impact of financial leverage, we shall examine two financial plans for a firm, each employing a significantly different amount of debt in the capital structure. Financing totaling $200,000 is required to carry the assets of the firm. Here are the facts:

	Total Assets—$200,000			
	Plan A (*leveraged*)		**Plan B** (*conservative*)	
Debt (8% interest)	$150,000	($12,000 interest)	$ 50,000	($4,000 interest)
Common stock	50,000	(8,000 shares at $6.25)	150,000	(24,000 shares at $6.25)
Total financing	$200,000		$200,000	

Under *leveraged* Plan A we will borrow $150,000 and sell 8,000 shares of stock at $6.25 to raise an additional $50,000, whereas *conservative* Plan B calls for borrowing only $50,000 and acquiring an additional $150,000 in stock with 24,000 shares.

In Table 5-5, we compute earnings per share for the two plans at various levels of "earnings before interest and taxes" (EBIT). These earnings (EBIT) represent the operating income of the firm—before deductions have been made for financial charges or taxes. We assume EBIT levels of 0, $12,000, $16,000, $36,000, and $60,000.

The impact of the two financing plans is dramatic. Although both plans assume the same operating income, or EBIT, for comparative purposes at each level (say, $36,000 in calculation 4), the reported income per share is vastly different ($1.50 versus $0.67). It is also evident that the *conservative* Plan A will produce better results at low income levels—but the *leveraged* Plan B will generate much better earnings per share as operating income, or EBIT, goes up. The firm would be indifferent between the two plans at an EBIT level of $16,000, as shown in Table 5-5.

In Figure 5-4, we graphically demonstrate the effect of the two financing plans on earnings per share and the indifference point at an EBIT of $16 (thousand).

With an EBIT of $16,000, we are earning 8 percent on total assets of $200,000—precisely the percentage cost of borrowed funds to the firm. The use or nonuse of debt does not influence the answer. Beyond $16,000, Plan A, employing heavy financial

Table 5-5   Impact of financing plan on earnings per share

	Plan A *(leveraged)*	Plan B *(conservative)*
1. EBIT (0)		
Earnings before interest and taxes (EBIT)	0	0
– Interest (*I*)	$(12,000)	$ (4,000)
Earnings before taxes (EBT)	$(12,000)	$ (4,000)
– Taxes (*T*)*	(6,000)	(2,000)
Earnings after taxes (EAT)	$ (6,000)	$ (2,000)
Shares	8,000	24,000
Earnings per share (EPS)	$ (0.75)	$ (0.08)
2. EBIT ($12,000)		
Earnings before interest and taxes (EBIT)	$ 12,000	$12,000
– Interest (*I*)	12,000	4,000
Earnings before taxes (EBT)	$ 0	$ 8,000
– Taxes (*T*)	0	4,000
Earnings after taxes (EAT)	$ 0	$ 4,000
Shares	8,000	24,000
Earnings per share (EPS)	$ 0	$ 0.17
3. EBIT ($16,000)		
Earnings before interest and taxes (EBIT)	$ 16,000	$16,000
– Interest (*I*)	12,000	4,000
Earnings before taxes (EBT)	$ 4,000	$12,000
– Taxes (*T*)	2,000	6,000
Earnings after taxes (EAT)	$ 2,000	$ 6,000
Shares	8,000	24,000
Earnings per share (EPS)	$ 0.25	$ 0.25
4. EBIT ($36,000)		
Earnings before interest and taxes (EBIT)	$ 36,000	$36,000
– Interest (*I*)	12,000	4,000
Earnings before taxes (EBT)	$ 24,000	$32,000
– Taxes (*T*)	12,000	16,000
Earnings after taxes (EAT)	$ 12,000	$16,000
Shares	8,000	24,000
Earnings per share (EPS)	$ 1.50	$ 0.67
5. EBIT ($60,000)		
Earnings before interest and taxes (EBIT)	$ 60,000	$60,000
– Interest (*I*)	12,000	4,000
Earnings before taxes (EBT)	$ 48,000	$56,000
– Taxes (*T*)	24,000	28,000
Earnings after taxes (EAT)	$ 24,000	$28,000
Shares	8,000	24,000
Earnings per share (EPS)	$ 3.00	$ 1.17

*The assumption is that large losses can be written off against other income, perhaps in future years, thus providing the firm with a tax savings benefit. The tax rate is 50 percent for ease of computation.

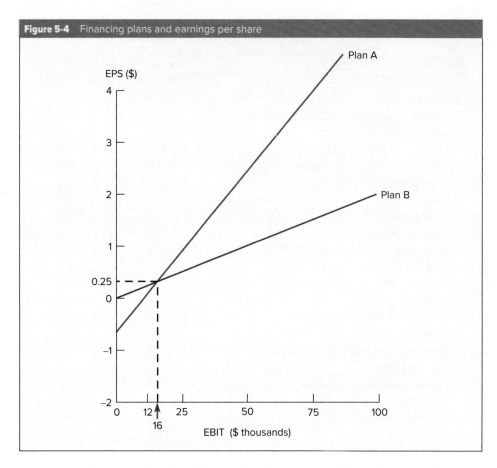

Figure 5-4   Financing plans and earnings per share

leverage, really goes to work, allowing the firm to expand earnings per share as a result of a change in EBIT. For example, at the EBIT level of $36,000, an 18 percent return on assets of $200,000 takes place—and financial leverage is clearly working to our benefit as earnings greatly expand.

Degree of Financial Leverage

As was true of operating leverage, degree of financial leverage measures the effect of a change in one variable on another variable. **Degree of financial leverage (DFL)** may be defined as the percent change in earnings (EPS) that occurs as a result of a percent change in earnings before interest and taxes (EBIT).

$$DFL = \frac{\text{Percent change in EPS}}{\text{Percent change in EBIT}} \tag{5-4}$$

For computation, the formula for DFL may be conveniently restated:

$$DFL = \frac{EBIT}{EBIT - I} \tag{5-5}$$

Let's compute the degrees of financial leverage for Plan A and Plan B, previously presented in Table 5-5, at an EBIT level of $36,000. Plan A calls for $12,000 of interest at all levels of financing, and Plan B requires $4,000.

Plan A (Leveraged)

$$DFL = \frac{EBIT}{EBIT - I} = \frac{\$36,000}{\$36,000 - \$12,000} = \frac{\$36,000}{\$24,000} = 1.5$$

Plan B (Conservative)

$$DFL = \frac{EBIT}{EBIT - I} = \frac{\$36,000}{\$36,000 - \$4,000} = \frac{\$36,000}{\$32,000} = 1.1$$

As expected, Plan A has a much higher degree of financial leverage. At an EBIT level of $36,000, a 1 percent increase in earnings will produce a 1.5 percent increase in earnings per share under Plan A, but only a 1.1 percent increase under Plan B. DFL may be computed for any level of operation, and it will change from point to point, but Plan A will always exceed Plan B.

Limitations to Use of Financial Leverage

Alert students may quickly observe that if debt is such a good thing, why sell any stock? (Perhaps one share to yourself.) With exclusive debt financing at an EBIT level of $36,000, we would have a degree of financial leverage factor (DFL) of 1.8.

$$DFL = \frac{EBIT}{EBIT - I} = \frac{\$36,000}{\$36,000 - \$16,000} = \frac{\$36,000}{\$20,000} = 1.8$$

(With no stock, we would borrow the full $200,000.)

$$(8\% \times \$200,000 = \$16,000 \text{ interest})$$

As stressed throughout the text, debt financing and financial leverage offer unique advantages, but only up to a point—beyond that point, debt financing may be detrimental to the firm. For example, as we expand the use of debt in our capital structure, lenders will perceive a greater financial risk for the firm. For that reason, they may raise the average interest rate to be paid and may demand that certain restrictions be placed on the corporation. Furthermore, concerned common stockholders may drive down the price of the stock—forcing us away from the *objective of maximizing the firm's overall value* in the market. The impact of financial leverage must be carefully weighed by firms with high debt such as United Airlines.

This is not to say that financial leverage does not work to the benefit of the firm—it does if properly used. Further discussion of appropriate debt-equity mixes is covered in Chapter 11, "Cost of Capital." For now, we accept the virtues of financial leverage, knowing that all good things must be used in moderation. For firms that are in industries that offer some degree of stability, are in a positive stage of growth, and are operating in favorable economic conditions, the use of debt is recommended.

Combining Operating and Financial Leverage

If both operating and financial leverage allow us to magnify our returns, then we will get maximum leverage through their combined use in the form of **combined leverage**. We have said that operating leverage affects primarily the asset structure of the firm, while financial leverage affects the debt-equity mix. From an income statement viewpoint, operating leverage determines return from operations, while financial leverage determines how the "fruits of our labor" will be allocated to debt holders and, more importantly, to stockholders in the form of earnings per share. Table 5-6 shows the combined influence of operating and financial leverage on the income statement. The values in Table 5-6 are drawn from earlier material in the chapter (Tables 5-2 and 5-5). We assumed in both cases a high degree of operating and financial leverage (i.e., the leveraged firm). The sales volume is 80,000 units.

Table 5-6 Income statement	
Sales (total revenue) (80,000 units @ $2)	$160,000
− Fixed costs	60,000
− Variable costs ($0.80 per unit)	64,000
Operating income	$ 36,000
Earnings before interest and taxes	$ 36,000
− Interest	12,000
Earnings before taxes	$ 24,000
− Taxes	12,000
Earnings after taxes	$ 12,000
Shares	8,000
Earnings per share	$1.50

(Sales through Operating income bracketed as Operating leverage; Earnings before interest and taxes through Earnings per share bracketed as Financial leverage)

You will observe, first, that operating leverage influences the top half of the income statement—determining operating income. The last item under operating leverage, operating income, then becomes the initial item for determining financial leverage.

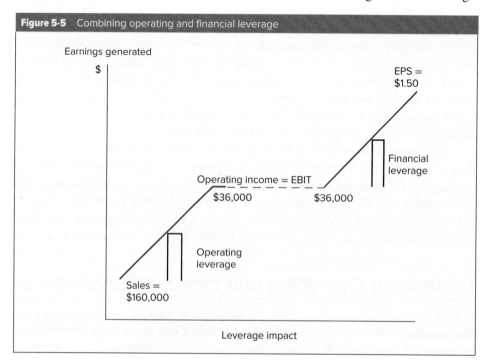

Figure 5-5   Combining operating and financial leverage

"Operating income" and "Earnings before interest and taxes" are one and the same, representing the return to the corporation after production, marketing, and so forth—but before interest and taxes are paid. In the second half of the income statement, we show the extent to which earnings before interest and taxes are translated into earnings per share. A graphical representation of these points is presented in Figure 5-5.

Degree of Combined Leverage

Degree of combined leverage (DCL) uses the entire income statement and shows the impact of a change in sales or volume on bottom-line earnings per share. Degree of operating leverage and degree of financial leverage are, in effect, being combined. Table 5-7 shows what happens to profitability as the firm's sales go from $160,000 (80,000 units) to $200,000 (100,000 units).

Table 5-7 Operating and financial leverage		
	80,000 Units	**100,000 Units**
Sales—$2 per unit	$160,000	$200,000
– Fixed costs	60,000	60,000
– Variable costs ($0.80 per unit)	64,000	80,000
Operating income = EBIT	$ 36,000	$ 60,000
– Interest	12,000	12,000
Earnings before taxes	$ 24,000	$ 48,000
– Taxes	12,000	24,000
Earnings after taxes	$ 12,000	$ 24,000
Shares	8,000	8,000
Earnings per share	$ 1.50	$ 3.00

The formula for degree of combined leverage is stated as

$$\frac{\text{Degree of combined}}{\text{leverage (DCL)}} = \frac{\text{Percent change in EPS}}{\text{Percent change in sales (or volume)}} \quad (5\text{-}6)$$

Using data from Table 5-7,

$$\frac{\text{Percent change in EPS}}{\text{Percent change in sales}} = \frac{\dfrac{\$1.50}{\$1.50} \times 100}{\dfrac{\$40,000}{\$160,000} \times 100} = \frac{100\%}{25\%} = 4$$

we find that every percentage point change in sales will be reflected in a 4 percent change in earnings per share at this level of operation (quite an impact).

An algebraic statement of the formula is

$$\text{DCL} = \frac{Q(P - \text{VC})}{Q(P - \text{VC}) - \text{FC} - I} \quad (5\text{-}7)$$

From Table 5-7: Beginning Q (Quantity) = 80,000; P (Price per unit) = $2.00; VC (Variable costs per unit) = $0.80; FC (Fixed costs) = $60,000; and I (Interest) = $12,000.

$$DCL = \frac{80{,}000(\$2.00 - \$0.80)}{80{,}000(\$2.00 - \$0.80) - \$60{,}000 - \$12{,}000}$$

$$= \frac{80{,}000(\$1.20)}{80{,}000(\$1.20) - \$72{,}000}$$

$$DCL = \frac{\$96{,}000}{\$96{,}000 - \$72{,}000} = \frac{\$96{,}000}{\$24{,}000} = 4$$

The answer is once again shown to be 4.[3]

A Word of Caution

In a sense, we are piling risk on risk as the two different forms of leverage are combined. Perhaps a firm carrying heavy operating leverage may wish to moderate its position financially, and vice versa. One thing is certain—the decision will have a major impact on the operations of the firm.

---

[3]The formula for DCL may also be rewritten as

$$DCL = \frac{Q(P - VC)}{Q(P - VC) - FC - I} = \frac{Q(P) - Q(VC)}{Q(P) - Q(VC) - FC - I}$$

We can rewrite the second terms as

$Q(P) = S$, or Sales (Quantity × Price)

$Q(VC) = TVC$, or Total variable costs (Quantity × Variable costs per unit)

FC = Total fixed costs (remains the same term)

I = Interest (remains the same term)

We then have

$$DCL = \frac{S - TVC}{S - TVC - FC - I}, \text{ or } \frac{\$160{,}000 - \$64{,}000}{\$160{,}000 - \$64{,}000 - \$60{,}000 - \$12{,}000} = \frac{\$96{,}000}{\$24{,}000} = 4$$

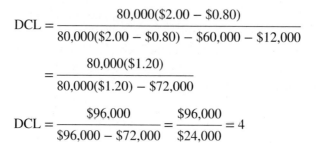

Finance in ACTION

Give Shareholders a Slice of the Apple and Leverage Rises

Managerial

Apple Computer Company was founded in 1976 and its first product was the Apple-1 computer, designed and built by one man, Steve Wozniak. Wozniak's little computer hit like a bolt of lightning. Steve Jobs, Wozniak's partner, then led the company to great early success through rapid innovation and brilliant marketing. Unfortunately, Microsoft proved to be a tough competitor, and Apple fell on tough times. Jobs was fired by Apple's board in 1985, only to be rehired a decade later as the company struggled to find direction.

Then, lightning struck a second time, and it kept on striking. In 2001 Apple debuted the iPod, a small digital audio player that allowed the owner to carry "1,000 songs in your pocket." In 2003, the iTunes Store came online. The iPhone was released in 2007, the iPad in 2010. With this series of blockbusters came a great wave of cash. As can be seen in the

(continued)

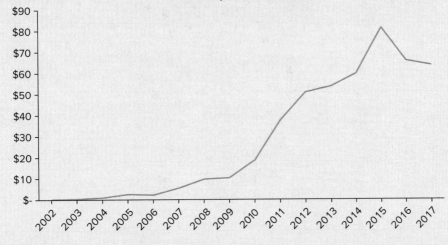

Cash from operations ($ billions)

accompanying chart, Apple grew its cash flow from operations from just over $80 million in 2002 to over $80 billion in 2015. Apple Inc. entered 2018 as the most valuable company in the world.

Once Apple began to generate reliable profits, its management decided to change its capital structure. To achieve this, the company instituted a "capital return program" for its stockholders. Between 2012 and 2017, the firm issued $61 billion in dividends and repurchased $166 billion in stock. In the 2017 annual report, management stated that "the Company plans to continue to access the domestic and international debt markets to assist in funding its capital return program."

Prior to beginning the capital return program, Apple's debt-to-assets ratio was less than 33 percent; by 2017, the ratio had risen above 64 percent.

SUMMARY

Leverage may be defined as the use of fixed cost items to magnify returns at high levels of operation. Operating leverage primarily affects fixed versus variable cost utilization in the operation of the firm. An important concept—degree of operating leverage (DOL)—measures the percent change in operating income as a result of a percent change in volume. The heavier the utilization of fixed cost assets, the higher DOL is likely to be.

Financial leverage reflects the extent to which debt is used in the capital structure of the firm. Substantial use of debt will place a great burden on the firm at low levels of profitability, but it will help magnify earnings per share as volume or operating income increases. We combine operating leverage and financial leverage to assess the impact of all types of fixed costs on the firm. There is a multiplier effect when we use the two different types of leverage.

Because leverage is a two-edged sword, management must be sure the level of risk assumed is in accord with its desires for risk and its perceptions of the future. High operating leverage may be balanced off against lower financial leverage if this is deemed desirable, and vice versa.

REVIEW OF FORMULAS

1. $BE = \dfrac{FC}{P - VC}$ (5-1)

> BE is break-even point.
> FC is fixed costs.
> P is price per unit.
> VC is variable cost per unit.

2. $DOL = \dfrac{Q(P - VC)}{Q(P - VC) - FC}$ (5-3)

> DOL is degree of operating leverage.
> Q is quantity at which DOL is computed.
> P is price per unit.
> VC is variable cost per unit.
> FC is fixed costs.

3. $DOL = \dfrac{S - TVC}{S - TVC - FC}$ (Footnote 2)

> DOL is degree of operating leverage.
> S is sales (QP) at which DOL is computed.
> TVC is total variable costs.
> FC is fixed costs.

4. $DFL = \dfrac{EBIT}{EBIT - I}$ (5-5)

> DFL is degree of financial leverage.
> EBIT is earnings before interest and taxes.
> I is interest.

5. $DCL = \dfrac{Q(P - VC)}{Q(P - VC) - FC - I}$ (5-7)

> DCL is degree of combined leverage.
> Q is quantity at which DCL is computed.
> P is price per unit.
> VC is variable cost per unit.
> FC is fixed costs.
> I is interest.

6. $DCL = \dfrac{S - TVC}{S - TVC - FC - I}$ (Footnote 3)

> DCL is degree of combined leverage.
> S is sales (QP) at which DCL is computed.
> TVC is total variable costs.
> FC is fixed costs.
> I is interest.

LIST OF TERMS

DISCUSSION QUESTIONS

1. Discuss the various uses for break-even analysis. *(LO5-2)*
2. What factors would cause a difference in the use of financial leverage for a utility company and an automobile company? *(LO5-1)*
3. Explain how the break-even point and operating leverage are affected by the choice of manufacturing facilities (labor intensive versus capital intensive). *(LO5-2)*
4. What role does depreciation play in break-even analysis based on accounting flows? based on cash flows? Which perspective is longer-term in nature? *(LO5-2)*
5. What does risk taking have to do with the use of operating and financial leverage? *(LO5-6)*
6. Discuss the limitations of financial leverage. *(LO5-4)*
7. How does the interest rate on new debt influence the use of financial leverage? *(LO5-4)*
8. Explain how combined leverage brings together operating income and earnings per share. *(LO5-5)*
9. Explain why operating leverage decreases as a company increases sales and shifts away from the break-even point. *(LO5-3)*
10. When you are considering two different financing plans, does being at the level where earnings per share are equal between the two plans always mean you are indifferent as to which plan is selected? *(LO5-4)*

PRACTICE PROBLEMS AND SOLUTIONS

1. Meyer Appliance Company makes cooling fans. The firm's income statement is as follows:

Degree of leverage
(LO5-2 & 5-5)

Sales (7,000 fans at $20)	$140,000
Less: Variable costs (7,000 fans at $8)	56,000
Fixed costs	44,000
Earnings before interest and taxes (EBIT)	$ 40,000
– Interest (*I*)	10,000
Earnings before taxes (EBT)	$ 30,000
– Taxes (*T*)	6,000
Earnings after taxes (EAT)	$ 24,000

Compute the following:

a. Degree of operating leverage.

b. Degree of financial leverage.

c. Degree of combined leverage.

d. The break-even point.

2. Hubball Resources has the following capital structure.

Debt @ 8%	$300,000
Common stock, $10 par (shares 50,000)	500,000
Total	$800,000

a. Compute earnings per share if earnings before interest and taxes are $64,000. (Assume a 20 percent tax rate.)

b. Assume debt goes up by $200,000, common stock goes down by $200,000, and the interest rate on the new debt is 10 percent. The tax rate remains at 20 percent. The par value on the common stock is still $10. Compute earnings per share if earnings before interest and taxes is $80,000.

Solutions

1. a. $$\text{DOL} = \frac{Q(P - \text{VC})}{Q(P - \text{VC}) - \text{FC}} = \frac{7,000(\$20 - \$8)}{7,000(\$20 - \$8) - \$44,000}$$

$$= \frac{7,000(\$12)}{7,000(\$12) - \$44,000} = \frac{84,000}{\$84,000 - \$44,000} = \frac{\$84,000}{\$40,000} = 2.10\text{x}$$

b. $$\text{DFL} = \frac{\text{EBIT}}{\text{EBIT} - I} = \frac{\$40,000}{\$40,000 - \$10,000} = \frac{\$40,000}{\$30,000} = 1.33\text{x}$$

c. $$\text{DCL} = \frac{Q(P - \text{VC})}{Q(P - \text{VC}) - \text{FC} - I} = \frac{7,000(\$20 - \$8)}{7,000(\$20 - \$8) - \$44,000 - \$10,000}$$

$$= \frac{7,000(\$12)}{7,000(\$12) - \$54,000} = \frac{\$84,000}{\$84,000 = \$54,000}$$

$$= \frac{\$84,000}{\$30,000} = 2.80\text{x}$$

d. $$\text{BE} = \frac{\text{FC}}{P - \text{VC}} = \frac{\$44,000}{\$20 - \$8} = \frac{\$44,000}{\$12} = 3,667 \text{ fans}$$

2. *a.*

Earnings before interest and taxes (EBIT)	$64,000
− Interest (*I*)	24,000*
Earnings before taxes (EBT)	$40,000
− Taxes (*T*) 20%	8,000
Earnings after taxes (EAT)	$32,000
Shares	50,000
Earnings per share (EPS)	$ 0.64

*8 percent interest × $300,000 debt = $24,000.

b.

Earnings before interest and taxes (EBIT)	$80,000
− Interest (*I*)	44,000*
Earnings before taxes (EBT)	$36,000
− Taxes (*T*) 20%	7,200
Earnings after taxes (EAT)	$28,800
Shares	30,000†
Earnings per share (EPS)	$ 0.96

*Interest on old debt ($24,000) + interest on new debt ($20,000). 10 percent × $200,000.
The total is $44,000.
†50,000 shares reduced by ($200,000/$10 par value) = 50,000 − 20,000 = 30,000.

PROBLEMS

≡ connect **Selected problems are available with Connect. Please see the preface for more information.**

Basic Problems

1. Shock Electronics sells portable heaters for $35 per unit, and the variable cost to produce them is $22. Mr. Amps estimates that the fixed costs are $97,500.

    Break-even analysis (LO5-2)

    a. Compute the break-even point in units.

    b. Fill in the table (in dollars) to illustrate the break-even point has been achieved.

Sales	_____
− Fixed costs	_____
− Total variable costs	_____
Net profit (loss)	_____

2. The Hartnett Corporation manufactures baseball bats with Pudge Rodriguez's autograph stamped on them. Each bat sells for $35 and has a variable cost of $22. There are $97,500 in fixed costs involved in the production process.

    Break-even analysis (LO5-2)

    a. Compute the break-even point in units.

    b. Find the sales (in units) needed to earn a profit of $262,500.

Break-even analysis
(LO5-2)

3. Therapeutic Systems sells its products for $13 per unit. It has the following costs:

Rent	$145,000
Factory labor	$4.00 per unit
Executives under contract	$186,500
Raw material	$1.20 per unit

Separate the expenses between fixed and variable costs per unit. Using this information and the sales price per unit of $13, compute the break-even point.

✖
Break-even
analysis
(LO5-2)

4. Draw two break-even graphs—one for a conservative firm using labor-intensive production and another for a capital-intensive firm. Assuming these companies compete within the same industry and have identical sales, explain the impact of changes in sales volume on both firms' profits.

Break-even
analysis
(LO5-2)

5. Eaton Tool Company has fixed costs of $255,000, sells its units for $66, and has variable costs of $36 per unit.

   a. Compute the break-even point.

   b. Ms. Eaton comes up with a new plan to cut fixed costs to $200,000. However, more labor will now be required, which will increase variable costs per unit to $39. The sales price will remain at $66. What is the new break-even point?

   c. Under the new plan, what is likely to happen to profitability at very high volume levels (compared to the old plan)?

Break-even
analysis
(LO5-2)

6. Shawn Pen & Pencil Sets Inc. has fixed costs of $80,000. Its product currently sells for $5 per unit and has variable costs of $2.50 per unit. Mr. Bic, the head of manufacturing, proposes to buy new equipment that will cost $400,000 and drive up fixed costs to $120,000. Although the price will remain at $5 per unit, the increased automation will reduce costs per unit to $2.

   As a result of Bic's suggestion, will the break-even point go up or down? Compute the necessary numbers.

Cash break-even
analysis
(LO5-2)

7. Calloway Cab Company determines its break-even strictly on the basis of cash expenditures related to fixed costs. Its total fixed costs are $450,000, but 5 percent of this value is represented by depreciation. Its contribution margin (price minus variable cost) for each unit is $4.10. How many units does the firm need to sell to reach the cash break-even point?

Cash break-even
analysis
(LO5-2)

8. Air Purifier Inc. computes its break-even point strictly on the basis of cash expenditures related to fixed costs. Its total fixed costs are $2,450,000, but 15 percent of this value is represented by depreciation. Its contribution margin (price minus variable cost) for each unit is $40. How many units does the firm need to sell to reach the cash break-even point?

Cash break-even
analysis
(LO5-2)

9. Boise Timber Co. computes its break-even point strictly on the basis of cash expenditures related to fixed costs. Its total fixed costs are $6,500,000, but 10 percent of this value is represented by depreciation. Its contribution margin (price minus variable cost) for each unit is $9. How many units does the firm need to sell to reach the cash break-even point?

Intermediate Problems

10. The Sterling Tire Company's income statement for 20X1 is as follows:

Degree of leverage
(LO5-2 & 5-5)

STERLING TIRE COMPANY	
Income Statement	
For the Year Ended December 31, 20X1	
Sales (20,000 tires at $60 each)	$1,200,000
Less: Variable costs (20,000 tires at $30)	600,000
Fixed costs	400,000
Earnings before interest and taxes (EBIT)	$ 200,000
Interest expense	50,000
Earnings before taxes (EBT)	$ 150,000
Income tax expense (30%)	45,000
Earnings after taxes (EAT)	$ 105,000

Given this income statement, compute the following:
- a. Degree of operating leverage.
- b. Degree of financial leverage.
- c. Degree of combined leverage.
- d. Break-even point in units.

11. The Harding Company manufactures skates. The company's income statement for 20X1 is as follows:

Degree of leverage
(LO5-2 & 5-5)

HARDING COMPANY	
Income Statement	
For the Year Ended December 31, 20X1	
Sales (10,500 skates @ $60 each)	$630,000
Less: Variable costs (10,500 skates at $25)	262,500
Fixed costs	200,000
Earnings before interest and taxes (EBIT)	$167,500
Interest expense	62,500
Earnings before taxes (EBT)	$105,000
Income tax expense (30%)	31,500
Earnings after taxes (EAT)	$ 73,500

Given this income statement, compute the following:
- a. Degree of operating leverage.
- b. Degree of financial leverage.
- c. Degree of combined leverage.
- d. Break-even point in units (number of skates).

12. Healthy Foods Inc. sells 50-pound bags of grapes to the military for $10 a bag. The fixed costs of this operation are $80,000, while the variable costs of grapes are $0.10 per pound.

Break-even point and
degree of leverage
(LO5-2 & 5-5)

- a. What is the break-even point in bags?
- b. Calculate the profit or loss on 12,000 bags and on 25,000 bags.

c. What is the degree of operating leverage at 20,000 bags and at 25,000 bags? Why does the degree of operating leverage change as the quantity sold increases?

d. If Healthy Foods has an annual interest expense of $10,000, calculate the degree of financial leverage at both 20,000 and 25,000 bags.

e. What is the degree of combined leverage at both sales levels?

Break-even point and degree of leverage (LO5-2 & 5-5)

13. United Snack Company sells 50-pound bags of peanuts to university dormitories for $20 a bag. The fixed costs of this operation are $176,250, while the variable costs of peanuts are $0.15 per pound.

a. What is the break-even point in bags?

b. Calculate the profit or loss on 7,000 bags and on 20,000 bags.

c. What is the degree of operating leverage at 19,000 bags and at 24,000 bags? Why does the degree of operating leverage change as the quantity sold increases?

d. If United Snack Company has an annual interest expense of $15,000, calculate the degree of financial leverage at both 19,000 and 24,000 bags.

e. What is the degree of combined leverage at both sales levels?

Nonlinear breakeven analysis (LO5-2)

14. International Data Systems' information on revenue and costs is relevant only up to a sales volume of 105,000 units. After 105,000 units, the market becomes saturated and the price per unit falls from $14.00 to $8.80. Also, there are cost overruns at a production volume of over 105,000 units, and variable cost per unit goes up from $7.00 to $8.00. Fixed costs remain the same at $55,000.

a. Compute operating income at 105,000 units.

b. Compute operating income at 205,000 units.

Use of different formulas for operating leverage (LO5-3)

15. U.S. Steal has the following income statement data:

Units Sold	Total Variable Costs	Fixed Costs	Total Costs	Total Revenue	Operating Income (Loss)
60,000	$120,000	$50,000	$170,000	$360,000	$190,000
80,000	160,000	50,000	210,000	480,000	270,000

a. Compute DOL based on the following formula (see page 131 for an example):

$$DOL = \frac{\text{Percent change in operating income}}{\text{Percent change in units sold}}$$

b. Confirm that your answer to part *a* is correct by recomputing DOL using Formula 5-3. There may be a slight difference due to rounding.

$$DOL = \frac{Q(P - VC)}{Q(P - VC) - FC}$$

Q represents beginning units sold (all calculations should be done at this level). *P* can be found by dividing total revenue by units sold. VC can be found by dividing total variable costs by units sold.

16. Lenow Drug Stores and Hall Pharmaceuticals are competitors in the discount drug chain store business. The separate capital structures for Lenow and Hall are presented here:

Lenow		Hall	
Debt @ 10%	$100,000	Debt @ 10%	$200,000
Common stock, $10 par	200,000	Common stock, $10 par	100,000
Total	$300,000	Total	$300,000
Shares	20,000	Common shares	10,000

  a. Compute earnings per share if earnings before interest and taxes are $20,000, $30,000, and $120,000 (assume a 30 percent tax rate).

  b. Explain the relationship between earnings per share and the level of EBIT.

  c. If the cost of debt went up to 12 percent and all other factors remained equal, what would be the break-even level for EBIT?

17. The capital structure for Cain Supplies is presented below. Compute the stock price for Cain if it sells at 19 times earnings per share and EBIT is $50,000. The tax rate is 20 percent.

Cain	
Debt @ 9%	$100,000
Common stock, $10 par	200,000
Total	$300,000
Common shares	20,000

Advanced Problems

18. Sterling Optical and Royal Optical both make glass frames and each is able to generate earnings before interest and taxes of $132,000. The separate capital structures for Sterling and Royal are shown here:

Sterling		Royal	
Debt @ 12%	$ 660,000	Debt @ 12%	$ 220,000
Common stock, $5 par	440,000	Common stock, $5 par	880,000
Total	$1,100,000	Total	$1,100,000
Common shares	88,000	Common shares	176,000

  a. Compute earnings per share for both firms. Assume a 25 percent tax rate.

  b. In part *a,* you should have gotten the same answer for both companies' earnings per share. Assuming a P/E ratio of 22 for each company, what would its stock price be?

c. Now as part of your analysis, assume the P/E ratio would be 16 for the riskier company in terms of heavy debt utilization in the capital structure and 24 for the less risky company. What would the stock prices for the two firms be under these assumptions? (Note: Although interest rates also would likely be different based on risk, we will hold them constant for ease of analysis.)

d. Based on the evidence in part *c,* should management be concerned only about the impact of financing plans on earnings per share, or should stockholders' wealth maximization (stock price) be considered as well?

Japanese firm and combined leverage
(LO5-5)

19. Firms in Japan often employ both high operating and financial leverage because of the use of modern technology and close borrower–lender relationships. Assume the Mitaka Company has a sales volume of 130,000 units at a price of $30 per unit; variable costs are $10 per unit, and fixed costs are $1,850,000. Interest expense is $405,000. What is the degree of combined leverage for this Japanese firm?

Combining operating and financial leverage
(LO5-5)

20. Sinclair Manufacturing and Boswell Brothers Inc. are both involved in the production of brick for the homebuilding industry. Their financial information is as follows:

Capital Structure		
	Sinclair	**Boswell**
Debt @ 11%	$ 900,000	0
Common stock, $10 per share	600,000	$ 1,500,000
Total	$ 1,500,000	$ 1,500,000
Common shares	60,000	150,000
Operating Plan		
Sales (55,000 units at $20 each)..	$ 1,100,000	$ 1,100,000
Less: Variable costs	880,000	550,000
	($16 per unit)	($10 per unit)
Fixed costs	0	305,000
Earnings before interest and taxes (EBIT)	$ 220,000	$ 245,000

a. If you combine Sinclair's capital structure with Boswell's operating plan, what is the degree of combined leverage? (Round to two places to the right of the decimal point.)

b. If you combine Boswell's capital structure with Sinclair's operating plan, what is the degree of combined leverage?

c. Explain why you got the results you did in part *b.*

d. In part *b,* if sales double, by what percentage will EPS increase?

Expansion and leverage
(LO5-5)

21. DeSoto Tools Inc. is planning to expand production. The expansion will cost $300,000, which can be financed either by bonds at an interest rate of 14 percent or by selling 10,000 shares of common stock at $30 per share. The current income statement before expansion is as follows:

DeSOTO TOOLS, INC. Income Statement 20X1		
Sales		$1,500,000
Less: Variable costs	$450,000	
Fixed costs	550,000	1,000,000
Earnings before interest and taxes		$ 500,000
Less: Interest expense		100,000
Earnings before taxes		$ 400,000
Less: Taxes @ 34%		136,000
Earnings after taxes		$ 264,000
Shares		100,000
Earnings per share		$ 2.64

After the expansion, sales are expected to increase by $1,000,000. Variable costs will remain at 30 percent of sales, and fixed costs will increase to $800,000. The tax rate is 34 percent.

a. Calculate the degree of operating leverage, the degree of financial leverage, and the degree of combined leverage before expansion. (For the degree of operating leverage, use the formula developed in footnote 2; for the degree of combined leverage, use the formula developed in footnote 3. These instructions apply throughout this problem.)

b. Construct the income statement for the two alternative financing plans.

c. Calculate the degree of operating leverage, the degree of financial leverage, and the degree of combined leverage, after expansion.

d. Explain which financing plan you favor and the risks involved with each plan.

22. Using Standard & Poor's data or annual reports, compare the financial and operating leverage of Chevron, Eastman Kodak, and Delta Air Lines for the most current year. Explain the relationship between operating and financial leverage for each company and the resultant combined leverage. What accounts for the differences in leverage of these companies?

Leverage analysis with actual companies (LO5-6)

23. Dickinson Company has $12 million in assets. Currently half of these assets are financed with long-term debt at 10 percent and half with common stock having a par value of $8. Ms. Smith, vice president of finance, wishes to analyze two refinancing plans, one with more debt (D) and one with more equity (E). The company earns a return on assets before interest and taxes of 10 percent. The tax rate is 45 percent.

Leverage and sensitivity analysis (LO5-6)

Under Plan D, a $3 million long-term bond would be sold at an interest rate of 12 percent and 375,000 shares of stock would be purchased in the market at $8 per share and retired.

Under Plan E, 375,000 shares of stock would be sold at $8 per share and the $3,000,000 in proceeds would be used to reduce long-term debt.

a. How would each of these plans affect earnings per share? Consider the current plan and the two new plans.

b. Which plan would be most favorable if return on assets fell to 5 percent? increased to 15 percent? Consider the current plan and the two new plans.

c. If the market price for common stock rose to $12 before the restructuring, which plan would then be most attractive? Continue to assume that $3 million in debt will be used to retire stock in Plan D and $3 million of new equity will be sold to retire debt in Plan E. Also assume for calculations in part *c* that return on assets is 10 percent.

Leverage and sensitivity analysis (LO5-6)

24. Edsel Research Labs has $27 million in assets. Currently half of these assets are financed with long-term debt at 5 percent and half with common stock having a par value of $10. Ms. Edsel, the vice president of finance, wishes to analyze two refinancing plans, one with more debt (D) and one with more equity (E). The company earns a return on assets before interest and taxes of 5 percent. The tax rate is 30 percent.

Under Plan D, a $6.75 million long-term bond would be sold at an interest rate of 11 percent and 675,000 shares of stock would be purchased in the market at $10 per share and retired. Under Plan E, 675,000 shares of stock would be sold at $10 per share and the $6,750,000 in proceeds would be used to reduce long-term debt.

a. How would each of these plans affect earnings per share? Consider the current plan and the two new plans. Which plan(s) would produce the highest EPS?

b. Which plan would be most favorable if return on assets increased to 8 percent? Compare the current plan and the two new plans. What has caused the plans to give different EPS numbers?

c. Assuming return on assets is back to the original 5 percent, but the interest rate on new debt in Plan D is 7 percent, which of the three plans will produce the highest EPS? Why?

Leverage and sensitivity analysis (LO5-6)

25. The Lopez-Portillo Company has $10.6 million in assets, 80 percent financed by debt and 20 percent financed by common stock. The interest rate on the debt is 9 percent and the par value of the stock is $10 per share. President Lopez-Portillo is considering two financing plans for an expansion to $18 million in assets.

Under Plan A, the debt-to-total-assets ratio will be maintained, but new debt will cost a whopping 12 percent! Under Plan B, only new common stock at $10 per share will be issued. The tax rate is 40 percent.

a. If EBIT is 9 percent on total assets, compute earnings per share (EPS) before the expansion and under the two alternatives.

b. What is the degree of financial leverage under each of the three plans?

c. If stock could be sold at $20 per share due to increased expectations for the firm's sales and earnings, what impact would this have on earnings per share for the two expansion alternatives? Compute earnings per share for each.

> *d.* Explain why corporate financial officers are concerned about their stock values.

26. Mr. Gold is in the widget business. He currently sells 1.5 million widgets a year at $6 each. His variable cost to produce the widgets is $4 per unit, and he has $1,550,000 in fixed costs. His sales-to-assets ratio is six times, and 30 percent of his assets are financed with 10 percent debt, with the balance financed by common stock at $10 par value per share. The tax rate is 35 percent.

Operating leverage
and ratios
(LO5-6)

His brother-in-law, Mr. Silverman, says Mr. Gold is doing it all wrong. By reducing his price to $5 a widget, he could increase his volume of units sold by 60 percent. Fixed costs would remain constant, and variable costs would remain $4 per unit. His sales-to-assets ratio would be 7.5 times. Furthermore, he could increase his debt-to-assets ratio to 50 percent, with the balance in common stock. It is assumed that the interest rate would go up by 1 percent and the price of stock would remain constant.

a. Compute earnings per share under the Gold plan.

b. Compute earnings per share under the Silverman plan.

c. Mr. Gold's wife, the chief financial officer, does not think that fixed costs would remain constant under the Silverman plan but that they would go up by 15 percent. If this is the case, should Mr. Gold shift to the Silverman plan, based on earnings per share?

27. Delsing Canning Company is considering an expansion of its facilities. Its current income statement is as follows:

Expansion, break-
even analysis, and
leverage
(LO5-2, 5-3, & 5-4)

Sales	$5,500,000
Less: Variable expense (50% of sales)	2,750,000
Fixed expense	1,850,000
Earnings before interest and taxes (EBIT)	$ 900,000
Interest (10% cost)	300,000
Earnings before taxes (EBT)	$ 600,000
Tax (40%)	240,000
Earnings after taxes (EAT)	$ 360,000
Shares of common stock—250,000	
Earnings per share	$ 1.44

The company is currently financed with 50 percent debt and 50 percent equity (common stock, par value of $10). In order to expand the facilities, Mr. Delsing estimates a need for $2.5 million in additional financing. His investment banker has laid out three plans for him to consider:

1. Sell $2.5 million of debt at 13 percent.

2. Sell $2.5 million of common stock at $20 per share.

3. Sell $1.25 million of debt at 12 percent and $1.25 million of common stock at $25 per share.

Variable costs are expected to stay at 50 percent of sales, while fixed expenses will increase to $2,350,000 per year. Delsing is not sure how much this expansion will add to sales, but he estimates that sales will rise by $1.25 million per year for the next five years.

Delsing is interested in a thorough analysis of his expansion plans and methods of financing. He would like you to analyze the following:

a. The break-even point for operating expenses before and after expansion (in sales dollars).

b. The degree of operating leverage before and after expansion. Assume sales of $5.5 million before expansion and $6.5 million after expansion. Use the formula in footnote 2 of the chapter.

c. The degree of financial leverage before expansion and for all three methods of financing after expansion. Assume sales of $6.5 million for this question.

d. Compute EPS under all three methods of financing the expansion at $6.5 million in sales (first year) and $10.5 million in sales (last year).

e. What can we learn from the answer to part *d* about the advisability of the three methods of financing the expansion?

COMPREHENSIVE PROBLEM

Ryan Boot Company
(Review of Chapters 2 through 5)
(*Multiple LOs from Chapters 2–5*)

a. Analyze Ryan Boot Company, using ratio analysis. Compute the Ryan ratios and compare them to the industry data that are given. Discuss the weak points, strong points, and what you think should be done to improve the company's performance.

b. In your analysis, calculate the overall break-even point in sales dollars and the cash break-even point. Also compute the degree of operating leverage, degree of financial leverage, and degree of combined leverage. (Use footnote 2 for DOL and footnote 3 for DCL.)

c. Use the information in parts *a* and *b* to discuss the risk associated with this company. Given the risk, decide whether a bank should lend funds to Ryan Boot.

Ryan Boot Company is trying to plan the funds needed for 20X2. The management anticipates an increase in sales of 20 percent, which can be absorbed *without increasing fixed assets.*

d. What would be Ryan's needs for external funds based on the current balance sheet? Compute RNF (required new funds). Notes payable (current) and bonds are not part of the liability calculation.

e. What would be the required new funds if the company brings its ratios into line with the industry average during 20X2? Specifically examine receivables turnover, inventory turnover, and the profit margin. Use the new values to recompute the factors in RNF (assume liabilities stay the same).

RYAN BOOT COMPANY
Balance Sheet
December 31, 20X1

Assets		Liabilities and Stockholders' Equity	
Cash	$ 50,000	Accounts payable	$2,200,000
Marketable securities	80,000	Accrued expenses	150,000
Accounts receivable	3,000,000	Notes payable (current)	400,000
Inventory	1,000,000	Bonds (10%)	2,500,000
Gross plant and equipment	6,000,000	Common stock (1.7 million shares, par value $1)	1,700,000
Less: Accumulated depreciation	2,000,000	Retained earnings	1,180,000
Total assets	$8,130,000	Total liabilities and stockholders' equity	$8,130,000

Income Statement—20X1

Sales (credit)	$7,000,000
Fixed costs*	2,100,000
Variable costs (0.60)	4,200,000
Earnings before interest and taxes	$ 700,000
Less: Interest	250,000
Earnings before taxes	$ 450,000
Less: Taxes @ 35%	157,500
Earnings after taxes	$ 292,500
Dividends (40% payout)	117,000
Increased retained earnings	$ 175,500

*Fixed costs include (a) lease expense of $200,000 and (b) depreciation of $500,000.

Note: Ryan Boot also has $65,000 per year in sinking fund obligations associated with its bond issue. The sinking fund represents an annual repayment of the principal amount of the bond. It is not tax-deductible.

Ratios

	Ryan Boot (to be filled in)	Industry
Profit margin	_____	5.75%
Return on assets	_____	6.90%
Return on equity	_____	9.20%
Receivables turnover	_____	4.35 ×
Inventory turnover	_____	6.50 ×
Fixed asset turnover	_____	1.85 ×
Total asset turnover	_____	1.20 ×
Current ratio	_____	1.45 ×
Quick ratio	_____	1.10 ×
Debt to total assets	_____	25.05%
Interest coverage (times interest earned)	_____	5.35 ×
Fixed charge coverage	_____	4.62 ×

f.   Do not calculate—only comment on these questions. How would required new funds change if the company

(1) Were at full capacity?

(2) Raised the dividend payout ratio?

(3) Suffered a decreased growth in sales?

(4) Faced an accelerated inflation rate?

WEB EXERCISE

1.   At the start of the chapter, we talked about how risky and volatile airlines' operations are. Let us examine this further. Go to finance.yahoo.com. Enter "UAL" for United Continental Holdings in the "Quote Lookup" box. Scroll down to "United Continental Holdings" and click.

2.   Click on "Profile" under the stock price and to the right of "Summary." Write a one-paragraph description of the company.

3.   Now click on "Financials." Look at the Income Statement and describe the pattern of change for "Total Revenue" and "Operating Income or Loss" in one paragraph.

4.   Go to "Balance Sheet." In one sentence, describe the pattern of change in stockholders' equity and indicate whether this does or does not appear to be a matter of concern.

5.   Click on "Analysts." Do UAL's earnings estimates appear to be more or less promising for the future?

Note: Occasionally a topic we have listed may have been deleted, updated, or moved into a different location on a website. If you click on the site map or site index, you will be introduced to a table of contents that should aid you in finding the topic you are looking for.

Working Capital Management

6

Working Capital and the Financing Decision

LEARNING OBJECTIVES

LO 6-1 Working capital management involves financing and controlling the current assets of the firm.

LO 6-2 Management must distinguish between current assets that are easily converted to cash and those that are more permanent.

LO 6-3 The financing of an asset should be tied to how long the asset is likely to be on the balance sheet.

LO 6-4 Long-term financing is usually more expensive than short-term financing based on the theory of the term structure of interest rates.

LO 6-5 Risk, as well as profitability, determines the financing plan for current assets.

LO 6-6 Expected value analysis may sometimes be employed in working capital management.

The rapid growth of business firms in the last two decades has challenged the ingenuity of financial managers to provide adequate financing. Rapidly expanding sales may cause intense pressure for inventory and receivables buildup—draining the cash resources of the firm. As indicated in Chapter 4, "Financial Forecasting," a large sales increase creates an expansion of current assets, especially accounts receivable and inventory. Some of the increased current assets can be financed through the firm's retained earnings, but in most cases internal funds will not provide enough financing and some external sources of funds must be found. In fact, the faster the growth in sales, the more likely it is that an increasing percentage of financing will be external to the firm. These funds could come from the sale of common stock, preferred stock, long-term bonds, short-term securities, and bank loans or from a combination of short- and long-term sources of funds.

There is also the problem of seasonal sales that affects many industries such as soft drinks, toys, retail sales, and textbook publishing. Seasonal demand for products makes forecasting cash flows and receivables and inventory management difficult. The Internet and cloud computing are beginning to alleviate some of these problems and help management make better plans.

If you have had a marketing course, you have heard about supply chain management. Well, financial executives are also interested in the supply chain as an area where the Internet can help control working capital through online software. McDonald's Corporation of Big Mac fame formed eMac Digital to explore opportunities in business-to-business (B2B) online ventures. One of the first things on the agenda was to have eMac Digital help McDonald's reduce costs. McDonald's wanted to create an online marketplace where restaurants can buy supplies online from food companies. McDonald's, like Walmart, Harley-Davidson, and Ericsson, has embraced supply chain management using web-based procedures. The goal is to squeeze out inefficiencies in the supply chain and thereby lower costs. One of the big benefits is a reduction in inventory through online communications between the buyer and supplier, which speeds up the ordering and delivery process and reduces the amount of inventory needed on hand. These systems may also be able to attract a large number of suppliers to bid on the company's business at more competitive prices.

Retailers like Walmart require suppliers to ship their goods with radio frequency identification (RFID) chips embedded in their shipments. These chips eliminate processing delays, reduce theft, and result in better inventory management. From the financial manager's viewpoint, anything that can reduce inventory levels without creating out-of-stock situations will reduce the amount of money needed to finance inventory. You can read more about Walmart and RFID chips in the nearby Finance in Action box.

Working capital management involves the financing and management of the current assets of the firm. The financial executive probably devotes more time to working capital management than to any other activity. Current assets, by their very nature, are changing daily, if not hourly, and managerial decisions must be made. "How much inventory is to be carried, and how do we get the funds to pay for it?" Unlike long-term decisions, there can be no deferral of action. While long-term decisions involving plant and equipment or market strategy may well determine the eventual success of the firm, short-term decisions on working capital determine whether the firm gets to the long term.

In this chapter, we examine the nature of asset growth, the process of matching sales and production, the financial aspects of working capital management, and the factors that go into development of an optimum policy.

The Nature of Asset Growth

Any company that produces and sells a product, whether the product is consumer or manufacturer oriented, will have current assets and fixed assets. If a firm grows, those assets are likely to increase over time. The key to current asset planning is the ability of management to forecast sales accurately and then to match the production schedules with the sales forecast. Whenever actual sales are different from forecast sales, unexpected buildups or reductions in inventory will occur that will eventually affect receivables and cash flow.

In the simplest case, all of the firm's current assets will be **self-liquidating assets** (sold at the end of a specified time period). Assume that at the start of the summer you buy 100 tires to be disposed of by September. It is your intention that all tires will be sold, receivables collected, and bills paid over this time period. In this case, your working capital (current asset) needs are truly short term.

Now let us begin to expand the business. In stage two, you add radios, seat covers, and batteries to your operation. Some of your inventory will again be completely liquidated, while other items will form the basic stock for your operation. To stay in business, you must maintain floor displays and multiple items for selection. Furthermore, not all items will sell. As you eventually grow to more than one store, this "permanent" aggregate stock of current assets will continue to increase. Problems of inadequate financing arrangements are often the result of the business-person's failure to realize the firm is carrying not only self-liquidating inventory but also the anomaly of **"permanent" current assets**.

A Great Inventory Tracking System May Be Helping You

RFID (radio frequency identification) technology, a system that has been around since World War II and was used by the military to keep track of airplanes, continues to gain traction in inventory/supply chain management. RFID chips have been used in trains, ships, and trucks to track shipment containers. They are also used in automatic toll systems that allow drivers to pass through tolling areas without stopping. The state of Michigan has used these chips to track livestock; marathon officials have used them to track a runner's time; and the Defense Department has used them to track the shelf life of food rations. Additionally, they are now being used to make sure that shipping containers entering U.S. ports have not been tampered with after inspection.

Hewlett-Packard, in a business briefing paper, indicates that there may be as much as $45 billion of excess inventory in the retail supply chain that is unaccounted for at any given time. In short, RFID chips can help a company track goods and make sure that the right goods get to the right places on time. More sophisticated chips can be reused and can even record a sale. For example, if an expensive piece of jewelry is sold with a chip attached, when the chip is decommissioned, the sale automatically shows up in the store's computer system.

In 2005, Walmart mandated that by the end of 2007, its 300 largest suppliers must have RFID chips in each pallet of goods shipped to its distribution centers. Procter & Gamble (P&G) was one of the first companies to comply and found the system beneficial in managing its own inventory, reducing out-of-stock inventory levels, and preventing inventory theft or theft of goods in transit. For manufacturers of expensive products such as pharmaceuticals, theft reduction can be a significant cost saving. P&G noted that when comparing bar codes to RFID chips, it took 20 seconds to manually tally bar-code data on a pallet versus five seconds to read RFID technology. P&G states that it earned a return on its RFID investment in the millions of dollars.

The largest U.S. retailers now use RFID chips for many of their products, but a rather unique use of these chips is for high-value poker chips at casinos. In 2010, a robber entered the Bellagio in Las Vegas and left with $1.5 million in poker chips. Little did he know that the chips had embedded RFID chips, and as soon as he walked out of the casino, the chips became worthless and unable to be used anywhere.

The movement from stage one to stage two of growth for a typical business is depicted in Figure 6-1. In panel A, the buildup in current assets is **temporary**—while in panel B, part of the growth in current assets is temporary and part is permanent. (Fixed assets are included in the illustrations, but they are not directly related to the present discussion.)

Controlling Assets—Matching Sales and Production

In most firms, fixed assets grow slowly as productive capacity is increased and old equipment is replaced, but current assets fluctuate in the short run, depending on the level of production versus the level of sales. When the firm produces more than it sells, inventory rises. When sales rise faster than production, inventory declines and receivables rise.

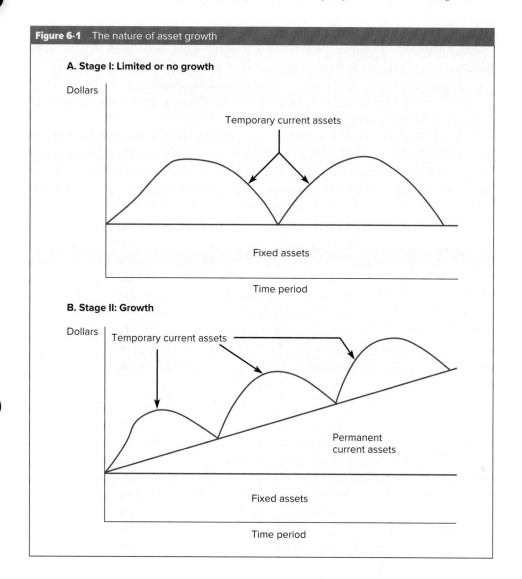

Figure 6-1 The nature of asset growth

A. Stage I: Limited or no growth

Dollars

Temporary current assets

Fixed assets

Time period

B. Stage II: Growth

Dollars

Temporary current assets

Permanent current assets

Fixed assets

Time period

As discussed in the treatment of the cash budgeting process in Chapter 4, some firms employ **level production** methods to smooth production schedules and use manpower and equipment efficiently at a lower cost. One consequence of level production is that current assets go up and down when sales and production are not equal. Other firms may try to match sales and production as closely as possible in the short run. This allows current assets to increase or decrease with the level of sales and eliminates the large seasonal bulges or sharp reductions in current assets that occur under level production.

Seasonal industries can be found in manufacturing, retailing, electricity, and natural gas. Demand is uneven in these industries, and many exhibit a seasonal demand. For example, electricity producers have more demand in the summer for air conditioning, while natural gas companies have more demand in the winter for heating. One small manufacturing company that exhibits this type of seasonal demand is Briggs & Stratton Corporation from Wauwatosa, Wisconsin.

Briggs & Stratton is the largest maker of 3.5- to 25-horsepower air-cooled gasoline engines. If you've ever mowed a lawn, there is a good chance your lawnmower had a Briggs & Stratton engine. Its motors can be found in pressure washers, compressors and pumps, garden tillers, generators, small tractors, lawnmowers, and outboard marine engines, and about 30 percent of the company's overall sales are in the international market.

Briggs & Stratton's fiscal year ends in June, and Figure 6 2 demonstrates both the seasonality of sales and the leverage impact on earnings per share that we discussed in Chapter 5. Because Briggs sells most of its products to other manufacturers, who use the engines as part of their finished products, a large percentage of sales must occur

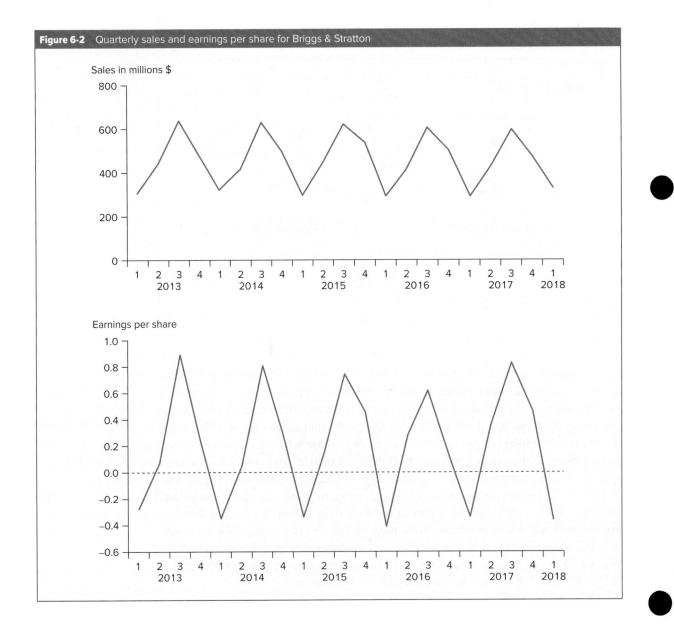

Figure 6-2   Quarterly sales and earnings per share for Briggs & Stratton

early in the year in order to produce the garden equipment that would be in demand in spring and summer. We can see from Figure 6-2 that sales are lowest in the July to September quarter, followed by the September to December quarter. Peak sales are in the third quarter, beginning in January and ending in March. There are carryover sales in the April to June quarter, which is the second-best period for Briggs & Stratton.

Notice that the first quarter of the year always generates negative earnings per share as the costs of production outweigh the revenue produced. This is most likely caused by the costs of building inventory. Earnings in the second and fourth quarters are small, with most of the earnings coming in the peak sales period of the third quarter. For example, in 2016, Briggs & Stratton earned $57 million for the year with $36 million coming in the third quarter; in 2017 the firm earned $27 million with all of it coming in the third quarter. The seasonal nature of the company's sales can be exacerbated by inventory buildup at the end user and a fall in orders for the next season.

Retail firms such as Target and Macy's also have seasonal sales patterns. Figure 6-3 on the next page shows the quarterly sales and earnings per share of these two companies, with the quarters ending in April, July, October, and January. These retail companies do not stock a year or more of inventory at one time. They are selling products that are either manufactured for them by others or manufactured by their subsidiaries. Most retail stores are not involved in deciding on level versus seasonal production but rather in matching sales and inventory. Their suppliers must make the decision to produce on either a level or a seasonal basis. Since the selling seasons are very much affected by the weather and holiday periods, the suppliers and retailers cannot avoid inventory risk. The fourth quarter for retailers, which begins in November and ends in January, is their biggest quarter and accounts for more than half of their earnings. You can be sure that inventory not sold during the Christmas season will be put on sale during January.

Both Target and Macy's show seasonal peaks and troughs in sales that will also be reflected in their cash balances, accounts receivable, and inventory. Notice that Target has higher sales than Macy's. Even so, Macy's peak earnings per share are often higher than Target's earnings per share when the fourth quarter sales peak out. Both companies illustrate the impact of leverage on earnings as discussed in Chapter 5, but we can tell that Macy's has higher leverage because its EPS rises and falls with sales more than Target's EPS (bottom of Figure 6-3). We shall see as we go through the chapter that seasonal sales can cause asset management problems. A financial manager must be aware of these problems to avoid getting caught short of cash or unprepared to borrow when necessary.

Many retail-oriented firms have been more successful in matching sales and orders in recent years because of computerized inventory control systems linked to online point-of-sales terminals. These **point-of-sales terminals** allow either digital input or use of optical scanners to record the inventory code numbers and the amount of each item sold. Managers can continuously examine sales and inventory levels item by item and, if need be, adjust orders or production schedules. The predictability of the market will influence the speed with which the manager reacts to this information, while the length and complexity of the production process will dictate how fast production levels can be changed.

Figure 6-3   Quarterly sales and earnings per share, Target and Macy's

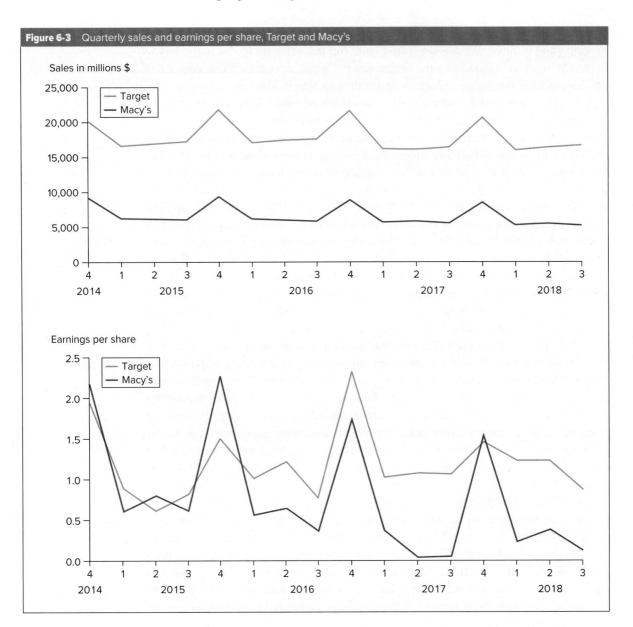

Temporary Assets under Level Production—an Example

To get a better understanding of how current assets fluctuate, let us use the example of the Yawakuzi Motorcycle Company, which manufactures and sells in the snowy U.S. Midwest. Not too many people will be buying motorcycles during October through March, but sales will pick up in early spring and summer and will again trail off during the fall. Because of the fixed assets and the skilled labor involved in the production process, Yawakuzi decides that level production is the least expensive and the most efficient production method. The marketing department provides a 12-month sales forecast for October through September (Table 6-1).

Table 6-1 Yawakuzi sales forecast (in units)			
1st Quarter	**2nd Quarter**	**3rd Quarter**	**4th Quarter**
October 300	January 0	April 1,000	July 2,000
November 150	February 0	May 2,000	August 1,000
December 50	March 600	June 2,000	September 500

Total sales of 9,600 units at $3,000 each = $28,800,000 in sales.

After reviewing the sales forecast, Yawakuzi decides to produce 800 motorcycles per month, or one year's production of 9,600 divided by 12. A look at Table 6-2 shows how level production and seasonal sales combine to create fluctuating inventory. Assume that October's beginning inventory is one month's production of 800 units. The ending inventory level is computed for each month and then multiplied by the production cost per unit of $2,000.

Table 6-2 Yawakuzi's production schedule and inventory					
	Beginning Inventory	**+ Production (level production)**	**– Sales**	**= Ending Inventory**	**Inventory (at cost of $2,000 per unit)**
October	800	 800	 300	 1,300	.... $2,600,000
November	1,300	 800	 150	 1,950	 3,900,000
December	1,950	 800	 50	 2,700	 5,400,000
January	2,700	 800	 0	 3,500	 7,000,000
February	3,500	 800	 0	 4,300	 8,600,000
March	4,300	 800	 600	 4,500	 9,000,000
April	4,500	 800	 1,000	 4,300	 8,600,000
May	4,300	 800	 2,000	 3,100	 6,200,000
June	3,100	 800	 2,000	 1,900	 3,800,000
July	1,900	 800	 2,000	 700	 1,400,000
August	700	 800	 1,000	 500	 1,000,000
September	500	 800	 500	 800	 1,600,000

The inventory level at cost fluctuates from a high of $9 million in March, the last consecutive month in which production is greater than sales, to a low of $1 million in August, the last month in which sales are greater than production. Table 6-3 combines a sales forecast, a cash receipts schedule, a cash payments schedule, and a brief cash budget to examine the buildup in accounts receivable and cash.

In Table 6-3, the *sales forecast* is based on assumptions in Table 6-1. The unit volume of sales is multiplied by a sales price of $3,000 to get sales dollars in millions. Next, *cash receipts* represent 50 percent collected in cash during the month of sale and 50 percent from the prior month's sales. For example, in October this would represent $0.45 million from the current month plus $0.75 million from the prior month's sales.

Table 6-3 Sales forecast, cash receipts and payments, and cash budget

	Oct.	Nov.	Dec.	Jan.	Feb.	March	April	May	June	July	Aug.	Sept.
Sales Forecast ($ millions)												
Sales (units)........	300	150	50	0	0	600	1,000	2,000	2,000	2,000	1,000	500
Sales (unit price, $3,000)...........	$0.9	$0.45	$0.15	$ 0	$ 0	$1.8	$3.0	$6.0	$6.0	$6.0	$3.0	$1.5
Cash Receipts Schedule ($ millions)												
50% cash	$0.45	$0.225	$0.075	$ 0	$ 0	$0.9	$1.5	$3.0	$3.0	$3.0	$1.5	$0.75
50% from prior month's sales	0.75*	0.450	0.225	0.075	0	0	0.9	1.5	3.0	3.0	3.0	1.50
Total cash receipts	$1.20	$0.675	$0.300	$0.075	0	$0.9	$2.4	$4.5	$6.0	$6.0	$4.5	$2.25

*Assumes September sales of $1.5 million.

	Oct.	Nov.	Dec.	Jan.	Feb.	March	April	May	June	July	Aug.	Sept.
Cash Payments Schedule ($ millions)												
Constant production of 800 units/ month (cost, $2,000 per unit).................	$1.6	$1.6	$1.6	$1.6	$1.6	$1.6	$1.6	$1.6	$1.6	$1.6	$1.6	$1.6
Overhead...........	0.4	0.4	0.4	0.4	0.4	0.4	0.4	0.4	0.4	0.4	0.4	0.4
Dividends and interest	—	—	—	—	—	—	—	—	—	—	1.0	—
Taxes...................	0.3	—	—	0.3	—	—	0.3	—	—	0.3	—	—
Total cash payments	$2.3	$2.0	$2.0	$2.3	$2.0	$2.0	$2.3	$2.0	$2.0	$2.3	$3.0	$2.0

Cash Budget ($ millions; required minimum balance is $0.25 million)												
Cash flow...........	$(1.1)	$(1.325)	$(1.7)	$(2.225)	$(2.0)	$(1.1)	$0.1	$2.5	$4.0	$3.7	$1.5	$0.25
Beginning cash	0.25*	0.25	0.25	0.250	0.25	0.25	0.25	0.25	0.25	0.25	1.1	2.60
Cumulative cash balance...........	$(0.85)	$(1.075)	$(1.45)	$(1.975)	$(1.75)	$(0.85)	$0.35	$2.75	$4.25	$3.95	$2.6	$2.85
Monthly loan or (repayment)...	1.1	1.325	1.7	2.225	2.0	1.1	(0.1)	(2.5)	(4.0)	(2.85)	0	0
Cumulative loan	1.1	2.425	4.125	6.350	8.35	9.45	9.35	6.85	2.85	0	0	0
Ending cash balance...........	0.25	0.25	0.25	0.25	0.25	0.25	0.25	0.25	0.25	1.1	2.6	2.85

*Assumes a cash balance of $0.25 million at the beginning of October and that this is the desired minimum cash balance.

Cash payments in Table 6-3 are based on an assumption of level production of 800 units per month at a cost of $2,000 per unit, or $1.6 million, plus payments for overhead, dividends, interest, and taxes.

Finally, the *cash budget* in Table 6-3 represents a comparison of the cash receipts and cash payments schedules to determine cash flow. We further assume the firm desires a minimum cash balance of $0.25 million. Thus in October, a negative cash flow of $1.1 million brings the cumulative cash balance to a negative $0.85 million and $1.1 million must be borrowed to provide an ending cash balance of $0.25 million. Similar negative cash flows in subsequent months necessitate expanding the bank loan. For example, in November there is a negative cash flow of $1.325 million. This brings the cumulative cash balance to −$1.075 million, requiring additional borrowings of $1.325 million to ensure a minimum cash balance of $0.25 million. The cumulative loan through November (October and November borrowings) now adds up to $2.425 million. Our cumulative bank loan is highest in the month of March.

We now wish to ascertain our total current asset buildup as a result of level production and fluctuating sales for October through September. The analysis is presented in Table 6-4. The cash figures come directly from the last line of Table 6-3. The accounts receivable balance is based on the assumption that accounts receivable represent 50 percent of sales in a given month, as the other 50 percent is paid for in cash. Thus the accounts receivable figure in Table 6-4 represents 50 percent of the sales figure from the second numerical line in Table 6-3. Finally, the inventory figure in Table 6-4 is taken directly from the last column of Table 6-2, which presented the production schedule and inventory data.

Table 6-4 Total current assets, first year ($ millions)			
	Cash	**Accounts Receivable**	**Inventory**	**Total Current Assets**
October	$0.25	$0.450	$2.6	$ 3.30
November	0.25	0.225	3.9	4.375
December	0.25	0.075	5.4	5.725
January	0.25	0.00	7.0	7.25
February	0.25	0.00	8.6	8.85
March	0.25	0.90	9.0	10.15
April	0.25	1.50	8.6	10.35
May	0.25	3.00	6.2	9.45
June	0.25	3.00	3.8	7.05
July	1.10	3.00	1.4	5.50
August	2.60	1.50	1.0	5.10
September	2.85	0.75	1.6	5.20

Total current assets (last column in Table 6-4) start at $3.3 million in October and rise to $10.35 million in the peak month of April. From April through August, sales are larger than production, and inventory falls to its low of $1 million in August, but accounts receivable peak at $3 million in the highest sales months of May, June, and July. The cash budget in Table 6-3 explains the cash flows and external funds borrowed to finance asset accumulation. From October to March, Yawakuzi borrows more and more money to finance the inventory buildup, but from April forward it eliminates all borrowing as inventory is liquidated and cash balances rise to complete the cycle. In October, the cycle starts over again; but now the firm has accumulated cash it can use to finance next year's asset accumulation, pay a larger dividend, replace old

Table 6-5   Cash budget and assets for second year with no growth in sales ($ millions)

| | End of First Year | Second Year | | | | | | | | | | | |
	Sept.	Oct.	Nov.	Dec.	Jan.	Feb.	March	April	May	June	July	Aug.	Sept.
Cash flow	$0.25	$(1.1)	$(1.325)	$(1.7)	$(2.225)	$(2.0)	$ (1.1)	$ 0.1	$2.5	$4.0	$ 3.7	$1.5	$0.25
Beginning cash	2.60	2.85	1.750	0.425	0.25	0.25	0.25	0.25	0.25	0.25	0.25	3.7	5.2
Cumulative cash balance		1.75	0.425	(1.275)	(1.975)	(1.75)	(0.85)	0.35	2.75	4.25	3.95	5.2	5.45
Monthly loan (or repayment)		—	—	1.525	2.225	2.0	1.1	(0.1)	(2.5)	(4.0)	(0.25)	—	—
Cumulative loan		—	—	1.525	3.750	5.75	6.85	6.75	4.25	0.25	0	—	—
Ending cash balance	$2.85	$ 1.75	$0.425	$ 0.25	$ 0.25	$ 0.25	$ 0.25	$ 0.25	$0.25	$0.25	$ 3.70	$5.2	$5.45
Total Current Assets													
Ending cash balance	$2.85	$ 1.75	$0.425	$ 0.25	$ 0.25	$ 0.25	$ 0.25	$ 0.25	$0.25	$0.25	$ 3.70	$5.2	$5.45
Accounts receivable	0.75	0.45	0.225	0.075	0	0	0.95	1.50	3.0	3.0	3.0	1.5	0.75
Inventory	1.6	2.6	3.9	5.4	7.0	8.6	9.0	8.6	6.2	3.8	1.4	1.0	1.60
Total current assets	$5.2	$4.8	$ 4.55	$5.725	$ 7.25	$ 8.85	$10.20	$10.35	$9.45	$7.05	$ 8.1	$7.7	$7.80

equipment, or—if growth in sales is anticipated—invest in new equipment to increase productive capacity. Table 6-5 presents the cash budget and total current assets for the second year. Under a simplified no-growth assumption, the monthly cash flow is the same as that of the first year, but beginning cash in October is much higher than the first year's beginning cash balance, and this lowers the borrowing requirement and increases the ending cash balance and total current assets at year-end. Higher current assets are present despite the fact that accounts receivable and inventory do not change.

Figure 6-4 is a graphic presentation of the current asset cycle. It includes the two years covered in Tables 6-4 and 6-5 assuming level production and no sales growth.

Patterns of Financing

The financial manager's selection of external sources of funds to finance assets may be one of the firm's most important decisions. The axiom that all current assets should be financed by current liabilities (accounts payable, bank loans, commercial paper, etc.) is subject to challenge when one sees the permanent buildup that can occur in current assets. In the Yawakuzi example, the buildup in inventory was substantial at $9 million. The example had a logical conclusion in that the motorcycles were sold, cash was generated, and current assets became very liquid. What if a much smaller level of sales had occurred? Yawakuzi would be sitting on a large inventory that needed to be financed and would be generating no cash. Theoretically, the firm could be declared technically insolvent (bankrupt) if short-term sources of funds were used but were unable to be renewed when they came due. How would the interest and

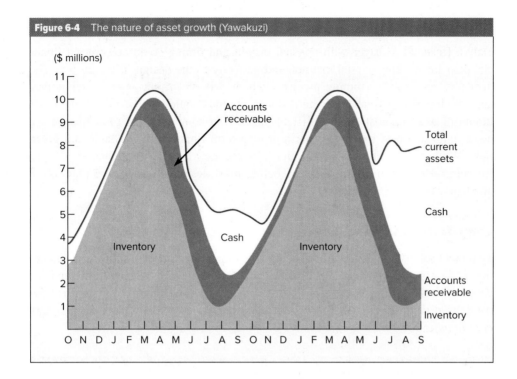

Figure 6-4   The nature of asset growth (Yawakuzi)

principal be paid without cash flow from inventory liquidation? The most appropriate financing pattern would be one in which asset buildup and length of financing terms are perfectly matched, as indicated in Figure 6-5.

In the upper part of Figure 6-5, we see that the temporary buildup in current assets (represented by teal) is financed by short-term funds. More importantly, however, permanent current assets and fixed assets (both represented by blue) are financed with long-term funds from the sale of stock, the issuance of bonds, or the retention of earnings.

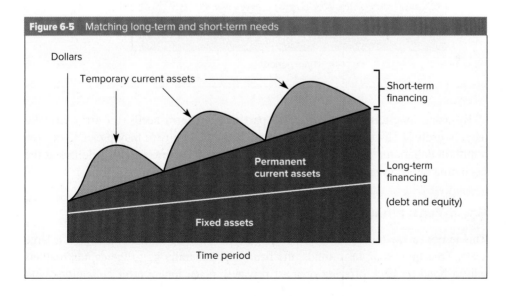

Figure 6-5   Matching long-term and short-term needs

Alternative Plans

Only a financial manager with unusual insight and timing could construct a financial plan for working capital that adhered perfectly to the design in Figure 6-5. The difficulty rests in determining precisely which part of current assets is temporary and which part is permanent. Even if dollar amounts could be ascertained, the exact timing of asset liquidation is a difficult matter. To compound the problem, we are never quite sure how much short-term or long-term financing is available at a given time. While the precise synchronization of temporary current assets and short-term financing depicted in Figure 6-5 may be the most desirable and logical plan, other alternatives must be considered.

Long-Term Financing

To protect against the danger of not being able to provide adequate short-term financing in tight money periods, the financial manager may rely on long-term funds to cover some short-term needs. As indicated in Figure 6-6, long-term capital is now being used to finance fixed assets, permanent current assets, and part of *temporary current assets.*

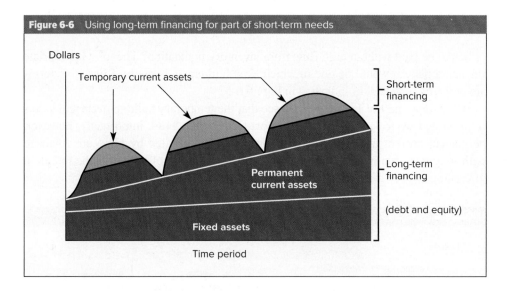

Figure 6-6   Using long-term financing for part of short-term needs

By using long-term capital to cover part of short-term needs, the firm virtually assures itself of having adequate capital at all times. The firm may prefer to borrow a million dollars for 10 years—rather than attempt to borrow a million dollars at the beginning of each year for 10 years and pay it back at the end of each year.

Short-Term Financing (Opposite Approach)

This is not to say that all financial managers utilize long-term financing on a large scale. To acquire long-term funds, the firm must generally go to the capital markets with a bond or stock offering or must privately place longer-term obligations with insurance companies, wealthy individuals, and so forth. Many small businesses do not have access to such long-term capital and are forced to rely heavily on short-term bank and trade credit.

Furthermore, short-term financing offers some advantages over more extended financial arrangements. As a general rule, the interest rate on short-term funds is lower than that on long-term funds. We might surmise, then, that a firm could develop a working capital financing plan in which short-term funds are used to finance not only temporary current assets but also part of the permanent working capital needs of the firm. As depicted in Figure 6-7, bank and trade credit as well as other sources of short-term financing are now supporting part of the permanent capital asset needs of the firm.

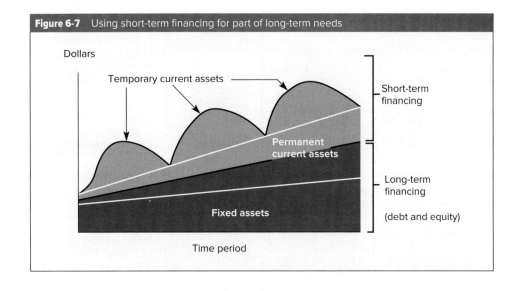

Figure 6-7 Using short-term financing for part of long-term needs

The Financing Decision

Some corporations are more flexible than others because they are not locked into a few available sources of funds. Corporations would like many financing alternatives in order to minimize their cost of funds at any point. Unfortunately, not many firms are in this enviable position through the duration of a business cycle. During an economic boom period, a shortage of low-cost alternatives exists, and firms often minimize their financing costs by raising funds in advance of forecast asset needs.

Not only does the financial manager encounter a timing problem, but he or she also needs to select the right type of financing. Even for companies having many alternative sources of funds, there may be only one or two decisions that will look good in retrospect. At the time the financing decision is made, the financial manager is never sure it is the right one. Should the financing be long term or short term, debt or equity, and so on?

Figure 6-8 is a decision-tree diagram that shows many of the financing choices available to a chief financial officer. A decision is made at each point until a final financing method is chosen. In most cases, a corporation will use a combination of these financing methods. At all times, the financial manager will balance short-term versus long-term considerations against the composition of the firm's assets and the firm's willingness to accept risk. The ratio of long-term financing to short-term financing at any point in time will be greatly influenced by the *term structure of interest rates.*

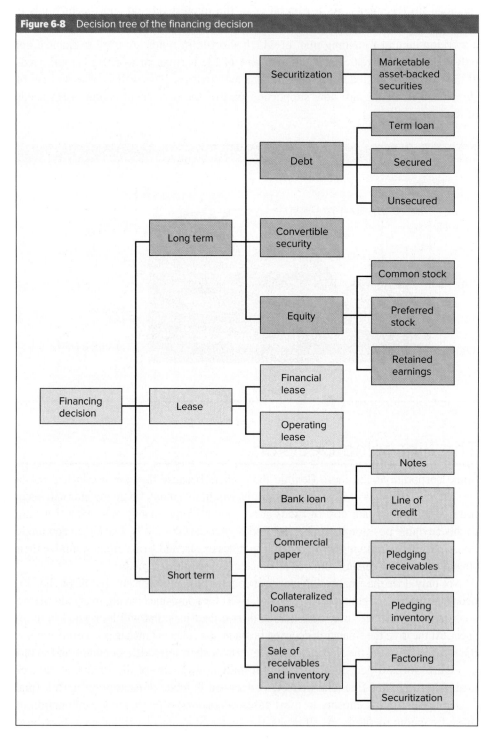

Figure 6-8   Decision tree of the financing decision

Term Structure of Interest Rates

The **term structure of interest rates** is often referred to as a **yield curve**. It shows the relative level of short-term and long-term interest rates at a point in time. Knowledge of changing interest rates and interest rate theory is extremely valuable to corporate executives making decisions about how to time and structure their borrowing between short- and long-term debt. Generally, U.S. government securities are used to construct yield curves because they are free of default risk and the large number of maturities creates a fairly continuous curve. Yields on corporate debt securities will move in the same direction as government securities but will have higher interest rates because of their greater financial risk. Yield curves for both corporations and government securities change daily to reflect current competitive conditions in the money and capital markets, expected inflation, and changes in economic conditions.

Three basic theories describe the shape of the yield curve. The first theory is called the **liquidity premium theory** and states that long-term rates should be higher than short-term rates. This premium of long-term rates over short-term rates exists because short-term securities have greater liquidity and therefore higher rates have to be offered to potential long-term bond buyers to entice them to hold these less liquid and more price-sensitive securities. The **market segmentation theory** (the second theory) states that Treasury securities are divided into market segments by the various financial institutions investing in the market. Commercial banks prefer short-term securities of one year or less to match their short-term lending strategies. Savings and loans and other mortgage-oriented financial institutions prefer the intermediate-length securities of between 5 and 7 years, while pension funds and life insurance companies prefer long-term 20- to 30-year securities to offset the long-term nature of their commitments to policyholders. The changing needs, desires, and strategies of these investors tend to strongly influence the nature and relationship of short-term and long-term interest rates.

The third theory describing the term structure of interest rates is called the **expectations hypothesis**. This theory explains the yields on long-term securities as a function of short-term rates. The expectations theory says long-term rates reflect the average of short-term expected rates over the time period that the long-term security is outstanding. Using a four-year example and simple averages, we demonstrate this theory in Table 6-6. In the left-hand panel of the table, we show the anticipated one-year rate on T-bill (Treasury bill) securities at the beginning of each of four years in the future. Treasury bills are short-term securities issued by the government. In the right-hand panel, we show the two-, three- and four-year averages of the one-year anticipated rates.

Table 6-6 The expectations theory	
1-year T-bill at beginning of year 1 = 4%	
1-year T-bill at beginning of year 2 = 5%	2-year security (4% + 5%)/2 = 4.5%
1-year T-bill at beginning of year 3 = 6%	3-year security (4% + 5% + 6%)/3 = 5.0%
1-year T-bill at beginning of year 4 = 7%	4-year security (4% + 5% + 6% + 7%)/4 = 5.5%

For example, the two-year security rate is the average of the expected yields of two one-year T-bills, while the rate on the four-year security is the average of all four one-year rates.[1] In this example, the progressively higher rates for two-, three-, and four-year securities represent a reflection of higher anticipated one-year rates in the future. The expectations hypothesis is especially useful in explaining the shape and movement of the yield curve. The result of the expectations hypothesis is that when long-term rates are much higher than short-term rates, the market is saying it expects short-term rates to rise. When long-term rates are lower than short-term rates, the market is expecting short-term rates to fall. This theory is useful to financial managers in helping them set expectations for the cost of financing over time and, especially, in making choices about when to use short-term debt or long-term debt.

In fact, all three theories of the term structure just discussed have some impact on interest rates. At times the liquidity premium or segmentation theory dominates the shape of the curve, and at other times the expectations theory is the most important.

Figure 6-9 shows a Treasury yield curve that is published by the St. Louis Federal Reserve Bank in *National Economic Trends,* a weekly online publication that can be directly accessed on www.stlouisfed.org. The bottom axis shows time periods (months and years) and the vertical axis indicates rates. In this figure, there are three curves: January 2016, January 2017, and January 2018. We can see that short-term yields rose during 2017. However, 10-year yields did not rise very much during 2016 and 2017. Using the January 2016 curve (the red line), we can see that yields rose from less than 0.25 percent for three-month Treasury bills to approximately 1.75 percent for 5-year Treasury notes and continued up to almost 2.25 percent for 10-year Treasury bonds.

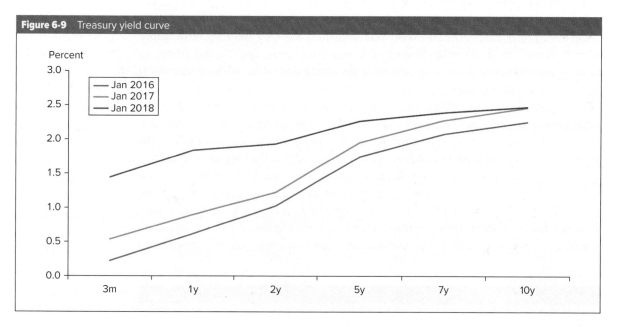

Figure 6-9   Treasury yield curve

---

[1]Using a geometric mean return rather than a simple average return creates a more exact rate of return. For example, for the four-year security a geometric return would provide a return of 5.494 percent rather than the 5.5 percent simple average in Table 6-6. The calculation would be as follows:

$$[(1.04) \times (1.05) \times (1.06) \times (1.07)]^{1/4} - 1 = 0.05494$$

This upward-sloping yield curve has the normal shape. The increase in rates from the three-month to the 10-year yield was 2.02 percent, or 202 **basis points**. (A basis point represents 1/100th of 1 percent.) Over the last decade, the Federal Reserve has kept all interest rates low, with short-term rates extremely low. This action by the Fed was intended to help the economy recover from the most serious recession since the Great Depression. By keeping the cost of borrowing low, the Federal Reserve helps stimulate the economy. As the economy recovers, the yield curve will shift up and become less steep, as we were already seeing in January 2018.

An *upward-sloping* yield curve is considered normal, but the difference between short-term and long-term rates has often been quite wide, as in October 1993 when short-term rates were less than 3 percent and long-term rates were close to 7 percent. Generally, the more upward-sloping the yield curve, the greater the expectation that interest rates will rise. When faced with a *downward-sloping,* or inverted, yield curve, the expectation would be the opposite. A good example of this occurred in September 1981 when short-term rates were over 17 percent and long-term rates were close to 15 percent. A little over one year later, in December 1982, short-term rates were 8 percent and long-term rates were about 10.5 percent. This example also illustrates that interest rates can move dramatically in a relatively short time (in this case, 15 months).

In designing working capital policy, the astute financial manager is interested in not only the term structure of interest rates but also the relative volatility and the historical level of short-term and long-term rates. Figure 6-10 covers a 20-year period and demonstrates that short-term rates (green) are more volatile than long-term rates (red). This volatility is what makes a short-term financing strategy risky. Figure 6-10 also shows that interest rates follow the general trend of inflation as measured by the consumer price index (blue). Note that rates declined during the recession of

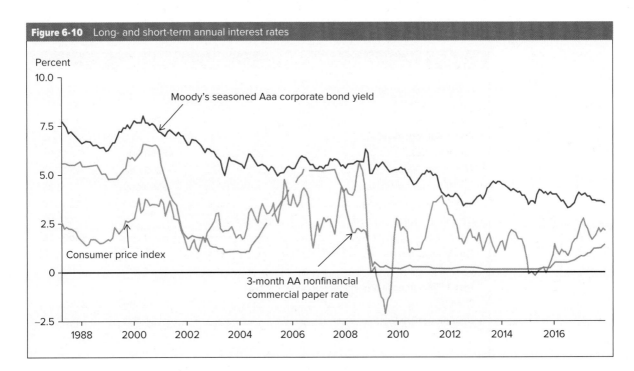

Figure 6-10   Long- and short-term annual interest rates

2007–2009, which is what is expected as demand declines. As inflation goes up or down, so do interest rates. While we can see that short- and long-term interest rates are closely related to each other and to inflation, the record of the professionals for accurate interest rate predictions for periods longer than a few months is spotty at best.

How should the financial manager respond to fluctuating interest rates and changing term structures? When interest rates are high and expected to decline, the financial manager generally tries to borrow short term (if funds are available). As rates decline, the chief financial officer will try to lock in the lower rates with heavy long-term borrowing. Some of these long-term funds will be used to reduce short-term debt, and the rest will be available for future expansion of plant and equipment and working capital if necessary.

A Decision Process

Assume we are comparing alternative financing plans for working capital. As indicated in Table 6-7, $500,000 of working capital (current assets) must be financed for the Edwards Corporation. Under Plan A, we will finance all our current asset needs with short-term funds (fourth line), while under Plan B we will finance only a relatively small portion of current assets with short-term money—relying heavily on long-term funds. In either case, we will carry $100,000 of fixed assets with long-term financing commitments. As indicated in part 3 of Table 6-7, under Plan A we will finance total needs of $600,000 with $500,000 of short-term financing and $100,000 of long-term financing, whereas with Plan B we will finance $150,000 short term and $450,000 long term.

Table 6-7 Alternative financing plans		
EDWARDS CORPORATION		
	Plan A	**Plan B**
Part 1. Current assets		
Temporary	$250,000	$250,000
Permanent	250,000	250,000
Total current assets	$500,000	$500,000
Short-term financing (6%)	500,000	150,000
Long-term financing (10%)	0	350,000
	$500,000	$500,000
Part 2. Fixed assets		
Long-term financing (10%)	$100,000	$100,000
Part 3. Total financing (summary of parts 1 and 2)		
Short-term (6%)	$500,000	$150,000
Long-term (10%)	100,000	450,000
	$600,000	$600,000

Plan A carries the lower cost of financing, with interest of 6 percent on $500,000 of the $600,000 required. We show the impact of both plans on bottom-line earnings in Table 6-8.[2] Assuming the firm generates $200,000 in earnings before interest and taxes, Plan A will provide aftertax earnings of $120,000, while Plan B will generate only $109,500.

Table 6-8 Impact of financing plans on earnings	
EDWARDS CORPORATION	
Plan A	
Earnings before interest and taxes	$200,000
Interest (short term), 6% × $500,000	30,000
Interest (long term), 10% × $100,000	10,000
Earnings before taxes	$160,000
Taxes (25%)	40,000
Earnings after taxes	$120,000
Plan B	
Earnings before interest and taxes	$200,000
Interest (short term), 6% × $150,000	9,000
Interest (long term), 10% × $450,000	45,000
Earnings before taxes	$146,000
Taxes (25%)	36,500
Earnings after taxes	$109,500

Introducing Varying Conditions

Although Plan A, employing cheaper short-term sources of financing, appears to provide $10,500 more in return, this is not always the case. During **tight money** periods, when capital is scarce, short-term financing may be difficult to find or may carry exorbitant rates. Furthermore, inadequate financing may mean lost sales or financial embarrassment. For these reasons, the firm may wish to evaluate Plans A and B based on differing assumptions about the economy and the money markets.

Expected Value

History combined with economic forecasting may indicate an 80 percent probability of normal events and a 20 percent chance of extremely tight money. Using Plan A, under normal conditions the Edwards Corporation will enjoy a $10,500 superior return over Plan B (as previously indicated in Table 6-8). Let us now assume that under disruptive tight money conditions, Plan A would provide a $15,000 lower return than Plan B because of high short-term interest rates. These conditions are summarized in Table 6-9, and an expected value of return is computed. The **expected value** represents the sum of the expected outcomes under the two conditions.

---

[2]Common stock is eliminated from the example to simplify the analysis.

Table 6-9   Expected returns under different economic conditions

EDWARDS CORPORATION					
1. Normal conditions	Expected higher return under Plan A		Probability of normal conditions		Expected outcome
	$10,500	×	0.80	=	$8,400
2. Tight money	Expected lower return under Plan A		Probability of tight money		
	($15,000)	×	0.20	=	(3,000)
Expected value of return for Plan A versus Plan B				=	+$5,400

We see that even when downside risk is considered, Plan A carries a higher expected return of $5,400. For another firm, XYZ, in the same industry that might suffer $50,000 lower returns during tight money conditions, Plan A becomes too dangerous to undertake, as indicated in Table 6-10. Plan A's expected return is now $1,600 less than that of Plan B.

Table 6-10   Expected returns for high-risk firm

XYZ CORPORATION					
1. Normal conditions	Expected higher return under Plan A		Probability of normal conditions		Expected outcome
	$10,500	×	0.80	=	$8,400
2. Tight money	Expected lower return under Plan A		Probability of tight money		
	($50,000)	×	0.20	=	(10,000)
Negative expected value of return for Plan A versus Plan B				=	($1,600)

Shifts in Asset Structure

For large U.S. nonfinancial corporations as represented by Standard & Poor's, the percentage of net working capital [(Current assets − Current liabilities) divided by sales] has varied over time.

Figure 6-11 depicts the combined net working capital ratio and the current ratio for five large industrial companies: Caterpillar, United Technologies, 3M, Boeing, and ExxonMobil. These financially strong companies exhibit the same pattern as that of the S&P industrials. During a recession, sales decline or stay even, but cash, receivables, and inventory fall and short-term debt may rise, causing a large decline in the net working capital to sales ratio. As the firm's profitability increases during the upswing, cash, receivables, and inventory rise, and short-term debt may fall or be replaced by low-cost long-term debt in the low-interest rate environment of a recession. These two effects cause the ratio to rise. Figure 6-11 clearly shows the cyclical nature of working capital to sales. The ratio bottoms out in the recession of 2008 and makes a steady

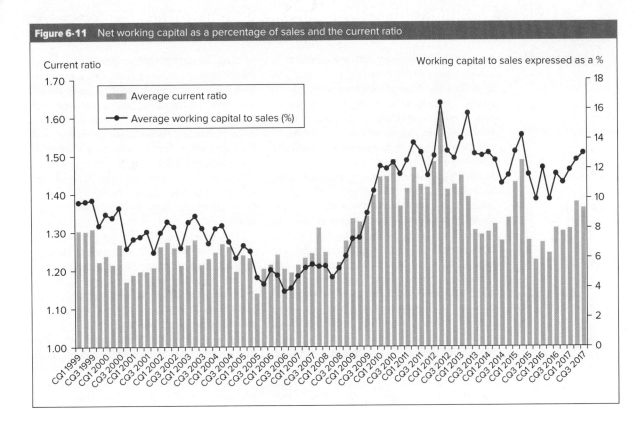

Figure 6-11 Net working capital as a percentage of sales and the current ratio

increase as these companies build up their cash balances and inventories. Because of the uncertainty surrounding the economy, many companies opted to hold larger cash balances for future stock repurchases, mergers, or dividend increases.

However, the low current ratios in recent years (right scale) can be traced to more efficient inventory management such as just-in-time inventory programs, point-of-sales terminals, more efficient cash management, electronic cash flow transfer systems, and the ability to sell accounts receivable through the securitization of assets (more fully explained in the next chapter).

Toward an Optimal Policy

As previously indicated, the firm should attempt to relate asset liquidity to financing patterns, and vice versa. In Table 6-11, a number of working capital alternatives are presented. Along the top of the table, we show asset liquidity; along the side, the type of financing arrangement. The combined impact of the two variables is shown in each of the four panels of the table.

In Table 6-11, each firm must decide how it wishes to combine asset liquidity and financing needs. The aggressive, risk-oriented firm in panel 1 will borrow short term and maintain relatively low levels of liquidity, hoping to increase profit. It will benefit from low-cost financing and high-return assets, but it will be vulnerable to a credit crunch. The more conservative firm, following the plan in panel 4, will utilize established long-term financing and maintain a high degree of liquidity. In panels 2 and 3,

Managerial

Many small businesses that are seasonal in nature have difficult financing problems. This is particularly true of retail nursery (plants) stores, greeting card shops, boating stores, and so on. The problem is that each of these businesses has year-round fixed commitments, but the business is seasonal. For example, Calloway's Nursery, located in the Dallas–Fort Worth Metroplex, as well as in Houston, does approximately half of its business in the April to June quarter, yet it must make lease payments for its 18 retail outlets every month of the year. The problem is compounded by the fact that during seasonal peaks it must compete with large national retail chains such as Lowe's and Home Depot that can easily convert space allocated to nursery products to other purposes when winter comes. While Calloway's Nursery can sell garden-related arts and crafts in its off-season, the potential volume is small compared to the boom periods of April, May, and June.

Seasonality is not a problem that is exclusive to small businesses. However, its effects can be greater because of the difficulty that small businesses have in attracting large pools of permanent funds through the use of equity capital. The smaller business firm is likely to be more dependent on suppliers, commercial banks, and others to provide financing needs. Suppliers are likely to provide the necessary funds during seasonal peaks but are not a good source of financing during the off-season. Banks may provide a line

www.calloways.com

of credit (a commitment to provide funds) for the off-season, but the small firm can sometimes find it difficult to acquire bank financing. This has become particularly true with the consolidation of the banking industry through mergers. Twenty years ago, the small businessperson was usually on a first-name basis with the local banker, who knew every aspect of his or her business. Now a loan request may have to go to North Carolina, Ohio, California, New York, or elsewhere for final approval.

The obvious answer to seasonal working capital problems is sufficient financial planning to ensure that profits produced during the peak season are available to cover losses during the off-season. Calloway's Nursery and many other small firms literally predict at the beginning of their fiscal period the movement of cash flow for every week of the year. This includes the expansion and reduction of the workforce during peak and slow periods, as well as the daily tracking of inventory. However, even such foresight cannot fully prepare a firm for an unexpected freeze, a flood, the entrance of a new competitor into the marketplace, a zoning change that redirects traffic in the wrong direction, and so on.

Thus the answer lies not just in planning, but in flexible planning. If sales are down by 10 percent, then a similar reduction in employees, salaries, fringe benefits, inventory, and other areas must take place. Plans for expansion must be changed into plans for contraction.

Table 6-11 Asset liquidity and financing assets

	Asset Liquidity	
Financing Plan	**Low Liquidity**	**High Liquidity**
Short Term	1 High profit High risk	2 Moderate profit Moderate risk
Long Term	3 Moderate profit Moderate risk	4 Low profit Low risk

we see more moderate positions in which the firm compensates for short-term financing with highly liquid assets (2) or balances off low liquidity with precommitted, long-term financing (3).

Each financial manager must structure his or her working capital position and the associated risk-return trade-off to meet the company's needs. For firms whose cash flow patterns are predictable, typified by the public utilities sector, a low degree of liquidity can be maintained. Immediate access to capital markets, such as that enjoyed by large, prestigious firms, also allows a greater risk-taking capability. In each case, the ultimate concern must be for maximizing the overall valuation of the firm through a judicious consideration of risk-return options.

In the next two chapters, we will examine the various methods for managing the individual components of working capital. In Chapter 7, we consider the techniques for managing cash, marketable securities, receivables, and inventory. In Chapter 8, we look at trade and bank credit and at other sources of short-term funds.

SUMMARY

Working capital management involves the financing and controlling of the current assets of the firm. These current assets include cash, marketable securities, accounts receivable, and inventory. A firm's ability to properly manage current assets and the associated liability obligations may determine how well it is able to survive in the short run.

Because a firm with continuous operations will always maintain minimum levels of current assets, management must be able to distinguish between current assets that are permanent and those that are temporary or cyclical. To determine the permanent or cyclical nature of current assets, the financial manager must give careful attention to the growth in sales and the relationship of the production process to sales. Level production in a seasonal sales environment increases operating efficiency, but it also calls for more careful financial planning.

In general, we advocate tying the maturity of the financing plan to the maturity of the current assets. That is, finance short-term cyclical current assets with short-term liabilities and permanent current assets with long-term sources of funds. In order to carry out the company's financing plan with minimum cost, the financial manager must keep an eye on the general cost of borrowing, the term structure of interest rates, and the relative volatility of short- and long-term rates and must predict, if possible, any change in the direction of interest rate movements.

Because the yield curve is usually upward sloping, long-term financing is generally more expensive than short-term financing. This lower cost in favor of short-term financing must be weighed against the risk that short-term rates are more volatile than long-term rates. Additionally, if long-term rates are expected to rise, the financial manager may want to lock in long-term financing needs before they do.

The firm has a number of risk-return decisions to consider. Though long-term financing provides a safety margin for the availability of funds, its higher cost may reduce the profit potential of the firm. On the asset side, carrying highly liquid current assets assures the bill-paying capability of the firm—but detracts from profit potential. Each firm must tailor the various risk-return trade-offs to meet its own needs. The peculiarities of a firm's industry will have a major impact on the options open to its management.

LIST OF TERMS

DISCUSSION QUESTIONS

1. Explain how rapidly expanding sales can drain the cash resources of a firm. *(LO6-3)*

2. Discuss the relative volatility of short- and long-term interest rates. *(LO6-4)*

3. What is the significance to working capital management of matching sales and production? *(LO6-3)*

4. How is a cash budget used to help manage current assets? *(LO6-1)*

5. "The most appropriate financing pattern would be one in which asset buildup and length of financing terms are perfectly matched." Discuss the difficulty involved in achieving this financing pattern. *(LO6-5)*

6. By using long-term financing to finance part of temporary current assets, a firm may have less risk but lower returns than a firm with a normal financing plan. Explain the significance of this statement. *(LO6-5)*

7. A firm that uses short-term financing methods for a portion of permanent current assets is assuming more risk but expects higher returns than a firm with a normal financing plan. Explain. *(LO6-3)*

8. What does the *term structure of interest rates* indicate? *(LO6-4)*

9. What are three theories for describing the shape of the term structure of interest rates (the yield curve)? Briefly describe each theory. *(LO6-4)*

10. Since the mid-1960s, corporate liquidity has been declining. What reasons can you give for this trend? *(LO6-1)*

PRACTICE PROBLEMS AND SOLUTIONS

Expected value
(LO6-6)

1. Meyer Electronics expects sales next year to be $3,000,000 if the economy is strong, $1,200,000 if the economy is steady, and $800,000 if the economy is weak. Mr. Meyer believes there is a 30 percent probability the economy will be strong, a 60 percent probability of a steady economy, and a 10 percent probability of a weak economy. What is the expected level of sales for the next year?

2. Otis Resources is trying to develop an asset financing plan. The firm has $200,000 in temporary current assets and $500,000 in permanent current assets. Otis also has $300,000 in fixed assets. Alternative financing plans *(LO6-5)*

   a. Construct two alternative financing plans for the firm. One of the plans should be conservative, with 70 percent of assets financed by long-term sources and the rest financed by short-term sources. The other plan should be aggressive, with only 20 percent of assets financed by long-term sources and the remaining assets financed by short-term sources. The current interest rate is 12 percent on long-term funds and 5 percent on short-term financing. Compute the annual interest payments under each plan.

   b. Given that Otis's earnings before interest and taxes are $234,000, calculate earnings after taxes for each of your alternatives. Assume a tax rate of 35 percent.

Solutions

1.

State of Economy	Expected Sales	×	Probability	=	Expected Outcome
Strong	$3,000,000		0.30		$ 900,000
Steady	1,200,000		0.60		720,000
Weak	800,000		0.10		80,000
			Expected level of sales =		$1,700,000

2. *a.*

Temporary current assets	$ 200,000
Permanent current assets	500,000
Fixed assets	300,000
Total assets	$1,000,000

Conservative Plan

Total Assets	Percent of Total	Dollar Amount	×	Interest Rate	=	Interest Expense
$1,000,000	Long term (0.70)	$700,000		0.12		$84,000
1,000,000	Short term (0.30)	300,000		0.05		15,000
				Total interest expense		$99,000

Aggressive Plan

Total Assets	Percent of Total	Dollar Amount	×	Interest Rate	=	Interest Expense
$1,000,000	Long term (0.20)	$200,000		0.12		$24,000
1,000,000	Short term (0.80)	800,000		0.05		40,000
				Total interest expense		$64,000

b.

	Conservative	Aggressive
EBIT	$234,000	$234,000
I	99,000	64,000
EBT	$135,000	$170,000
Tax 35%	47,250	59,500
EAT	$ 87,750	$110,500

PROBLEMS

■ connect Selected problems are available with Connect. Please see the preface for more information.

Basic Problems

Expected value
(LO6-6)

1. Gary's Pipe and Steel Company expects sales next year to be $800,000 if the economy is strong, $500,000 if the economy is steady, and $350,000 if the economy is weak. Gary believes there is a 20 percent probability the economy will be strong, a 50 percent probability of a steady economy, and a 30 percent probability of a weak economy. What is the expected level of sales for next year?

Expected value
(LO6-6)

2. Sharpe Knife Company expects sales next year to be $1,550,000 if the economy is strong, $825,000 if the economy is steady, and $550,000 if the economy is weak. Ms. Sharpe believes there is a 30 percent probability the economy will be strong, a 40 percent probability of a steady economy, and a 30 percent probability of a weak economy. What is the expected level of sales for the next year?

External financing
(LO6-1)

3. Tobin Supplies Company expects sales next year to be $500,000. Inventory and accounts receivable will increase $90,000 to accommodate this sales level. The company has a steady profit margin of 12 percent with a 40 percent dividend payout. How much external financing will Tobin Supplies Company have to seek? Assume there is no increase in liabilities other than that which will occur with the external financing.

External financing
(LO6-1)

4. Antivirus Inc. expects its sales next year to be $2,500,000. Inventory and accounts receivable will increase $480,000 to accommodate this sales level. The company has a steady profit margin of 15 percent with a 35 percent dividend payout. How much external financing will the firm have to seek? Assume there is no increase in liabilities other than that which will occur with the external financing.

Level versus seasonal
production
(LO6-1)

5. Antonio Banderos & Scarves makes headwear that is very popular in the fall–winter season. Units sold are anticipated as follows:

October	1,250
November	2,250
December	4,500
January	3,500
	11,500 units

If seasonal production is used, it is assumed that inventory will directly match sales for each month and there will be no inventory buildup.

However, Antonio decides to go with level production to avoid being out of merchandise. He will produce the 11,500 items over four months at a level of 2,875 per month.

a.   What is the ending inventory at the end of each month? Compare the units sales to the units produced and keep a running total.

b.   If the inventory costs $8 per unit and will be financed at the bank at a cost of 12 percent, what is the monthly financing cost and the total for the four months? (Use 1 percent or the monthly rate.)

6.   Bambino Sporting Goods makes baseball gloves that are very popular in the spring and early summer season. Units sold are anticipated as follows:

Level versus seasonal production
(LO6-1)

March	3,250
April	7,250
May	11,500
June	9,500
	31,500 units

If seasonal production is used, it is assumed that inventory will directly match sales for each month and there will be no inventory buildup.

The production manager thinks the preceding assumption is too optimistic and decides to go with level production to avoid being out of merchandise. He will produce the 31,500 units over four months at a level of 7,875 per month.

a.   What is the ending inventory at the end of each month? Compare the unit sales to the units produced and keep a running total.

b.   If the inventory costs $12 per unit and will be financed at the bank at a cost of 12 percent, what is the monthly financing cost and the total for the four months? (Use 0.01 as the monthly rate.)

7.   Boatler Used Cadillac Co. requires $850,000 in financing over the next two years. The firm can borrow the funds for two years at 12 percent interest per year. Ms. Boatler decides to do forecasting and predicts that if she utilizes short-term financing instead, she will pay 7.75 percent interest in the first year and 13.55 percent interest in the second year. Determine the total two-year interest cost under each plan. Which plan is less costly?

Short-term versus longer-term borrowing
(LO6-3)

8.   Biochemical Corp. requires $550,000 in financing over the next three years. The firm can borrow the funds for three years at 10.60 percent interest per year. The CEO decides to do a forecast and predicts that if she utilizes short-term financing instead, she will pay 8.75 percent interest in the first year, 13.25 percent interest in the second year, and 10.15 percent interest in the third year. Determine the total interest cost under each plan. Which plan is less costly?

Short-term versus longer-term borrowing
(LO6-3)

Intermediate Problems

9.   Sauer Food Company has decided to buy a new computer system with an expected life of three years. The cost is $150,000. The company can borrow $150,000 for three years at 10 percent annual interest or for one year at 8 percent annual interest.

𝒳

Short-term versus longer-term borrowing
(LO6-3)

How much would Sauer Food Company save in interest over the three-year life of the computer system if the one-year loan is utilized and the loan is rolled over (reborrowed) each year at the same 8 percent rate? Compare this to the 10 percent three-year loan. What if interest rates on the 8 percent loan go up to 13 percent in year 2 and 18 percent in year 3? What would be the total interest cost compared to the 10 percent, three-year loan?

Optimal policy mix
(LO6-5)

10. Assume that Hogan Surgical Instruments Co. has $2,500,000 in assets. If it goes with a low-liquidity plan for the assets, it can earn a return of 18 percent, but with a high-liquidity plan, the return will be 14 percent. If the firm goes with a short-term financing plan, the financing costs on the $2,500,000 will be 10 percent, and with a long-term financing plan, the financing costs on the $2,500,000 will be 12 percent. (Review Table 6-11 for parts *a*, *b*, and *c* of this problem.)

   a. Compute the anticipated return after financing costs with the most aggressive asset financing mix.

   b. Compute the anticipated return after financing costs with the most conservative asset financing mix.

   c. Compute the anticipated return after financing costs with the two moderate approaches to the asset financing mix.

   d. Would you necessarily accept the plan with the highest return after financing costs? Briefly explain.

Optimal policy mix
(LO6-5)

11. Assume that Atlas Sporting Goods Inc. has $840,000 in assets. If it goes with a low-liquidity plan for the assets, it can earn a return of 15 percent, but with a high-liquidity plan the return will be 12 percent. If the firm goes with a short-term financing plan, the financing costs on the $840,000 will be 9 percent, and with a long-term financing plan the financing costs on the $840,000 will be 11 percent. (Review Table 6-11 for parts *a*, *b*, and *c* of this problem.)

   a. Compute the anticipated return after financing costs with the most aggressive asset financing mix.

   b. Compute the anticipated return after financing costs with the most conservative asset financing mix.

   c. Compute the anticipated return after financing costs with the two moderate approaches to the asset financing mix.

   d. If the firm used the most aggressive asset financing mix described in part *a* and had the anticipated return you computed for part *a,* what would earnings per share be if the tax rate on the anticipated return was 30 percent and there were 20,000 shares outstanding?

   e. Now assume the most conservative asset financing mix described in part *b* will be utilized. The tax rate will be 30 percent. Also assume there will only be 5,000 shares outstanding. What will earnings per share be? Would it be higher or lower than the earnings per share computed for the most aggressive plan computed in part *d*?

12. Colter Steel has $4,200,000 in assets.

Matching asset mix
and financing plans
(LO6-3)

Temporary current assets	$1,000,000
Permanent current assets	2,000,000
Fixed assets	1,200,000
Total assets	$4,200,000

Short-term rates are 8 percent. Long-term rates are 13 percent. Earnings before interest and taxes are $996,000. The tax rate is 40 percent.

If long-term financing is perfectly matched (synchronized) with long-term asset needs, and the same is true of short-term financing, what will earnings after taxes be? For a graphical example of perfectly matched plans, see Figure 6-5.

13. In Problem 12, assume the term structure of interest rates becomes inverted, with short-term rates going to 11 percent and long-term rates 5 percentage points lower than short-term rates. If all other factors in the problem remain unchanged, what will earnings after taxes be?

Impact of term
structure of interest
rates on financing
plans
(LO6-4)

14. Guardian Inc. is trying to develop an asset financing plan. The firm has $400,000 in temporary current assets and $300,000 in permanent current assets. Guardian also has $500,000 in fixed assets. Assume a tax rate of 40 percent.

Conservative versus
aggressive financing
(LO6-5)

   a. Construct two alternative financing plans for Guardian. One of the plans should be conservative, with 75 percent of assets financed by long-term sources, and the other should be aggressive, with only 56.25 percent of assets financed by long-term sources. The current interest rate is 15 percent on long-term funds and 10 percent on short-term financing.

   b. Given that Guardian's earnings before interest and taxes are $200,000, calculate earnings after taxes for each of your alternatives.

   c. What would happen if the short- and long-term rates were reversed?

15. Lear Inc. has $840,000 in current assets, $370,000 of which are considered permanent current assets. In addition, the firm has $640,000 invested in fixed assets.

Alternative
financing plans
(LO6-5)

   a. Lear wishes to finance all fixed assets and half of its permanent current assets with long-term financing costing 8 percent. The balance will be financed with short-term financing, which currently costs 7 percent. Lear's earnings before interest and taxes are $240,000. Determine Lear's earnings after taxes under this financing plan. The tax rate is 30 percent.

   b. As an alternative, Lear might wish to finance all fixed assets and permanent current assets plus half of its temporary current assets with long-term financing and the balance with short-term financing. The same interest rates apply as in part *a.* Earnings before interest and taxes will be $240,000. What will be Lear's earnings after taxes? The tax rate is 30 percent.

   c. What are some of the risks and cost considerations associated with each of these alternative financing strategies?

16. Using the expectations hypothesis theory for the term structure of interest rates, determine the expected return for securities with maturities of two, three, and four years based on the following data. Do an analysis similar to that in Table 6-6.

1-year T-bill at beginning of year 1	6%
1-year T-bill at beginning of year 2	7%
1-year T-bill at beginning of year 3	9%
1-year T-bill at beginning of year 4	11%

17. Using the expectations hypothesis theory for the term structure of interest rates, determine the expected return for securities with maturities of two, three, and four years based on the following data. Do an analysis similar to that in the right-hand portion of Table 6-6.

1-year T-bill at beginning of year 1	5%
1-year T-bill at beginning of year 2	8%
1-year T-bill at beginning of year 3	7%
1-year T-bill at beginning of year 4	10%

Advanced Problems

18. Carmen's Beauty Salon has estimated monthly financing requirements for the next six months as follows:

January	$8,500	April	$8,500
February	2,500	May	9,500
March	3,500	June	4,500

Short-term financing will be utilized for the next six months. Here are the projected annual interest rates:

January	9.0%	April	16.0%
February	10.0%	May	12.0%
March	13.0%	June	12.0%

   a. Compute total dollar interest payments for the six months. To convert an annual rate to a monthly rate, divide by 12. Then multiply this value times the monthly balance. To get your answer, add up the monthly interest payments.

   b. If long-term financing at 12 percent had been utilized throughout the six months, would the total-dollar interest payments be larger or smaller? Compute the interest owed over the six months and compare your answer to that in part *a.*

19. In Problem 18, what long-term interest rate would represent a break-even point between using short-term financing as described in part *a* and long-term financing? (Hint: Divide the interest payments in 18*a* by the amount of total funds provided for the six months and multiply by 12.)

20. Eastern Auto Parts Inc. has 15 percent of its sales paid for in cash and 85 percent on credit. All credit accounts are collected in the following month. Assume the following sales:

January	$ 65,000
February	55,000
March	100,000
April	45,000

Sales in December of the prior year were $75,000.

Prepare a cash receipts schedule for January through April.

21. Bombs Away Video Games Corporation has forecasted the following monthly sales:

January	$100,000	July	$ 45,000
February	93,000	August	45,000
March	25,000	September	55,000
April	25,000	October	85,000
May	20,000	November	105,000
June	35,000	December	123,000
	Total annual sales = $756,000		

Bombs Away Video Games sells the popular Strafe and Capture video game. It sells for $5 per unit and costs $2 per unit to produce. A level production policy is followed. Each month's production is equal to annual sales (in units) divided by 12.

Of each month's sales, 30 percent are for cash and 70 percent are on account. All accounts receivable are collected in the month after the sale is made.

a. Construct a monthly production and inventory schedule in units. Beginning inventory in January is 25,000 units. (Note: To do part *a*, you should work in terms of units of production and units of sales.)

b. Prepare a monthly schedule of cash receipts. Sales in the December before the planning year are $100,000. Work part *b* using dollars.

c. Determine a cash payments schedule for January through December. The production costs of $2 per unit are paid for in the month in which they occur. Other cash payments, besides those for production costs, are $45,000 per month.

d. Prepare a monthly cash budget for January through December using the cash receipts schedule from part *b* and the cash payments schedule from part *c*. The beginning cash balance is $5,000, which is also the minimum desired.

22. Esquire Products Inc. expects the following monthly sales:

January	$28,000	May	$ 8,000	September	$29,000
February	19,000	June	6,000	October	34,000
March	12,000	July	22,000	November	42,000
April	14,000	August	26,000	December	24,000
		Total sales = $264,000			

Cash sales are 40 percent in a given month, with the remainder going into accounts receivable. All receivables are collected in the month following the sale. Esquire sells all of its goods for $2 each and produces them for $1 each. Esquire uses level production, and average monthly production is equal to annual production divided by 12.

a. Generate a monthly production and inventory schedule in units. Beginning inventory in January is 12,000 units. (Note: To do part *a,* you should work in terms of units of production and units of sales.)

b. Determine a cash receipts schedule for January through December. Assume that dollar sales in the prior December were $20,000. Work part *b* using dollars.

c. Determine a cash payments schedule for January through December. The production costs ($1 per unit produced) are paid for in the month in which they occur. Other cash payments (besides those for production costs) are $7,400 per month.

d. Construct a cash budget for January through December using the cash receipts schedule from part *b* and the cash payments schedule from part *c.* The beginning cash balance is $3,000, which is also the minimum desired.

e. Determine total current assets for each month. Include cash, accounts receivable, and inventory. Accounts receivable equal sales minus 40 percent of sales for a given month. Inventory is equal to ending inventory (part *a*) times the cost of $1 per unit.

WEB EXERCISE

1. Target was mentioned in the chapter as a company that has a high degree of seasonality (and associated working capital issues). Let us use the Internet to examine the seasonality. Go to www.target.com. Scroll to the bottom of the page, and under the "more" heading, click on "Investor Relations." Click on "Annual Report." Find the option for the 10-K and download the 10-K. Search for "Quarterly Results (unaudited)," which is a footnote to the 10-K. You will see historical data for both quarterly and annual periods.

2. Based on the observed data, which of the four quarters is normally best for Target? Why?

3. Which quarter is normally the worst? This may be a close call.

4. Taking the most recent year in which four quarters of data are shown, what percentage of total fiscal year earnings does the best quarter represent?

Note: Occasionally a topic we have listed may have been deleted, updated, or moved into a different location on a website. If you click on the site map or site index, you will be introduced to a table of contents that should aid you in finding the topic you are looking for.

7

Current Asset Management

LEARNING OBJECTIVES

LO 7-1 Current asset management is an extension of concepts discussed in the previous chapter and involves the management of cash, marketable securities, accounts receivable, and inventory.

LO 7-2 Cash management involves control over the receipt and payment of cash to minimize nonearning cash balances.

LO 7-3 The management of marketable securities involves selecting between various short-term investments.

LO 7-4 Accounts receivable management requires credit policy decisions aimed at maximizing profitability.

LO 7-5 Inventory management requires determining the level of inventory necessary to enhance sales and profitability.

LO 7-6 An overriding concept is that the less liquid an asset is, the higher the required return.

Retailing is one of the most challenging industries for managing current assets. Weather, economic conditions, changing customer tastes, and seasonal purchasing influence retail industry sales. The industry reports monthly sales figures and so becomes a barometer of consumers' spending attitudes. Forecasting inventory needs and cash flows is extremely difficult when sales don't go according to plan.

The Christmas selling season is the biggest time of the year for most retailers, and the economy, as well as the weather, has a large impact on how much consumers will spend. In 2006, retail stores were concerned about the continuing effects of Hurricane Katrina and Hurricane Rita. Again, in 2007, the housing market collapse and subprime mortgage problems created concerns about Christmas spending. As the economy crawled out of a deep recession in 2009, the Christmas season for retailers was again in jeopardy. In 2012, Hurricane Sandy, as well as Congress's inability to solve the problem of taxes and spending cuts, had retailers worrying. As the economy recovered, so did holiday sales, showing positive increases each year between 2014 and 2017. Even in 2017, with four major hurricanes causing over $200 billion in damages, sales grew 3.8 percent. Each year brings new problems forecasting inventory and its impact on cash and receivables.

Many retailers carry light inventories into the holiday periods with low expectations, trying to avoid large after-Christmas discounts. This strategy doesn't always work well because consumers are often not predictable. Sometimes stores such as Abercrombie & Fitch do so well that they run out of popular merchandise, while other stores suffer subpar sales and end up with more merchandise than they need.

These retail companies have their hands full managing their current assets. Those that do it well, such as Walmart, establish a competitive advantage that helps increase their market share and often creates an increase in shareholder value through a rising stock price. This is why financial managers must carefully allocate resources among the current assets of the firm—cash, marketable securities, accounts receivable, and inventory. In managing cash and marketable securities, the primary concern should be for safety and liquidity—with secondary attention placed on maximizing profitability. As we move to accounts receivable and inventory, a stiffer profitability test must be met. The investment level should not be a result of happenstance or historical determination but must meet the same return-on-investment criteria applied to any decision. We may need to choose between a 20 percent increase in inventory and a new plant location or a major research program. We shall examine the decision techniques that are applied to the various forms of current assets.

Cash Management

Managing cash is becoming ever more sophisticated in the global and electronic age of the 21st century as financial managers try to squeeze the last dollar of profit out of their cash management strategies. Despite whatever lifelong teachings you might have learned about the virtues of cash, the corporate financial manager actively seeks to keep this nonearning asset to a minimum. The less cash you have, generally the better off you are, but still you do not want to get caught without cash when you need it. Minimizing cash balances as well as having accurate knowledge of when cash moves into and out of the company can improve overall corporate profitability. First we discuss the reasons for holding cash and then examine the cash flow cycle for the typical firm.

Reasons for Holding Cash Balances

There are several reasons for holding cash: for transactions balances, for compensating balances for banks, and for precautionary needs. The transactions motive involves the use of cash to pay for planned corporate expenses, such as supplies, payrolls, and taxes, but also can include planned acquisitions of long-term fixed assets. The second major reason for holding cash results from the practice of holding balances to compensate a bank for services provided rather than paying directly for those services.

Holding cash for precautionary motives assumes management wants cash for emergency purposes when cash inflows are less than projected. Precautionary cash balances are more likely to be important in seasonal or cyclical industries where cash inflows are more uncertain. Firms with precautionary needs usually rely on untapped lines of bank credit. For most firms, the primary motive for holding cash is the transactions motive.

Cash Flow Cycle

Cash balances are largely determined by cash flowing through the company on a daily, weekly, and monthly basis as determined by the **cash flow cycle**. As discussed in Chapter 4, the cash budget is a common tool used to track cash flows and resulting cash balances. Cash flow relies on the payment pattern of customers, the speed at which suppliers and creditors process checks, and the efficiency of the banking system. The primary consideration in managing the cash flow cycle is to ensure that inflows and outflows of cash are properly synchronized for transaction purposes. In Chapter 6, we discussed the cyclical nature of asset growth and its impact on cash, receivables, and inventory, and we now expand on that by examining the cash flow process more fully.

Figure 7-1 illustrates the simple cash flow cycle where the sale of finished goods or services produces either a cash sale or an account receivable for future collection.

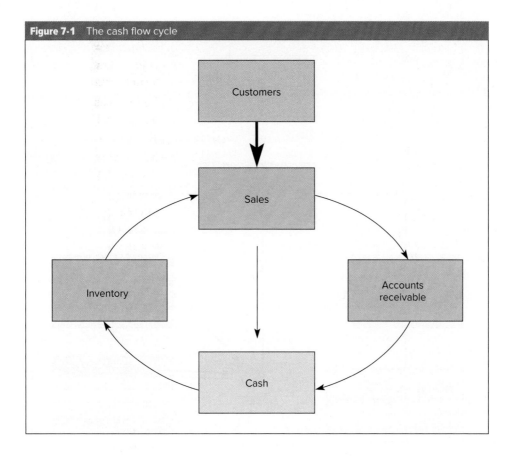

Figure 7-1 The cash flow cycle

Eventually the accounts receivable are collected and become cash, which is used to buy or produce inventory that is then sold. Thus the cash-generating process is continuous, even though the cash flow may be unpredictable and uneven.

Sales, receivables, and inventory form the basis for cash flow, but other activities in the firm can also affect cash inflows and outflows. The cash flow cycle presented in Figure 7-2 expands the detail and activities that influence cash. Cash inflows are driven by sales and influenced by the type of customers, their geographical location, the product being sold, and the industry.

A sale can be made for cash (Dairy Queen) or on credit (Target). Some industries, like textbook publishing, will grant credit terms of 60 days to bookstores; others, like department stores, will grant customers credit for 30 days.

One trend that is having a positive effect on cash flow is the rise of e-commerce sales. Most retailers have shopping websites, but you can only shop Amazon.com on the web. You can go to a search engine and type in the name of a retail chain and be directed to its website, where most likely you can sign up for the gift registry or create a wish list. One of the benefits of selling on the Internet is that customers have to buy with credit or debit cards, which generate cash flow much faster than a sale made with the retailer's own credit card that has 30-day payment terms. The credit card companies advance the cash to the retailer within 7–10 days. Because cash flow starts with the sale, financial managers have to pay attention to the percentage of sales generated by cash, by outside credit cards, and by the company's own credit cards.

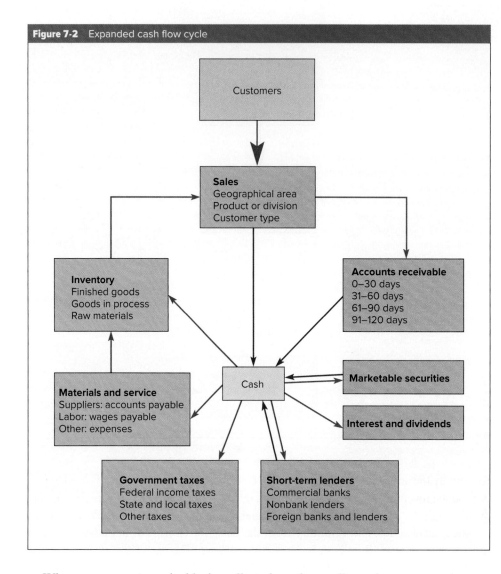

Figure 7-2   Expanded cash flow cycle

When an account receivable is collected or the credit card company advances payment, cash balances increase and the firm uses cash to pay interest to lenders, dividends to stockholders, taxes to the government, accounts payable to suppliers, and wages to workers and to replace inventory. When the firm has excess cash, it will invest in marketable securities, and when it needs cash for current assets, it will usually either sell marketable securities or borrow funds from short-term lenders.

Collections and Disbursements

Managing the cash inflows and payment outflows is one of the critical functions of the financial manager. New electronic transfer mediums are changing the time period between the mailing of a check and the collection period (float). While the cash flow cycle is still affected by collection mechanisms such as lockboxes, the U.S. mail system, and international sales, to name a few, the use of float became much

Information technology has a significant effect on the way companies manage the purchase of their inventory, the way they sell their goods, how they collect their money, and how they manage their cash. Electronic funds transfer systems, discussed later in the chapter, have been around for over 20 years, although their growth has accelerated in the last several years.

Two major trends will affect corporate practices and profitability for decades to come. The first trend is the creation and use of business-to-business (B2B) industry supply exchanges usually initiated by the "old" economy companies. The second trend is the use of auction markets, which have been created by "new" economy companies to allow businesses to buy and sell goods among themselves.

There are several examples of supply exchanges that will have a major impact on the industry. Covisint (www.covisint.com) is one of the highest-profile B2B exchanges and was launched in 2000. It is an industry-specific exchange originally supported by five of the largest automobile manufacturers in the world, including founders Ford, General Motors, Chrysler, Nissan, and Renault. "Covisint" stands for "cooperation, vision, and integration" and is an online marketplace where original equipment manufacturers (OEMs) and suppliers come together to do business in a single business environment using the same tools and user interface. It was created to reduce costs and increase efficiencies through its purchasing and bidding system.

At the beginning of 2018, Covisint—part of Open Text, a leader in Enterprise Information Management—had over 2,000 global customers and accounted for over $1 trillion with more than 212,000 clients. Covisint's customers included global automotive, health care, oil and gas, manufacturing, life sciences, and food and beverage industries.

The second trend in working capital management is the use of online auction companies for business-to-business markets such as Perfect Commerce (www.perfect.com) and Ariba (www.ariba.com).

Ariba got into the business in 2003 by acquiring FreeMarkets, a pioneer in the online auction market for industry. FreeMarkets developed specialties and qualified buyers and suppliers for more than 70 product categories such as coal, injection molded plastic parts, metal fabrications, chemicals, printed circuit boards, and more. Ariba is now part of SAP AG of Germany, an international technology, software, and consulting company. By the end of 2017, Ariba had connected with over 2.5 million companies in more than 190 countries. Its network executed over $2.5 billion in transactions daily, and the firm estimates that it saves customers millions of dollars in supply costs daily.

Perfect Commerce started out as a B2B auction site but like the others has broadened its scope to include what has developed into the word "spend policy." In other words, these companies help other companies spend their money wisely and efficiently through the use of e-commerce technology. Perfect Commerce has a stellar client list that includes Microsoft, Johnson Controls, ITT, Michelin, CEMEX, and the states of Missouri, New York, Idaho, and North Carolina. It serves over 2 million users in 100 countries with 20 languages. It works with major industries like chemical, energy, food products, hospitality, technology, education, retail, financial services, medical, manufacturing, transportation, and more.

The advantage of these auction sites is that they eliminate geographical barriers and allow suppliers from all over the world to bid on business that they would never have thought of soliciting before the Internet. The bidding processes have a time limit, which can be several hours or days. Just like any other auction, the participants get feedback on the bids made and can compete on price. The suppliers are prequalified so that they meet the manufacturing standards of the purchaser.

www.ariba.com

www.covisint.com

www.opentext.com

www.perfect.com

www.sap.com

less significant when the U.S. Congress passed the Check 21 Act in 2003. These issues are presented in detail in the following section.

Float

Some people are shocked to realize that cash listed on a balance sheet does not necessarily represent the company's actual cash in the bank. There are actually two cash balances of importance: the corporation's recorded amount and the amount credited to the corporation by the bank. The difference between the two is called **float**.

There are two kinds of float: mail float and clearing float. Mail float occurs because of the time it takes to deliver the mail. For example, say it takes three days for a check to arrive and the check clears on the day of arrival. That means there will be at least three days that the balance on the company's books is different from the balance on the bank's books. Clearing float takes place because of the time it takes to clear a check once a payment is made. Once a check is received in the mail and a deposit is made, the deposited funds may not be available for use until the check has cleared the banking system and has been credited to the corporate account.

Mail float may still exist for individuals and small businesses that use mail for their payments, but for most large corporations, mail float and clearing float don't exist anymore because of the widespread use of electronic payments made possible by the **Check Clearing for the 21st Century Act of 2003** (referred to as the **Check 21 Act**). This act allows banks and others to process checks electronically.[1]

When companies wire deposits and make payments electronically through the banking system, float is eliminated altogether. As part of the Federal Reserve Board's long-term strategy to respond to the declining use of checks in favor of electronic check processing, the Cleveland Federal Reserve Bank became the only clearing location in the Federal Reserve System on March 2, 2010. This is down from 45 locations in 2003 and reflects the impact of the Check 21 Act.

Improving Collections

A firm may further expedite the collection and check-clearing process through a number of strategies. A popular method is to utilize a variety of collection centers throughout the marketing area. An insurance company such as Allstate, with headquarters in Chicago, may have 75 collection offices dispersed throughout the country, each performing billing and collection-deposit functions.

For those who wish to enjoy the benefits of expeditious check clearance at lower costs, a **lockbox system** may replace the network of regional collection offices. A lockbox is usually a post office box close to the company's bank. The customer sends the check to the bank, and a bank employee picks up the check and processes the check electronically through Check 21 and credits the company's account with a deposit. The information is then electronically sent to the company's finance center to record the payment.

Extending Disbursements

Perhaps you have heard of the multimillion-dollar corporation with its headquarters located in the most exclusive office space in downtown Manhattan, but with its

---

[1]From www.federalreserve.gov/paymentsystems.

primary check disbursement center in Fargo, North Dakota. Though the firm may engage in aggressive speedup techniques in the processing of incoming checks, a slowdown pattern more aptly describes the payment procedures. While the preceding example represents an extreme case, the slowing of disbursements is not uncommon in cash management. It has even been given the title "extended disbursement float."

Cost-Benefit Analysis

An efficiently maintained cash management program can be an expensive operation. The use of remote collection and disbursement centers involves additional costs, and banks involved in the process will require that the firm maintain adequate deposit balances or pay sufficient fees to justify the services.

These expenses must be compared to the benefits that may accrue through the use of **cost-benefit analysis**. If a firm has an average daily remittance of $2 million and 1.5 days can be saved in the collection process by establishing a sophisticated collection network, the firm has freed $3 million for investment elsewhere. Also, through stretching the disbursement schedule by one day, perhaps another $2 million will become available for other uses. An example of this process is shown in Figure 7-3. If the firm is able to earn 10 percent on the $5 million that is freed up, as much as $500,000 may be expended on the administrative costs of cash management before the new costs are equal to the generated revenue.

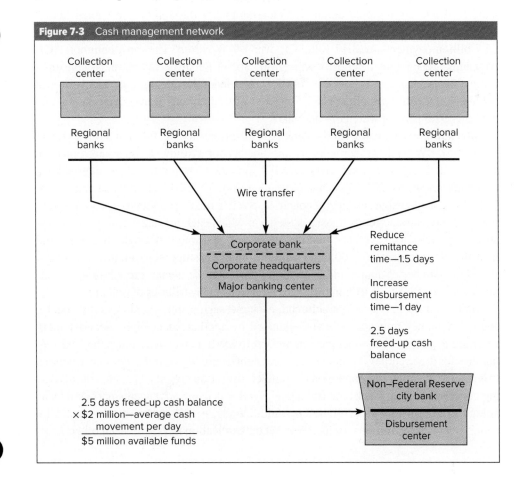

Figure 7-3   Cash management network

Electronic Funds Transfer

As previously mentioned, the techniques of delaying payment and using float are being reduced through the techniques of **electronic funds transfer**, a system in which funds are moved between computer terminals without the use of a "check." Through the use of terminal communication between the store and the bank, your debit card payment to the supermarket is automatically charged against your account at the bank before you walk out the door. Individuals can also use a bill pay service provided by their financial institution that allows bills to be paid electronically directly from their checking account. More recently some financial institutions have created mobile applications for cell phones that allow cash transfers between individuals.

Most large corporations have computerized cash management systems. For example, a firm may have 55 branch offices and 56 banks—one bank or branch of the same bank for each branch office and a lead bank in which the major corporate account is kept. At the end of each day, the financial manager can check all the company's bank accounts online. He or she can then electronically transfer all excess cash balances from each branch or regional bank to the corporate lead bank for overnight investment in money market securities.

Automated clearinghouses (ACHs) are an important element in electronic funds transfers. An ACH transfers information between one financial institution and another and from account to account. The ACH network universally connects all U.S. financial institutions and moves money and information directly from one bank account to another. There are regional automated clearinghouses throughout the United States, claiming total membership of over 10,000 financial institutions and processing over 25.7 billion payments in 2017 valued at over $46.8 trillion. The most common ACH payments are for direct deposits of payroll, Social Security, tax refunds, consumer bill payment, business-to-business transfers, and federal, state, and local government payments. In 2017 approximately 7.5 percent of transactions were governmental and the other 92.5 percent were commercial.

International electronic funds transfer is mainly carried out through SWIFT (www. swift.com). SWIFT is an acronym for the Society for Worldwide Interbank Financial Telecommunications. During 2017, SWIFT provided around-the-clock international payments on its SWIFT Financial Network (SWIFTNET FIN) between more than 11,353 financial institutions in 200 countries. SWIFT uses a proprietary secure messaging system (electronic funds transfer system) in which each message represents a transfer of currencies for payments, treasury, securities, and trade. A single message could be instructions to transfer $100 or $1 billion from one institution to another. Figure 7-4 shows the number of annual messages in millions and the annual growth in messages. Total volume of over 7.1 trillion messages represents many trillions of dollars.

Rigid security standards are enforced, each message is encrypted (secretly coded), and every money transaction is authenticated by another code. These security measures are important to the members as well as to SWIFT, which assumes the financial liability for the accuracy, completeness, and confidentiality of transaction instructions from and to the point of connection to member institution circuits. One area of increasing concern has been electronic fraud, and SWIFT is using advanced smart card technology to improve its security system. Additionally, it will automate the process by which financial institutions exchange secret authentication keys with each other.

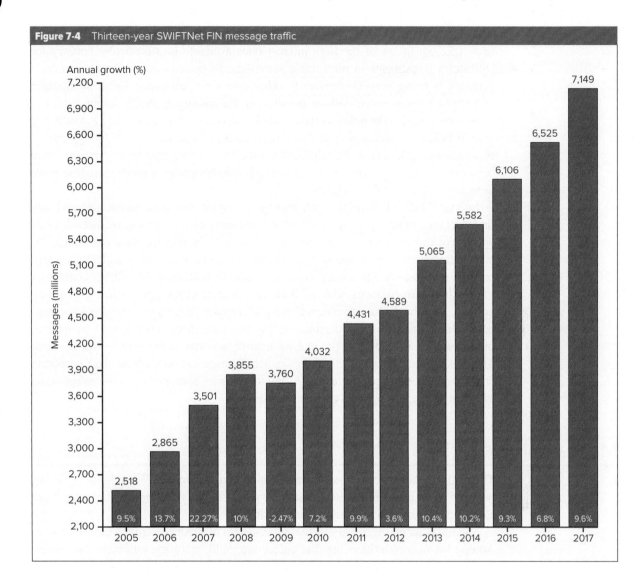

Figure 7-4   Thirteen-year SWIFTNet FIN message traffic

International Cash Management

Multinational corporations can shift funds from country to country much as a firm may transfer funds from regional banks to the lead bank. Just as financial institutions in the United States have become more involved in electronic funds transfer, an international payments system has also developed. However, international cash management has many differences from domestic cash management systems. Payment methods differ from country to country. In some countries, electronic payments are more common than in the United States. International cash management is more complex because liquidity management, involving short-term cash balances and deficits, has to be managed across international boundaries and time zones and is subject to the risks of currency fluctuations and interest rate changes in all countries. There are also differences in banking systems and check-clearing processes, account balance management, information reporting systems, and cultural, tax, and accounting differences.

A company may prefer to hold cash balances in one currency rather than another or to take advantage of the high interest rates available in a particular country for short-term investments in marketable securities. In periods in which one country's currency is rising in value relative to other currencies, an astute financial manager will try to keep as much cash as possible in the country with the strong currency. In periods in which the dollar is rising relative to other currencies, many balances are held in U.S. bank accounts or in dollar-denominated bank accounts in foreign banks, more commonly known as Eurodollar deposits. The international money markets have been growing in scope and size, so these markets have become a much more important aspect of efficient cash management.

International and domestic cash managers employ the same techniques and rely on forecasting methods using cash budgets and daily cash reports to predict cash balances. For those companies that are unable to actively manage their cash balances, banks often provide them special accounts to manage their cash flow and earn a return on their excess cash. The **sweep account** is one such account that allows companies to maintain zero balances with all their excess cash swept into an interest-earning account. Most banks have accounts that allow corporate clients to write checks on zero balance accounts with the understanding that when the check is presented for payment, money will be moved from the interest-bearing account to the appropriate account. These examples illustrate the way banks help manage excess cash for their corporate customers. The next section explains how companies manage their own excess cash balances by purchasing marketable securities.

Marketable Securities

The firm may hold excess funds in anticipation of a cash outlay. When funds are being held for other than immediate transaction purposes, they should be converted from cash into interest-earning marketable securities.[2]

The financial manager has a virtual supermarket of securities from which to choose. Among the factors influencing that choice are yield, maturity, minimum investment required, safety, and marketability. Under normal conditions, the longer the maturity period of the security, the higher the yield, as indicated in Figure 7-5.

The problem in "stretching out" the maturity of your investment is that you may have to take a loss. A $5,000 Treasury note issued initially at 5.5 percent, with three years to run, may be worth only $4,800 if the going interest rate climbs to 7 percent and the investor has to cash in before maturity. This risk is considerably greater as the maturity date is extended. A complete discussion of the "interest rate risk" is presented in Chapter 16, "Long-Term Debt and Lease Financing."

The various forms of marketable securities and investments, emphasizing the short term, are presented in Table 7-1. The key characteristics of each investment will be reviewed along with examples of yields at six different time periods.

As shown in Table 7-1, yields are given for six periods starting with March 22, 1980, when interest rates were extremely high because of double-digit inflation, and

---

[2]The one possible exception to this principle is found in the practice of holding compensating balances at commercial banks—a topic for discussion in Chapter 8.

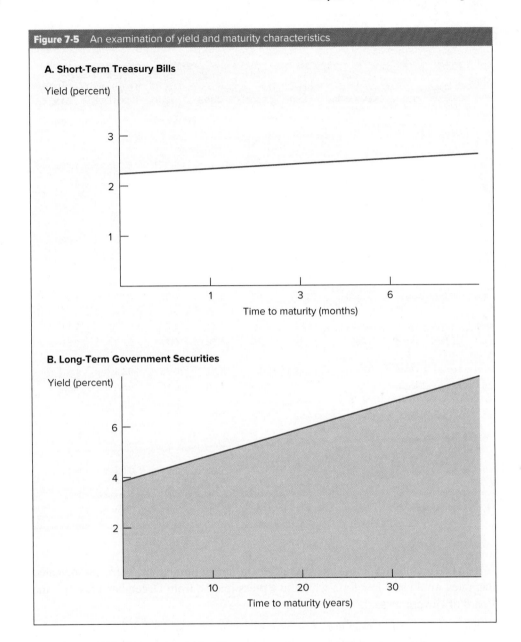

Figure 7-5   An examination of yield and maturity characteristics

A. Short-Term Treasury Bills

Yield (percent)

Time to maturity (months)

B. Long-Term Government Securities

Yield (percent)

Time to maturity (years)

ending with January 12, 2018. The Federal Reserve raised rates twice in 2016 and three times in 2017. Perhaps the July 2000 rates represent more normal rates than any of the other six periods. The low rates in 2003 represented an attempt by the Federal Reserve Board to stimulate an economy that had gone into recession during March 2001 and whose recovery was uncertain due to the terrorist attacks of 9/11/2001. Interest rates in 2010 through 2015 were even lower than in 2003 as the Federal Reserve kept rates low to help the economy recover from the worst financial crisis and longest recession since the Great Depression of the 1930s. As the economy improved in 2016 and 2017, rates were allowed to rise. The 2017 Tax Cuts and Jobs Act is expected to increase GDP in 2018, and as a result the Federal Reserve may step in to raise rates again if inflation approaches their 2 percent limit.

Table 7-1   Types of short-term investments

	Maturity	Minimum Amount	Safety	Marketability	Yield March 22, 1980	Yield July 14, 2000	Yield January 9, 2003	Yield May 14, 2010	Yield January 9, 2015	Yield January 12, 2018
Federal government securities:										
Treasury bills	3 months	$100	Excellent	Excellent	14.76%	6.06%	1.18%	0.16%	0.03%	1.43%
Treasury bills	6 months	$100	Excellent	Excellent	13.85	6.34	1.24	0.23	0.09	1.57
Federal agency securities:										
Federal Home Loan Bank	1 year	5,000	Excellent	Excellent	14.40	6.78	1.40	0.25	0.43	1.52
Nongovernment securities:										
Certificates of deposit (large)	3 months	100,000	Good	Good	16.97	6.65	1.29	0.38	0.27	1.31
Certificates of deposit (small)	3 months	500	Good	Poor	15.90	6.00	1.31	0.35	0.21	1.11
Commercial paper	3 months	25,000	Good	Fair	17.40	6.50	1.28	0.21	0.17	1.61
Banker's acceptances	3 months	None	Good	Good	17.22	6.51	1.31	0.35	0.23	1.62
Savings accounts	Open	None	Excellent	None	5.25	3.00	1.25	0.40	0.06	1.35
Money market funds	Open	500	Good	None	14.50	6.00	0.96	0.72	0.40	1.40
Money market deposit accounts (financial institutions)	Open	1,000	Excellent	None	—	5.50	1.20	0.57	0.08	1.35

Several of the above securities can be purchased with maturities longer than those indicated. The above are the most commonly quoted.

Sources: Various issues of *The Wall Street Journal, Barron's* magazine, and *Bank Rate Monitor*, and the St. Louis Federal Reserve Bank.

The Fed maintained a low interest rate environment throughout 2015 and indicated that rates would stay low for a while. In a press release from December 17, 2014, the Board of Governors said,

> When the Committee decides to begin to remove policy accommodation, it will take a balanced approach consistent with its longer-run goals of maximum employment and inflation of 2 percent. The Committee currently anticipates that, even after employment and inflation are near mandate-consistent levels, economic conditions may, for some time, warrant keeping the target federal funds rate below levels the Committee views as normal in the longer run.

Note that interest rates for various securities fell significantly between 1980 and 2015. Table 7-1 may very well show the high and low of interest rates for the post–World War II period.

Let us examine the characteristics of each security in Table 7-1. **Treasury bills** are short-term obligations of the federal government and are a popular place to "park funds" because of a large and active market. Although these securities are originally issued with maturities of 91 days and 182 days, the investor may buy an outstanding

T-bill with as little as one day remaining (perhaps two prior investors have held it for 45 days each).

With the government issuing new Treasury bills weekly, a wide range of choices is always available. Treasury bills are unique in that they trade on a discount basis— meaning the yield you receive occurs as a result of the difference between the price you pay and the maturity value.

Federal agency securities represent the offerings of such governmental organizations as the Federal Home Loan Bank and the Student Loan Marketing Association. Though lacking the direct backing of the U.S. Treasury, they are guaranteed by the issuing agency and provide all the safety that one would normally require. There is an excellent secondary market for agency securities that allows investors to sell an outstanding issue in an active and liquid market before the maturity date. Government agency issues pay slightly higher yields than direct Treasury issues.

Another outlet for investment is a **certificate of deposit (CD)**, offered by commercial banks, savings and loans, and other financial institutions. The investor places his or her funds on deposit at a specified rate over a given time period as evidenced by the certificate received. This is a two-tier market, with small CDs ($500 to $10,000) carrying lower interest rates, while larger CDs ($100,000 and more) have higher interest provisions and a degree of marketability for those who wish to sell their CDs before maturity. The CD market became fully deregulated by the federal government in 1986. CDs are normally insured (guaranteed) by the federal government for up to $250,000.

Comparable in yield and quality to large certificates of deposit, **commercial paper** represents unsecured promissory notes issued to the public by large business corporations. When Ford Motor Credit Corporation needs short-term funds, it may choose to borrow at the bank or expand its credit resources by issuing its commercial paper to the general public in minimum units of $25,000. Commercial paper is usually held to maturity by the investor, with no active secondary market in existence.

Banker's acceptances are short-term securities that generally arise from foreign trade. The acceptance is a draft drawn on a bank for payment when presented to the bank. The difference between a draft and a check is that a company does not have to deposit funds at the bank to cover the draft until the bank has accepted the draft for payment and presented it to the company. In the case of banker's acceptances arising from foreign trade, the draft may be accepted by the bank for *future* payment of the required amount. This means the exporter who now holds the banker's acceptance may have to wait 30, 60, or 90 days to collect the money. Because there is an active market for banker's acceptances, the exporter can sell the acceptance on a discount basis to any buyer and in this way receive the money before the importer receives the goods. This provides a good investment opportunity in banker's acceptances. Banker's acceptances rank close behind Treasury bills and certificates of deposit as vehicles for viable short-term investments.

Another popular international short-term investment arising from foreign trade is the **Eurodollar certificate of deposit**. The rate on this investment is usually higher than the rates on U.S. Treasury bills and bank certificates of deposit at large U.S. banks. Eurodollars are U.S. dollars held on deposit by foreign banks and in turn lent by those banks to anyone seeking dollars. Since the U.S. dollar is the only international currency accepted worldwide, any country can use it to help pay for goods purchased through international trade. Therefore, there is a large market for Eurodollar deposits and loans.

The lowest-yielding investment may well be a **passbook savings account** at a bank or a savings and loan. Although rates on savings accounts are no longer prescribed by federal regulation, they are still a relatively unattractive form of investment in terms of yield.

Of particular interest to the smaller investor is the **money market fund**—a product of the tight money periods of the 1970s and early 1980s. For as little as $500 or $1,000, an investor may purchase shares in a money market fund, which in turn reinvests the proceeds in higher-yielding $100,000 bank CDs, $25,000 to $100,000 commercial paper, and other large-denomination, higher-yielding securities. The investor then receives his or her pro rata portion of the interest proceeds daily as a credit to his or her shares.

Money market funds allow the small businessperson or investor to participate directly in higher-yielding securities. All too often in the past, the small investor was forced to place funds in low-yielding savings accounts while "smart" money was parked at higher yields in large-unit investments. Examples of money market funds are Dreyfus Liquid Assets Inc. and Fidelity Daily Income Trust. The investor can normally write checks on a money market fund.

Commercial banks, savings and loans, and credit unions are permitted by the regulatory agencies and Congress to offer **money market accounts** modeled after the money market funds. Due to deregulation, financial institutions are able to pay competitive market rates on money market deposit accounts. While there is not a federally prescribed minimum balance, the normal minimum is $1,000. Terms do vary from institution to institution. Generally these accounts may have only three deposits and three withdrawals per month and are not meant to be transaction accounts but a place to keep excess cash balances. They may be used by individuals or corporations but are more attractive to smaller firms than to larger firms (which have many more alternatives available). These accounts are insured up to $100,000 by federal agencies, which makes them slightly less risky than money market funds.

Although not a short-term investment as such, most financial institutions also offer NOW accounts. NOW accounts are checking accounts that pay interest. (These accounts are not included in Table 7-1 because their primary purpose is for check writing.)

Management of Accounts Receivable

An increasing portion of the investment in corporate assets has been in accounts receivable as expanding sales, fostered at times by inflationary pressures, have placed additional burdens on firms to carry larger balances for their customers. Frequently, recessions have also stretched out the terms of payment as small customers have had to rely on suppliers for credit. Accounts receivable as a percentage of total assets have increased relative to inventory, and this is a matter of concern for some corporations in their management of current assets.

Accounts Receivable as an Investment

As is true of other current assets, accounts receivable should be thought of as an investment. The level of accounts receivable should not be judged too high or too low based on historical standards of industry norms, but rather the test should be whether the level of return we are able to earn from this asset equals or exceeds the potential gain from other investments. For example, if we allow our customers five extra days to clear their accounts, our accounts receivable balance will increase—draining funds from marketable securities and perhaps drawing down the inventory level. We must ask whether we are optimizing our return, in light of appropriate risk and liquidity considerations.

An example of a buildup in accounts receivable is presented in Figure 7-6, with supportive financing provided through reducing lower-yielding assets and increasing lower-cost liabilities.

Credit Policy Administration

In considering the extension of credit, there are three primary policy variables to consider in conjunction with our profit objective:

1. Credit standards
2. Terms of trade
3. Collection policy

Credit Standards   The firm must determine the nature of the credit risk on the basis of prior records of payment, financial stability, current net worth, and other factors. When an account receivable is created, credit has been extended to the customer who is expected to repay according to the terms of trade. Bankers sometimes refer to the

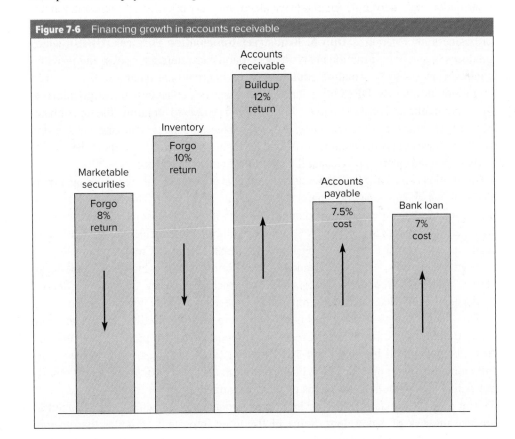

Figure 7-6 Financing growth in accounts receivable

5 Cs of credit (character, capital, capacity, conditions, and collateral) as an indication of whether a loan will be repaid on time, late, or not at all. *Character* refers to the moral and ethical quality of the individual who is responsible for repaying the loan. A person of principle or a company run by people of high ethical standards is expected to be a good credit risk. A decision on character is a judgment call on the part of the lender and is considered one of the most significant considerations when making a loan. *Capital* is the level of financial resources available to the company seeking the loan and involves an analysis of debt to equity and the firm's capital structure. *Capacity* refers to the availability and sustainability of the firm's cash flow at a level high enough to pay off the loan. *Conditions* refers to the sensitivity of the operating income and cash flows to the economy. Some industries such as automobiles, chemicals, and paper are quite cyclical and exhibit wide fluctuations in cash flows as the economy moves through the economic cycle of contraction and expansion. The more sensitive the cash flow to the economy, the greater the credit risk of the firm. When the economy is in a recession, business health in general is weaker, and most firms are riskier. *Collateral* is determined by the assets that can be pledged against the loan. Much as an automobile serves as collateral for a car loan or a house for a mortgage, companies can pledge assets that are available to be sold by the lender if the loan is not repaid. Obviously, the better the quality of the collateral, the lower the risk of the loan.

The assessment of credit risk and the setting of reasonable credit standards that allow marketing and finance to set goals and objectives together are based on the ability to get information and analyze it. An extensive electronic network of credit information has been developed by credit agencies throughout the country. The most prominent source of business information is **Dun & Bradstreet Information Services (DBIS)**, which produces business information analysis tools, publishes reference books, and provides computer access to information contained in its international database of more than 40 million businesses. DBIS has a large staff of analysts constantly updating information from public and private sources. Information is gathered, detailing the line of business, net worth, size of the company, years in business, management, and much more. DBIS produces many different reports, but its Business Information Report (BIR) is its cornerstone information product and a credit decision support tool.

In addition to the BIR, Dun & Bradstreet is known for a variety of credit scoring reports that rank a company's payment habits relative to its peer group. This is very important when, for example, a company is doing business with a new customer and there is no track record of orders and payment. Some of the other reports include a Supplier Evaluation, a Commercial Credit Scoring Report, a Small Business Credit Scoring Report, a Payment Analysis Report, a Financial Stress Report, and an Industry Credit Score Report. Table 7-2 presents the first page of the Trucking Industry Credit Score Report. Understanding the details is not as important as understanding the general concept.

Dun & Bradstreet's Credit Scoring products help facilitate credit decisions on more than 10 million U.S. businesses. Credit Score reports can help predict the likelihood that a company will become severely delinquent (90+ days past term) in paying its bills for a 12-month period. Small business and industry-specific credit score reports are available, and the information is continuously updated.

The credit scores are based on D&B's statistical models, which are designed to analyze the risk of a bad debt. Some of the more important variables that go into these models include the age of the company in years, negative public records (suits,

Table 7-2 Dun & Bradstreet report

Trucking Industry Credit Score Level 2: ■
Gorman Manufacturing Company*

COPYRIGHT 1999 DUN & BRADSTREET INC. - PROVIDED UNDER CONTRACT
FOR THE EXCLUSIVE USE OF SUBSCRIBER 230-151290

TRUCKING INDUSTRY CREDIT SCORE REPORT
LEVEL TWO

D-U-N-S: 80-473-5132			DATE PRINTED:	January 20, 1999
			BUSINESS RECORD DATE:	October 12, 1998
GORMAN MANUFACTURING COMPANY, INC				
(AND BRANCH(ES) OR DIVISION(S))			BUSINESS SUMMARY	
			CONTROL:	1965
492 KOLLER STREET			EMPLOYS:	105
SAN FRANCISCO, CA 94110			NET WORTH:	$2,838,982
TEL: 650-555-0000				
			SIC:	27 52
			LOB:	COMMERCIAL PRINTING

PAYMENTS REPORTED FROM MEMBERS OF THE TRUCKING INDUSTRY
(amounts may be rounded to nearest figure in prescribed ranges)

Antic	- Anticipated	(Payments received prior to date of invoice)
Disc	- Discounted	(Payments received within trade discount period)
Ppt	- Prompt	(Payments received within terms granted)

REPORTED	PAYING RECORD	HIGH CREDIT	NOW OWES	PAST DUE	SELLING TERMS	LAST SALE WITHIN
06/98	Ppt	1,000	500	0	N30	
04/98	(002)	0	0	0		
	Satisfactory					
03/98	Ppt	100,000	20,000	0	N30	1 mo
	Slow 15	90,000	70,000	0	N30	1 mo
	Slow 210	2,500	2,500	2,500		1 mo
	(006)	7,500	7,500	7,500		1 mo
	Placed for collection					
	(007)	2,500	1,000	1,000	N30	1 mo

Accounts are sometimes placed for collection even though the existence or amount of the debt is disputed.

Payment experiences reflect how bills are met in relation to the terms granted. In some instances payment beyond terms can be the result of disputes over merchandise, skipped invoices etc.

Each experience shown represents a separate account reported by a supplier. Updated trade experiences replace those previously reported.

The TRUCKING INDUSTRY CREDIT RISK SCORE predicts the likelihood of a firm paying trucking bills in a delinquent manner (90 Days Past Terms) during the next 12 months, based on the information in Dun & Bradstreet's files. The score was calculated using statistically valid models derived from D&B's extensive information files and includes analysis of the trucking industry payment information.

The PERCENTILE ranks the firm relative to all businesses who use trucking services. For example, a firm in the 80th percentile is a better risk than 79% of all trucking customers.

The INCIDENCE OF DELINQUENT PAYMENT is the proportion of trucking customers with scores in this range that were reported 90 days past due by members of the trucking industry. The incidence of delinquent payment for the entire population of trucking customers was 11.8% over the past year.

TRUCKING INDUSTRY CREDIT RISK SCORE: (1 HIGHEST RISK – 100 LOWEST RISK)	24
PERCENTILE:	1
INCIDENCE OF DELINQUENT PAYMENT FOR TRUCKING CUSTOMERS WITH SCORES 21 – 25:	74.2%

Source: Dun & Bradstreet.
*This is a fictitious company used by D&B for demonstration purposes.

liens, judgments, and virtually all business bankruptcy filing, etc.), total number of employees, facility ownership, financial statement data, payment index information, and satisfactory or slow payment experiences. The model is intended to predict payment problems as much as 12 months before they occur.

Given that the world is doing more and more business on a global scale, being able to track companies around the world using a database containing over 40 million listings is a big advantage. The companies in the database can be verified through a D-U-N-S® Number, which is accepted by the United Nations and other international organizations as a global business identification standard. The **Data Universal Number System (D-U-N-S)** is a unique nine-digit code assigned by Dun & Bradstreet Information Services (DBIS) to each business in its information base. The D-U-N-S number can be used to track whole families of companies that are related through ownership. Subsidiaries, divisions, and branches can be linked to their ultimate parent company at the top of the family pyramid. For example, this tracking ability could be useful to identify additional sales opportunities within a corporate family. An example of this hierarchical relationship is shown in Figure 7-7 for Gorman Printing Company Inc. Clearly the use of information databases will continue to save companies time and money in their credit decisions.

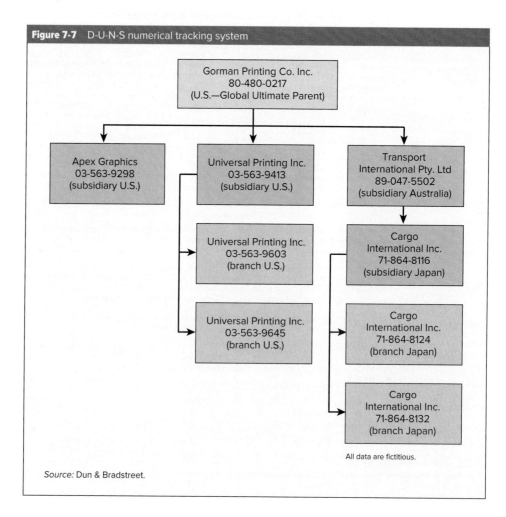

Figure 7-7   D-U-N-S numerical tracking system

Source: Dun & Bradstreet.

Terms of Trade   The stated terms of credit extension will have a strong impact on the eventual size of the accounts receivable balance. If a firm averages $5,000 in daily credit sales and allows 30-day terms, the average accounts receivable balance will be $150,000. If customers are carried for 60 days, we must maintain $300,000 in receivables and much additional financing will be required.

In establishing credit terms, the firm should also consider the use of a cash discount. Offering the terms 2/10, net 30, enables the customer to deduct 2 percent from the face amount of the bill when paying within the first 10 days; but if the discount is not taken, the customer must remit the full amount within 30 days.

Collection Policy   In assessing collection policy, a number of quantitative measures may be applied to the credit department of the firm.

a.   Average collection period $= \dfrac{\text{Accounts receivable}}{\text{Average daily credit sales}}$

An increase in the **average collection period** may be the result of a predetermined plan to expand credit terms or the consequence of poor credit administration.

b.   Ratio of bad debts to credit sales.

An increasing ratio may indicate too many weak accounts or an aggressive market expansion policy.

c.   Aging of accounts receivables.

Aging of accounts receivable is one way of finding out if customers are paying their bills within the time prescribed in the credit terms. If there is a buildup in receivables beyond normal credit terms, cash inflows will suffer, and more stringent credit terms and collection procedures may have to be implemented. An aging schedule is presented to illustrate the concept.

	Age of Receivables, May 31, 20X1		
Month of Sales	**Age of Account (days)**	**Amounts**	**Percent of Account Due**
May	0–30	$ 60,000	60%
April	31–60	25,000	25
March	61–90	5,000	5
February	91–120	10,000	10
Total receivables		$100,000	100%

If the normal credit terms are 30 days, the firm is doing something wrong because 40 percent of accounts are overdue with 10 percent over 90 days outstanding.

An Actual Credit Decision

We now examine a credit decision that brings together the various elements of accounts receivable management. Assume a firm is considering selling to a group of customers that will bring $10,000 in new annual sales, of which 10 percent will be uncollectible. While this is a very high rate of nonpayment, the critical question is, What is the potential contribution to profitability?

Assume the collection cost on these accounts is 5 percent and the cost of producing and selling the product is 77 percent of the sales dollar. We are in a 40 percent tax bracket. The profit on new sales is as follows:

Additional sales	$10,000
Accounts uncollectible (10% of new sales)	1,000
Annual incremental revenue	$ 9,000
Collection costs (5% of new sales)	500
Production and selling costs (77% of new sales)	7,700
Annual income before taxes	$ 800
Taxes (40%)	320
Annual incremental income after taxes	$ 480

Though the return on sales is only 4.8 percent ($480/$10,000), the return on invested dollars may be considerably higher. Let us assume the only new investment in this case is a buildup in accounts receivable. (Present inventory and fixed assets are sufficient to support the higher sales level.) Assume an analysis of our accounts indicates a turnover ratio of 6 to 1 between sales and accounts receivable. Our new accounts receivable balance will average $1,667.

$$\text{Accounts receivable} = \frac{\text{Sales}^3}{\text{Turnover}} = \frac{\$10,000}{6} = \$1,667$$

Thus we are committing an average investment of only $1,667 to provide an aftertax return of $480, so that the yield is a very attractive 28.8 percent. If the firm had a minimum required aftertax return of 10 percent, this would clearly be an acceptable investment. We might ask next if we should consider taking on 12 percent or even 15 percent in uncollectible accounts—remaining loyal to our concept of maximizing return on investment and forsaking any notion about risky accounts being inherently good or bad.

Inventory Management

In a manufacturing company, inventory is usually divided into the three basic categories: raw materials used in the product; work in process, which reflects partially finished products; and finished goods, which are ready for sale. All these forms of inventory need to be financed, and their efficient management can increase a firm's profitability. The amount of inventory is not always totally controlled by company management because it is affected by sales, production, and economic conditions.

Because of its cyclical sales that are highly sensitive to the U.S. economic business climate, the automobile industry is a good case study in inventory management. The automakers have often suffered from inventory buildups when sales declined because adjusting production levels requires time.

Because inventory is the least liquid of current assets, it should provide the highest yield to justify the investment. While the financial manager may have direct control over cash management, marketable securities, and accounts receivable, control over

---

[3]We could actually argue that our out-of-pocket commitment to sales is 82 percent (77 percent production and sales costs plus 5 percent collection costs) times $10,000, or $8,200. This would indicate an even smaller commitment to receivables.

inventory policy is generally shared with production management and marketing. Let us examine some key factors influencing inventory management.

Level versus Seasonal Production

A manufacturing firm must determine whether a plan of level or seasonal production should be followed. Level production was discussed in Chapter 6. While level (even) production throughout the year allows for maximum efficiency in the use of manpower and machinery, it may result in unnecessarily high inventory buildups before shipment, particularly in a seasonal business. For example, a bathing suit manufacturer would not want excess suits in stock in November.

If we produce on a seasonal basis, the inventory problem is eliminated, but we will then have unused capacity during slack periods. Furthermore, as we shift to maximum operations to meet seasonal needs, we may be forced to pay overtime wages to labor and to sustain other inefficiencies as equipment is overused.

We have a classic problem in financial analysis. Are the cost savings from level production sufficient to justify the extra expenditure in carrying inventory? Let us look at a typical case.

	Production	
	Level	Seasonal
Average inventory	$100,000	$70,000
Operating costs—aftertax	50,000	60,000

Though $30,000 more will have to be invested in average inventory under level production (first line), $10,000 will be saved in operating costs (second line). This represents a 33 percent return on investment. If the required rate of return is 10 percent, this is clearly an acceptable alternative.

Inventory Policy in Inflation (and Deflation)

The price of copper went from $3.00 to $0.50 a pound and back to $4.00 during the last two decades. Similar price instability has occurred in wheat, sugar, lumber, and a number of other commodities. Only the most astute inventory manager can hope to prosper in this type of environment. The problem can be partially controlled by taking moderate inventory positions (not fully committing at one price).

Another way of protecting an inventory position is by hedging with a futures contract to buy or sell at a stipulated price some months from now.

Rapid price movements in inventory may also have a major impact on the reported income of the firm, a process described in Chapter 3, "Financial Analysis." A firm using FIFO (first-in, first-out) accounting may experience large inventory profits when old, less expensive inventory is written off against new, high prices in the marketplace. The benefits may be transitory, as the process reverses itself when prices decline.

The Inventory Decision Model

Substantial research has been devoted to determining optimum inventory size, order quantity, usage rate, and similar considerations. An entire branch in the field of operations research is dedicated to the subject.

In developing an inventory model, we must evaluate the two basic costs associated with inventory: the carrying costs and the ordering costs. Through a careful analysis of both of these variables, we can determine the optimum order size that minimizes costs.

Carrying Costs   Carrying costs include interest on funds tied up in inventory and the costs of warehouse space, insurance premiums, and material handling expenses. There is also an implicit cost associated with the dangers of obsolescence or perishability and rapid price change. The larger the order we place, the greater the average inventory we will have on hand, and the higher the carrying costs.

Ordering Costs   As a second factor, we must consider the **cost of ordering and processing inventory into stock. If we maintain a relatively low average inventory in stock, we must order many times, and total ordering costs will be high. The opposite patterns associated with the two costs are portrayed in Figure 7-8.

As the order size increases, carrying costs go up because we have more inventory on hand. With larger orders, of course, we will order less frequently and overall ordering costs will go down. We can best judge the trade-off between the two by examining the total cost curve. At point *M* on that curve, we have appropriately played the advantages and disadvantages of the respective costs against each other. With larger orders,

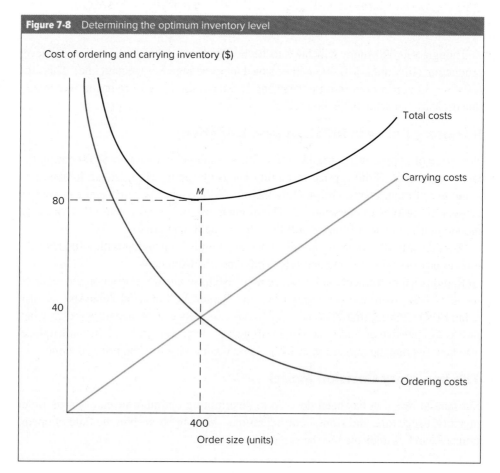

Figure 7-8   Determining the optimum inventory level

carrying costs will be excessive, while at a reduced order size, constant ordering will put us at an undesirably high point on the ordering cost curve.

Economic Ordering Quantity

The question becomes this: How do we mathematically determine the minimum point (*M*) on the total cost curve? We may use the following formula:

$$EOQ = \sqrt{\frac{2SO}{C}} \qquad (7\text{-}1)$$

EOQ is the **economic ordering quantity**, the most advantageous amount for the firm to order each time. We will determine this value, translate it into average inventory size, and determine the minimum total cost amount (*M*). The terms in the EOQ formula are defined as follows:

$S =$ Total sales in units.

$O =$ Ordering cost for each order.

$C =$ Carrying cost per unit in dollars.

Let us assume that we anticipate selling 2,000 units; it will cost us $8 to place each order; and the price per unit is $1, with a 20 percent carrying cost to maintain the average inventory, resulting in a carrying charge per unit of $0.20. Plugging these values into our formula, we show

$$EOQ = \sqrt{\frac{2SO}{C}} = \sqrt{\frac{2 \times 2{,}000 \times \$8}{\$0.20}} = \sqrt{\frac{\$32{,}000}{\$0.20}} = \sqrt{160{,}000}$$
$$= 400 \text{ units}$$

The optimum order size is 400 units. On the assumption that we will use up inventory at a constant rate throughout the year, our average inventory on hand will be 200 units, as indicated in Figure 7-9. Average inventory equals EOQ/2.

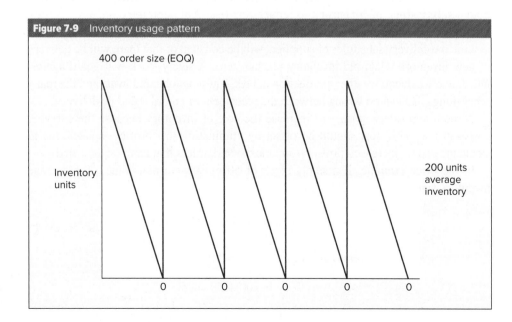

Figure 7-9   Inventory usage pattern

400 order size (EOQ)

Inventory units

200 units average inventory

Our total costs with an order size of 400 and an average inventory size of 200 units are computed in Table 7-3.

Table 7-3   Total costs for inventory

1. Ordering $= \dfrac{2,000}{400} = \dfrac{\text{Units}}{\text{Order size}} = 5$ orders

5 orders at $8 per order = $40

2. Carrying costs = Average inventory in units × Carrying cost per unit

200 × $0.20 = $40

3. Order cost	$ 40
Carrying cost	+ 40
Total cost	$ 80

Point *M* in Figure 7-8 can be equated to a total cost of $80 at an order size of 400 units. At no other order point can we hope to achieve lower costs. The same basic principles of total cost minimization that we have applied to inventory can be applied to other assets as well. For example, we may assume cash has a carrying cost (opportunity cost of lost interest on marketable securities as a result of being in cash) and an ordering cost (transaction costs of shifting in and out of marketable securities) and then work toward determining the optimum level of cash. In each case, we are trying to minimize the overall costs and increase profit.

Safety Stock and Stockouts

In our analysis thus far, we have assumed we would use inventory at a constant rate and would receive new inventory when the old level of inventory reached zero. We have not specifically considered the problem of being out of stock.

A stockout occurs when a firm is out of a specific inventory item and is unable to sell or deliver the product. The risk of losing sales to a competitor may cause a firm to hold a **safety stock of inventory** to reduce this risk. Although the company may use the EOQ model to determine the optimum order quantity, management cannot always assume the delivery schedules of suppliers will be constant or that there will be delivery of new inventory when old inventory reaches zero. A safety stock will guard against late deliveries due to weather, production delays, equipment breakdowns, and the many other things that can go wrong between the placement of an order and its delivery.

A minimum safety stock will increase the cost of inventory because the carrying cost will rise. This cost should be offset by eliminating lost profits on sales due to stockouts and by increased profits from unexpected orders that can now be filled.

In the prior example, if a safety stock of 50 units were maintained, the average inventory figure would be 250 units.

$$\text{Average inventory} = \frac{\text{EOQ}}{2} + \text{Safety stock} \qquad (7\text{-}2)$$

$$\text{Average inventory} = \frac{400}{2} = 50$$

$$= 200 + 50 = 250$$

NASA Experiments with Inventory Tracking on the International Space Station (ISS)

Normally when we think about inventory control, we think about corporations that have a product to sell, but that doesn't mean that governmental agencies, like the National Aeronautics and Space Administration (NASA), can't use the same technology used by Walmart and other companies to manage and track inventory. On earth, many companies use radio frequency ID (RFID) systems to track inventory through the supply chain. Usually, RFID chips are quite inexpensive and can be attached to large shipments of everything from pharmaceuticals to household products. Many trucking companies use this technology to keep track of their shipments and estimate the time of arrival at their destinations.

The International Space Station (ISS) is the size of a football field, and gravity does not hold items down to the floor. Items are stored in containers attached to walls or piles of cargo bags secured to the floor; otherwise, they would float around and cause serious damage. So NASA is experimenting with RFID chips on the ISS to track supplies and to help the astronauts find everything from personal supplies to equipment for scientific experiments. NASA is developing a system, called RFID-Enabled Autonomous Logistics Management (REALM) (RFID Logistics Awareness), that tests a radio-based inventory control system in space. One goal of this system is to reduce the time it takes for the crew to perform inventory audits. Since the space station is supplied infrequently by rocket ships carrying supplies, it is extremely important for the astronauts to know their precise needs.

While much of the technology is similar to that used on earth, it includes new adaptations to deal with the concept of microgravity. In 2008, the crew began by using handheld RFID readers that replaced the optical bar-code readers they had been using. The use of RFID has become more sophisticated and now includes smaller antennas and more automated methods augmented by intelligent software, which NASA hopes will free up the crew from having to use the handheld devices to inventory items individually. Because many items may be in the same container or bag, the readers can get a little confused, so what is required in space is a very high read accuracy of 100 percent. At least that is the goal.

One way of achieving 100 percent accuracy is to use zone-based RFID, so that items are stored in zones, as well as intelligent software with which they can infer where the items are located when real-time reads are not available. NASA is also experimenting with "smart" enclosures and containers; two smart drawers are currently in use on the space station. These smart containers contain radio antennas and are able to enhance the accuracy of the RFID reader. It is hoped that this new system will be successful and save time, will record the consumption of important supplies, and will provide accurate information so that supply shipments will include everything the astronauts need for six or more months in space.

Source: "RFID-Enabled Autonomous Logistics Management (REALM) (RFID Logistics Awareness)," December 13, 2017, www.nasa.gov/mission_pages/station/research/experiments/2137.html (accessed January 15, 2018).

www.nasa.gov

The inventory carrying cost will now increase to $50.

$$\text{Carrying costs} = \text{Average inventory in units} \times \text{Carrying cost per unit}$$
$$= 250 \times \$0.20 = \$50$$

The amount of safety stock that a firm carries is likely to be influenced by the predictability of inventory usage and the time period necessary to fill inventory orders. The following discussion indicates that safety stock may be reduced in the future.

Just-in-Time Inventory Management

Just-in-time inventory management (JIT) was designed for Toyota by the Japanese firm Shigeo Shingo and found its way to the United States. Just-in-time inventory management is part of a total production concept that often interfaces with a total quality control program. A JIT program has several basic requirements: (1) quality production that continually satisfies customer requirements; (2) close ties among suppliers, manufacturers, and customers; and (3) minimization of the level of inventory.

Usually suppliers are located near manufacturers and are able to fill orders in small lot sizes because of short delivery times. One side effect has been for manufacturers to reduce their number of suppliers to assure quality as well as to ease the complexity of ordering and delivery. Computerized ordering/inventory tracking systems both on the assembly line and in the supplier's production facility are necessary for JIT to work.

Cost Savings from Lower Inventory   Cost savings from lower levels of inventory and reduced financing costs are supposed to be the major benefits of JIT. On average, it is estimated that over the last decade just-in-time inventory systems have reduced inventory-to-sales ratios by over 10 percent. Some individual cases are more dramatic.

Harley-Davidson reduced its in-process and in-transit inventory by $20 million at a single plant and lowered overall inventory by 75 percent. In one sense, the manufacturer pushes some of the cost of financing onto the supplier. If the supplier also imposes JIT on its suppliers, these efficiencies work their way down the supplier chain to create a leaner production system for the whole economy.

Other Benefits   There are other, not so obvious cost savings to just-in-time inventory systems. Because of reduced warehouse space for inventory, some plants in the automotive industry have reduced floor space by 70 percent over the more traditional plants that warehoused inventory. This saves construction costs and reduces overhead expenses for utilities and manpower. The JIT systems have been aided in the last few years by the development of the Internet and electronic data interchange (EDI) systems between suppliers and production and manufacturing departments. EDI reduces rekeying errors and duplication of forms for the accounting and finance functions. Xerox implemented a quality process along with JIT and reduced its supplier list to 450, which provided a $15 million savings in quality control programs. Reductions in costs from quality control are often overlooked by financial analysts because JIT prevents defects rather than detecting poor quality; therefore, no cost savings are recognized. One last item is the elimination of waste, which is one of the side benefits of a total quality control system coupled with just-in-time inventory systems.

It is important to realize that the just-in-time inventory system is very compatible with the concept of economic ordering quantity. The focus is to balance reduced carrying costs from maintaining less inventory with increased ordering costs. Fortunately, electronic data interchange minimizes the impact of having to place orders more often.

The Downside of JIT   Major U.S. companies such as Walmart, Harley-Davidson, McDonald's, Dell, Cisco, and Hewlett-Packard use just-in-time inventory management.

When JIT methods work as planned, firms are able to maintain very little inventory, reduce warehouse storage space, and reduce the cost of financing a large inventory. Some JIT management systems allow inventory levels ranging from 1 hour's worth of parts to a maximum of 16 hours' worth. However, there are costs associated with an integrated JIT system. These costs should not be overlooked.

When JIT works, it saves money, but there can be problems. This is a lesson the electronics market learned painfully in 2000. Parts shortages led to lost sales and slowing growth for the electronics industry. Parts that took 4 weeks to get in 1998 and 1999 were taking 40 weeks in July of 2000. Some high-frequency cell phone transistors needed to be ordered 18 months in advance. Industry experts said that the huge multinationals used to have one month's supplies of inventory. The industry got caught short without the capacity to produce parts for the hot growth items of cell phones, computers, handheld devices, and more. The failure of JIT was that sales increased much more rapidly than forecast, and manufacturers could not keep up with the demand.

The opposite happened during the recession and the slow economies of 2001–2002 and 2007–2009. Sales dropped so fast that even with JIT systems, inventory piled up at suppliers and manufacturers. Eventually sales forecasts and production schedules were adjusted and inventory levels changed. The tsunami in Japan during 2011 created JIT problems but probably not as many as the October 2011 floods in Thailand that shut down half the world's supply of computer hard drives. The floods resulted in a shortage of computers, and it took more than six months to get production back on track. This one event gave solid state drives a chance to take market share away from disk drives. More recently, Hurricane Maria in Puerto Rico in the fall of 2017 caused a shortage of intravenous bags used for transfusions of blood, saline solutions, and other medical uses. One lesson learned is to have a diverse geographical set of suppliers.

SUMMARY

This chapter on current asset management extends our discussion of Chapter 6 by focusing on the management of cash, marketable securities, accounts receivable, and inventory. An overriding concept in current asset management is that the less liquid an asset, the higher the required return.

In cash management, the primary goal should be to keep the cash balances as low as possible, consistent with the notion of maintaining adequate funds for transactions purposes and compensating balances. Cash moves through the firm in a cycle as customers make payments and the firm pays its bills. We try to speed the inflow of funds and defer their outflow in managing the company's cash balances. The increased use of electronic funds transfer systems both domestically and internationally is reducing float and making collections and disbursements more timely. The use of electronic payment mechanisms, such as automated clearinghouses and the Check 21 Act, have changed the way management manages collections and payments. We are moving toward a checkless society.

One principle of cash management is not to let excess cash sit in banks and checking accounts when those cash balances could be earning a higher rate of return. Excess short-term funds may be placed in marketable securities—with a wide selection of issues, maturities, and yields from which to choose. The choices are summarized in Table 7-1.

The management of accounts receivable calls for the determination of credit standards and the forms of credit to be offered as well as the development of an effective collection policy. There is no such thing as bad credit—only unprofitable credit extension. It should also be understood that the accounts receivable policy is related to the inventory management policy.

Inventory is the least liquid of the current assets, so it should provide the highest yield. We recognize three inventory types: raw materials, work in process, and finished goods. We manage inventory levels through models such as the economic ordering quantity (EOQ) model, which helps us determine the optimum average inventory size that minimizes the total cost of ordering and carrying inventory. The just-in-time inventory management model (JIT) focuses on minimizing inventory, through quality production techniques and close ties between manufacturers and suppliers. Both EOQ and JIT models are compatible and can work together in the management of inventory.

It seems like a simple concept, but it needs to be stated that the company that manages its current assets efficiently will minimize (or optimize) its investment in them, thereby freeing up funds for other corporate uses. The result will be higher profitability and return on total assets for the firm.

LIST OF TERMS

cash flow cycle   192
float   196
Check Clearing for the 21st Century
   Act of 2003 (Check 21 Act)   196
lockbox system   196
cost-benefit analysis   197
electronic funds transfer   198
automated clearinghouses (ACHs)   198
international electronic funds
   transfer   198
sweep account   200
Treasury bills   202
federal agency securities   203
certificate of deposit (CD)   203
commercial paper   203
banker's acceptances   203
Eurodollar certificate of deposit   203

passbook savings account   204
money market fund   204
money market accounts   204
5 Cs of credit   206
Dun & Bradstreet Information
   Services (DBIS)   206
Data Universal Number System
   (D-U-N-S)   208
average collection period   209
aging of accounts receivable   209
carrying costs   212
cost of ordering   212
economic ordering quantity
   (EOQ)   213
safety stock of inventory   214
just-in-time inventory management
   (JIT)   216

DISCUSSION QUESTIONS

1. In the management of cash and marketable securities, why should the primary concern be for safety and liquidity rather than maximization of profit? *(LO7-2 & 7-3)*

2. Explain the similarities and differences of lockbox systems and regional collection offices. *(LO7-2)*

3. Why would a financial manager want to slow down disbursements? *(LO7-2)*

4. Use *The Wall Street Journal* or some other financial publication to find the going interest rates for the list of marketable securities in Table 7-1. Which security would you choose for a short-term investment? Why? *(LO7-3)*

5. Why are Treasury bills a favorite place for financial managers to invest excess cash? *(LO7-3)*

6. Explain why the bad debt percentage or any other similar credit-control percentage is not the ultimate measure of success in the management of accounts receivable. What is the key consideration? *(LO7-4)*

7. What are three quantitative measures that can be applied to the collection policy of the firm? *(LO7-4)*

8. What are the 5 Cs of credit that are sometimes used by bankers and others to determine whether a potential loan will be repaid? *(LO7-4)*

9. What does the EOQ formula tell us? What assumption is made about the usage rate for inventory? *(LO7-5)*

10. Why might a firm keep a safety stock? What effect is it likely to have on carrying cost of inventory? *(LO7-5)*

11. If a firm uses a just-in-time inventory system, what effect is that likely to have on the number and location of suppliers? *(LO7-5)*

PRACTICE PROBLEMS AND SOLUTIONS

1. Abbott Communications has annual credit sales of $1,800,000 and accounts receivable of $190,000. What is the average collection period?

Average collection period
(LO7-4)

2. Archer Chemical is thinking about extending trade credit to new customers. Sales would increase by $80,000 if credit were extended to these customers. Of the new accounts receivable related to these sales, 8 percent would be uncollectible. Additional collection costs would be 4 percent of sales, and selling and collection costs would be 80 percent of sales. The firm is in a 30 percent tax bracket.

Credit policy decision
(LO7-4)

   a. Compute the new income after taxes.

   b. What will be the percentage return on the new sales?

   c. If accounts receivable are turned over four times a year, what will be the new investment in accounts receivable?

   d. What will be the return on investment assuming the only new investment will be in accounts receivable?

Solutions

1. Average collection period $= \dfrac{\text{Accounts receivable}}{\text{Average daily credit sales}}$

   Accounts receivable $= \$190,000$

   Average daily credit sales $= \dfrac{\text{Credit sales}}{360} = \dfrac{\$1,800,000}{360} = \$5,000$

   Average collection period $= \dfrac{\$190,000}{5,000} = 38$ days

2. *a.*

Additional sales	$80,000
Accounts uncollectible (8% of new sales)	6,400
Annual incremental revenue	$73,600
Collection costs (4% of new sales)	3,200
Production and selling costs (80% of new sales)	64,000
Annual income before taxes	$ 6,400
Taxes (30%)	1,920
Annual incremental income after taxes	$ 4,480

b. $\dfrac{\text{Incremental income}}{\text{Sales}} = \dfrac{\$4,480}{80,000} = 5.6\%$

c. $\text{Accounts receivable} = \dfrac{\text{Sales}}{\text{Accounts receivable turnover}}$

$$= \dfrac{\$80,000}{4} = \$20,000$$

d. $\text{Return on investment} = \dfrac{\text{Incremental income}}{\text{Accounts receivable}} = \dfrac{\$4,480}{20,000} = 22.40\%$

PROBLEMS

≡ connect Selected problems are available with Connect. Please see the preface for more information.

Basic Problems

Ӿ

Cost-benefit analysis
of cash management
(LO7-2)

1. City Farm Insurance has collection centers across the country to speed up collections. The company also makes its disbursements from remote disbursement centers, so the firm's checks will take longer to clear the bank. Collection time has been reduced by two days and disbursement time increased by one day because of these policies. Excess funds are being invested in short-term instruments yielding 12 percent per annum.

    a. If City Farm has $5 million per day in collections and $3 million per day in disbursements, how many dollars has the cash management system freed up?

    b. How much can City Farm earn in dollars per year on short-term investments made possible by the freed-up cash?

Cost-benefit analysis
of cash management
(LO7-2)

2. Neon Light Company of Kansas City ships lamps and lighting appliances throughout the country. Ms. Neon has determined that through the establishment of local collection centers around the country, she can speed up the collection of payments by three days. Furthermore, the cash management department of her bank has indicated to her that she can defer her payments on her accounts by one-half day without affecting suppliers. The bank has a remote disbursement center in Florida.

    a. If Neon Light Company has $2.25 million per day in collections and $1.05 million per day in disbursements, how many dollars will the cash management system free up?

    b.   If Neon Light Company can earn 6 percent per annum on freed-up funds, how much will the income be?

    c.   If the total cost of the new system is $400,000, should it be implemented?

3. Orbital Communications has operating plants in over 100 countries. It also keeps funds for transactions purposes in many foreign countries. Assume in 2010 it held 150,000 kronas in Norway worth $40,000. The funds drew 13 percent interest, and the krona increased 6 percent against the dollar.

      What is the value of the holdings, based on U.S. dollars, at year-end? (Hint: Multiply $40,000 times 1.13 and then multiply the resulting value by 106 percent.)

International cash management
(LO7-2)

4. Postal Express has outlets throughout the world. It also keeps funds for transactions purposes in many foreign countries. Assume in 2010 it held 240,000 reals in Brazil worth 170,000 dollars. It drew 12 percent interest, but the Brazilian real declined 24 percent against the dollar.

International cash management
(LO7-2)

    a.   What is the value of its holdings, based on U.S. dollars, at year-end? (Hint: Multiply $170,000 times 1.12 and then multiply the resulting value by 76 percent.)

    b.   What is the value of its holdings, based on U.S. dollars, at year-end if instead it drew 9 percent interest and the real went up by 13 percent against the dollar?

5. Thompson Wood Products has credit sales of $2,160,000 and accounts receivable of $288,000. Compute the value of the average collection period.

Average collection period
(LO7-4)

6. Oral Roberts Dental Supplies has annual sales of $5,200,000. Ninety percent are on credit. The firm has $559,000 in accounts receivable. Compute the value of the average collection period.

Average collection period
(LO7-4)

7. Knight Roundtable Co. had annual credit sales of $1,080,000 and an average collection period of 32 days in 2018. Assume a 360-day year. What were the company's average accounts receivable balance? Accounts receivable are equal to the average daily credit sales times the average collection period.

Accounts receivable balance
(LO7-4)

8. Darla's Cosmetics had annual credit sales of $1,440,000 and an average collection period of 45 days in 2018. Assume a 360-day year.

      What was the company's average accounts receivable balance? Accounts receivable are equal to the average daily credit sales times the average collection period.

Accounts receivable balance
(LO7-4)

9. Barney's Antique Shop has annual credit sales of $1,620,000 and an accounts receivable balance of $157,500. Calculate the average collection period (use 360 days in a year).

Credit policy
(LO7-4)

10. Mervyn's Fine Fashions has an average collection period of 50 days. The accounts receivable balance is $95,000. What is the value of its credit sales?

Determination of credit sales
(LO7-4)

Intermediate Problems

11. Route Canal Shipping Company has the following schedule for aging of accounts receivable:

    a.   Fill in column (4) for each month.

%

Aging of accounts receivable
(LO7-4)

	Age of Receivables April 30, 20X1		
(1)	**(2)**	**(3)**	**(4)**
			Percent of
Month of Sales	**Age of Account**	**Amounts**	**Amount Due**
April	0–30	$ 131,250	_____
March	31–60	93,750	_____
February	61 90	112,500	_____
January	91–120	37,500	_____
Total receivables		$ 375,000	100%

b.   If the firm had $1,500,000 in credit sales over the four-month period, compute the average collection period. Average daily sales should be based on a 120-day period.

c.   If the firm likes to see its bills collected in 35 days, should it be satisfied with the average collection period?

d.   Disregarding your answer to part c and considering the aging schedule for accounts receivable, should the company be satisfied?

e.   What additional information does the aging schedule bring to the company that the average collection period may not show?

Economic ordering quantity
(LO7-5)

12.   Nowlin Pipe & Steel has projected sales of 72,000 pipes this year, an ordering cost of $6 per order, and carrying costs of $2.40 per pipe.

a.   What is the economic ordering quantity?

b.   How many orders will be placed during the year?

c.   What will the average inventory be?

Economic ordering quantity
(LO7-5)

13.   Fisk Corporation is trying to improve its inventory control system and has installed an online computer at its retail stores. Fisk anticipates sales of 49,000 units per year, an ordering cost of $8 per order, and carrying costs of $1.60 per unit.

a.   What is the economic ordering quantity?

b.   How many orders will be placed during the year?

c.   What will the average inventory be?

d.   What is the total cost of ordering and carrying inventory?

Economic ordering quantity
(LO7-5)

14.   (See Problem 13 for basic data.) In the second year, Fisk Corporation finds that it can reduce ordering costs to $2 per order but that carrying costs stay the same at $1.60 per unit. Also, volume remains at 49,000 units per year.

a.   What is the economic ordering quantity?

b.   How many orders will be placed during the year?

c.   What will the average inventory be?

d.   What is the total cost of ordering and carrying inventory?

Economic ordering quantity with safety stock
(LO7-5)

15.   Diagnostic Supplies has expected sales of 84,100 units per year, carrying costs of $5 per unit, and an ordering cost of $10 per order.

a.   What is the economic order quantity?

b.   What is the average inventory? What is the total carrying cost?

    c.   Assume an additional 80 units of inventory will be required as safety stock. What will the new average inventory be? What will the new total carrying cost be?

16.   Wisconsin Snowmobile Corp. is considering a switch to level production. Cost efficiencies would occur under level production, and aftertax costs would decline by $36,000, but inventory would increase by $300,000. Wisconsin Snowmobile would have to finance the extra inventory at a cost of 13.5 percent.

> *Level versus seasonal production (LO7-5)*

    a.   Determine the extra cost or savings of switching over to level production. Should the company go ahead and switch to level production?

    b.   How low would interest rates need to fall before level production would be feasible?

17.   Johnson Electronics is considering extending trade credit to some customers previously considered poor risks. Sales would increase by $150,000 if credit were extended to these new customers. Of the new accounts receivable generated, 5 percent will prove to be uncollectible. Additional collection costs will be 2 percent of sales, and production and selling costs will be 74 percent of sales. The firm is in the 35 percent tax bracket.

> *Credit policy decision (LO7-4)*

    a.   Compute the incremental income after taxes.

    b.   What will Johnson's incremental return on sales be if these new credit customers are accepted?

    c.   If the receivables turnover ratio is 3 to 1 and no other asset buildup is needed to serve the new customers, what will Johnson's incremental return on new average investment be?

Advanced Problems

18.   Henderson Office Supply is considering a more liberal credit policy to increase sales but expects that 9 percent of the new accounts will be uncollectible. Collection costs are 6 percent of new sales, production and selling costs are 74 percent, and accounts receivable turnover is four times. Assume income taxes of 20 percent and an increase in sales of $65,000. No other asset buildup will be required to service the new accounts.

> *Credit policy decision—receivables and inventory (LO7-4 & 7-5)*

    a.   What is the level of accounts receivable to support this sales expansion?

    b.   What would be Henderson's incremental aftertax return on investment?

    c.   Should Henderson liberalize credit if a 16 percent aftertax return on investment is required?

Assume that Henderson also needs to increase its level of inventory to support new sales and that inventory turnover is two times.

    d.   What would be the total incremental investment in accounts receivable and inventory to support a $65,000 increase in sales?

    e.   Given the income determined in part *b* and the investment determined in part *d,* should Henderson extend more liberal credit terms?

19.   Fast Turnstiles Co. is evaluating the extension of credit to a new group of customers. Although these customers will provide $180,000 in additional credit sales, 12 percent are likely to be uncollectible. The company will also incur

> *Credit policy decision with changing variables (LO7-4)*

$16,200 in additional collection expense. Production and marketing costs represent 72 percent of sales. The firm is in a 34 percent tax bracket and has a receivables turnover of four times. No other asset buildup will be required to service the new customers. The firm has a 10 percent desired return.

a. Calculate the incremental income after taxes and the return on incremental investment. Should Fast Turnstiles Co. extend credit to these customers?

b. Calculate the incremental income after taxes and the return on incremental investment if 15 percent of the new sales prove to be uncollectible. Should credit be extended if 15 percent of the new sales prove uncollectible?

c. Calculate the return on incremental investment if the receivables turnover drops to 1.6 and 12 percent of the accounts are uncollectible. Should credit be extended if the receivables turnover drops to 1.6 and 12 percent of the accounts are uncollectible (as in part a)?

Credit policy decision with changing variables
(LO7-4)

20. Slow Roll Drum Co. is evaluating the extension of credit to a new group of customers. Although these customers will provide $180,000 in additional credit sales, 12 percent are likely to be uncollectible. The company will also incur $16,200 in additional collection expense. Production and marketing costs represent 72 percent of sales. The firm is in a 34 percent tax bracket. No other asset buildup will be required to service the new customers. The firm has a 10 percent desired return. Assume the average collection period is 120 days.

a. Compute the return on incremental investment.

b. Should credit be extended?

Credit policy and return on investment
(LO7-4)

21. Global Services is considering a promotional campaign that will increase annual credit sales by $450,000. The company will require investments in accounts receivable, inventory, and plant and equipment. The turnover for each is as follows:

Accounts receivable	2x
Inventory	6x
Plant and equipment	1x

All $450,000 of the sales will be collectible. However, collection costs will be 6 percent of sales, and production and selling costs will be 71 percent of sales. The cost to carry inventory will be 4 percent of inventory. Depreciation expense on plant and equipment will be 5 percent of plant and equipment. The tax rate is 30 percent.

a. Compute the investments in accounts receivable, inventory, and plant and equipment based on the turnover ratios. Add the three together.

b. Compute the accounts receivable collection costs and production and selling costs and add the two figures together.

c. Compute the costs of carrying inventory.

d. Compute the depreciation expense on new plant and equipment.

e. Add together all the costs in parts b, c, and d.

f. Subtract the answer from part *e* from the sales figure of $450,000 to arrive at income before taxes. Subtract taxes at a rate of 30 percent to arrive at income after taxes.

g. Divide the aftertax return figure in part *f* by the total investment figure in part *a*. If the firm has a required return on investment of 8 percent, should it undertake the promotional campaign described throughout this problem?

Problems 22–25 are a series and should be completed in order.

22. Dome Metals has credit sales of $180,000 yearly with credit terms of net 60 days, which is also the average collection period. Dome does not offer a discount for early payment, so its customers take the full 60 days to pay. What is the average receivables balance? receivables turnover?

23. If Dome offers a 3 percent discount for payment in 18 days, what will the new average receivables balance be? Use the credit sales of $180,000 for your calculation of receivables.

24. What will be the net gain or loss to the firm if Dome offers a 3 percent discount for payment in 18 days, every customer takes advantage of the new terms, and Dome reduces its bank loans, which cost 12 percent, by the cash generated from its reduced receivables? Should it offer the discount? Use the credit sales of $180,000 yearly with credit terms of net 60 days for your calculation.

25. Now assume that the new trade terms of 3/18, net 60 will increase Dome's sales by 15 percent because the discount makes Dome's price competitive. If Dome earns 20 percent on sales before discounts, what will be the net change in income? Should it offer the discount?

Credit policy decision with changing variables (LO7-4)

COMPREHENSIVE PROBLEM

Logan Distributing Company of Atlanta sells fans and heaters to retail outlets throughout the Southeast. Joe Logan, the president of the company, is thinking about changing the firm's credit policy to attract customers away from competitors. The present policy calls for a 1/10, net 30 cash discount. The new policy would call for a 3/10, net 50 cash discount. Currently 30 percent of Logan customers are taking the discount, and it is anticipated that this number would go up to 50 percent with the new discount policy. It is further anticipated that annual sales would increase from a level of $400,000 to $600,000 as a result of the change in the cash discount policy.

Logan Distributing Company (Receivables and inventory policy) (LO7-4 & 7-5)

The increased sales would also affect the inventory level. The average inventory carried by Logan is based on a determination of an EOQ. Assume sales of fans and heaters increase from 15,000 to 22,500 units. The ordering cost for each order is $200, and the carrying cost per unit is $1.50 (these values will not change with the discount). The average inventory is based on EOQ/2. Each unit in inventory has an average cost of $12.

Cost of goods sold is equal to 65 percent of net sales; general and administrative expenses are 15 percent of net sales; and interest payments of 14 percent will only be necessary for the increase in the accounts receivable and inventory balances. Taxes will be 40 percent of before-tax income.

a. Compute the accounts receivable balance before and after the change in the cash discount policy. Use the net sales (total sales minus cash discounts) to determine the average daily sales.

b. Determine the EOQ before and after the change in the cash discount policy. Translate this into average inventory (in units and dollars) before and after the change in the cash discount policy.

c. Complete the following income statement:

	Before Policy Change	After Policy Change
Net sales (Sales – Cash discounts)		
Cost of goods sold		
Gross profit		
General and administrative expense		
Operating profit		
Interest on increase in accounts receivable and inventory (14%)		
Income before taxes		
Taxes		
Income after taxes		

d. Should the new cash discount policy be utilized? Briefly comment.

WEB EXERCISE

1. One of the items discussed in this chapter was the impact of the Internet on working capital management. Ariba and Perfect Commerce are two companies at the forefront of the B2B trend. Go to the Perfect Commerce website at www.perfect.com.

2. Under the heading "Company," select "About Us." Read the description, and in one short paragraph, describe what Perfect Commerce does.

3. Under the heading "Company," click on "Customers" and list five of its key customers.

4. Under the heading "Solutions," you will find "Public Sector," "Private Sector," and "eCommerce." Click on "B2B Commerce" and read about eNabler; explain how this system can save companies money.

Note: Occasionally a topic we have listed may have been deleted, updated, or moved into a different location on a website. If you click on the site map or site index, you will be introduced to a table of contents that should aid you in finding the topic you are looking for.

8

LEARNING OBJECTIVES

LO 8-1 Trade credit from suppliers is normally the most available form of short-term financing.

LO 8-2 Bank loans are usually short term and should be paid off from funds from the normal operations of the firm.

LO 8-3 Commercial paper represents a short-term, unsecured promissory note issued by the firm.

LO 8-4 By using accounts receivable and inventory as collateral for a loan, the firm may be able to borrow larger amounts.

LO 8-5 Hedging may be used to offset the risk of interest rates rising.

Sources of Short-Term Financing

In this chapter we examine the cost and availability of the various sources of short-term funds, with primary attention to trade credit from suppliers, bank loans, corporate promissory notes, foreign borrowing, and loans against receivables and inventory. It is sometimes said the only way to be sure a bank loan will be approved is to convince the banker that you don't really need the money. The learning objective of this chapter is the opposite—namely, to demonstrate how badly needed funds can be made available on a short-term basis from the various credit suppliers.

For example, Yum! Brands, the company that owns KFC, Pizza Hut, and Taco Bell, entered a credit agreement in 2012 with a consortium of banks. The $1.3 billion agreement was syndicated by 24 banks, was unsecured, and matured in 2017. In June 2017 Yum! was able to extend the maturity date of its credit agreement to June 2022. It ended up with $1 billion on one agreement and $500 million on a second credit facility while reducing the interest rate. These loans usually are renewed unless the economy nose-dives as it did in late 2008 and 2009. During this most recent credit crisis, bank lending dried up, but if a firm had a credit agreement, banks were obligated to meet the terms of the agreement. However, banks were not obligated to renew credit agreements that had matured.

Yum! Brands had agreements with 24 banks because this reduces its dependence on any one bank. From the banks' point of view, this spreads out their risk. The commitments from the banks ranged from $23 million to $115 million. The interest rate for borrowings under this new credit agreement ranged from 1.25 percent to 1.75 percent over the London Interbank Offered Rate (LIBOR). The interest rate is contingent on Yum! Brands meeting certain financial targets for financial leverage and fixed charge coverage, and it limits additional indebtedness, liens, and other transactions specified in the agreement. In tight credit markets, the lenders have the upper hand in restricting the behavior of the borrower.

We now look at various forms of credit.

Trade Credit

The largest provider of short-term credit is usually at the firm's doorstep—the manufacturer or seller of goods and services. Approximately 40 percent of short-term financing is in the form of accounts payable or trade credit. Accounts payable are a **spontaneous source of funds**, growing as the business expands on a seasonal or long-term basis and contracting in a like fashion when business declines.

Payment Period

Trade credit is usually extended for 30 to 60 days. Many firms attempt to "stretch the payment period" to receive additional short-term financing. This is an acceptable form of financing as long as it is not carried to an abusive extent. Going from a 30- to a 35-day average payment period may be tolerated within the trade, while stretching payments to 65 days might alienate suppliers and cause a diminishing credit rating with Dun & Bradstreet and local credit bureaus. A major variable in determining the payment period is the possible existence of a cash discount.

Cash Discount Policy

A **cash discount** allows a reduction in price if payment is made within a specified time period. A 2/10, net 30 cash discount means we can deduct 2 percent if we remit our funds 10 days after billing, but failing this, we must pay the full amount by the 30th day.

On a $100 billing, we could pay $98 up to the 10th day or $100 at the end of 30 days. If we fail to take the cash discount, we will get to use $98 for 20 more days at a $2 fee or 2 percent of the $100 transaction. The cost is a high 36.72 percent. Note that we first consider the interest cost and then convert this to an annual basis. Here's the standard formula for this example:

$$\begin{matrix} \text{Cost of failing to} \\ \text{take a cash discount} \end{matrix} = \frac{\text{Discount percent}}{100 \text{ percent} - \text{Discount percent}} \times \frac{360}{\text{Final due date} - \text{Discount period}} \qquad (8\text{-}1)$$

$$\frac{2\%}{100\% - 2\%} \times \frac{360}{(30 - 10)} = 2.04\% \times 18 = 36.72\%$$

Cash discount terms may vary. For example, on a 2/10, net 90 basis, it would cost us only 9.18 percent not to take the discount and to pay the full amount after 90 days.

$$\frac{2\%}{100\% - 2\%} \times \frac{360}{(90 - 10)} = 2.04\% \times 4.5 = 9.18\%$$

In each case, we must ask ourselves whether bypassing the discount and using the money for a longer period is the cheapest means of financing. In the first example, with an annualized cost of 36.72 percent, it probably is not. We would be better off borrowing $98 for 20 days at some lower rate. For example, at 10 percent interest we would pay

54 cents[1] in interest, as opposed to $2 under the cash discount policy. With the 2/10, net 90 arrangement, the cost of missing the discount is only 9.18 percent and we may choose to let our suppliers carry us for an extra 80 days.

Net Credit Position

In Chapter 2, "Review of Accounting," we defined accounts receivable as a use of funds and accounts payable as a source of funds. The firm should closely watch the relationship between the two to determine its **net trade credit** position. Net trade credit is positive when accounts receivable are greater than accounts payable and negative when the opposite is true. If a firm has average daily sales of $5,000 and collects in 30 days, the accounts receivable balance will be $150,000. If this is associated with average daily purchases of $4,000 and a 25-day average payment period, the average accounts payable balance is $100,000—indicating $50,000 more in credit is extended than received. Changing this situation to an average payment period of 40 days increases the accounts payable to $160,000 ($4,000 × 40). Accounts payable now exceed accounts receivable by $10,000, thus leaving these funds for other needs. Larger firms tend to be net providers of trade credit (relatively high receivables), with smaller firms in the user position (relatively high payables).

Bank Credit

Banks may provide funds for the financing of seasonal needs, product line expansion, and long-term growth. The typical banker prefers a **self-liquidating loan** in which the use of funds will ensure a built-in or automatic repayment scheme. Actually, two-thirds of bank loans are short term. Nevertheless, through the process of renewing old loans, many of these 90- or 180-day agreements take on the characteristics of longer-term financing.

Major changes occurring in banking today are centered on the concept of "full-service banking." The modern banker's function is much broader than merely accepting deposits, making loans, and processing checks. A banking institution may provide trust and investment services, a credit card operation, real estate lending, data processing services, cash management services both domestically and internationally, pension fund management, and many other services for large and small businesses.

The banking scene has become more international to accommodate increased world trade and the rise of international corporations. The largest international banks are expanding into the United States through bank acquisitions and branch offices. Every major financial center from New York to San Francisco has experienced an increase in the number of foreign banks.

However, the recession of 2007–2009, which was the most severe since the Great Depression of the 1930s, caused hundreds of bank failures. The Federal Reserve and the Federal Deposit Insurance Corporation forced many large banks on the verge of collapse, like Wachovia and National City Bank, to be taken over by healthy banks, like

---

[1] $\frac{20}{360} \times 10\% \times \$98 = 0.54$

Wells Fargo and PNC Bank. With the enactment of the Gramm–Leach–Bliley Act in 1999, commercial banks and investment banks were allowed to merge. Many economists and politicians think that these combinations were responsible for banks taking on more risk than they could manage, and that this excess risk taking led to the credit problems that started to show up in 2007. In 2011, Congress passed the Dodd–Frank Act, which created more stringent regulations for financial institutions. (For more coverage of Dodd–Frank, see Chapter 1.)

We will look at a number of terms generally associated with banking (and other types of lending activity) and consider the significance of each. Attention is directed to the prime interest rate, LIBOR, compensating balances, the term loan arrangement, and methods of computing interest.

Prime Rate and LIBOR

The **prime rate** is the rate a bank charges its most creditworthy customers, and a premium is added as a customer's credit risk gets higher. At certain slack loan periods in the economy, or because of international competition, banks may actually charge top customers less than the published prime rate; however, such activities are difficult to track. The average customer can expect to pay one or two percentage points above prime, while in tight money periods a builder in a speculative construction project might have to pay five or more percentage points over prime.

Since the U.S. dollar is the world's international currency, and because the United States has run up huge foreign trade deficits over the last several decades, there are several trillion dollars floating around the world's money markets. London is the center of Eurodollar deposits, and a majority of these U.S. dollars can be found there. Because U.S. companies can borrow dollars from London banks quite easily, large borrowers shop for the lowest interest rate in London, New York, or any other major money market center. This means that the U.S. prime rate competes with the **London Interbank Offered Rate (LIBOR)** for companies with an international presence or those sophisticated enough to use the London Eurodollar market for loans. For example, in March 2018, LIBOR one-month loans were at 1.80 percent versus a U.S. prime rate of 4.75 percent. A loan at 1.0 or 2.0 percent above LIBOR would still be less than the U.S. prime rate.

Figure 8-1 shows the relationship between LIBOR and the prime rate between December 1997 and March 1, 2018. Notice that during this period the prime rate was always higher than LIBOR.

Compensating Balances

In providing loans and other services, a bank may require that *business* customers either pay a fee for the service or maintain a minimum average account balance, referred to as a **compensating balance**. In some cases, both fees and compensating balances are required. When interest rates are in the 8.5 percent range, large commercial banks may require compensating balances of over $20,000 to offset $100 in service fees. As interest rates go down, this compensating balance rises; so under the 2007 prime rate of 7.75 percent, the compensating balances could be over $40,000 per $100 in service fees. Because the funds do not generate as much revenue at lower

Figure 8-1   The prime rate versus the London Interbank Offered Rate on U.S. dollar deposits

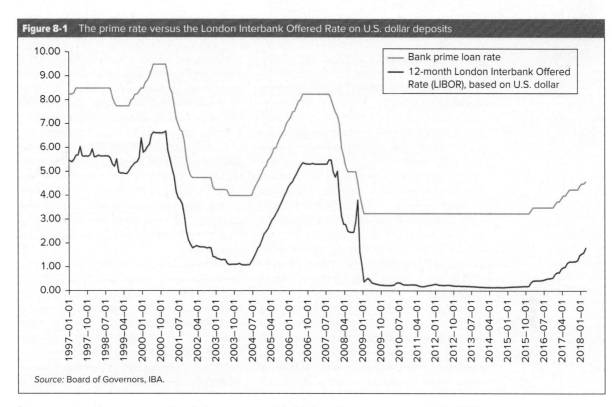

Source: Board of Governors, IBA.

interest rates, the compensating balance amount is higher. It was even greater in 2015 with the 3.25 percent prime rate.

When compensating balances are required to obtain a loan, the required amount is usually computed as a percentage of customer loans outstanding, or as a percentage of bank commitments toward future loans to a given account. A common ratio is 20 percent against outstanding loans or 10 percent against total future commitments, though market conditions tend to influence the percentages.

Some view the compensating balance requirement as an unusual arrangement. Where else would you walk into a business establishment, buy a shipment of goods, and then be told you could not take 20 percent of the purchase home with you? If you borrow $100,000, paying 8 percent interest on the full amount with a 20 percent compensating balance requirement, you will be paying $8,000 for the use of $80,000 in funds, or an effective rate of 10 percent.

The amount that must be borrowed to end up with the desired sum of money is simply figured by taking the needed funds and dividing by $(1 - c)$, where c is the compensating balance expressed as a decimal. For example, if you need $100,000 in funds, you must borrow $125,000 to ensure the intended amount will be available. This would be calculated as follows:

$$\text{Amount to be borrowed} = \frac{\text{Amount needed}}{(1 - c)}$$

$$= \frac{\$100,000}{(1 - 0.2)}$$

$$= \$125,000$$

A check on this calculation can be done to see if you actually end up with the use of $100,000:

$125,000	Loan
− 25,000	20% compensating balance requirement
$100,000	Available funds

The intent here is not to suggest that the compensating balance requirement represents an unfair or hidden cost. If it were not for compensating balances, quoted interest rates would be higher or gratuitous services now offered by banks would carry a price tag.

In practice, some corporate clients pay a fee for cash management or similar services, while others eliminate the direct fee with compensating balances. Fees and compensating balances vary widely among banks. As the competition heats up among the providers of financial services, corporations can be expected to selectively shop for high-quality, low-cost institutions.

Maturity Provisions

As previously indicated, bank loans have been traditionally short term and usually renewable. In the last decade there has been an increase in the use of the **term loan**, in which credit is extended for one to seven years. The loan is usually repaid in monthly or quarterly installments over its life rather than in one payment. Only superior credit applicants, as measured by working capital strength, potential profitability, and competitive position, can qualify for term loan financing. Here the banker and the business firm are said to be stuck together at the hip because of the length of the loan.

Bankers are hesitant to fix a single interest rate to a term loan. The more common practice is to allow the interest rate to change with market conditions. Thus the interest rate on a term loan may be tied to the prime rate or LIBOR. Often loans will be priced at a premium over one of these two rates reflecting the risk of the borrower. For example, a loan may be priced at 1.5 percentage points above LIBOR, as in the Yum! example at the beginning of the chapter, and the rate will move up and down with changes in the base rate.

Cost of Commercial Bank Financing

The effective interest rate on a loan is based on the loan amount, the dollar interest paid, the length of the loan, and the method of repayment. It is easy enough to observe that $60 interest on a $1,000 loan for one year would carry a 6 percent interest rate, but what if the same loan were for 120 days? We use this formula:

$$\text{Effective rate} = \frac{\text{Interest}}{\text{Principal}} \times \frac{\text{Days in the year (360)}}{\text{Days loan is outstanding}} \qquad (8\text{-}2)$$

$$= \frac{\$60}{\$1,000} \times \frac{360}{120} = 6\% \times 3 = 18\%$$

Since we have use of the funds for only 120 days, the effective rate is 18 percent. To highlight the impact of time, if you borrowed $20 for only 10 days and paid back $21, the effective interest rate would be 180 percent—a violation of almost every usury law.

$$\frac{\$1}{\$20} \times \frac{360}{10} = 5\% \times 36 = 180\%$$

In addition to the time dimension of a loan, the way interest is charged is also important. We have assumed that interest would be paid when the loan came due. If the bank uses a **discounted loan** and deducts the interest in advance, the effective rate of interest increases. For example, a $1,000 one-year loan with $60 of interest deducted in advance represents the payment of interest on only $940, or an effective rate of 6.38 percent.

$$\text{Effective rate on} \atop \text{discounted loan} = \frac{\text{Interest}}{\text{Principal} - \text{Interest}} \times \frac{\text{Days in the year (360)}}{\text{Days loan is outstanding}} \qquad (8\text{-}3)$$

$$= \frac{\$60}{\$1,000 - \$60} \times \frac{360}{360} = \frac{\$60}{\$940} = 6.38\%$$

Interest Costs with Compensating Balances

When a loan is made with compensating balances, the effective interest rate is the stated interest rate divided by $(1 - c)$, where c is the compensating balance expressed as a decimal. Assume that 6 percent is the stated annual rate and that a 20 percent compensating balance is required.

$$\text{Effective rate with} \atop \text{compensating balances} = \frac{\text{Interest}}{(1 - c)} \qquad (8\text{-}4)$$

$$= \frac{6\%}{(1 - 0.2)}$$

$$= 7.5\%$$

In the prior examples, if dollar amounts are used and the stated rate is unknown, Formula 8-5 can be used. The assumption is that we are paying $60 interest on a $1,000 loan but are able to use only $800 of the funds. The loan is for a year.

$$\text{Effective rate with} \atop \text{compensating} \atop \text{balances} = \frac{\text{Interest}}{\text{Principal} - \text{Compensating} \atop \text{balance in dollars}} \times \frac{\text{Days in the} \atop \text{year (360)}}{\text{Days loan is} \atop \text{outstanding}} \qquad (8\text{-}5)$$

$$= \frac{60}{\$1,000 - \$200} \times \frac{360}{360} = \frac{\$60}{\$800} = 7.5\%$$

Only when a firm has idle cash balances that could be used to cover compensating balance requirements would the firm not use the higher effective-cost formulas (Formulas 8-4 and 8-5).

Rate on Installment Loans

The most confusing borrowing arrangement to the average bank customer or a consumer is the installment loan. An **installment loan** calls for a series of equal payments over the life of the loan. Though federal legislation prohibits a misrepresentation of interest rates on loans to customers, a loan officer or an overanxious salesperson may quote a rate on an installment loan that is approximately half the true rate.

Assume that you borrow $1,000 on a 12-month installment basis, with regular monthly payments to apply to interest and principal, and the interest requirement is $60. While it might be suggested that the rate on the loan is 6 percent, this is clearly not the case. Though you are paying a total of $60 in interest, you do not have the use of $1,000 for one year—rather, you are paying back the $1,000 on a monthly basis, with an average outstanding loan balance for the year of approximately $500. The effective rate of interest is 11.08 percent.

$$\text{Effective rate on installment loan} = \frac{2 \times \text{Annual no. of payments} \times \text{Interest}}{(\text{Total no. of payments} + 1) \times \text{Principal}} \qquad (8\text{-}6)$$

$$= \frac{2 \times 12 \times \$60}{13 \times \$1,000} = \frac{\$1,440}{\$13,000} = 11.08\%$$

Annual Percentage Rate

Because the way interest is calculated often makes the effective rate different from the stated rate, Congress passed the Truth in Lending Act in 1968. This act required that the actual **annual percentage rate (APR)** be given to the borrower. The APR is really a measure of the effective rate we have presented. Congress was primarily trying to protect the unwary consumer from paying more than the stated rate without his or her knowledge. For example, the stated rate on an installment loan might be 6 percent but the APR might be 11.08 percent. It has always been assumed that businesses should be well versed in business practices and financial matters; therefore, the Truth in Lending Act was intended to protect individual borrowers but not business borrowers.

The annual percentage rate requires the use of the actuarial method of compounded interest when calculating the APR. This requires knowledge of the time-value-of-money techniques presented in Chapter 9. For our purposes in this chapter, it is enough to know that the lender must calculate interest for the period on the outstanding loan balance at the beginning of the period. Any payments are first credited against interest due, and any amount left is used to reduce the principal or loan balance. Because there are so many ways to structure loan repayment schedules, no one formula is applicable for computing the APR. For example, loans do not all have a full year—some have only 10 or 15 days or other portions of a year.

Since most consumer loans are installment types, the APR is usually based on the assumption of amortization. Amortization means an equal dollar amount is paid each period to retire principal and interest. According to the law, a loan amortization schedule is the final authority in the calculation of the APR. The amortization schedule always has an annual percentage rate that diminishes the principal to zero over the loan period. You will learn how to develop an amortization schedule in Chapter 9.

The Credit Crunch Phenomenon

In 1969–1970, 1973–1974, 1979–1981, and 2007– 2009, the economy went through periods of extreme credit shortages. We seem to find ourselves in the midst of a tight money situation every few years. The anatomy of a credit crunch is as follows. The Federal Reserve tightens the growth in the money supply in its battle against inflation, causing a decrease in lendable funds and an increase in interest rates. To compound the difficulty, business requirements for funds may be increasing to carry inflation-laden inventory and receivables. A third problem is the massive withdrawal of savings deposits at banking and thrift institutions, all in search of higher returns. There simply are not enough lendable funds.

Recent history has taught us that the way *not* to deal with credit shortages is to impose artificial limits on interest rates in the form of restrictive usury laws or extreme governmental pressure. In 1969–1970, the prime rate went to 8.5 percent in a tight money period—a level not high enough to bring the forces of demand and supply together, and little credit was available. In 1974, the prime rose to 12 percent, a rate truly reflecting market conditions, and funds were available. The same was true in 1980 and 1981 as the prime went to 20 percent and higher, but lendable funds were available.

In the late 1980s and early 1990s, the financial system suffered from bad loans made to real estate investors, Third World countries, and high-risk corporations. These bad loans resulted in the partial collapse of the savings and loan industry, and it created problems for many banks and insurance companies. Credit conditions can change dramatically and suddenly because of unexpected defaults, causing changes in monetary policy, economic recessions, and other shocks to economies around the world. Available funds can simply dry up as lenders become more risk-averse and refuse to lend to high-risk borrowers or even borrowers of moderate risk.

Not all credit crunches are caused by high interest rates. In the summer of 2007, a credit crunch of a different kind hit the United States and eventually infected the major international financial markets in Europe and Asia. The cause was subprime lending. As the mortgage market grew by leaps and bounds in the early 2000s, many high-risk loans were made (thus the term *subprime*—less than good quality). To compound the problem, many of these loans were made with adjustable rate mortgages; as interest rates moved up, some borrowers were unable to make their higher monthly payments, and defaults grew. As the mortgage market collapsed, the Federal Reserve added tens of billions of dollars to keep the markets liquid, and also cut interest rates. Commercial banks, investment banks, and hedge funds reported losses in the billions, and Countrywide Financial, the largest mortgage banker in the United States, couldn't sell commercial paper. It was forced to rely on an $11 billion credit from a consortium of banks and a $2 billion equity infusion by Bank of America, which eventually bought Countrywide. Loans were difficult to get for most firms, and the problems persisted into 2012 as banks repaired their capital structures in response to the recession and the Dodd–Frank Act, which requires a higher percentage of equity capital in banks' balance sheets. Banks also became more risk-averse and restricted loans to high-quality borrowers.

Financing through Commercial Paper

For large and prestigious firms, commercial paper may provide an outlet for raising funds. **Commercial paper** represents a short-term, unsecured promissory note issued to the public in minimum units of $25,000.[2] As Figure 8-2 indicates, the total amount of commercial paper outstanding (top line) has fluctuated dramatically. The overall amount of commercial paper outstanding reflects the willingness of qualified

---

[2]An exception to this definition is asset-backed commercial paper, which is covered later in this discussion.

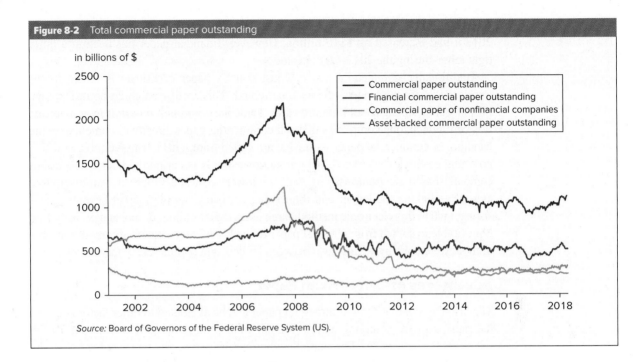

Figure 8-2   Total commercial paper outstanding

in billions of $

Legend:
— Commercial paper outstanding
— Financial commercial paper outstanding
— Commercial paper of nonfinancial companies
— Asset-backed commercial paper outstanding

Source: Board of Governors of the Federal Reserve System (US).

companies to borrow at the lowest rate available. The size of the market has made it easier for corporations to raise short-term funds.

Commercial paper falls into three categories. First, there are finance companies, such as General Motors Acceptance Corporation (GMAC) and General Electric Capital Corporation, that issue paper primarily to institutional investors such as pension funds, insurance companies, and money market mutual funds. The growth of money market mutual funds has increased the ability of companies to sell commercial paper. Paper sold by financial firms such as GMAC is referred to as **finance paper**, and because it is usually sold directly to the lender by the finance company, it is also referred to as **direct paper**. The second type of commercial paper is sold by industrial companies, utility firms, and financial companies too small to have their own selling network. These firms use an intermediate dealer network to distribute their paper, and so this type of paper is referred to as **dealer paper** or nonfinancial paper.

A third type of commercial paper and a relative newcomer on the block is **asset-backed commercial paper**. An inspection of Figure 8-2 shows a dramatic increase in the amount in this category from approximately $610 billion in 2001 to $1,210 billion at its peak in 2007. Notice the huge drop in asset-backed commercial paper in the third quarter of 2007 and its continued decline to the end of 2017.

The huge increase in the amount of asset-backed securities between 2005 and 2007 was primarily the result of mortgage-backed securities being bundled up and sold in the markets. During this time, asset-backed securities ballooned by more than $500 billion, but when the banking crisis hit full speed, many of these mortgage-backed securities had to be written off the investing bank's books. The drop in value between 2007 and 2017 was $975 billion. At the same time, the commercial paper markets froze, and you can see that both financial and nonfinancial commercial paper funds fell by hundreds of billions of dollars. A pickup in nonfinancial commercial paper could be seen as the economy went into the fourth quarter of 2009, and by the end of 2017 it had increased by $110 billion. However, financial paper has been in a fairly tight range during the 2013–2017 period.

Traditionally, commercial paper is just that. A paper certificate is issued to the lender to signify the lender's claim to be repaid. This certificate could be lost, stolen, misplaced, or damaged, and, in rare cases, someone could fail to cash it in at maturity. It is common among companies that sell commercial paper directly to computerize the handling of commercial paper with what are called **book-entry transactions**, in which no actual certificate is created. All transactions simply occur on the books. The use of computer-based electronic issuing methods lowers cost and simplifies administration, as well as linking the lender and the issuing company. As the market becomes more accustomed to this electronic method, large users ($500 million or more) will likely find it profitable to switch from physical paper to the book-entry system, where all transfers of money are done by wiring cash between lenders and commercial paper issuers.

Advantages of Commercial Paper

The growing popularity of commercial paper can be attributed to other factors besides the rapid growth of money market mutual funds and their need to find short-term securities for investment. For example, commercial paper may be issued at below the prime interest rate. As indicated in the last column of Table 8-1, this rate differential is normally 2 to 3 percent.

A second advantage of commercial paper is that no compensating balance requirements are associated with its issuance, though the firm is generally required to maintain commercial bank lines of approved credit equal to the amount of the paper outstanding (a procedure somewhat less costly than compensating balances). Finally, a number of firms enjoy the prestige associated with being able to float their commercial paper in what is considered a "snobbish market" for funds.

Limitations on the Issuance of Commercial Paper

The commercial paper market is not without its problems. Recessions, a series of corporate bankruptcies, major corporate fraud, and other events cause lenders in the commercial paper market to become risk-averse. Because only high-quality companies with good credit ratings can access this market, many firms that have had their credit quality downgraded by credit rating agencies can no longer sell their commercial paper. These companies are then forced to draw down more expensive lines of credit at their banks to replace the commercial paper they couldn't roll over with new paper. This is why companies like Yum! Brands, mentioned at the beginning of this chapter, get a revolving line of credit. The credit lines become funds available in case of need.

Although the funds provided through the issuance of commercial paper are cheaper than bank loans, they are also less predictable. While a firm may pay a higher rate for a bank loan, it is also buying a degree of loyalty and commitment that is unavailable in the commercial paper market. Table 8-1 demonstrates that the difference between the cost of commercial paper and the prime rate is fairly consistent over time. Also note that the prime rate remained low and constant from 2008 to 2014. Toward the end of 2015, the prime went to 3.5 percent, and by 2018 it was 4.5 percent.

Table 8-1   Comparison of commercial paper rate to prime rate (annual rate*)

	Finance Co. Paper (directly placed) 3 Months	Average Bank Prime Rate	Prime Rate Minus Finance Paper
1997	5.72	8.5	2.78
1998	4.94	7.75	2.81
1999	5.73	8.5	2.77
2000	6.34	9.5	3.16
2001	1.81	4.75	2.94
2002	1.31	4.25	2.94
2003	1.07	4.00	2.93
2004	2.48	5.25	2.77
2005	4.46	7.25	2.79
2006	5.31	8.25	2.94
2007	4.82	7.25	2.43
2008	1.54	3.25	1.71
2009	0.24	3.25	3.01
2010	0.37	3.25	2.88
2011	0.58	3.25	2.67
2012	0.35	3.25	2.9
2013	0.20	3.25	3.05
2014	0.23	3.25	3.02
2015	0.23	3.26	3.03
2016	0.64	3.51	2.87
2017	1.15	4.10	2.95
Average	2.36	5.18	2.83

*Averages for the year.

Source: St. Louis Federal Reserve Bank (FRED).

Foreign Borrowing

An increasing source of funds for U.S. firms has been overseas banks. This trend started several decades ago with the Eurodollar market centered in London. A **Eurodollar loan** is a loan denominated in dollars and made by a foreign bank holding dollar deposits. Such loans are usually short term to intermediate term in maturity. LIBOR is the base interest rate paid on such loans for companies of the highest quality. Loans are often priced at LIBOR plus X percent, as opposed to prime plus X percent. As Figure 8-1 on page 231 shows, Eurodollar loans at LIBOR (rather than the prime interest rate) can be cheaper than U.S. domestic loans. International companies are always looking at foreign markets for cheaper ways of borrowing.

One approach to borrowing has been to borrow from international banks in foreign currencies either directly or through foreign subsidiaries. In using a subsidiary to borrow, the companies may convert the borrowed currencies to dollars, which are then sent to the United States to be used by the parent company. While international borrowing can often be done at lower interest rates than domestic loans, the borrowing firm may suffer from currency risk. That is, the value of the foreign funds borrowed may rise against the dollar so that the loan will take more dollars to repay. Companies generating foreign revenue streams may borrow in those same currencies and thereby reduce or avoid any currency risk. Currency risk will be given greater coverage later in the chapter.

McDonald's, with its widespread international operations, borrows money in many currencies. McDonald's states in its SEC 10-Q quarterly report ending September 30, 2017, that "a significant part of the Company's operating income is generated outside the U.S., and about 35 percent of its total debt is denominated in foreign currencies. Accordingly, earnings are affected by changes in foreign currency exchange rates, particularly the Euro, British Pound, Australian Dollar, and Canadian Dollar. Collectively, these currencies represent approximately 70 percent of the Company's operating income outside the U.S. If all four of these currencies moved by 10 percent in the same direction, the Company's annual diluted earnings per share would change by about 25 cents." This example illustrates that the financial markets have become more international and so must financial managers.

Use of Collateral in Short-Term Financing

Almost any firm would prefer to borrow on an unsecured (no-collateral) basis; but if the borrower's credit rating is too low or its need for funds too great, the lending institution will require that certain assets be pledged. A secured credit arrangement might help the borrower obtain funds that would otherwise be unavailable.

In any loan, the lender's primary concern, however, is whether the borrower's capacity to generate cash flow is sufficient to liquidate the loan as it comes due. Few lenders would make a loan strictly on the basis of collateral. Collateral is merely a stopgap device to protect the lender when all else fails. The bank or finance company is in business to collect interest, not to repossess and resell assets.

Though a number of different types of assets may be pledged, our attention will be directed to accounts receivable and inventory. All states have now adopted the Uniform Commercial Code, which standardizes and simplifies the procedures for establishing security on a loan.

Accounts Receivable Financing

Accounts receivable financing may include **pledging accounts receivable** as collateral for a loan or an outright *sale* (**factoring**) of receivables. Receivables financing is popular because it permits borrowing to be tied directly to the level of asset expansion at any point in time. As the level of accounts receivable goes up, a firm is able to borrow more.

A drawback is that this is a relatively expensive method of acquiring funds, so it must be carefully compared to other forms of credit. Accounts receivable represent one of the firm's most valuable short-term assets, and they should be committed only where the appropriate circumstances exist. An ill-advised accounts receivable financing plan may exclude the firm from a less expensive bank term loan.

Pledging Accounts Receivable

The lending institution will generally stipulate which of the accounts receivable is of sufficient quality to serve as collateral for a loan. On this basis, we may borrow 60 to 90 percent of the value of the acceptable collateral. The loan percentage will depend on the financial strength of the borrowing firm and on the creditworthiness of its accounts. The lender will have full recourse against the borrower if any of the accounts go bad. The interest rate in a receivables borrowing arrangement is generally well in excess of the prime rate.

The interest is computed against the loan balance outstanding, a figure that may change quite frequently, as indicated in Table 8-2. In the illustration, interest is assumed to be 12 percent annually, or 1 percent per month. In month 1, we are able to borrow $8,000 against $10,000 in acceptable receivables and we must pay $80 in interest. Similar values are developed for succeeding months.

Table 8-2 Receivables loan balance				
	Month 1	**Month 2**	**Month 3**	**Month 4**
Total accounts receivable	$11,000	$15,100	$19,400	$16,300
Acceptable accounts receivable (to finance company)	10,000	14,000	18,000	15,000
Loan balance (80%)	8,000	11,200	14,400	12,000
Interest 12% annual—1% per month	80	112	144	120

Factoring Receivables

When we factor receivables, they are sold outright to a finance company. Our customers may be instructed to remit the proceeds directly to the purchaser of the account. The factoring firm generally does not have recourse against the seller of the receivables. As a matter of practice, the finance company may do part or all of the credit analysis directly to ensure the quality of the accounts. As a potential sale is being made, the factoring firm may give immediate feedback to the seller on whether the account will be purchased.

When the factoring firm accepts an account, it may forward funds immediately to the seller, in anticipation of receiving payment 30 days later as part of the normal billing process. The factoring firm is not only absorbing risk but also actually advancing funds to the seller a month earlier than the seller would normally receive them.

For taking the risk, the factoring firm is generally paid on a fee or commission equal to 1 to 3 percent of the invoices accepted. In addition, it is paid a lending rate for advancing the funds early. If $100,000 a *month* is processed at a 1 percent commission and a 12 percent annual borrowing rate, the total effective cost will be 24 percent on an *annual* basis.

1% Commission

<u>1%</u> Interest for one month (12% annual/12)

2% Total fee monthly

2% Monthly × 12 = 24% annual rate

If one considers that the firm selling the accounts is transferring risk as well as receiving funds early, which may allow it to take cash discounts, the rate may not be considered exorbitant. Also, the firm is able to pass on much of the credit-checking cost to the factor.

Asset-Backed Public Offerings of Receivables

While factoring has long been one way of selling receivables, public offerings of securities backed by receivables as collateral gained respectability when General Motors Acceptance Corporation (GMAC) made a public offering of $500 million of asset-backed securities in December 1985. However, you can see by referring back to Figure 8-2 on page 237 that asset-backed securities have fallen out of favor since the financial crisis.

These **asset-backed securities** are nothing more than the sale of receivables. In former years, companies that sold receivables were viewed as short of cash, financially shaky, or in some financial trouble. This negative perception has been diminished by new issues of receivables-backed securities by large, creditworthy companies like IBM.

These asset-backed public offerings of receivables have continued to be marketable, and IBM added a new wrinkle by selling a public offering of receivables due from state and municipal governments. The interest paid to the owners of these securities is not taxable by the federal government. This allows IBM to raise cash at below-market rates. This strategy may be available only to large companies having significant business with state and local government units. Investment bankers continue to develop new types of asset-backed securities, and they are optimistic that the use of all asset-backed securities will continue to grow.

One of the benefits to the issuer is that they trade future cash flows for immediate cash. The asset-backed security is likely to carry a high credit rating of AA or better, even when the issuing firm may have a low credit rating. This allows the issuing firm to acquire lower-cost funds than it could with a bank loan or a bond offering. While this short-term market is still relatively small by money market standards, it can provide an important avenue for corporate liquidity and short-term financing.

However, several problems face the public sale of receivables. One consideration for the buyer of these securities is the probability that the receivables will actually be paid. Even though the loss rate on loans was about one-half of 1 percent in the past, bad debts can be much more than that in times of recession. For example, a serious recession might cause many car owners to default on their car payments to GMAC, thus leaving the owners of the asset-backed security without the promised cash flows. This happened quite often in 2007–2009. To counteract these fears, many issuers set up a loan-loss reserve fund to partially insure against the possibility of a loss.

Inventory Financing

We may also borrow against inventory to acquire funds. The extent to which inventory financing may be employed is based on the marketability of the pledged goods, their associated price stability, and the perishability of the product. Another significant factor is the degree of physical control that can be exercised over the product by the lender. We can relate some of these factors to the stages of inventory production and the nature of lender control.

Stages of Production

Raw materials and finished goods are likely to provide the best collateral, while goods in process may qualify for only a small percentage loan. To the extent that a firm is holding such widely traded raw materials as lumber, metals, grain, cotton, and wool, a loan of 70 to 80 percent or higher is possible. The lender may have to place only a few quick phone calls to dispose of the goods at market value if the borrower fails to repay the loan. For standardized finished goods, such as tires, canned goods, and building products, the same principle would apply. Goods in process, representing altered but unfinished raw materials, may qualify for a loan of only one-fourth of their value or less.

Nature of Lender Control

The methods for controlling pledged inventory go from the simple to the complex, providing ever greater assurances to the lender but progressively higher administrative costs. Typical arrangements are as follows.

Blanket Inventory Liens   The simplest method is for the lender to have a general claim against the inventory of the borrower through **blanket inventory liens**. Specific items are not identified or tagged, and there is no physical control.

Trust Receipts   A **trust receipt** is an instrument acknowledging that the borrower holds the inventory and proceeds from sales in trust for the lender. Each item is carefully marked and specified by serial number. When the items are sold, the proceeds are transferred to the lender and the trust receipt is canceled. Also known as *floor planning,* this financing device is popular among auto and industrial equipment dealers and in the television and home appliance industries. Although it provides tighter control than does the blanket inventory lien, it still does not give the lender direct physical control over inventory—only a better and more legally enforceable system of tracing the goods.

Warehousing   Under this arrangement, goods are physically identified, segregated, and stored under the direction of an independent warehousing company. The firm issues a warehouse receipt to the lender, and goods can be moved only with the lender's approval.

The goods may be stored on the premises of the warehousing firm, an arrangement known as **public warehousing**, or on the *borrower's premises*—under a **field warehousing** agreement. When field warehousing is utilized, it is still an independent warehousing company that exercises control over inventory.

Technology

For small borrowers tired of paying exorbitant interest rates to traditional lenders, here's a new idea for that college loan or automobile loan. Try www.prosper.com, an eBay-type online lender–borrower setup for the Internet age. If you don't want to borrow, you might decide to become a minibanker (lender) online.

Here's how it all works. People who want to borrow go to the prosper.com site and list their borrowing needs. They indicate the amount they want to borrow and the maximum interest rate they are willing to pay. This might be $1,000 to pay off credit card debt at a maximum rate of 10 percent. To help lenders decide whether to forward the funds, the borrower must have his or her credit record checked and receive a credit grade. The borrowers can remain anonymous to everyone but the central facilitator, prosper.com. In most cases, the borrower is not likely to be an AAA individual on the upside or a deadbeat on the downside, but rather an average person in need of funds who is looking for the best possible deal. In this day and time, people look to the Internet to trade in used clothing, so why not money?

The good news for potential lenders is that they do not have to provide the full amount of the loan. They merely submit a small amount of the funds the borrower wishes to acquire. In the prior $1,000 example, a lender may indicate he or she will provide $50 at a rate of 9 percent. There could be 20 to 25 other potential lenders willing to lend anywhere from $25 to $100 each with interest rates varying from 6 to 10 percent.

www.prosper.com
www.lendingclub.com

The borrower then chooses the lenders with the lowest rates to provide funds up to $1,000. It's possible that the loan request will not get fully funded and the borrower will accept 60 to 70 percent of the funds needed on the consolidated loan. On the website, there is a constant update of how much of the loan has been funded, much as on eBay, where there is a constant update on the number of bids on an item and the current high bid.

Once the loan arrangement is completed, Prosper.com facilitates the repayment from the borrower's bank account to the various lenders. This may take place over many months or years depending on the terms of the loan. For doing its part, Prosper.com charges the borrower 1 percent of the loan amount for arranging the loan and the seller 0.5 percent for servicing the loan (transferring the funds, etc.). The total charge is normally less than that involved in hidden fees to a credit card provider.

Some critics of online borrowing say it's too risky to lend money to people you do not know or have never met. But keep in mind people buy $5,000 autographed baseballs on the Internet or accept dates with people they have never met through online arrangements. Could the risk here be much greater?

Perhaps online lending came of age in December 2014 as one of Prosper's competitors, LendingClub, raised over $850 million in an initial public offering. This firm's stock is listed on the New York Stock Exchange under the ticker symbol LC. The stock hit a high of $25.74 and was trading at $4.02 in January 2018. You can follow LendingClub on Yahoo! Finance.

Appraisal of Inventory Control Devices

While the more structured methods of inventory financing appear somewhat restrictive, they are well accepted in certain industries. For example, field warehousing is popular in grain storage and food canning. Well-maintained control measures involve substantial administrative expenses, and they raise the overall costs of borrowing. The costs of inventory financing may run 15 percent or higher. However, as is true of accounts receivable financing, the extension of funds is well synchronized with the need.

Hedging to Reduce Borrowing Risk

Those who are in continual need of borrowed funds to operate their firms are exposed to the risk of interest rate changes. One way to partially reduce that risk is through interest rate hedging activities in the financial futures market. **Hedging** means to engage in a transaction that partially or fully reduces a prior risk exposure.

The **financial futures market** is set up to allow for the trading of a financial instrument at a future point in time. For example, in January 2019 one might sell a Treasury bond contract that is to be closed out in June 2019. The sales price of the June 2019 contract is established by the initial January transaction. However, a subsequent purchase of a June 2019 contract at a currently unknown price will be necessary to close out the transaction. In the financial futures market, you do not physically deliver the goods; you merely execute a later transaction that reverses your initial position. Thus if you initially sell a futures contract, you later buy a contract that covers your initial sale. If you initially buy a futures contract, the opposite is true and you later sell a contract that covers your initial purchase position.

In the case of selling a Treasury bond futures contract, the subsequent pattern of interest rates will determine whether it is profitable or not. If interest rates go up, Treasury bond prices will go down, and you will be able to buy a subsequent contract at a lower price than the sales value you initially established. This will result in a profitable transaction. Note the following example:

Sales price, June 2019 Treasury bond contract* (sale occurs in January 2019)	$100,000
Purchase price, June 2019 Treasury bond contract (purchase occurs in June 2019)	95,000
Profit on futures contract	$ 5,000

*Only a small percentage of the actual dollars involved must be invested to initiate the contract. This is known as margin.

The reason Treasury bond prices went down is that interest rates and bond prices move in opposite directions, and interest rates went up. The lesson to be learned from this example is that rising interest rates can mean profits in the financial futures market if you initially sell a contract and later buy it back.

The financial manager who continually needs to borrow money and fears changes in interest rates can partially hedge his or her position by engaging in the type of futures contract just described. If interest rates rise, the extra cost of borrowing money to actually finance the business can be offset by the profit on a futures contract. If interest rates go down, there will be a loss on the futures contract as bond prices go up, but this will be offset by the more desirable lower borrowing costs of financing the firm.

The financial futures market can be used to partially or fully hedge against almost any financial event. In addition to Treasury bonds, trades may be initiated in Treasury bills, certificates of deposit, GNMA certificates,[3] and many other instruments. The trades may be executed on such exchanges as the Chicago Mercantile Exchange or the New York Futures Exchange.

---

[3]GNMA stands for Government National Mortgage Association, also known as Ginnie Mae.

Large, international firms such as Procter & Gamble or ExxonMobil may also need to hedge against foreign exchange risk. For example, if a company borrows money in Japanese yen and intends to repay the loan using U.S. dollars, it has some concern that the exchange rate between the Japanese yen and the U.S. dollar may change in a way that would make the loan more expensive. If the value of the Japanese yen increases against the U.S. dollar, more dollars will be needed to repay the loan. This movement in the exchange rate increases the total cost of the loan by making the principal repayment more expensive than the original amount of the loan.

The company could hedge against a rise in the Japanese yen by using the Chicago Mercantile Exchange's International Monetary Market where Japanese yen futures contracts are traded, as well as those in euros, Canadian dollars, Mexican pesos, and other currencies. If a ¥100-million Japanese loan were due in six months, the company could buy a Japanese yen futures contract that could be closed out six months in the future. The purchase price on the futures contract is established at the time of the initial purchase transaction. The eventual sales price for the contract will be determined later. If the value of the Japanese yen increases against the dollar, profit will be made on the futures contract. The money made on the futures contract can offset the higher cost of the company's loan payment. The currency exposure has thus been effectively hedged.[4]

SUMMARY

A firm in search of short-term financing must be aware of all the institutional arrangements that are available. Trade credit from suppliers is normally the most available form of short-term financing and is a natural outgrowth of the buying and reselling of goods. Larger firms tend to be net providers of trade credit, while smaller firms are net users.

Bank loans are usually short term and self-liquidating, being paid back from funds from the normal operations of the firm. A financially strong customer will be offered the lowest rate, with the rates to other customers scaled up to reflect their risk category. Bankers use either the prime rate or LIBOR as their base rate and add to that depending on the creditworthiness of the customer. Banks also use compensating balances as well as fees to increase the effective yield to the bank.

An alternative to bank credit for the large, prestigious firm is the use of commercial paper, which represents a short-term, unsecured promissory note issued by the firm. Though generally issued at a rate below prime, it is an impersonal means of financing that may "dry up" during difficult financing periods.

Firms are increasingly turning to foreign markets for lower-cost sources of funds. They may borrow in the Eurodollar market (foreign dollar loans) or borrow foreign currency directly from banks in an attempt to lower their borrowing costs.

By using accounts receivable and inventory as collateral for a loan, the firm may be able to turn these current assets into cash more quickly than by waiting for the normal cash flow cycle. By using a secured form of financing, the firm ties its borrowing requirements directly to its asset buildup. The firm may also sell its accounts receivable to a factor. These secured forms of borrowing may be expensive but may fit the

---

[4]For a more complete discussion of corporate hedging in the futures market, see "Commodities and Financial Futures" in Chapter 15 of Geoffrey Hirt and Stanley Block, *Fundamentals of Investment Management,* 10th ed. (New York: McGraw-Hill, 2012).

credit needs of the firm, particularly the needs of a small firm that cannot qualify for lower-cost bank financing or the commercial paper market.

Finally, the financial manager may wish to consider the use of hedging through the financial futures market. The consequences of rapid interest rate or currency changes can be reduced through participation in the futures market.

LIST OF TERMS

DISCUSSION QUESTIONS

1. Under what circumstances would it be advisable to borrow money to take a cash discount? *(LO8-1)*

2. Discuss the relative use of credit between large and small firms. Which group is generally in the net creditor position, and why? *(LO8-1)*

3. How have new banking laws influenced competition? *(LO8-2)*

4. What is the prime interest rate? How does the average bank customer fare in regard to the prime interest rate? *(LO8-2)*

5. What does LIBOR mean? Is LIBOR normally higher or lower than the U.S. prime interest rate? *(LO8-2)*

6. What advantages do compensating balances have for banks? Are the advantages to banks necessarily disadvantages to corporate borrowers? *(LO8-2)*

7. Commercial paper may show up on corporate balance sheets as either a current asset or a current liability. Explain this statement. *(LO8-3)*

8. What are the advantages of commercial paper in comparison with bank borrowing at the prime rate? What is a disadvantage? *(LO8-3)*

9. What is the difference between pledging accounts receivable and factoring accounts receivable? *(LO8-4)*

10. What is an asset-backed public offering? *(LO8-4)*

11. Briefly discuss three types of lender control used in inventory financing. *(LO8-4)*

12. What is meant by hedging in the financial futures market to offset interest rate risks? *(LO8-5)*

PRACTICE PROBLEMS AND SOLUTIONS

Cash discount
decision
(LO8-1)

1. Automatic Machinery is being offered a 2/10, net 50 cash discount. The firm will have to borrow the funds at 12 percent to take the discount. Should it proceed with the discount?

Computation
of rates
(LO8-2)

2. A company plans to borrow $2 million for a year. The stated interest rate is 12 percent. Compute the effective interest rate under each of these assumptions. Each part stands alone.

   a. The interest is discounted.

   b. There is a 20 percent compensating balance requirement.

   c. It is a 12-month installment loan.

   d. Assume the interest is only $45,000 and the loan is for 90 days.

Solutions

1. First compute the cost of not taking the cash discount.

$$\text{Cost of failing to take a cash discount} = \frac{\text{Discount \%}}{100\% - \text{Discount \%}}$$

$$\times \frac{360}{\text{Final due date} - \text{Discount period}}$$

$$= \frac{2\%}{100\% - 2\%} \times \frac{360}{50 - 10}$$

$$= 2.04\% \times 9 = 18.36\%$$

Since money can be borrowed at 12 percent, the firm should borrow the funds and take the discount.

2. *a.* Effective rate on discounted loan $= \dfrac{\text{Interest}}{\text{Principal} - \text{Interest}}$

$$\times \frac{\text{Days in the year (360)}}{\text{Days loan is outstanding}}$$

$$= \frac{\$240,000}{\$2,000,000 - 240,000} \times \frac{360}{360}$$

$$= \frac{\$240,000}{1,760,000} \times 1 = 13.64\%$$

   b. Effective rate with compensating balances

$$= \frac{\text{Interest}}{\text{Principal} - \text{Compensating balance in dollars}} \times \frac{\text{Days in the year (360)}}{\text{Days loan is outstanding}}$$

Compensating balance $= 20\% \times \$2,000,000 = \$400,000$

$$\text{Effective rate} = \frac{\$240,000}{1,600,000} \times 1 = 15\%$$

   c. Effective rate on installment loan

$$= \frac{2 \times \text{Annual number of payments} \times \text{Interest}}{(\text{Total number of payments} + 1) \times \text{Principal}}$$

$$= \frac{2 \times 12 \times \$240,000}{(12 + 1) \times \$2,000,000} \times \frac{\$576,000}{2,600,000} = 22.15\%$$

d.   Effective rate = $\dfrac{\text{Interest}}{\text{Principal}} \times \dfrac{\text{Days in the year (360)}}{\text{Days loan is outstanding}}$

$$= \dfrac{\$45,000}{\$2,000,000} \times \dfrac{360}{90} = 2.25\% \times 4 = 9\%$$

PROBLEMS

connect Selected problems are available with Connect. Please see the preface for more information.

Basic Problems

1. Compute the cost of not taking the following cash discounts:
   a.   2/10, net 40
   b.   2/15, net 30
   c.   2/10, net 45
   d.   3/10, net 90

   Cash discount decision (LO8-1)

2. Regis Clothiers can borrow from its bank at 17 percent to take a cash discount. The terms of the cash discount are 3/19, net 45. Should the firm borrow the funds?

   Cash discount decision (LO8-1)

3. Simmons Corp. can borrow from its bank at 17 percent to take a cash discount. The terms of the cash discount are 1.5/10, net 45. Should the firm borrow the funds?

   Cash discount decision (LO8-1)

4. Your bank will lend you $4,000 for 45 days at a cost of $50 interest. What is your effective rate of interest?

   Effective rate of interest (LO8-2)

5. A pawnshop will lend $2,500 for 45 days at a cost of $35 interest. What is the effective rate of interest?

   Effective rate of interest (LO8-2)

6. Sol Pine borrows $5,000 for one year at 13 percent interest. What is the effective rate of interest if the loan is discounted?

   Effective rate on discounted loan (LO8-2)

7. Mary Ott is going to borrow $10,400 for 120 days and pay $150 interest. What is the effective rate of interest if the loan is discounted?

   Effective rate on discounted loan (LO8-2)

8. Dr. Ruth is going to borrow $5,000 to help write a book. The loan is for one year and the money can be borrowed at either the prime rate or the LIBOR rate. Assume the prime rate is 11 percent and LIBOR 1.5 percent less. Also assume there will be a $45 transaction fee with LIBOR (this amount must be added to the interest cost with LIBOR). Which loan has the lower effective interest cost?

   Prime vs. LIBOR (LO8-2)

9. Gulliver Travel Agency thinks interest rates in Europe are low. The firm borrows euros at 9 percent for one year. During this time period, the dollar falls 14 percent against the euro. What is the effective interest rate on the loan for one year? (Consider the 14 percent fall in the value of the dollar as well as the interest payment.)

   Foreign borrowing (LO8-2)

10. Talmud Book Company borrows $24,900 for 60 days at 12 percent interest. What is the dollar cost of the loan?

$$\begin{array}{c} \text{Dollar cost} \\ \text{of loan} \end{array} = \begin{array}{c} \text{Amount} \\ \text{borrowed} \end{array} \times \begin{array}{c} \text{Interest} \\ \text{rate} \end{array} \times \frac{\text{Days loan is outstanding}}{\text{Days in the year (360)}}$$

11. McGriff Dog Food Company normally takes 27 days to pay for average daily credit purchases of $9,530. Its average daily sales are $10,680, and it collects accounts in 32 days.

    a.   What is its net credit position? That is, compute its accounts receivable and accounts payable and subtract the latter from the former.

$$\text{Accounts receivable} = \frac{\text{Average daily credit sales} \times}{\text{Average collection period}}$$

$$\text{Accounts payable} = \frac{\text{Average daily credit purchases} \times}{\text{Average payment period}}$$

    b.   If the firm extends its average payment period from 27 days to 37 days (and all else remains the same), what is the firm's new net credit position? Has it improved its cash flow?

12. Maxim Air Filters Inc. plans to borrow $300,000 for one year. Northeast National Bank will lend the money at 10 percent interest and requires a compensating balance of 20 percent. What is the effective rate of interest?

13. Digital Access Inc. needs $400,000 in funds for a project.

    a.   With a compensating balance requirement of 20 percent, how much will the firm need to borrow?

    b.   Given your answer to part a and a stated interest rate of 9 percent on the *total* amount borrowed, what is the effective rate on the $400,000 actually being used?

Intermediate Problems

14. Carey Company is borrowing $200,000 for one year at 12 percent from Second Intrastate Bank. The bank requires a 20 percent compensating balance. What is the effective rate of interest? What would the effective rate be if Carey were required to make 12 equal monthly payments to retire the loan? The principal, as used in Formula 8-6, refers to funds the firm can utilize effectively (Amount borrowed − Compensating balance).

15. Randall Corporation plans to borrow $233,000 for one year at 20 percent from the Waco State Bank. There is a 21 percent compensating balance requirement. Randall Corporation keeps minimum transaction balances of $17,500 in the normal course of business. This idle cash counts toward meeting the compensating balance requirement. What is the effective rate of interest?

16. The treasurer for the Macon Blue Sox baseball team is seeking a $23,600 loan for one year from the 4th National Bank of Macon. The stated interest rate is 10 percent, and there is a 15 percent compensating balance requirement. The

treasurer always keeps a minimum of $2,280 in the baseball team's checking accounts. These funds count toward meeting any compensating balance requirements. What will be the effective rate of interest on this loan?

17. Your company plans to borrow $13 million for 12 months, and your banker gives you a stated rate of 24 percent interest. You would like to know the effective rate of interest for the following types of loans. (Each of the following parts stands alone.)

    a.   Simple 24 percent interest with a 10 percent compensating balance.

    b.   Discounted interest.

    c.   An installment loan (12 payments).

    d.   Discounted interest with a 5 percent compensating balance.

Effective rate under different terms (LO8-2)

18. If you borrow $5,300 at $400 interest for one year, what is your effective interest rate for the following payment plans?

    a.   Annual payment

    b.   Semiannual payments

    c.   Quarterly payments

    d.   Monthly payments

Effective rate under different terms (LO8-2)

Advanced Problems

19. Zerox Copying Company plans to borrow $172,000. New Jersey National Bank will lend the money at one-half percentage point over the prime rate at the time of 17½ percent (18 percent total) and requires a compensating balance of 21 percent. The principal in this case will be funds that the firm can effectively use in the business. This loan is for one year. What is the effective rate of interest? What would the effective rate be if Zerox were required to make four quarterly payments to retire the loan?

Effective rate under different terms (LO8-2)

20. Lewis and Clark Camping Supplies Inc. is borrowing $51,000 from Western State Bank. The total interest is $15,700. The loan will be paid by making equal monthly payments for the next three years. What is the effective rate of interest on this installment loan?

Installment loan for multiyears (LO8-2)

21. Mr. Hugh Warner is a very cautious businessman. His supplier offers trade credit terms of 3/15, net 85. Mr. Warner never takes the discount offered, but he pays his suppliers in 75 days rather than the 85 days allowed so that he is sure the payments are never late. What is Mr. Warner's cost of not taking the cash discount?

Cash discount under special circumstance (LO8-2)

22. The Reynolds Corporation buys from its suppliers on terms of 3/17, net 45. Reynolds has not been utilizing the discounts offered and has been taking 45 days to pay its bills.

    Ms. Duke, Reynolds Corporation vice president, has suggested that the company begin to take the discounts offered. Duke proposes that the company borrow from its bank at a stated rate of 16 percent. The bank requires a 27 percent

Bank loan to take cash discount (LO8-1 & 8-2)

compensating balance on these loans. Current account balances would not be available to meet any of this compensating balance requirement.

Do you agree with Duke's proposal?

Bank loan to take cash discount
(LO8-1 & 8-2)

23. In Problem 22, if the compensating balance were 20 percent instead of 27 percent, would your answer change? Do the appropriate calculation.

Bank loan to take cash discount
(LO8-1 & 8-2)

24. Neveready Flashlights Inc. needs $340,000 to take a cash discount of 3/17, net 72. A banker will lend the money for 55 days at an interest cost of $10,400.

   a.   What is the effective rate on the bank loan?

   b.   How much would it cost (in percentage terms) if the firm did not take the cash discount but paid the bill in 72 days instead of 17 days?

   c.   Should the firm borrow the money to take the discount?

   d.   If the banker requires a 20 percent compensating balance, how much must the firm borrow to end up with the $340,000?

   e.   What would be the effective interest rate in part *d* if the interest charge for 55 days were $13,000? Should the firm borrow with the 20 percent compensating balance? (The firm has no funds to count against the compensating balance requirement.)

Bank loan to take cash discount
(LO8-1 & 8-2)

25. Harper Engine Company needs $631,000 to take a cash discount of 2.5/20, net 75. A banker will lend the money for 55 days at an interest cost of $13,300.

   a.   What is the effective rate on the bank loan?

   b.   How much would it cost (in percentage terms) if Harper did not take the cash discount but paid the bill in 75 days instead of 20 days?

   c.   Should Harper borrow the money to take the discount?

   d.   If another banker requires a 10 percent compensating balance, how much must Harper borrow to end up with $631,000?

   e.   What would be the effective interest rate in part *d* if the interest charge for 55 days were $10,100? Should Harper borrow with the 10 percent compensating balance? (There are no funds to count against the compensating balance requirement.)

Competing terms from banks
(LO8-2)

26. Summit Record Company is negotiating with two banks for a $151,000 loan. Fidelity Bank requires a 28 percent compensating balance, discounts the loan, and wants to be paid back in four quarterly payments. Southwest Bank requires a 14 percent compensating balance, does not discount the loan, but wants to be paid back in 12 monthly installments. The stated rate for both banks is 10 percent. Compensating balances will be subtracted from the $151,000 in determining the available funds in part *a*.

   a.   Calculate the effective interest rate for Fidelity Bank and Southwest Bank. Which loan should Summit accept?

   b.   Recompute the effective cost of interest, assuming that Summit ordinarily maintains $42,280 at each bank in deposits that will serve as compensating balances.

   c.   Does your choice of banks change if the assumption in part *b* is correct?

27. Charming Paper Company sells to the 12 accounts listed here:

Ӿ
Accounts receivable
financing
(LO8-1)

Account	Receivable Balance Outstanding	Average Age of the Account over the Last Year
A	$ 60,800	22
B	168,000	43
C	78,300	19
D	24,300	55
E	58,900	42
F	238,000	39
G	30,400	16
H	374,000	72
I	41,400	32
J	96,500	58
K	292,000	17
L	67,700	37

Capital Financial Corporation will lend 90 percent against account balances that have averaged 30 days or less, 80 percent for account balances between 31 and 40 days, and 70 percent for account balances between 41 and 45 days. Customers that take over 45 days to pay their bills are not considered acceptable accounts for a loan.

The current prime rate is 15.5 percent, and Capital charges 4.5 percent over prime to Charming as its annual loan rate.

a. Determine the maximum loan for which Charming Paper Company could qualify.

b. Determine how much one month's interest expense would be on the loan balance determined in part *a.*

28. The treasurer for Pittsburgh Iron Works wishes to use financial futures to hedge her interest rate exposure. She will sell five Treasury futures contracts at $138,000 per contract. It is July, and the contracts must be closed out in December of this year. Long-term interest rates are currently 13.3 percent. If they increase to 14.5 percent, assume the value of the contracts will go down by 5 percent. Also, if interest rates do increase by 1.2 percent, assume the firm will have additional interest expense on its business loans and other commitments of $53,000. This expense, of course, will be separate from the futures contracts.

Hedging to
offset risk
(LO8-5)

a. What will be the profit or loss on the futures contract if interest rates increase to 14.5 percent by December when the contract is closed out?

b. Explain why a profit or loss took place on the futures contracts.

c. After considering the hedging in part *a,* what is the net cost to the firm of the increased interest expense of $53,000? What percentage of this $53,000 cost did the treasurer effectively hedge away?

d. Indicate whether there would be a profit or loss on the futures contracts if interest rates dropped.

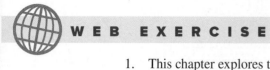

1. This chapter explores the various sources of financing working capital needs. It also mentions General Electric Capital as a competitor to the banking community. This exercise examines General Electric Capital's various services. Go to General Electric's website at www.ge.com.

    Go to "GE Capital" on the home page. Click on "GE Businesses."

2. Scroll down and list three types of services GE Capital provides.

3. Explain the benefits of GE Capital's Aviation Finance.

4. Based on the information you have seen, does it appear that GE Capital competes with more traditional financial institutions?

Note: Occasionally a topic we have listed may have been deleted, updated, or moved into a different location on a website. If you click on the site map or site index, you will be introduced to a table of contents that should aid you in finding the topic you are looking for.

The Capital Budgeting Process

FOUR

>>> RELATED WEBSITES

finance.yahoo.com
www.microsoft.com
www.cisco.com
www.oracle.com

www.intel.com
www.genecor.com
www.lexicon-genetics.com
www.celera.com

www.deltagen.com
www.marvell.com
www.ciena.com
www.alcoa.com

The Time Value of Money

The time value of money can have a dramatic effect over time. The best way to demonstrate this point is to give an example that directly applies to you. When you graduate from college and secure a job, you will have the opportunity to put money in an individual retirement account (IRA). The part of your salary that you put in the IRA will not be taxed at that time and will be allowed to grow tax-free for 40–50 years. You can repeat this process every year. Only when you withdraw the money in retirement are your annual contributions to the IRA and yearly gains taxed (perhaps in 2050 or 2060).

Suppose you set aside $2,000 annually for 50 years (that will be the typical work life span in the future as people are continuing to live longer according to the Department of Labor). Your total contributions will be $100,000. Keep in mind that each annual contribution is assumed to grow in value if you invest it wisely. If you get a 6 percent return on your annual contribution over 50 years, you will have accumulated $580,680 (at which point the government will probably take one-third in taxes). The huge gain in value from $100,000 to $580,680 is all due to the time value of money compounding effect.

While not all examples are this dramatic, the time value of money applies to many day-to-day decisions. Understanding the effective rate on a business loan, the mortgage payment in a real estate transaction, or the true return on an investment depends on understanding the time value of money. As long as an investor can make a positive return on idle dollars, distinctions must be made between money received today and money received in the future. The investor/lender essentially demands that a financial "rent" be paid on his or her funds as current dollars are set aside today in anticipation of higher returns in the future.

Relationship to the Capital Outlay Decision

The decision to purchase new plant and equipment or to introduce a new product in the market requires using capital allocating or capital budgeting techniques. Essentially we must determine whether future benefits are sufficiently large to justify current outlays. It is important that we develop the mathematical tools for the time value of money as the first step toward making capital allocation decisions. Let us now examine the basic terminology of "time value of money."

Future Value—Single Amount

In determining the **future value**, we measure the value of an amount that is allowed to grow at a given interest rate over a period of time. Assume an investor has $1,000 and wishes to know its worth after four years if it grows at 10 percent per year. At the end of the first year, the investor will have $1,000 × 1.10, or $1,100. By the end of year 2, the $1,100 will have grown to $1,210 ($1,100 × 1.10). This process of earning more interest on a previous period's interest is called compounding. The four-year pattern is indicated here:

1st year	$1,000 × 1.10 = $1,100
2nd year	$1,100 × 1.10 = $1,210
3rd year	$1,210 × 1.10 = $1,331
4th year	$1,331 × 1.10 = $1,464.10

After the fourth year, the investor has accumulated $1,464. Because compounding scenarios often cover a long period, a more generalized formula is necessary to describe the compounding procedure. We shall let

$$FV = \text{Future value}$$
$$PV = \text{Present value}$$
$$i = \text{Interest value}$$
$$n = \text{Number of periods}$$

The simple formula is:

$$FV = PV(1 + i)^n \qquad (9\text{-}1)$$

In this case, PV = $1,000, $i = 10$ percent, $n = 4$, so we have:

$$FV = \$1,000(1.10)^4, \text{ or } \$1,000 \times 1.4641 = \$1,464.10$$

The term $(1.10)^4$ is found to equal 1.4641 by multiplying 1.10 four times itself (the fourth power).

Because the future value equation is simple, you will probably find that calculating the future value of a single amount can be done easily using this equation. However, some students will prefer to use a financial calculator or a spreadsheet to do these calculations.

Although the future value of a single amount is straightforward, we will encounter cash flow patterns that are more complicated. To organize those cash flows and other information in a useful manner, you will need to use a timeline. Using timelines is an excellent habit to form. Many of the early examples shown will probably seem so simple that a timeline adds little to your organizational abilities. However, by forming this good habit early, you will be much more competent and confident when you begin to encounter more difficult concepts.

With this in mind, consider the following timeline:

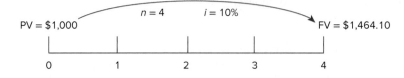

The intervals between each of the periods represent the number of years. The number "2" labels the end of the second year, and the label "4" marks the end of the fourth year. Notice that the period markers are at the end of each year.

Cash flows are shown above the timeline. The present value of $1,000 grows at 10% for 4 years to the future value of $1,464.10.

One concept that may be difficult to grasp is that a number marks the end of a period, but it also marks the beginning of another period. For example, the number "2" marks the end of the second year, but this is also the beginning of the third year. Likewise, the end of the third year will coincide with the beginning of the fourth year. Therefore, the beginning of the fourth year is labeled "3" on the timeline.

A financial calculator is useful for solving common time-value-of-money problems. Financial calculators usually have five keys that represent the variables used in most common problems. You have already seen four of these variables in Formula 9-1:

The keys $\boxed{\text{N}}$ and $\boxed{\text{I/Y}}$ represent the number of periods and the interest rate as described in each of the prior equations, but note that some calculators use $\boxed{\text{I}}$ rather than $\boxed{\text{I/Y}}$. For calculations involving the present value or future value of a single payment, the $\boxed{\text{PV}}$ and $\boxed{\text{FV}}$ keys represent present value and future value. These are the only keys needed to solve for problems involving future values of a single payment. The $\boxed{\text{PMT}}$ key is used for annuity problems, which we address later in this chapter.

Financial Calculator Hints

Students often encounter problems using a financial calculator because they have values stored in the calculator from previous calculations. There are always two things to do before starting your calculations: Clear the calculator and set the decimal point. Below are the keystrokes for accomplishing both of these tasks using the Texas Instruments BAII Plus, which is used for all of the examples in the margins of this chapter. Further information is offered in Appendix 9C. Also, the website www.tvmcalcs.com has instructions for numerous other commonly used financial calculators.

FINANCIAL CALCULATOR

Clearing the Calculator

Function	*Function*		
CE/C	CE/C		Clears the screen
2nd	CLR WORK		Clears regular memory
2nd	CLR TVM		Clears TVM memory
CF	2nd	CLR WORK	Clears cash flow values

FINANCIAL CALCULATOR

Setting the Decimal Point

Function
2nd
FORMAT
Value
4
Function
Enter

We will address a few details concerning how to use the financial calculator after we see an example. Let's consider the future value problem we saw in this chapter: What is the future value of $1,000 if it is invested at 10% and compounds for 4 years?

$$FV = PV(1 + i)^n$$

The keystrokes for this calculator example are presented in the margin. Notice that we enter the appropriate value for each variable prior to pressing the appropriate function key. The calculator assumes that either the PV key or the FV key is a cash outflow, and the solution will have the opposite sign. Because we enter a negative value for PV , the final solution is positive. If you enter a positive value for PV , the FV solution will have a negative sign. Also notice that we enter the interest rate as a whole number, 10. With a nonfinancial calculator you would need to enter the value as 0.10, but most financial calculators assume that the number entered for the I/Y key is a percentage. To enter the value 0.065 or 6.5%, you would enter 6.5 before striking the I/Y key. In the margin example, the CPT key shown above FV stands for "compute." Not all financial calculators use a CPT key.

Time value of money problems can also be solved using Excel functions. There are dozens of financial functions available in Excel, but a student who can use five basic functions can solve almost any problem. These functions are the **FV, PV, RATE, NPER,** and **PMT** functions. Each of these functions requires inputs (called arguments) that correspond to the variables in the time value equations. Since we are currently interested in solving for future values as in Formula 9-1, we will discuss Excel's **FV** function.

FV(rate, nper, pmt, [pv], [type])

The **FV** function syntax (similar to the other four basic time-value functions) has the following arguments:

- **rate** The interest rate per period.
- **nper** The total number of periods.
- **pmt** The payment made each period for an annuity. (Since this problem does not involve an annuity, pmt = 0.)
- **pv** The present value.
- **type** An optional argument that can be omitted for this problem.

Excel's **FV** function can be used to calculate the future value of a single payment. The following Excel spreadsheet shows two examples of the **FV** function. In cell D1, the **FV** function references cells B1 to B4 for each argument. When a user begins to type the **FV** function, Excel provides some help by displaying a screen tip showing the arguments required in the function. Here you see the on-screen tip provided by Excel as a banner in cell D2. Cells D1 and D2 (in combination) show how the function appears as you type in the required arguments. Cell D3 shows the calculated answer for cell D1 after the enter key has been pressed. Once the enter key is pressed, the tip in cell D2 will disappear.

The **FV** function in cell D5 uses numerical values for each argument rather than cell references. The method used in cell D5 is called *hardcoding*. In general, cell references are preferred to hardcoded solutions. Excel's ability to accept cell references in formulas is one of its greatest strengths as a spreadsheet tool.

Excel's on-screen help is shown in cell D6, and the ultimate value produced after striking the enter key is shown in cell D7. Of course, the values in D3 and D7 are identical to the calculator solution.

FINANCIAL CALCULATOR

Future Value

Enter	Function
4	N
10	I/Y
−1000	PV
0	PMT

Function	Solution
CPT	
FV	1,464.10

	A	B	C	D	E	F
1	rate	10.00%		=FV(B1,B2,B3,B4)		
2	nper	4		**FV**(rate, nper, pmt, [pv], [type])		
3	pmt	0		$1,464.10		
4	pv	−1000				
5				━ı FV(0.1,4,0, 1000)		
6				**FV**(rate, nper, pmt, [pv], [type])		
7				$1,464.10		

As in the calculator keystroke example, Excel's **FV** solution has the opposite sign of the **pv** argument. Since we invested $1,000 initially, **pv** equals −1000, and the **FV** returned has the opposite (positive) value.

Present Value—Single Amount

In recent years, the sports pages have been filled with stories of athletes who receive multimillion-dollar contracts for signing with sports organizations. Perhaps you have wondered how the New York Yankees or Los Angeles Lakers can afford to pay such fantastic sums. The answer may lie in the concept of present value—a sum payable in the future is worth less today than the stated amount.

The **present value** is the exact opposite of the future value. For example, earlier we determined that the future value of $1,000 for four periods at 10 percent was $1,464.10. We could reverse the process to state that $1,464.10 received four years into the future, with a 10 percent interest or **discount rate**, is worth only $1,000 today—its present value.

A timeline for this problem is presented as follows:

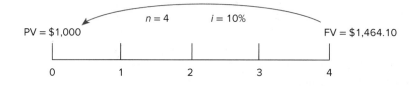

You will notice that this timeline looks similar to the first one. In fact, only the direction of the arrow is reversed. This reflects the close relationship between present values and future values. Figure 9-1 depicts this relationship. When the interest rate is 10%, $1,000 at the time zero has the same value as $1,464.10 at time 4. Also, every point along the red line in Figure 9-1 shows the value at other points in time. Every value along the red line has the same value at a different time, given that i is equal to 10% ($i = 10\%$).

The formula for present value is derived from the original formula for future value:

$$FV = PV(1 + i)^n \qquad \text{Future value}$$

$$PV = FV\left[\frac{1}{(1 + i)^n}\right] \qquad \text{Present value} \qquad (9\text{-}2)$$

The present value can be determined by finding the mathematical solution to this formula:

$$PV = \$1,464.10 \times \left[\frac{1}{(1.10)^4}\right] = \$1,000$$

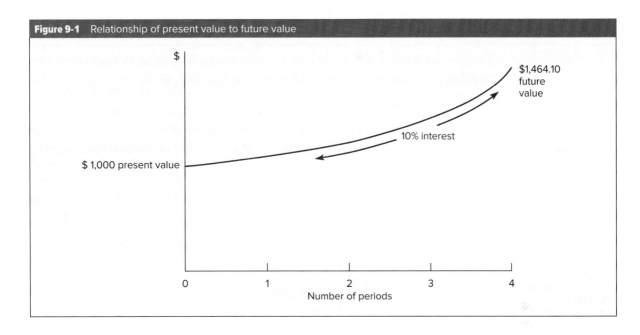

Figure 9-1   Relationship of present value to future value

To help you feel comfortable with the various methods of writing the present value formula, here are several alternatives that all have the same algebraic meaning:

$$PV = FV\left(\frac{1}{(1+i)^n}\right) = FV\left(\frac{1}{(1+i)}\right)^n = \frac{FV}{(1+i)^n} = FV(1+i)^{-n}$$

With a little practice, you will be completely comfortable using Formula 9-2, but we will also cover the use of financial calculators and spreadsheet functions.

Let's consider the present value version of the above problem: What is the present value of $1,464.10 if it is discounted at 10% for 4 years?

$$PV = FV\,\frac{1}{(1+i)^n}$$

Again the calculator keystrokes are shown in the margin. Because we enter a negative value for **FV**, the final solution is positive. If you enter a positive value for **FV**, your **PV** solution will be −$1,000.

Excel's **PV** function produces the present value of a single payment. The function in cell D1 uses cell references. The function in cell D5 uses hardcoded inputs. In both cases, the values produced by the **PV** function are identical to the calculator solution, but using cell references is preferred where possible.

FINANCIAL CALCULATOR

Present Value

Enter	Function
4	N
10	I/Y
−1464.1	FV
0	PMT

Function	Solution
CPT	
PV	1,000.00

	A	B	C	D	E	F
1	rate	10.00%		=+PV(B1,B2,B3,B4)		
2	nper	4		**PV**(rate, nper, pmt, [fv], [type])		
3	pmt	0		$1,000.00		
4	fv	−1464.1				
5				=+PV(0.1,4,0,−1464.1)		
6				**PV**(rate, nper, pmt, [fv], [type])		
7				$1,000.00		

Interest Rate—Single Amount

Thus far, we have seen that we can solve for the present value in Formula 9-1 by rewriting the equation to isolate PV on the left side of the equation to form Formula 9-2. Both Formula 9-1 and 9-2 use the same four variables: FV, PV, *i,* and *n.* In fact, if we know any three of these variables, we can always solve for the fourth.

Suppose we want to know the return on an investment that we have made, and we know the future value, present value, and the number of compounding periods. The return on the investment would be the interest rate that relates all of these variables.[1]

$$i = \left(\frac{\text{FV}}{\text{PV}}\right)^{\frac{1}{n}} - 1 \qquad (9\text{-}3)$$

When we substitute the values from our previous example, we find

$$i = \left(\frac{\$1,464.10}{\$1,000}\right)^{\frac{1}{4}} - 1 = 10\%$$

FINANCIAL CALCULATOR

Interest Value

Enter	Function
4	N
1000	PV
−1464.1	FV
0	PMT

Function	Solution
CPT	
I/Y	10

How do we solve for the interest rate using a financial calculator?

In this example, shown in the margin, you should notice that the $\boxed{\text{FV}}$ and $\boxed{\text{PV}}$ keys must be assigned different signs. The solution value is shown as 10, but this means that the interest rate is 10%.

Excel's **RATE** function calculates the interest rate that equates a present value to a future value over *n* periods. The function in cell D1 below references the arguments in cells B1 to B4. The function in cell D5 is hardcoded. Although cell references are preferred, in both cases the values produced by the **RATE** function are identical to the calculator solution.

	A	B	C	D	E	F	G
1	nper	4		=RATE(B1,B2,B3,B4)			
2	pmt	0		**RATE**(nper, pmt, pv, [fv], [type], [guess])			
3	pv	1000		10.00%			
4	fv	−1464.1					
5				=+RATE(4,0,1000,−1464.1)			
6				**RATE**(nper, pmt, pv, [fv], [type], [guess])			
7				10.00%			

---

[1]Because $(x^n)^{\frac{1}{n}} = x$, we can derive Formula 9-3 starting with Formula 9-1:

$$\text{FV} = \text{PV}(1 + i)^n$$

$$\frac{\text{FV}}{\text{PV}} = (1 + i)^n$$

$$\left(\frac{\text{FV}}{\text{PV}}\right)^{\frac{1}{n}} = [(1 + i)^n]^{\frac{1}{n}}$$

$$\left(\frac{\text{FV}}{\text{PV}}\right)^{\frac{1}{n}} = 1 + i$$

$$\left(\frac{\text{FV}}{\text{PV}}\right)^{\frac{1}{n}} - 1 = i$$

Number of Periods—Single Amount

Assume that an investment can earn 10% per year. If we wanted to know how many years it would take for a $1,000 investment to grow to be $1,464.10, we can make use of the log function, denoted in Formula 9-4 as ln(x), to find the solution.[2]

$$n = \frac{\ln\left(\dfrac{FV}{PV}\right)}{\ln(1 + i)} \tag{9-4}$$

If we substitute the values from our previous example, we find

$$n = \frac{\ln\left(\dfrac{\$1,464.10}{\$1,000}\right)}{\ln(1 + 10\%)} = \frac{\ln(1.4641)}{\ln(1.10)}$$

$$n = \frac{0.381241}{0.09531} = 4$$

The financial calculator does not require us to use the log function, as you can see in the keystroke solution for the number of periods in the margin.

Excel's **NPER** function calculates the interest rate that equates a present value to a future value given the periodic interest rate, *i*. The function in cell D1 references the arguments in cells B1 to B4. The function in cell D5 is hardcoded. Cell references are preferred, but in both cases, the values produced by the **NPER** function are identical to the calculator solution.

	A	B	C	D	E	F
1	rate	10.00%		=NPER(B1,B2,B3,B4)		
2	pmt	0		NPER(rate, pmt, pv, [fv], [type])		
3	pv	1000		4		
4	fv	−1464.1				
5				=+NPER(0.1,0,1000,−1464.1)		
6				NPER(rate, pmt, pv, [fv], [type])		
7				4		

While the algebra required to find the present value and the future value of a single amount is very straightforward, the algebra needed to find the interest rate or compounding periods is more complex. For this reason, many students choose to use the formulas to solve for PV and FV, but they use the financial calculator function keys or Excel to solve for the interest rate or the number of periods.

FINANCIAL CALCULATOR

Number of Periods

Enter	Function
10	I/Y
1000	PV
−1464.1	FV
0	PMT

Function	Solution
CPT	
N	4

---

[2]To derive Formula 9-4 from Formula 9-1, we must know something about natural logarithms.

$$\ln(x^n) = n \times \ln(x)$$

Starting with Formula 9-1

$$FV = PV(1 + i)^n$$

$$\frac{FV}{PV} = (1 + i)^n$$

$$\ln\frac{FV}{PV} = \ln[(1 + i)^n] = n \times \ln[(1 + i)]$$

$$\frac{\ln\left(\dfrac{FV}{PV}\right)}{\ln(1 + i)} = n$$

Future Value—Annuity

Our calculations up to now have dealt with single amounts rather than an **annuity**, which is defined as a series of consecutive payments or receipts of equal amount. Ordinary annuity payments are assumed to occur at the end of each period. If we invest $1,000 at the end of each year for four years and our funds grow at 10 percent, what is the future value of this annuity?

First let's draw a timeline to organize the information.

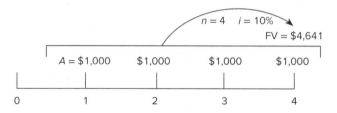

Notice that the annuity payments are of equal size, and they occur *at the end* of each year. When payments occur at the end of each year, the payment stream is called an **ordinary annuity**. Shortly we will discuss equations that calculate the future value and present value of annuities. However, these equations only apply when the annuity payments occur *at the end* of each period. Students often overlook this point, so it is worth repeating. *Unless otherwise stated, annuity payments are assumed to come at the end of each period.*

We may find the future value for each payment and then total them to find the **future value of an annuity** (Figure 9-2). The future value for the annuity in Figure 9-2

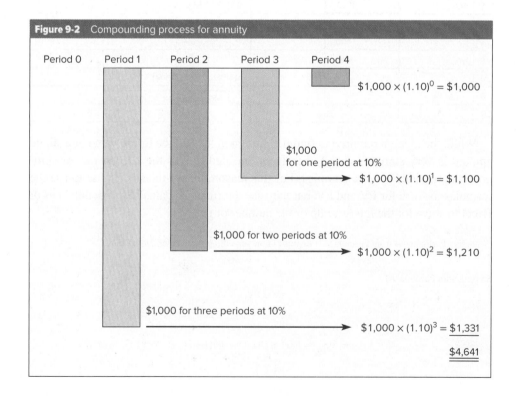

Figure 9-2   Compounding process for annuity

is \$4,641. Although this is a four-period annuity, the first \$1,000 comes at the *end* of the first period and has but three periods to run, the second \$1,000 at the *end* of the second period, with two periods remaining—and so on down to the last \$1,000 at the end of the fourth period. The final payment (period 4) earns no return at all.

The calculations presented in Figure 9-2 can be tedious when the number of payments becomes very large, but the future value of an annuity can be calculated using an algebraic formula:

$$FV_A = A(1 + i)^{n-1} + A(1 + i)^{n-2} \ldots A(1 + i)^1 + A(1 + i)^0$$

$$FV_A = A \left[\frac{(1 + i)^n - 1}{i} \right] \tag{9-5}$$

where

FV_A = future value of an annuity

A = the annuity payment

i = the interest rate

n = the number of payments

Using Formula 9-5 to calculate the future value of our annuity payments,

$A = \$1,000$

$i = 10\%$

$n = 4$

$$FV_A = \$1,000 \left[\frac{(1 + 0.10)^4 - 1}{0.10} \right] = \$4,641$$

Because this problem involves an annuity rather than a single payment, when solving with a financial calculator, the value that we enter for the $\boxed{\text{PMT}}$ key is −\$1,000. Now we enter a zero for the $\boxed{\text{PV}}$ key. As we computed earlier using the future value of an annuity equation, we find that when the interest rate is 10%, the future value of a 4-year, \$1,000 annuity is \$4,641.

Excel's **FV** function can also produce the future value of an annuity stream. The **FV** function assumes that each payment is at the end of a period as shown in the previous timeline. The annuity amount is entered as the **pmt** argument. The function in cell D1 uses cell references for the arguments in cells B1 to B4. The function in cell D5 uses hardcoded values. The values produced by the **FV** function are identical to the calculator solution, but hardcoded solutions should be avoided in preference to cell referenced solutions.

FINANCIAL CALCULATOR

FV of Annuity

Enter	Function
4	N
10	I/Y
−1000	PMT
0	PV

Function	Solution
CPT	
FV	4,641.00

	A	B	C	D	E	F
1	rate	10.00%		=FV(B1,B2,B3,B4)		
2	nper	4.00		**FV**(rate, nper, pmt, [pv], [type])		
3	pmt	−1000		\$4,641.00		
4	pv	0				
5				=+FV(0.1,4,−1000,0)		
6				**FV**(rate, nper, pmt, [pv], [type])		
7				\$4,641.00		

The largest single Powerball jackpot winner to date is Mavis Wanczyk, who won a reported $758.7 million in August 2017. She bought the winning ticket at a convenience store in Massachusetts.

The Powerball lottery is jointly played in 44 states, plus Washington, D.C., and the overall odds of winning the Powerball jackpot are about 1 in 292 million, according to the Multi-State Lottery Association. If you win the jackpot, one of the first choices you must make is whether to take your winnings in a single lump sum or to spread them out in annual installments over 30 years.

Wanczyk opted to take the lump sum cash payout. It turns out that holding the golden ticket did not entitle Ms. Wanczyk to $758.7 million. The prize is actually a growing annuity, which means that the payout rises each year (in this case by 5 percent to keep up

with expected inflation) to equal $758.7 million spread over 30 years. If a winner selects the lump sum, she gets only the present value of the growing annuity.

Ms. Wanczyk does not appear to have been outraged at being "shortchanged," despite the fact that she received only $480.5 million—63 percent of the advertised prize. If the discount rate had been higher (it was approximately 3 percent), her lump sum would have been even less. If she had chosen the annuity, she would have received $11.4 million in the first year, but almost $47 million in the final year.

Deciding which option to take in these circumstances is complicated. If you win the Powerball grand prize, contact your finance instructor for advice. You will probably discover that you are remembered as his or her favorite student.

Present Value—Annuity

To find the **present value of an annuity**, we reverse the process. In theory, each individual payment is discounted back to the present and then all of the discounted payments are added up, yielding the present value of the annuity. Notice that the present value of an annuity is always less than the sum of the cash flows, unless the discount rate is zero.

Here is a timeline that depicts the cash flows:

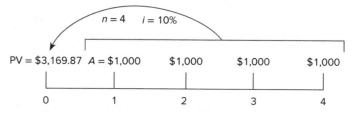

The present value of this annuity, which we label "PV_A," could be calculated by discounting each payment individually as follows:

$$PV_A = A \left(\frac{1}{1+i}\right)^1 + A \left(\frac{1}{1+i}\right)^2 + \ldots A \left(\frac{1}{1+i}\right)^n$$

But the formula actually simplifies to

$$PV_A = A \times \left(\frac{1 - \frac{1}{(1+i)^n}}{i}\right)$$

(9-6)

Once again, assume $A = \$1,000$, $n = 4$, and $i = 10$ percent—only now we want to know the present value of the annuity. Using Formula 9-6:

$$PV_A = \$1,000 \times \left(\frac{1 - \dfrac{1}{(1 + 0.10)^4}}{0.10} \right) = \$3,169.87$$

When calculating the present value of an annuity using a financial calculator, we should remember to enter a zero using the $\boxed{\text{FV}}$ key; all other inputs remain the same as when calculating the future value of an annuity. As we found before, the present value of the annuity stream, using an interest rate of 10%, is $3,169.87.

Excel's **PV** function can calculate the present value of an annuity stream. The **PV** function assumes that each payment is at the end of a period as shown in the previous timeline. The annuity amount is entered as the **pmt** argument. The function in cell D1 uses cell references for the arguments in cells B1 to B4. The function in cell D5 uses hardcoded values. The values produced by the **PV** function are identical to the calculator solution, but hardcoded solutions should be avoided in preference to cell referenced solutions.

	A	B	C	D	E	F
1	rate	10.00%		=+PV(B1,B2,B3,B4)		
2	nper	4		PV(rate, nper, pmt, [fv], [type])		
3	pmt	−1000		$3,169.87		
4	fv	0				
5				=+PV(0.1,4,−1000,0)		
6				PV(rate, nper, pmt, [fv], [type])		
7				$3,169.87		

Alternative Calculations: Using TVM Tables

We have learned to calculate present values and future values using (1) formulas, (2) financial calculator keystrokes, and (3) Excel functions. A fourth technique involves the use of time-value-of-money tables. Versions of the four standard TVM tables can be found in the appendixes at the end of this book. A full discussion of the use of these tables to solve for PV, FV, FV_A, and PV_A can be found at the end of this chapter in Appendix 9A.

Graphical Presentation of Time Value Relationships

This section is designed to supplement the previous discussion of future value, present value, and annuities and to reinforce your understanding of these concepts before you continue into the next sections. This material is nonmathematical and focuses on time value concepts using a visual approach.

The Relationship between Present Value and Future Value

Earlier in this chapter, we presented the future value of a single amount as well as the present value of a single amount and applied the concept of annuities to both

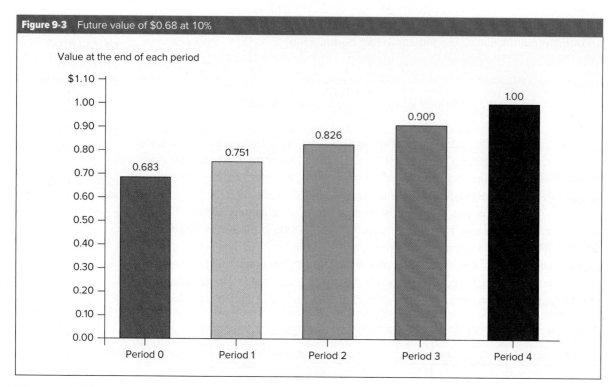

Figure 9-3   Future value of $0.68 at 10%

Value at the end of each period

Log in to Connect to access an interactive version of this figure

future value and present value. In this section, we use color coding to help clarify the relationships between future and present value.

In Figures 9-3 and 9-4, we show how the future value and present value of a single amount are mirror images of each other; in other words, they are inversely related. Future value takes a value today, such as $0.68, and computes its value in the future assuming that it earns a rate of return each period. In Figure 9-3, the $0.68 is invested at 10 percent and grows to $1.00 at the end of period 4. Because we want to avoid large mathematical rounding errors, we actually carry the decimal points three places. The $0.683 that we invest today (period 0), grows to $0.751 after one period, $0.826 after two periods, $0.909 after three periods, and $1.00 at the end of the fourth period. In this example, the $0.68 is the present value and the $1.00 is the future value.

Notice in Figure 9-4, that the future value and present value graphs are a reflection of each other. In the present value table, it becomes clear that if I have $1.00 in period 0, it is worth its present value of $1.00. However, if I have to wait one period to receive my dollar, it is worth only $0.909 if I can earn a 10 percent return on my money. We can see that Figures 9-3 and 9-4 are mirror images of one another. The $0.909 at the end of period 3 will grow to $1.00 during period 4. Or by letting $0.909 compound at a 10 percent rate for one period, you have $1.00.

Because you can earn a return on your money, $1.00 received in the future is worth less than $1.00 today, and the longer you have to wait to receive the dollar, the less it is worth. For example, if you are to receive $1.00 at the end of four periods, how much is its present value? In Figure 9-4 you see that the answer is $0.68,

Figure 9-4   Present value of $1.00 at 10%

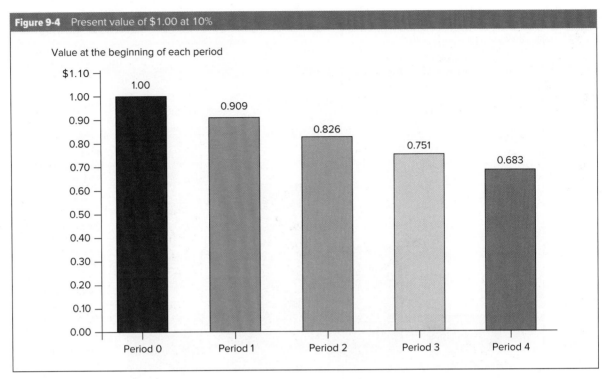

Log in to Connect to access an interactive version of this figure

the same value that we started with in period 0 in the future value graph in Figure 9-3. As you change the rate of return that can be earned, the values in Figure 9-3 and 9-4 will change, but the relationship will remain the same as presented in this example.

The Relationship between the Present Value of a Single Amount and the Present Value of an Annuity

Figure 9-5 shows the relationship between the present value of $1.00 and the present value of a $1.00 annuity. The assumption is that you will receive $1.00 at the end of each period. This is the same concept as a lottery, where you win $2 million over 20 years and receive $100,000 per year for 20 years. In this example, we receive only four payments of $1.00 each and we use color coding to build up one year at a time.

Looking at Figure 9-5, you see the present value of $1.00 to be received at the end of period 1 is $0.909; $1.00 received at the end of period 2 is $0.826; $1.00 received at the end of period 3 is $0.751; and $1.00 received at the end of period 4 is $0.683. These numbers should look familiar. Figure 9-5 has the same values as Figure 9-4, except there is no period 0.

Looking at the second column for two periods, you see that if you receive two $1.00 payments, the first at the end of period 1 and the second at the end of period 2, the total present value will simply be the sum of the present value of each $1.00 payment. You can see that the total present value of $1.74 represents the present value of $1.00 to be received at the end of the first period ($0.909) and the present value of $1.00 to

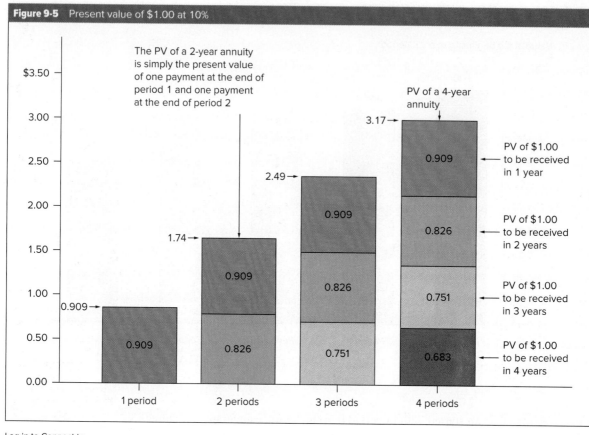

Figure 9-5   Present value of $1.00 at 10%

The PV of a 2-year annuity is simply the present value of one payment at the end of period 1 and one payment at the end of period 2

PV of a 4-year annuity

3.17→

2.49→

1.74→

0.909→

0.909

0.909

0.909

0.826

0.909

0.826

0.751

0.826

0.751

0.683

$3.50

3.00

2.50

2.00

1.50

1.00

0.50

0.00

1 period   2 periods   3 periods   4 periods

PV of $1.00 ← to be received in 1 year

PV of $1.00 ← to be received in 2 years

PV of $1.00 ← to be received in 3 years

PV of $1.00 ← to be received in 4 years

Log in to Connect to access an interactive version of this figure

be received at the end of the second period. In the third column we add the present value of $0.751, received at the end of the third year, to end up with the present value of a three-period annuity equaling $2.49. The fourth column adds another $0.683 to column 3 and illustrates the present value of four $1.00 payments equaling $3.17.

This $3.17 is the sum of each present value. The color coding helps illustrate the relationships. The top box is always $0.909 and represents the present value of $1.00 received at the end of the first period; the second box from the top is always $0.826 and is the present value of the $1.00 received at the end of the second year; the box third from the top is $0.751 and is the present value of the $1.00 received at the end of the third year; and finally, the present value of the $1.00 received at the end of the fourth year is $0.683.

Future Value Related to the Future Value of an Annuity

The next relationship is between the future value of a single sum and the future value of an annuity. We start with Figure 9-6, which graphically depicts the future value of $1.00 that is growing at a 10 percent rate of return each period. If we start with a present value of $1.00 today (period 0), at the end of period 1 we will have $1.10; at the end of period 2 we will have $1.21; and at the end of period 3 the $1.00 will have grown to $1.33.

One of the confusing features between the future value of $1.00 and the future value of a $1.00 annuity is that they have different assumptions concerning the timing of

Figure 9-6   Future value of $1.00 at 10%

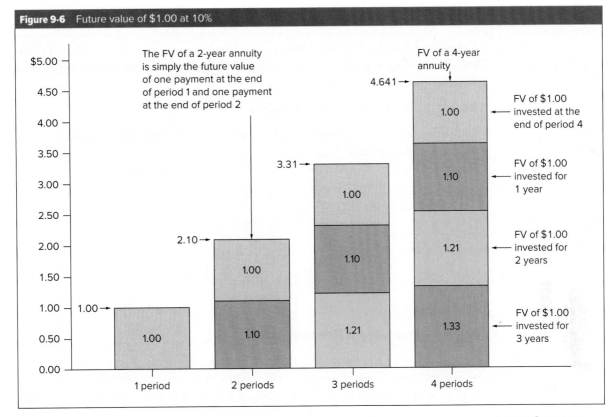

cash flows. **The future value of $1.00 assumes the $1.00 is invested at the beginning of the period and grows to the end of the period. The future value of an ordinary annuity assumes $1.00 is invested at the end of the period and grows to the end of the next period.** This means the last $1.00 invested has no time to increase its value by earning a return. This relationship is shown in Figure 9-6 by adding a period 0 to the future value graph.

The calculation for the future value of a $1.00 annuity simply adds together the future value of a series of equal $1.00 investments. Since the last $1.00 invested does not have a chance to compound, the future value of a two-period annuity equals $2.10. This $2.10 comes from adding the $1.00 invested at the end of period 2 plus the first $1.00 that has grown to $1.10. When you look at column three, notice the future value of a three-period annuity is $3.31. This $3.31 is a combination of the $1.00 invested at the end of period 3, the $1.10 from the second $1.00 invested, and $1.21 from the first dollar invested.

Finally, the last column demonstrates that the future value of a four-period annuity totals $4.64. The explanation of how each value creates the total is given in the figure. Since Figure 9-6 is color-coded, you might notice the pattern that exists. The $1.00 amount is always the top box and is the same color. This is the $1.00 that is always invested at the end of the period and has no time to compound. The $1.10 is always the second box from the top and represents the $1.00 that has been invested for only one period, while the $1.21 is always the third box from the top and represents the $1.00 invested for two periods. The $1.33 is the fourth box from the top and represents $1.00 invested for three periods.

Determining the Annuity Value

Formulas 9-7 and 9-8 in this section are presented for completeness. Most students will choose to use a financial calculator or Excel to solve problems that require determining an annuity value.

Annuity Equaling a Future Value

Assume that we wish to accumulate $4,641 after four years at a 10 percent interest rate, how much must be set aside at the end of each of the four periods? We can reorganize Formula 9-5 so that we solve for the annuity amount (*A*) rather than FV_A:

$$A = \frac{FV_A}{\left[\dfrac{(1+i)^n - 1}{i}\right]} \tag{9-7}$$

$$A = \frac{\$4,641}{\left[\dfrac{1.10^4 - 1}{0.10}\right]} = \$1,000$$

Annuity Equaling a Present Value

Next assume you know the present value and you wish to determine what size annuity can be equated to that amount. Suppose your wealthy uncle presents you with $10,000 now to help you get through the next four years of college. If you are able to earn 6 percent on deposited funds, how many equal payments can you withdraw at the end of each year for four years? We need to know the value of an annuity equal to a given present value. We can reorganize Formula 9-6 so that we solve for the annuity value *A* rather than PV_A:

$$A = \frac{PV_A}{\left[\dfrac{1 - \dfrac{1}{(1+i)^n}}{i}\right]} \tag{9-8}$$

$$A = \frac{\$10,000}{\left[\dfrac{1 - \dfrac{1}{1.06^4}}{0.06}\right]} = \$2,885.91$$

The flow of funds would follow the pattern in Table 9-1. Annual interest is based on the beginning balance for each year.

Table 9-1   Relationship of present value to annuity

Year	Beginning Balance	Annual Interest (6%)	Annual Withdrawal	Ending Balance
1	$10,000.00	$600.00	$2,885.91	$7,714.09
2	7,714.09	462.85	2,885.91	5,291.03
3	5,291.03	317.46	2,885.91	2,722.58
4	2,722.58	163.35	2,885.91	0.00

The same process can be used to indicate necessary repayments on a loan. Suppose a homeowner signs an $80,000 mortgage to be repaid over 20 years at 8 percent interest. How much must he or she pay annually to eventually liquidate the loan? In other words, what annuity paid over 20 years is the equivalent of an $80,000 present value with an 8 percent interest rate?[3]

$$A = \frac{PV_A}{\left[\dfrac{1 - \dfrac{1}{(1+i)^n}}{i} \right]} = \frac{\$80,000}{\left[\dfrac{1 - \dfrac{1}{1.08^{20}}}{0.08} \right]} = \$8,148.18$$

Part of the payments to the mortgage company will go toward the payment of interest, with the remainder applied to debt reduction, as indicated in Table 9-2.

Table 9-2   Payoff table for loan (amortization table)

Period	Beginning Balance	Annual Payment	Annual Interest (8%)	Repayment on Principal	Ending Balance
1	$80,000	$8,148	$6,400	$1,748	$78,252
2	78,252	8,148	6,260	1,888	76,364
3	76,364	8,148	6,109	2,039	74,325

Notice in this table that each year's annual payment is $8,148. Each payment is split between interest and repayment of the loan principal. The interest (8 percent of each line's beginning balance) is paid first, and the remainder of the payment reduces the outstanding balance on the loan. For each line, the difference between the beginning balance and the ending balance is the repayment amount.

If this same process is followed over 20 years, the balance will be reduced to zero. You might note that the homeowner will pay over $82,964 of *interest* during the term of the loan:

Total payments (for 20 years)	$ 162,964
Repayment of principal	−80,000
Payments applied to interest	$ 82,964

Let's continue with a calculator example of finding the annuity amount.

Finding Annuity Payments with a Financial Calculator or Excel

Suppose that you have $3,169.87 in a bank account when you start college, and you intend to take out an equal payment amount at the end of each year for four years when interest rates are 10 percent. How much can you take out at the end of each year? Answering this question requires that you recognize you are trying to find the $\boxed{\text{PMT}}$ for an annuity. As expected, the financial calculator solution shows that the annuity amount is $1,000 per year.

FINANCIAL CALCULATOR

Annuity Payment

Enter	Function
4	N
10	I/Y
−3169.87	PV
0	FV
Function	*Solution*
CPT	
PMT	1,000.00

---

[3]The actual mortgage could be further refined into monthly payments of approximately $680.

Excel's **PMT** function can calculate the annuity payment amount given the present value or future value of an annuity. The **PMT** function assumes that each payment is at the end of a period as shown in the previous timeline. Either the **pv** or **fv** argument must be entered. The function in cell D1 references the arguments in cells B1 to B4. The function in cell D5 uses numerical inputs instead. In both cases, the values produced by the **PMT** function are identical to the calculator solution.

	A	B	C	D	E	F
1	rate	10.00%		=+PMT(B1,B2,B3,B4)		
2	nper	4		**PMT**(rate, nper, pv, [fv], [type])		
3	pv	−3169.87		$1,000.00		
4	fv	0				
5				=+PMT(0.1,4,−3169.87,0)		
6				**PMT**(rate, nper, pv, [fv], [type])		
7				$1,000.00		

Finding Interest Rates and the Number of Payments

Both a financial calculator and Excel are useful for finding the interest rate and the number of periods in annuity problems.

Finding Annuity Interest Rates

Now suppose that an insurance company offers to pay you an annuity of $1,000 per year for 4 years in exchange for $3,169.87 today. To compare this offer to what you could earn in a bank account, you must determine what interest rate of return you are being offered. Calculator keystrokes in the margin show that the rate of return being offered is 10%.

In this example, the $\boxed{\text{PMT}}$ key and the $\boxed{\text{PV}}$ key *must be assigned different signs.* If both are assigned a positive value, the calculator will return an error alert.

Excel's **RATE** function can calculate the interest rate that equates the value of an annuity payment stream with the present value or future value of an annuity. The **RATE** function assumes that each payment is at the end of a period as shown in the previous timeline. Either the **pv** or **fv** argument must be entered, as well as a **pmt** argument. The function in cell D1 references the arguments in cells B1 to B4. The function in cell D5 uses hardcoded numerical inputs instead. In both cases, the values produced by the **RATE** function are identical to the calculator solution.

FINANCIAL CALCULATOR

Interest Rate

Enter	Function
4	N
−3169.87	PV
1000	PMT
0	FV

Function	Solution
CPT	
I/Y	10.00

	A	B	C	D	E	F	G
1	nper	4.00		=+RATE(B1,B2,B3,B4)			
2	pmt	1000		**RATE**(nper, pmt, pv, [fv], [type], [guess])			
3	pv	−3169.87		10.00%			
4	fv	0					
5				=+RATE(4,1000,−3169.87,0)			
6				**RATE**(nper, pmt, pv, [fv], [type], [guess])			
7				10.00%			

Finding the Number of Annuity Payments

As our final example, suppose that an insurance company offers to pay you an annuity of $1,000 per year in exchange for $3,169.87 today. They promise you a 10% return until the money runs out. How many years will you receive payments?

Making sure that the PMT key and the PV key are given opposite signs, we find on the right that the annuity will last for 4 years.

Excel's **NPER** function calculates the interest rate that equates the annuity payment stream with the present value or future value of the annuity. The **NPER** function assumes that each payment is at the end of a period as shown in the previous timeline. Either the **pv** or **fv** argument must be entered, as well as a **pmt** argument. The function in cell D1 references the arguments in cells B1 to B4. The function in cell D5 uses hardcoded numbers instead of cell references. In both cases, the values produced by the **NPER** function are identical to the calculator solution.

	A	B	C	D	E	F
1	rate	10.00%		=+NPER(B1,B2,B3,B4)		
2	pmt	1000		**NPER**(rate, pmt, pv, [fv], [type])		
3	pv	−3169.87		4		
4	fv	0				
5				=+NPER(0.1,1000,−3169.87,0)		
6				**NPER**(rate, pmt, pv, [fv], [type])		
7				4		

Compounding over Additional Periods

We have assumed interest was compounded or discounted on an annual basis. This assumption will now be relaxed. Contractual arrangements, such as an installment purchase agreement or a corporate bond contract, may call for semiannual, quarterly, or monthly compounding periods. The adjustment to the normal formula is simple. **To determine n, multiply the number of years by the number of compounding periods during the year. The factor for i is then determined by dividing the quoted annual interest rate by the number of compounding periods**.

Case 1 Find the future value of a $1,000 investment after five years at 8 percent annual interest, **compounded semiannually**.

$$n = 5 \times 2 = 10 \quad i = 8\%/2 = 4\%$$

Since the problem calls for the future value of a single amount, the formula is

$$FV = PV \times (1 + i)^n$$
$$FV = \$1,000 \times (1.04)^{10} = \$1,480.24$$

Case 2 Find the present value of 20 quarterly payments of $2,000 each to be received over the next five years. The stated interest rate is 8 percent per annum. The problem calls for the present value of an annuity. We again follow the same procedure as in Case 1 in regard to n and i.

$$A = 2,000 \qquad n = 20 \qquad i = 8\%/4 = 2\%$$

$$PV_A = A \times \frac{1 - \dfrac{1}{(1+i)^n}}{i}$$

$$PV_A = \$2,000 \times \frac{1 - \dfrac{1}{(1.02)^{20}}}{0.02} = \$32,702.87$$

Patterns of Payment with a Deferred Annuity

Time value of money problems may revolve around a number of different payment or receipt patterns. Not every situation will involve a single amount or an annuity. For example, a contract may call for the payment of a different amount each year over a three-year period. To determine present value, each payment is discounted to the present and then summed.

(Assume 8% discount rate)

n	Payment	×	PV Factor $\dfrac{1}{(1+i)^n}$	=	PV
1.	$1,000	×	0.926	=	$ 926
2.	2,000	×	0.857	=	1,714
3.	3,000	×	0.794	=	2,382
			PV at time = 0		$5,022

A more involved problem might include a combination of single amounts and an annuity. If the annuity will be paid at some time in the future, it is referred to as a deferred annuity and requires special treatment. Assume the same problem as above, but with an annuity of $1,000 that will be paid at the end of each year from the fourth through the eighth years. With a discount rate of 8 percent, what is the present value of the cash flows?

1. $1,000 ⎫
2. 2,000 ⎬ Present value = $5,022
3. 3,000 ⎭
4. 1,000 ⎫
5. 1,000 ⎪
6. 1,000 ⎬ Five-year annuity
7. 1,000 ⎪
8. 1,000 ⎭

We know the present value of the first three payments is $5,022 from our previous calculation, but what about the annuity? Let's diagram the five annuity payments.

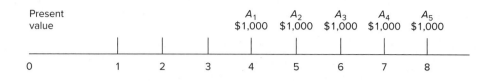

Notice that the annuity begins at the *end* of year 4. This detail is extremely impor-tant because the present value of an annuity formula (Formula 9-6) provides the value of an annuity at the *beginning* of the year. *The beginning of year 4 is the end of year 3.* In the following diagram, we see that the first annuity payment is at time 4, but the PV$_A$ is at time 3. For $n = 5$ and $i = 8\%$, the PV$_A$ is $3,993.

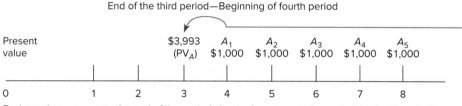

Each number represents the end of the period; that is, 4 represents the end of the fourth period.

The $3,993 must finally be discounted back to the present. Since this single amount falls at the beginning of the fourth period—in effect, the equivalent of the end of the third period—we discount back for three periods at the stated 8 percent interest rate. Using Formula 9-2, we have:

$$PV = FV \times \frac{1}{(1 + i)^n}$$

$$PV = \$3,993 \times \frac{1}{(1.08)^3} = \$3,170$$

The last step in this discounting process for the annuity is shown here:

End of the third period—Beginning of the fourth period

$3,170
Present
value

$3,993
(single A_1 A_2 A_3 A_4 A_5
amount) $1,000 $1,000 $1,000 $1,000 $1,000

```
  |      |      |      |      |      |      |      |
  0      1      2      3      4      5      6      7      8
```

The present value of the five-year annuity may now be added to the present value of the inflows over the first three years to arrive at the total value:

$ 5,022	Present value of the first three period flows
+ 3,170	Present value of the five-year annuity
$ 8,192	Total present value

Annuities Due

As stated earlier in the chapter, annuity payments are assumed to come at the end of each payment period. An annuity payment stream of this type is referred to as an ordinary annuity. However, we should also address how to value annuity payments that come at the beginning of each period (called an **annuity due**). As an example, rental payments are usually required at the beginning of each month. Consider the following timelines:

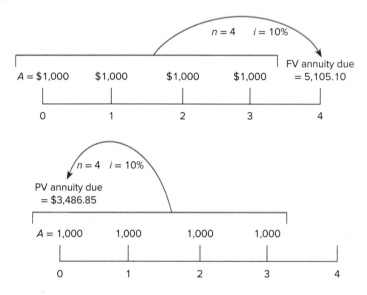

The first timeline depicts the future value of an annuity due. The second timeline depicts the present value of the same annuity due. There are formulas for both of these calculations:

$$FV_{AD} = A \times \left(\frac{(1 + i)^{n + 1} - 1}{i} - 1 \right)$$

$$PV_{AD} = A \times \left(\frac{1 - \dfrac{1}{(1 + i)^{n - 1}}}{i} + 1 \right)$$

Both of these are slight variations on the previous formulas shown for ordinary annuities.

When using a financial calculator, modifications must be made so that the calculator recognizes that the annuity payments are being made at the beginning of each period. These adjustments differ for various calculators. The website www.tvmcalcs.com has examples of the appropriate calculator adjustments for numerous commonly used financial calculators.

Using Excel to solve for the future value or present value of an annuity due is straightforward. To this point, we have ignored the **[type]** argument in Excel's **PV** and **FV** functions. When the **[type]** argument is ignored (or [type = 0]), Excel regards the annuity payments as ordinary. If [type = 1], Excel values the cash flows as an annuity due. The following spreadsheet illustrates this point. Notice that the last argument is **[type]**.

	A	B	C	D	E	F	G
1	**Future Value of an Annuity Due**						
2	*i*	*n*	pmt	FV$_{AD}$			
3	10.00%	4	−1000	$5,105.10	=+**FV**(A3,B3,C3,0,1)		
4				FV(rate, nper, **pmt**, [pv], [type])			
5							
6	**Present Value of an Annuity Due**						
7	*i*	*n*	pmt	PV$_{AD}$			
8	10.00%	4	−1000	$3,486.85	=+**PV**(A8,B8,C8,0,1)		
9				PV(rate, **nper**, pmt, [fv], [type])			

LIST OF TERMS

DISCUSSION QUESTIONS

1. How is the future value related to the present value of a single sum? *(LO9-1)*
2. How is the present value of a single sum related to the present value of an annuity? *(LO9-3)*
3. Why does money have a time value? *(LO9-1)*
4. Does inflation have anything to do with making a dollar today worth more than a dollar tomorrow? *(LO9-1)*
5. Adjust the annual formula for a future value of a single amount at 12 percent for 10 years to a semiannual compounding formula. What are the interest factors (FV$_{IF}$) before and after? Why are they different? *(LO9-5)*
6. If, as an investor, you had a choice of daily, monthly, or quarterly compounding, which would you choose? Why? *(LO9-5)*
7. What is a deferred annuity? *(LO9-4)*
8. List five different financial applications of the time value of money. *(LO9-1)*

PRACTICE PROBLEMS AND SOLUTIONS

1. *a.* You invest $12,000 today at 9 percent per year. How much will you have after 15 years?

   b. What is the current value of $100,000 after 10 years if the discount rate is 12 percent?

   c. You invest $2,000 a year for 20 years at 11 percent. How much will you have after 20 years?

Future value
Present value
(LO9-2 & 9-3)

Solving for an
annuity
(LO9-4)

2. *a.* How much must Katie Wilson set aside each year to accumulate $80,000
after 15 years? The interest rate is 10 percent.

   b. How much must Josh Thompson repay each year for five years to pay off a
$20,000 loan that he just took out? The interest rate is 8 percent.

Solutions

1. *a.* $FV = PV \times (1 + i)^n$

   $FV = \$12,000 \times (1.09)^{15}$

   $FV = \$43,709.79$

**FINANCIAL
CALCULATOR**

Enter	Function
15	N
9	I/Y
−12,000	PV
0	PMT
Function	Solution
CPT	
FV	43,709.79

	A	B	C	D	E	F
1	rate	9.00%		=FV(B1,B2,B3,B4)		
2	nper	15		FV(rate, nper, pmt, [pv], [type])		
3	pmt	0		$43,709.79		
4	pv	−12,000				

   b. $PV = FV \times \left(\dfrac{1}{(1 + i)^n} \right)$

   $PV = \$100,000 \times \left(\dfrac{1}{(1.12)^{10}} \right)$

   $PV = \$32,197.32$

**FINANCIAL
CALCULATOR**

Enter	Function
10	N
12	I/Y
−100,000	FV
0	PMT
Function	Solution
CPT	
PV	32,197.32

	A	B	C	D	E	F
1	rate	12.00%		=PV(B1,B2,B3,B4)		
2	nper	10		PV(rate, nper, pmt, [fv], [type])		
3	pmt	0		$32,197.32		
4	fv	−100,000				

   c. $FV_A = A \times \left(\dfrac{(1 + i)^n - 1}{i} \right)$

   $FV_A = \$2,000 \times \left(\dfrac{(1.11)^{20} - 1}{0.11} \right)$

   $FV_A = \$128,405.66$

**FINANCIAL
CALCULATOR**

Enter	Function
20	N
11	I/Y
0	PV
−2,000	PMT
Function	Solution
CPT	
FV	128,405.66

	A	B	C	D	E	F
1	rate	11.00%		=FV(B1,B2,B3,B4)		
2	nper	20		FV(rate, nper, pmt, [pv], [type])		
3	pmt	−2,000		$128,405.66		
4	pv	0				

2. *a.* $FV_A = A \times \left(\dfrac{(1 + i)^n - 1}{i} \right)$

   $\$80,000 = A \times \left(\dfrac{(1.10)^{15} - 1}{0.10} \right)$

   $A = \left(\dfrac{\$80,000}{\left(\dfrac{(1.10)^{15} - 1}{0.10} \right)} \right)$

   $A = \$2,517.90$

	A	B	C	D	E	F
1	rate	10.00%		=PMT(B1,B2,B3,B4)		
2	nper	15		PMT(rate, nper, pv, [fv], [type])		
3	pv	0		$2,517.90		
4	fv	−80,000				

FINANCIAL CALCULATOR

Enter	Function
15	N
10	I/Y
−80,000	PV
0	FV

Function	Solution
CPT	
PMT	2,517.90

b.
$$PV_A = A \times \left(\frac{\left(1 - \dfrac{1}{(1+i)^n}\right)}{i} \right)$$

$$\$20,000 = A \times \left(\frac{\left(1 - \dfrac{1}{(1.08)^5}\right)}{0.08} \right)$$

$$A = \frac{\$20,000}{\left(\dfrac{\left(1 - \dfrac{1}{(1.08)^n}\right)}{0.08} \right)}$$

$$A = \$5,009.13$$

	A	B	C	D	E	F
1	rate	8.00%		=PMT(B1,B2,B3,B4)		
2	nper	5		PMT(rate, nper, pv, [fv], [type])		
3	pv	−20,000		$5,009.13		
4	fv	0				

FINANCIAL CALCULATOR

Enter	Function
5	N
8	I/Y
0	PV
−20,000	FV

Function	Solution
CPT	
PMT	5,009.13

PROBLEMS

≡ connect· Selected problems are available with Connect. Please see the preface for more information.

Basic Problems

1. You invest $3,000 for three years at 12 percent.

   Future value
   (LO9-2)

   a. What is the value of your investment after one year? Multiply $3,000 × 1.12.

   b. What is the value of your investment after two years? Multiply your answer to part *a* by 1.12.

   c. What is the value of your investment after three years? Multiply your answer to part *b* by 1.12. This gives your final answer.

   d. Combine these steps using the formula FV = PV × $(1 + i)^n$ to find the future value of $3,000 in three years at 12 percent interest.

2. What is the present value of

   Present value
   (LO9-3)

   a. $7,900 in 10 years at 11 percent?

   b. $16,600 in 5 years at 9 percent?

   c. $26,000 in 14 years at 6 percent?

3. *a.* What is the present value of $140,000 to be received after 30 years with a 14 percent discount rate?

   Present value
   (LO9-3)

   b. Would the present value of the funds in part *a* be enough to buy a $2,900 concert ticket?

Present value
(LO9-4)

4. You will receive $6,800 three years from now. The discount rate is 10 percent.
   a. What is the value of your investment two years from now? Multiply $6,800 × (1/1.10) or divide by 1.10 (one year's discount rate at 10 percent).
   b. What is the value of your investment one year from now? Multiply your answer to part *a* by (1/1.10).
   c. What is the value of your investment today? Multiply your answer to part *b* by (1/1.10).
   d. Use the formula PV = FV × $\frac{1}{(1 + i)^n}$ to find the present value of $6,600 received three years from now at 10 percent interest.

Future value
(LO9-2)

5. If you invest $9,000 today, how much will you have
   a. In 2 years at 9 percent?
   b. In 7 years at 12 percent?
   c. In 25 years at 14 percent?
   d. In 25 years at 14 percent (compounded semiannually)?

Present value
(LO9-3)

6. Your aunt offers you a choice of $20,100 in 20 years or $870 today. If money is discounted at 17 percent, which should you choose?

Present value
(LO9-3)

7. Your uncle offers you a choice of $105,000 in 10 years or $47,000 today. If money is discounted at 9 percent, which should you choose?

Present value
(LO9-3)

8. Your father offers you a choice of $105,000 in 12 years or $47,000 today.
   a. If money is discounted at 8 percent, which should you choose?
   b. If money is still discounted at 8 percent, but your choice is between $105,000 in 9 years or $47,000 today, which should you choose?

Present value
(LO9-3)

9. You are going to receive $205,000 in 18 years. What is the difference in present value between using a discount rate of 12 percent versus 9 percent?

Present value
(LO9-3)

10. How much would you have to invest today to receive
    a. $15,000 in 8 years at 10 percent?
    b. $20,000 in 12 years at 13 percent?
    c. $6,000 each year for 10 years at 9 percent?
    d. $50,000 each year for 50 years at 7 percent?

Future value
(LO9-2)

11. If you invest $8,500 per period for the following number of periods, how much would you have?
    a. 12 years at 10 percent.
    b. 50 years at 9 percent.

Future value
(LO9-2)

12. You invest a single amount of $10,000 for 5 years at 10 percent. At the end of 5 years you take the proceeds and invest them for 12 years at 15 percent. How much will you have after 17 years?

Present value
(LO9-3)

13. Mrs. Crawford will receive $7,600 a year for the next 19 years from her trust. If a 14 percent interest rate is applied, what is the current value of the future payments?

Present value
(LO9-3)

14. Phil Goode will receive $175,000 in 50 years. His friends are very jealous of him. If the funds are discounted back at a rate of 14 percent, what is the present value of his future "pot of gold"?

Present value
(LO9-3)

15. Sherwin Williams will receive $18,500 a year for the next 25 years as a result of a picture he has painted. If a discount rate of 12 percent is applied, should he be willing to sell out his future rights now for $165,000?

Present value
(LO9-3)

16. Carrie Tune will receive $19,500 for the next 20 years as a payment for a new song she has written. If a 10 percent rate is applied, should she be willing to sell out her future rights now for $160,000?

17. The Clearinghouse Sweepstakes has just informed you that you have won $1 million. The amount is to be paid out at the rate of $20,000 a year for the next 50 years. With a discount rate of 10 percent, what is the present value of your winnings?

    Present value (LO9-3)

18. Rita Gonzales won the $41 million lottery. She is to receive $1.5 million a year for the next 19 years plus an additional lump sum payment of $12.5 million after 19 years. The discount rate is 14 percent. What is the current value of her winnings?

    Present value (LO9-3)

19. Al Rosen invests $25,000 in a mint condition 1952 Mickey Mantle Topps baseball card. He expects the card to increase in value 12 percent per year for the next 10 years. How much will his card be worth after 10 years?

    Future value (LO9-2)

20. Christy Reed made a $2,000 deposit in her savings account on her 21st birthday, and she has made another $2,000 deposit on every birthday since then. Her account earns 7 percent compounded annually. How much will she have in the account after she makes the deposit on her 32nd birthday?

    Future value (LO9-2)

21. At a growth (interest) rate of 10 percent annually, how long will it take for a sum to double? to triple? Select the year that is closest to the correct answer.

    Future value (LO9-2)

22. If you owe $35,000 payable at the end of eight years, what amount should your creditor accept in payment immediately if she could earn 13 percent on her money?

    Present value (LO9-3)

Intermediate Problems

23. Jack Hammer invests in a stock that will pay dividends of $2.00 at the end of the first year; $2.20 at the end of the second year; and $2.40 at the end of the third year. Also, he believes that at the end of the third year he will be able to sell the stock for $33. What is the present value of all future benefits if a discount rate of 11 percent is applied? (Round all values to two places to the right of the decimal point.)

    Present value (LO9-3)

24. Les Moore retired as president of Goodman Snack Foods Company but is currently on a consulting contract for $35,000 per year for the next 10 years.

    Present value (LO9-3)

    a. If Mr. Moore's opportunity cost (potential return) is 10 percent, what is the present value of his consulting contract?

    b. Assuming Mr. Moore will not retire for two more years and will not start to receive his 10 payments until the end of the third year, what would be the value of his deferred annuity?

25. Juan Garza invested $20,000 10 years ago at 12 percent, compounded quarterly. How much has he accumulated?

    Quarterly compounding (LO9-5)

26. Determine the amount of money in a savings account at the end of 10 years, given an initial deposit of $5,500 and a 12 percent annual interest rate when interest is compounded (a) annually, (b) semiannually, and (c) quarterly.

    Special compounding (LO9-5)

27. As stated in the chapter, annuity payments are assumed to come at the end of each payment period (termed an ordinary annuity). However, an exception occurs when the annuity payments come at the beginning of each period (termed an annuity due). To find the present value of an annuity due, the annuity formula must be adjusted as to the following:

    Annuity due (LO9-4)

$$PV_{AD} = A \times \left(\frac{1 - \dfrac{1}{(1+i)^{n-1}}}{i} + 1 \right)$$

Likewise, the formula for the future value of an annuity due requires a modification:

$$FV_{AD} = A \times \left(\frac{(1+i)^{n+1}-1}{i} - 1 \right)$$

What is the future value of a 15-year annuity of $1,800 per period where payments come at the beginning of each period? The interest rate is 12 percent.

Annuity due
(LO9-4)

28. What is the present value of a 10-year annuity of $3,000 per period in which payments come at the beginning of each period? The interest rate is 12 percent.

$$PV_{AD} = A \times \left(\frac{1 - \dfrac{1}{(1+i)^{n-1}}}{i} + 1 \right)$$

Advanced Problems

Present value
alternative
(LO9-3)

29. Your grandfather has offered you a choice of one of the three following alternatives: $7,500 now; $2,200 a year for nine years; or $31,000 at the end of nine years. Assuming you could earn 10 percent annually, which alternative should you choose? If you could earn 11 percent annually, would you still choose the same alternative?

Payments required
(LO9-4)

30. You need $28,974 at the end of 10 years, and your only investment outlet is an 8 percent long-term certificate of deposit (compounded annually). With the certificate of deposit, you make an initial investment at the beginning of the first year.

    a. What single payment could be made at the beginning of the first year to achieve this objective?

    b. What amount could you pay at the end of each year annually for 10 years to achieve this same objective?

Quarterly
compounding
(LO9-5)

31. Beverly Hills started a paper route on January 1. Every three months, she deposits $550 in her bank account, which earns 8 percent annually but is compounded quarterly. Four years later, she used the entire balance in her bank account to invest in an investment at 7 percent annually. How much will she have after three more years?

Yield
(LO9-4)

32. Franklin Templeton has just invested $9,260 for his son (age one). This money will be used for his son's education 18 years from now. He calculates that he will need $71,231 by the time the boy goes to school. What rate of return will Mr. Templeton need in order to achieve this goal?

Yield on investment
(LO9-4)

33. Mr. Dow bought 100 shares of stock at $14 per share. Three years later, he sold the stock for $20 per share. What is his annual rate of return?

Yield on investment
(LO9-4)

34. C. D. Rom has just given an insurance company $35,000. In return, he will receive an annuity of $3,700 for 20 years. At what rate of return must the insurance company invest this $35,000 in order to make the annual payments?

Solving for an annuity
(LO9-4)

35. Betty Bronson has just retired after 25 years with the electric company. Her total pension funds have an accumulated value of $180,000, and her life expectancy

is 15 more years. Her pension fund manager assumes he can earn a 9 percent return on her assets. What will be her yearly annuity for the next 15 years?

36. Morgan Jennings, a geography professor, invests $50,000 in a parcel of land that is expected to increase in value by 12 percent per year for the next five years. He will take the proceeds and provide himself with a 10-year annuity. Assuming a 12 percent interest rate, how much will this annuity be?

Solving for an annuity (LO9-4)

37. You wish to retire in 14 years, at which time you want to have accumulated enough money to receive an annual annuity of $17,000 for 19 years after retirement. During the period before retirement you can earn 8 percent annually, while after retirement you can earn 10 percent on your money.

    What annual contributions to the retirement fund will allow you to receive the $17,000 annuity?

Solving for an annuity (LO9-4)

38. Del Monty will receive the following payments at the end of the next three years: $2,000, $3,500, and $4,500. Then from the end of the 4th year through the end of the 10th year, he will receive an annuity of $5,000 per year. At a discount rate of 9 percent, what is the present value of all three future benefits?

Deferred annuity (LO9-3)

39. Bridget Jones has a contract in which she will receive the following payments for the next five years: $1,000, $2,000, $3,000, $4,000, and $5,000. She will then receive an annuity of $8,500 a year from the end of the 6th through the end of the 15th year. The appropriate discount rate is 14 percent. If she is offered $30,000 to cancel the contract, should she do it?

Present value (LO9-3)

40. Mark Ventura has just purchased an annuity to begin payment two years from today. The annuity is for $8,000 per year and is designed to last 10 years. If the interest rate for this problem calculation is 13 percent, what is the most he should have paid for the annuity?

Deferred annuity (LO9-3)

41. If you borrow $9,441 and are required to pay back the loan in five equal annual installments of $2,750, what is the interest rate associated with the loan?

Yield (LO9-4)

42. Cal Lury owes $10,000 now. A lender will carry the debt for five more years at 10 percent interest. That is, in this particular case, the amount owed will go up by 10 percent per year for five years. The lender then will require that Cal pay off the loan over the next 12 years at 11 percent interest. What will his annual payment be?

Loan repayment (LO9-4)

43. If your uncle borrows $60,000 from the bank at 10 percent interest over the seven-year life of the loan, what equal annual payments must be made to discharge the loan, plus pay the bank its required rate of interest (round to the nearest dollar)? How much of his first payment will be applied to interest? to principal? How much of his second payment will be applied to each?

Loan repayment (LO9-4)

44. Larry Davis borrows $80,000 at 14 percent interest toward the purchase of a home. His mortgage is for 25 years.

    a. How much will his annual payments be? (Although home payments are usually on a monthly basis, we shall do our analysis on an annual basis for ease of computation. We will get a reasonably accurate answer.)

    b. How much interest will he pay over the life of the loan?

    c. How much should he be willing to pay to get out of a 14 percent mortgage and into a 10 percent mortgage with 25 years remaining on the mortgage?

Loan repayment (LO9-4)

Assume current interest rates are 10 percent. Carefully consider the time value of money. Disregard taxes.

45. You are chairperson of the investment fund for the Continental Soccer League. You are asked to set up a fund of semiannual payments to be compounded semiannually to accumulate a sum of $250,000 after nine years at a 10 percent annual rate (18 payments). The first payment into the fund is to take place six months from today, and the last payment is to take place at the end of the ninth year.

    a. Determine how much the semiannual payment should be. (Round to whole numbers.)

    On the day after the sixth payment is made (the beginning of the fourth year), the interest rate goes up to a 12 percent annual rate, and you can earn a 12 percent annual rate on funds that have been accumulated as well as all future payments into the fund. Interest is to be compounded semiannually on all funds.

    b. Determine how much the revised semiannual payments should be after this rate change (there are 12 payments and compounding dates). The next payment will be in the middle of the fourth year. (Round all values to whole numbers.)

46. Your younger sister, Linda, will start college in five years. She has just informed your parents that she wants to go to Hampton University, which will cost $17,000 per year for four years (cost assumed to come at the end of each year). Anticipating Linda's ambitions, your parents started investing $2,000 per year five years ago and will continue to do so for five more years. How much more will your parents have to invest each year (A?) for the next five years to have the necessary funds for Linda's education? Use 10 percent as the appropriate interest rate throughout this problem (for discounting or compounding).

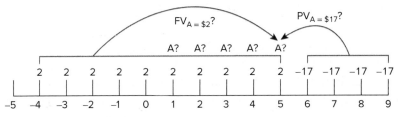

47. This problem is available only in Connect.

COMPREHENSIVE PROBLEM

Dr. Harold Wolf of Medical Research Corporation (MRC) was thrilled with the response he had received from drug companies for his latest discovery, a unique electronic stimulator that reduces the pain from arthritis. The process had yet to pass rigorous Federal Drug Administration (FDA) testing and was still in the early stages of development, but the interest was intense. He received the three offers described in the following paragraph. (A 10 percent interest rate should be used throughout this analysis unless otherwise specified.)

Offer I $1,000,000 now plus $200,000 from year 6 through 15. Also if the product did over $100 million in cumulative sales by the end of year 15, he would receive an additional $3,000,000. Dr. Wolf thought there was a 70 percent probability this would happen.

Offer II   Thirty percent of the buyer's gross profit on the product for the next four years. The buyer in this case was Zbay Pharmaceutical. Zbay's gross profit margin was 60 percent. Sales in year 1 were projected to be $2 million and then expected to grow by 40 percent per year.

Offer III   A trust fund would be set up for the next eight years. At the end of that period, Dr. Wolf would receive the proceeds (and discount them back to the present at 10 percent). The trust fund called for semiannual payments for the next eight years of $200,000 (a total of $400,000 per year).

The payments would start immediately. Since the payments are coming at the beginning of each period instead of the end, this is an annuity due. Assume the annual interest rate on this annuity is 10 percent annually (5 percent semiannually). Determine the present value of the trust fund's final value. Hint: See the section "Annuities Due."

Required: Find the present value of each of the three offers and indicate which one has the highest present value.

W E B   E X E R C I S E

1. As you have seen in this chapter, a dollar today does not have the same value as a dollar in the future or a dollar received in the past. At the time of his death in 1937, John D. Rockefeller was estimated to be worth $1.4 billion.

    Go to the Bureau of Labor Statistics at www.bls.gov. Highlight "Data Tools" at the top of the page, and select "Calculators" in the drop-down menu. Click the calculator icon next to "Inflation." How much would Rockefeller's fortune be worth in today's dollars?

2. Now let's consider a hypothetical situation where you are worth $1 million at the end of World War II. Using the same CPI tool, calculate how much you would need today to maintain the same purchasing power as in 1945.

3. Assume that the rate of inflation for the next 30 years is the same as the last 30 years. How much will you need to have the same purchasing power as you have today?

Note: Occasionally a topic we have listed may have been deleted, updated, or moved into a different location on a website. If you click on the site map or site index, you will be introduced to a table of contents that should aid you in finding the topic you are looking for.

Alternative Calculations: Using TVM Tables

So far we have learned to calculate present values and future values using (1) time-value-of-money formulas, (2) financial calculator keystrokes, and (3) Excel functions. A fourth technique involves the use of time-value-of-money tables. In particular, using Formulas 9-5 and 9-6 to find the future value of an annuity or the present value of an annuity is cumbersome. These formulas are complex. To deal with this complexity, tables have been created to simplify the computations required.

We will present four tables. Each table contains a set of **interest factors** that collapse the interest rate (i) information and the number of periods (n) into a single number that can be used in a simplified time-value-of-money formula.

Formula Number	Formula	Substitution	Table Formula	Table
(9-1)	$FV = PV \times (1 + i)^n$	$(1 + i)^n = FV_{IF}$	$FV = PV \times FV_{IF}$	9A-1
(9-2)	$PV = FV \times \dfrac{1}{(1 + i)^n}$	$\dfrac{1}{(1 + i)^n} = PV_{IF}$	$PV = FV \times PV_{IF}$	9A-2
(9-5)	$FV_A = A \times \dfrac{(1 + i)^n - 1}{i}$	$\dfrac{(1 + i)^n - 1}{i} = FV_{IFA}$	$FV_A = A \times FV_{IFA}$	9A-3
(9-6)	$PV_A = A \times \dfrac{1 - \dfrac{1}{(1+i)^n}}{i}$	$\dfrac{1 - \dfrac{1}{(1+i)^n}}{i} = PV_{IFA}$	$PV_A = A \times PV_{IFA}$	9A-4

Future Value of a Single Amount

Let's return to the example that was presented immediately after Formula 9-1.

If $1,000 were invested for four years at 10 percent, what would the future value be? Using Formula 9-1,

$$FV = PV \times (1 + i)^n$$
$$FV = \$1,000(1.10)^4 = \$1,464.10$$

Alternatively, let us use Table 9A-1 to solve the problem.

$$FV = PV \times FV_{IF} \qquad (i = 10\% \text{ and } n = 4)$$
$$FV = \$1,000 \times 1.464 = \$1.464$$

Table 9A-1 shows the future value of $1. The term FV_{IF} is found to equal 1.464 in the table when $n = 4$ and $i = 10$. Because the table gives the future value of only $1, we find the future value of $1,000 by multiplying the FV_{IF} by $1,000.

Notice that the solution using equation Table 9A-1 ($1,464) deviates from the original solution ($1,464.10) by 0.10. This deviation occurs because the table values in Table 9A-1 are rounded to three significant digits. For the example given, this difference is very small. However, the rounding error can be large if and when n or i is large.

Table 9A-1   Future value of $1, $FV_{IF} = (1 + i)^n$

Periods	1%	2%	3%	4%	6%	8%	10%
1	1.010	1.020	1.030	1.040	1.060	1.080	1.100
2	1.020	1.040	1.061	1.082	1.124	1.166	1.210
3	1.030	1.061	1.093	1.125	1.191	1.260	1.331
4	1.041	1.082	1.126	1.170	1.262	1.360	1.464
5	1.051	1.104	1.159	1.217	1.338	1.469	1.611
10	1.105	1.219	1.344	1.480	1.791	2.159	2.594
20	1.220	1.486	1.806	2.191	3.207	4.661	6.727

An expanded table is presented in Appendix A.

Present Value of a Single Amount

Return to the example that was presented immediately after Formula 9-2.

What is the present value of $1,464.10 received in four years if the discount rate is 10 percent? Using Formula 9-2,

$$PV = FV \times \left[\frac{1}{(1 + i)^n} \right]$$

$$PV = \$1,464.10 \times \left[\frac{1}{(1.10)^4} \right] = \$1,000$$

Alternatively, let us use Table 9A-2 to solve the problem.

$$PV = FV \times PV_{IF} \qquad (i = 10\% \text{ and } n = 4)$$
$$PV = \$1,464.10 \times 0.683 = \$999.98$$

Table 9A-2   Present value of $1, $PV_{IF} = 1/(1 + i)^n$

Periods	1%	2%	3%	4%	6%	8%	10%
1	0.990	0.980	0.971	0.962	0.943	0.926	0.909
2	0.980	0.961	0.943	0.925	0.890	0.857	0.826
3	0.971	0.942	0.915	0.889	0.840	0.794	0.751
4	0.961	0.924	0.888	0.855	0.792	0.735	0.683
5	0.951	0.906	0.863	0.822	0.747	0.681	0.621
10	0.905	0.820	0.744	0.676	0.558	0.463	0.386
20	0.820	0.673	0.554	0.456	0.312	0.215	0.149

An expanded table is presented in Appendix B.

Table 9A-2 shows the present value of $1. Thus, as we did when using Table 9A-1, we find the future value of $1,464.10 by multiplying the PV_{IF} by $1,464.10. Again the solution using Table 9A-2 ($999.98) deviates from the original solution ($1,000) very slightly. The equation value is the exact solution, but the table provides a close approximation.

Future Value of an Annuity

Now let us turn to the time value of annuity payments. Annuity equations are cumbersome, but table values are easy to use. Let us return to the example following Formula 9-5.

What is the future value of an annuity that pays $1,000 each year for four years, beginning at the end of the first year? Using Formula 9-5,

$$FV_A = A \left[\frac{(1 + i)^n - 1}{i} \right]$$

$$FV_A = \$1,000 \left[\frac{(1 + 0.10)^4 - 1}{0.10} \right] = \$4,641$$

Alternatively, we use Table 9A-3 to solve the problem.

$$FV_A = A \times FV_{IFA} \qquad (i = 10\% \text{ and } n = 4)$$
$$FV_A = \$1,000 \times 4.641 = \$4,641$$

Table 9A-3 shows the future value of a $1 annuity ($FV_{IFA}$), so we find the future value of the $1,000 annuity by multiplying the FV_{IFA} by $1,000. In this case, the table solution and the equation are identical, but that will not always be the case. The equation value will be exact, and the table will provide an approximation.

Table 9A-3   Future value of an annuity of $1, $FV_{IFA} = [(1 + i)^n - 1]/i$

Periods	1%	2%	3%	4%	6%	8%	10%
1	1.000	1.000	1.000	1.000	1.000	1.000	1.000
2	2.010	2.020	2.030	2.040	2.060	2.080	2.100
3	3.030	3.060	3.091	3.122	3.184	3.246	3.310
4	4.060	4.122	4.184	4.246	4.375	4.506	4.641
5	5.101	5.204	5.309	5.416	5.637	5.867	6.105
10	10.462	10.950	11.464	12.006	13.181	14.487	15.937
20	22.019	24.297	26.870	29.778	36.786	45.762	57.275
30	34.785	40.568	47.575	56.085	79.058	113.283	164.494

An expanded table is presented in Appendix C.

Present Value of an Annuity

Finally, we return to the example following Formula 9-6.

What is the present value of an annuity that pays $1,000 each year for four years, beginning at the end of the first year? Using Formula 9-6,

$$PV_A = A \left[\frac{1 - \dfrac{1}{(1 + i)^n}}{i} \right]$$

$$PV_A = \$1,000 \left[\frac{1 - \dfrac{1}{(1.10)^4}}{0.10} \right] = \$3,169.87$$

Alternatively, we use Table 9A-4 to solve the problem.

$$PV_A = A \times PV_{IFA} \qquad (i = 10\% \text{ and } n = 4)$$
$$PV_A = \$1,000 \times 3.170 = \$3,170$$

Table 9A-4 shows the present value of a $1 annuity ($PV_{IFA}$) that must be multiplied by the $1,000 annuity amount to find the future value of the annuity. Again we see a minor difference between the equation solution and the table solution due to a small rounding effect in the table.

Table 9A-4 Present value of an annuity of $1, $PV_{IFA} = \{1 - [1/(1 + i)^n]\}/i$

Periods	1%	2%	3%	4%	6%	8%	10%
1	0.990	0.980	0.971	0.962	0.943	0.926	0.909
2	1.970	1.942	1.913	1.886	1.833	1.783	1.736
3	2.941	2.884	2.829	2.775	2.673	2.577	2.487
4	3.902	3.808	3.717	3.630	3.465	3.312	3.170
5	4.853	4.713	4.580	4.452	4.212	3.993	3.791
10	9.471	8.983	8.530	8.111	7.360	6.710	6.145
20	18.046	16.351	14.877	13.590	11.470	9.818	8.514
30	25.808	22.396	19.600	17.292	13.765	11.258	9.427

An expanded table is presented in Appendix D.

APPENDIX | 9B

Yield and Payment Examples Using TVM Tables

Annuity Equaling a Future Value

If we wish to accumulate $4,641 after four years at a 10 percent interest rate, how much must be set aside at the end of each of the four periods? We take the previously developed statement for the future value of an annuity and solve for A.

$$FV_A = A \times FV_{IFA}$$
$$A = \frac{FV_A}{FV_{IFA}} \qquad \qquad (9B\text{-}1)$$

The future value of an annuity (FV_A) is given as $4,641, and FV_{IFA} may be determined from Appendix C (future value for an annuity). Whenever you are working with an annuity problem relating to future value, you can use Appendix C regardless of the variable that is unknown. For $n = 4$, and $i = 10$ percent, FV_{IFA} is 4.641. Thus A equals \$1,000.

$$A = \frac{FV_A}{FV_{IFA}} = \frac{\$4,641}{4.641} = \$1,000$$

The solution is the exact reverse of that previously presented under the discussion of the future value of an annuity. As a second example, assume the director of the Women's Tennis Association must set aside an equal amount for each of the next 10 years to accumulate \$1,000,000 in retirement funds and the return on deposited funds is 6 percent. Solve for the annual contribution, A, using Appendix C.

$$A = \frac{FV_A}{FV_{IFA}} \quad (n = 10, i = 6\%)$$

$$A = \frac{\$1,000,000}{13.181} = \$75,867$$

Annuity Equaling a Present Value

In this instance, we assume you know the present value and you wish to determine what size annuity can be equated to that amount. Suppose your wealthy uncle presents you with \$10,000 now to help you get through the next four years of college. If you are able to earn 6 percent on deposited funds, how many equal payments can you withdraw at the end of each year for four years? We need to know the value of an annuity equal to a given present value. We take the previously developed statement for the present value of an annuity and reverse it to solve for A.

$$PV_A = A \times PV_{IFA} \tag{9B-2}$$

$$A = \frac{PV_A}{PV_{IFA}}$$

The appropriate table is in Appendix D (present value of an annuity). We determine an answer of \$2,886.

$$A = \frac{PV_A}{PV_{IFA}} \quad (n = 4, i = 6\%)$$

$$A = \frac{\$10,000}{3.465} = \$2,886$$

The same process can be used to indicate necessary repayments on a loan. Suppose a homeowner signs an \$80,000 mortgage to be repaid over 20 years at 8 percent interest. How much must he or she pay annually to eventually liquidate the loan? In other words, what annuity paid over 20 years is the equivalent of an \$80,000 present value with an 8 percent interest rate?[4]

$$A = \frac{PV_A}{PV_{IFA}} \quad (n = 20, i = 8\%)$$

$$A = \frac{\$80,000}{9.818} = \$8,148$$

---

[4]The actual mortgage could be further refined into monthly payments of approximately \$340.

Yield—Present Value of a Single Amount

An investment producing $1,464 after four years has a present value of $1,000. What is the interest rate, or **yield**, on the investment?

We take the basic formula for the present value of a single amount and rearrange the terms.

$$PV \times FV \times PV_{IF}$$

$$PV_{IF} = \frac{PV}{FV} = \frac{\$1,000}{\$1,464} = 0.683 \qquad (9B\text{-}3)$$

The determination of PV_{IF} does not give us the final answer—but it scales down the problem so we may ascertain the answer from the table in Appendix B, the present value of $1. A portion of Appendix B is reproduced here:

Periods	1%	2%	3%	4%	5%	6%	8%	10%
2	0.980	0.961	0.943	0.925	0.907	0.890	0.857	0.826
3	0.971	0.942	0.915	0.889	0.864	0.840	0.794	0.751
4	0.961	0.924	0.888	0.855	0.823	0.792	0.735	0.683

Read down the left column of the previous table until you have located the number of periods in question (in this case, $n = 4$), and read across the table for $n = 4$ until you have located the computed value of PV_{IF} from Formula 9B-3. We see that for $n = 4$ and PV_{IF} equal to 0.683, the interest rate, or yield, is 10 percent. This is the rate that will equate $1,464 received in four years to $1,000 today.

If a PV_{IF} value does not fall under a given interest rate, an approximation is possible. For example, with $n = 3$ and $PV_{IF} = 0.861$, using the table on the prior page, 5 percent may be suggested as an approximate answer.

Interpolation may also be used to find a more precise answer. In the above example, we write out the two PV_{IF} values that the designated PV_{IF} (0.861) falls between and take the difference between the two.

PV_{IF} at 5%	0.864
PV_{IF} at 6%	0.840
	0.024

We then find the difference between the PV_{IF} value at the lowest interest rate and the designated PV_{IF} value.

PV_{IF} at 5%	0.864
PV_{IF} designated	0.861
	0.003

We next express this value (0.003) as a fraction of the preceding value (0.024) and multiply by the difference between the two interest rates (6 percent minus 5 percent). The value is added to the lower interest rate (5 percent) to get a more exact answer of 5.125 percent rather than the estimated 5 percent.

$$5\% + \frac{0.003}{0.024}(1\%) =$$

$$5\% + 0.125\,(1\%) =$$

$$5\% + 0.125\% \qquad = 5.125\%$$

Yield—Present Value of an Annuity

We may also find the yield related to any other problem. Let's look at the present value of an annuity. Take the basic formula for the present value of an annuity, and rearrange the terms.

$$PV_A = A \times PV_{IFA}$$

$$PV_{IFA} = \frac{PV_A}{A} \tag{9B-4}$$

The appropriate table is in Appendix D (the present value of an annuity of $1). Assuming a $10,000 investment will produce $1,490 a year for the next 10 years, what is the yield on the investment?

$$PV_{IFA} = \frac{PV_A}{A} = \frac{\$10,000}{\$1,490} = 6.710$$

If you flip to Appendix D and read across the columns for $n = 10$ periods, you will see that the yield is 8 percent.

The same type of approximated or interpolated yield that applied to a single amount can also be applied to an annuity when necessary.

APPENDIX | 9C

Using Calculators for Financial Analysis

This appendix is designed to help you use either an algebraic calculator (Texas Instruments BAII Plus Business Analyst) or the Hewlett-Packard 12C Financial Calculator. We realize that most calculators come with comprehensive instructions, and this appendix is meant only to provide basic instructions for commonly used financial calculations.

There are always two things to do before starting your calculations as indicated in the first table: Clear the calculator and set the decimal point. If you do not want to lose data stored in memory, do not perform steps 2 and 3 in the first box on the next page.

Each step is listed vertically as a number followed by a decimal point. After each step you will find either a number or a calculator function denoted by a box [   ]. Entering the number on your calculator is one step and entering the function is another. Notice that the HP 12C is color coded. When two boxes are found one after another, you may have an [f] or a [g] in the first box. An [f] is orange coded and refers to the orange functions above the keys. After typing the [f] function, you will automatically look for

	Texas Instruments BAII Plus		Hewlett-Packard 12C
First clear the calculator	*Function* *Function* CE/C CE/C 2nd CLR WORK 2nd CLR TVM CF 2nd CLR WORK	Clears the screen Clears regular memory Clears TVM memory Clears cash flow values	1. CLX Clears screen 2. f 3. REG Clears memory
Set the decimal point	*Function* 2nd FORMAT *Value* 4 *Function* ENTER		1. f 2. 4 (# of decimals)

an orange-coded key to punch. For example, after f in the first Hewlett-Packard box (right-hand panel), you will punch in the orange-color-coded REG. If the f function is not followed by another box, you merely type in f and the value indicated.

The g is coded blue and refers to the functions on the bottom of the function keys. After the g function key, you will automatically look for blue-coded keys. The TI BAII Plus is also color coded. The gold 2nd key, located near the top left corner of the calculator, refers to the gold functions above the keys. Upon pressing the 2nd key, the word "2nd" appears in the top left corner, indicating the gold function keys are active.

Familiarize yourself with the keyboard before you start. In the more complicated calculations, keystrokes will be combined into one step.

In the first four calculations, we solve for the future value (FV), present value (PV), future value of an ordinary annuity (FV_A), and present value of an ordinary annuity (PV_A), each for $100.

On the following pages, you can determine bond valuation, yield to maturity, net present value of an annuity, net present value of an uneven cash flow, internal rate of return for an annuity, and internal rate of return for an uneven cash flow.

Future Value—Single Amount (FV) of $100 in 5 years				
	Texas Instruments BAII Plus		**Hewlett-Packard 12C**	
Future Value of $100	*Value*	*Function*	*Value*	*Function*
$i = 9\%$ or 0.09	5	N	5	n
$n = 5$ years	9	I/Y	9	i
$FV = PV(1 + i)^n$	−100	PV	−100	PV
	0	PMT	0	PMT
	Function	*Solution*	*Function*	*Solution*
	CPT		FV	153.8624
	FV	153.8624		

Present Value—Single Amount (PV) of $100 in 5 years

Present Value of $100	Texas Instruments BAII Plus		Hewlett-Packard 12C	
	Value	Function	Value	Function
$i = 9\%$ or 0.09	5	N	5	n
$n = 5$ years	9	I/Y	9	i
$PV = FV\left[\dfrac{1}{(1+i)^n}\right]$	−100	FV	−100	FV
	0	PMT	0	PMT
	Function	Solution	Function	Solution
	CPT		PV	64.9931
	PV	64.9931		

Future Value of an Annuity (FV$_A$) of $100 for 5 years

Future Value of $100 Annuity	Texas Instruments BAII Plus		Hewlett-Packard 12C	
	Value	Function	Value	Function
$i = 9\%$ or 0.09	5	N	5	n
$n = 5$ years	9	I/Y	9	i
$FV_A = A\left[\dfrac{(1+i)^n - 1}{i}\right]$	−100	PMT	0	PV
	0	PV	−100	PMT
	Function	Solution	Function	Solution
	CPT		FV	598.4711
	FV	598.4711		

Present Value of an Annuity (PV$_A$) of $100 for 5 years

Present Value of $100 Annuity	Texas Instruments BAII Plus		Hewlett-Packard 12C	
	Value	Function	Value	Function
$i = 9\%$ or 0.09	5	N	5	n
$n = 5$ years	9	I/Y	9	i
$PV_A = A \times \left[\dfrac{1 - \dfrac{1}{(1+i)^n}}{i}\right]$	0	FV	0	FV
	−100	PMT	−100	PMT
	Function	Solution	Function	Solution
	CPT		PV	388.9651
	PV	388.9651		

Bond Valuation Using Both the TI BAII Plus and the HP 12C

Solve for V = Price of the bond
   Given:

       C_t = \$80 annual coupon payments or 8% coupon (\$40 semiannually)
       P_n = \$1,000 principal (par value)
        n = 10 years to maturity (20 periods semiannually)
         i = 9.0% rate in the market (4.5% semiannually)

You may choose to refer to Chapter 10 for a complete discussion of bond valuation.

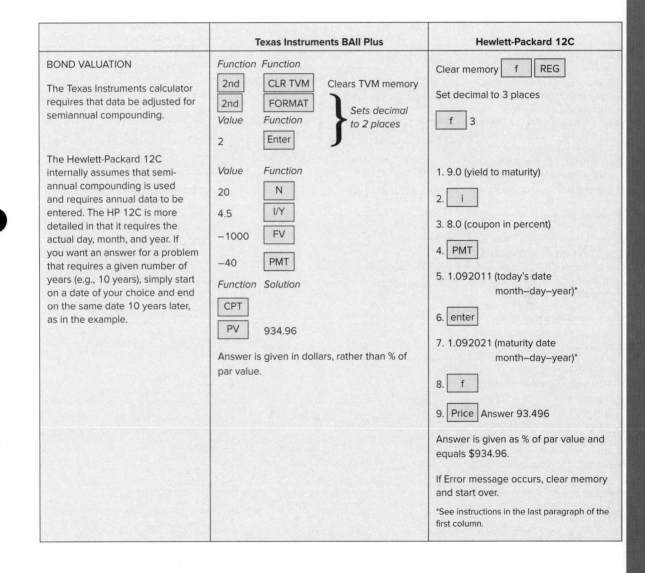

	Texas Instruments BAII Plus	Hewlett-Packard 12C

BOND VALUATION
 	
The Texas Instruments calculator requires that data be adjusted for semiannual compounding.
 	
The Hewlett-Packard 12C internally assumes that semi-annual compounding is used and requires annual data to be entered. The HP 12C is more detailed in that it requires the actual day, month, and year. If you want an answer for a problem that requires a given number of years (e.g., 10 years), simply start on a date of your choice and end on the same date 10 years later, as in the example.
	Function Function
	[2nd] [CLR TVM] Clears TVM memory
	[2nd] [FORMAT]
	Value Function } Sets decimal to 2 places
	2 [Enter]
	
	Value Function
	20 [N]
	4.5 [I/Y]
	−1000 [FV]
	−40 [PMT]
	
	Function Solution
	[CPT]
	[PV] 934.96
	
	Answer is given in dollars, rather than % of par value.
		Clear memory [f] [REG]
		
		Set decimal to 3 places
		
		[f] 3
		
		1. 9.0 (yield to maturity)
		
		2. [i]
		
		3. 8.0 (coupon in percent)
		
		4. [PMT]
		
		5. 1.092011 (today's date
		              month–day–year)*
		
		6. [enter]
		
		7. 1.092021 (maturity date
		              month–day–year)*
		
		8. [f]
		
		9. [Price] Answer 93.496

		Answer is given as % of par value and equals \$934.96. If Error message occurs, clear memory and start over. *See instructions in the last paragraph of the first column.

Yield to Maturity on Both the TI BAII Plus and HP 12C

Solve for Y = Yield to maturity
> Given:

> V = \$895.50 price of bond
> C_t = \$80 annual coupon payments or 8% coupon (\$40 semiannually)
> P_n = \$1,000 principal (par value)
> n = 10 years to maturity (20 periods semiannually)

You may choose to refer to Chapter 10 for a complete discussion of yield to maturity.

	Texas Instruments BAII Plus	Hewlett-Packard 12C

YIELD TO MATURITY
 	
The payment for a bond is normally an outflow of cash, while the receipt of the periodic interest payments and the repayment of the bond is an inflow of cash. The TI BAII Plus requires that inflows be entered as a positive number while outflows as a negative number. Before entering the current value of the bond, be sure to change the sign to negative.
 	
The Texas Instruments BAII Plus does not internally compute to a semiannual rate, so that data must be adjusted to reflect semiannual payments and periods. The answer received in step 11 is a semiannual rate, which must be multiplied by 2 to reflect an annual yield.
 	
The Hewlett-Packard 12C internally assumes that semiannual payments are made and, therefore, the answer in step 9 is the annual yield to maturity based on semiannual coupons. If you want an answer on the HP for a given number of years (e.g., 10 years), simply start on a date of your choice and end on the same date 10 years later, as in the example.
	Function Function
	[2nd] [CLR TVM] Clears TVM memory
	[2nd] [FORMAT] ⎫
	Value Function ⎬ *Sets decimal to 2 places*
	2 [Enter] ⎭
	
	Value Function
	20 [N]
	1000 [FV]
	40 [PMT]
	−895.5 [PV]
	
	Function Solution
	[CPT]
	[I/Y] 4.83 (semiannual rate)
	
	Function Value
	[×] 2
	[=]
	
	Solution
	9.65 (annual rate)
		Clear the memory [f] [REG]
		
		Set decimal [f] 2
		
		1. 89.55 (bond price as a percent of par)
		
		2. [PV]
		
		3. 8.0 (annual coupon in %)
		
		4. [PMT]
		
		5. 1.092011 (today's date
		            month–day–year)*
		
		6. [enter]
		
		7. 1.092021 (maturity date
		            month–day–year)*
		
		8. [f]
		
		9. [YTM] Answer 9.65%
		
		In case you receive an Error message, you have probably made a keystroke error. Clear the memory
		
		[f] [REG]
		
		and start over.
		
		*See instructions in the last paragraph of the first column.

Net Present Value of an Annuity on Both the TI BAII Plus and the HP 12C

Solve for A = Present value of annuity

Given:

n = 10 years (number of years cash flow will continue)

PMT = $5,000 per year (amount of the annuity)

i = 12% (cost of capital K_a)

Cost = $20,000

You may choose to refer to Chapter 12 for a complete discussion of net present value.

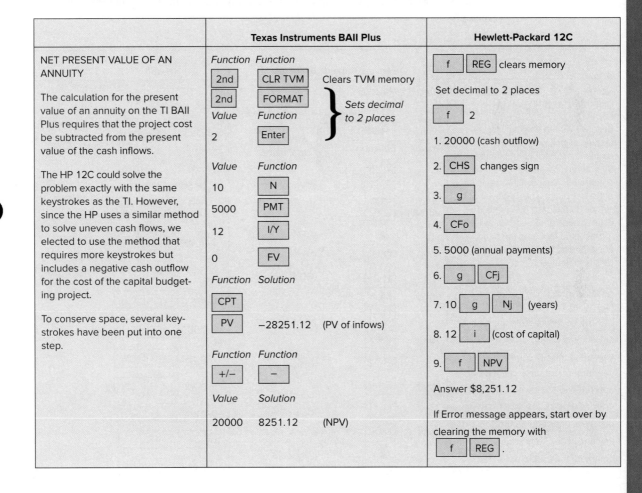

Net Present Value of an Uneven Cash Flow on Both the TI BAII Plus and the HP 12C

Solve for NPV = Net present value
   Given:

$$n = 5 \text{ years (number of years cash flow will continue)}$$
$$\text{PMT} = \$5,000 \text{ (yr. 1); } \$6,000 \text{ (yr. 2); } \$7,000 \text{ (yr. 3); } \$8,000 \text{ (yr. 4); } \$9,000 \text{ (yr. 5)}$$
$$i = 12\% \text{ (cost of capital } K_a)$$
$$\text{Cost} = \$25,000$$

You may choose to refer to Chapter 12 for a complete discussion of net present value concepts.

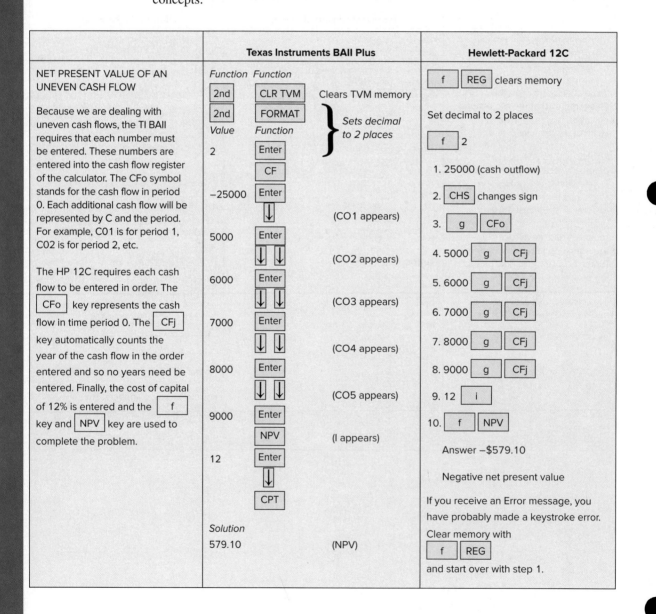

NET PRESENT VALUE OF AN UNEVEN CASH FLOW	Texas Instruments BAII Plus	Hewlett-Packard 12C
Because we are dealing with uneven cash flows, the TI BAII requires that each number must be entered. These numbers are entered into the cash flow register of the calculator. The CFo symbol stands for the cash flow in period 0. Each additional cash flow will be represented by C and the period. For example, C01 is for period 1, C02 is for period 2, etc.	*Function Function* 2nd CLR TVM Clears TVM memory 2nd FORMAT } Sets decimal to 2 places *Value Function* 2 Enter CF −25000 Enter (CO1 appears) 5000 Enter (CO2 appears)	f REG clears memory Set decimal to 2 places f 2 1. 25000 (cash outflow) 2. CHS changes sign 3. g CFo 4. 5000 g CFj
The HP 12C requires each cash flow to be entered in order. The CFo key represents the cash flow in time period 0. The CFj key automatically counts the year of the cash flow in the order entered and so no years need be entered. Finally, the cost of capital of 12% is entered and the f key and NPV key are used to complete the problem.	6000 Enter (CO3 appears) 7000 Enter (CO4 appears) 8000 Enter (CO5 appears) 9000 Enter NPV (I appears) 12 Enter CPT *Solution* 579.10 (NPV)	5. 6000 g CFj 6. 7000 g CFj 7. 8000 g CFj 8. 9000 g CFj 9. 12 i 10. f NPV Answer −\$579.10 Negative net present value If you receive an Error message, you have probably made a keystroke error. Clear memory with f REG and start over with step 1.

Internal Rate of Return for an Annuity on Both the TI BAII Plus and the HP 12C

Solve for IRR = Internal rate of return

Given:

$n = 10$ years (number of years cash flow will continue)

PMT = $10,000 per year (amount of the annuity)

Cost = $50,000 (this is the present value of the annuity)

You may choose to refer to Chapter 12 for a complete discussion of internal rate of return.

	Texas Instruments BAII Plus	Hewlett-Packard 12C
INTERNAL RATE OF RETURN ON AN ANNUITY The calculation for the internal rate of return on an annuity on the TI BAII Plus requires relatively few keystrokes. The HP 12C requires more keystrokes than the TI BAII Plus because it needs to use the function keys [f] and [g] to enter data into the internal programs. Both calculators require that the cash outflow be expressed as a negative. To conserve space, several keystrokes have been put into one step.	*Function Function* [2nd] [CLR TVM] Clears TVM memory [2nd] [FORMAT] } Sets decimal to 2 places *Value Function* 2 [Enter] 10 [N] −50000 [PV] 10000 [PMT] 0 [FV] *Function Solution* [CPT] [I/Y] 15.10 At an internal rate of return of 15.10%, the present value of the $50,000 outflow is equal to the present value of $10,000 cash inflows over the next 10 years.	[f] [REG] clears memory 1. 50000 (cash outflow) 2. [CHS] changes sign 3. [g] 4. [CFo] 5. 10000 (annual payments) 6. [g] [CFj] 7. 10 [g] [Nj] (years) 8. [f] [IRR] Answer is 15.10% If an Error message appears, start over by clearing the memory with [f] [REG].

Internal Rate of Return with an Uneven Cash Flow on Both the TI BAII Plus and the HP 12C

Solve for IRR = Internal rate of return (return that causes present value of outflows to equal present value of the inflows)

Given:

$n = 5$ years (number of years cash flow will continue)

PMT = $5,000 (yr. 1); $6,000 (yr. 2); $7,000 (yr. 3); $8,000 (yr. 4); $9,000 (yr. 5)

Cost = $25,000

You may choose to refer to Chapter 12 for a complete discussion of internal rate of return.

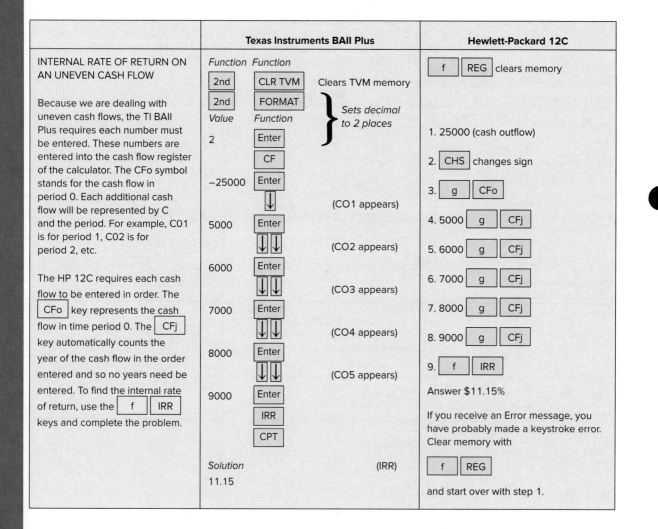

Valuation and Rates of Return

LEARNING OBJECTIVES

LO 10-1 The valuation of a financial asset is based on the present value of future cash flows.

LO 10-2 The required rate of return in valuing an asset is based on the risk involved.

LO 10-3 Bond valuation is based on the process of determining the present value of interest payments plus the present value of the principal payment at maturity.

LO 10-4 Preferred stock valuation is based on the dividend paid and the market required return.

LO 10-5 Stock valuation is based on determining the present value of the future benefits of equity ownership.

Valuation appears to be a fickle process to stockholders of some corporations. For example, if you held The Coca-Cola Company common stock in January 2018, you would be pleased to see that stockholders were valuing your stock at 46 times earnings. Certainly there was some justification for such a high valuation. Coca-Cola is sold in more than 200 countries, and it is the best-known brand in the world. But keep in mind that the company's earnings were lower in 2017 than in 2012, although dividends were up 45 percent from $1.02 to $1.48 per share.

If stockholders of Coca-Cola were happy with the firm's strong P/E (price-earnings ratio) valuation in January 2018, those who were invested in Ford were not. The automotive giant was trading at a P/E ratio of 10.4, even though both its earnings and its dividends had grown more rapidly than Coke's (140 percent and 160 percent, respectively). Keep in mind that while its competitors required government assistance to survive, Ford rode out the Great Recession that began in 2007 without needing a government bailout. Ford's debt had even returned to investment-grade status by 2012. After this record of resilience and success, shareholders were probably frustrated that the 2018 price of the stock produced a P/E ratio below 11.

The question then becomes, why are P/E ratios so different and why do they change so much? Informed investors care about their money and vote with their dollars. The factors that influence valuation are many and varied, and you will be exposed to many of them in this chapter.

In Chapter 9, we considered the basic principles of the time value of money. In this chapter, we will use many of those concepts to determine how financial assets (bonds, preferred stock, and common stock) are valued and how investors establish the rates of return they demand. In the next chapter, we will use material from this chapter to determine the overall cost of financing to the firm. We merely turn the coin over. Once we know how much bondholders and stockholders demand in rates of return, we will observe what the corporation is required to pay them to attract their funds.

The cost of corporate financing (capital) is subsequently used in analyzing whether a project is acceptable for investment. These relationships are depicted in Figure 10-1.

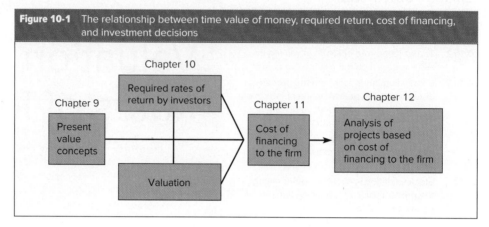

Figure 10-1   The relationship between time value of money, required return, cost of financing, and investment decisions

Valuation Concepts

The valuation of a financial asset is based on determining the present value of future cash flows. Thus we need to know the value of future cash flows and the discount rate to be applied to the future cash flows to determine the current value.

The market-determined **required rate of return**, which is the discount rate, depends on the market's perceived level of risk associated with the individual security. Also important is the idea that required rates of return are competitively determined among the many companies seeking financial capital. For example, Microsoft, due to its low financial risk, relatively high return, and strong market position, is likely to raise debt capital at a significantly lower cost than can United Airlines, a firm with high financial risk. This implies that investors are willing to accept low return for low risk, and vice versa. The market allocates capital to companies based on risk, efficiency, and expected returns—which are based to a large degree on past performance. The reward to the financial manager for efficient use of capital in the past is a lower required return for investors than that of competing companies that did not manage their financial resources as well.

Throughout the balance of this chapter, we apply concepts of valuation to corporate bonds, preferred stock, and common stock. Although we describe the basic characteristics of each form of security as part of the valuation process, extended discussion of each security is deferred until later chapters.

Valuation of Bonds

As previously stated, the value of a financial asset is based on the concept of the present value of future cash flows. Let's apply this approach to bond valuation. A bond provides an annuity stream of interest payments and a $1,000 principal payment at maturity.[1] These cash flows are discounted at Y, the yield to maturity. The value of Y is determined in the bond market and represents the required rate of return for bonds of a given risk and maturity. More will be said about the concept of yield to maturity in the next section.

---

[1]The assumption is that the bond has a $1,000 par value. If the par value is higher or lower, then this value would be discounted to the present from the maturity date.

The price of a bond is thus equal to the present value of regular interest payments discounted by the yield to maturity added to the present value of the principal (also discounted by the yield to maturity).

The following timeline depicts a bond's cash flows:

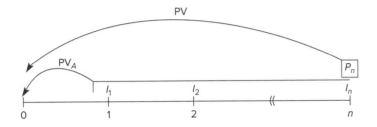

This relationship can be expressed mathematically as follows:

$$P_b = \sum_{t=1}^{n} \frac{I_t}{(1 + Y)^t} + \frac{P_n}{(1 + Y)^n} \tag{10-1}$$

where

P_b = Price of the bond

I_t = Interest payments

P_n = Principal payment at maturity

t = Number corresponding to a period; running from 1 to n

n = Number of periods

Y = Yield to maturity (or required rate of return)

The first term in the equation says to take the sum of the present values of the interest payments (I_t); the second term directs you to take the present value of the principal payment at maturity (P_n). The discount rate used throughout the analysis is the yield to maturity (Y). The answer derived is referred to as P_b (the price of the bond). The analysis is carried out for n periods.

Let's look at an example:

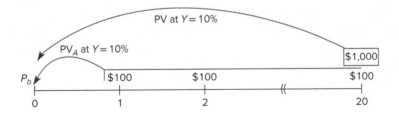

In this timeline, each interest payment (I_t) equals $100; P_n (principal payment at maturity) equals $1,000; Y (yield to maturity) is 10 percent; and n (total number of periods) equals 20. We could say that P_b (the price of the bond) equals:

$$P_b = \sum_{t=1}^{n} \frac{\$100}{(1 + 0.10)^t} + \frac{\$1,000}{(1 + 0.10)^{20}}$$

We take the present value of the interest payments and then add this value to the present value of the principal payment at maturity.

Present Value of Interest Payments   In this case, we determine the present value of a $100 annuity for 20 years.[2] The discount rate is 10 percent. We can use Formula 9-6 to find the following:

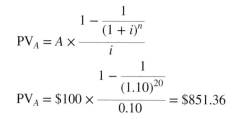

$$PV_A = A \times \frac{1 - \dfrac{1}{(1 + i)^n}}{i}$$

$$PV_A = \$100 \times \frac{1 - \dfrac{1}{(1.10)^{20}}}{0.10} = \$851.36$$

Present Value of Principal Payment (Par Value) at Maturity   This single value of $1,000 will be received after 20 years. Note the term *principal payment at maturity* is used interchangeably with *par value* or *face value* of the bond. We discount $1,000 back to the present at 10 percent.

We can use Formula 9-2 to find the following:

$$PV = FV \times \frac{1}{(1 + i)^n}$$

$$PV = \$1,000 \times \frac{1}{(1.10)^{20}} = \$148.64$$

The current price of the bond, based on the present value of interest payments and the present value of the principal payment at maturity, is $1,000.

Present value of interest payments	$ 851.40
Present value of principal payment at maturity	148.64
Total present value, or price, of the bond	$1,000.00

The price of the bond in this case is essentially the same as its par, or stated, value to be received at maturity of $1,000. This is because the annual interest rate is 10 percent (the annual interest payment of $100 divided by $1,000) and the yield to maturity, or discount rate, is also 10 percent. When the interest rate on the bond and the yield to maturity are equal, the bond will trade at par value. Later we will examine the mathematical effects of varying the yield to maturity above or below the interest rate on the bond.

Bond Valuation Using a Financial Calculator

Bond values can be found using the $\boxed{\text{PV}}$ function on a financial calculator. The first calculator solution box in the margin shows the present value of the twenty $100 coupon

---

[2]For now, we are using *annual* interest payments for simplicity. Later in the discussion, we will shift to semi-annual payments, and more appropriately determine the value of a bond.

payments. The calculator keystrokes are identical to those used to find the present value of an annuity. Notice that the PMT value is entered as a negative number. As we found earlier, the present value of the coupon payment annuity stream is $851.36.

The second calculator solution shows the present value of the $1,000 principal payment that will be received at the end of 20 years. The calculator keystrokes are identical to those used to find the present value of a single amount. If the FV value is entered as a negative number, the present value of the principal will be $148.64. This is the value found using the present value equation earlier. Of course, the value of the bond ($1,000) is the sum of the present values in panel A and panel B.

Finally, the third calculator solution demonstrates how we calculate the bond value when entering the principal and coupon payments simultaneously. Again, the coupon amounts are entered as a negative value using the PMT key, and the principal is entered as a negative value using the FV key. The value of the bond is $1,000.

Using Excel's PV Function to Calculate a Bond Price

Excel's **PV** function can calculate the price of a bond. In order to produce a positive bond price, the coupon payment annuity amount is input as a negative value for the **pmt** argument. The principal payment (−1000) is entered as the **fv** argument. The function in cell D1 references the arguments in cells B1 to B4. The function in cell D5 uses hard-coded numerical values. In both cases, the bond values produced by the **PV** function are identical to the calculator solution.

	A	B	C	D	E	F
1	rate	10.00%		=+PV(B1,B2,B3,B4)		
2	nper	20		PV(**rate**, nper, pmt, [fv], [type])		
3	pmt	−100		$1,000.00		
4	fv	−1000				
5				=+PV(0.1,20,−100,−1000)		
6				PV(**rate**, nper, pmt, [fv], [type])		
7				$1,000.00		

Concept of Yield to Maturity

In the previous example, the yield to maturity that was used as the discount rate was 10 percent. The **yield to maturity**, or discount rate, is the rate of return required by bondholders. The bondholder, or any investor for that matter, will allow *three* factors to influence his or her required rate of return:

1. The required **real rate of return**—This is the rate of return the investor demands for giving up the current use of the funds on a noninflation-adjusted basis. It is the financial "rent" the investor charges for using his or her funds for one year, five years, or any given period. Although it varies from time to time, historically the real rate of return demanded by investors has been about 2 to 3 percent.

2. **Inflation premium**—In addition to the real rate of return discussed above, the investor requires a premium to compensate for the eroding effect of inflation on the value of the dollar. It would hardly satisfy an investor to have a

3 percent total rate of return in a 5 percent inflationary economy. Under such circumstances, the lender (investor) would be paying the borrower 2 percent for use of the funds, or in other words, losing 2 percent in purchasing power. This would represent an irrational action. No one wishes to *pay* another party to use his or her fund. The inflation premium added to the real rate of return ensures that this will not happen. The size of the inflation premium will be based on the investor's expectations about future inflation. In the last two decades, the inflation premium has been 1 to 4 percent. In the late 1970s, it was in excess of 10 percent.

If one combines the real rate of return (part 1) and the inflation premium (part 2), the **risk-free rate of return** is determined. This is the rate that compensates the investor for the current use of his or her funds and for the loss in purchasing power due to inflation, but not for taking risks. As an example, if the real rate of return were 3 percent and the inflation premium were 4 percent, we would say the risk-free rate of return is 7 percent.[3]

3. **Risk premium**—We must now add the risk premium to the risk-free rate of return. This is a premium associated with the special risks of a given investment. Of primary interest to us are two types of risk: **business risk** and **financial risk**. Business risk relates to the inability of the firm to hold its competitive position and maintain stability and growth in its earnings. Financial risk relates to the inability of the firm to meet its debt obligations as they come due. In addition to the two forms of risk mentioned above, the risk premium will be greater or less for different types of investments. For example, because bonds possess a contractual obligation for the firm to pay interest to bondholders, they are considered less risky than common stock where no such obligation exists.[4]

The risk premium of an investment may range from as low as zero on a very-short-term U.S. government–backed security to 10 to 15 percent on a gold mining expedition. The typical risk premium is 2 to 6 percent. Just as the required real rate of return and the inflation premium change over time, so does the risk premium. For example, high-risk corporate bonds (sometimes referred to as junk bonds) normally require a risk premium of about 5 percentage points over the risk-free rate. However, in September 1989 the bottom fell out of the junk bond market as Campeau Corp., International Resources, and Resorts International began facing difficulties in making their payments. Risk premiums almost doubled. The same phenomenon took place in the fall of 2008 in reaction to the U.S. financial crisis and in the spring of 2010 in reaction to the debt crisis in Greece, Portugal, Ireland, Italy, and Spain. As is emphasized in many parts of the text, there is a strong correlation between the risk the investor is taking and the return the investor demands. Supposedly, in finance as in other parts of business, "There is no such thing as a free lunch." As you take more risk hoping for higher returns, you also expose yourself to the possibility of lower or negative returns on the other end of the probability curve.

---

[3]Actually a slightly more accurate representation would be this: Risk-free rate = (1 + Real rate of return) (1 + Inflation premium) − 1. We would show: (1.03)(1.04) − 1 = 1.0712 − 1 = 0.0712 = 7.12 percent.
[4]On the other hand, common stock carries the potential for very high returns when the corporation is quite profitable.

We shall assume that in the investment we are examining the risk premium is 3 percent. If we add this risk premium to the two components of the risk-free rate of return developed in parts 1 and 2, we arrive at an overall required rate of return of 10 percent.

+ Real rate of return	3%
+ Inflation premium	4
= Risk-free rate	7%
+ Risk premium	3
= Required rate of return	10%

In this instance, we assume we are evaluating the required return on a bond issued by a firm. If the security had been the common stock of the same firm, the risk premium might be 5 to 6 percent and the required rate of return 12 to 13 percent.

Finally, in concluding this section, you should recall that the required rate of return on a bond is effectively the same concept as required yield to maturity.

Changing the Yield to Maturity and the Impact on Bond Valuation

In the earlier bond value calculation, we assumed the interest rate was 10 percent ($100 annual interest on a $1,000 par value bond) and the yield to maturity was also 10 percent. Under those circumstances, the price of the bond was basically equal to par value. Now let's assume conditions in the market cause the yield to maturity to change.

Increase in Inflation Premium   For example, assume the inflation premium goes up from 4 to 6 percent. All else remains constant. The required rate of return would now be 12 percent.

+ Real rate of return	3%
+ Inflation premium	6
= Risk-free rate	9%
+ Risk premium	3
= Required rate of return	12%

With the required rate of return, or yield to maturity, now at 12 percent, the price of the bond will change.[5] A bond that pays only 10 percent interest when the required rate of return (yield to maturity) is 12 percent will fall below its current value of approximately $1,000. The new price of the bond is $850.61.

We can calculate the bond price by using the calculator keystrokes shown in the margin or by using the time-value equations as follows:

Present Value of Interest Payments   We take the present value of a $100 annuity for 20 years. The discount rate is 12 percent.

$$PV_A = A \times \frac{1 - \dfrac{1}{(1+i)^n}}{i}$$

$$PV_A = \$100 \times \frac{1 - \dfrac{1}{(1.12)^{20}}}{0.12} = \$746.94$$

FINANCIAL CALCULATOR

Bond Price

Value	Function
20	N
12	I/Y
1000	FV
100	PMT
Function	Solution
CPT	
PV	−850.61

---

[5]Of course the required rate of return on all other financial assets will also go up proportionally.

Present Value of Principal Payment at Maturity   We take the present value of $1,000 after 20 years. The discount rate is 12 percent.

$$PV = FV \times \frac{1}{(1 + i)^n}$$

$$PV = \$1,000 \times \frac{1}{(1.12)^{20}} = \$103.67$$

Total Present Value

Present value of interest payments	$746.94
Present value of principal payment at maturity	103.67
Total present value, or price, of the bond	$850.61

In this example, we assumed increasing inflation caused the required rate of return (yield to maturity) to go up and the bond price to fall by approximately $150. The same effect would occur if the business risk increased or the demanded level for the *real* rate of return became higher.

Decrease in Inflation Premium   The opposite effect would happen if the required rate of return went down because of lower inflation, less risk, or other factors. Let's assume the inflation premium declines and the required rate of return (yield to maturity) goes down to 8 percent.

The 20-year bond with the 10 percent interest rate (coupon rate) would now sell for $1,196.36 as shown in the calculator keystrokes in the margin or using the following calculations:

Present Value of Interest Payments

$$PV_A = A \times \frac{1 - \dfrac{1}{(1 + i)^n}}{i}$$

$$PV_A = \$100 \times \frac{1 - \dfrac{1}{(1.08)^{20}}}{0.08} = \$981.81$$

Present Value of Principal Payment at Maturity

$$PV = FV \times \frac{1}{(1 + i)^n}$$

$$PV = \$1,000 \times \frac{1}{(1.08)^{20}} = \$214.55$$

Total Present Value

Present value of interest payments	$ 981.81
Present value of principal payment at maturity	214.55
Total present value, or price, of the bond	$1,196.36

The bond is now trading at $196.36 over par value. This is certainly the expected result because the bond is paying 10 percent interest when the yield required in the market is only 8 percent. The 2 percentage point differential on a $1,000 par value bond represents $20 per year. The investor will receive this differential for the next 20 years. The present value of $20 for the next 20 years at the current market rate of

---

FINANCIAL CALCULATOR

Bond Price

Value	Function
20	N
8	I/Y
1000	FV
100	PMT

Function	Solution
CPT	
PV	−1196.36

interest of 8 percent is approximately $196.36. This explains why the bond is trading at $196.36 over its stated, or par, value.

The further the yield to maturity on a bond changes from the stated interest rate on the bond, the greater the price change effect will be. This is illustrated in Table 10-1 for the 10 percent coupon rate, 20-year bonds discussed in this chapter.

Table 10-1	Bond price table				
(10% Interest Payment, 20 Years to Maturity)					
Yield to Maturity	PV of Coupons		PV of Principal		Bond Price
2%	$1,635.14	+	$672.97	=	$2,308.11
4%	1,359.03	+	456.39	=	1,815.42
6%	1,146.99	+	311.80	=	1,458.80
7%	1,059.40	+	258.42	=	1,317.82
8%	981.81	+	214.55	=	1,196.36
9%	912.85	+	178.43	=	1,091.29
10%	851.36	+	148.64	=	1,000.00
11%	796.33	+	124.03	=	920.37
12%	746.94	+	103.67	=	850.61
13%	702.48	+	86.78	=	789.26
14%	662.31	+	72.76	=	735.07
16%	592.88	+	51.39	=	644.27
20%	486.96	+	26.08	=	513.04
25%	395.39	+	11.53	=	406.92

We clearly see the impact that different yields to maturity have on the price of a bond.

Time to Maturity

The impact of a change in yield to maturity on valuation is also affected by the remaining time to maturity. The effect of a bond paying 2 percentage points more or less than the going rate of interest is quite different for a 20-year bond than it is for a 1-year bond. In the latter case, the investor will be gaining or giving up only $20 for one year. That is certainly not the same as having this $20 differential for an extended period. Let's once again return to the 10 percent interest rate bond and show the impact of a 2 percentage point decrease or increase in yield to maturity for varying *times* to maturity. The values are shown in Table 10-2 and graphed in Figure 10-2. The upper part of Figure 10-2 shows how the amount (premium) above par value is reduced as the number of years to maturity becomes smaller and smaller. Figure 10-2 should be read from left to right. The lower part of the figure shows how the amount (discount) below par value is reduced with progressively fewer years to maturity. Clearly, the longer the maturity, the greater the impact of changes in yield.

Determining Yield to Maturity from the Bond Price

Until now we have used yield to maturity as well as other factors, such as the interest rate on the bond and number of years to maturity, to compute the price of the bond. We shall now assume we know the price of the bond, the interest rate on the bond, and the

Table 10-2   Impact of time to maturity on bond prices

(10% Interest Payment, Various Times to Maturity)		
Time Period in Years to Maturity	Bond Price with 8% Yield to Maturity	Bond Price with 12% Yield to Maturity
0	$1,000.00	$1,000.00
1	1,018.52	982.14
5	1,079.85	927.90
10	1,134.20	887.00
15	1,171.19	863.78
20	1,196.36	850.61
25	1,213.50	843.14
30	1,225.16	838.90

Figure 10-2   Relationship between time to maturity and bond price*

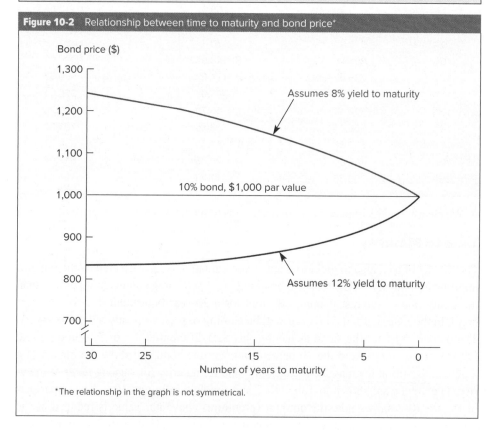

*The relationship in the graph is not symmetrical.

years to maturity, and we wish to determine the yield to maturity. Once we have computed this value, we have determined the rate of return that investors are demanding in the marketplace to provide for inflation, risk, and other factors.

Let's once again present Formula 10-1:

$$P_b = \sum_{t=1}^{n} \frac{I_t}{(1 + Y)^t} + \frac{P_n}{(1 + Y)^n}$$

We now determine the value of Y, the yield to maturity, that will equate the interest payments (I_t) and the principal payment (P_n) to the price of the bond (P_b).

Consider the following timeline for payments on a 15-year bond that pays $110 per year (11 percent of the face amount) in interest and $1,000 in principal repayment after 15 years. The current price of the bond is $931.89.

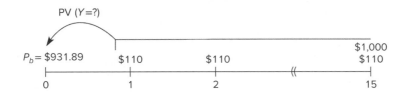

We wish to compute the yield to maturity, or discount rate, that equates future flows with the current price. It turns out that there is no algebraic formula that allows us to solve for the yield to maturity directly. Once upon a time, this presented a difficult puzzle that required tedious trial-and-error estimations to be checked before a solution could be found.

Fortunately, our tools have improved. Both Excel and financial calculators are able to do these calculations so rapidly that the user is frequently left unaware that they are using the same trial-and-error process that was once done by hand.

Let us start by reorganizing the timeline in an Excel spreadsheet as shown in Table 10-3. The Excel function **RATE(n,pmt,pv,fv)** shown at the bottom of the spreadsheet can also be used to find the yield to maturity, but the full spreadsheet has the advantage of making all the steps transparent to the reader. The spreadsheet also introduces Excel's very flexible Goal Seek feature, which has many uses in addition to finding yields to maturity.

In the spreadsheet, the time (n) of each payment is shown in column B, and each payment amount is shown in column C. The last two payments are at time $n = 15$ when both the last coupon payment and the principal are paid. In column D, we see a "PV factor" that is used to find the present value of each payment. The general equation for each factor is shown in the first comment box that points to cell D2. The comment box pointing to cell D4 shows the actual Excel equation and syntax for that cell. Each of the PV factor cells references the discount rate in cell D$1, which is also the yield to maturity. The dollar sign in the cell ensures that each row in the D column is referencing cell D1. Column E shows the present value of each payment, and the sum of the present value of all these payments is shown in cell E20. This is the bond price. Once you have created the spreadsheet and entered the data and appropriate equations, you are ready to use Goal Seek.

The yield to maturity of $Y = 12.00\%$ is shown in red in cell D1. This cell was calculated using the Goal Seek function in Excel. Goal Seek is used when you know the result that you want for a formula, but you are not sure what input value the formula needs to get the result. In the case of the yield to maturity, we know the bond price should be $931.89, but we do not know the discount rate that produces that price.

The Goal Seek function can be found in the most recent version of Excel on the **Data** tab, in the **Data Tools** group, under **What-If Analysis.** See Figure 10-3 for a picture of the Excel Ribbon location. Earlier versions of Excel also include Goal Seek, but the feature may be in a menu or toolbar instead of on the Excel Ribbon.

FINANCIAL CALCULATOR

Bond Yield

Value	Function
15	N
−931.89	PV
110	PMT
1000	FV

Function	Solution
CPT	
I/Y	12.00

Table 10-3   Excel functions for YTM

	A	B	C	D	E	F	G	H
1			$Y=$	12.00%		PV Factor = $1/(1+Y)^n$		
2		n	Payment	PV factor	PV			
3		1	110	0.893	$98.21	=$1/(1+D\$1)^B4$		
4		2	110	0.797	$87.69	=C5*D5		
5		3	110	0.712	$78.30			
6		4	110	0.636	$69.91			
7		5	110	0.567	$62.42			
8		6	110	0.507	$55.73			
9		7	110	0.452	$49.76			
10		8	110	0.404	$44.43			
11		9	110	0.361	$39.67			
12		10	110	0.322	$35.42			
13		11	110	0.287	$31.62			
14		12	110	0.257	$28.23			
15		13	110	0.229	$25.21			
16		14	110	0.205	$22.51			
17		15	110	0.183	$20.10			
18					$749.19	PV of coupons		
19	Face Amount	15	1000	0.183	$182.70	PV of face		
20					$931.89	P_b = Bond price		
21								
22	=Rate(15,110,−931.89,1000)							
23	RATE (nper, pmt, pv, [fv], [type], [guess])							

(Coupon Payments (I_t) — vertical label spanning rows 3–17, column A)

Goal Seek

Set cell:	E20
To value:	931.89
By changing cell:	D1

[OK]   [Cancel]

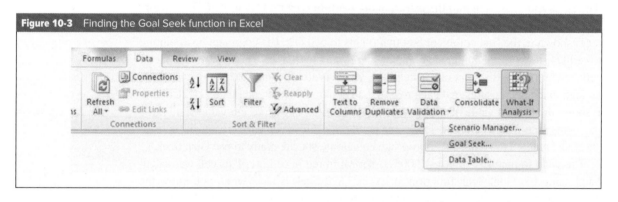

Figure 10-3   Finding the Goal Seek function in Excel

The financial calculator keystrokes function much like Excel's **RATE(nper,pmt,pv,(fv))** function. These keystrokes are shown in the margin near Table 10-3.

These are the steps used to find the yield to maturity:

1. Make sure that you have calculated an arbitrary bond price by putting an interest rate in cell D1. Any rate should work, but using 11% is a good place to

start because you already know that, at 11%, the price of the bond should be $1,000 since the coupon payment of $110 is 11% of the principal.

2. Open the Goal Seek feature.

3. In the "Set cell" box, enter the reference for the cell containing the formula for the bond price.

4. In the "To value" box, type the value 931.89, which is the price of the bond.

5. In the "By changing cell" box, enter the reference for the cell that contains the discount rate that you wish to find. This is cell D1 for this example.

6. Click "OK."

Goal Seek runs and produces the result in cell D1: $Y = 12\%$. The **RATE (nper,pmt,pv,(fv))** function in cell A22 also produces a value of 12%.

Semiannual Interest and Bond Prices

We have been assuming that interest was paid annually in our bond analysis. In actuality, most bonds pay interest semiannually. Thus a 10 percent interest rate bond may actually pay $50 twice a year instead of $100 annually. To make the conversion from an annual to semiannual analysis, we follow three steps:

1. Divide the annual interest rate by 2.

2. Multiply the number of years by 2.

3. Divide the annual yield to maturity by 2.

Assume a 10 percent, $1,000 par value bond has a maturity of 20 years. The annual yield to maturity is 12 percent. In following the three steps above, we would show this:

1. 10%/2 = 5% semiannual interest rate; therefore, 5% × $1,000 = $50 semiannual interest.

2. 20 × 2 = 40 periods to maturity.

3. 12%/2 = 6% yield to maturity, expressed on a semiannual basis.

The calculator solution for this problem is shown in the margin.

The answer of $849.54 is slightly below what we found previously for the same bond, assuming an annual interest rate ($850.61). This value was initially shown on page 309. In terms of accuracy, the semiannual analysis is a more acceptable method and is the method used in bond tables. As is true in many finance texts, we present the annual interest rate approach first for ease of presentation, and then the semiannual basis is given. In the problems at the back of the chapter, you will be asked to do problems on both an annual and semiannual interest payment basis.

FINANCIAL CALCULATOR	
Bond Price	
Value	*Function*
40	N
6	I/Y
50	PMT
1000	FV
Function	*Solution*
CPT	
PV	−849.54

Valuation and Preferred Stock

Preferred stock usually represents a **perpetuity** or, in other words, has no maturity date. It is valued in the market without any principal payment since it has no ending life. If preferred stock had a maturity date, the analysis would be similar to that of the preceding bond example. Preferred stock has a fixed dividend payment carrying a higher order of precedence than common stock dividends, but not the binding contractual obligation of interest on debt. Preferred stock, being a hybrid security, has neither the ownership privilege of common stock nor the legally enforceable provisions of debt. To value a perpetuity such as preferred stock, we first consider this formula:

$$P_p = \frac{D_p}{(1 + K_p)^1} + \frac{D_p}{(1 + K_p)^2} + \frac{D_p}{(1 + K_p)^3} + \ldots + \frac{D_p}{(1 + K_p)^\infty} \qquad (10\text{-}2)$$

where

P_p = the price of preferred stock

D_p = the annual dividend for preferred stock (a constant value)

K_p = the required rate of return, or discount rate, applied to preferred stock dividends

Notice that, unlike a bond, the preferred stock never matures. Because the dividend payments are promised to continue forever, a preferred stock is valued as a perpetuity. A perpetuity is described by a timeline that stretches to infinity as shown here:

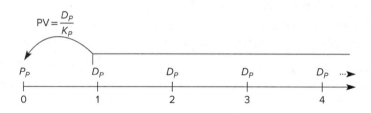

The preferred stock is easily valued as

$$P_p = \frac{D_p}{K_p} \qquad (10\text{-}3)$$

Actually, Formula 10-3 can be used to value any perpetuity, as long as the first payment occurs one year from the valuation date. All we have to do to find the price of preferred stock (P_p) is to divide the constant annual dividend payment (D_p) by the required rate of return that preferred stockholders are demanding (K_p). For example, if the annual dividend were $10 and the stockholder required a 10 percent rate of return, the price of preferred stock would be $100.

$$P_p = \frac{D_p}{K_p} = \frac{\$10}{0.10} = \$100$$

As was true in our bond valuation analysis, if the rate of return required by security holders changes, the value of the financial asset (in this case, preferred stock) will change. You may also recall that the longer the life of an investment, the greater the impact of a change in required rate of return. It is one thing to be locked into a low-paying security for one year when the rate goes up; it is quite another to be locked in for 10 or 20 years. With preferred stock, you have a *perpetual* security, so the impact is at a maximum. Assume in the prior example that because of higher inflation or increased business risk, K_p (the required rate of return) increases to 12 percent. The new value for the preferred stock shares is:

$$P_p = \frac{D_p}{K_p} = \frac{\$10}{0.12} = \$83.33$$

If the required rate of return were reduced to 8 percent, the opposite effect would occur. The preferred stock price would be computed as:

$$P_p = \frac{D_p}{K_p} = \frac{\$10}{0.08} = \$125$$

It is not surprising that the preferred stock is now trading well above its original price of $100. It is still offering a $10 dividend (10 percent of the original offering price of $100), and the market is demanding only an 8 percent yield. To match the $10 dividend with the 8 percent rate of return, the market price will advance to $125.

Determining the Required Rate of Return (Yield) from the Market Price

In our analysis of preferred stock, we have used the value of the annual dividend (D_p) and the required rate of return (K_p) to solve for the price of preferred stock (P_p). We could change our analysis to solve for the required rate of return (K_p) as the unknown, given that we know the annual dividend (D_p) and the preferred stock price (P_p). We take Formula 10-3 and rewrite it as Formula 10-4, where the unknown is the required rate of return (K_p).

$$P_p = \frac{D_p}{K_p} \text{ (reverse the position of } K_p \text{ and } P_p) \qquad (10\text{-}3)$$

$$K_p = \frac{D_p}{P_p} \qquad (10\text{-}4)$$

Using Formula 10-4, if the annual preferred dividend (D_p) is $10 and the price of preferred stock (P_p) is $100, the required rate of return (yield) would be 10 percent as follows:

$$K_p = \frac{D_p}{P_P} = \frac{\$10}{\$100} = 10\%$$

If the price goes up to $130, the yield will be only 7.69 percent:

$$K_p = \frac{\$10}{\$130} = 7.69\%$$

We see the higher market price provides quite a decline in the yield.

Valuation of Common Stock

The value of a share of common stock may be interpreted by the shareholder as the *present value* of an expected stream of *future dividends*. Although in the short run stockholders may be influenced by a change in earnings or other variables, the ultimate value of any holding rests with the distribution of earnings in the form of dividend payments. Though the stockholder may benefit from the retention and reinvestment of earnings by the corporation, at some point the earnings must be translated into cash flow for the stockholder. A stock valuation model based on future expected dividends, which is termed a **dividend valuation model**, can be stated as:

$$P_0 = \frac{D_1}{(1 + K_e)^1} + \frac{D_2}{(1 + K_e)^2} + \frac{D_3}{(1 + K_e)^3} + \ldots + \frac{D_\infty}{(1 + K_e)^\infty} \qquad (10\text{-}5)$$

where

P_0 = Price of stock today

D = Dividend for each year

K_e = Required rate of return for common stock (discount rate)

This formula, with modification, is generally applied to three different circumstances:

1. No growth in dividends.
2. Constant growth in dividends.
3. Variable growth in dividends.

No Growth in Dividends

Under the no-growth circumstance, common stock is very similar to preferred stock. The common stock pays a constant dividend each year. For that reason, we merely translate the terms in Formula 10-3, which applies to preferred stock, to apply to common stock. This is shown as new Formula 10-6:

$$P_0 = \frac{D_1}{K_e} \qquad (10\text{-}6)$$

P_0 = Price of common stock today

D_1 = Current annual common stock dividend (a constant value)

K_e = Required rate of return for common stock

Assume D_1 = \$1.87 and K_e = 12 percent; the price of the stock would be \$15.58:

$$P_0 = \frac{\$1.87}{0.12} = \$15.58$$

A no-growth policy for common stock dividends does not hold much appeal for investors and so is seen infrequently in the real world.[6]

Constant Growth in Dividends

A firm that increases dividends at a constant rate is a more likely circumstance. Perhaps a firm decides to increase its dividends by 7 percent per year. The general valuation approach is shown in Formula 10-7:

---

[6]Since this is a no-growth stock, D_1 equals D_0. Formula 10-6 uses D_1 to emphasize that the first dividend payment comes at the end of year 1.

$$P_0 = \frac{D_0(1 + g)^1}{(1 + K_e)^1} + \frac{D_0(1 + g)^2}{(1 + K_e)^2} + \frac{D_0(1 + g)^3}{(1 + K_e)^3} + \ldots + \frac{D_0(1 + g)^\infty}{(1 + K_e)^\infty} \qquad (10\text{-}7)$$

where

P_0 = Price of common stock today

$D_0(1 + g)^1$ = Dividend in year 1, D_1

$D_0(1 + g)^2$ = Dividend in year 2, D_2, and so on

g = Constant growth rate in dividends

K_e = Required rate of return for common stock (discount rate)

As shown in Formula 10-7, the current price of the stock is the present value of the future stream of dividends growing at a constant rate. If we can anticipate the growth pattern of future dividends and determine the discount rate, we can ascertain the price of the stock.

For example, assume the following information:

D_0 = Last 12-month's dividend (assume $1.87)

D_1 = First year, $2.00 (growth rate, 7%)

D_2 = Second year, $2.14 (growth rate, 7%)

D_3 = Third year, $2.29 (growth rate, 7%), etc.

K_e = Required rate of return (discount rate), 12%

then

$$P_0 = \frac{\$2.00}{(1.12)^1} + \frac{\$2.14}{(1.12)^2} + \frac{\$2.29}{(1.12)^3} + \ldots + \frac{\text{Infinite dividend}}{(1.12)^\infty}$$

To find the price of the stock, we take the present value of each year's dividend. This is no small task when the formula calls for us to take the present value of an *infinite* stream of growing dividends. Fortunately, Formula 10-7 can be compressed into a much more usable form if two circumstances are satisfied:

1. The firm must have a constant dividend growth rate (g).
2. The discount rate (K_e) must be higher than the growth rate (g).

For most introductory courses in finance, these assumptions are usually made to reduce the complications in the analytical process. This allows us to reduce or rewrite Formula 10-7 as Formula 10-8. Formula 10-8 is the basic equation for finding the value of common stock and is referred to as the constant growth dividend valuation model:

$$P_0 = \frac{D_1}{K_e - g} \qquad (10\text{-}8)$$

This is an extremely easy formula to use in which:

P_0 = Price of the stock today

D_1 = Dividend at the end of the first year

K_e = Required rate of return (discount rate)

g = Constant growth rate in dividends

In this formula, P_0 is sometimes referred to as the value of a "growing perpetuity" because it is a perpetuity that grows at a constant rate. In order for Formula 10-8 to work, it is critical that the first dividend come at the end of the first year. Based on the current example:

$$D_1 = \$2.00$$
$$K_e = 0.12$$
$$g = 0.07$$

and P_0 is computed as:

$$P_0 = \frac{D_1}{K_e - g} = \frac{\$2.00}{0.12 - 0.07} = \frac{\$2.00}{0.05} = \$40$$

Thus, given that the stock has a $2 dividend at the end of the first year, a discount rate of 12 percent, and a constant growth rate of 7 percent, the current price of the stock is $40.

Let's take a closer look at Formula 10-8 shown earlier and the factors that influence valuation. For example, what is the anticipated effect on valuation if K_e (the required rate of return, or discount rate) increases as a result of inflation or increased risk? Intuitively, we would expect the stock price to decline if investors demand a higher return and the dividend and growth rate remain the same. This is precisely what happens.

If D_1 remains at $2.00 and the growth rate (g) is 7 percent, but K_e increases from 12 percent to 14 percent, using Formula 10-8, the price of the common stock will now be $28.57 as shown below. This is considerably lower than its earlier value of $40:

$$P_0 = \frac{D_1}{K_e - g} = \frac{\$2.00}{0.14 - 0.07} = \frac{\$2.00}{0.07} = \$28.57$$

Similarly, if the growth rate (g) increases while D_1 and K_e remain constant, the stock price can be expected to increase. Assume $D_1 = \$2.00$, K_e is set at its earlier level of 12 percent, and g increases from 7 percent to 9 percent. Using Formula 10-8 once again, the new price of the stock would be $66.67:

$$P_0 = \frac{D_1}{K_e - g} = \frac{\$2.00}{0.12 - 0.09} = \frac{\$2.00}{0.03} = \$66.67$$

We should not be surprised to see that an increasing growth rate has enhanced the value of the stock.

Stock Valuation Based on Future Stock Value   The discussion of stock valuation to this point has related to the concept of the present value of future dividends. This is a valid concept, but suppose we wish to approach the issue from a slightly different viewpoint. Assume we are going to buy a stock and hold it for three years and then sell it. We wish to know the present value of our investment. This is somewhat like the bond valuation analysis. We will receive a dividend for three years (D_1, D_2, D_3) and then a price (payment) for the stock at the end of three years (P_3). What is the present value of the benefits? To solve this, we add the present value of three years of dividends and the present value of the stock price after three years. Assuming a constant growth dividend analysis, the stock price after three years is simply the present value of all future dividends after the third year (from the fourth year on). Thus the current price of the stock in this case is nothing other than the present value of the first three dividends, plus the present value of all future dividends (which is equivalent to the stock price after the third year). Saying the price of the stock is the present value of all future dividends is also the equivalent of saying it is the present value of a dividend stream for a number of years, plus the present value of the price of the stock after that time period. The appropriate formula would be Formula 10-7, where the fourth term would be replaced by $P_3 = D_4/(K_e - g)$.

Determining the Required Rate of Return from the Market Price

In our analysis of common stock, we have used the first year's dividend (D_1), the required rate of return (K_e), and the growth rate (g) to solve for the stock price (P_0) based on Formula 10-8.

$$P_0 = \frac{D_1}{K_e - g}$$

We could change the analysis to solve for the required rate of return (K_e) as the unknown, given that we know the first year's dividend (D_1), the stock price (P_0), and the growth rate (g). We take the preceding formula and algebraically change it to provide Formula 10-9.

$$P_0 = \frac{D_1}{K_e - g} \tag{10-8}$$

$$K_e = \frac{D_1}{P_0} + g \tag{10-9}$$

Formula 10-9 allows us to compute the required return (K_e) for the investment. Returning to the basic data from the common stock example:

K_e = Required rate of return (to be solved)

D_1 = Dividend at the end of the first year, $2.00

P_0 = Price of the stock today, $40

g = Constant growth rate 0.07, or 7%

$$K_e = \frac{\$2.00}{\$40} + 7\% = 5\% + 7\% = 12\%$$

In this instance, we would say the stockholder demands a 12 percent return on the common stock investment. Of particular interest are the individual parts of the formula for K_e that we have been discussing. Let's write out Formula 10-9 again.

$$K_e = \frac{\text{First year's dividend}}{\text{Common stock price}}\left(\frac{D_1}{P_0}\right) + \text{Growth } (g)$$

The first term represents the **dividend yield** the stockholder will receive, and the second term represents the anticipated growth in dividends, earnings, and stock price. While we have been describing the growth rate primarily in terms of dividends, it is assumed the earnings and stock price will also grow at that same rate over the long term if all else holds constant. You should also observe that the preceding formula represents a total-return concept. The stockholder is receiving a current dividend plus anticipated growth in the future. If the dividend yield is low, the growth rate must be high to provide the necessary return. Conversely, if the growth rate is low, a high dividend yield will be expected. The concepts of dividend yield and growth are clearly interrelated.

The Price-Earnings Ratio Concept and Valuation

In Chapter 2, we introduced the concept of the price-earnings ratio. The **price-earnings (P/E) ratio** represents a multiplier applied to current earnings to determine the value of a share of stock in the market. It is considered a pragmatic, everyday approach to valuation. If a stock has earnings per share of $3 and a P/E ratio of 15 times, it will carry a market value of $45. Another company with the same earnings but a P/E ratio of 20 times will enjoy a market price of $60.

The price-earnings ratio is influenced by the earnings and sales growth of the firm, the risk (or volatility in performance), the debt-equity structure of the firm, the dividend policy, the quality of management, and a number of other factors. Firms that have bright expectations for the future tend to trade at high P/E ratios while the opposite is true for low P/E firms.

For example, the average P/E for the S&P 500 Index firms was 26 in early 2018, but Amazon.com traded at a P/E of 351 because its earnings were expected to grow dramatically, and Ford traded at a P/E of just above 10 because auto sales were expected to decline after several good years.

P/E ratios can be looked up in *Barron's*, at finance.yahoo.com, and a number of other publications and Internet sites. Quotations from *Barron's* are presented in Table 10-4. The first column after the company's name shows the ticker symbol and is followed by the yield (dividends per share divided by stock price). The third column is the item of primary interest and it indicates the current price-earnings (P/E) ratio. The remaining columns cover the stock price (last), the weekly price change, and dividend data.

For IBM, which is highlighted in white in Table 10-4, the P/E ratio is 14, indicating that the company's stock price of $162.37 represents 14 times earnings (of approximately $11.60) for the past 12 months. Firms that are operating at a loss (deficit) have the symbol dd in the P/E ratio column.

The dividend valuation approach (based on the present value of dividends) that we have been using throughout the chapter is more theoretically sound than P/E ratios and more likely to be used by sophisticated financial analysts. To some extent, the two concepts of P/E ratios and dividend valuation models can be brought together. A stock that has a high required rate of return (K_e) because it's risky will generally have a low P/E ratio. Similarly, a stock with a low required rate of return (K_e) because of the predictability of positive future performance will normally have a

Table 10-4   Quotations from *Barron's*

52-Wk High	Low	Name	Tick Sym	Yld	P/E	–Week's– Last	Chg.	Div Amt.
23.22	16.00	InfraREIT	HIFR	5.2	16	19.07	+1.28	.25
96.23	77.00	Ingersoll-Rand	IR	2.0	23	90.93	−0.17	.45
80.18	52.25	Ingevity	NGVT	...	35	76.63	+2.08	...
142.64	113.07	Ingredion	INGR	1.8	20	137.13	+1.17	.60
36.88	15.45	InnovativeIndProp	IIPR	3.5	dd	28.17	−2.08	.25
51.78	31.97	Inphi	IPHI	...	dd	32.07	−6.56	...
62.30	34.78	Insperity	NSP	2.0	33	60.70	+1.65	2.00
79.40	40.00	InstalledBldg	IBP	...	57	74.40	+1.40	...
36.60	21.40	Instructure	INST	...	dd	33.80	−0.45	...
55.20	29.60	IntegerHoldings	ITGR	...	78	49.05	+0.50	...
7.47	2.63	Intelsat	I	...	1	3.02	−0.26	...
75.79	56.69	ICE	ICE	1.1	27	75.60	+0.82	.20
68.61	48.08	InterContinentl	IHG	...	32	68.56	+2.90	.33
182.79	139.13	IBM	IBM	3.7	14	162.37	−0.77	1.50
157.40	114.81	IntlFlavors	IFF	1.8	30	155.19	+1.49	.69
29.36	17.25	IntlGameTech	IGT	2.9	dd	27.33	−0.46	.20
63.71	49.60	IntlPaper	IP	3.0	29	63.50	+1.24	.475
23.43	16.37	IntlSeaways	INSW	...	dd	18.47	−0.23	...
25.71	18.30	Interpublic	IPG	3.4	15	21.35	−0.39	.18
60.50	36.94	InterXion	INXN	...	95	59.87	+1.72	...
5.12	1.24	IntrepidPotash	IPI	...	dd	4.20	−0.12	...
26.99	10.26	Intrexon	XON	...	dd	13.00	−1.71	...
17.95	9.90	Invacare	IVC	.3	dd	16.91	−0.14	.0125
18.86	14.15	InvescoMtg	IVR	9.6	5	17:59	−0.16	.42
23.96	17.63	InvestmentTech	ITG	1.3	dd	21.23	+0.27	.07
6.99	5.49	InvRlFst	IRET	4.9	dd	5.71	+0.10	.07

Source: *Barron's*, February 9, 2015, p. M18.

high P/E ratio. These are generalized relationships. There are, of course, exceptions to every rule of thumb.

Variable Growth in Dividends

In the discussion of common stock valuation, we have considered procedures for firms that had no growth in dividends and for firms that had a constant growth. Most of the discussion and literature in finance assumes a constant growth dividend model. However, there is also a third case, and that is one of variable growth in dividends. The most common variable growth model is one in which the firm experiences supernormal (very rapid) growth for a number of years and then levels off to more normal, constant growth. The **supernormal growth** pattern is often

An Important Question—What's a Small Business Really Worth?

The value of a small, privately held business takes on importance when the business is put up for sale, is part of a divorce settlement, or is being valued for estate purposes at the time of the owner's death. The same basic principles that establish valuation for *Fortune* 500 companies apply to small businesses as well. However, there are important added considerations.

One factor is that private businesses often lack liquidity. Unlike a firm trading in the public securities market, there is no ready market for a local clothing goods store, a bowling alley, or even a doctor's clinic. Therefore, after the standard value has been determined, it is usually reduced for lack of liquidity. Although circumstances vary, the normal reduction is in the 30 percent range. Thus a business that is valued at $100,000 on the basis of earnings or cash flow may be assigned a value of $70,000 for estate valuation purposes.

There are other factors that are important to small business valuation as well. For example, how important was a key person to the operation of a business? If the founder of the business was critical to its functioning, the firm may have little or no value in his or her absence. For example, a bridal consulting shop or a barber shop may have minimal value upon the death of the owner. On the other hand, a furniture company with established brand names or a small TV station with programming under contract may retain most of its value.

Another consideration that is important in valuing a small business is the nature of the company's earnings. They are often lower than they would be in a publicly traded company. Why? First of all, the owners of many small businesses intermingle personal expenses with business expenses. Thus family cars, health insurance, travel, and so on may be charged as business expenses when, in fact, they have a personal element to them. While the IRS tries to restrict such practices, there are fine lines in distinguishing between personal and business uses. As a general rule, small, private businesses try to report earnings as low as possible to minimize taxes. Contrast this with public companies that report earnings quarterly with the intent of showing ever-growing profitability. For this reason, in valuing a small, privately held company, analysts often rework stated earnings in an attempt to demonstrate earning power that is based on income less necessary expenditures. The restated earnings are usually higher.

After these and many other factors are taken into consideration, the average small, private company normally sells at 5 to 10 times average adjusted earnings for the previous three years. It is also important to identify recent sale prices of comparable companies, and business brokers may be able to supply such information. When establishing final value, many people often look to their CPA or a business consultant to determine the true worth of a firm.

experienced by firms in emerging industries, such as in the early days of electronics or microcomputers.

In evaluating a firm with an initial pattern of supernormal growth, we first take the present value of dividends during the exceptional growth period. We then determine the price of the stock at the end of the supernormal growth period by taking the present value of the normal, constant dividends that follow the supernormal growth period. We discount this price to the present and add it to the present value of the supernormal dividends. This gives us the current price of the stock.

A numerical example of a supernormal growth rate evaluation model is presented in Appendix 10A at the end of this chapter.

Finally, in the discussion of common stock valuation models, readers may ask about the valuation of companies that currently pay no dividends. Since virtually all our discussion has been based on values associated with dividends, how can this "no dividend" circumstance be handled? One approach is to assume that even for the firm that pays no current dividends, at some point in the future, stockholders will be rewarded with cash dividends. We then take the present value of their deferred dividends.

A second approach to valuing a firm that pays no cash dividends is to take the present value of earnings per share for a number of periods and add that to the present value of a future anticipated stock price. The discount rate applied to future earnings is generally higher than the discount rate applied to future dividends.

SUMMARY AND REVIEW OF FORMULAS

The primary emphasis in this chapter is on valuation of financial assets: bonds, preferred stock, and common stock. Regardless of the security being analyzed, valuation is normally based on the concept of determining the present value of future cash flows. Thus we draw on many of the time-value-of-money techniques developed in Chapter 9. Inherent in the valuation process is a determination of the rate of return that investors demand. When we have computed this value, we have also identified what it will cost the corporation to raise new capital. Let's specifically review the valuation techniques associated with bonds, preferred stock, and common stock.

Bonds

The price, or current value, of a bond is equal to the present value of interest payments (I_t) over the life of the bond plus the present value of the principal payment (P_n) at maturity. The discount rate used in the analytical process is the yield to maturity (Y). The yield to maturity (required rate of return) is determined in the marketplace by such factors as the real rate of return, an inflation premium, and a risk premium.

The equation for bond valuation was presented as Formula 10-1.

$$P_b = \sum_{t=1}^{n} \frac{I_t}{(1 + Y)^t} + \frac{P_n}{(1 + Y)^n} \qquad (10\text{-}1)$$

The actual terms in the equation are solved by the use of present value tables. We say the present value of interest payments is:

$$PV_A = A \times \frac{1 - \dfrac{1}{(1 + i)^n}}{i}$$

The present value of the principal payment at maturity is:

$$PV = FV \times \frac{1}{(1 + i)^n}$$

We add these two values together to determine the price of the bond. We use annual or semiannual analysis.

FINANCIAL CALCULATOR

Bond Price

Value	Function
n	N
Y	I/Y
P_n	FV
I_t	PMT
Function	Solution
CPT	
PV	P_b

The value of the bond will be strongly influenced by the relationship of the yield to maturity in the market to the interest rate on the bond and also the length of time to maturity.

If you know the price of the bond, the size of the interest payments, and the maturity of the bond, you can solve for the yield to maturity through a trial and error approach, by an approximation approach, or by using financially oriented calculators (in Appendix 9C in Chapter 9) or appropriate computer software.

Preferred Stock

In determining the value of preferred stock, we are taking the present value of an infinite stream of level dividend payments. This would be a tedious process if the mathematical calculations could not be compressed into a simple formula. The appropriate equation is Formula 10-3.

$$P_p = \frac{D_p}{K_p} \qquad (10\text{-}3)$$

According to Formula 10-3, to find the preferred stock price (P_p) we take the constant annual dividend payment (D_p) and divide this value by the rate of return that preferred stockholders are demanding (K_p).

If, on the other hand, we know the price of the preferred stock and the constant annual dividend payment, we can solve for the required rate of return on preferred stock as:

$$K_p = \frac{D_p}{P_p} \qquad (10\text{-}4)$$

Common Stock

The value of common stock is also based on the concept of the present value of an expected stream of future dividends. Unlike preferred stock, the dividends are not necessarily level. The firm and shareholders may experience:

1. No growth in dividends.
2. Constant growth in dividends.
3. Variable or supernormal growth in dividends.

It is the second circumstance that receives most of the attention in the financial literature. If a firm has constant growth (g) in dividends (D) and the required rate of return (K_e) exceeds the growth rate, Formula 10-8 can be utilized.

$$P_0 = \frac{D_1}{K_e - g} \qquad (10\text{-}8)$$

In using Formula 10-8, all we need to know is the value of the dividend at the end of the first year, the required rate of return, and the discount rate. Most of our valuation calculations with common stock utilize Formula 10-8.

If we need to know the required rate of return (K_e) for common stock, Formula 10-9 can be employed.

$$K_e = \frac{D_1}{P_0} + g \qquad (10\text{-}9)$$

The first term represents the dividend yield on the stock and the second term the growth rate. Together they provide the total return demanded by the investor.

LIST OF TERMS

required rate of return   304
yield to maturity   307
real rate of return   307
inflation premium   307
risk-free rate of return   308
risk premium   308

business risk   308
financial risk   308
perpetuity   315
dividend valuation model   318
dividend yield   322
price-earnings (P/E) ratio   322
supernormal growth   323

DISCUSSION QUESTIONS

1. How is valuation of any financial asset related to future cash flows? *(LO10-2)*
2. Why might investors demand a lower rate of return for an investment in Microsoft as compared to United Airlines? *(LO10-2)*
3. What are the three factors that influence the required rate of return by investors? *(LO10-2)*
4. If inflationary expectations increase, what is likely to happen to the yield to maturity on bonds in the marketplace? What is also likely to happen to the price of bonds? *(LO10-2)*
5. Why is the remaining time to maturity an important factor in evaluating the impact of a change in yield to maturity on bond prices? *(LO10-4)*
6. What are the three adjustments that have to be made in going from annual to semiannual bond analysis? *(LO10-4)*
7. Why is a change in required yield for preferred stock likely to have a greater impact on price than a change in required yield for bonds? *(LO10-4)*
8. What type of dividend pattern for common stock is similar to the dividend payment for preferred stock? *(LO10-1)*
9. What two conditions must be met to go from Formula 10-7 to Formula 10-8 in using the dividend valuation model? *(LO10-5)*

$$P_0 = \frac{D_1}{K_e - g} \qquad (10\text{-}8)$$

10. What two components make up the required rate of return on common stock? *(LO10-5)*
11. What factors might influence a firm's price-earnings ratio? *(LO10-3)*

12. How is the supernormal growth pattern likely to vary from the normal, constant growth pattern? *(LO10-5)*

13. What approaches can be taken in valuing a firm's stock when there is no cash dividend payment? *(LO10-5)*

PRACTICE PROBLEMS AND SOLUTIONS

Bond value
(LO10-3)

1. The Titan Corp. issued a $1,000 par value bond paying 8 percent interest with 15 years to maturity. Assume the current yield to maturity on such bonds is 10 percent. What is the price of the bond? Do annual analysis.

Common stock value
(LO10-5)

2. Host Corp. will pay a $2.40 dividend (D_1) in the next 12 months. The required rate of return (K_e) is 13 percent and the constant growth rate (g) is 5 percent.
   a. Compute the stock price (P_0).
   b. If K_e goes up to 15 percent, and all else remains the same, what will be the stock price (P_0)?
   c. Now assume in the next year, $D_1 = \$2.70$, $K_e = 12$ percent, and g is equal to 6 percent. What is the price of the stock?

Solutions

1. **Present Value of Interest Payments**

$$PV_A = \$80 \times \frac{1 - \dfrac{1}{(1 + 0.10)^{15}}}{0.10} = \$608.49$$

Present Value of the Principal Payment at Maturity

$$PV = \$1,000 \times \frac{1}{(1 + 0.10)^{15}} = \$237.39$$

Total Present Value (Bond Price)

Present value of interest payments	$608.49
Present value of principal payment at maturity	237.39
Bond price	$847.88

FINANCIAL CALCULATOR

Bond Price

Value	Function
15	N
10	I/Y
1000	FV
80	PMT

Function	Solution
CPT	
PV	−847.88

2.

$$P_0 = \frac{D_1}{K_e - g} \qquad (10\text{-}8)$$

a. $P_0 = \dfrac{\$2.40}{0.13 - 0.05} = \dfrac{\$2.40}{0.08} = \$30.00$

b. $P_0 = \dfrac{\$2.40}{0.15 - 0.05} = \dfrac{\$2.40}{0.10} = \$24.00$

c. $P_0 = \dfrac{\$2.70}{0.12 - 0.06} = \dfrac{\$2.70}{0.06} = \$45.00$

PROBLEMS

connect Selected problems are available with Connect. Please see the preface for more information.

Basic Problems

For the first 20 bond problems, assume interest payments are on an annual basis.

1. The Lone Star Company has $1,000 par value bonds outstanding at 10 percent interest. The bonds will mature in 20 years. Compute the current price of the bonds if the present yield to maturity is

    a.   6 percent.

    b.   9 percent.

    c.   13 percent.

    Bond value (LO10-3)

2. Midland Oil has $1,000 par value bonds outstanding at 8 percent interest. The bonds will mature in 25 years. Compute the current price of the bonds if the present yield to maturity is

    a.   7 percent.

    b.   10 percent.

    c.   13 percent.

    Bond value (LO10-3)

3. Exodus Limousine Company has $1,000 par value bonds outstanding at 10 percent interest. The bonds will mature in 50 years. Compute the current price of the bonds if the percent yield to maturity is

    a.   5 percent.

    b.   15 percent.

    Bond value (LO10-3)

4. Barry's Steroids Company has $1,000 par value bonds outstanding at 16 percent interest. The bonds will mature in 40 years. If the percent yield to maturity is 13 percent, what percent of the total bond value does the repayment of principal represent?

    Bond value (LO10-3)

5. Essex Biochemical Co. has a $1,000 par value bond outstanding that pays 15 percent annual interest. The current yield to maturity on such bonds in the market is 17 percent. Compute the price of the bonds for these maturity dates:

    a.   30 years.

    b.   20 years.

    c.   4 years.

    Bond value (LO10-3)

6. Kilgore Natural Gas has a $1,000 par value bond outstanding that pays 9 percent annual interest. The current yield to maturity on such bonds in the market is 12 percent. Compute the price of the bonds for these maturity dates:

    a.   30 years.

    b.   15 years.

    c.   1 year.

    Bond value (LO10-3)

7. Toxaway Telephone Company has a $1,000 par value bond outstanding that pays 6 percent annual interest. If the yield to maturity is 8 percent, and remains

    Bond maturity effect (LO10-3)

so over the remaining life of the bond, the bond will have the following values over time:

Remaining Maturity	Bond Price
15	$795.67
10	$830.49
5	$891.86
1	$973.21

Graph the relationship in a manner similar to the bottom half of Figure 10-2. Also explain why the pattern of price change takes place.

Interest rate effect
(LO10-3)

8. Go to Table 10-1, which is based on bonds paying 10 percent interest for 20 years. Assume interest rates *in the market* (yield to maturity) decline from 11 percent to 8 percent:

   a. What is the bond price at 11 percent?

   b. What is the bond price at 8 percent?

   c. What would be your percentage return on investment if you bought when rates were 11 percent and sold when rates were 8 percent?

Interest rate effect
(LO10-3)

9. Look at Table 10-1 again, and now assume interest rates in the market (yield to maturity) increase from 9 to 12 percent.

   a. What is the bond price at 9 percent?

   b. What is the bond price at 12 percent?

   c. What would be your percentage return on the investment if you bought when rates were 9 percent and sold when rates were 12 percent?

Interest rate effect
(LO10-3)

10. Using Table 10-1, assume interest rates in the market (yield to maturity) are 14 percent for 20 years on a bond paying 10 percent.

   a. What is the price of the bond?

   b. Assume 5 years have passed and interest rates in the market have gone down to 12 percent. Now, using Table 10-2 for 15 years, what is the price of the bond?

   c. What would your percentage return be if you bought the bonds when interest rates in the market were 14 percent for 20 years and sold them 5 years later when interest rates were 12 percent?

Effect of maturity on bond price
(LO10-3)

11. Using Table 10-2:

   a. Assume the interest rate in the market (yield to maturity) goes down to 8 percent for the 10 percent bonds. Using column 2, indicate what the bond price will be with a 10-year, a 15-year, and a 20-year time period.

   b. Assume the interest rate in the market (yield to maturity) goes up to 12 percent for the 10 percent bonds. Using column 3, indicate what the bond price will be with a 10-year, a 15-year, and a 20-year period.

   c. Based on the information in part *a,* if you think interest rates in the market are going down, which bond would you choose to own?

   d. Based on information in part *b,* if you think interest rates in the market are going up, which bond would you choose to own?

Intermediate Problems

12. Jim Busby calls his broker to inquire about purchasing a bond of Disk Storage Systems. His broker quotes a price of $1,180. Jim is concerned that the bond might be overpriced based on the facts involved. The $1,000 par value bond pays 14 percent interest, and it has 25 years remaining until maturity. The current yield to maturity on similar bonds is 12 percent. Compute the new price of the bond and comment on whether you think it is overpriced in the marketplace.

    Bond value (LO10-3)

13. Tom Cruise Lines Inc. issued bonds 5 years ago at $1,000 per bond. These bonds had a 25-year life when issued and the annual interest payment was then 15 percent. This return was in line with the required returns by bondholders at that point as described next:

    Effect of yield to maturity on bond price (LO10-3)

Real rate of return	4%
Inflation premium	6
Risk premium	5
Total return	15%

    Assume that 5 years later the inflation premium is only 3 percent and is appropriately reflected in the required return (or yield to maturity) of the bonds. The bonds have 20 years remaining until maturity. Compute the new price of the bond.

14. Katie Pairy Fruits Inc. has a $1,000 20-year bond outstanding with a nominal yield of 15 percent (coupon equals 15% × $1,000 = $150 per year). Assume that the current market required interest rate on similar bonds is now only 12 percent.

    Analyzing bond price changes (LO10-3)

    a. Compute the current price of the bond.

    b. Find the present value of 3 percent × $1,000 (or $30) for 20 years at 12 percent. The $30 is assumed to be an annual payment. Add this value to $1,000.

    c. Explain why the answers in parts *a* and *b* are basically the same. (There is a slight difference due to rounding in the tables.)

15. Media Bias Inc. issued bonds 10 years ago at $1,000 per bond. These bonds had a 40-year life when issued and the annual interest payment was then 12 percent. This return was in line with the required returns by bondholders at that point in time as described next:

    Effect of yield to maturity on bond price (LO10-2 & 10-3)

Real rate of return	2%
Inflation premium	5
Risk premium	5
Total return	12%

    Assume that 10 years later, due to good publicity, the risk premium is now 2 percent and is appropriately reflected in the required return (or yield to maturity) of the bonds. The bonds have 30 years remaining until maturity. Compute the new price of the bond.

Effect of yield to maturity on bond price
(LO10-2 & 10-3)

16. Wilson Oil Company issued bonds 5 years ago at $1,000 per bond. These bonds had a 25-year life when issued and the annual interest payment was then 15 percent. This return was in line with the required returns by bondholders at that point in time as described next:

Real rate of return	8%
Inflation premium	3
Risk premium	4
Total return	15%

Assume that 10 years later, due to bad publicity, the risk premium is now 7 percent and is appropriately reflected in the required return (or yield to maturity) of the bonds. The bonds have 15 years remaining until maturity. Compute the new price of the bond.

Deep discount bonds
(LO10-3)

17. Lance Whittingham IV specializes in buying deep discount bonds. These represent bonds that are trading at well below par value. He has his eye on a bond issued by the Leisure Time Corporation. The $1,000 par value bond pays 4 percent annual interest and has 18 years remaining to maturity. The current yield to maturity on similar bonds is 14 percent.

   a. What is the current price of the bonds?

   b. By what percentage will the price of the bonds increase between now and maturity?

   c. What is the annual compound rate of growth in the value of the bonds? (An approximate answer is acceptable.)

Yield to maturity— calculator or Excel required
(LO10-3)

18. Bonds issued by the Coleman Manufacturing Company have a par value of $1,000, which of course is also the amount of principal to be paid at maturity. The bonds are currently selling for $690. They have 10 years remaining to maturity. The annual interest payment is 13 percent ($130). Compute the yield to maturity.

Yield to maturity— calculator or Excel required
(LO10-3)

19. Stilley Resources bonds have four years left to maturity. Interest is paid annually, and the bonds have a $1,000 par value and a coupon rate of 5 percent. If the price of the bond is $841.51, what is the yield to maturity?

Yield to maturity— calculator or Excel required
(LO10-3)

20. Evans Emergency Response bonds have six years to maturity. Interest is paid semiannually. The bonds have a $1,000 par value and a coupon rate of 8 percent. If the price of the bond is $1,073.55, what is the annual yield to maturity?

For the next two problems, assume interest payments are on a semiannual basis.

Bond value— semiannual analysis
(LO10-3)

21. Heather Smith is considering a bond investment in Locklear Airlines. The $1,000 par value bonds have a quoted annual interest rate of 11 percent and the interest is paid semiannually. The yield to maturity on the bonds is 14 percent annual interest. There are seven years to maturity. Compute the price of the bonds based on semiannual analysis.

Bond value— semiannual analysis
(LO10-3)

22. You are called in as a financial analyst to appraise the bonds of Olsen's Clothing Stores. The $1,000 par value bonds have a quoted annual interest rate of

10 percent, which is paid semiannually. The yield to maturity on the bonds is 10 percent annual interest. There are 15 years to maturity.

   a. Compute the price of the bonds based on semiannual analysis.

   b. With 10 years to maturity, if yield to maturity goes down substantially to 8 percent, what will be the new price of the bonds?

23. The preferred stock of Denver Savings and Loan pays an annual dividend of $5.70. It has a required rate of return of 6 percent. Compute the price of the preferred stock.

                                       Preferred stock value *(LO10-4)*

24. North Pole Cruise Lines issued preferred stock many years ago. It carries a fixed dividend of $6 per share. With the passage of time, yields have soared from the original 6 percent to 14 percent (yield is the same as required rate of return).

                                       Preferred stock value *(LO10-4)*

   a. What was the original issue price?

   b. What is the current value of this preferred stock?

   c. If the yield on the Standard & Poor's Preferred Stock Index declines, how will the price of the preferred stock be affected?

25. X-Tech Company issued preferred stock many years ago. It carries a fixed dividend of $12 per share. With the passage of time, yields have soared from the original 10 percent to 17 percent (yield is the same as required rate of return).

                                       Preferred stock value *(LO10-4)*

   a. What was the original issue price?

   b. What is the current value of this preferred stock?

   c. If the yield on the Standard & Poor's Preferred Stock Index declines, how will the price of the preferred stock be affected?

26. Analogue Technology has preferred stock outstanding that pays a $9 annual dividend. It has a price of $76. What is the required rate of return (yield) on the preferred stock?

                                       Preferred stock rate of return *(LO10-4)*

All of the following problems pertain to the common stock section of the chapter.

27. Stagnant Iron and Steel currently pays a $12.25 annual cash dividend (D_0). The company plans to maintain the dividend at this level for the foreseeable future as no future growth is anticipated. If the required rate of return by common stockholders (K_e) is 18 percent, what is the price of the common stock?

                                       𝕏 Common stock value *(LO10-5)*

28. BioScience Inc. will pay a common stock dividend of $3.20 at the end of the year (D_1). The required return on common stock (K_e) is 14 percent. The firm has a constant growth rate (g) of 9 percent. Compute the current price of the stock (P_0).

                                       Common stock value *(LO10-5)*

Advanced Problems

29. Ecology Labs Inc. will pay a dividend of $6.40 per share in the next 12 months (D_1). The required rate of return (K_e) is 14 percent and the constant growth rate is 5 percent.

                                       𝕏 Common stock value under different market conditions *(LO10-5)*

   a. Compute P_0.

   (For parts *b, c,* and *d* in this problem, all variables remain the same except the one specifically changed. Each question is independent of the others.)

   b. Assume K_e, the required rate of return, goes up to 18 percent. What will be the new value of P_0?

c. Assume the growth rate (g) goes up to 9 percent. What will be the new value of P_0? K_e goes back to its original value of 14 percent.

d. Assume D_1 is $7. What will be the new value of P_0? Assume K_e is at its original value of 14 percent and g goes back to its original value of 5 percent.

Common stock value under different market conditions *(LO10-5)*

30. Maxwell Communications paid a dividend of $3 last year. Over the next 12 months, the dividend is expected to grow at 8 percent, which is the constant growth rate for the firm (g). The new dividend after 12 months will represent D_1. The required rate of return (K_e) is 14 percent. Compute the price of the stock (P_0).

Common stock value based on determining growth rate *(LO10-5)*

31. Justin Cement Company has had the following pattern of earnings per share over the last five years:

Year	Earnings per Share
20X1	$5.00
20X2	5.30
20X3	5.62
20X4	5.96
20X5	6.32

The earnings per share have grown at a constant rate (on a rounded basis) and will continue to do so in the future. Dividends represent 40 percent of earnings. Project earnings and dividends for the next year (20X6).

If the required rate of return (K_e) is 13 percent, what is the anticipated stock price (P_0) at the beginning of 20X6?

Common stock required rate of return *(LO10-5)*

32. A firm pays a $4.80 dividend at the end of year 1 (D_1), has a stock price of $80, and a constant growth rate (g) of 5 percent. Compute the required rate of return (K_e).

Common stock required rate of return *(LO10-5)*

33. A firm pays a $1.50 dividend at the end of year 1 (D_1), has a stock price of $155 ($P_0$), and a constant growth rate (g) of 10 percent.

a. Compute the required rate of return (K_e).

Indicate whether each of the following changes would make the required rate of return (K_e) go up or down. (Each question is separate from the others. That is, assume only one variable changes at a time.) No actual numbers are necessary.

b. The dividend payment increases.

c. The expected growth rate increases.

d. The stock price increases.

Common stock value based on PV calculations *(LO10-5)*

34. Martin Office Supplies paid a $3 dividend last year. The dividend is expected to grow at a constant rate of 7 percent over the next four years. The required rate of return is 14 percent (this will also serve as the discount rate in this problem). Round all values to three places to the right of the decimal point where appropriate.

a. Compute the anticipated value of the dividends for the next four years. That is, compute D_1, D_2, D_3, and D_4—for example, D_1 is $3.21 ($3.00 × 1.07).

b. Discount each of these dividends back to present at a discount rate of 14 percent and then sum them.

c. Compute the price of the stock at the end of the fourth year (P_4).

$$P_4 = \frac{D_5}{K_e - g}$$

(D_5 is equal to D_4 times 1.07)

d. After you have computed P_4, discount it back to the present at a discount rate of 14 percent for four years.

e. Add together the answers in part *b* and part *d* to get P_0, the current value of the stock. This answer represents the present value of the four periods of dividends, plus the present value of the price of the stock after four periods (which, in turn, represents the value of all future dividends).

f. Use Formula 10-8 to show that it will provide approximately the same answer as part *e*.

$$P_0 = \frac{D_1}{K_e - g}$$

For Formula 10-8, use $D_1 = \$3.21$, $K_e = 14$ percent, and $g = 7$ percent. (The slight difference between the answers to part *e* and part *f* is due to rounding.)

g. If current EPS were equal to $5.32 and the P/E ratio is 1.1 times higher than the industry average of 8, what would the stock price be?

h. By what dollar amount is the stock price in part *g* different from the stock price in part *f*?

i. In regard to the stock price in part *f*, indicate which direction it would move if (1) D_1 increases, (2) K_e increases, and (3) g increases.

35. Beasley Ball Bearings paid a $4 dividend last year. The dividend is expected to grow at a constant rate of 2 percent over the next four years. The required rate of return is 15 percent (this will also serve as the discount rate in this problem). Round all values to three places to the right of the decimal point where appropriate.

Common stock value based on PV calculations (LO10-5)

a. Compute the anticipated value of the dividends for the next four years. That is, compute D_1, D_2, D_3, and D_4; for example, D_1 is $4.08 ($4 × 1.02).

b. Discount each of these dividends back to present at a discount rate of 15 percent and then sum them.

c. Compute the price of the stock at the end of the fourth year (P_4).

$$P_4 = \frac{D_5}{K_e - g}$$

(D_5 is equal to D_4 times 1.02.)

d. After you have computed P_4, discount it back to the present at a discount rate of 15 percent for four years.

e. Add together the answers in part *b* and part *d* to get P_0, the current value of the stock. This answer represents the present value of the four periods of dividends, plus the present value of the price of the stock after four periods (which in turn represents the value of all future dividends).

f. Use Formula 10-8 to show that it will provide approximately the same answer as part *e*.

$$P_0 = \frac{D_1}{K_e - g}$$

For Formula 10-8, use D_1 = \$4.08, K_e = 15 percent, and g = 2 percent. (The slight difference between the answers to part *e* and part *f* is due to rounding.)

g. If current EPS were equal to \$4.98 and the P/E ratio is 1.2 times higher than the industry average of 6, what would the stock price be?

h. By what dollar amount is the stock price in part *g* different from the stock price in part *f*?

i. In regard to the stock price in part *f*, indicate which direction it would move if (1) D_1 increases, (2) K_e increases, and (3) *g* increases.

COMPREHENSIVE PROBLEM

Preston Resources

(Dividend valuation model, P/E ratio)

(LO10-5)

Mel Thomas, the chief financial officer of Preston Resources, has been asked to do an evaluation of Dunning Chemical Company by the president and chair of the board, Sarah Reynolds. Preston Resources was planning a joint venture with Dunning (which was privately traded), and Sarah and Mel needed a better feel for what Dunning's stock was worth because they might be interested in buying the firm in the future.

Dunning Chemical paid a dividend at the end of year 1 of \$1.30, the anticipated growth rate was 10 percent, and the required rate of return was 14 percent.

a. What is the value of the stock based on the dividend valuation model (Formula 10-8)?

b. Indicate that the value you computed in part *a* is correct by showing the value of D_1, D_2, and D_3 and by discounting each back to the present at 14 percent. D_1 is \$1.30, and it increases by 10 percent (*g*) each year. Also discount the anticipated stock price at the end of year 3 back to the present and add it to the present value of the three dividend payments.

The value of the stock at the end of year 3 is:

$$P_3 = \frac{D_4}{K_e - g} \qquad D_4 = D_3(1 + g)$$

If you have done all these steps correctly, you should get an answer approximately equal to the answer in part *a*.

c. As an alternative measure, you also examine the value of the firm based on the price-earnings (P/E) ratio times earnings per share.

Since the company is privately traded (not in the public stock market), you will get your anticipated P/E ratio by taking the average value of five publicly traded chemical companies. The P/E ratios were as follows during the time period under analysis:

	P/E Ratio
Dow Chemical	15
DuPont	18
Georgia Gulf	7
3M	19
Olin Corp	21

Assume Dunning Chemical has earnings per share of $2.10. What is the stock value based on the P/E ratio approach? Multiply the average P/E ratio you computed times earnings per share. How does this value compare to the dividend valuation model values that you computed in parts *a* and *b?*

d. If in computing the industry average P/E, you decide to weight Olin Corp. by 40 percent and the other four firms by 15 percent, what would be the new weighted average industry P/E? (Note: You decided to weight Olin Corp. more heavily because it is similar to Dunning Chemical.) What will the new stock price be? Earnings per share will stay at $2.10.

e. By what percentage will the stock price change as a result of using the weighted average industry P/E ratio in part *d* as opposed to that in part *c?*

W E B   E X E R C I S E

1. When the price of oil fell in 2014 and 2015, ExxonMobil's stock price dropped in expectation that earnings would also eventually fall. The P/E ratio was below 10 for some time. Go to finance.yahoo.com and type "XOM" into the "Quote Lookup" box. Scroll down and click on "ExxonMobil Corporation."

    Click on "Profile" and write a one-paragraph description of the company's activities. Return to the summary page and write down the company's P/E ratio. Is it still relatively low (under 15)?

    Compare ExxonMobil to others in the industry (Chevron, BP, etc.) based on the P/E ratio and the PEG ratio (the P/E ratio divided by annual growth).

2. Go back to the summary page. Is the stock up or down from the prior day? (See the number in parentheses next to the share price.)

3. What is its 52-week range?

4. Click on the "Analysts" heading. What are the Average Earnings Estimate, Low Earnings Estimate, and High Earnings Estimate? How many analysts follow earnings?

APPENDIX | 10A

Valuation of a Supernormal Growth Firm

The equation for the valuation of a supernormal growth firm is:

$$P_0 = \sum_{t=1}^{n} \frac{D_t}{(1 + K_e)^t} + P_n \left(\frac{1}{1 + K_e} \right)^n \tag{10A-1}$$

(Supernormal   (After supernormal
growth period)   growth period)

The formula is not difficult to use. The first term calls for determining the present value of the dividends during the supernormal growth period. The second term calls for computing the present value of the future stock price as determined at the end of the supernormal growth period. If we add the two, we arrive at the current stock price. We are adding together the present value of the two benefits the stockholder will receive: a future stream of dividends during the supernormal growth period and the future stock price.

Let's assume the firm paid a dividend over the last 12 months of $1.67; this represents the current dividend rate. Dividends are expected to grow by 20 percent per year over the supernormal growth period (n) of three years. They will then grow at a normal constant growth rate (g) of 5 percent. The required rate of return (discount rate) as represented by K_e is 9 percent. We first find the present value of the dividends during the supernormal growth period.

1. Present Value of Supernormal Dividends

$D_0 = \$1.67$. We allow this value to grow at 20 percent per year over the
three years of supernormal growth.
$D_1 = D_0 (1 + 0.20) = \$1.67(1.20) = \$2.00$
$D_2 = D_1 (1 + 0.20) = \$2.00(1.20) = \$2.40$
$D_3 = D_2 (1 + 0.20) = \$2.40(1.20) = \$2.88$

We then discount these values back at 9 percent to find the present value of dividends during the supernormal growth period.

	Supernormal Dividends	Discount Rate $K_e = 9\%$	Present Value of Dividends during the Supernormal Period
D_1	$2.00	0.917	$1.83
D_2	2.40	0.842	2.02
D_3	2.88	0.772	2.22
			$6.07

The present value of the supernormal dividends is $6.07. We now turn to the future stock price.

2. Present Value of Future Stock Price

We first find the future stock price at the end of the supernormal growth period. This is found by taking the present value of the dividends that will be growing at a normal, constant rate after the supernormal period. This will begin *after* the third (and last) period of supernormal growth.

Since after the supernormal growth period the firm is growing at a normal, constant rate ($g = 5$ percent) and K_e (the discount rate) of 9 percent exceeds the new, constant growth rate of 5 percent, we have fulfilled the two conditions for using the constant dividend growth model after three years. That is, we can apply Formula 10-8 (without subscripts for now).

$$P = \frac{D}{K_e - g}$$

In this case, however, D is really the dividend at the end of the fourth period because this phase of the analysis starts at the beginning of the fourth period and D is supposed to fall at the *end* of the first period of analysis in the formula. Also the price we are solving for now is the price at the beginning of the fourth period, which is the same concept as the price at the end of the third period (P_3).

We thus say:

$$P_3 = \frac{D_4}{K_e - g} \tag{10A-2}$$

D_4 is equal to the previously determined value for D_3 of $2.88 compounded for one period at the constant growth rate of 5 percent.

$$D_4 = \$2.88(1.05) = \$3.02$$

Also:

$K_e = 0.09$ discount rate (required rate of return)

$g = 0.05$ constant growth rate

$$P_3 = \frac{D_4}{K_e - g} = \frac{\$3.02}{0.09 - 0.05} = \frac{\$3.02}{0.04} = \$75.50$$

This is the value of the stock at the end of the third period. We discount this value back to the present.

Stock Price after Three Years	Discount Rate* $K_e = 9\%$	Present Value of Future Price
$75.50	0.772	$58.29

*Note: n is equal to 3.

The present value of the future stock price (P_3) of $75.50 is $58.29.

By adding together the answers in parts (1) and (2) of this appendix, we arrive at the total present value, or price, of the supernormal growth stock.

(1) Present value of dividends during the normal growth period	$ 6.07
(2) Present value of the future stock price	58.29
Total present value, or price	$64.36

The process is also illustrated in Figure 10A-1.

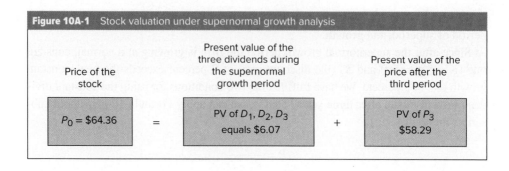

Figure 10A-1 Stock valuation under supernormal growth analysis

Price of the stock		Present value of the three dividends during the supernormal growth period		Present value of the price after the third period
$P_0 = \$64.36$	=	PV of D_1, D_2, D_3 equals $6.07	+	PV of P_3 $58.29

Problem

Valuation of supernormal growth firm
(LO10-5)

10A-1. Surgical Supplies Corporation paid a dividend of $1.12 per share over the last 12 months. The dividend is expected to grow at a rate of 25 percent over the next three years (supernormal growth). It will then grow at a normal, constant rate of 7 percent for the foreseeable future. The required rate of return is 12 percent (this will also serve as the discount rate).

a. Compute the anticipated value of the dividends for the next three years $(D_1, D_2,$ and $D_3)$.

b. Discount each of these dividends back to the present at a discount rate of 12 percent and then sum them.

c. Compute the price of the stock at the end of the third year (P_3).

$$P_3 = \frac{D_4}{K_e - g}$$

d. After you have computed P_3, discount it back to the present at a discount rate of 12 percent for three years.

e. Add together the answers in part *b* and part *d* to get the current value of the stock. (This answer represents the present value of the first three periods of dividends plus the present value of the price of the stock after three periods.)

LEARNING OBJECTIVES

LO 11-1 The cost of capital represents the weighted average cost of the source of financing to the firm.

LO 11-2 The cost of capital is normally the discount rate to use in analyzing an investment.

LO 11-3 The cost of capital is based on the valuation techniques from the previous chapter and is applied to bonds, preferred stock, and common stock.

LO 11-4 A firm attempts to find a minimum cost of capital through varying the mix of its sources of financing.

LO 11-5 The cost of capital may eventually increase as larger amounts of financing are utilized.

Cost of Capital

Throughout the previous two chapters, a number of references were made to discounting future cash flows in solving for the present value. How do you determine the appropriate interest rate or discount rate in a real situation? Suppose that a young doctor is rendered incapable of practicing medicine due to an auto accident in the last year of his residency. The court determines that he could have made $100,000 a year for the next 30 years. What is the present value of these inflows? We must know the appropriate discount rate. If 10 percent is used, the value is $942,700; with 5 percent, the answer is $1,537,300—over half a million dollars is at stake.

In the corporate finance setting, the more likely circumstance is that an investment will be made today—promising a set of inflows in the future—and we need to know the appropriate discount rate. This chapter describes the methods and procedures for making such a determination.

First, you should observe that if we invest money today to receive benefits in the future, we must be absolutely certain we are earning at least as much as it costs us to acquire the funds for investment—that, in essence, is the minimum acceptable return. If funds cost the firm 10 percent, then all projects must be tested to make sure they earn at least 10 percent. By using this as the discount rate, we can ascertain whether we have earned the financial cost of doing business.

The Overall Concept

How does the firm determine the cost of its funds or, more properly stated, the **cost of capital**? Suppose the plant superintendent wishes to borrow money at 6 percent to purchase a conveyor system, while a division manager suggests stock be sold at an effective cost of 12 percent to develop a new product. Not only would it be foolish for each investment to be judged against the specific means of financing used to implement it, but this would also make investment selection decisions inconsistent. For example, imagine financing a conveyor system having an 8 percent return with 6 percent debt and also evaluating a new product having an 11 percent return but financed with 12 percent common stock. If projects and financing are matched in this way, the project with the lower return would be accepted and the project with the higher return would be rejected. In reality, if stock and debt are sold in equal proportions, the average cost of financing would be 9 percent (one-half debt at 6 percent and one-half stock at 12 percent). With a 9 percent average cost of financing, we would now reject the 8 percent conveyor system and accept the 11 percent new product. This would be a rational and consistent decision. Though an investment financed by low-cost debt might appear acceptable at first glance, the use of debt might increase the overall risk of the firm and eventually make all forms of financing more expensive. Each project must be measured against the overall cost of funds to the firm. We now consider cost of capital in a broader context.

We can best understand how to determine the cost of capital by examining the capital structure of a hypothetical firm, the Baker Corporation, in Table 11-1. Note that the after-tax costs of the individual sources of financing are shown, then weights are assigned to each, and finally a weighted average cost is determined. (The costs under consideration are those related to new funds that can be used for future financing, rather than historical costs.) In the remainder of the chapter, each of these procedural steps is examined.

Table 11-1   Cost of capital—Baker Corporation

		(1) Cost (aftertax)	(2) Weights	(3) Weighted Cost
Debt	K_d	7.05%	30%	2.12%
Preferred stock	K_p	10.94	10	1.09
Common equity (retained earnings)	K_e	12.00	60	7.20
Weighted average cost of capital	K_a			10.41%

Each element in the capital structure has an explicit, or opportunity, cost associated with it, herein referred to by the symbol K. These costs are directly related to the valuation concepts developed in the previous chapter. If we understand how a security is valued, then there is little problem in determining its cost. The mathematics involved in the cost of capital are not difficult. We begin our analysis with a consideration of the cost of debt.

Cost of Debt

The cost of debt is measured by the interest rate at which a company can raise new capital. For companies that do not issue bonds but simply borrow from a bank, this rate will be the rate at which they can borrow from the bank. The more interesting case arises when the cost of debt is measured by the interest rate, or yield, paid to bondholders. The simplest case would be a $1,000 bond paying $100 annual interest, thus providing a 10 percent yield. The computation may be more difficult if the bond is priced at a discount or premium from par value. Techniques for computing such bond yields were presented in Chapter 10.

Assume the firm is preparing to issue new debt. To determine the likely cost of the new debt in the marketplace, the firm will compute the yield on its currently outstanding debt. This is not the rate at which the old debt was issued, but the rate that investors are demanding today. Assume the debt issue pays $90 per year in interest, has a 15-year life (at which time the principal amount of $1,000 will be paid), and is currently selling for $968.50. The yield to maturity is the interest rate that the market uses to price the bond. In Table 10-3, we saw how the yield to maturity can be obtained using Excel's Goal Seek function or Excel's **RATE** function. Using the **RATE** function, as shown in Table 11-2, we find that the yield to maturity for this bond is 9.40 percent. Calculator keystrokes shown in the margin produce the same result.

FINANCIAL CALCULATOR	
Bond YTM	
Value	*Function*
15	**N**
−968.50	**PV**
90	**PMT**
1000	**FV**
Function	*Solution*
CPT	
I/Y	9.40

Table 11-2 Yield to maturity						
	A	B	C	D	E	F	G
1	nper	15		=+RATE (B1,B2,B3,B4)			
2	pmt	90		RATE(nper, pmt, pv, [fv], [type], [guess])			
3	pv	−968.50		9.40%			
4	fv	1000					
5				=RATE(15,90,−968.50, 1000)			
6				RATE(nper, pmt, pv, [fv], [type], [guess])			
7				9.40%			

In many cases, you will not have to compute the yield to maturity. It will simply be given to you. The practicing corporate financial manager also can normally consult a source such as *S&P Capital IQ Net Advantage* to determine the yield to maturity on the firm's outstanding debt. An excerpt from this bond guide is presented in Table 11-3. If the firm involved is Keyspan Corp., for example, the financial manager could observe that debt maturing in 2030 would have a yield to maturity of 4.71 percent as highlighted in Table 11-3.

Once the bond yield is determined through the formula, a calculator, or the tables (or is given to you), you must adjust the yield for tax considerations. Yield to maturity indicates how much the corporation has to pay on a *before-tax* basis. But keep in mind the interest payment on debt is a tax-deductible expense. Since interest is tax-deductible, its true cost is less than its stated cost because the government is picking up part of the tab by allowing the firm to pay less tax. The aftertax cost of debt is actually the yield to maturity times 1 minus the tax rate.[1] This is presented as Formula 11-1.

$$K_d \text{ (Cost of debt)} = Y(1 - T) \qquad (11\text{-}1)$$

The term Y (*yield*) in the formula is interchangeable with yield to maturity. Earlier in this section, we determined that the existing yield on the debt was 9.40 percent. We shall assume new debt can be issued at the same going market rate,[2] and that the firm

---

[1]The yield may also be thought of as representing the interest cost to the firm after considering all selling and distribution costs, though no explicit representation is given above to these costs in relationship to debt. These costs are usually quite small, and they are often bypassed entirely in some types of loans. For those who wish to explicitly include this factor in Formula 11-1, we would have:

$$K_d = [\text{Yield}/(1 - \text{Distribution costs})] \, (1 - T)$$

[2]Actually the rate might be slightly lower to reflect that bonds trading at a discount from par ($968.50 in this case) generally pay a lower yield to maturity than par value bonds because of potential tax advantages and higher leverage potential. This is not really a major issue in this case.

Table 11-3   Excerpt from *S&P Capital IQ Net Advantage*

Maturity Date	Issue	Security Type	Seniority	Coupon	Offer Date	Amt. Outstdg. ($mm)	Current Price	Current YTM	S&P Rating
Nov-15-2030	KeySpan Corporation	Corporate Debentures	Senior Unsecured	8.000	Nov-15-2000	250.00	131.285	4.710	BBB+
Apr-01-2033	KeySpan Corporation	Corporate Debentures	Senior Unsecured	5.875	Apr-01-2003	150.00	117.973	4.250	BBB+
Apr-01-2035	KeySpan Corporation	Corporate Debentures	Senior Unsecured	5.803	Mar-29-2005	307.20	117.973	4.021	BBB+

is paying a 25 percent tax (a nice, easy rate with which to work). Applying the tax adjustment factor, the aftertax cost of debt would be 7.05 percent.

$$K_d \text{ (Cost of debt)} = Y(1 - T)$$
$$= 9.40\%(1 - 0.25)$$
$$= 9.40\%(0.75)$$
$$= 7.05\%$$

Please refer back to Table 11-1 and observe in column 1 that the aftertax cost of debt is the 7.05 percent that we have just computed.

The 2017 Tax Cuts and Jobs Act introduced complexity in calculating the cost of debt for companies with high interest expense. Beginning in 2022, a company can only deduct interest of up to 30 percent of its earnings before interest and taxes (EBIT). Until then a more generous limitation applies; the company can deduct interest up to 30 percent of earnings before interest, taxes, depreciation, and amortization (EBITDA). EBITDA is higher than EBIT as long as the company has depreciation or amortization expenses.

For companies with very high interest expense, or very low EBIT, the interest expense limitation will remove the tax advantage to issuing debt, and Equation 11-1 would need to be adjusted to reflect the fact that the pretax and aftertax costs are the same for these firms.

Cost of Preferred Stock

The cost of preferred stock is similar to the cost of debt in that a constant annual payment is made, but dissimilar in that there is no maturity date on which a principal payment must be made. Determining the yield on preferred stock is simpler than determining the yield on debt. All you have to do is divide the annual dividend by the current price (this process was discussed in Chapter 10). This represents the rate of return to preferred stockholders as well as the annual cost to the corporation for the preferred stock issue.

We need to make one slight alteration to this process by dividing the dividend payment by the net price or proceeds received by the firm. Since a new share of preferred stock has a selling cost (**flotation cost**), the proceeds to the firm are equal to the selling price in the market minus the flotation cost. The cost of preferred stock is presented as Formula 11-2.[3]

---

[3]Note that in Chapter 10, K_p was presented without any adjustment for flotation costs. The instructor may wish to indicate that we have altered the definition slightly. Some may wish to formally add an additional subscript to K_p to indicate we are now talking about the cost of *new* preferred stock. The adjusted symbol would be K_{pn}.

$$K_p \text{ (Cost of preferred stock)} = \frac{D_p}{P_p - F} \tag{11-2}$$

where

K_p = Cost of preferred stock

D_p = Annual dividend on preferred stock

P_p = Price of preferred stock

F = Flotation, or selling cost

In the case of the Baker Corporation, we shall assume the annual dividend is $10.50, the preferred stock price is $100, and the flotation, or selling cost, is $4. The effective cost is:

$$K_p = \frac{D_p}{P_p - F} = \frac{\$10.50}{\$100 - \$4} = \frac{\$10.50}{\$96} = 10.94\%$$

Because a preferred stock dividend is not a tax-deductible expense, there is no downward tax adjustment.

Please refer back to Table 11-1 and observe in column 1 that 10.94 percent is the value we used for the cost of preferred stock.

Cost of Common Equity

Determining the cost of common stock in the capital structure is a more involved task. The out-of-pocket cost is the cash dividend, but is it prudent to assume the percentage cost of common stock is simply the current year's dividend divided by the market price?

$$\frac{\text{Current dividend}}{\text{Market price}}$$

If such an approach were followed, the common stock costs for selected U.S. corporations in February 2018 would be as follows: Target (3.25 percent), Microsoft (1.82 percent), Walmart (1.91 percent), and PepsiCo (2.66 percent). Ridiculous, you say! If new common stock costs were assumed to be so low, the firms would have no need to issue other securities and could profitably finance projects that earned only 2 or 3 percent. How then do we find the correct theoretical cost of common stock to the firm?

Valuation Approach

In determining the cost of common stock, the firm must be sensitive to the pricing and performance demands of current and future stockholders. An appropriate approach is to develop a model for valuing common stock and to extract from this model a formula for the required return on common stock.

In Chapter 10, we discussed the constant growth **dividend valuation model** and said the current price of common stock could be stated to equal:

$$P_0 = \frac{D_1}{K_e - g}$$

where

P_0 = Price of the stock today

D_1 = Dividend at the end of the first year (or period)

K_e = Required rate of return

g = Constant growth rate in dividends

We then stated we could arrange the terms in the formula to solve for K_e instead of P_0. This was presented in Formula 10-9. We present the formula once again and relabel it Formula 11-3.

$$K_e = \frac{D_1}{P_0} + g \tag{11-3}$$

The required rate of return (K_e) is equal to the dividend at the end of the first year (D_1), divided by the price of the stock today (P_0), plus a constant growth rate (g). Although the growth rate basically applies to dividends, it is also assumed to apply to earnings and stock price over the long term.

If $D_1 = \$2$, $P_0 = \$40$, and $g = 7\%$, we would say K_e equals 12 percent.

$$K_e = \frac{D_1}{P_0} + g = \frac{\$2}{\$40} + 7\% = 5\% + 7\% = 12\%$$

This means stockholders expect to receive a 5 percent dividend yield on the stock price plus a 7 percent growth in their investment, making a total return of 12 percent.

Required Return on Common Stock Using the Capital Asset Pricing Model

The required return on common stock can also be calculated by an alternate approach called the capital asset pricing model. This topic is covered in Appendix 11A, so only brief mention will be made at this point. Some accept the capital asset pricing model as an important approach to common stock valuation, while others suggest it is not a valid description of how the real world operates.

Under the **capital asset pricing model (CAPM)**, the required return for common stock (or other investments) can be described by the following formula:

$$K_j = R_f + \beta(K_m - R_f) \tag{11-4}$$

where

K_j = Required return on common stock

R_f = Risk-free rate of return; usually the current rate on Treasury bill securities

β = Beta coefficient. The beta measures the historical volatility of an individual stock's return relative to a stock market index. A beta greater than 1 indicates greater volatility (price movements) than the market, while the reverse would be true for a beta less than 1.

K_m = Return expected in the market as measured by an appropriate index

For the Baker Corporation example, we might assume the following values:

$R_f = 5.5\%$

$K_m = 12\%$

$\beta = 1.0$

K_j, based on Formula 11-4, would then equal:

$$K_j = 5.5\% + 1.0(12\% - 5.5\%) = 5.5\% + 1.0(6.5\%)$$
$$= 5.5\% + 6.5\% = 12\%$$

In this calculation, we have assumed that K_j (the required return under the capital asset pricing model) would equal K_e (the required return under the dividend valuation model). They are both computed to equal 12 percent. Under this equilibrium circumstance, the dividend valuation model and the capital asset pricing model would produce the same answer.

For now we shall use the dividend valuation model exclusively; that is, we shall use $K_e = (D_1/P_0) + g$ in preference to $K_j = R_f + \beta(K_m - R_f)$.

Those who wish to study the capital asset pricing model further are referred to Appendix 11A. This appendix is optional and not required for further reading in the text.

Cost of Retained Earnings

Up to this point, we have discussed the cost (required return) of common stock in a general sense. We have not really specified who is supplying the funds. One obvious supplier of **common stock equity** capital is the purchaser of new shares of common stock. But this is not the only source. For many corporations the most important source of ownership or equity capital is in the form of retained earnings, an internal source of funds.

Accumulated retained earnings represent the past and present earnings of the firm minus previously distributed dividends. Retained earnings, by law, belong to the current stockholders. They can be either paid out to the current stockholders in the form of dividends or reinvested in the firm. As current funds are retained in the firm for reinvestment, they represent a source of equity capital that is being supplied by the current stockholders. However, they should not be considered free. An opportunity cost is involved. As previously indicated, the funds could be paid out to the current stockholders in the form of dividends, and then redeployed by the stockholders in other stocks, bonds, real estate, and so on. What is the expected rate of return on these alternative investments? That is, what is the opportunity cost? We assume stockholders could at least earn an equivalent return to that provided by their present investment in the firm (on an equal risk basis). This represents $D_1/P_0 + g$. In the security markets, there are thousands of investments from which to choose, so it is not implausible to assume the stockholder could take dividend payments and reinvest them for a comparable yield.

Thus when we compute the cost of retained earnings, this takes us back to the point at which we began our discussion of the cost of common stock. The cost of retained earnings is equivalent to the rate of return on the firm's common stock.[4] This is the opportunity cost. Thus we say the cost of common equity in the form of retained earnings is equal to the required rate of return on the firm's stock as follows:

$$K_e \begin{pmatrix} \text{Cost of common equity in the} \\ \text{form of retained earnings} \end{pmatrix} = \frac{D_1}{P_0} + g \qquad (11\text{-}5)$$

---

[4]One could logically suggest this is not a perfectly equivalent relationship. For example, if stockholders receive a distribution of retained earnings in the form of dividends, they will have to pay taxes on the dividends before they can reinvest them in equivalent yield investments. Also the stockholder may incur brokerage costs in the process. For these reasons, one might suggest the opportunity cost of retained earnings is less than the rate of return on the firm's common stock. The authors have generally supported this position in the past. However, the current predominant view is that the appropriate cost for retained earnings is equal to the rate of return on the firm's common stock. The strongest argument for this equality position is that, in a publicly traded company, a firm always has the option of buying back its stock in the market. Given that this is the case, it is assured a return of K_e. Thus, the firm should not make a physical asset investment that has an expected equity return of less than K_e. Having presented both sides of the argument, the authors have adopted the equality position in recent editions and have used it throughout this chapter. Nevertheless, some instructors may wish to discuss both sides of the issue.

Thus K_e represents not only the required return on common stock as previously defined but also the cost of equity in the form of retained earnings. It is a symbol that has double significance.

For ease of reference, the terms in Formula 11-5 are reproduced in the box that follows. They are based on prior values presented in this section on the cost of common equity.

> K_e = Cost of common equity in the form of retained earnings
>
> D_1 = Dividend at the end of the first year, $2
>
> P_0 = Price of the stock today, $40
>
> g = Constant growth rate in dividends, 7%
>
> We arrive at the value of 12%.
>
> $$K_e = \frac{D_1}{P_0} + g = \frac{\$2}{\$40} + 7\% = 5\% + 7\% = 12\%$$

The cost of common equity in the form of retained earnings is equal to 12 percent. Please refer back to Table 11-1 and observe in column 1 that 12 percent is the value we have used for common equity.

Cost of New Common Stock

Let's now consider the other source of equity capital, new common stock. If we are issuing *new* common stock, we must earn a slightly higher return than K_e, which represents the required rate of return of *present* stockholders. The higher return is needed to cover the distribution costs of the new securities. Assume the required return for present stockholders is 12 percent and shares are quoted to the public at $40. A new distribution of securities must earn slightly more than 12 percent to compensate the corporation for not receiving the full $40 because of sales commissions and other expenses. The formula for K_e is restated as K_n (the cost of new common stock) to reflect this requirement.

Common stock $\qquad K_e = \dfrac{D_1}{P_0} + g$

New common stock $\qquad K_n = \dfrac{D_1}{P_0 - F} + g \qquad$ (11-6)

The only new term is F (flotation, or selling costs).

Assume the following:

$$D_1 = \$2$$
$$P_0 = \$40$$
$$F = \$4$$
$$g = 7\%$$

then

$$K_n = \frac{\$2}{\$40 - \$4} + 7\%$$

$$= \frac{\$2}{\$36} + 7\%$$

$$= 5.6\% + 7\% = 12.6\%$$

The cost of new common stock to the Baker Corporation is 12.6 percent. This value will be used more extensively later in the chapter. New common stock is not assumed to be in the original capital structure for the Baker Corporation presented in Table 11-1.

Overview of Common Stock Costs

For our purposes, there are only two common stock formulas that you will be using in the rest of the chapter and in the problems at the end of the chapter.

$$K_e \text{ (Cost of common equity in the form of retained earnings)} = \frac{D_1}{P_0} + g$$

$$K_n \text{ (Cost of new common stock)} = \frac{D_1}{P_0 - F} + g$$

The primary emphasis will be on K_e for now, but later in the chapter we will also use K_n when we discuss the marginal cost of capital.

Optimum Capital Structure—Weighting Costs

Having established the techniques for computing the cost of the various elements in the capital structure, we must now discuss methods of assigning weights to these costs. We will attempt to weight capital components in accordance with our desire to achieve a minimum overall cost of capital. This represents an **optimum capital structure**. For the purpose of this discussion, Table 11-1 (cost of capital for the Baker Corporation) is reproduced.

		Cost (aftertax)	Weights	Weighted Cost
Debt	K_d	7.05%	30%	2.12%
Preferred stock	K_p	10.94	10	1.09
Common equity (retained earnings)	K_e	12.00	60	7.20
Weighted average cost of capital	K_a			10.41%

How does the firm decide on the appropriate weights for debt, preferred stock, and common stock financing? Though debt is the cheapest form of financing, it should be used only within reasonable limits. In the Baker Corporation example, debt carried an aftertax cost of 7.05 percent, while other sources of financing cost at least 10.94 percent. Why not use more debt? The answer is that the use of debt beyond a reasonable point may greatly increase the firm's financial risk and thereby drive up the costs of all sources of financing.

Assume you are going to start your own company and are considering three different capital structures. For ease of presentation, only debt and equity (common stock) are being considered. The costs of the components in the capital structure change each time we vary the debt-assets mix (weights).

	Cost (aftertax)	Weights	Weighted Cost
Financial Plan A:			
Debt	6.5%	20%	1.3%
Equity	12.0	80	9.6
			10.9%
Financial Plan B:			
Debt	7.0%	40%	2.8%
Equity	12.5	60	7.5
			10.3%
Financial Plan C:			
Debt	9.0%	60%	5.4%
Equity	15.0	40	6.0
			11.4%

The firm is able to initially reduce the **weighted average cost of capital** with debt financing, but beyond Plan B the continued use of debt becomes unattractive and greatly increases the costs of the sources of financing. Traditional financial theory maintains that there is a U-shaped cost-of-capital curve relative to debt utilization by the firm, as illustrated in Figure 11-1. In this example, the optimum capital structure occurs at a 40 percent debt-to-assets ratio. The weighted average cost of capital is such a fundamental concept that finance professionals often referred to it simply as "the WACC."

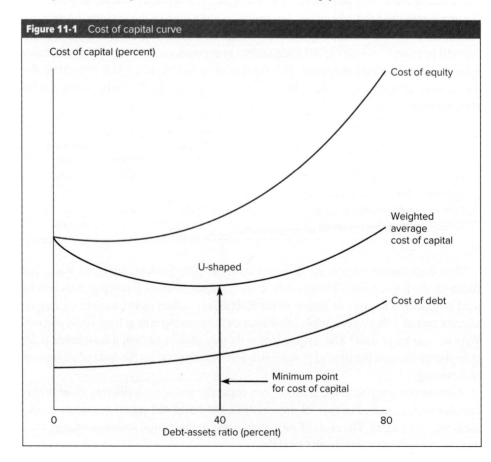

Figure 11-1   Cost of capital curve

The weights that are used to calculate the WACC should be market-value weights. This is consistent with our use of market-based costs of capital for the WACC's component costs.

The optimal level of corporate debt depends on the business risks faced by the firm and the nature of the assets that the firm employs. As discussed in Chapter 5, "Operating and Financial Leverage," a growth firm in a reasonably stable industry can afford to absorb more debt than its counterparts in cyclical industries. In determining the appropriate capital mix, the firm generally begins with its present capital structure and ascertains whether its current position is optimal. If not, subsequent financing should carry the firm toward a mix that is deemed more desirable. Only the costs of new or incremental financing should be considered.

Examples of debt levels by companies in various industries are presented in Table 11-4. Despite the fact that low interest rates have encouraged firms to issue more debt, for most of these firms the 2018 percent debt is less than the 2015 percentage. This happened because equity market values rose dramatically from late 2016 to early 2018, and firms usually move gradually toward their optimal debt-equity mix.

Table 11-4 2015 and 2018 long-term debt as a percentage of debt + equity (MV)		
Selected Companies with Industry Designations	**2015 Percent**	**2018 Percent**
Microsoft (computers)	9%	10%
Intel (semiconductors)	11	8
Home Depot (home repair products)	11	8
Merck & Co. (pharmaceuticals)	16	13
PepsiCo (soft drinks and snacks)	19	15
ExxonMobil (integrated oil)	22	8
Hyatt Hotels (lodging)	22	13
Pfizer (pharmaceuticals)	25	13
Delta Air Lines (air travel)	42	14
Gannett (newspapers and publishing)	43	23

Capital Acquisition and Investment Decision Making

So far the various costs of financial capital and the optimum capital structure have been discussed. **Financial capital**, as you may have figured out, consists of bonds, preferred stock, and common equity. These forms of financial capital appear on the corporate balance sheet under liabilities and equity. The money raised by selling these securities and retaining earnings is invested in the real capital of the firm, the long-term productive assets of plant and equipment.

Long-term funds are usually invested in long-term assets, with several asset-financing mixes possible over the business cycle. Obviously a firm wants to provide all of the necessary financing at the lowest possible cost. This means selling common stock when prices are relatively high to minimize the cost of equity. The financial manager also wants to sell debt at low interest rates. Since there is short-term and long-term debt, the manager needs to know how interest rates move over the business cycle and when to use short-term versus long-term debt.

A firm has to find a balance between debt and equity to achieve its minimum cost of capital. Although we discussed minimizing the overall cost of capital (K_a) at a single debt-to-equity ratio, in reality a firm operates within a relevant range of debt to equity before it becomes penalized with a higher overall cost because of increased risk.

Figure 11-2 shows a theoretical cost-of-capital curve at three different points. As we move from time period t to time period $t + 2$, falling interest rates and rising stock prices cause a downward shift in K_a. This graph illuminates two basic points: (1) The firm wants to keep its debt-to-assets ratio between x and y along the bottom axis at all times because this is the lowest area on each of the three curves; and (2) the firm would like to finance its long-term needs at time period $t + 2$ rather than the other two time periods because overall costs are lowest during this time frame.

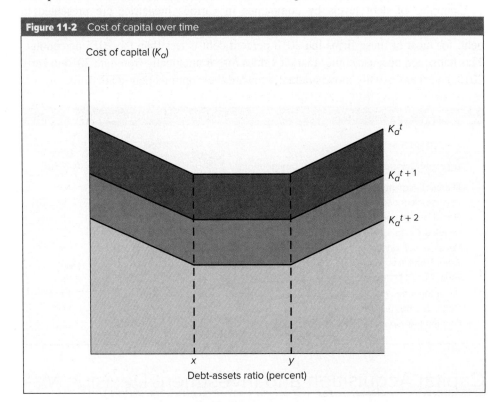

Figure 11-2   Cost of capital over time

Cost of capital (K_a)

$K_a{}^t$

$K_a{}^{t+1}$

$K_a{}^{t+2}$

x y

Debt-assets ratio (percent)

Corporations are allowed some leeway in the money and capital markets, and it is not uncommon for the debt-to-equity ratio to fluctuate between x and y over a business cycle. The firm that is at point y has lost the flexibility of increasing its debt-to-assets ratio without incurring the penalty of higher capital costs.

Cost of Capital in the Capital Budgeting Decision

The current cost of capital for each source of funds is important when making a capital budgeting decision. Historical costs for past fundings may have very little to do with current costs against which present returns must be measured. When raising new financial capital, a company will tap the various sources of financing over a reasonable time. Regardless of the particular source of funds the company is using for the purchase of an asset, the required rate of return, or discount rate, will be the weighted average cost of capital. As long as the company earns its cost of capital, the common stock value of the firm will be maintained or will increase, since stockholder expectations are being met. For example, assume the Baker Corporation was considering making an investment in eight projects with the returns and costs shown in Table 11-5.

Table 11-5	Investment projects available to the Baker Corporation	
Projects	Expected Returns	Cost ($ millions)
A	16.00%	$10
B	14.00	5
C	13.50	4
D	11.80	20
E	10.65	11
F	9.50	20
G	8.60	15
H	7.00	10
		$95 million

These projects in Table 11-5 could be viewed graphically and merged with the weighted average cost of capital to make a capital budgeting decision, as indicated in Figure 11-3.

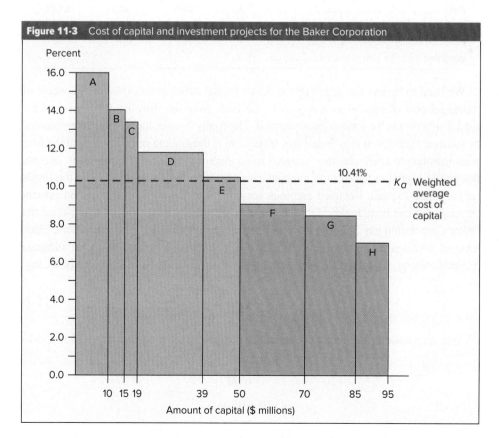

Figure 11-3 Cost of capital and investment projects for the Baker Corporation

Notice in Figure 11-3 that the Baker Corporation is considering $95 million in potential projects, but given the weighted average cost of capital of 10.41 percent, it will choose only projects A through E, or $50 million in new investments. Selecting assets F, G, and H would probably reduce the market value of the common stock because these projects do not provide a return equal to the overall costs of raising funds. The use of the weighted average cost of capital assumes the Baker Corporation is in its optimum capital structure range.

The Marginal Cost of Capital

Nothing guarantees the Baker Corporation that its cost of capital will stay constant for as much money as it wants to raise even if a given capital structure is maintained. If a large amount of financing is desired, the market may demand a higher cost of capital for each amount of funds desired. The point is analogous to the fact that you may be able to go to your relatives and best friends and raise funds for an investment at 10 percent. After you have exhausted the lending or investing power of those closest to you, you will have to look to other sources and the marginal cost of your capital will go up.

As a background for this discussion, the cost of capital table for the Baker Corporation is reproduced again as follows:

		Cost (aftertax)	Weights	Weighted Cost
Debt	K_d	7.05%	30%	2.12%
Preferred stock	K_p	10.94	10	1.09
Common equity (retained earnings)	K_e	12.00	60	7.20
Weighted average cost of capital	K_a			10.41%

We need to review the nature of the firm's capital structure to explain the concept of **marginal cost of capital** as it applies to the firm. Note the firm has 60 percent of the capital structure in the form of equity capital. The equity (ownership) capital is represented by retained earnings. It is assumed that 60 percent is the amount of equity capital the firm must maintain to keep a balance between fixed income securities and ownership interest. But equity capital in the form of retained earnings cannot grow indefinitely as the firm's capital needs expand. Retained earnings are limited to the amount of past and present earnings that can be redeployed into the investment projects of the firm. Let's assume the Baker Corporation has $23.40 million of retained earnings available for investment. Since retained earnings are to represent 60 percent of the capital structure, there are adequate retained earnings to support a capital structure of up to $39 million. More formally, we say:

$$X = \frac{\text{Retained earnings}}{\text{Percent of retained earnings in the capital structure}} \qquad (11\text{-}7)$$

(Where X represents the size of the capital structure that retained earnings will support.)

$$X = \frac{\$23.40 \text{ million}}{0.60}$$

$$= \$39 \text{ million}$$

Big Bonds Are "Liquid" Bonds

Corporate bond buyers have found that there can be safety in bigger bond deals amid a pullback in bond trading by big Wall Street banks. The Dodd–Frank law's "Volcker Rule" bans U.S. banks from some proprietary trading. This ban makes it harder for the big banks to hold inventory for "making markets" in illiquid corporate bonds.

The difficulty in trading junk bonds has long been a factor in the high yield-to-maturity paid on these debt instruments. Certainly, junk bonds require high interest rates because they have credit risk, but they also often have liquidity risk. Credit risk is the risk that the bond's issuer will go bankrupt before the bond matures. Liquidity risk is the risk that if a bondholder wants to sell the bond prior to maturity, no one else will be eager to buy it.

Researchers Amihud and Mendelson (1986) showed that the most illiquid *stocks* have yielded monthly returns that are over 0.5 percent higher than the most liquid stocks. That is over 6 percent per year! Similarly, buyers of illiquid bonds require a higher return than liquid bonds. Simply put, many investors don't want to buy a bond if selling it later will be difficult.

The Wall Street Journal has reported that "investors are flocking to investment-grade bonds issued in amounts of $500 million or more, which are called benchmark deals. Bonds sold in big batches are performing better than smaller debt issued as part of smaller deals, data show. Some companies have taken note and are boosting offerings in order to pass the $500 million threshold."* One such company is Ventas, a publicly traded real estate investment trust.

In August 2012, Ventas issued $275 million in senior debt due in August 2022. Because of the low interest rate environment at the time, the yield on these 10-year bonds was only 3.25 percent. Then Ventas realized that issuing more of the same bonds might not cost them much more. In December 2012, Ventas issued another $225 million of the same bonds, taking the total to the $500 million benchmark. Ventas has acknowledged that it is "clearly wanting to create liquidity for our investors" by increasing the total size of its individual bond issuances.

*"For Bonds, Bigger Is Better," *The Wall Street Journal*, February 12, 2012, p. C4.

www.ventas.com

After the first $39 million of capital is raised, retained earnings will no longer be available to provide the 60 percent equity position in the capital structure. Nevertheless, lenders and investors will still require that 60 percent of the capital structure be in the form of common equity (ownership) capital. Because of this, *new* common stock will replace retained earnings to provide the 60 percent common equity component for the firm. That is, after $39 million, common equity capital will be in the form of new common stock rather than retained earnings.

In the left portion of Table 11-6 on the next page, we see the original cost of capital that we have been discussing throughout the chapter. This applies up to $39 million. After $39 million, the concept of marginal cost of capital becomes important. The cost of capital then goes up as shown on the right portion of the table.

K_{mc} in the bottom right portion of the table represents the *marginal* cost of capital, and it is 10.77 percent after $39 million. The meaning of K_{mc} is basically the same as K_a; they both represent the cost of capital, but the *mc* subscript after K indicates the (marginal) cost of capital is going up.

The marginal cost of capital has increased after $39 million because common equity is now in the form of new common stock rather than retained earnings. The aftertax (A/T) cost of new common stock is slightly more expensive than retained earnings

Table 11-6   Costs of capital for different amounts of financing

First $39 Million				Next $11 Million			
	A/T Cost	Wts.	Weighted Cost		A/T Cost	Wts.	Weighted Cost
Debt .... K_d	7.05%	0.30	2.12%	Debt .... K_d	7.05%	0.30	2.12%
Preferred .... K_p	10.94	0.10	1.09	Preferred .... K_p	10.94	0.10	1.09
Common equity* .... K_e	12.00	0.60	7.20	Common equity† .... K_n	12.60	0.60	7.56
*Retained earnings.			$K_a = 10.41\%$	†New common stock.			$K_{mc} = 10.77\%$

because of flotation costs (F). The equation for the cost of new common stock was shown earlier in the chapter as Formula 11-6 and now we are using it:

$$K_n = \frac{D_1}{P_0 - F} + g = \frac{\$2}{\$40 - \$4} + 7\%$$

$$= \frac{\$2}{\$36} + 7\% = 5.6\% + 7\% = 12.6\%$$

The flotation cost (F) is $4 and the cost of new common stock is 12.60 percent. This is higher than the 12 percent cost of retained earnings that we have been using and causes the increase in the marginal cost of capital.

To carry the example a bit further, we will assume the cost of debt of 7.05 percent applies to the first $15 million of debt the firm raises. After that the aftertax cost of debt will rise to 8.60 percent. Since debt represents 30 percent of the capital structure for the Baker Corporation, the cheaper form of debt can be used to support the capital structure up to $50 million. We derive the $50 million by using Formula 11-8.

$$Z = \frac{\text{Amount of lower-cost debt}}{\text{Percent of debt in the capital structure}} \qquad (11\text{-}8)$$

(Here Z represents the size of the capital structure in which lower-cost debt can be utilized.)

$$Z = \frac{\$15 \text{ million}}{0.30}$$

$$= \$50 \text{ million}$$

After the first $50 million of capital is raised, lower-cost debt will no longer be available to provide 30 percent of the capital structure. After $50 million in total financing, the aftertax cost of debt will go up to the previously specified 8.60 percent. The marginal cost of capital for over $50 million in financing is shown in Table 11-7.

The change in the cost of debt gives way to a new marginal cost of capital (K_{mc}) of 11.23 percent after $50 million of financing. You should observe that the capital structure with over $50 million of financing reflects not only the change in the cost of debt, but also the continued exclusive use of new common stock to represent common

Table 11-7   Cost of capital for increasing amounts of financing

		Over $50 Million		
		Cost (aftertax)	Weights	Weighted Cost
Debt (higher cost)	K_d	8.60%	0.30	2.58%
Preferred stock	K_p	10.94	0.10	1.09
Common equity (new common stock)	K_n	12.60	0.60	7.56
				$K_{mc} = 11.23\%$

equity capital. This change occurred at $39 million, but must be carried on indefinitely as the capital structure expands.

We could continue this process by next indicating a change in the cost of preferred stock, or by continually increasing the cost of debt or new common stock as more capital is used. For now it is sufficient that you merely observe the basic process. To summarize, we have said the Baker Corporation has a basic weighted average cost of capital of 10.41 percent. This value was developed throughout the chapter and was originally presented in Table 11-1. However, as the firm began to substantially expand its capital structure, the weighted average cost of capital increased. This gave way to the term *marginal cost of capital*. The first increase or break point was at $39 million in which the marginal cost of capital went up to 10.77 percent as a result of replacing retained earnings with new common stock. The second increase or break point was at $50 million in which the marginal cost of capital increased to 11.23 percent as a result of the utilization of more expensive debt. The changes are summarized in Figure 11-4.

Amount of Financing	Marginal Cost of Capital
0–$39 million	10.41%
$39–50 million	10.77
Over $50 million	11.23

In previously presented Figure 11-3, we showed returns from investments A through H. In Figure 11-4, we reproduce the returns originally shown in Figure 11-3 but include the concept of marginal cost of capital. Observe the increasing cost of capital (dotted lines) in relationship to the decreasing returns (straight lines).

In Figure 11-3, the Baker Corporation was justified in choosing projects A through E for a capital expenditure of $50 million. This is no longer the case in Figure 11-4. Because of the increasing marginal cost of capital, the returns exceed the cost of capital only up to $39 million and now only projects A through D are acceptable.

Although the concept of marginal cost of capital is very important, for most of our capital budgeting decisions in the next chapter, we will assume we are operating on the initial flat part of the marginal cost of capital curve in Figure 11-4, and most of our decisions can be made based on the initial weighted average cost of capital.

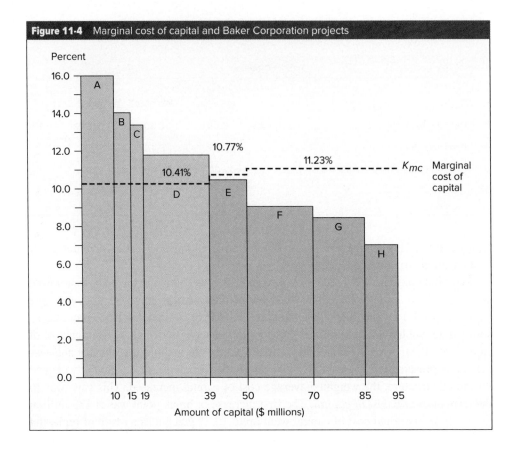

Figure 11-4 Marginal cost of capital and Baker Corporation projects

SUMMARY

The cost of capital for the firm is determined by computing the costs of various sources of financing and weighting them in proportion to their representation in the capital structure. The cost of each component in the capital structure is closely associated with the valuation of that source, which we studied in the prior chapter. For debt and preferred stock, the cost is directly related to the current yield, with debt adjusted downward to reflect the tax-deductible nature of interest.

For common stock, the cost of retained earnings (K_e) is the current dividend yield on the security plus an anticipated rate of growth for the future. Minor adjustments are made to the formula to determine the cost of new common stock. A summary of Baker Corporation's capital costs is presented in Table 11-8.

We weight the elements in the capital structure in accordance with our desire to achieve a minimum overall cost. While debt is usually the "cheapest" form of financing, excessive debt use may increase the financial risk of the firm and drive up the costs of all sources of financing. The wise financial manager attempts to ascertain what debt component will result in the lowest overall cost of capital. Once this has been determined, the weighted average cost of capital is the discount rate we use in present-valuing future flows to ensure we are earning at least the cost of financing.

Table 11-8   Cost of components in the capital structure

1. Cost of debt	$K_d = Y(1 - T) = 7.05\%$	Y (Yield) = 9.40%
		T = Corporate tax rate, 25%
2. Cost of preferred stock	$K_p = \dfrac{D_p}{P_p - F} = 10.94\%$	D_p = Preferred dividend, \$10.50
		P_p = Price of preferred stock, \$100
		F = Flotation costs, \$4
3. Cost of common equity (retained earnings)	$K_e = \dfrac{D_1}{P_0} + g = 12\%$	D_1 = First year common dividend, \$2
		P_0 = Price of common stock, \$40
		g = Growth rate, 7%
4. Cost of new common stock	$K_n = \dfrac{D_1}{P_0 - F} + g = 12.60\%$	Same as above, with F = Flotation costs, \$4

The marginal cost of capital is also introduced to explain what happens to a company's cost of capital as it tries to finance a large amount of funds. First the company will use up retained earnings, and the cost of financing will rise as higher-cost new common stock is substituted for retained earnings in order to maintain the optimum capital structure with the appropriate debt-to-equity ratio. Larger amounts of financial capital can also cause the individual means of financing to rise by raising interest rates or by depressing the price of the stock because more is sold than the market wants to absorb.

REVIEW OF FORMULAS

1. K_d (cost of debt) $= Y(1 - T)$ (11-1)
    Y is yield
    T is corporate tax rate

2. K_p (cost of preferred stock) $= \dfrac{D_p}{P_p - F}$ (11-2)

    D_p is the annual dividend on preferred stock
    P_p is the price of preferred stock
    F is flotation, or selling, cost

3. K_e (cost of common equity) $= \dfrac{D_1}{P_0} + g$ (11-3)

    D_1 is dividend at the end of the first year (or period)
    P_0 is the price of the stock today
    g is growth rate in dividends

4. K_j (required return on common stock) $= R_f + \beta(K_m - R_f)$ (11-4)
    R_f is risk-free rate of return
    β is beta coefficient
    K_m is return in the market as measured by the appropriate index

5. K_e (cost of common equity in the form of retained earnings) $= \dfrac{D_1}{P_0} + g$ (11-5)
    D_1 is dividend at the end of the first year (or period)
    P_0 is price of the stock today
    g is growth rate in dividends

6. K_n (cost of new common stock) $= \dfrac{D_1}{P_0 - F} + g$ (11-6)

   Same as above with:

   F as flotation, or selling, cost

7. X (size of capital structure that retained earnings will support) $= \dfrac{\text{Retained earnings}}{\text{\% of retained earnings in the capital structure}}$ (11-7)

8. Z (size of capital structure that lower-cost debt will support) $= \dfrac{\text{Amount of lower-cost debt}}{\text{\% of debt in the capital structure}}$ (11-8)

LIST OF TERMS

cost of capital   341
flotation cost   344
dividend valuation model   345
capital asset pricing
   model (CAPM)   346

common stock equity   347
optimum capital structure   349
weighted average cost of capital   350
financial capital   351
marginal cost of capital   354

DISCUSSION QUESTIONS

1. Why do we use the overall cost of capital for investment decisions even when only one source of capital will be used (e.g., debt)? *(LO11-1)*

2. How does the cost of a source of capital relate to the valuation concepts presented previously in Chapter 10? *(LO11-3)*

3. In computing the cost of capital, do we use the historical costs of existing debt and equity or the current costs as determined in the market? Why? *(LO11-3)*

4. Why is the cost of debt less than the cost of preferred stock if both securities are priced to yield 10 percent in the market? *(LO11-3)*

5. What are the two sources of equity (ownership) capital for the firm? *(LO11-3)*

6. Explain why retained earnings have an associated opportunity cost. *(LO11-3)*

7. Why is the cost of retained earnings the equivalent of the firm's own required rate of return on common stock (K_e)? *(LO11-3)*

8. Why is the cost of issuing new common stock (K_n) higher than the cost of retained earnings (K_e)? *(LO11-3)*

9. How are the weights determined to arrive at the optimal weighted average cost of capital? *(LO11-4)*

10. Explain the traditional, U-shaped approach to the cost of capital. *(LO11-4)*

11. It has often been said that if the company can't earn a rate of return greater than the cost of capital it should not make investments. Explain. *(LO11-2)*

12. What effect would inflation have on a company's cost of capital? (*Hint:* Think about how inflation influences interest rates, stock prices, corporate profits, and growth.) *(LO11-3)*

13. What is the concept of marginal cost of capital? *(LO11-5)*

PRACTICE PROBLEMS AND SOLUTIONS

1. *a.* A $1,000 par value bond issued by Conseco Electronics has 16 years to
   maturity. The bond pays $78 a year in interest and is selling for $884. What
   is the yield to maturity?

   b. If the firm is in a 25 percent tax bracket, what is the aftertax cost of the
   debt?

2. *a.* Assume the following capital structure for the Morgan Corp.:

Yield to maturity
and cost of debt
(LO11-3)

Debt	35%
Preferred stock	15%
Common equity	50%

Weighted average
cost of capital
(LO11-1)

The following facts are also provided:

Bond yield to maturity	9%
Corporate tax rate	25%
Dividend, preferred stock	$ 8.50
Price, preferred stock	$100.00
Flotation cost, preferred stock	$ 2.00
Dividend, common stock	$ 1.20
Price, common stock	$ 30.00
Growth rate, common stock	9%

Compute the weighted average cost of capital.

   b. If there are $30 million in retained earnings, at what dollar value will the
   marginal cost of capital go up? If the flotation cost on common stock is
   $1.50, what will be the cost of new common stock?

Solutions

1. *a.* Yield to maturity (YTM)

	A	B	C	D
1	nper	16		
2	pmt	78		
3	pv	−884		
4	fv	1000		
5				
6	=+RATE(B1,B2,B3,B4)		9.21%	
7	**RATE**(nper, pmt, pv, [fv], [type], [guess])			

The yield to maturity is 9.21 percent.

   b. K_d (aftertax cost of debt) $= Y$ (yield)$(1 - T)$

$$= 9.21\% \ (1 - 0.25)$$

$$= 9.21\% \ (0.75)$$

$$= 6.91\%$$

**FINANCIAL
CALCULATOR**

Bond YTM

Value	Function
16	N
−884	PV
78	PMT
1000	FV
Function	*Solution*
CPT	
I/Y	9.21

2. *a.* First compute the cost of the components in the capital structure.

$$K_d \text{ (aftertax cost of debt)} = \text{Yield } (1 - T)$$
$$= 9\% \ (1 - 0.25) = 6.75\% \qquad (11\text{-}1)$$

$$K_p \text{ (cost of preferred stock)} = \frac{D_p}{P_p - F} \qquad (11\text{-}2)$$

D_p = Dividend, preferred stock = $8.50
P_p = Price, preferred stock = $100
F = Flotation cost, preferred stock = $2

$$K_p = \frac{\$8.50}{\$100 - \$2} = \frac{\$8.50}{\$98} = 8.67\%$$

$$K_e \text{ (cost of common equity in the form of retained earnings)} = \frac{D_1}{P_0} + g \qquad (11\text{-}5)$$

D_1 = Dividend, common stock = $1.20
P_0 = Price, common stock = $30
g = Growth rate, common stock = 9%

$$K_e = \frac{\$1.20}{\$30} + 9\% = 4\% + 9\% = 13\%$$

Now combine these with the weights in the capital structure to compute the weighted average cost of capital.

		Cost	Weights	Weighted Cost
Debt	K_d	6.75%	35%	2.36%
Preferred stock	K_p	8.67	15	1.30
Common equity (retained earnings)	K_e	13.00	50	6.50
Weighted average cost of capital (K_a)				10.16%

b. The marginal cost of capital will go up when there are no longer enough retained earnings to support the capital structure. This is point *X*.

Solve for *X*:

$$X = \frac{\text{Retained earnings}}{\text{Percent of retained earnings in the capital structure}}$$

$$= \frac{\$30 \text{ million}}{0.50} = \$60 \text{ million}$$

At this point, new common stock will be *used* instead of retained earnings in the capital structure. The cost of the new common stock is:

$$K_n = \frac{D_1}{P_0 - F} + g \qquad (11\text{-}6)$$

$$K_n = \text{Cost of new common stock}$$

The only new term is *F:*

D_1 = $1.20

$P_0 = \$30$

F = Flotation cost, new common stock $1.50

$g = 9\%$

$K_n = \dfrac{\$1.20}{\$30 - \$1.50} + 9\% = \dfrac{\$1.20}{\$28.50} + 9\% = 4.21\% + 9\% = 13.21\%$

PROBLEMS

■ **connect** Selected problems are available with Connect. Please see the preface for more information.

Basic Problems

1. In March 2010, Hertz Pain Relievers bought a massage machine that provided a return of 8 percent. It was financed by debt costing 7 percent. In August, Mr. Hertz came up with a heating compound that would have a return of 14 percent. The chief financial officer, Mr. Smith, told him it was impractical because it would require the issuance of common stock at a cost of 16 percent to finance the purchase. Is the company following a logical approach to using its cost of capital?
    Cost of capital (LO11-2)

2. Speedy Delivery Systems can buy a piece of equipment that is anticipated to provide an 11 percent return and can be financed at 6 percent with debt. Later in the year, the firm turns down an opportunity to buy a new machine that would yield a 9 percent return but would cost 15 percent to finance through common equity. Assume debt and common equity each represent 50 percent of the firm's capital structure.
    Cost of capital (LO11-2)

    a. Compute the weighted average cost of capital.

    b. Which project(s) should be accepted?

3. A brilliant young scientist is killed in a plane crash. It is anticipated that he could have earned $240,000 a year for the next 50 years. The attorney for the plaintiff's estate argues that the lost income should be discounted back to the present at 4 percent. The lawyer for the defendant's insurance company argues for a discount rate of 8 percent. What is the difference between the present value of the settlement at 4 percent and 8 percent? Compute each one separately.
    Effect of discount rate (LO11-2)

4. Telecom Systems can issue debt yielding 9 percent. The company is in a 30 percent bracket. What is its aftertax cost of debt?
    Aftertax cost of debt (LO11-3)

5. Calculate the aftertax cost of debt under each of the following conditions:
    Aftertax cost of debt (LO11-3)

	Yield	Corporate Tax Rate
a.	8.0%	18%
b.	12.0	34
c.	10.6	15

6. Calculate the aftertax cost of debt under each of the following conditions:
    Aftertax cost of debt (LO11-3)

	Yield	Corporate Tax Rate
a.	8.0%	26%
b.	9.0	35
c.	8.0	0

Aftertax cost of debt
(LO11-3)

7. The Goodsmith Charitable Foundation, which is tax-exempt, issued debt last year at 9 percent to help finance a new playground facility in Los Angeles. This year the cost of debt is 25 percent higher; that is, firms that paid 11 percent for debt last year will be paying 13.75 percent this year.

    a. If the Goodsmith Charitable Foundation borrowed money this year, what would the aftertax cost of debt be, based on their cost last year and the 25 percent increase?

    b. If the receipts of the foundation were found to be taxable by the IRS (at a rate of 25 percent because of involvement in political activities), what would the aftertax cost of debt be?

Aftertax cost of debt
(LO11-3)

8. Royal Jewelers Inc. has an aftertax cost of debt of 7 percent. With a tax rate of 25 percent, what can you assume the yield on the debt is?

Yield to maturity
and cost of debt
(LO11-3)

9. Airborne Airlines Inc. has a $1,000 par value bond outstanding with 25 years to maturity. The bond carries an annual interest payment of $88 and is currently selling for $950. Airborne is in a 25 percent tax bracket. The firm wishes to know what the aftertax cost of a new bond issue is likely to be. The yield to maturity on the new issue will be the same as the yield to maturity on the old issue because the risk and maturity date will be similar.

    a. Compute the yield to maturity on the old issue and use this as the yield for the new issue.

    b. Make the appropriate tax adjustment to determine the aftertax cost of debt.

Yield to maturity
and cost of debt
(LO11-3)

10. Russell Container Corporation has a $1,000 par value bond outstanding with 30 years to maturity. The bond carries an annual interest payment of $105 and is currently selling for $880 per bond. Russell Corp. is in a 25 percent tax bracket. The firm wishes to know what the aftertax cost of a new bond issue is likely to be. The yield to maturity on the new issue will be the same as the yield to maturity on the old issue because the risk and maturity date will be similar.

    a. Compute the yield to maturity on the old issue and use this as the yield for the new issue.

    b. Make the appropriate tax adjustment to determine the aftertax cost of debt.

Changing rates
and cost of debt
(LO11-3)

11. Terrier Company is in a 40 percent tax bracket and has a bond outstanding that yields 10 percent to maturity.

    a. What is Terrier's aftertax cost of debt?

    b. Assume that the yield on the bond goes down by 1 percentage point, and due to tax reform, the corporate tax rate falls to 25 percent. What is Terrier's new aftertax cost of debt?

    c. Has the aftertax cost of debt gone up or down from part *a* to part *b?* Explain why.

Real-world example
and cost of debt
(LO11-3)

12. KeySpan Corp. is planning to issue debt that will mature in 2035. In many respects, the issue is similar to currently outstanding debt of the corporation.

    a. Using Table 11-3, identify the yield to maturity on similarly outstanding debt for the firm in terms of maturity.

    b. Assume that because the new debt will be issued at par, the required yield to maturity will be 0.15 percent higher than the value determined in part *a.* Add this factor to the answer in *a.* (New issues sold at par sometimes require a slightly higher yield than older seasoned issues because there are fewer tax advantages and more financial leverage that increase company risk.)

    c.   If the firm is in a 25 percent tax bracket, what is the aftertax cost of debt?

13. Medco Corporation can sell preferred stock for $90 with an estimated flotation cost of $2. It is anticipated the preferred stock will pay $8 per share in dividends.

    a.   Compute the cost of preferred stock for Medco Corp.

    b.   Do we need to make a tax adjustment for the issuing firm?

Cost of preferred stock
(LO11-3)

14. Wallace Container Company issued $100 par value preferred stock 12 years ago. The stock provided a 9 percent yield at the time of issue. The preferred stock is now selling for $72. What is the current yield or cost of the preferred stock? (Disregard flotation costs.)

Cost of preferred stock
(LO11-3)

15. The treasurer of Riley Coal Co. is asked to compute the cost of fixed income securities for her corporation. Even before making the calculations, she assumes the aftertax cost of debt is at least 3 percent less than that for preferred stock. Based on the following facts, is she correct?

    Debt can be issued at a yield of 11.0 percent, and the corporate tax rate is 21 percent. Preferred stock will be priced at $60 and pay a dividend of $6.40. The flotation cost on the preferred stock is $6.

Comparison of the costs of debt and preferred stock
(LO11-3)

16. Murray Motor Company wants you to calculate its cost of common stock. During the next 12 months, the company expects to pay dividends (D_1) of $2.50 per share, and the current price of its common stock is $50 per share. The expected growth rate is 8 percent.

    a.   Compute the cost of retained earnings (K_e). Use Formula 11-5.

    b.   If a $3 flotation cost is involved, compute the cost of new common stock (K_n). Use Formula 11-6.

Costs of retained earnings and new common stock
(LO11-3)

17. Compute K_e and K_n under the following circumstances:

    a. $D_1 = \$5.00$, $P_0 = \$70$, $g = 8\%$, $F = \$7.00$.

    b. $D_1 = \$0.22$, $P_0 = \$28$, $g = 7\%$, $F = \$2.50$.

    c. E_1 (earnings at the end of period 1) $= \$7$, payout ratio equals 40 percent, $P_0 = \$30$, $g = 6.0\%$, $F = \$2.20$.

    d. D_0 (dividend at the beginning of the first period) $= \$6$, growth rate for dividends and earnings (g) $= 7\%$, $P_0 = \$60$, $F = \$3$.

Costs of retained earnings and new common stock
(LO11-3)

Intermediate Problems

18. Business has been good for Keystone Control Systems, as indicated by the four-year growth in earnings per share. The earnings have grown from $1.00 to $1.63.

    a.   Determine the compound annual rate of growth in earnings ($n = 4$).

    b.   Based on the growth rate determined in part *a*, project earnings for next year (E_1). Round to two places to the right of the decimal point.

    c.   Assume the dividend payout ratio is 40 percent. Compute D_1. Round to two places to the right of the decimal point.

    d.   The current price of the stock is $50. Using the growth rate (g) from part *a* and (D_1) from part *c*, compute K_e.

    e.   If the flotation cost is $3.75, compute the cost of new common stock (K_n).

Ⓧ

Growth rates and common stock valuation
(LO11-3)

X

Weighted average
cost of capital
(LO11-1)

19. Global Technology's capital structure is as follows:

Debt	35%
Preferred stock	15
Common equity	50

The aftertax cost of debt is 6.5 percent; the cost of preferred stock is 10 percent; and the cost of common equity (in the form of retained earnings) is 13.5 percent. Calculate Global Technology's weighted average cost of capital in a manner similar to Table 11-1.

Weighted average
cost of capital
(LO11-1)

20. Evans Technology has the following capital structure:

Debt	40%
Common equity	60

The aftertax cost of debt is 6 percent, and the cost of common equity (in the form of retained earnings) is 13 percent.

a. What is the firm's weighted average cost of capital?

b. An outside consultant has suggested that because debt is cheaper than equity, the firm should switch to a capital structure that is 50 percent debt and 50 percent equity. Under this new and more debt-oriented arrangement, the aftertax cost of debt is 7 percent, and the cost of common equity (in the form of retained earnings) is 15 percent. Recalculate the firm's weighted average cost of capital.

c. Which plan is optimal in terms of minimizing the weighted average cost of capital?

Weighted average
cost of capital
(LO11-1)

21. Sauer Milk Inc. wants to determine the minimum cost of capital point for the firm. Assume it is considering the following financial plans:

	Cost (aftertax)	Weights
Plan A		
Debt	4.0%	30%
Preferred stock	8.0	15
Common equity	12.0	55
Plan B		
Debt	4.5%	40%
Preferred stock	8.5	15
Common equity	13.0	45
Plan C		
Debt	5.0%	45%
Preferred stock	18.7	15
Common equity	12.8	40
Plan D		
Debt	12.0%	50%
Preferred stock	19.2	15
Common equity	14.5	35

a.   Which of the four plans has the lowest weighted average cost of capital? (Round to two places to the right of the decimal point.)

b.   Briefly discuss the results from Plan C and Plan D, and why one is better than the other.

22.   Given the following information, calculate the weighted average cost of capital for Hamilton Corp. Line up the calculations in the order shown in Table 11-1.

Weighted average cost of capital *(LO11-1)*

Percent of capital structure:

Debt	35%
Preferred stock	20
Common equity	45

Additional information:

Bond coupon rate	11%
Bond yield to maturity	9%
Dividend, expected common	$ 5.00
Dividend, preferred	$ 12.00
Price, common	$ 60.00
Price, preferred	$106.00
Flotation cost, preferred	$ 4.50
Growth rate	6%
Corporate tax rate	25%

23.   Given the following information, calculate the weighted average cost of capital for Digital Processing Inc. Line up the calculations in the order shown in Table 11-1.

Weighted average cost of capital *(LO11-1)*

Percent of capital structure:

Preferred stock	20%
Common equity	40
Debt	40

Additional information:

Corporate tax rate	24%
Dividend, preferred	$ 8.50
Dividend, expected common	$ 2.50
Price, preferred	$105.00
Growth rate	7%
Bond yield	9.5
Flotation cost, preferred	$ 3.60
Price, common	$ 75.00

Advanced Problems

24.   Brook's Window Shields Inc. is trying to calculate its cost of capital for use in a capital budgeting decision. Mr. Glass, the vice president of finance, has given you the following information and has asked you to compute the weighted average cost of capital.

Changes in costs and weighted average cost of capital *(LO11-1)*

The company currently has outstanding a bond with a 12.2 percent coupon rate and another bond with a 9.5 percent coupon rate. The firm has been informed by its investment banker that bonds of equal risk and credit rating are now selling to yield 13.4 percent.

The common stock has a price of $58 and an expected dividend (D_1) of $5.30 per share. The firm's historical growth rate of earnings and dividends per share has been 9.5 percent, but security analysts on Wall Street expect this growth to slow to 7 percent in future years.

The preferred stock is selling at $54 per share and carries a dividend of $6.75 per share. The corporate tax rate is 25 percent. The flotation cost is 2.1 percent of the selling price for preferred stock. The optimum capital structure is 40 percent debt, 25 percent preferred stock, and 35 percent common equity in the form of retained earnings.

Compute the cost of capital for the individual components in the capital structure, and then calculate the weighted average cost of capital (similar to Table 11-1).

Changes in cost and weighted average cost of capital
(LO11-1)

25. A-Rod Manufacturing Company is trying to calculate its cost of capital for use in making a capital budgeting decision. Mr. Jeter, the vice president of finance, has given you the following information and has asked you to compute the weighted average cost of capital.

The company currently has outstanding a bond with a 10.6 percent coupon rate and another bond with an 8.2 percent rate. The firm has been informed by its investment banker that bonds of equal risk and credit rating are now selling to yield 11.5 percent. The common stock has a price of $65 and an expected dividend (D_1) of $1.50 per share. The historical growth pattern (g) for dividends is as follows:

$1.40
1.54
1.69
1.85

Compute the historical growth rate, round it to the nearest whole number, and use it for g.

The preferred stock is selling at $85 per share and pays a dividend of $8.50 per share. The corporate tax rate is 25 percent. The flotation cost is 2.6 percent of the selling price for preferred stock. The optimum capital structure for the firm is 35 percent debt, 5 percent preferred stock, and 60 percent common equity in the form of retained earnings.

Compute the cost of capital for the individual components in the capital structure, and then calculate the weighted average cost of capital (similar to Table 11-1).

Impact of credit ratings on cost of capital
(LO11-3)

26. Northwest Utility Company faces increasing needs for capital. Fortunately, it has an Aa3 credit rating. The corporate tax rate is 25 percent. Northwest's treasurer is trying to determine the corporation's current weighted average cost of capital in order to assess the profitability of capital budgeting projects.

Historically, the corporation's earnings and dividends per share have increased about 8.2 percent annually and this should continue in the future.

Northwest's common stock is selling at $64 per share, and the company will pay a $6.50 per share dividend (D_1).

The company's $96 preferred stock has been yielding 8 percent in the current market. Flotation costs for the company have been estimated by its investment banker to be $6.00 for preferred stock.

The company's optimum capital structure is 55 percent debt, 20 percent preferred stock, and 25 percent common equity in the form of retained earnings. Refer to the following table on bond issues for comparative yields on bonds of equal risk to Northwest:

Data on Bond Issues

Issue	Moody's Rating	Price	Yield to Maturity
Utilities:			
Southwest Electric Power—7¼ 2023	Aa2	$ 895.18	8.74%
Pacific Bell—7⅜ 2025	Aa3	891.25	8.73
Pennsylvania Power & Light—8½ 2022	A2	970.66	8.77
Industrials:			
Johnson & Johnson—6¾ 2023	Aaa	880.24	8.55%
Dillard's Department Stores—7⅛ 2023	A2	960.92	8.22
Marriott Corp.—10 2015	B2	1,035.10	9.77

Compute the answers to the following questions from the information given:

a.   Cost of debt, K_d. (Use the accompanying table—relate to the utility bond credit rating for yield.)

b.   Cost of preferred stock, K_p.

c.   Cost of common equity in the form of retained earnings, K_e.

d.   Weighted average cost of capital.

27.   Delta Corporation has the following capital structure:

Marginal cost of capital (LO11-5)

	Cost (aftertax)	Weights	Weighted Cost
Debt	8.1%	35%	2.84%
Preferred stock (K_p)	9.6	5	0.48
Common equity (K_e) (retained earnings)	10.1	60	6.06
Weighted average cost of capital (K_a)			9.38%

a.   If the firm has $18 million in retained earnings, at what size capital structure will the firm run out of retained earnings?

b.   The 8.1 percent cost of debt referred to earlier applies only to the first $14 million of debt. After that the cost of debt will go up. At what size capital structure will there be a change in the cost of debt?

28.   The Nolan Corporation finds it is necessary to determine its marginal cost of capital. Nolan's current capital structure calls for 50 percent debt, 30 percent preferred stock, and 20 percent common equity. Initially, common equity will be in the form of retained earnings (K_e) and then new common stock (K_n). The costs of the various sources of financing are as follows: debt, 9.6 percent;

Marginal cost of capital (LO11-5)

preferred stock, 9 percent; retained earnings, 10 percent; and new common stock, 11.2 percent.

a. What is the initial weighted average cost of capital? (Include debt, preferred stock, and common equity in the form of retained earnings, K_e.)

b. If the firm has $18 million in retained earnings, at what size capital structure will the firm run out of retained earnings?

c. What will the marginal cost of capital be immediately after that point? (Equity will remain at 20 percent of the capital structure, but will all be in the form of new common stock, K_n.)

d. The 9.6 percent cost of debt previously referred to applies only to the first $29 million of debt. After that, the cost of debt will be 11.2 percent. At what size capital structure will there be a change in the cost of debt?

e. What will the marginal cost of capital be immediately after that point? (Consider the facts in both parts c and d.)

Marginal cost of capital
(LO11-5)

29. The McGee Corporation finds it is necessary to determine its marginal cost of capital. McGee's current capital structure calls for 40 percent debt, 30 percent preferred stock, and 30 percent common equity. Initially, common equity will be in the form of retained earnings (K_e) and then new common stock (K_n). The costs of the various sources of financing are as follows: debt, 9.6 percent; preferred stock, 9.0 percent; retained earnings, 10.0 percent; and new common stock, 11.4 percent.

a. What is the initial weighted average cost of capital? (Include debt, preferred stock, and common equity in the form of retained earnings, K_e.)

b. If the firm has $28.5 million in retained earnings, at what size capital structure will the firm run out of retained earnings?

c. What will the marginal cost of capital be immediately after that point? (Equity will remain at 30 percent of the capital structure, but will all be in the form of new common stock, K_n.)

d. The 9.6 percent cost of debt referred to earlier applies only to the first $30 million of debt. After that, the cost of debt will be 11.2 percent. At what size capital structure will there be a change in the cost of debt?

e. What will the marginal cost of capital be immediately after that point? (Consider the facts in both parts c and d.)

Capital asset pricing model and dividend valuation model
(LO11-3)

30. Eaton Electronic Company's treasurer uses both the capital asset pricing model and the dividend valuation model to compute the cost of common equity (also referred to as the required rate of return for common equity).

Assume the following:

$$R_f = 7\%$$
$$K_m = 10\%$$
$$\beta = 1.6$$
$$D_1 = \$.70$$
$$P_0 = \$19$$
$$g = 8\%$$

a. Compute K_i (required rate of return on common equity based on the capital asset pricing model).

b. Compute K_e (required rate of return on common equity based on the dividend valuation model).

COMPREHENSIVE PROBLEM

Medical Research Corporation is expanding its research and production capacity to introduce a new line of products. Current plans call for the expenditure of $100 million on four projects of equal size ($25 million each), but different returns. Project A is in blood clotting proteins and has an expected return of 18 percent. Project B relates to a hepatitis vaccine and carries a potential return of 14 percent. Project C, dealing with a cardiovascular compound, is expected to earn 11.8 percent, and Project D, an investment in orthopedic implants, is expected to show a 10.9 percent return.

Medical Research Corporation
(Marginal cost of capital and investment returns)
(LO11-5)

The firm has $15 million in retained earnings. After a capital structure with $15 million in retained earnings is reached (in which retained earnings represent 60 percent of the financing), all additional equity financing must come in the form of new common stock.

Common stock is selling for $25 per share and underwriting costs are estimated at $3 if new shares are issued. Dividends for the next year will be $0.90 per share ($D_1$), and earnings and dividends have grown consistently at 11 percent per year.

The yield on comparative bonds has been hovering at 11 percent. The investment banker feels that the first $20 million of bonds could be sold to yield 11 percent while additional debt might require a 2 percent premium and be sold to yield 13 percent. The corporate tax rate is 25 percent. Debt represents 40 percent of the capital structure.

a. Based on the two sources of financing, what is the initial weighted average cost of capital? (Use K_d and K_e.)

b. At what size capital structure will the firm run out of retained earnings?

c. What will the marginal cost of capital be immediately after that point?

d. At what size capital structure will there be a change in the cost of debt?

e. What will the marginal cost of capital be immediately after that point?

f. Based on the information about potential returns on investments in the first paragraph and information on marginal cost of capital (in parts *a, c,* and *e*), how large a capital investment budget should the firm use?

g. Graph the answer determined in part *f*.

COMPREHENSIVE PROBLEM

Masco Oil and Gas Company is a very large company with common stock listed on the New York Stock Exchange and bonds traded over the counter. As of the current balance sheet, it has three bond issues outstanding:

Masco Oil and Gas
(Cost of capital with changing financial needs)
(LO11-1)

$150 million of 10 percent series	2026
$50 million of 7 percent series	2020
$75 million of 5 percent series	2016

The vice president of finance is planning to sell $75 million of bonds next year to replace the debt due to expire in 2016. Present market yields on similar Baa-rated bonds are 12.1 percent. Masco also has $90 million of 7.5 percent noncallable preferred stock outstanding, and it has no intentions of selling any preferred stock at any time in the future. The preferred stock is currently priced at $80 per share, and its dividend per share is $7.80.

The company has had very volatile earnings, but its dividends per share have had a very stable growth rate of 8 percent and this will continue. The expected dividend (D_1) is $1.90 per share, and the common stock is selling for $40 per share. The company's investment banker has quoted the following flotation costs to Masco: $2.50 per share for preferred stock and $2.20 per share for common stock.

On the advice of its investment banker, Masco has kept its debt at 50 percent of assets and its equity at 50 percent. Masco sees no need to sell either common or preferred stock in the foreseeable future as it has generated enough internal funds for its investment needs when these funds are combined with debt financing. Masco's corporate tax rate is 25 percent.

Compute the cost of capital for the following:

a. Bond (debt) (K_d).

b. Preferred stock (K_p).

c. Common equity in the form of retained earnings (K_e).

d. New common stock (K_n).

e. Weighted average cost of capital.

 WEB EXERCISE

1. In Table 11-4, Intel was shown to have a low debt ratio. Let's learn more about this company. Go to its website at www.intel.com, and follow these steps: Scroll down and click on "Investor Relations" at the bottom of the home page. Click on "Financials and Filings." Click on "Trended Financial." Download the most current annual financial statements.

2. Compute the $ change in "Total Assets" over the last two years.

3. Do the same computation for "Stockholders' Equity."

4. Do the same computation for "Long-Term Debt."

5. In a brief paragraph, describe the change in long-term obligations (debt) that has taken place relative to the changes in total assets and stockholders' equity. Does it appear to be good or bad?

Note: Occasionally a topic we have listed may have been deleted, updated, or moved into a different location on a website. If you click on the site map or site index, you will be introduced to a table of contents that should aid you in finding the topic you are looking for.

APPENDIX | 11A

Cost of Capital and the Capital Asset Pricing Model

The Capital Asset Pricing Model

The **capital asset pricing model (CAPM)** relates the risk-return trade-offs of individual assets to market returns. Common stock returns over time have generally been used to test this model since stock prices are widely available and efficiently priced, as are market indexes of stock performance. In theory, the CAPM encompasses all assets, but in practice it is difficult to measure returns on all types of assets or to find an all-encompassing market index. For our purposes, we will use common stock returns to explain the model and occasionally we will generalize about other assets.

The basic form of the CAPM is a linear relationship between returns on individual stocks and stock market returns over time. By using least squares regression analysis, the return on an individual stock, K_j, is expressed in Formula 11A-1:

$$K_j = \alpha + \beta K_m + e \qquad (11A\text{-}1)$$

where

K_j = Return on individual common stock of a company

α = Alpha, the intercept on the y-axis

β = Beta, the coefficient

K_m = Return on the stock market (an index of stock returns is used, usually the Standard & Poor's 500 Index)

e = Error term of the regression equation

As indicated in Table 11A-1 and Figure 11A-1, this equation uses historical data to generate the beta coefficient (β), a measurement of the return performance of a given stock versus the return performance of the market. Assume that we want to calculate a beta for Parts Associates Inc. (PAI), and that we have the performance data for that company and the market shown in Table 11A-1. The relationship between PAI and the market appears graphically in Figure 11A-1.

Table 11A-1 Performance of PAI and the market

Year	Rate of Return on Stock	
	PAI	Market
1	12.0%	10.0%
2	16.0	18.0
3	20.0	16.0
4	16.0	10.0
5	6.0	8.0
Mean return	14.0%	12.4%
Standard deviation	4.73%	3.87%

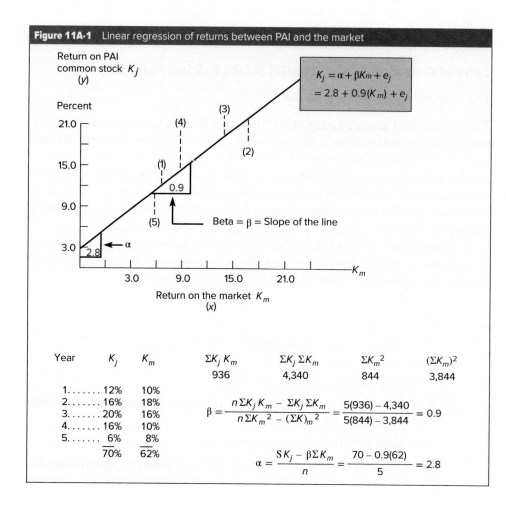

Figure 11A-1 Linear regression of returns between PAI and the market

Return on PAI common stock K_j (y)

$$K_j = \alpha + \beta K_m + e_j$$
$$= 2.8 + 0.9(K_m) + e_j$$

Percent

Beta = β = Slope of the line

α

2.8

Return on the market K_m (x)

Year	K_j	K_m	$\Sigma K_j K_m$	$\Sigma K_j \Sigma K_m$	ΣK_m^2	$(\Sigma K_m)^2$
			936	4,340	844	3,844
1.	12%	10%				
2.	16%	18%				
3.	20%	16%				
4.	16%	10%				
5.	6%	8%				
	70%	62%				

$$\beta = \frac{n\Sigma K_j K_m - \Sigma K_j \Sigma K_m}{n\Sigma K_m^2 - (\Sigma K)_m^2} = \frac{5(936) - 4,340}{5(844) - 3,844} = 0.9$$

$$\alpha = \frac{S K_j - \beta \Sigma K_m}{n} = \frac{70 - 0.9(62)}{5} = 2.8$$

The alpha term in Figure 11A-1 of 2.8 percent is the *y* intercept of the linear regression. It is the expected return on PAI stock if returns on the market are zero. However, if the returns on the market are expected to approximate the historical rate of 11.6 percent, the expected return on PAI would be $K_j = 2.8 + 0.9(11.6) = 13.2$ percent. This maintains the historical relationship. If the returns on the market are expected to rise to 18 percent next year, expected return on PAI would be $K_j = 2.8 + 0.9(18.0) = 19$ percent.

Notice that we are talking in terms of expectations. The CAPM is an expectational (ex ante) model, and there is no guarantee historical data will reoccur. One area of empirical testing involves the stability and predictability of the beta coefficient based on historical data. Research has indicated that betas are more useful in a portfolio context (for groupings of stocks) because the betas of individual stocks are less stable from period to period than portfolio betas. In addition, research indicates betas of individual common stocks have the tendency to approach 1.0 over time.

The Security Market Line   The capital asset pricing model evolved from Formula 11A-1 into a **market risk premium** model where the basic assumption is that for investors to take more risk, they must be compensated by larger expected returns. Investors should also not accept returns that are less than they can get from a riskless asset. For CAPM purposes, it is assumed that short-term U.S. Treasury bills may be considered a riskless asset.[1] When viewed in this context, an investor must achieve an extra return above that obtainable from a Treasury bill in order to induce the assumption of more risk. This brings us to the more common and theoretically useful model:

$$K_j = R_f + \beta(K_m - R_f) \qquad\qquad (11A\text{-}2)$$

where

$R_f =$ Risk-free rate of return

$\beta =$ Beta coefficient from Formula 11A-1

$K_m =$ Return on the market index

$K_m - R_f =$ Premium or excess return of the market versus the risk-free rate (since the market is riskier than R_f, the assumption is that the expected K_m will be greater than R_f)

$\beta(K_m - R_f) =$ Expected return above the risk-free rate for the stock of Company *j*, given the level of risk

The model centers on "beta," the coefficient of the premium demanded by an investor to invest in an individual stock. For each individual security, **beta** measures the sensitivity (volatility) of the security's return to the market. By definition, the market has a beta of 1.0, so that if an individual company's beta is 1.0, it can expect to have returns as volatile as the market and total returns equal to the market. A company with a beta of 2.0 would be twice as volatile as the market and would be expected to generate more returns, whereas a company with a beta of 0.5 would be half as volatile as the market.

The term $(K_m - R_f)$ indicates common stock is expected to generate a rate of return higher than the return on a U.S. Treasury bill. This makes sense since common stock has more risk. Research by Roger Ibbotson shows that this risk premium over the last 83 years is close to 6.5 percent on average but exhibits a wide standard deviation.[2] In the actual application of the CAPM to cost of capital, companies often will use this historical risk premium in their calculations. In our example, we use 6.5 percent to represent the expected $(K_m - R_f)$.

For example, assuming the risk-free rate is 5.5 percent and the market risk premium $(K_m - R_f)$ is 6.5 percent, the following returns would occur with betas of 2.0, 1.0, and 0.5:

$$K_2 = 5.5\% + 2.0(6.5\%) = 5.5\% + 13.0\% = 18.5\%$$
$$K_1 = 5.5\% + 1.0(6.5\%) = 5.5\% + 6.5\% = 12.0\%$$
$$K_{.5} = 5.5\% + 0.5(6.5\%) = 5.5\% + 3.25\% = 8.75\%$$

---

[1] A number of studies have also indicated that longer-term government securities may appropriately represent R_f (the risk-free rate).

[2] Ibbotson Associates, *Stocks, Bonds, Bills and Inflation: 2007 Yearbook* (Chicago: Ibbotson Associates and Capital Market Research Center, 2010).

The beta term measures the riskiness of an investment relative to the market. To outperform the market, one would have to assume more risk by selecting assets with betas greater than 1.0. Another way of looking at the risk-return trade-off would be that if less risk than the market is desired, an investor would choose assets with a beta of less than 1.0. Beta is a good measure of a stock's risk when the stock is combined into a portfolio, and therefore it has some bearing on the assets that a company acquires for its portfolio of real capital.

In Figure 11A-1, individual stock returns were compared to market returns and the beta from Formula 11A-1 was shown. From Formula 11A-2, the risk-premium model, a generalized risk-return graph called the **security market line (SML)** can be constructed that identifies the risk-return trade-off of any common stock (asset) relative to the company's beta. This is shown in Figure 11A-2.

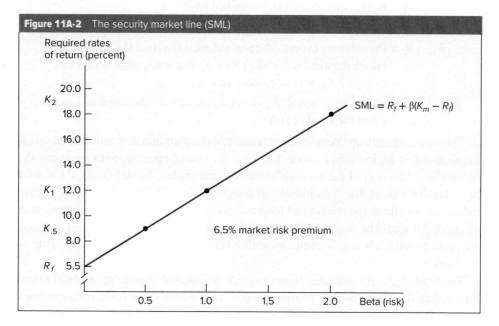

Figure 11A-2   The security market line (SML)

The required return for all securities can be expressed as the risk-free rate plus a premium for risk. Thus we see that a stock with a beta of 1.0 would have a risk premium of 6.5 percent added to the risk-free rate of 5.5 percent to provide a required return of 12 percent. Since a beta of 1.0 implies risk equal to the stock market, the return is also at the overall market rate. If the beta is 2.0, twice the market risk premium of 6.5 percent must be earned, and we add 13 percent to the risk-free rate of 5.5 percent to determine the required return of 18.5 percent. For a beta of 0.5, the required return is 8.75 percent.

Cost of Capital Considerations   When calculating the cost of capital for common stock, remember that K_e is equal to the expected total return from the dividend yield and capital gains.

$$K_e = \frac{D_1}{P_0} + g$$

K_e is the return required by investors based on expectations of future dividends and growth. The SML provides the same information, but in a market-related risk-return model. As required returns rise, prices must fall to adjust to the new equilibrium return level, and as required returns fall, prices rise. Stock markets are generally efficient, and when stock prices are in equilibrium, the K_e derived from the dividend model will be equal to K_j derived from the SML.

The SML helps us to identify several circumstances that can cause the cost of capital to change. Figure 11-2 in Chapter 11 examined required rates of returns over time with changing interest rates and stock prices. Figure 11A-3 does basically the same thing, only through the SML format.

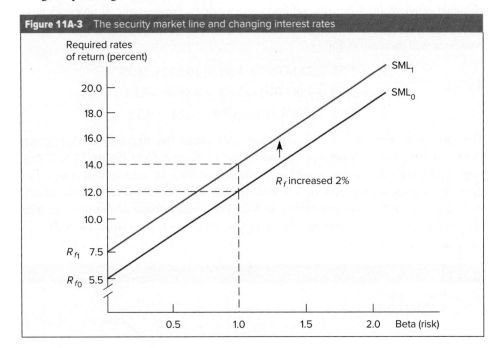

Figure 11A-3   The security market line and changing interest rates

When interest rates increase from the initial period (R_{f1} versus R_{f0}), the security market line in the next period is parallel to SML_0, but higher. What this means is that required rates of return have risen for every level of risk, as investors desire to maintain their risk premium over the risk-free rate.

One very important variable influencing interest rates is the rate of inflation. As inflation increases, lenders try to maintain their real dollar purchasing power, so they increase the required interest rates to offset inflation. The risk-free rate can be thought of as

$$R_f = RR + IP$$

where

RR is the real rate of return on a riskless government security when inflation is zero.

IP is an inflation premium that compensates lenders (investors) for loss of purchasing power.

An upward shift in the SML indicates that the prices of all assets will shift downward as interest rates move up. In Chapter 10, "Valuation and Rates of Return," this was demonstrated in the discussion that showed that when market interest rates went up, bond prices adjusted downward to make up for the lower coupon rate (interest payment) on the old bonds.

Another factor affecting the cost of capital is a change in risk preferences by investors. As investors become more pessimistic about the economy, they require larger premiums for assuming risks. Even though the historical average market risk premium may be close to 6.5 percent, this is not stable and investors' changing attitudes can have a big impact on the market risk premium. For example, the 1987 stock market crash on October 19 (a 22.6 percent decline in one day) had to be somewhat influenced by investors' quick moves to a more risk-averse attitude. This risk aversion shows up in higher required stock returns and lower stock prices. For example, if investors raise their market risk premium to 8 percent, the required rates of return from the original equations will increase as follows:

$$K_2 = 5.5\% + 2.0(8.0\%) = 5.5\% + 16.0\% = 21.5\%$$
$$K_1 = 5.5\% + 1.0(8.0\%) = 5.5\% + 8.0\% = 13.5\%$$
$$K_{.5} = 5.5\% + 0.5(8.0\%) = 5.5\% + 4.0\% = 9.5\%$$

The change in the market risk premium will cause the required market return (beta = 1.00) to be 13.5 percent instead of the 12 percent from Figure 11A-2. Any asset riskier than the market would have a larger increase in the required return. For example, a stock with a beta of 2.0 would need to generate a 21.5 percent return, instead of the 18.5 percent in Figure 11A-2. The overall shape of the new security market line (SML_1) is shown in Figure 11A-4. Note the higher slope for SML_1, in comparison to SML_0.

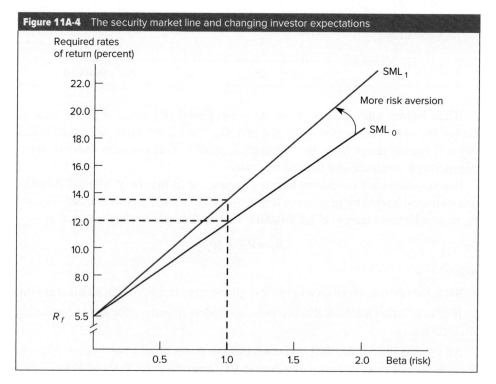

Figure 11A-4   The security market line and changing investor expectations

In many instances rising interest rates and pessimistic investors go hand-in-hand, so the SML may change its slope and intercept at the same time. This combined effect would cause severe drops in the prices of risky assets and much larger required rates of return for such assets.

The capital asset pricing model and the security market line have been presented to further your understanding of market-related events that impact the firm's cost of capital, such as market returns and risk, changing interest rates, and changing risk preferences.

While the capital asset pricing model has received criticism because of the difficulties of dealing with the betas of individual securities and because of the problems involved in consistently constructing the appropriate slope of the SML to represent reality, it provides some interesting insights into risk-return measurement.

	List of Terms
capital asset pricing model (CAPM) 373 **beta** 375	
market risk premium 374 **security market line (SML)** 376	

Discussion Questions

11A–1. How does the capital asset pricing model help explain changing costs of capital? *(LO11-1)*

11A–2. How does the SML react to changes in the rate of interest, changes in the rate of inflation, and changing investor expectations? *(LO11-2)*

Problems

Capital asset pricing model *(LO11-3)*

11A-1. Assume that $R_f = 5$ percent and $K_m = 10.5$ percent. Compute K_j for the following betas, using Formula 11A-2.

   a.   0.6

   b.   1.3

   c.   1.9

Capital asset pricing model *(LO11-3)*

11A-2. Assume that $R_f = 6$ percent and the market risk premium $(K_m - R_f)$ is 7.0 percent. Compute K_j for the following betas, using Formula 11A-2.

   a.   0.6

   b.   1.3

   c.   1.9

12

The Capital Budgeting Decision

LEARNING OBJECTIVES

LO 12-1   A capital budgeting decision represents a long-term investment decision.

LO 12-2   Cash flow rather than earnings is used in the capital budgeting decision.

LO 12-3   The payback method considers the importance of liquidity, but fails to consider the time value of money.

LO 12-4   The net present value and internal rate of return are generally the preferred methods of capital budgeting analysis.

LO 12-5   The discount or cutoff rate is normally the cost of capital.

The decision on capital outlays is among the most significant a firm has to make. A decision to build a new plant or expand into a foreign market may influence the performance of the firm over the next decade. The airline industry has shown a tendency to expand in excess of its needs, while other industries have insufficient capacity. The auto industry has often miscalculated its product mix and has had to shift down from one car size to another at an enormous expense.

The capital budgeting decision involves the planning of expenditures for a project with a life of at least one year, and usually considerably longer. In the public utilities sector, a time horizon of 25 years is not unusual. The capital expenditure decision requires extensive planning to ensure that engineering and marketing information is available, product design is completed, necessary patents are acquired, and the capital markets are tapped for the necessary funds. Throughout this chapter we will use techniques developed under the discussion of the time value of money to equate future cash flows to the present, while using the cost of capital as the basic discount rate.

As the time horizon moves farther into the future, uncertainty becomes a greater hazard. The manager is uncertain about annual costs and inflows, product life, interest rates, economic conditions, and technological change. A good example of the vagueness of the marketplace can be observed in the pocket calculator industry going back to the 1970s. A number of firms tooled up in the early 1970s in the hope of being first to break through the $100 price range for pocket calculators, assuming that penetration of the $100 barrier would bring a larger market share and high profitability. However, technological advancement, price cutting, and the appearance of Texas Instruments in the consumer market drove prices down by 60 to 90 percent and made the $100 pocket calculator a museum piece. Rapid Data Systems, the first entry into the under-$100 market, went into bankruptcy. The same type of change, though less dramatic, can be viewed in the personal computer industry over the last 20 years. IBM and Apple took the early lead in product development and had no difficulty selling their products in the $2,000 to $5,000 range. As Compaq, Dell, and foreign competitors moved into the market, prices dropped by 50 percent and consumer demand for quality went up. Not all new developments are so perilous, and a number of techniques, which will be treated in the next chapter, have been devised to cope with the impact of uncertainty on decision making.

Not only is capital budgeting important to people in finance or accounting, it is essential to people throughout the business organization. For example, a marketing or production manager who is proposing a new product must be familiar with the capital budgeting procedures of the firm. If he or she is not familiar with the concepts presented in this chapter, the best idea in the world may not be approved because it has not been properly evaluated and presented. You must be familiar not only with your product but also with its financial viability.

In this chapter, capital budgeting is studied under the following major topical headings: administrative considerations, accounting flows versus cash flows, methods of ranking investment proposals, selection strategy, capital rationing, combining cash flow analysis and selection strategy, and the replacement decision. Later in the chapter, taxes and their impact on depreciation and capital budgeting decisions are emphasized.

Administrative Considerations

A good capital budgeting program requires that a number of steps be taken in the decision-making process:

1. Search for and discovery of investment opportunities.
2. Collection of data.
3. Evaluation and decision making.
4. Reevaluation and adjustment.

The search for new opportunities is often the least emphasized, though perhaps the most important, of the four steps. The collection of data should go beyond engineering data and market surveys and should attempt to capture the relative likelihood of the occurrence of various events. The probabilities of increases or slumps in product demand may be evaluated from statistical analysis, while other outcomes may be estimated subjectively.

After all data have been collected and evaluated, the final decision must be made. Generally, determinations involving relatively small amounts of money will be made at the department or division level, while major expenditures can be approved only by top management. A constant monitoring of the results of a given decision may indicate that a new set of probabilities must be developed, based on first-year experience, and the initial decision to choose Product A over Product B must be reevaluated and perhaps reversed. The preceding factors are illustrated in Figure 12-1.

Accounting Flows versus Cash Flows

In most capital budgeting decisions the emphasis is on **cash flow**, rather than reported income. Let us consider the logic of using cash flow in the capital budgeting process. Because depreciation does not represent an actual expenditure of funds in arriving at profit, it is added back to profit to determine the amount of cash flow

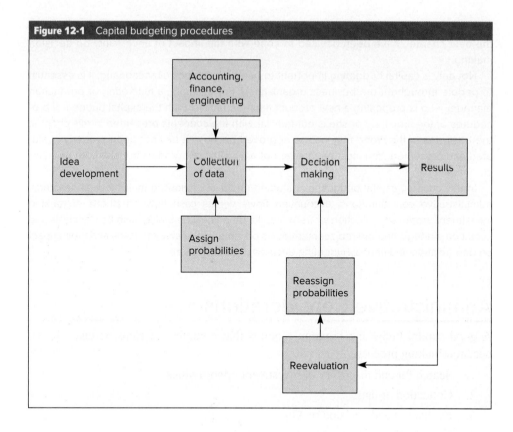

Figure 12-1   Capital budgeting procedures

generated.[1] Assume the Alston Corporation has $50,000 of new equipment to be depreciated at $5,000 per year. The firm has $20,000 in earnings before depreciation and taxes and pays 25 percent in taxes. The information is presented in Table 12-1 to illustrate the key points involved.

The firm shows $11,250 in earnings after taxes, but it adds back the noncash deduction of $5,000 in depreciation to arrive at a cash flow figure of $16,250. The logic of

Table 12-1   Cash flow for Alston Corporation

Earnings before depreciation and taxes (cash inflow)	$20,000
Depreciation (noncash expense)	5,000
Earnings before taxes	$15,000
Taxes (cash outflow)	3,750
Earnings after taxes	$11,250
Depreciation	+5,000
Cash flow	$16,250

---

[1]As explained in Chapter 2, depreciation is not a new source of funds (except in tax savings) but represents a noncash outlay to be added back.

adding back depreciation becomes even greater if we consider the impact of $20,000 in depreciation for the Alston Corp. (Table 12-2). Net earnings before and after taxes are zero, but the company has $20,000 cash in the bank.

Table 12-2 Revised cash flow for Alston Corporation	
Earnings before depreciation and taxes	$20,000
Depreciation	20,000
Earnings before taxes	$ 0
Taxes	0
Earnings after taxes	$ 0
Depreciation	20,000
Cash flow	$20,000

To the capital budgeting specialist, the use of cash flow figures is well accepted. However, top management does not always take a similar viewpoint. Assume you are the president of a firm listed on the New York Stock Exchange and must select between two alternatives. Proposal A will provide zero in aftertax earnings and $100,000 in cash flow, while Proposal B, calling for no depreciation, will provide $50,000 in aftertax earnings and cash flow. As president of a publicly traded firm, you have security analysts constantly penciling in their projections of your earnings for the next quarter, and you fear your stock may drop dramatically if earnings are too low by even a small amount. Although Proposal A is superior, you may be more sensitive to aftertax earnings than to cash flow and you may therefore select Proposal B. Perhaps you are overly concerned about the short-term impact of a decision rather than the long-term economic benefits that might accrue.

You must be sensitive to executives' concessions to short-term pressures. Nevertheless in the material that follows, the emphasis is on the use of proper evaluation techniques to make the best economic choices and ensure long-term wealth maximization.

Methods of Ranking Investment Proposals

In order to choose among competing capital projects, we must understand the methods commonly used to rank investment proposals. Let us consider two projects whose cash flows are presented as follows:

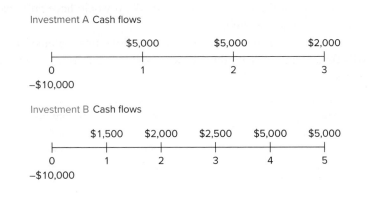

Three widely used methods for evaluating capital expenditures will be considered, along with the shortcomings and advantages of each:

1. Payback method.
2. Internal rate of return.
3. Net present value.

The first method, while not conceptually sound, is often used. Approaches 2 and 3 are more acceptable, and one or the other should be applied to most situations.

Payback Method

Under the **payback** method, we compute the time required to recoup the initial investment. Assume we are called on to select between Investments A and B in Table 12-3. Notice that the values in this table match the preceding timeline.

Table 12-3	Investment alternatives		
		Cash Inflows (of $10,000 investment)	
Year		Investment A	Investment B
1		$5,000	$1,500
2		5,000	2,000
3		2,000	2,500
4			5,000
5			5,000

The payback period for Investment A is 2 years, while Investment B requires 3.8 years. In the latter case, we recover $6,000 in the first 3 years, leaving us with the need for another $4,000 to recoup the full $10,000 investment. Since the fourth year has a total inflow of $5,000, $4,000 represents 0.8 of that value. Thus the payback period for Investment B is 3.8 years.

In using the payback method to select Investment A, we ignore two important considerations. First there is no consideration of inflows after the cutoff period. The $2,000 in year 3 for Investment A in Table 12-3 is ignored, as is the $5,000 in year 5 for Investment B. Even if the $5,000 were $50,000, it would have no impact on the decision under the payback method.

Second, the method fails to consider the concept of the time value of money. If we had two $10,000 investments with the following inflow patterns, the payback method would rank them equally.

Year	Early Returns	Late Returns
1	$9,000	$1,000
2	1,000	9,000
3	1,000	1,000

Although both investments have a payback period of two years, the first alternative is clearly superior because the $9,000 comes in the first year rather than the second.

The payback method does have some features that help to explain its use by U.S. corporations. It is easy to understand, and it emphasizes liquidity. An investment must recoup the initial investment quickly or it will not qualify (most corporations use a maximum time horizon of three to five years). A rapid payback may be particularly important to firms in industries characterized by rapid technological developments.

Nevertheless the payback method, concentrating as it does on only the initial years of investment, fails to discern the optimum or most economic solution to a capital budgeting problem. The analyst is therefore required to consider more theoretically correct methods.

Net Present Value

Net present value (NPV) is often the preferred investment selection method for two important reasons. First, it is a theoretically valid method. Second, it is well understood and used by real-world finance professionals. In other words, not only is NPV a theoretically correct method, it is also often the preferred method in practice. The net present value is the sum of the present values of all outflows and inflows related to a project. The present value of each inflow and outflow is usually discounted using the weighted average cost of capital, K_a, for the firm. Thus inflows that arrive in later years must provide a return that at least equals the cost of the invested capital.

In Table 12-4, we calculate the NPVs for Investments A and B using an assumed cost of capital, or discount rate, of 10 percent.

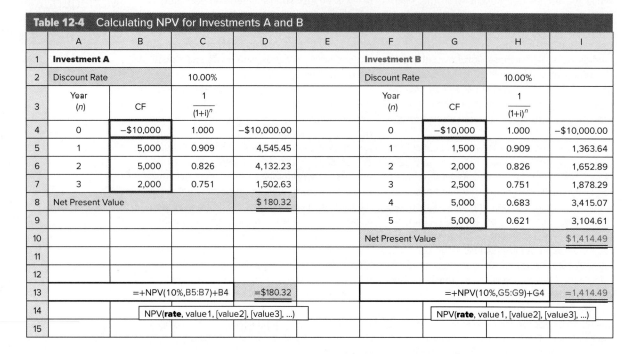

Table 12-4   Calculating NPV for Investments A and B

	A	B	C	D	E	F	G	H	I
1	**Investment A**					**Investment B**			
2	Discount Rate		10.00%			Discount Rate		10.00%	
3	Year (n)	CF	$\frac{1}{(1+i)^n}$			Year (n)	CF	$\frac{1}{(1+i)^n}$	
4	0	−$10,000	1.000	−$10,000.00		0	−$10,000	1.000	−$10,000.00
5	1	5,000	0.909	4,545.45		1	1,500	0.909	1,363.64
6	2	5,000	0.826	4,132.23		2	2,000	0.826	1,652.89
7	3	2,000	0.751	1,502.63		3	2,500	0.751	1,878.29
8	Net Present Value			$ 180.32		4	5,000	0.683	3,415.07
9						5	5,000	0.621	3,104.61
10						Net Present Value			$1,414.49
11									
12									
13		=+NPV(10%,B5:B7)+B4		=$180.32			=+NPV(10%,G5:G9)+G4		=1,414.49
14		NPV(**rate**, value1, [value2], [value3], ...)					NPV(**rate**, value1, [value2], [value3], ...)		
15									

For Investment A, the timing of each cash flow is shown in column A with the amount of each cash flow shown in column B. Together these columns produce a vertical time-line of cash flows. The discount rate of 10 percent is shown in cell C2, and each of the values in cells C4 to C7 is the present value factor needed to convert the values in column B into the present values in column D. The net present value is simply the sum of all the individual present values in column D. The NPV of $180.32 is highlighted in cell D8.

Excel also provides an **NPV** function, which is shown in cell C13. Unfortunately, when the initial cash flow occurs at time zero (as the $10,000 investment outflow does in our example), the **NPV** function does not provide an accurate calculation unless the user conducts a slight manipulation. Excel's **NPV** function behaves badly because it assumes that the first cash flow comes at the end of the first year. To treat the initial outlay properly, we must leave the initial outlay out of the **NPV** function. Then we must subtract the initial outlay separately. Also note that because the initial outlay is entered as a negative number in cell B4, we must actually *add* the outlay to the **NPV** calculation. For Investment A, the cash flows in cells B5 through B7 are entered inside the **NPV** function, and the initial outlay in cell B4 must be added to the **NPV** function value. Unless you look carefully at cell C13, you may overlook this subtle but important point.

The NPV for Investment B is calculated in an identical manner. The cash flow timeline is inserted in columns F and G. Present value factors are computed in column H using the 10 percent discount rate from cell H2, and the present value of each cash flow is shown in column I. The sum of the present values is the NPV of $1,414.49 value highlighted in cell I10. Using the Excel **NPV** function yields the same result in cell H13.

The standard decision rule for NPV analysis is as follows:

> **NPV > 0; Accept** the project because the project increases firm value.
> **NPV < 0; Reject** the project because the project reduces firm value.

While both proposals here are acceptable, Investment B has a considerably higher net present value than Investment A.[2]

Internal Rate of Return

The **internal rate of return (IRR)** is another important metric used to make capital budgeting decisions. While NPV measures the attractiveness of a project in dollar (i.e., currency) terms, the IRR measures the profitability of investments as a return percentage—much like finding the interest rate (i) in a time value of money problem. The key to fully understanding the meaning of the internal rate of return is to understand how IRR relates to NPV: The internal rate of return on an investment or project is the "rate of return" that makes the net present value of the project equal to zero.

> The IRR is the interest rate (i) that makes NPV = 0.

Let us return to our analysis of Investment A and Investment B. At the top of Table 12-5, the cash flows for Investment A are set up exactly as before when we calculated the NPV of the investment. However, you will notice that instead of using a discount rate of 10 percent, the discount rate is 11.16 percent. This is the discount rate that forces the NPV value shown in cell D8 to be exactly zero! Because the NPV is zero when the discount rate is 11.16 percent, we have found the IRR. The internal rate of return is 11.16 percent.

An inquisitive student like you may not be satisfied with simply understanding this definition of the IRR (the rate that makes NPV = 0). Instead, you would probably like to know *how* the IRR was found. Unfortunately, there is usually no simple equation to find the IRR. However, once again we can make use of the Goal Seek function that was introduced in Chapter 10. Recall that Goal Seek was used in Chapter 10 to find the yield to maturity of a bond (YTM). In fact, the concept behind IRR is almost identical to the YTM concept.

> YTM equates the present value of inflows (bond payments) to an outflow (the bond's cost).
>
> IRR equates the present value of inflows (project returns) to an outflow (the project's cost).

Excel's Goal Seek feature doesn't use an equation. It operates by using an iterative method to find a solution. Specifically, it tries an initial input value to see whether that

---

[2]A further possible refinement under the net present value method is to compute a profitability index.

$$\text{Profitability index} = \frac{\text{Present value of the inflows}}{\text{Present value of the outflows}} = \frac{\text{NPV} + \text{PV of outflows}}{\text{PV of outflows}}$$

For Investment A the profitability index is 1.0180 ($10,180/$10,000), and for Investment B it is 1.1414 ($11,414/$10,000). The profitability index can be helpful in comparing returns from different-size investments by placing them on a common measuring standard. This was not necessary in this example.

FINANCIAL CALCULATOR

IRR (Uneven Inflows)

Function

CF

2nd

CLR WORK

Value	*Function*
−10000	ENTER
	↓
5000	ENTER
	↓ ↓
5000	ENTER
	↓ ↓
2000	ENTER

Function	*Solution*
IRR	
CPT	11.1635

Table 12-5   Calculating IRR for Investments A and B

	A	B	C	D	E	F	G
1	**Investment A**						
2	IRR		11.16%				
3	Year (n)	CF	$\dfrac{1}{(1+IRR)^n}$				
4	0	−$10,000	1.000	−$10,000.00			
5	1	5,000	0.900	4,497.88			
6	2	5,000	0.809	4,046.18			
7	3	2,000	0.728	1,455.94			
8	Net Present Value			$0.00			
9							
10		=+IRR(B4:B7)		=11.16%			
11			IRR (values, [guess])				
12							
13	**Investment B**						
14	IRR		14.33%				
15	Year (n)	CF	$\dfrac{1}{(1+IRR)^n}$				
16	0	−$10,000	1.000	−$10,000.00			
17	1	1,500	0.875	1,311.96			
18	2	2,000	0.765	1,529.99			
19	3	2,500	0.669	1,672.73			
20	4	5,000	0.585	2,926.07			
21	5	5,000	0.512	2,559.25			
22	Net Present Value			$0.00			
23							
24		=+IRR(B16:B21)		=14.33%			
25			IRR (values, [guess])				
26							

Goal Seek   ?   ✕

Set cell: D8

To value: 0

By changing cell: C2

OK   Cancel

FINANCIAL CALCULATOR

IRR (Uneven Inflows)

Function
CF
2nd
CLR WORK

Value	*Function*
−10000	ENTER
	↓
1500	ENTER
	↓ ↓
2000	ENTER
	↓ ↓
2500	ENTER
	↓ ↓
5000	ENTER
	↓ ↓
5000	ENTER
Function	*Solution*
IRR	
CPT	14.3329

value produces the result you want. If it doesn't, Goal Seek tries other input values until it converges on a solution.

Returning to Table 12-5, you will notice that the inputs in the Goal Seek dialog box tell Excel to set the NPV value in cell D8 to the value 0 by changing the cell C2. When Excel finds the solution that satisfies the requirement, it has found the IRR. This value is 11.16 percent.

The IRR can also be calculated using Excel's **IRR** function. See cell C10 for the proper syntax. Fortunately, the **IRR** function is more straightforward than the **NPV** function. Unlike the **NPV** function, the **IRR** function treats the first value entered as occurring at the beginning of the first period. Therefore, the **IRR** function only requires us to enter the range of values from B4 to B7. You will see that the IRR calculated using the **IRR** function is 11.16 percent, the same as that found using Goal Seek. The calculator keystrokes are shown in the margin.

The IRR can be found for Investment B in an identical manner. The IRR for Investment B is 14.33 percent because this is the value that produces NPV = 0. The IRR is shown in cell C14 using Goal Seek, and the identical value is shown in cell D24 using the **IRR** function.

Now that we have determined the IRR of each investment, we will need to assess whether these returns are high enough to justify investing in the firm. The final selection of any project under the internal rate of return method will depend on whether the yield exceeds some minimum threshold, such as the firm's cost of capital. You will recall that we assumed that the firm has a 10 percent weighted average cost of capital (WACC) in the preceding NPV analysis. Given this threshold, both projects are expected to produce returns in excess of the WACC.

Under most circumstances, both the net present value and the internal rate of return methods give theoretically correct answers. Payback is simple, and it *may* produce useful insights, but it is not theoretically sound. Payback's usefulness depends on rules of thumb that differ from firm to firm, and it has serious shortcomings when applied to complicated cash flow patterns. Therefore, subsequent discussion will be restricted to further examination of the NPV and the IRR methods. A summary of the various conclusions reached under the three methods is presented in Table 12-6.

Table 12-6 Capital budgeting results			
	Investment A	**Investment B**	**Selection**
Payback method	2 years	3.8 years	Quicker payback: Investment A
Net present value	$180	$1,414	Higher net present value: Investment B
Internal rate of return	11.17%	14.33%	Higher yield: Investment B

Selection Strategy

In both the internal rate of return and net present value methods, the profitability must equal or exceed the cost of capital for the project to be potentially acceptable. However, other distinctions are necessary—namely, *whether the projects are mutually exclusive or not.* If investments are **mutually exclusive**, the selection of one alternative will preclude the selection of any other alternative. Assume we are going to build a specialized assembly plant, and four major international cities are under consideration, only one of which will be picked. In this situation, we select the alternative with the highest acceptable yield or the highest net present value and disregard all others. Even if certain other locations provide a marginal return in excess of the cost of capital, assumed to be 10 percent, they will be rejected. In the table below, the possible alternatives are presented.

Mutually Exclusive Alternatives	**IRR**	**Net Present Value**
Bangkok	15%	$300
Beijing	12	200
Mexico City	11	100
Cost of capital	*10*	—
Singapore	9	(100)

Among the mutually exclusive alternatives, only Bangkok would be selected. If the alternatives were not mutually exclusive (for example, much-needed multiple retail outlets), we would accept all of the alternatives that provide a return in excess of our cost of capital, and only Singapore would be rejected.

Applying this logic to Investments A and B in the prior discussion and assuming a cost of capital of 10 percent, only Investment B would be accepted if the alternatives were mutually exclusive, while both would clearly qualify if they were not mutually exclusive.

	Investment A	Investment B	Accepted If Mutually Exclusive	Accepted If Not Mutually Exclusive
Internal rate of return	11.17%	14.33%	B	A, B
Net present value	$180	$1,414	B	A, B

The discussion to this point has assumed the internal rate of return and net present value methods will call for the same decision. Although this is generally true, there are exceptions. Two rules may be stated:

1. Both methods will accept or reject the same investments based on minimum return or cost of capital criteria. If an investment has a positive net present value, it will also have an internal rate of return in excess of the cost of capital.

2. In certain limited cases, however, the two methods may give different answers in selecting the best investment from a range of acceptable alternatives.

Reinvestment Assumption

It is only under this second state of events that a preference for one method over the other must be established. A prime characteristic of the internal rate of return is the **reinvestment assumption** that all inflows can be reinvested at the yield from a given investment. For example, in the case of the aforementioned Investment A yielding 11.17 percent, the assumption is made that the dollar amounts coming in each year can be reinvested at that rate. For Investment B, with a 14.33 percent internal rate of return, the new funds are assumed to be reinvested at this high rate. The relationships are presented in Table 12-7.

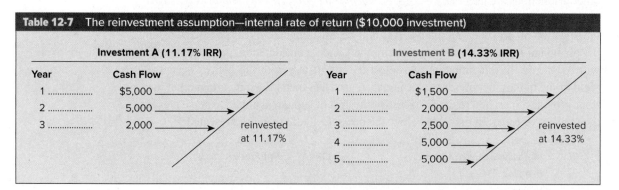

Table 12-7   The reinvestment assumption—internal rate of return ($10,000 investment)

Investment A (11.17% IRR)		Investment B (14.33% IRR)	
Year	Cash Flow	Year	Cash Flow
1	$5,000	1	$1,500
2	5,000	2	2,000
3	2,000 reinvested at 11.17%	3	2,500 reinvested at 14.33%
		4	5,000
		5	5,000

For investments with a very high IRR, it may be unrealistic to assume that reinvestment can occur at an equally high rate. The net present value method, depicted in Table 12-8, makes the more conservative assumption that each inflow can be reinvested at the cost of capital or discount rate.

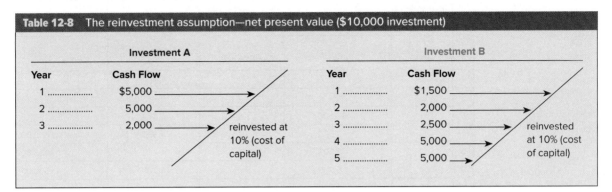

Table 12-8 The reinvestment assumption—net present value ($10,000 investment)

	Investment A			Investment B	
Year	**Cash Flow**		**Year**	**Cash Flow**	
1	$5,000		1	$1,500	
2	5,000		2	2,000	
3	2,000	reinvested at 10% (cost of capital)	3	2,500	reinvested at 10% (cost of capital)
			4	5,000	
			5	5,000	

The reinvestment assumption under the net present value method allows for a certain consistency. Inflows from each project are assumed to have the same (though conservative) investment opportunity. Although this may not be an accurate picture for all firms, net present value is generally the preferred method.

Modified Internal Rate of Return You should also be aware of an alternative methodology that combines the reinvestment assumption of the net present value method (cost of capital) with the internal rate of return. This process is termed the **modified internal rate of return (MIRR)**. The analyst searches for the discount rate that will equate the future value of the inflows, each growing at the cost of capital, with the investment. Here is the formula:

$$\text{Investment} = \frac{\text{FV of inflows}}{(1 + \text{MIRR})^n} \qquad (12\text{-}1)$$

As can be seen in this equation, the MIRR is the discount rate that equates the future value of inflows with the value of the original investment. As an example, we will return to the cash flow stream from our NPV valuation of Investment B. Notice in the MIRR spreadsheet shown in Table 12-9 that for each of the cash inflows, we have calculated a future value in column E. As an example, in line 6 we calculate the future value of the $1,500 inflow by assuming it is reinvested for four years at the 10 percent cost of capital. Specifically, $1,500 \times 1.464 = \$2,196.15$, the value in cell E6. The sum of these future values ($18,383.15) in cell E11 represents the numerator in Formula 12-1.

Since we now know both the future value of the cash inflows and the present value of the outflows (the investment), we can use Excel's **RATE** function to find the MIRR. Being careful to enter a zero for the **pmt** argument in the **RATE** function, we find that the MIRR is 12.95 percent.

Excel also offers an **MIRR** function that produces the same result, shown at the bottom of Table 12-9. The list of value arguments in the **MIRR** function are the same as those used in Excel's **IRR** function, but a finance rate and reinvestment rate must be entered also. In most instances, including our example, these rates are the same.

Recall that the conventional internal rate of return for Investment B was 14.33 percent. The modified internal rate of return, using the more realistic assumption of reinvestment

	A	B	C	D	E
	Table 12-9 Calculating MIRR for Investment B				
	A	B	C	D	E
1	**Investment B**				
2	Reinvestment Rate (*i*)			10.00%	
3	Year	CF	Periods of Growth (*n*)	$(1+i)^n$	Future Value
4	0	−$10,000			
5					
6	1	$1,500	4	1.464	$2,196.15
7	2	2,000	3	1.331	2662.00
8	3	2,500	2	1.210	3025.00
9	4	5,000	1	1.100	5500.00
10	5	5,000	0	1.000	5,000.00
11				(FV of inflows)	$18,383.15
12					
13	Investment (PV of outflows)				−$10,000
14	MIRR (using RATE function)		=+RATE(A10,0,E13,E11)		=12.95%
15				RATE(nper, pmt, pv, [fv], [type], [guess])	
16					
17	Year	CF			
18	0	−$10,000			
19	1	1,500			
20	2	2,000			
21	3	2,500			
22	4	5,000	Reinvestment Rate		
23	5	5,000	10.00%		
24					
25		=+MIRR(B18:B23,C23,C23)		=12.95%	
26		MIRR(values, finance_rate, reinvest_rate)			

at the cost of capital, gives a more conservative, and more theoretically correct, answer. For that reason you should be familiar with it. However, both NPV and IRR are used more often by financial analysts than is the MIRR. Therefore, we will end our discussion of MIRR here and continue the analyses in this chapter using IRR where an internal return measure is needed. The MIRR indicates that when you have an IRR higher than the cost of capital, the MIRR will be smaller than the IRR. In the case of Investment A, the difference between the 11.17 percent IRR and the 10 percent cost of capital is small, and while the MIRR would fall below the cost of capital, it would not decline as much as Investment B.

Capital Rationing

At times management may place an artificial constraint on the amount of funds that can be invested in a given period. This is known as **capital rationing**. The executive planning committee may emerge from a lengthy capital budgeting session to announce that only $5 million may be spent on new capital projects this year. Although $5 million may represent a large sum, it is still an artificially determined constraint and not the product of marginal analysis, in which the return for each proposal is related to the cost of capital for the firm, and projects with positive net present values are accepted.

A firm may adopt a posture of capital rationing because it is fearful of too much growth or hesitant to use external sources of financing (perhaps there is a fear of debt). In a strictly economic sense, capital rationing hinders a firm from achieving maximum profitability. With capital rationing, as indicated in Table 12-10, acceptable projects must be ranked, and only those with the highest positive net present value are accepted.

Table 12-10 Capital rationing				
	Project	**Investment**	**Total Investment**	**Net Present Value**
Capital rationing solution	A	$2,000,000		$400,000
	B	2,000,000		380,000
	C	1,000,000	$5,000,000	150,000
	D	1,000,000		100,000
Best solution	E	800,000		40,000
	F	800,000		(30,000)

Under capital rationing, only Projects A through C, calling for $5 million in investment, will be accepted. Although Projects D and E have returns exceeding the cost of funds, as evidenced by a positive net present value, they will not be accepted with the capital rationing assumption.

Net Present Value Profile

An interesting way to summarize the characteristics of an investment is through the use of the **net present value profile**. The profile allows us to graphically portray the net present value of a project at different discount rates. Let's apply the profile to the investments we discussed earlier in the chapter. The projects are summarized again here:

	Cash Inflows (of $10,000 investment)	
Year	**Investment A**	**Investment B**
1	$5,000	$1,500
2	5,000	2,000
3	2,000	2,500
4		5,000
5		5,000

To apply the net present value profile, you need to know three characteristics about an investment:

1. *The net present value at a zero discount rate.* That is easy to determine. A zero discount rate means no discount rate. The values simply retain their original

value. For Investment A, the net present value would be $2,000 ($5,000 + $5,000 + $2,000 − $10,000). For Investment B, the answer is $6,000 ($1,500 + $2,000 + $2,500 + $5,000 + $5,000 − $10,000).

2. *The net present value as determined by a normal discount rate* (such as the cost of capital). For these two investments, we use a discount rate of 10 percent. As previously summarized in Table 12-6, the net present values for the two investments at that discount rate are $180 for Investment A and $1,414 for Investment B.

3. *The internal rate of return for the investments.* Once again referring to Table 12-6, we see the internal rate of return is 11.17 percent for Investment A and 14.33 percent for Investment B. The reader should also realize the internal rate of return is the discount rate that allows the project to have a net present value of zero. This characteristic will become more apparent when we discuss our graphic display.

We summarize the information about discount rates and net present values for each investment here:

Investment A		Investment B	
Discount Rate	**Net Present Value**	**Discount Rate**	**Net Present Value**
0	$2,000	0	$6,000
10%	180	10%	1,414
11.17% (IRR)	0	14.33% (IRR)	0

Note that in Figure 12-2, we have graphed the three points for each investment. For Investment A we showed a $2,000 net present value at a zero discount rate, a $180 net present value at a 10 percent discount rate, and a zero net present value at an 11.17 percent discount rate. We then connected the points. The same procedure was applied to Investment B. The reader can also visually approximate what the net present value for the investment projects would be at other discount rates (such as 5 percent).

In the current example, the net present value of Investment B was superior to Investment A at every point. This is not always the case in comparing various projects. To illustrate, let's introduce a new project, Investment C, and then compare it with Investment B.

Investment C ($10,000 Investment)	
Year	**Cash Inflows**
1	$9,000
2	3,000
3	1,200

Characteristics of Investment C

1. The net present value at a zero discount rate for this project is $3,200 ($9,000 + $3,000 + $1,200 − $10,000).
2. The net present value at a 10 percent discount rate is $1,560.
3. The internal rate of return is 22.51 percent.

Figure 12-2   Net present value profile

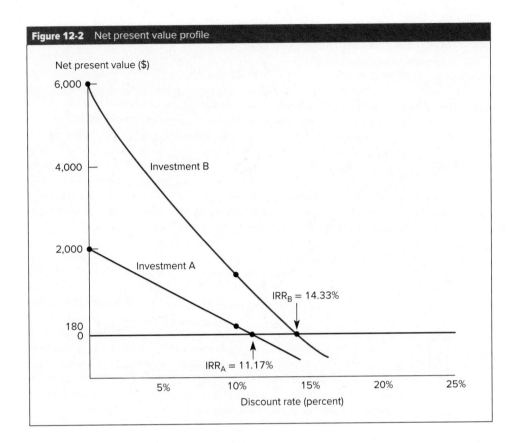

Comparing Investment B to Investment C in Figure 12-3, we observe that at low discount rates, Investment B has a higher net present value than Investment C. However, at high discount rates, Investment C has a higher net present value than Investment B. The actual crossover point can be viewed as approximately 8.7 percent. At lower rates (below 8.7 percent), you would choose Investment B. At higher rates (above 8.7 percent), you would select Investment C. Since the cost of capital is presumed to be 10 percent, you would probably prefer Investment C.

Why does Investment B do well compared to Investment C at low discount rates and relatively poorly compared to Investment C at high discount rates? This difference is related to the timing of inflows. Let's examine the inflows as reproduced in the following table.

Year	Cash Inflows (of $10,000 investment)	
	Investment B	**Investment C**
1	$1,500	$9,000
2	2,000	3,000
3	2,500	1,200
4	5,000	
5	5,000	

Investment B has heavy late inflows ($5,000 in both the fourth and fifth years), and these are more strongly penalized by high discount rates. Investment C has extremely high early inflows, and these hold up well with high discount rates.

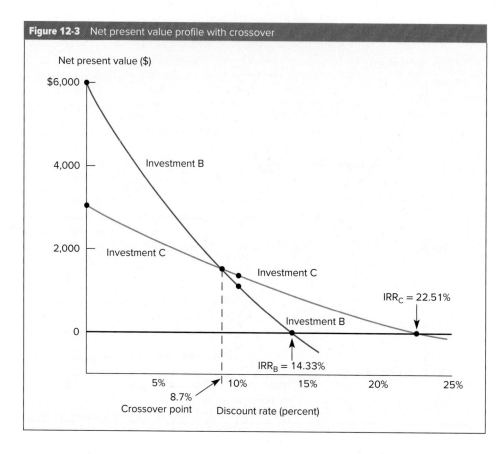

Figure 12-3   Net present value profile with crossover

As previously mentioned in the chapter, if the investments are nonmutually exclusive or there is no capital rationing, we would probably accept both Investments B and C at discount rates below 14.33 percent because they both would have positive net present values. If we can select only one, the decision may well turn on the discount rate. Observe in Figure 12-3 at a discount rate of 5 percent we would select Investment B, at 10 percent we would select Investment C, and so on. The net present value profile helps us make such decisions. Now back to basic capital budgeting issues.

Combining Cash Flow Analysis and Selection Strategy

Many of the points we have covered thus far will be reviewed in the context of a capital budgeting decision, in which we determine the annual cash flows from an investment and compare them to the initial outlay. To be able to analyze a wide variety of cash flow patterns, we shall first consider the types of allowable depreciation.

The Rules of Depreciation

Tax law changes in 2017 have complicated how depreciation is calculated for tax purposes. Congress wants businesses to invest more in long-lived assets, so it temporarily allows companies to take 100 percent bonus depreciation in the first year that an asset is placed in service. This bonus will phase out, beginning in 2023, and it is set to expire by 2027.

While bonus depreciation is temporarily in place, the **modified accelerated cost recovery system**, often referred to as **MACRS**, also remains in place. MACRS is expected to remain applicable even after the current bonus depreciation program sunsets, and we will use the MACRS rules to continue our discussion of depreciation and cash flows.

Under MACRS, assets are classified according to nine categories that determine the allowable rate of depreciation write-off. MACRS categories reference an older system called **ADR**, which stands for **asset depreciation range**, or the expected physical life of the asset or class of assets. MACRS categories generally have shorter lives than the midpoint of the matched ADR ranges that MACRS categories are built upon— meaning MACRS is designed for faster depreciation. Table 12-11 shows the various categories for depreciation, linking the depreciation write-off period to the midpoint of the ADR.

It is not necessary that you become an expert in determining the category of an asset. In problems at the end of this material you will be given enough information to easily make a determination.

Each of the nine categories in Table 12-11 has its own rate of depreciation that can be applied to the purchase price of the asset. We will direct our attention to the first six categories in the table, which apply to assets normally used in business transactions. The last three categories relate to real estate investments and, for purposes of simplicity, will not be covered.

Table 12-11 Categories for depreciation write-off	
Class	
3-year MACRS	All property with ADR midpoints of 4 years or less. Autos and light trucks are excluded from this category.
5-year MACRS	Property with ADR midpoints of more than 4, but less than 10 years. Key assets in this category include automobiles, light trucks, and technological equipment such as computers and research-related properties.
7-year MACRS	Property with ADR midpoints of 10 years or more, but less than 16 years. Most types of manufacturing equipment would fall into this category, as would office furniture and fixtures.
10-year MACRS	Property with ADR midpoints of 16 years or more, but less than 20 years. Petroleum refining products, railroad tank cars, and manufactured homes fall into this group.
15-year MACRS	Property with ADR midpoints of 20 years or more, but less than 25 years. Land improvement, pipeline distribution, telephone distribution, and sewage treatment plants all belong in this category.
20-year MACRS	Property with ADR midpoints of 25 years or more (with the exception of real estate, which is treated separately). Key investments in this category include electric and gas utility property and sewer pipes.
27.5-year MACRS	Residential rental property if 80 percent or more of the gross rental income is from nontransient dwelling units (e.g., an apartment building); low-income housing.
31.5-year MACRS	Nonresidential real property that has no ADR class life or whose class life is 27.5 years or more.
39-year MACRS	Nonresidential real property placed in service after May 12, 1993.

The rates of depreciation that apply to the first six classes in Table 12-11 are shown in Table 12-12. The rates shown in Table 12-12 are developed with the use of the half-year convention, which treats all property as if it were put in service in midyear. The half-year convention is also extended to the sale or retirement of an asset. Thus for three-year MACRS depreciation, there are four years of depreciation to be taken, as demonstrated below:

Year 1	½ year
Year 2	1 year
Year 3	1 year
Year 4	½ year
	3-year MACRS depreciation

For five-year depreciation, there are six years to be taken, and so on.

Table 12-12   Depreciation percentages (expressed in decimals)

Depreciation Year	3-Year MACRS	5-Year MACRS	7-Year MACRS	10-Year MACRS	15-Year MACRS	20-Year MACRS
1	0.333	0.200	0.143	0.100	0.050	0.038
2	0.445	0.320	0.245	0.180	0.095	0.072
3	0.148	0.192	0.175	0.144	0.086	0.067
4	0.074	0.115	0.125	0.115	0.077	0.062
5		0.115	0.089	0.092	0.069	0.057
6		0.058	0.089	0.074	0.062	0.053
7			0.089	0.066	0.059	0.045
8			0.045	0.066	0.059	0.045
9				0.065	0.059	0.045
10				0.065	0.059	0.045
11				0.033	0.059	0.045
12					0.059	0.045
13					0.059	0.045
14					0.059	0.045
15					0.059	0.045
16					0.030	0.045
17						0.045
18						0.045
19						0.045
20						0.045
21						0.017
	1.000	1.000	1.000	1.000	1.000	1.000

Let's return to Table 12-12 and assume you purchase a $50,000 asset that falls in the five-year MACRS category. How much would your depreciation be for the next six years? (Don't forget that we get an extra year because of the half-year convention.) The depreciation schedule is shown in Table 12-13.

	Table 12-13 Depreciation schedule		
(1)	**(2)**	**(3)**	**(4)**
Year	Depreciation Base	Percentage Depreciation (Table 12-12)	Annual Depreciation
1	$50,000	0.200	$10,000
2	50,000	0.320	16,000
3	50,000	0.192	9,600
4	50,000	0.115	5,750
5	50,000	0.115	5,750
6	50,000	0.058	2,900
		Total depreciation:	$50,000

The Tax Rate

In analyzing investment decisions, a corporate tax rate must be considered. Tax rates have changed five times since 1980, and they are almost certain to be changed again in the future. The Tax Cuts and Jobs Act of 2017 dramatically cut corporate tax rates. Prior to the law, the tax rate was graduated with a top rate of 35 percent. The new law imposed a flat 21 percent rate on corporate profits. In addition to federal taxes, most U.S. states impose corporate income taxes ranging from 3 percent to 12 percent.[3] Large corporations with foreign tax obligations may pay higher or lower effective rates. In the following examples, we shall use a combined federal and state tax rate of 25 percent, but remember, the rate varies from situation to situation and from time period to time period. In the problems at the back of the chapter, you will be given a variety of tax rates with which to work.

Actual Investment Decision

Assume in the $50,000 depreciation analysis shown in Table 12-13 that we are given additional facts and asked to make an investment decision about whether an asset should be purchased or not. We shall assume we are purchasing a piece of machinery that will have a six-year productive life. It will produce income of $18,500 for the first three years before deductions for depreciation and taxes. In the last three years, the income before depreciation and taxes will be $12,000. Furthermore, we will assume a corporate tax rate of 25 percent and a cost of capital of 10 percent for the analysis. The annual cash flow related to the machinery is presented in Table 12-14. For each year we subtract depreciation from "earnings before depreciation and taxes" to arrive at earnings before taxes. We then subtract the taxes to determine earnings after taxes. Finally, depreciation is added to earnings after taxes to arrive at cash flow. The cash flow starts at $16,375 in the first year and ends at $9,725 in the last year.

---

[3]Four states have no income tax; instead, they tax gross receipts. Only South Dakota and Wyoming have neither a corporate income nor a gross receipts tax.

Table 12-14 Cash flow related to the purchase of machinery

	Year 1	Year 2	Year 3	Year 4	Year 5	Year 6
Earnings before depreciation and taxes (EBDT)	$18,500	$18,500	$18,500	$12,000	$12,000	$12,000
Depreciation (from Table 12-13)	10,000	16,000	9,600	5,750	5,750	2,900
Earnings before taxes	8,500	2,500	8,900	6,250	6,250	9,100
Taxes (25%)	2,125	625	2,225	1,563	1,563	2,275
Earnings after taxes	6,375	1,875	6,675	4,687	4,687	6,825
+ Depreciation	10,000	16,000	9,600	5,750	5,750	2,900
Cash flow	$16,375	$17,875	$16,275	$10,437	$10,437	$ 9,725

Having determined the annual cash flows, we now are in a position to discount the values back to the present at the previously specified cost of capital, 10 percent. The analysis is presented in Table 12-15. At the bottom of the same table, the present value of the inflows is compared to the present value of the outflows (simply the cost of the asset) to arrive at a net present value of $10,986. On the basis of the analysis, it appears that the asset should be purchased.

Table 12-15 Net present value

Year	Cash Flow (inflows)	Present Value Factor (10%)	Present Value
1	$16,375	0.909	$14,886
2	17,875	0.826	14,773
3	16,275	0.751	12,228
4	10,437	0.683	7,129
5	10,437	0.621	6,481
6	9,725	0.564	5,490
			$60,986
Present value of inflows..			$60,986
Present value of outflows (cost)			50,000
Net present value			$10,986

Note: PV factors rounded to three decimal places.

The Replacement Decision

So far our analysis has centered on an investment that is being considered as a net addition to the present plant and equipment. However, many investment decisions occur because of new technology, and these are considered **replacement decisions**. The financial manager often needs to determine whether a new machine with advanced technology can do the job better than the machine being used at present.

These replacement decisions include several additions to the basic investment situation. For example, we need to include the sale of the old machine in our analysis.

This sale will produce a cash inflow that partially offsets the purchase price of the new machine. In addition, the sale of the old machine will usually have tax consequences. Some of the cash inflow from the sale will be taxable if the old machine is sold for more than book value. If it is sold for less than book value, this will be considered a loss and will provide a tax benefit.

The replacement decision can be analyzed by using a total analysis of both the old and new machines or by using an incremental analysis that emphasizes the changes in cash flows between the old and the new machines. We will emphasize the incremental approach.

Assume the Bradley Corporation purchased a computer two years ago for $120,000. The asset is being depreciated under the five-year MACRS schedule previously shown in Table 12-12, which implies a six-year write-off because of the half-year convention. We will assume the old computer can be sold for $37,600. A new computer will cost $180,000 and will also be written off using the five-year MACRS schedule in Table 12-12.

The new computer will provide cost savings and operating benefits, compared to the old computer, of $42,000 per year for the next six years. These cost savings and operating benefits are the equivalent of increased earnings before depreciation and taxes. The firm has a 25 percent tax rate and a 10 percent cost of capital. First we need to determine the net cost of the new computer. We will take the purchase price of the new computer ($180,000) and subtract the cash inflow from the sale of the old computer.

Sale of Old Asset

The cash inflow from the sale of the old computer is based on the sales price as well as the related tax factors. To determine these tax factors, we first compute the book value of the old computer and compare this figure to the sales price to determine if there is a taxable gain or loss. The book value of the old computer is shown in Table 12-16.

Table 12-16   Book value of old computer

Year	Depreciation Base	Percentage Depreciation (Table 12-12)	Annual Depreciation
1	$120,000	0.200	$ 24,000
2	120,000	0.320	38,400
Total depreciation to date			$ 62,400
Purchase price			$120,000
Total depreciation to date			62,400
Book value			$ 57,600

Since the book value of the old computer is $57,600 and the sales price (previously given) is $37,600, there will be a $20,000 loss.

Book value	$57,600
Sales price	37,600
Tax loss on sale	$20,000

This loss can be written off against other income for the corporation.[4] The Bradley Corporation has a 25 percent tax rate, so the tax write-off is worth $7,000.

Tax loss on sale	$20,000
Tax rate	25%
Tax benefit	$ 5,000

We now add the tax benefit to the sale price to arrive at the cash inflow from the sale of the old computer.

Sale price of old computer	$37,600
Tax benefit from sale	5,000
Cash inflow from sale of old computer	$42,600

The computation of the cash inflow figure from the old computer allows us to compute the net cost of the new computer. The purchase price of $180,000, minus the cash inflow from the sale of the old computer, provides a value of $137,400 as indicated in Table 12-17.

Table 12-17   Net cost of new computer

Price of new computer	$180,000
− Cash flow from sale of old computer	42,600
Net cost of new computer	$137,400

The question then becomes this: Are the incremental gains from the new computer compared to those of the old computer large enough to justify the net cost of $137,400? We will assume that both will be operative over the next six years, although the old computer will run out of depreciation in four more years. We will base our cash flow analysis on (*a*) the incremental gain in depreciation and the related tax shield benefits and (*b*) cost savings.

Incremental Depreciation

The annual depreciation on the new computer will be:

Year	Depreciation Base	Percentage Depreciation (Table 12-12)	Annual Depreciation
1	$180,000	0.200	$ 36,000
2	180,000	0.320	57,600
3	180,000	0.192	34,560
4	180,000	0.115	20,700
5	180,000	0.115	20,700
6	180,000	0.058	10,440
			$180,000

---

[4]Note that had there been a capital gain instead of a loss, it would have been automatically taxed at the corporation's normal tax rate.

The annual depreciation on the old computer for the remaining four years would be:

Year*	Depreciation Base	Percentage Depreciation (Table 12-12)	Annual Depreciation
1	$120,000	0.192	$23,040
2	120,000	0.115	13,800
3	120,000	0.115	13,800
4	120,000	0.058	6,960

*The next four years represent the last four years for the old computer, which is already two years old.

In Table 12-18, we bring together the depreciation on the old and new computers to determine **incremental depreciation** and the related tax shield benefits. Since depreciation shields other income from being taxed, the benefits of the tax shield are worth the amount being depreciated times the tax rate. For example, in year 1, $12,960 (third column below) in incremental depreciation will keep $12,960 from being taxed, and with the firm in a 25 percent tax bracket, this represents a tax savings of $3,240. The same type of analysis applies to each subsequent year.

Table 12-18 Analysis of incremental depreciation benefits

(1) Year	(2) Depreciation on New Computer	(3) Depreciation on Old Computer	(4) Incremental Depreciation	(5) Tax Rate	(6) Tax Shield Benefits
1	$36,000	$23,040	$12,960	0.25	$ 3,240
2	57,600	13,800	43,800	0.25	10,950
3	34,560	13,800	20,760	0.25	5,190
4	20,700	6,960	13,740	0.25	3,435
5	20,700		20,700	0.25	5,175
6	10,440		10,440	0.25	2,610

Cost Savings

The second type of benefit relates to the incremental cost savings from the new computer. As previously stated, these savings are assumed to be $42,000 for the next six years. The aftertax benefits are shown in Table 12-19.

Table 12-19 Analysis of incremental cost savings benefits

(1) Year	(2) Cost Savings	(3) (1 – Tax Rate)	(4) Aftertax Savings
1	$42,000	0.75	$31,500
2	42,000	0.75	31,500
3	42,000	0.75	31,500
4	42,000	0.75	31,500
5	42,000	0.75	31,500
6	42,000	0.75	31,500

As indicated in Table 12-19, we take the cost savings in column 2 and multiply by one minus the tax rate. This indicates the value of the savings on an aftertax basis.

We now combine the incremental tax shield benefits from depreciation (Table 12-18) and the aftertax cost savings (Table 12-19) to arrive at total annual benefits in Table 12-20 (column 4). These benefits are discounted to the present at a 10 percent cost of capital. The present value of the inflows is $160,118 as indicated at the bottom of column 6 in Table 12-20.

Table 12-20   Present value of the total incremental benefits

(1) Year	(2) Tax Shield Benefits from Depreciation (from Table 12-18)	(3) Aftertax Cost Savings (from Table 12-19)	(4) Total Annual Benefits	(5) Present Value Factor (10%)	(6) Present Value
1	$ 3,240	$31,500	$34,740	0.909	$ 31,582
2	10,950	31,500	42,450	0.826	35,083
3	5,190	31,500	36,690	0.751	27,566
4	3,435	31,500	34,935	0.683	23,861
5	5,175	31,500	36,675	0.621	22,772
6	2,610	31,500	34,110	0.564	19,254
		Present value of incremental benefits			$160,118

Note: PV factors are rounded to three decimal places.

We now are in a position to compare the present value of incremental benefits of $160,118 from Table 12-20 to the net cost of the new computer of $137,400 from Table 12-17. The answer of $22,718 is shown here:

Present value of incremental benefits	$160,118
Net cost of new computer	137,400
Net present value	$ 22,718

Clearly there is a positive net present value, and the purchase of the computer should be recommended on the basis of the financial analysis.

Elective Expensing

We have stressed throughout the chapter the importance of taking deductions as early in the life of the asset as possible. Since a tax deduction produces cash flow, the earlier you can get the cash flow the better. Businesses can actually write off tangible property, such as equipment, furniture, tools, and computers, *in the year* they are purchased for up to $1 million. This is clearly superior to depreciating the asset when the write-off must take place over a number of years. This tax provision, called Section 179 **elective expensing** is primarily beneficial to small businesses because the allowance is phased out dollar for dollar when total property purchases exceed $2.5 million in a year. Thus, a business that purchases $3.5 million in assets for the year no longer has this option. However, until the 100 percent bonus depreciation deduction begins to phase out in 2023, even larger capital purchases can be fully written off in the first year.

SUMMARY

The capital budgeting decision involves the planning of expenditures for a project with a life of at least one year and usually considerably longer. Although top management is often anxious about the impact of their decisions on short-term reported income, the planning of capital expenditures dictates a longer time horizon.

Because capital budgeting deals with actual dollars rather than reported earnings, cash flow instead of operating income is used in the decision.

Three primary methods are used to analyze capital investment proposals: the payback method, the internal rate of return, and the net present value. The first method is normally unsound, while the last two are acceptable, with net present value deserving our greatest attention. The net present value method uses the cost of capital as the discount rate. In using the cost of capital as the discount, or hurdle, rate, we affirm that a project must at least earn the cost of funding to be acceptable as an investment.

As demonstrated in the chapter, the two forms of benefits attributed to an investment are (*a*) aftertax operating benefits and (*b*) the tax shield benefits of depreciation. The present value of these inflows must exceed the investment for a project to be acceptable.

LIST OF TERMS

cash flow 381	**capital rationing** 392
payback 384	**net present value profile** 393
net present value (NPV) 385	**modified accelerated cost recovery
internal rate of return (IRR) 387	system (MACRS)** 397
mutually exclusive 389	**asset depreciation range (ADR)** 397
reinvestment assumption 390	**replacement decisions** 400
modified internal rate of return	**incremental depreciation** 403
(MIRR) 391	**elective expensing** 404

DISCUSSION QUESTIONS

1. What are the important administrative considerations in the capital budgeting process? *(LO12-1)*

2. Why does capital budgeting rely on analysis of cash flows rather than on net income? *(LO12-2)*

3. What are the weaknesses of the payback method? *(LO12-3)*

4. What is normally used as the discount rate in the net present value method? *(LO12-5)*

5. What does the term *mutually exclusive investments* mean? *(LO12-4)*

6. How does the modified internal rate of return include concepts from both the traditional internal rate of return and the net present value methods? *(LO12-4)*

7. If a corporation has projects that will earn more than the cost of capital, should it ration capital? *(LO12-5)*

8. What is the net present value profile? What three points should be determined to graph the profile? *(LO12-4)*

9. How does an asset's ADR (asset depreciation range) relate to its MACRS category? *(LO12-2)*

Cash flow
(LO12-2)

Depreciation and
net present value
(LO12-4)

PRACTICE PROBLEMS AND SOLUTIONS

1. Systems Software has earnings before depreciation and taxes of $180,000, depreciation of $60,000, and a tax rate of 25 percent. Compute its cash flow.

2. Archer Chemical Corp. is considering purchasing new equipment that falls under the three-year MACRS category. The cost is $200,000. Earnings before depreciation and taxes for the next four years will be:

Year 1	$ 90,000
Year 2	105,000
Year 3	85,000
Year 4	35,000

The firm is in a 25 percent tax bracket and has a 12 percent cost of capital. Should it purchase the new equipment?

Solutions

1.

Earnings before depreciation and taxes	$180,000
Depreciation	60,000
Earnings before taxes	$120,000
Taxes @ 25%	30,000
Earnings after taxes	$ 90,000
Depreciation	60,000
Cash flow	$150,000

2. First determine annual depreciation based on the $200,000 purchase price. Use Table 12-12 for the annual depreciation rate for three-year MACRS depreciation.

Year	Depreciation Base	Percentage Depreciation (Table 12-12)	Annual Depreciation
1	$200,000	0.333	$66,600
2	200,000	0.445	89,000
3	200,000	0.148	29,600
4	200,000	0.074	14,800

Then determine the annual cash flow for each year.

	Year 1	Year 2	Year 3	Year 4
Earnings before depreciation and taxes	$90,000	$105,000	$85,000	$35,000
Depreciation	66,600	89,000	29,600	14,800
Earnings before taxes	$23,400	$16,000	$55,400	$20,200
Taxes @ 25%	5,850	4,000	13,850	5,050
Earnings after taxes	$17,550	$12,000	$41,550	$15,150
Depreciation	66,600	89,000	29,600	14,800
Cash flow	$84,150	$101,000	$71,150	$29,950

Finally, determine the present value of the cash flows and compare that to the $200,000 cost to determine the net present value.

Year	Cash Flow (inflows)	Present Value Factor (12%)	Present Value
1	$ 84,150	0.893	$ 75,134
2	101,000	0.797	80,517
3	71,150	0.712	50,643
4	29,950	0.636	19,034
			$225,327

Present value of inflows	$225,327
Present value of outflows (cost)	200,000
Net present value	$ 25,327

The net present value is positive, and the new equipment should be purchased.

PROBLEMS

■ connect Selected problems are available with Connect. Please see the preface for more information.

Basic Problems

1. Assume a corporation has earnings before depreciation and taxes of $90,000, depreciation of $40,000, and a 25 percent tax bracket. Compute its cash flow using the following format:

Cash flow (LO12-2)

Earnings before depreciation and taxes	_____
Depreciation	_____
Earnings before taxes	_____
Taxes @ 25%	_____
Earnings after taxes	_____
Depreciation	_____
Cash flow	_____

2. Assume a corporation has earnings before depreciation and taxes of $100,000, depreciation of $40,000, and a 24 percent tax bracket.

Cash flow (LO12-2)

   a. Compute its cash flow using the following format:

Earnings before depreciation and taxes	_____
Depreciation	_____
Earnings before taxes	_____
Taxes @ 24%	_____
Earnings after taxes	_____
Depreciation	_____

   b. Compute the cash flow for the company if depreciation is only $20,000.

   c. How much cash flow is lost due to the reduced depreciation from $40,000 to $20,000?

<table>
<tr><td>Cash flow
(LO12-2)</td><td>3.</td><td>Assume a firm has earnings before depreciation and taxes of $200,000 and no depreciation. It is in a 25 percent tax bracket.</td></tr>
</table>

Cash flow
(LO12-2)

3. Assume a firm has earnings before depreciation and taxes of $200,000 and no depreciation. It is in a 25 percent tax bracket.

   a. Compute its cash flow.

   b. Assume it has $200,000 in depreciation. Recompute its cash flow.

   c. How large a cash flow benefit did the depreciation provide?

Cash flow
(LO12-2)

4. Assume a firm has earnings before depreciation and taxes of $440,000 and depreciation of $140,000.

   a. If it is in a 35 percent tax bracket, compute its cash flow.

   b. If it is in a 20 percent tax bracket, compute its cash flow.

Cash flow versus
earnings
(LO12-2)

5. Al Quick, the president of a New York Stock Exchange–listed firm, is very short-term oriented and interested in the immediate consequences of his decisions. Assume a project that will provide an increase of $2 million in cash flow because of favorable tax consequences, but carries a two-cent decline in earnings per share because of a write-off against first-quarter earnings. What decision might Mr. Quick make?

Payback method
(LO12-3)

6. Assume a $250,000 investment and the following cash flows for two products:

Year	Product X	Product Y
1	$90,000	$50,000
2	90,000	80,000
3	60,000	60,000
4	20,000	70,000

Which alternatives would you select under the payback method?

Payback method
(LO12-3)

7. Assume a $40,000 investment and the following cash flows for two alternatives:

Year	Investment X	Investment Y
1	$ 6,000	$15,000
2	8,000	20,000
3	9,000	10,000
4	17,000	—
5	20,000	—

Which of the alternatives would you select under the payback method?

Payback method
(LO12-3)

8. Assume a $90,000 investment and the following cash flows for two alternatives:

Year	Investment A	Investment B
1	$25,000	$40,000
2	30,000	40,000
3	25,000	28,000
4	19,000	—
5	25,000	—

   a. Calculate the payback for Investments A and B.

   b. If the inflow in the fifth year for Investment A was $25,000,000 instead of $25,000, would your answer change under the payback method?

9. The Short-Line Railroad is considering a $140,000 investment in either of two companies. The cash flows are as follows:

Payback method
(LO12-3)

Year	Electric Co.	Water Works
1	$85,000	$30,000
2	25,000	25,000
3	30,000	85,000
4–10	10,000	10,000

   a. Using the payback method, what will the decision be?

   b. Explain why the answer in part *a* can be misleading.

10. X-treme Vitamin Company is considering two investments, both of which cost $10,000. The cash flows are as follows:

Payback and net present value
(LO12-3 & 12-4)

Year	Project A	Project B
1	$12,000	$10,000
2	8,000	6,000
3	6,000	16,000

   a. Which of the two projects should be chosen based on the payback method?

   b. Which of the two projects should be chosen based on the net present value method? Assume a cost of capital of 10 percent.

   c. Should a firm normally have more confidence in answer *a* or answer *b*?

11. You buy a new piece of equipment for $16,230, and you receive a cash inflow of $2,500 per year for 12 years. What is the internal rate of return?

Internal rate of return
(LO12-4)

12. King's Department Store is contemplating the purchase of a new machine at a cost of $22,802. The machine will provide $3,500 per year in cash flow for nine years. King's has a cost of capital of 10 percent. Using the internal rate of return method, evaluate this project and indicate whether it should be undertaken.

Internal rate of return
(LO12-4)

13. Home Security Systems is analyzing the purchase of manufacturing equipment that will cost $50,000. The annual cash inflows for the next three years will be:

Internal rate of return
(LO12-4)

Year	Cash Flow
1	$25,000
2	23,000
3	18,000

   a. Determine the internal rate of return.

   b. With a cost of capital of 18 percent, should the machine be purchased?

14. Aerospace Dynamics will invest $110,000 in a project that will produce the following cash flows. The cost of capital is 11 percent. Should the project be undertaken? (Note that the fourth year's cash flow is negative.)

Net present value method
(LO12-4)

Year	Cash Flow
1	$36,000
2	44,000
3	38,000
4	(44,000)
5	81,000

Net present value
method
(LO12-4)

15. The Horizon Company will invest $60,000 in a temporary project that will generate the following cash inflows for the next three years:

Year	Cash Flow
1	$15,000
2	25,000
3	40,000

The firm will also be required to spend $10,000 to close down the project at the end of the three years. If the cost of capital is 10 percent, should the investment be undertaken?

Net present value
method
(LO12-4)

16. Skyline Corp. will invest $130,000 in a project that will not begin to produce returns until after the third year. From the end of the third year until the end of the 12th year (10 periods), the annual cash flow will be $34,000. If the cost of capital is 12 percent, should this project be undertaken?

Intermediate Problems

Net present value
and internal rate of
return methods
(LO12-4)

17. The Hudson Corporation makes an investment of $24,000 that provides the following cash flow:

Year	Cash Flow
1	$13,000
2	13,000
3	4,000

　　a.　What is the net present value at an 8 percent discount rate?

　　b.　What is the internal rate of return?

　　c.　In this problem, would you make the same decision under both parts *a* and *b*?

Net present value
and internal rate of
return methods
(LO12-4)

18. The Pan American Bottling Co. is considering the purchase of a new machine that would increase the speed of bottling and save money. The net cost of this machine is $60,000. The annual cash flows have the following projections:

Year	Cash Flow
1	$23,000
2	26,000
3	29,000
4	15,000
5	8,000

  a. If the cost of capital is 13 percent, what is the net present value of selecting a new machine?

  b. What is the internal rate of return?

  c. Should the project be accepted? Why?

19. You are asked to evaluate the following two projects for the Norton Corporation. Using the net present value method combined with the profitability index approach described in footnote 2 of this chapter, which project would you select? Use a discount rate of 14 percent.

Use of a profitability index (LO12-4)

Project X (videotapes of the weather report) ($20,000 investment)		Project Y (slow-motion replays of commercials) ($40,000 investment)	
Year	Cash Flow	Year	Cash Flow
1	$10,000	1	$20,000
2	8,000	2	13,000
3	9,000	3	14,000
4	8,600	4	16,000

20. Turner Video will invest $76,344 in a project. The firm's cost of capital is 10 percent. The investment will provide the following inflows:

Reinvestment rate assumption in capital budgeting (LO12-4)

Year	Inflow
1	$15,000
2	17,000
3	21,000
4	25,000
5	29,000

The internal rate of return is 11 percent.

  a. If the reinvestment assumption of the net present value method is used, what will be the total value of the inflows after five years? (Assume the inflows come at the end of each year.)

  b. If the reinvestment assumption of the internal rate of return method is used, what will be the total value of the inflows after five years?

  c. Generally is one investment assumption likely to be better than another?

21. The Caffeine Coffee Company uses the modified internal rate of return. The firm has a cost of capital of 11 percent. The project being analyzed is as follows ($26,000 investment):

Modified internal rate of return (LO12-4)

Year	Cash Flow
1	$12,000
2	11,000
3	9,000

    a.   What is the modified internal rate of return? An approximation from Appendix B is adequate. (You do not need to interpolate.)

    b.   Assume the traditional internal rate of return on the investment is 17.5 percent. Explain why your answer in part *a* would be lower.

Z

Capital rationing and mutually exclusive investments (LO12-4)

22.   The Suboptimal Glass Company uses a process of capital rationing in its decision making. The firm's cost of capital is 10 percent. It will invest only $77,000 this year. It has determined the internal rate of return for each of the following projects:

Project	Project Size	Internal Rate of Return
A	$10,500	21%
B	30,500	22
C	25,500	18
D	10,500	13
E	10,500	20
F	20,500	11
G	10,500	16

    a.   Select the projects that the firm should accept.

    b.   If Projects A and B are mutually exclusive, how would that affect your overall answer? That is, which projects would you accept in spending the $77,000?

Advanced Problems

Net present value profile (LO12-4)

23.   Keller Construction is considering two new investments. Project E calls for the purchase of earthmoving equipment. Project H represents an investment in a hydraulic lift. Keller wishes to use a net present value profile in comparing the projects. The investment and cash flow patterns are as follows:

Project E ($20,000 investment)		Project H ($20,000 investment)	
Year	Cash Flow	Year	Cash Flow
1	$5,000	1	$16,000
2	6,000	2	5,000
3	7,000	3	4,000
4	10,000		

    a.   Determine the net present value of the projects based on a zero percent discount rate.

    b.   Determine the net present value of the projects based on a 9 percent discount rate.

    c.   The internal rate of return on Project E is 13.25 percent, and the internal rate of return on Project H is 16.30 percent. Graph a net present value profile for the two investments similar to Figure 12-3. (Use a scale up to $8,000 on the vertical axis, with $2,000 increments. Use a scale up to 20 percent on the horizontal axis, with 5 percent increments.)

  d. If the two projects are not mutually exclusive, what would your accep-
      tance or rejection decision be if the cost of capital (discount rate) is
      8 percent? (Use the net present value profile for your decision; no actual
      numbers are necessary.)

  e. If the two projects are mutually exclusive (the selection of one precludes
      the selection of the other), what would be your decision if the cost of
      capital is (1) 6 percent, (2) 13 percent, (3) 18 percent? Once again, use the
      net present value profile for your answer.

24. Davis Chili Company is considering an investment of $35,000, which produces
     the following inflows:

Net present value
profile
(LO12-4)

Year	Cash Flow
1	$16,000
2	15,000
3	12,000

You are going to use the net present value profile to approximate the value for
the internal rate of return. Please follow these steps:

  a. Determine the net present value of the project based on a zero
      discount rate.

  b. Determine the net present value of the project based on a 10 percent
      discount rate.

  c. Determine the net present value of the project based on a 15 percent
      discount rate (it will be negative).

  d. Draw a net present value profile for the investment and observe the
      discount rate at which the net present value is zero. This is an approxima-
      tion of the internal rate of return based on the procedure presented in this
      chapter.

25. Telstar Communications is going to purchase an asset for $380,000 that will
     produce $180,000 per year for the next four years in earnings before deprecia-
     tion and taxes. The asset will be depreciated using the three-year MACRS
     depreciation schedule in Table 12-12. (This represents four years of deprecia-
     tion based on the half-year convention.) The firm is in a 25 percent tax bracket.
     Fill in the following schedule for the next four years:

Ⅺ

MACRS depreciation
and cash flow
(LO12-2)

Earnings before depreciation and taxes	_____
Depreciation	_____
Earnings before taxes	_____
Taxes	_____
Earnings after taxes	
+ Depreciation	_____
Cash flow	_____

MACRS depreciation categories
(LO12-4)

26. Assume $65,000 is going to be invested in each of the following assets. Using Tables 12-11 and 12-12, indicate the dollar amount of the first year's depreciation.

    a.   Office furniture.

    b.   Automobile.

    c.   Electric and gas utility property.

    d.   Sewage treatment plant.

MACRS depreciation and net present value
(LO12-4)

27. The Summit Petroleum Corporation will purchase an asset that qualifies for three-year MACRS depreciation. The cost is $160,000 and the asset will provide the following stream of earnings before depreciation and taxes for the next four years:

Year 1	$70,000
Year 2	85,000
Year 3	42,000
Year 4	40,000

The firm is in a 35 percent tax bracket and has an 8 percent cost of capital. Should it purchase the asset? Use the net present value method.

MACRS depreciation and net present value
(LO12-4)

28. Oregon Forest Products will acquire new equipment that falls under the five-year MACRS category. The cost is $300,000. If the equipment is purchased, the following earnings before depreciation and taxes will be generated for the next six years:

Year 1	$112,000
Year 2	105,000
Year 3	82,000
Year 4	53,000
Year 5	37,000
Year 6	32,000

The firm is in a 25 percent tax bracket and has a 14 percent cost of capital. Should Oregon Forest Products purchase the equipment? Use the net present value method.

MACRS depreciation and net present value
(LO12-4)

29. Universal Electronics is considering the purchase of manufacturing equipment with a 10-year midpoint in its asset depreciation range (ADR). Carefully refer to Table 12-11 to determine in what depreciation category the asset falls. (Hint: It is not 10 years.) The asset will cost $120,000, and it will produce earnings before depreciation and taxes of $37,000 per year for 3 years, and then $19,000 a year for 7 more years. The firm has a tax rate of 25 percent. With a cost of capital of 12 percent, should it purchase the asset? Use the net present value method. In doing your analysis, if you have years in which there is no depreciation, merely enter a zero for depreciation.

Working capital requirements in capital budgeting
(LO12-4)

30. The Spartan Technology Company has a proposed contract with the Digital Systems Company of Michigan. The initial investment in land and equipment

will be $120,000. Of this amount, $70,000 is subject to five-year MACRS depreciation. The balance is in nondepreciable property. The contract covers six years; at the end of six years, the nondepreciable assets will be sold for $50,000. The depreciated assets will have zero resale value.

The contract will require an additional investment of $55,000 in working capital at the beginning of the first year and, of this amount, $25,000 will be returned to the Spartan Technology Company after six years.

The investment will produce $50,000 in income before depreciation and taxes for each of the six years. The corporation is in a 25 percent tax bracket and has a 10 percent cost of capital. Should the investment be undertaken? Use the net present value method.

31. An asset was purchased three years ago for $120,000. It falls into the five-year category for MACRS depreciation. The firm is in a 25 percent tax bracket. Compute the following:

    a. Tax loss on the sale and the related tax benefit if the asset is sold now for $15,060.

    b. Gain and related tax on the sale if the asset is sold now for $56,060. (Refer to footnote 4 in the chapter.)

    Tax losses and gains in capital budgeting (LO12-2)

32. DataPoint Engineering is considering the purchase of a new piece of equipment for $240,000. It has an eight-year midpoint of its asset depreciation range (ADR). It will require an additional initial investment of $140,000 in nondepreciable working capital. Thirty-five thousand dollars of this investment will be recovered after the sixth year and will provide additional cash flow for that year. Here is the projected income before depreciation and taxes for the next six years:

    Capital budgeting with cost of capital computation (LO12-5)

Year	Amount
1	$185,000
2	160,000
3	130,000
4	115,000
5	95,000
6	85,000

The tax rate is 25 percent. The cost of capital must be computed based on the following (round the final value to the nearest whole number):

		Cost (aftertax)	Weights
Debt	K_d	9.5%	25%
Preferred stock	K_p	13.2	25
Common equity (retained earnings)	K_e	18.0	50

a. Determine the annual depreciation schedule.

b. Determine annual cash flow. Include recovered working capital in the sixth year.

    c.   Determine the weighted average cost of capital.

    d.   Determine the net present value. Should DataPoint purchase the new equipment?

Replacement decision analysis
(LO12-4)

33.   Hercules Exercise Equipment Co. purchased a computerized measuring device two years ago for $58,000. The equipment falls into the five-year category for MACRS depreciation and can currently be sold for $24,800.

     A new piece of equipment will cost $148,000. It also falls into the five-year category for MACRS depreciation. Assume the new equipment would provide the following stream of added cost savings for the next six years:

Year	Cost Savings
1	$62,000
2	54,000
3	52,000
4	50,000
5	47,000
6	36,000

The firm's tax rate is 25 percent and the cost of capital is 12 percent.

    a.   What is the book value of the old equipment?

    b.   What is the tax loss on the sale of the old equipment?

    c.   What is the tax benefit from the sale?

    d.   What is the cash inflow from the sale of the old equipment?

    e.   What is the net cost of the new equipment? (Include the inflow from the sale of the old equipment.)

    f.   Determine the depreciation schedule for the new equipment.

    g.   Determine the depreciation schedule for the remaining years of the old equipment.

    h.   Determine the incremental depreciation between the old and new equipment and the related tax shield benefits.

    i.   Compute the aftertax benefits of the cost savings.

    j.   Add the depreciation tax shield benefits and the aftertax cost savings, and determine the present value. (See Table 12-20 as an example.)

    k.   Compare the present value of the incremental benefits (j) to the net cost of the new equipment (e). Should the replacement be undertaken?

COMPREHENSIVE PROBLEM

Woodruff Corporation (Replacement decision analysis) (LO12-4)

The Woodruff Corporation purchased a piece of equipment three years ago for $230,000. It has an asset depreciation range (ADR) midpoint of eight years. The old equipment can be sold for $90,000.

    A new piece of equipment can be purchased for $320,000. It also has an ADR of eight years.

Assume the old and new equipment would provide the following operating gains (or losses) over the next six years:

Year	New Equipment	Old Equipment
1	$80,000	$25,000
2	76,000	16,000
3	70,000	9,000
4	60,000	8,000
5	50,000	6,000
6	45,000	(7,000)

The firm has a 25 percent tax rate and a 9 percent cost of capital. Should the new equipment be purchased to replace the old equipment?

WEB EXERCISE

1. Texas Instruments was referred to in the chapter as being an innovator in the calculator industry. But that is only one of its products. Let's see how this large company is doing today. Go to finance.yahoo.com and in the "Quote Lookup" box type "TXN" and select "Texas Instruments Incorporated."

2. Click on "Profile." Write a one-paragraph description of its major operations.

3. Returning to TXN's summary page, record the following:
   a. Last trade price
   b. 52-week low
   c. 52-week high

4. Now click on "Chart" and scroll down to see the pattern for the last year. Scroll up and click on "5Y" and scroll down to the summary data for five years. Finally, click on "Comparison" and select the S&P 500 (Standard & Poor's 500 Stock Index). Scroll down and review the summary data for that period. Write a paragraph describing TXN's stock performance.

Note: Occasionally a topic we have listed may have been deleted, updated, or moved into a different location on a website. If you click on the site map or site index, you will be introduced to a table of contents that should aid you in finding the topic you are looking for.

Risk and Capital Budgeting

Nobody understands the meaning of risk better than Apache Corp., a firm that drills for natural gas and oil on properties in the United States, Canada, Australia, Egypt, and the North Sea.

Over the last 20 years, the price of oil has vacillated from less than $11 per barrel to over $145 per barrel. Natural gas has been even more volatile. What appears to be a great opportunity for drilling and discovery when energy prices are at their peak can turn out to be a disaster when those prices drop by 25 to 50 percent or more.[1] An even greater threat to Apache Corp. is the proverbial "dry hole," in which millions of dollars are spent only to discover that there is no oil to be found. Apache's stock price performance reflects the price of oil. On February 1, 2008, the common stock sold for $134.68 and 10 years later on January 22, 2018, the price was $46.05.

Energy producers such as Apache Corp. are much more vulnerable to changing circumstances in the market than fully integrated oil companies such as ExxonMobil, which not only drills for oil and gas, but refines it and sells it at the retail level through its service stations. For ExxonMobile, lower profits at the discovery level are often offset by higher profits at the retail level and vice versa.

But the upside for oil producers such as Apache Corp. is enormous when they discover oil and gas in a previously untested area. The risk and rewards of this business exceed those in almost any other.

In this chapter, we examine definitions of risk, its measurement and its incorporation into the *capital budgeting* process, and the basic tenets of portfolio theory.

Definition of Risk in Capital Budgeting

Risk may be defined in terms of the variability of possible outcomes from a given investment. If funds are invested in a 30-day U.S. government obligation, the outcome is certain and there is no variability—hence no risk. If we invest the same funds in a

---

[1]This has happened many times worldwide.

deep-sea oil drilling venture above the Arctic Circle, the variability of possible outcomes is great and we say the project is extremely risky.

Risk is measured not only in terms of losses but also in terms of uncertainty.[2] We say gold mining carries a high degree of risk not just because you may lose your money but also because there is a wide range of possible outcomes. Observe in Figure 13-1 examples of three investments with different risk characteristics.

In each case, the distributions are centered on the same expected value of $20,000, but the variability (risk) increases as we move from Investment A to Investment C. Because you may gain or lose the most in Investment C, it is clearly the riskiest of the three.

Figure 13-1   Variability and risk

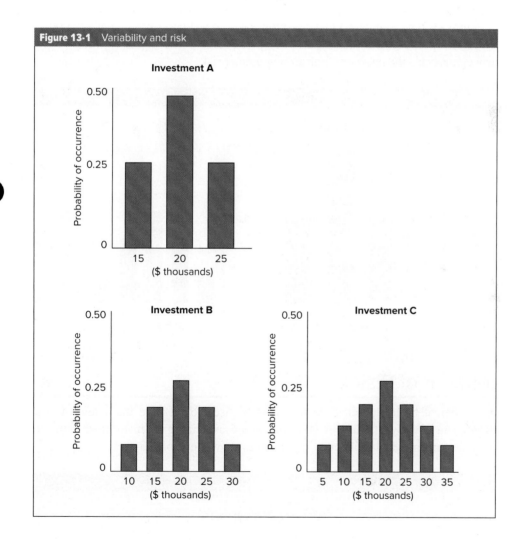

---

[2]We use the term *uncertainty* in its normal sense, rather than in the more formalized sense in which it is sometimes used in decision theory to indicate that insufficient evidence is available to estimate a probability distribution.

The Concept of Risk-Averse

A basic assumption in financial theory is that most investors and managers are **risk-averse**—that is, for a given situation they would prefer relative certainty to uncertainty. In Figure 13-1, they would prefer Investment A over Investments B and C, although all three investments have the same expected value of $20,000. You are probably risk-averse too. Assume you have saved $1,000 toward your last year in college and are challenged to flip a coin, double or nothing. Heads, you end up with $2,000; tails, you are broke. Given that you are not enrolled at the University of Nevada at Las Vegas or that you are not an inveterate gambler, you will probably stay with your certain $1,000.

This is not to say investors or businesspeople are unwilling to take risks—but rather that they will require a higher expected value or return for risky investments. In Figure 13-2, we compare a low-risk proposal with an expected value of $20,000 to a high-risk proposal with an expected value of $30,000. The higher expected return may compensate the investor for absorbing greater risk.

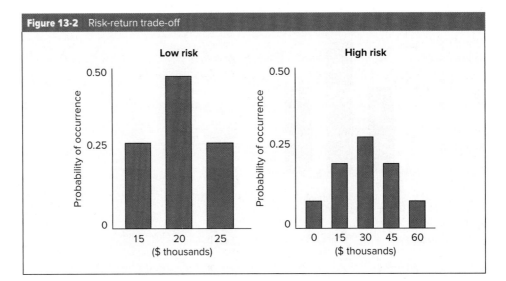

Figure 13-2   Risk-return trade-off

Actual Measurement of Risk

A number of basic statistical devices may be used to measure the extent of risk inherent in any given situation. Assume we are examining an investment with the possible outcomes and probability of outcomes shown in Table 13-1.

Table 13-1   Probability distribution of outcomes

Outcome	Probability of Outcome	Assumption
$300	0.2	Pessimistic
600	0.6	Moderately successful
900	0.2	Optimistic

The probabilities in Table 13-1 may be based on past experience, industry ratios and trends, interviews with company executives, and sophisticated simulation techniques. The probability values may be easy to determine for the introduction of a mechanical stamping process in which the manufacturer has 10 years of past data, but difficult to assess for a new product in a foreign market. In any event, we force ourselves into a valuable analytical process.

Based on the data in Table 13-1, we compute two important statistical measures—the expected value and the standard deviation. The **expected value** $(\overline{D})$ is a weighted average of the outcomes (D) times their probabilities (P).

$$\overline{D}\text{ (expected value)} = \Sigma DP \tag{13-1}$$

$$
\begin{array}{rll}
D & P & DP \\
300 \times 0.2 & = & \$\ 60 \\
600 \times 0.6 & = & 360 \\
900 \times 0.2 & = & \underline{180} \\
 & & \$600 \ = \Sigma DP = \overline{D}
\end{array}
$$

The expected value $(\overline{D})$ is $600. We then compute the **standard deviation**—the measure of dispersion or variability around the expected value:

$$\sigma \text{ (standard deviation)} = \sqrt{\Sigma (D - \overline{D})^2 P} \tag{13-2}$$

The following steps should be taken:

Step 1: Subtract the Expected Value $(\overline{D})$ from Each Outcome (D)		Step 2: Square $(D - \overline{D})$		Step 3: Multiply by P and Sum		Step 4: Determine the Square Root
D $\quad \overline{D}$	$(D - \overline{D})$	$(D - \overline{D})^2$		P	$(D - \overline{D})^2 P$	
$300 - 600 =$	-300	$90{,}000$	$\times$	$0.20 =$	$18{,}000$	
$600 - 600 =$	0	0	$\times$	$0.60 =$	0	
$900 - 600 =$	$+300$	$90{,}000$	$\times$	$0.20 =$	$\underline{18{,}000}$ $36{,}000$	$\sqrt{36{,}000} = \$190$

The standard deviation of $190 gives us a rough average measure of how far each of the three outcomes falls away from the expected value. Generally, the larger the standard deviation (or spread of outcomes), the greater is the risk, as indicated in Figure 13-3. You will note that in Figure 13-3 we compare the standard deviation of three investments with the same expected value of $600. If the expected values of the investments were different (such as $600 versus $6,000), a direct comparison of the standard deviations for each distribution would not be helpful in measuring risk. In Figure 13-4 we show such an occurrence.

The investment in panel A of Figure 13-4 appears to have a high standard deviation, but not when related to the expected value of the distribution. A standard deviation of $600 on an investment with an expected value of $6,000 may indicate less risk than a standard deviation of $190 on an investment with an expected value of only $600 (panel B).

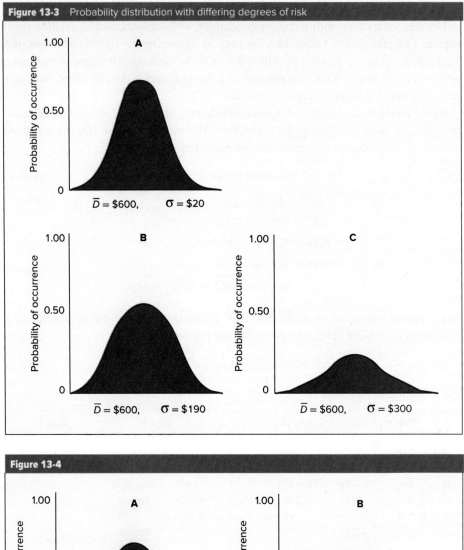

Figure 13-3   Probability distribution with differing degrees of risk

Figure 13-4

We can eliminate the size difficulty by developing a third measure, the **coefficient of variation** (*V*). This term calls for nothing more difficult than dividing the standard deviation of an investment by the expected value. Generally, the larger the coefficient of variation, the greater is the risk. The formula for the coefficient of variation is numbered 13-3.

$$\text{Coefficient of variation } (V) = \frac{\sigma}{\overline{D}} \qquad (13\text{-}3)$$

For the investments in panels A and B of Figure 13-4, we show:

$$\begin{array}{cc} \mathbf{A} & \mathbf{B} \\ V = \dfrac{600}{6,000} = 0.10 & V = \dfrac{190}{600} = 0.317 \end{array}$$

We have correctly identified Investment B as carrying the greater risk.

Another risk measure, **beta** (β), is widely used with portfolios of common stock. Beta measures the volatility of returns on an individual stock relative to the stock market index of returns, such as the Standard & Poor's 500 Stock Index.[3] A common stock with a beta of 1.0 is said to be of equal risk with the market. Stocks with betas greater than 1.0 are riskier than the market, while stocks with betas of less than 1.0 are less risky than the market. Table 13-2 presents a sample of betas for some well-known companies from 2013 to 2018. We note that betas are not stable over time.

Table 13-2 Average betas for a five-year period (ending January 2018)

Company Name	Beta
Walmart Stores Inc.	0.75
Philip Morris International	0.82
Exxon Mobil Corp.	0.98
Nike Inc. Cl B	0.99
Budweiser	1.00
The Walt Disney Co.	1.01
Starbucks Corp.	1.02
Apple Inc.	1.02
Intel Corp.	1.07
Boeing Co.	1.08
FedEx Corp.	1.11
Visa Inc.	1.12
Ford Motor Co.	1.14
Facebook Inc.	1.16
Amazon	1.19
Netflix	1.26
Apache Corp.	1.30
Bank of America	1.32
Alcoa	1.34

Risk and the Capital Budgeting Process

How can risk analysis be used effectively in the capital budgeting process? In Chapter 12 we made no distinction between risky and nonrisky events.[4] We showed the amount of the investment and the annual returns—making no comment about the riskiness or likelihood of achieving these returns. We know that investors and managers care about both risk and expected returns. A $1,400 investment that produces "certain" returns of $600 a year for three years is not the same as a $1,400 investment that produces returns with an expected value of $600 for three years, but with a high coefficient of variation.

---

[3]Other market measures may also be used.
[4]Our assumption was that the risk factor could be considered constant for various investments.

Investors, being risk-averse by nature, will apply a stiffer test to the second investment. How can this new criterion be applied to the capital budgeting process?

Risk-Adjusted Discount Rate

A favored approach to adjust for risk is to use different discount rates for proposals with different risk levels. Thus we use **risk-adjusted discount rates**. A project that carries a normal amount of risk and does not change the overall risk composure of the firm should be discounted at the cost of capital. Investments carrying greater than normal risk will be discounted at a higher rate, and so on. In Figure 13-5, we show a possible risk–discount rate trade-off scheme. We assume that risk is measured by the coefficient of variation (*V*).

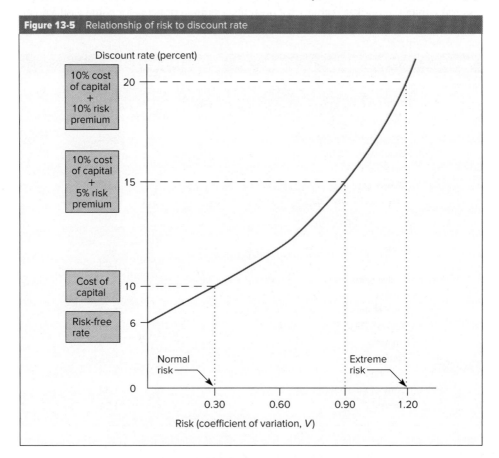

Figure 13-5   Relationship of risk to discount rate

The risk of the typical project undertaken by the firm is represented by a coefficient of variation of 0.30 (normal risk) on the bottom of Figure 13-5. An investment with this normal risk would be discounted at the firm's normal cost of capital of 10 percent. As the firm selects riskier projects, for example, with a *V* of 0.90, a risk premium of 5 percent is added to compensate for an increase in *V* of 0.60 (from 0.30 to 0.90). If the company selects a project with a coefficient of variation of 1.20, it will add another 5 percent risk premium for this additional *V* of 0.30. This is an example of being increasingly risk-averse at higher levels of risk and potential return. Management requires higher expected returns (by using higher discount rates) when the firm is considering projects with higher risks.

Increasing Risk over Time

Our ability to forecast accurately diminishes as we forecast farther out in time. As the time horizon becomes longer, more uncertainty enters the forecast. The decline in oil prices sharply curtailed the search for petroleum and left many drillers in serious financial condition in the 1980s after years of expanding drilling activity. Conversely, the users of petroleum products were hurt in 1990 when the conflict in the Middle East caused oil prices to skyrocket. Airlines and auto manufacturers had to reevaluate decisions made many years ago that were based on more stable energy prices. September 11, 2001, dealt another blow to the already fragile economy. The collapse of the housing market caused a terrible shock to the economy in 2007–2009. The inability of Congress to agree on tax reform and spending cuts lingered throughout Obama's presidency and caused a great deal of uncertainty for all businesses. Then oil prices again declined from $107 in June 2014 to $53 in July 2015. These unexpected events create a higher standard deviation in cash flows and increase the risk associated with long-lived projects. Figure 13-6 depicts the relationship between risk and time.

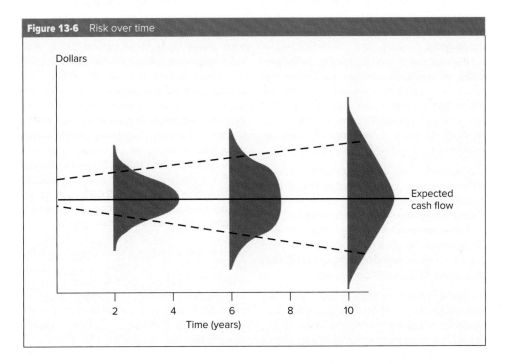

Figure 13-6   Risk over time

Even though a forecast of cash flows shows a constant expected value, Figure 13-6 indicates that the range of outcomes and probabilities increases as we move from year 2 to year 10. The standard deviations increase for each forecast of cash flow. If cash flows were forecast as easily for each period, all distributions would look like the first one for year 2.

Qualitative Measures

Rather than relate the discount rate—or required return—to the coefficient of variation or possibly the beta, management may wish to set up risk classes based on qualitative

One industry that affects world economies is energy. This industry includes coal, natural gas, oil, wind, solar, and even the Canadian tar sands. The prices of all these types of energy are important to every person and company that uses electricity, buses, cars, airplanes, trains, plastics, fertilizer, and more. The search for energy sources can be high risk and can result in either large deposits that generate high returns or no returns if nothing is found. Additionally, as companies search for oil in deeper and deeper waters, the technology used is more sophisticated and the chance of a disaster becomes higher. Just ask BP about the more than $20 billion in fines and claims that it will cost the company to settle the Gulf of Mexico Deepwater Horizon rig explosion that occurred in April 2010. Did it include the potential cost of disasters in its worldwide drilling program?

Besides the risk of a disaster, every producer of energy is affected by the cost of alternative energy sources. For example, the International Energy Agency now predicts that the United States will be energy independent by 2020. An article in *The Journal of the International Energy Agency* made this comment:

Five years ago no one would have been talking about the prospect of U.S. energy independence. But this year, domestic crude oil production should rise by 10%, and within five years the United States is likely to break the record output high reached more than two decades ago, to flirt with the position of top world producer.[5]

The amazing part of the story is that new technology, such as horizontal drilling and hydraulic fracturing, has found ways to get more oil and gas out of old deposits and to recover oil and gas from places that were previously unrecoverable. Estimates are that in the last five years, the United States has found enough natural gas for 50 years and is still finding more.

Natural gas is priced per one thousand cubic feet of natural gas or by its equivalent, 1 million BTUs (British thermal units). The price of natural gas has gone from $12 per thousand cubic feet in 2008, to $6 in 2011, to $2 in 2012, and $2.79 in 2015. Now if anyone could have predicted this price movement, capital budgeting decisions would have been greatly influenced. Go back and read the quote. Five years ago, no one knew that the United States would find so much natural gas in the Marcellus Shale of Pennsylvania and West Virginia and other shale formations in Texas, Colorado, North Dakota, and other western states.

Now this should all seem like good news, but environmentalists are worried that these low natural gas prices will set back wind and solar power projects as natural gas is now more cost competitive. This affects the capital budgeting projects for electric utilities and changes the balance between coal-, oil-, and gas-generating plants. It also affects the budding solar industry and companies like General Electric and Siemens that make electric generating wind turbines.

The ability of the United States to become energy independent also has a geopolitical impact as it reduces U.S. dependence on Middle East oil, which at times can be unpredictable and used as a political tool. The newfound sources of oil and gas will reduce some of the uncertainty of supply constraints. At its peak, the United States imported $300 billion of oil per year, and so more domestic oil production will help the country reduce its trade imbalance. This will affect the economy and the value of the dollar and other unpredictable benefits and costs.

We have presented an ever-changing picture of energy and its costs, which needs to be forecast by many companies around the world. The point is that even though we can try to put probabilities on potential outcomes, the accuracy of our forecasts is probably not too high. Given the economic interactions of energy on multiple industries, all the consequences are difficult to predict.

---

[5]Michael Cohen, "IEA Energy," *The Journal of the International Energy Agency*, © OECD/IEA 2012, Issue 3, p. 18, January 2013.

considerations. Examples are presented in Table 13-3. Once again we are raising the discount rate to reflect the perceived risk.

Table 13-3　Risk categories and associated discount rates

	Discount Rate
Low or no risk (repair to old machinery)	6%
Moderate risk (new equipment)	8
Normal risk (addition to normal product line)	10
Risky (new product in related market)	12
High risk (completely new market)	16
Highest risk (new product in foreign market)	20

Example—Risk-Adjusted Discount Rate　In Chapter 12, we compared two $10,000 investment alternatives and indicated that each had a positive net present value (at a 10 percent cost of capital). The analysis is reproduced in Table 13-4.

Table 13-4　Capital budgeting analysis

	A	B	C	D	E	F	G	H	I
1	Investment A					Investment B			
2	Discount Rate		10.00%			Discount Rate		10.00%	
3	Year (n)	CF	$\frac{1}{(1+i)^n}$			Year (n)	CF	$\frac{1}{(1+i)^n}$	
4	0	−$10,000	1.000	−$10,000.00		0	−$10,000	1.000	−$10,000.00
5	1	5,000	0.909	4,545.45		1	1,500	0.909	1,363.64
6	2	5,000	0.826	4,132.23		2	2,000	0.826	1,652.89
7	3	2,000	0.751	1,502.63		3	2,500	0.751	1,878.29
8	Net Present Value			$180.32		4	5,000	0.683	3,415.07
9						5	5,000	0.621	3,104.61
10						Net Present Value			$1,414.49
11									

Though both proposals are acceptable, if they were mutually exclusive, only Investment B would be undertaken. But what if we add a risk dimension to the problem? Assume Investment A calls for an addition to the normal product line and is assigned a discount rate of 10 percent. Further assume that Investment B represents a new product in a foreign market and must carry a 20 percent discount rate to adjust for the large risk component. As indicated in Table 13-5, our answers are reversed and Investment A is now the only acceptable alternative.

Other methods besides the risk-adjusted discount rate approach are also used to evaluate risk in the capital budgeting process. The spectrum runs from a seat-of-the-pants "executive preference" approach to sophisticated computer-based statistical analysis.

All methods, however, include a common approach—that is, they must recognize the riskiness of a given investment proposal and make an appropriate adjustment for risk.

Table 13-5 Capital budgeting decision adjusted for risk

	A	B	C	D	E	F	G	H	I
1	**Investment A**					**Investment B**			
2	Discount Rate		10.00%			Discount Rate		20.00%	
3	Year (n)	CF	$\frac{1}{(1+i)^n}$			Year (n)	CF	$\frac{1}{(1+i)^n}$	
4	0	−$10,000	1.000	−$10,000.00		0	−$10,000	1.000	−$10,000.00
5	1	5,000	0.909	4,545.45		1	1,500	0.833	1,250.00
6	2	5,000	0.826	4,132.23		2	2,000	0.694	1,388.89
7	3	5,000	0.751	1,502.63		3	2,500	0.579	1,446.76
8	Net Present Value			$ 180.32		4	5,000	0.482	2,411.27
9						5	5,000	0.402	2,009.39
10						Net Present Value			−$ 1,493.70
11									

Simulation Models

Computers make it possible to simulate various economic and financial outcomes, using a large number of variables. Thus **simulation** is one way of dealing with the uncertainty involved in forecasting the outcomes of capital budgeting projects or other types of decisions. A Monte Carlo simulation model uses random variables for inputs. By programming the computer to randomly select inputs from probability distributions, the outcomes generated by a simulation are distributed about a mean, and instead of generating one return or net present value, a range of outcomes with standard deviations is provided. A simulation model relies on repetition of the same random process as many as several hundred times. Since the inputs are representative of what one might encounter in the real world, many possible combinations of returns are generated.

One of the benefits of simulation is its ability to test various possible combinations of events. This sensitivity testing allows the planner to ask "what if" questions: What will happen to the returns on this project if oil prices go up? go down? What effect will a 2 percent increase in interest rates have on the net present value of this project? The analyst can use the simulation process to test possible changes in economic policy, sales levels, inflation, or any other variable included in the modeling process. Some simulation models are driven by sales forecasts with assumptions to derive income statements and balance sheets. Others generate probability acceptance curves for capital budgeting decisions by informing the analyst about the probabilities of having a positive net present value.

For example, each distribution in Figure 13-7 will have a value picked randomly and used for one simulation. The simulation will be run many times, each time selecting a new random variable to generate the final probability distribution for the net present value (at the bottom of Figure 13-7). For that probability distribution, the expected values are on the horizontal axis and the probability of occurrence is on the vertical axis. The outcomes also suggest something about the riskiness of the project, which is indicated by the overall dispersion.

Figure 13-7   Simulation flow chart

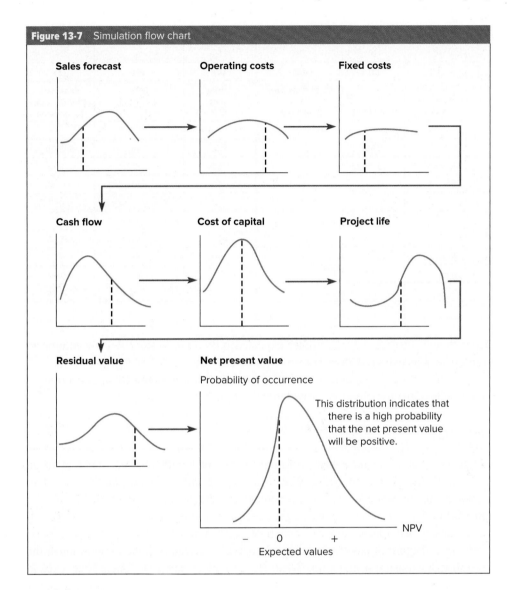

Decision Trees

Decision trees help lay out the sequence of decisions that can be made and present a tabular or graphical comparison resembling the branches of a tree, which highlights the differences between investment choices. In Table 13-6, we examine a retailer considering two choices: (*a*) opening additional physical stores in a new geographical region but using a format that has already proven successful elsewhere, or (*b*) developing a new online-only retail venture. The cost of both projects is the same, $60 million (column 4), but the net present value (NPV) and risk are different. If the firm expands its physical store count (Project A), it has a high likelihood of a modest positive rate of return. This market has some uncertainty, but long-run success seems to be likely. If the firm launches a new online store, it faces stiff competition from many established firms. It stands to lose more money if expected sales are lower than it would under option A, but it will make more if sales are high.

Table 13-6   Decision trees

	A	B	C	D	E	F	G	H
1			**(1)**	**(2)**	**(3)**	**(4)**	**(5)**	**(6)**
2	**Alternatives**		**Expected Sales**	**Probability**	**Cash Flow from Sales ($ millions)**	**Initial Cost ($ millions)**	**NPV (3) − (4) ($ millions)**	**Expected NPV (2) × (5) ($ millions)**
3								
4	**Project A**		High	0.50	$100	$60	$40	$20.00
5	Expand		Moderate	0.25	75	60	15	3.75
6	stores		Low	0.25	40	60	−20	−5.00
7							Expected NPV =	$18.75
8		Start						
9	**Project B**		High	0.20	$200	$60	$140	$28.00
10	Launch		Moderate	0.50	75	60	15	7.50
11	online		Low	0.30	25	60	−35	−10.50
12							Expected NPV =	$25.00

Even though Project B has a higher expected NPV than Project A (last column in Table 13-6), its extra risk does not make for an easy choice. More analysis would have to be done before management made the final decision between these two projects. Nevertheless, the decision tree provides an important analytical process.

The Portfolio Effect

Up to this point, we have been primarily concerned with the risk inherent in an *individual* investment proposal. While this approach is useful, we also need to consider the impact of a given investment on the overall risk of the firm—the **portfolio effect**. For example, we might undertake an investment in the building products industry that appears to carry a high degree of risk—but if our primary business is the manufacture of electronic components for industrial use, we may diminish the overall risk exposure of the firm. Why? Because electronic component sales expand when the economy does well and falter in a recession. The building products industry reacts in the opposite fashion—performing poorly in boom periods and generally reacting well in recessionary periods. By investing in the building products industry, an electronic components manufacturer could smooth the cyclical fluctuations inherent in its business and reduce overall risk exposure, as indicated in Figure 13-8.

The risk reduction phenomenon is demonstrated by a less dispersed probability distribution in panel C. We say the standard deviation for the entire company (the portfolio of investments) has been reduced.

Portfolio Risk

Whether or not a given investment will change the overall risk of the firm depends on its relationships to other investments. If one airline purchases another, there is very little risk reduction. Highly correlated investments—that is, projects that move in the same direction in good times as well as bad—do little or nothing to diversify away risk.

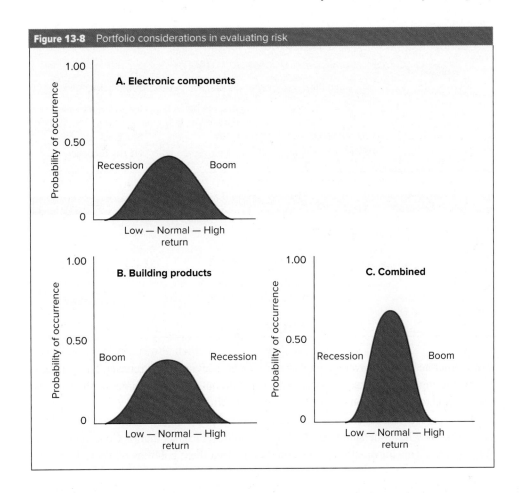

Figure 13-8 Portfolio considerations in evaluating risk

Projects moving in opposite directions (building products and electronic components) are referred to as being negatively correlated and provide a high degree of risk reduction.

Finally, projects that are totally uncorrelated provide some overall reduction in portfolio risk—though not as much as negatively correlated investments. For example, if a beer manufacturer purchases a textile firm, the projects are neither positively nor negatively correlated; but the purchase will reduce the overall risk of the firm simply through the "law of large numbers." If you have enough unrelated projects going on at one time, good and bad events will probably even out.

The extent of correlation among projects is represented by a new term called the **coefficient of correlation**—a measure that may take on values anywhere from −1 to +1.[6] Examples are presented in Table 13-7.

In the real world, few investment combinations take on values as extreme as −1 or +1, or for that matter exactly 0. The more likely case is a point somewhere between, such as −0.2 negative correlation or +0.3 positive correlation, as indicated along the continuum in Figure 13-9.

The fact that risk can be reduced by combining risky assets with low or negatively correlated assets can be seen in the example of Conglomerate Inc. in Table 13-8.

---

[6]Coefficient of correlation is not to be confused with coefficient of variation, a term used earlier in this chapter.

Table 13-7 Measures of correlation

Coefficient of Correlation	Condition	Example	Impact on Risk
−1	Negative correlation	Electronic components, building products	Large risk reduction
0	No correlation	Beer, textile	Some risk reduction
+1	Positive correlation	Two airlines	No risk reduction

Figure 13-9 Levels of risk reduction as measured by the coefficient of correlation

	Significant risk reduction		Some risk reduction		Minor risk reduction		
Extreme risk reduction	−1	−0.5	−0.2	0	+0.3	+0.5	+1	No risk reduction

Conglomerate has fairly average returns and standard deviations of returns. The company is considering the purchase of one of two separate but large companies with sales and assets equal to its own. Management is struggling with the decision since both companies have a 14 percent rate of return, which is 2 percentage points higher than that of Conglomerate, and they have the same standard deviation of returns as that of Conglomerate, at 2.82 percent. This information is presented in the first three columns of Table 13-8.

Table 13-8 Rates of return for Conglomerate Inc. and two merger candidates

	A	B	C	D	E	F
		(1)	**(2)**	**(3)**	**(4)** **(1) + (2)** Conglomerate Inc. + Positive Correlation Inc.	**(5)** **(1) + (3)** Conglomerate Inc. + Negative Correlation Inc.
1	Year	Conglomerate Inc.	Positive Correlation Inc. **+ 1.0**	Negative Correlation Inc. **− 0.9**		
2	1	14%	16%	10%	15%	12%
3	2	10	12	16	11	13
4	3	8	10	18	9	13
5	4	12	14	14	13	13
6	5	16	18	12	17	14
7	Mean return	12%	14%	14%	13%	13%
8	Standard deviation of returns (σ)	2.82%	2.82%	2.82%	2.82%	0.63%
9	Correlation coefficients with Conglomerate Inc.				+1.0	−0.9

Real Options Add a New Dimension to Capital Budgeting

According to traditional net present value analysis, the expected yearly inflows are discounted back to the present at the cost of capital, and their present value is compared to the cost of the investment. If the present value of the inflows is larger than the investment, the investment is considered acceptable; if not, it is rejected.

But some would argue this process is incomplete because it fails to consider the flexibility to revise decisions after a project has begun. For example, assume an oil company decides to drill for oil in 10 adjacent sites over the next five years. Under traditional capital budgeting analysis, the present value of expected cash flows would be discounted back for five years and compared to the cost of the venture. But traditional capital budgeting does not consider the intermittent decisions that can be made during the life of the project.

Let's initially assume that the oil drilling project has a negative net present value. But in further analyzing the project, we include the option that if after hitting two successful oil wells, we encounter three dry holes, we will abandon the project and cut the size of our investment. This could lead to a positive net present value, especially if the last five drilling attempts were going to be particularly expensive.

Alternatively, let's assume that if the first two sites turn out to be much more productive than initially anticipated, we expand the project to 15 sites by including other nearby potential oil wells. We might also have two or three other options. By including these options in the initial planning, a negative net value project may take on a positive return.

The options discussed here are termed *real* options because they involve assets as opposed to financial options, which relate to stocks and bonds.

Real options might include the flexibility of terminating a project, taking a more desirable route once initial results are in, greatly expanding the project if there is unexpected success, and so on. Such elements are particularly likely to be present in natural resource discovery, technology-related investments, and new product introductions. But the list does not stop there. Almost every capital budgeting project contains a potential element of flexibility once it's put into place. There is a real option to change the course of action, and this real option has a monetary value just as a financial option does.

The value of the real option is the difference in the net present value of the project with the flexibility included in the analysis versus the traditional static net present value analysis. An analogy can be drawn to playing poker where you can return part of your hand and draw again in five-card draw, versus five-card stud in which you must stay with the cards that are initially dealt to you.

Including real options in a capital budgeting analysis sounds good, but the process is not widely used. A recent study showed that only 14.3 percent of the *Fortune* 1000 companies use real options in any form in their analysis.[7] The primary reasons for this low utilization are lack of sophistication and distrust that the options will actually be properly used in the future. This low utilization rate is likely to change in the future as sophistication increases.

---

[7]Stanley Block, "Are 'Real Options' Actually Used in the Real World?" *The Engineering Economist* 52, no. 3 (2007), pp. 255–267.

Since management desires to reduce risk (σ) and to increase returns at the same time, it decides to analyze the results of each combination.[8] These are shown in the last two columns in Table 13-8. A combination with Positive Correlation Inc. increases the mean return for Conglomerate Inc. to 13 percent (average of 12 percent

---

[8]In Chapter 20, you will evaluate a merger situation in which there is no increase in earnings, only a reduction in the standard deviation. Because the lower risk may mean a higher price-earnings ratio, this could be beneficial.

and 14 percent) but maintains the same standard deviation of returns (no risk reduction) because the coefficient of correlation is +1.0 and no diversification benefits are achieved. The +1.0 value is shown on the bottom line in black. A combination with Negative Correlation Inc. also increases the mean return to 13 percent, but it reduces the standard deviation of returns to 0.63 percent, a significant reduction in risk. This occurs because of the offsetting relationship of returns between the two companies, as evidenced by the coefficient of correlation of −0.9 (bottom line of Table 13-8 in black). When one company has high returns, the other has low returns, and vice versa. Thus a merger with Negative Correlation Inc. appears to be the best decision.

Evaluation of Combinations

The firm should evaluate all possible combinations of projects, determining which will provide the best trade-off between risk and return. In Figure 13-10, we see a number of alternatives that might be available to a given firm. Each point represents a combination of different possible investments. For example, point F might represent a semiconductor manufacturer combining three different types of semiconductors, plus two types of computers, and two products in unrelated fields. In choosing between the various points or combinations, management should have two primary objectives:

1. Achieve the highest possible return at a given risk level.
2. Provide the lowest possible risk at a given return level.

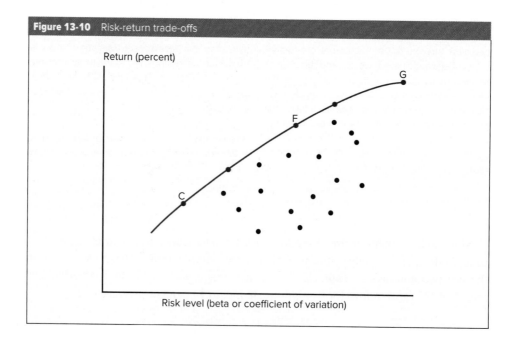

Figure 13-10   Risk-return trade-offs

Return (percent)

Risk level (beta or coefficient of variation)

All the best opportunities will fall along the leftmost sector of the diagram (line C–F–G). Each point on the line satisfies the two objectives of the firm. Any point to the right is less desirable.

After we have developed our best risk-return line, known in the financial literature as the "**efficient frontier**," we must determine where on the line our firm should be. There is no universally correct answer. To the extent we are willing to take large risks for superior returns, we will opt for some point on the upper portion of the line—such as G. However, a more conservative selection might be C.

The Share Price Effect

The firm must be sensitive to the wishes and demands of shareholders. To the extent that unnecessary or undesirable risks are taken, a higher discount rate and lower valuation may be assigned to the stock in the market. Higher profits, resulting from risky ventures, could have a result that is the opposite from that intended. In raising the firm's risk, we could be lowering the overall valuation of the firm.

The aversion of investors to nonpredictability (and the associated risk) is confirmed by observing the relative valuation given to cyclical stocks versus highly predictable growth stocks in the market. Metals, autos, and housing stocks generally trade at an earnings multiplier well below that for industries with level, predictable performances, such as drugs, soft drinks, and even alcohol or cigarettes. Each company must carefully analyze its own situation to determine the appropriate trade-off between risk and return. The changing desires and objectives of investors tend to make the task somewhat more difficult.

SUMMARY

Risk may be defined as the potential variability of the outcomes from an investment. The less predictable the outcomes, the greater is the risk. Both management and investors tend to be risk-averse—that is, all things being equal, they would prefer to take less risk, rather than greater risk.

The most commonly employed method to adjust for risk in the capital budgeting process is to alter the discount rate based on the perceived risk level. High-risk projects will carry a risk premium, producing a discount rate well in excess of the cost of capital.

In assessing the risk components in a given project, management may rely on simulation techniques to generate probabilities of possible outcomes and decision trees to help isolate the key variables to be evaluated.

Management must consider not only the risk inherent in a given project, but also the impact of a new project on the overall risk of the firm (the portfolio effect). Negatively correlated projects have the most favorable effect on smoothing business cycle fluctuations. The firm may wish to consider all combinations and variations of possible projects and to select only those that provide a total risk-return trade-off consistent with its goals.

REVIEW OF FORMULAS

1. $\overline{D}$ (expected value) $= \Sigma\, DP$ (13-1)
    D is outcome
    P is probability of outcome

2. σ (standard deviation) $= \sqrt{\Sigma(D - \overline{D})^2 P}$ (13-2)
    D is outcome
    $\overline{D}$ is expected value
    P is probability of outcome

3. V (coefficient of variation) $= \dfrac{\sigma}{\overline{D}}$ (13-3)
    σ is standard deviation
    $\overline{D}$ is expected value

LIST OF TERMS

risk   418
risk-averse   420
expected value   421
standard deviation   421
coefficient of variation   422
beta   423

risk-adjusted discount rates   424
simulation   428
decision trees   429
portfolio effect   430
coefficient of correlation   431
efficient frontier   435

DISCUSSION QUESTIONS

1. If corporate managers are risk-averse, does this mean they will not take risks? Explain. *(LO13-2)*

2. Discuss the concept of risk and how it might be measured. *(LO13-1)*

3. When is the coefficient of variation a better measure of risk than the standard deviation? *(LO13-1)*

4. Explain how the concept of risk can be incorporated into the capital budgeting process. *(LO13-3)*

5. If risk is to be analyzed in a qualitative way, place the following investment decisions in order from the lowest risk to the highest risk: *(LO13-1)*
    a. New equipment.
    b. New market.
    c. Repair of old machinery.
    d. New product in a foreign market.
    e. New product in a related market.
    f. Addition to a new product line.

6. Assume a company, correlated with the economy, is evaluating six projects, of which two are positively correlated with the economy, two are negatively correlated, and two are not correlated with it at all. Which two projects would it select to minimize the company's overall risk? *(LO13-5)*

7. Assume a firm has several hundred possible investments and that it wants to analyze the risk-return trade-off for portfolios of 20 projects. How should it proceed with the evaluation? *(LO13-5)*

8. Explain the effect of the risk-return trade-off on the market value of common stock. *(LO13-3)*

9. What is the purpose of using simulation analysis? *(LO13-4)*

PRACTICE PROBLEMS AND SOLUTIONS

1. Hanson Auto Supplies is examining the following probability distribution. What is the coefficient of variation?

Coefficient of variation *(LO13-1)*

Cash Flow	Probability
$20	0.30
40	0.40
60	0.30

2. Hanson Auto Supply in the prior problem uses the risk-adjusted discount rate and relates the discount rate to the coefficient of variation as follows:

Risk-adjusted discount rate decision *(LO13-3)*

Coefficient of Variation	Discount Rate
0–0.30	8%
0.31–0.60	10
0.61–0.90	12
0.91–1.20	16

It will invest $120 and receive the expected value of cash flows you computed in Problem 1 of $40. Assume those cash flows of $40 will be earned for the next 5 years and are discounted back at the appropriate discount rate based on the coefficient of variation computed in Problem 1. What is the net present value?

Solutions

1. The formula for the coefficient of variation (V) is:

$$V = \frac{\sigma}{D} \qquad (13\text{-}3)$$

First compute the expected value ($\bar{D}$).

$$\bar{D} = \Sigma\, DP \qquad (13\text{--}1)$$

D = Cash flow or outcome (in 000s)

P = Probability

D	P	DP
$20	0.30	6
40	0.40	16
60	0.30	18
		$40 = \Sigma DP$

$$\bar{D} = \$40$$

Then compute the standard deviation (σ).

$$\sigma = \sqrt{\Sigma(D - \overline{D})^2 P} \qquad (13\text{-}2)$$

D	$\overline{D}$	$(D - \overline{D})$	$(D - \overline{D})^2$	P	$(D - \overline{D})^2 P$
20	40	−20	400	0.30	120
40	0	0	0	0.40	0
60	40	+20	400	0.30	120
					$240 = \Sigma(D - \overline{D})^2 P$

$$\sigma = \sqrt{\Sigma(D - \overline{D})^2 P} = \sqrt{240} = 15.5$$

Next, divide the standard deviation (σ) by the expected value ($\overline{D}$) to determine the coefficient of variation (V).

$$V = \frac{\sigma}{\overline{D}} = \frac{15.5}{40} = 0.3875 \qquad (13\text{-}3)$$

2. First you must determine the appropriate discount rate based on the coefficient of variation. The coefficient of variation computed in the solution to practice Problem 1 is 0.3875. Using the table for this problem, the discount rate should be 10 percent since 0.3875 falls between 0.31 and 0.60.

Now take the present value of an annuity of $40 for five years and compare it to the investment of $120. The interest rate is the risk-adjusted discount rate of 10 percent identified above. The $40 is considered an annuity because it is an equal amount each year. This is not always the case, but eases the computation for this example.

PV of cash flows (inflows)	$151.63
Investment	−120.00
Net present value	$ 31.63

The investment has a positive net present value of $31.63.

FINANCIAL CALCULATOR

PV of Annuity

Enter	Function
5	N
10	I/Y
0	FV
−40	PMT

Function	Solution
CPT	
PV	151.63

PROBLEMS

connect Selected problems are available with Connect. Please see the preface for more information.

Basic Problems

Risk-averse *(LO13-2)*

1. Assume you are risk-averse and have the following three choices. Which project will you select? Compute the coefficient of variation for each.

	Expected Value	Standard Deviation
A	$2,200	$1,400
B	2,730	1,960
C	2,250	1,490

2. Myers Business Systems is evaluating the introduction of a new product. The possible levels of unit sales and the probabilities of their occurrence are given next:

Expected value and standard deviation (LO13-1)

Possible Market Reaction	Sales in Units	Probability
Low response	20	0.10
Moderate response	40	0.30
High response	55	0.40
Very high response	70	0.20

a. What is the expected value of unit sales for the new product?

b. What is the standard deviation of unit sales?

3. Sampson Corp. is evaluating the introduction of a new product. The possible levels of unit sales and the probabilities of their occurrence are shown next:

Expected value and standard deviation (LO13-1)

Possible Market Reaction	Sales in Units	Probability
Low response	30	0.10
Moderate response	50	0.20
High response	75	0.40
Very high response	90	0.30

a. What is the expected value of unit sales for the new product?

b. What is the standard deviation of unit sales?

4. Shack Homebuilders Limited is evaluating a new promotional campaign that could increase home sales. Possible outcomes and probabilities of the outcomes are shown next. Compute the coefficient of variation.

Coefficient of variation (LO13-1)

Possible Outcome	Additional Sales in Units	Probability
Ineffective campaign	40	0.30
Normal response	100	0.30
Extremely effective	120	0.40

5. Al Bundy is evaluating a new advertising program that could increase shoe sales. Possible outcomes and probabilities of the outcomes are shown next. Compute the coefficient of variation.

Coefficient of variation (LO13-1)

Possible Outcome	Additional Sales in Units	Probability
Ineffective campaign	40	0.20
Normal response	60	0.50
Extremely effective	140	0.30

Coefficient of variation (LO13-1)

6. Possible outcomes for three investment alternatives and their probabilities of occurrence are given next.

	Alternative 1		Alternative 2		Alternative 3	
	Outcome	Probability	Outcome	Probability	Outcome	Probability
Failure	50	0.2	90	0.3	95	0.2
Acceptable	90	0.4	190	0.3	215	0.6
Successful	135	0.4	225	0.4	380	0.2

Rank the three alternatives in terms of risk from lowest to highest (compute the coefficient of variation).

7. Five investment alternatives have the following returns and standard deviations of returns:

Alternative	Returns: Expected Value	Standard Deviation
A	$ 5,000	$1,200
B	4,000	600
C	4,000	800
D	8,000	3,200
E	10,000	900

Using the coefficient of variation, rank the five alternatives from the lowest risk to the highest risk.

8. Five investment alternatives have the following returns and standard deviations of returns:

Alternative	Returns: Expected Value	Standard Deviation
A	$ 1,980	$ 970
B	820	1,190
C	12,700	3,100
D	1,140	630
E	62,700	14,100

Using the coefficient of variation, rank the five alternatives from lowest risk to highest risk.

9. Digital Technology wishes to determine its coefficient of variation as a company over time. The firm projects the following data (in millions of dollars):

Year	Profits: Expected Value	Standard Deviation
1	$180	$ 62
3	240	104
6	300	166
9	400	292

a. Compute the coefficient of variation (V) for each time period.

b. Does the risk (V) appear to be increasing over a period of time? If so, why might this be the case?

10. Tim Trepid is highly risk-averse while Mike Macho actually enjoys taking a risk.   *Risk-averse*
    a. Which one of the four investments should Tim choose? Compute coeffi-   *(LO13-2)*
    cients of variation to help you in your choice.

Investment	Returns: Expected Value	Standard Deviation
Buy stocks	$ 9,140	$ 6,140
Buy bonds	7,680	2,560
Buy commodity futures	19,100	26,700
Buy options	17,700	18,200

    b. Which one of the four investments should Mike choose?

11. Mountain Ski Corp. was set up to take large risks and is willing to take the   *Risk-averse*
    greatest risk possible. Lakeway Train Co. is more typical of the average   *(LO13-2)*
    corporation and is risk-averse.
    a. Which of the following four projects should Mountain Ski Corp. choose?
    Compute the coefficients of variation to help you make your decision.
    b. Which one of the four projects should Lakeway Train Co. choose based on
    the same criteria of using the coefficient of variation?

Year	Returns Expected Value	Standard Deviation
A	$527,000	$834,000
B	682,000	306,000
C	74,000	135,000
D	140,000	89,000

12. Kyle's Shoe Stores Inc. is considering opening an additional suburban outlet.   *Coefficient of*
    An aftertax expected cash flow of $130 per week is anticipated from two stores   *variation and*
    that are being evaluated. Both stores have positive net present values.   *investment decision*
         Which store site would you select based on the distribution of these cash   *(LO13-1)*
    flows? Use the coefficient of variation as your measure of risk.

Site A		Site B	
Probability	Cash Flow	Probability	Cash Flow
0.3	$ 80	0.2	$ 50
0.3	130	0.2	80
0.1	160	0.3	130
0.3	170	0.1	180
		0.2	235

13. Waste Industries is evaluating a $70,000 project with the following cash flows: *Risk-adjusted*
                                                                                         discount rate

Year	Cash Flow
1	$11,000
2	16,000
3	21,000
4	24,000
5	30,000

(LO13-3)

The coefficient of variation for the project is 0.847.

Based on the following table of risk-adjusted discount rates, should the project be undertaken? Select the appropriate discount rate and then compute the net present value.

Coefficient of Variation	Discount Rate
0–0.25	6%
0.26–0.50	8
0.51–0.75	10
0.76–1.00	14
1.01–1.25	20

Intermediate Problems

Risk-adjusted discount rate
(LO13-3)

14. Dixie Dynamite Company is evaluating two methods of blowing up old buildings for commercial purposes over the next five years. Method one (implosion) is relatively low in risk for this business and will carry a 12 percent discount rate. Method two (explosion) is less expensive to perform but more dangerous and will call for a higher discount rate of 16 percent. Either method will require an initial capital outlay of $75,000. The inflows from projected business over the next five years are shown next. Which method should be selected using net present value analysis?

Year	Method 1	Method 2
1	$18,000	$20,000
2	24,000	25,000
3	34,000	35,000
4	26,000	28,000
5	14,000	15,000

Discount rate and timing
(LO13-1)

15. Fill in the following table from Appendix B. Does a high discount rate have a greater or lesser effect on long-term inflows compared to recent ones?

	Discount Rate	
Year	5%	20%
1	_____	_____
10	_____	_____
20	_____	_____

Expected value with net present value
(LO13-1)

16. Debby's Dance Studios is considering the purchase of new sound equipment that will enhance the popularity of its aerobics dancing. The equipment will cost $27,900. Debby is not sure how many members the new equipment will attract, but she estimates that her increased annual cash flows for each of the next five years will have the following probability distribution. Debby's cost of capital is 15 percent.

Cash Flow	Probability
$4,570	0.1
5,550	0.3
7,400	0.4
9,930	0.2

a. What is the expected value of the cash flow? The value you compute will apply to each of the five years.

b. What is the expected net present value?

c. Should Debby buy the new equipment?

Advanced Problems

17. Highland Mining and Minerals Co. is considering the purchase of two gold mines. Only one investment will be made. The Australian gold mine will cost $1,649,000 and will produce $353,000 per year in years 5 through 15 and $503,000 per year in years 16 through 25. The U.S. gold mine will cost $2,054,000 and will produce $282,000 per year for the next 25 years. The cost of capital is 13 percent.

Deferred cash flows and risk-adjusted discount rate *(LO13-1)*

a. Which investment should be made? (Note: In looking up present value factors for this problem, you need to work with the concept of a deferred annuity for the Australian mine. The returns in years 5 through 15 actually represent 11 years; the returns in years 16 through 25 represent 10 years.)

b. If the Australian mine justifies an extra 2 percent premium over the normal cost of capital because of its riskiness and relative uncertainty of cash flows, does the investment decision change?

18. Mr. Sam Golff desires to invest a portion of his assets in rental property. He has narrowed his choices down to two apartment complexes, Palmer Heights and Crenshaw Village. After conferring with the present owners, Mr. Golff has developed the following estimates of the cash flows for these properties:

Coefficient of variation and investment decision *(LO13-1)*

Palmer Heights		Crenshaw Village	
Yearly Aftertax Cash Inflow (in thousands)	Probability	Yearly Aftertax Cash Inflow (in thousands)	Probability
$ 70	0.2	$ 75	0.2
75	0.2	80	0.3
90	0.2	90	0.4
105	0.2	100	0.1
110	0.2		

a. Find the expected cash flow from each apartment complex.

b. What is the coefficient of variation for each apartment complex?

c. Which apartment complex has more risk?

19. Allison's Dresswear Manufacturers is preparing a strategy for the fall season. One alternative is to expand its traditional ensemble of wool sweaters. A second option would be to enter the cashmere sweater market with a new line of high-quality designer label products. The marketing department has determined that the wool and cashmere sweater lines offer the following probability of outcomes and related cash flows:

Decision tree analysis *(LO13-4)*

	Expand Wool Sweaters Line		Enter Cashmere Sweaters Line	
Expected Sales	**Probability**	**Present Value of Cash Flows from Sales**	**Probability**	**Present Value of Cash Flows from Sales**
Fantastic	0.5	$221,000	0.3	$341,000
Moderate	0.2	192,000	0.4	272,000
Low	0.3	88,600	0.3	0

The initial cost to expand the wool sweater line is $142,000. To enter the cashmere sweater line, the initial cost in designs, inventory, and equipment is $102,000.

a. Diagram a complete decision tree of possible outcomes similar to Table 13-6. Note that you are dealing with thousands of dollars rather than millions. Take the analysis all the way through the process of computing expected NPV (last column for each investment).

b. Given the analysis in part *a,* would you automatically make the investment indicated?

Probability analysis with a normal curve distribution
(LO13-4)

20. When returns from a project can be assumed to be normally distributed, such as those shown in Figure 13-6 (represented by a symmetrical, bell-shaped curve), the areas under the curve can be determined from statistical tables based on standard deviations. For example, 68.26 percent of the distribution will fall within one standard deviation of the expected value ($\overline{D} \pm 1\sigma$). Similarly, 95.44 percent will fall within two standard deviations ($\overline{D} \pm 2\sigma$), and so on. An abbreviated table of areas under the normal curve is shown next.

Number of σ's from Expected Value	**+ or −**	**+ and −**
0.5	0.1915	0.3830
1.0	0.3413	0.6826
1.5	0.4332	0.8664
1.65	0.4505	0.9010
2.0	0.4772	0.9544

Assume Project A has an expected value of $24,000 and a standard deviation (σ) of $4,800.

a. What is the probability that the outcome will be between $16,800 and $31,200?

b. What is the probability that the outcome will be between $14,400 and $33,600?

c. What is the probability that the outcome will be at least $14,400?

d. What is the probability that the outcome will be less than $31,900?

e. What is the probability that the outcome will be less than $19,200 or greater than $26,400?

21. The Oklahoma Pipeline Company projects the following pattern of inflows from an investment. The inflows are spread over time to reflect delayed benefits. Each year is independent of the others.

Increasing risk over time (LO13-1)

Year 1		Year 5		Year 10	
Cash Inflow	**Probability**	**Cash Inflow**	**Probability**	**Cash Inflow**	**Probability**
55	0.40	40	0.30	20	0.40
70	0.20	70	0.40	70	0.20
85	0.40	100	0.30	120	0.40

The expected value for all three years is $70.

a. Compute the standard deviation for each of the three years.

b. Diagram the expected values and standard deviations for each of the three years in a manner similar to Figure 13-6.

c. Assuming 6 percent and 12 percent discount rates, complete the following table for present value factors:

Year	PV$_{IF}$ 6%	PV$_{IF}$ 12%	Difference
1	0.943	0.893	0.050
5	_____	_____	_____
10	_____	_____	_____

d. Is the increasing risk over time, as diagrammed in part *b*, consistent with the larger differences in PV$_{IF}$s over time as computed in part *c*?

e. Assume the initial investment is $135. What is the net present value of the investment at a 12 percent discount rate? Should the investment be accepted?

22. Treynor Pie Co. is a food company specializing in high-calorie snack foods. It is seeking to diversify its food business and lower its risks. It is examining three companies—a gourmet restaurant chain, a baby food company, and a nutritional products firm. Each of these companies can be bought at the same multiple of earnings. The following table represents information about all the companies:

Portfolio effect of a merger (LO13-5)

Company	Correlation with Treynor Pie Company	Sales ($ millions)	Expected Earnings ($ millions)	Standard Deviation in Earnings ($ millions)
Treynor Pie Company	+1.0	$126	$10	$4.0
Gourmet restaurant	+0.4	63	9	1.4
Baby food company	+0.3	52	5	1.6
Nutritional products company	−0.7	77	7	3.2

a. Using the last two columns, compute the coefficient of variation for each of the four companies. Which company is the least risky? Which company is the most risky?

b. Discuss which of the acquisition candidates is most likely to reduce Treynor Pie Company's risk. Explain why.

Portfolio effect of a merger
(LO13-5)

23. Hooper Chemical Company, a major chemical firm that uses such raw materials as carbon and petroleum as part of its production process, is examining a plastics firm to add to its operations. Before the acquisition, the normal expected outcomes for the firm were as follows:

	Outcome ($ millions)	Probability
Recession	$20	0.30
Normal economy	40	0.40
Strong economy	60	0.30

After the acquisition, the expected outcomes for the firm would be:

	Outcome ($ millions)	Probability
Recession	$10	0.3
Normal economy	40	0.4
Strong economy	80	0.3

a. Compute the expected value, standard deviation, and coefficient of variation before the acquisition.

b. After the acquisition, these values are as follows:

Expected value	43.0 ($ millions)
Standard deviation	27.2 ($ millions)
Coefficient of variation	0.633

Comment on whether this acquisition appears desirable to you.

c. Do you think the firm's stock price is likely to go up as a result of this acquisition?

d. If the firm were interested in reducing its risk exposure, which of the following three industries would you advise it to consider for an acquisition? Briefly comment on your answer.

(1) Chemical company

(2) Oil company

(3) Computer company

Efficient frontier
(LO13-5)

24. Ms. Sharp is looking at a number of different types of investments for her portfolio. She identifies eight possible investments.

	Return	Risk		Return	Risk
(a)	11%	2%	(e)	14%	5.0%
(b)	11	2.5	(f)	16	5.0
(c)	13	3.0	(g)	15	5.8
(d)	13	4.2	(h)	18	7.0

a.   Graph the data in a manner similar to Figure 13-10. Use the following axes for your data:

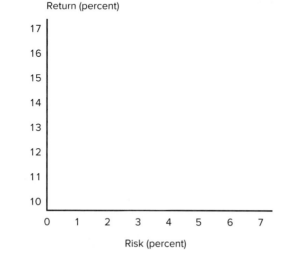

b.   Draw a curved line representing the efficient frontier.

c.   What two objectives do points on the efficient frontier satisfy?

d.   Is there one point on the efficient frontier that is best for all investors?

25. Sheila Goodman recently received her MBA from the Harvard Business School. She has joined the family business, Goodman Software Products Inc., as vice president of finance.

   She believes in adjusting projects for risk. Her father is somewhat skeptical but agrees to go along with her. Her approach is somewhat different than the risk-adjusted discount rate approach, but achieves the same objective.

   She suggests that the inflows for each year of a project be adjusted downward for lack of certainty and then be discounted back at a risk-free rate. The theory is that the adjustment penalty makes the inflows the equivalent of risk-less inflows, and therefore a risk-free rate is justified.

   A table showing the possible coefficient of variation for an inflow and the associated adjustment factor is shown next:

Certainty equivalent approach (LO13-1)

Coefficient of Variation	Adjustment Factor
0–0.25	0.90
0.26–0.50	0.80
0.51–0.75	0.70
0.76–1.00	0.60
1.01–1.25	0.50

Assume a $184,000 project provides the following inflows with the associated coefficients of variation for each year:

Year	Inflow	Coefficient of Variation
1	$32,200	0.12
2	59,500	0.28
3	79,900	0.45
4	59,200	0.79
5	65,600	1.15

a. Fill in the following table:

Year	Inflow	Coefficient of Variation	Adjustment Factor	Adjusted Inflow
1	$32,200	0.12	_____	_____
2	59,500	0.28	_____	_____
3	79,900	0.45	_____	_____
4	59,200	0.79	_____	_____
5	65,600	1.15	_____	_____

b. If the risk-free rate is 5 percent, should this $184,000 project be accepted? Compute the net present value of the adjusted inflows.

COMPREHENSIVE PROBLEM

Gibson Appliance Co.
(Portfolio effect of a merger)
(LO13-5)

Gibson Appliance Co. is a very stable billion-dollar company with a sales growth of about 7 percent per year in good or bad economic conditions. Because of this stability (a coefficient of correlation with the economy of +0.4, and a standard deviation of sales of about 5 percent from the mean), Mr. Hoover, the vice president of finance, thinks the company could absorb a small risky company that could add quite a bit of return without increasing the company's risk much. He is trying to decide which of the two companies he will buy, using the following figures. Gibson's cost of capital is 12 percent.

Genetic Technology Co. (cost $80 million)		Silicon Microchip Co. (cost $80 million)	
Cash Flow for 10 Years ($ millions)	**Probability**	**Cash Flow for 10 Years ($ millions)**	**Probability**
$ 2	0.2	$ 5	0.2
8	0.3	7	0.2
16	0.2	18	0.3
25	0.2	24	0.3
40	0.1		

a. What is the expected cash flow from both companies?

b. Which company has the lower coefficient of variation?

c. Compute the net present value of each company.

d. Which company would you pick, based on the net present values?

e. Would you change your mind if you added the risk dimensions to the problem? Explain.

f. What if Genetic Technology Co. had a coefficient of correlation with the economy of −0.2 and Silicon Microchip Co. had one of +0.5? Which of these companies would give you the best portfolio effects for risk reduction?

g. What might be the effect of the acquisitions on the market value of Gibson Appliance Co.'s stock?

COMPREHENSIVE PROBLEM

Five years ago, Kennedy Trucking Company was considering the purchase of 60 new diesel trucks that were 15 percent more fuel-efficient than the ones the firm was using. Mr. Hoffman, the president, had found that the company uses an average of 10 million gallons of diesel fuel per year at a price of $1.25 per gallon. If he can cut fuel consumption by 15 percent, he will save $1,875,000 per year (1,500,000 gallons times $1.25).

Mr. Hoffman assumed that the price of diesel fuel is an external market force that he cannot control and that any increased costs of fuel will be passed on to the shipper through higher rates endorsed by the Interstate Commerce Commission. If this is true, then fuel efficiency would save more money as the price of diesel fuel rises (at $1.35 per gallon, he would save $2,025,000 in total if he buys the new trucks). Mr. Hoffman has come up with two possible forecasts as shown next—each of which he feels has about a 50 percent chance of coming true. Under assumption 1, diesel prices will stay relatively low; under assumption 2, diesel prices will rise considerably. Sixty new trucks will cost Kennedy Trucking $5 million. Under a special provision from the Interstate Commerce Commission, the allowable depreciation will be 25 percent in year 1, 38 percent in year 2, and 37 percent in year 3. The firm has a tax rate of 40 percent and a cost of capital of 10 percent.

a. First compute the yearly expected costs of diesel fuel for both assumption 1 (relatively low prices) and assumption 2 (high prices) from the following forecasts.

Forecast for assumption 1 (low fuel prices):

Probability (same for each year)	Price of Diesel Fuel per Gallon		
	Year 1	Year 2	Year 3
0.1	$0.80	$0.90	$1.00
0.2	1.00	1.10	1.10
0.3	1.10	1.20	1.30
0.2	1.30	1.45	1.45
0.2	1.40	1.55	1.60

Forecast for assumption 2 (high fuel prices):

Probability (same for each year)	Price of Diesel Fuel per Gallon		
	Year 1	Year 2	Year 3
0.1	$1.20	$1.50	$1.70
0.3	1.30	1.70	2.00
0.4	1.80	2.30	2.50
0.2	2.20	2.50	2.80

Kennedy Trucking Company

(Investment decision based on probability analysis)

(LO13-1)

b. What will be the dollar savings in diesel expenses each year for assumption 1 and for assumption 2?

c. Find the increased cash flow after taxes for both forecasts.

d. Compute the net present value of the truck purchases for each fuel forecast assumption and the combined net present value (that is, weigh the NPVs by 0.5).

e. If you were Mr. Hoffman, would you go ahead with this capital investment?

f. How sensitive to fuel prices is this capital investment?

 WEB EXERCISE

1. Alcoa was listed in Table 13-2 as a company that has a relativity high beta (a measure of stock price volatility). Alcoa produces aluminum and aluminum products. Go to its website at www.alcoa.com, and follow these steps:

    Under "Investors" select "Financial Reports." Select "Annual Reports and Proxy Information." Download the latest annual report. Scroll all the way down to "Selected Financial Data."

2. One of the characteristics of high beta stocks is that they often have volatile earnings performances. Let's check out Alcoa. Compute the year-to-year percentage change in "Diluted-Income from Continuing Operations" for each of the five years. Do the earnings appear to be volatile?

3. Companies with high betas and inconsistent performance are encouraged to keep their debt ratios low (under 50 percent). Compute the ratio of long-term debt to total assets for each of the five years for Alcoa. What does the pattern look like to you?

Note: Occasionally a topic we have listed may have been deleted, updated, or moved into a different location on a website. If you click on the site map or site index, you will be introduced to a table of contents that should aid you in finding the topic you are looking for.

Long-Term Financing

>>> RELATED WEBSITES

www.nyse.com
www.nasdaq.com
www.google.com

finance.yahoo.com
www.cme.com
www.3m.com

www.cboe.com

14

Capital Markets

Security markets comprise myriad securities, from government bonds to corporate common stock. These markets are influenced by many variables such as interest rates, exchange rates, investors' confidence, economic growth, global crises, and more. Some of these influences are always present in the global economy and affect prices in the securities markets in either a positive or a negative way. For example, world stock markets have recovered substantially from the 2009 financial crisis, and although it took many years, at the beginning of 2018, all the world economies seemed to be running on all cylinders. Stock indexes around the world set new highs in 2017 and again in early 2018. The 2017 Tax Cuts and Jobs Act provided some impetus for the U.S. markets to continue their move into uncharted territory.

Capital markets provide a place both for governments and corporations to raise capital and for individuals to invest in promising business opportunities. Corporations come to capital markets for short-term sources of funds or long-term capital. When the markets are good, money is cheap and easy to find, and when the markets are bad, money is hard to find and often relatively expensive. The world markets frequently move back and forth between the two extremes.

Security markets are generally separated into short-term and long-term markets. The short-term markets comprise securities with maturities of one year or less and are referred to as **money markets**. The securities most commonly traded in these markets, such as Treasury bills, commercial paper, and negotiable certificates of deposit, were previously discussed under working capital and cash management in Chapter 7 and will not be covered again. The long-term markets are called **capital markets** and consist of securities having maturities greater than one year. The most common corporate securities in this category are bonds, common stock, preferred stock, and convertible securities. These securities are found on the firm's balance sheet under the designation long-term liabilities and equities. Taken together, these long-term securities comprise the firm's capital structure.

In this chapter, we will look at how the capital markets are organized and integrated into the corporate and economic system of the United States. Capital markets have become increasingly international as suppliers of financial capital seek out the best risk-return opportunities around the world.

The globalization of capital markets is particularly important for large U.S. multinational corporations that use these markets to raise capital for both domestic and international operations. We start with a global overview of markets and then discuss the U.S. capital markets more fully.

International Capital Markets

International capital markets have increased in importance during the last several decades and continue to become larger, and more efficient and competitive. The evolution and growth of these markets can be traced to several important economic trends over the last two decades. First, and perhaps foremost, all major economies around the world have adopted the basic principles of capitalism. Prior to 1991 this was not true. Both the Soviet Union and the People's Republic of China explicitly rejected capitalism's private ownership of productive property in favor of communism, which called for government control of productive assets. The Soviet Union disbanded in 1991, and China has moved along an increasingly capitalistic course for several decades. In the long run, capitalism has proven to be a more efficient system.

Even outside the Soviet Union and China, economies generally evolved toward capitalism. Central and Eastern European countries privatized many of their state industries during the 1990s as they moved toward market-based economies. Across the globe, countries sold off state-owned electric utilities, airlines, telephone systems, railroads, banks, and insurance companies. Privatization has been particularly important and successful in telecommunications where genuine competition has taken place. As state-owned companies lost their monopolies due to both legislation and technological change, prices for telecommunication services fell dramatically. Cheap and dependable telecommunication has allowed other technologies to be deployed rapidly.

Another important evolution for international capital markets has been the continuing development of international "free trade." In 1994 the North American Free Trade Agreement (NAFTA) was established among the United States, Canada, and Mexico. While this trade agreement has facilitated trade among these three countries, many, including President Trump, think that Canada and Mexico have gotten the better part of the deal. Because it is cheaper to manufacture in Mexico with lower labor costs, many manufacturing jobs have moved from the United States to Mexico. This has caused a problem in the Rust Belt states that have lost jobs. President Trump has vowed to renegotiate the deal, and time will tell if the United States ends up better off.

Other areas of the world have also seen trade barriers fall, and the European Union (EU) has grown to include 28 countries in this free trade zone. Nineteen countries have adopted the euro as their domestic currency, and the European Central Bank is in charge of monetary policy for these countries. This has caused some problems because not all countries are on the same economic level of development. For example, it is difficult to compare the Lithuanian or Greek economy to the German economy. However, because of the monetary union, the euro is the second most important international currency after the dollar. Once the Chinese yuan becomes convertible into world currencies, it most likely will take its place with the U.S. dollar, euro, and Japanese yen as a major currency.

On an even more global scale, the World Trade Organization (WTO) strives to further liberalize international trade. Russia, which was admitted to membership in 2012, is 1 of 164 countries in the WTO. Algeria, Ethiopia, Iraq, Iran, and dozens of other countries (mostly in northern Africa and central Asia) are seeking membership. Iran is currently the world's largest non-WTO economy, mostly because of its oil deposits.

All these events—the rise of capitalism, global privatizations, reduced telecommunication costs, and increased international trade—have combined to create an international demand and a need for capital worldwide. While the U.S. capital markets are still the largest and most important, other capital markets are increasing in size relative to the United States. In particular, European markets have changed markedly in the last decade, and the Asian markets of China, India, Indonesia, Thailand, and others have grown dramatically.

Taking advantage of free trade and improved global capital markets, companies search the international markets for opportunities to raise debt and equity capital at the lowest cost. Many corporations list their common stock worldwide to increase liquidity for their stockholders and to provide opportunities for the sale of new stock in foreign countries.

Figure 14-1 shows the market capitalization of each market—in other words, the total market value of all the companies listed on that exchange. This also gives us an idea of the size of the domestic economy and the size of the companies listed in U.S. dollars. Notice that the two largest markets, the NASDAQ and NYSE, are headquartered in the United States. However, both have significant international operations, and some foreign companies are listed on the U.S. exchanges as American Depository Receipts. What has changed since the last edition of this text three years ago is that there are now three Chinese exchanges listed—the Shanghai, the Shenzhen, and the Hong Kong exchanges. They have all grown, and combined they make up the second-largest market capitalization.

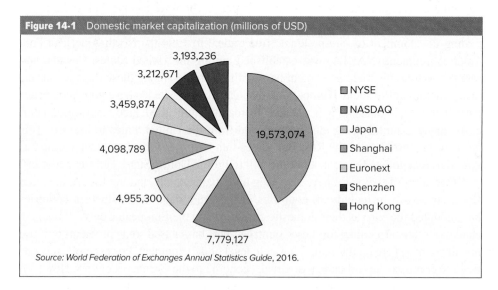

Figure 14-1   Domestic market capitalization (millions of USD)

- NYSE
- NASDAQ
- Japan
- Shanghai
- Euronext
- Shenzhen
- Hong Kong

19,573,074
7,779,127
4,955,300
4,098,789
3,459,874
3,212,671
3,193,236

Source: World Federation of Exchanges Annual Statistics Guide, 2016.

Table 14-1   World Federation of Exchanges members (2017)

The Americas	Europe, Middle East, and Africa	Asia-Pacific
Bermuda Stock Exchange	Abu Dhabi Securities Exchange	Australian Securities Exchange
Bolsa de Comercio de Buenos Aires	Amman Stock Exchange	BSE India Limited
Bolsa de Comercio de Santiago	Athens Stock Exchange (ATHEX)	Bursa Malaysia
Bolsa de Valores de Colombia	Bahrain Bourse	China Financial Futures Exchange
Bolsa de Valores de Lima	BME Spanish Exchanges	Colombo Stock Exchange
Bolsa Mexicana de Valores	Borsa Istanbul	Dalian Commodity Exchange
B3—Brasil Bolsa Balcao	Bourse de Casablanca	Dhaka Stock Exchange Ltd.
BATS Global Markets	Cyprus Stock Exchange	HoChiMinh Stock Exchange
CBOE Global Markets	Deutsche Börse AG	Hong Kong Exchanges and Clearing
CME Group	Dubai Financial Market	Indonesia Stock Exchange
The Depository Trust & Clearing Corporation	The Egyptian Stock Exchange	Japan Exchange Group, Inc.
Intercontinental Exchange, Inc. (NYSE)	EuroCCP	Johannesburg Stock Exchange
NASDAQ	Euronext	Korea Exchange
The Options Clearing Corporation	Irish Stock Exchange	National Stock Exchange of India Limited
TMX Group Inc. Toronto	Kazakhstan Stock Exchange	NZX Limited
	Luxembourg Stock Exchange	Philippine Stock Exchange
	Malta Stock Exchange	Shanghai Futures Exchange
	Moscow Exchange	Shanghai Stock Exchange
	Muscat Securities Market	Shenzhen Stock Exchange
	Nigerian Stock Exchange	Singapore Exchange
	Oslo Stock Exchange	Stock Exchange of Thailand
	Palestine Exchange	Taipei Exchange
	Qatar Stock Exchange	Taiwan Futures Exchange
	Saudi Stock Exchange (Tadawul)	Taiwan Stock Exchange
	SIX Swiss Exchange	Zhengzhou Commodity Exchange
	Stock Exchange of Mauritius	
	Tel-Aviv Stock Exchange	

Source: https://www.world-exchanges.org/home/index.php/members/wfe-members (accessed January 23, 2018).

Table 14-1 lists members of the World Federation of Exchanges. Not all are large but most are flourishing, with growing volume, new listings, and increased interest by investors worldwide.

The well-developed equity markets in the United States have facilitated investment in the U.S. economy by foreigners. This is not surprising since the United States is one of the most politically stable countries in the world. Not only do well-developed financial markets facilitate investment in the United States, but foreign investors also choose to invest in the United States because they believe that the U.S. economy will continue to prosper. Moreover, the U.S. government is not likely to confiscate foreigners' assets, an issue that is of considerable concern in some countries. For example, in recent years

Venezuela has confiscated assets from oil companies, cement producers, steel mills, and food processors. Between 2000 and 2010, Venezuela confiscated over 1,000 corporations from foreign and domestic owners. Unsurprisingly, and in contrast to the United States, foreign investors currently have almost no interest in investing in Venezuela.

A large percentage of foreign investments, especially by the Chinese and Japanese, has been invested in U.S. government securities. These investments help fund the large budget deficits the United States has been running. Much more has gone into corporate bonds, common stock, and direct investment in U.S. properties and companies.

Competition for Funds in the U.S. Capital Markets

Let's return to markets in the United States. In order to put U.S. corporate securities into perspective, it is necessary to look at other securities available in the capital markets. The federal government, government agencies, state governments, and local municipalities all compete with one another and corporations for a limited supply of financial capital. The capital markets serve as a way of allocating the available capital to the most efficient user. Therefore the ultimate investor must choose among many kinds of securities, both corporate and noncorporate. Before investors part with their money they desire to maximize their return for any given level of risk, and thus the expected return from the universe of securities acts as an allocating mechanism in the markets.

Government Securities

U.S. Government Securities   In accordance with government fiscal policy, the U.S. Treasury manages the federal government's debt in order to balance the flow of funds into and out of the U.S. Treasury. When deficits are incurred, the Treasury can sell short-term or long-term securities to finance the shortfall and when surpluses occur, the government can retire debt. When the U.S. government collects more in taxes than it is spending, it doesn't need to borrow and this frees up capital for the other sectors of the economy.

Federally Sponsored Credit Agencies   The **federally sponsored credit agencies** are governmental units that issue their securities on a separate basis from those securities sold directly by the U.S. Treasury. Some of the largest sponsored credit agencies are involved in mortgage lending to the U.S. housing market. Historically, the U.S. government did not directly guarantee securities issued by federally sponsored credit agencies. Instead, these guarantees were implicit. However, in 2008, the two largest agencies, the Federal National Mortgage Association (Fannie Mae) and the Federal Home Loan Mortgage Corporation (Freddie Mac), were placed into government conservatorship, and the implicit guarantee became explicit. The U.S. government also promised to buy an unlimited amount of debt issued by the Federal Home Loan Banks (FHLB), another sponsored agency, thereby guaranteeing that the FHLB could also raise as much capital as it needed. These actions were deemed necessary due to the collapse of residential real estate prices around the country in 2007 and 2008. The bailouts were highly controversial. Many blamed Fannie Mae and Freddie Mac, both of which are private stockholder-owned corporations, for promoting policies that led to the housing "price bubble" whose ultimate collapse drove these same companies to the brink of bankruptcy. Fortunately, as the economy recovered, so did these agencies.

Farm Credit Banks, the Student Loan Marketing Association (Sallie Mae), and the Federal Agricultural Mortgage Corporation (Farmer Mac) are other federally sponsored credit agencies. Like Fannie Mae and Freddie Mac, Sallie Mae and Farmer Mac are private companies whose stocks are traded on the New York Stock Exchange.

State and Local Securities   State and local issues are referred to as **municipal securities** or tax-exempt offerings. Interest payments from securities issued by state and local governments are exempt from federal income taxes and income taxes levied by the state of issue. (For example, if the state of California issues a bond that is bought by someone living in the state of California, the interest is not taxable by California. However if someone living in the state of California buys a bond issued by the state of New York, the interest will be taxable by California.) Because these securities are exempt from federal taxes, they tend to be purchased by investors in high marginal tax brackets. Unlike the federal government, most state governments are required by law to balance their budgets. Therefore, bonds issued by municipal governments or state entities are often supported by revenue-generating projects such as sewers, college dormitories, and toll roads.

Corporate Securities

Corporate Bonds   One misconception held by many investors is that the market for common stocks dominates the corporate bond markets in size. This is far from the truth. Bonds are debt instruments that have a fixed life and must be repaid at maturity. As bonds come due and are paid off, the corporation normally replaces this debt with new bonds. For this reason, corporate bond issuances have traditionally made up the majority of external financing transactions by corporations.

In general, when interest rates are expected to rise, financial managers try to lock in long-term financing at a low cost and balance the company's debt structure with more long-term debt and less short-term debt. This has been especially true in the 2012 to 2015 period that has seen historically low long-term rates. Rates began rising in 2017, and the market expects at least two more rate increases by the Fed in 2018. This is more motivation for companies to get in their last bit of low-cost debt. The amount of long-term debt a corporation chooses to employ as a percentage of total capital is also a function of several options. Management must decide about its willingness to accept risk and examine the amount of financing available from other sources, such as internal cash flow, common stock, and preferred stock.

Preferred Stock   Preferred stock is the least used of all long-term corporate securities. The major reason for the small amount of financing with preferred stock is that the dividend is not tax-deductible to the corporation, as is bond interest. Corporations that are at their maximum debt limit issue much of the preferred stock that is sold. These companies may also suffer from low common stock prices or want to issue preferred stock that may someday be convertible into common stock.

Common Stock   Companies seeking new equity capital sell common stock. As explained in the next chapter on investment banking, common stock is either sold as a new issue in an initial public offering (IPO) or as a secondary offering. A secondary offering means that shares are already being publicly traded in the markets and the new offering will be at least the second time the company has sold common stock to the public. When companies *purchase* their own shares in the market because they have excess cash, these shares are shown on the company's balance sheet as treasury stock. Because common stock has no maturity date like bonds, new common stock is never sold to replace old stock in the way that new bonds are used to refund old bonds.

Internal versus External Sources of Funds   So far we have discussed how corporations raise funds externally through long-term financing using bonds, common stock, and preferred stock. Another extremely important source of funds to the corporation is **internally generated funds** as represented by retained earnings and cash flow added back from depreciation. On average, during the last 30 years corporations raised about 40 percent of their funds internally and 60 percent of their funds externally through the sale of bonds, common and preferred stock.

What makes up the internal funds? The composition of internal funds is a function of corporate profitability, the dividends paid and the resultant retained earnings, and the depreciation tax shield firms get from making additions to plant and equipment.

To arrive at the internally generated funds of the firm, we usually begin with the firm's earnings and add back deducted depreciation expense. Depreciation is deducted from corporate income, but depreciation does not result in lower cash flows. Although we frequently refer to depreciation as "a source of cash flow," in reality, we refer to depreciation in this way because we have chosen to start the calculation of cash flows using corporate earnings as calculated by the firm's accountants. Those earnings include a noncash depreciation deduction, and we must add the depreciation back to reflect the actual cash generated. When companies invest heavily in new plant and equipment, depreciation can rise substantially in the following years.

Panel A in Figure 14-2 shows the relative importance of depreciation and retained earnings in providing internal financing. During the period covered in panel A in Figure 14-2, retained earnings provided less than a quarter of the internal funds while depreciation provided the rest. In times of recession when corporate profits fall, retained earnings decline as a percentage of internal funds while the opposite is true during economic expansions. Panel B shows the breakdown of corporate income, dividends paid, retained earnings, and depreciation. The graph gives a good depiction of the relative size of each, with corporate earnings generating the dividend payments and retained earnings. Notice that funds from depreciation are larger than corporate earnings.

The Supply of Capital Funds

Having discussed the major users of capital in the U.S. economy, we turn our attention to the suppliers of capital. In a **three-sector economy**, consisting of business, government, and households, the major supplier of funds for investment is the household sector. Corporations and the federal government have traditionally been net demanders of funds. Figure 14-3 diagrams the flow of funds through our basic three-sector economy.

The major suppliers of funds in the credit markets are traditionally mutual funds and exchange-traded funds, commercial banks, credit unions, insurance companies, and pension funds. These institutions get most of their funds from households, and they

Figure 14-2 Internally generated funds—corporate profits, dividends, and retained earnings

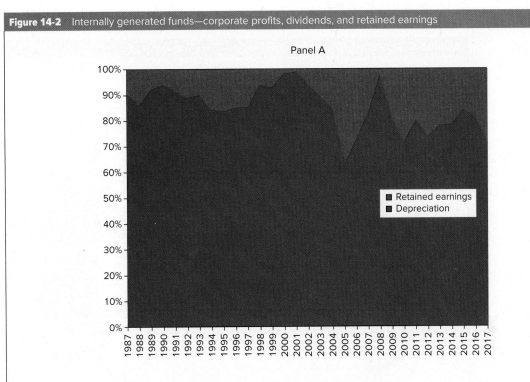

Panel A

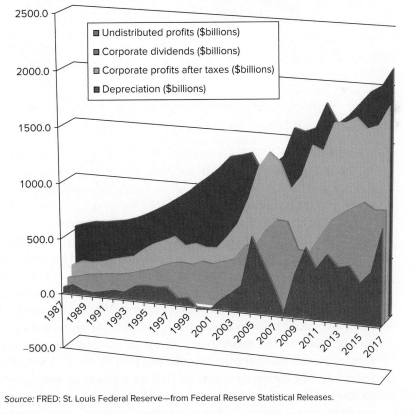

Panel B

Source: FRED: St. Louis Federal Reserve—from Federal Reserve Statistical Releases.

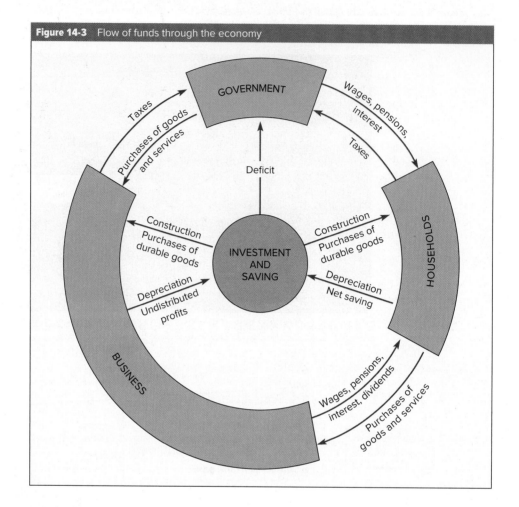

Figure 14-3 Flow of funds through the economy

are referred to as financial intermediaries. These intermediary lenders are discussed in the next paragraph. Funds supplied for mortgages are largely provided by government-sponsored agencies such as Fannie Mae and federally related mortgage pools. Foreign investors and governments are also an important source of credit funds.

As households receive wages and transfer payments from the government and wages and dividends from corporations, they generally save some portion of their income. These savings are usually funneled to **financial intermediaries** that, in turn, make investments in the capital markets with the funds received from the household sector. This is known as indirect investment. The types of financial institutions that channel funds into the capital markets are specialized and diverse. Funds may flow into commercial banks, mutual savings banks, and credit unions. Households may also purchase mutual fund shares, invest in life insurance, or participate in some form of private pension plan or profit sharing. All these financial institutions act as intermediaries; they help make the flow of funds from one sector of the economy to another very efficient and competitive. Without intermediaries, the cost of funds would be higher, and the efficient allocation of funds to the best users at the lowest cost would not occur.

The World's Biggest Exchange: Hatched from an Egg?

Almost everyone has heard of the New York Stock Exchange, but unless you are involved in sophisticated financial transactions you might not be familiar with the CME Group. The CME Group began life in 1898 as the Chicago Butter and Egg Board. The Board provided a place for traders to buy and sell eggs (and butter). At first, traders sold eggs and delivered them the same day, but eventually it occurred to these traders that it made sense to create contracts that called for delivery several days or weeks later. A buyer could lock in a price for eggs that he knew he would eventually need. Sellers could lock in a future selling price.

If a buyer wanted to hedge against prices rising in the future, he actually had two choices. He could negotiate a new contract with a seller for future delivery, or he could take over the contract of someone who had already negotiated to buy eggs in the future. These contracts were called "futures." Futures contracts became so popular that by 1915, 98 percent of the egg trades at the Board were futures. Only 2 percent were for immediate delivery.

World War I disrupted this system. During the war, the government imposed price controls on eggs. Since everyone knew what the price would be, there was no need for futures to lock in a price. Egg futures largely stopped trading, but when price controls were lifted after the war, futures trading took off again.

Turning the clock ahead, the Butter and Egg Board grew as it added futures trading in orange juice, wheat, pork bellies (bacon), and many other commodities. To reflect the broader activities, the Board's name was changed to the Chicago Mercantile Exchange (CME).

In 1972, a major economic event occurred. The world's major governments agreed to allow their currencies to trade freely. Until that time, each country tied its currency to gold in a fixed exchange rate, but fixed rates were too hard to manage. The "butter and egg" traders had seen this scenario before. They guessed that as price controls were lifted on currencies, there would be a big market for currency futures—probably bigger than for eggs. And they were right.

Within a few years, futures were introduced on many other financial products including government bonds and stock indexes. Just as companies used egg futures to hedge egg price risks, companies used financial futures to hedge against financial risks.

Today the volume of trading at the CME Group is hard for most people to imagine. The CME Group includes the CME, CBOT, NYMEX, and COMEX. According to the CME website, the "CME Group is the world's leading and most diverse derivatives marketplace, handling 3 billion contracts worth approximately $1 quadrillion annually (on average)."*

---

*http://www.cmegroup.com/company/history.

The Role of the Security Markets

Security markets exist to aid the allocation of capital among households, corporations, and governmental units, with financial institutions acting as intermediaries. Just as financial institutions specialize in their services and investments, the capital markets are divided into many functional subsets, with each specific market serving a certain type of security. For example, the common stocks of some of the largest corporations are traded on the New York Stock Exchange, and the NASDAQ whereas government securities are traded by government security dealers in the over-the-counter markets.

Once a security is sold for the first time as an original offering, the security trades in its appropriate market among all kinds of investors. This trading activity is known as **secondary trading**, since funds flow among investors, rather than to the corporation. Secondary trading provides liquidity to investors and keeps prices competitive among alternative security investments. It is very important to the functioning of the financial markets.

Security markets provide liquidity in two ways. First, they enable corporations to raise funds by selling new issues of securities rapidly at fair, competitive prices. Second, they allow the investor who purchases securities to sell them with relative ease and speed and thereby turn a paper asset into cash. Ask yourself, "Would I buy securities if there were no place to sell them?" You would probably think twice before committing funds to an illiquid investment. Without markets, corporations and governmental units would not be able to raise the large amounts of capital necessary for economic growth.

The Organization of the Security Markets

The structure of the security markets has changed drastically in the last decade, and markets are expected to continue evolving toward a global electronic structure. The most important change that markets have undergone may be the rise of **electronic communication networks (ECNs)**. ECNs are electronic trading systems that automatically match buy and sell orders at specific prices via computers. They have lowered trading costs and forced organized security exchanges to make significant changes in their operations and structure. These changes include mergers and alliances between traditional exchanges, their transformation from membership-owned organizations to public companies, and the acquisition of leading ECNs by the traditional exchanges.

In this chapter, we present the current organization of the markets and provide updates on significant events of the last few years. Historically, the markets have been divided into organized exchanges, which were floor-traded auction markets conducted by brokers, and over-the-counter (OTC) markets, which were traded through dealers using electronic quotes. Before discussing the important changes that ECNs have brought about, it first helps to understand the structure of traditional security markets.

Traditional Organized Exchanges

Traditional organized exchanges are either national or regional, but both are structured in a similar fashion. Historically, exchanges have had a central trading location where securities are bought and sold in an auction market by brokers acting as agents for the buyers and sellers. If a stock is not traded electronically and instead is traded on the floor of an exchange, it is traded at a physical location, a trading post, on the exchange's trading floor. Brokers are registered members of the exchanges, and their number is fixed by each exchange. The largest of the traditional exchanges with a physical location is the New York Stock Exchange (NYSE).

The regional exchanges began their existence trading securities of local firms. As the firms grew, they also were listed on the national exchanges but continued to be traded on the regionals. Many cities, such as Chicago, Cincinnati, Philadelphia, and Boston, have regional exchanges. Today most of the trading on these exchanges is done in nationally known companies. Trading in the same companies is common between the NYSE and such regionals as the Chicago Stock Exchange. More than 90 percent of the companies traded on the Chicago Stock Exchange are also listed on the NYSE. This is referred to as **dual trading**.

Listing Requirements for Firms   One of the major factors distinguishing an exchange is its **listing requirements**. The only way a firm's securities can be traded on an exchange is if the company meets the listing requirements and has been approved by the board of governors of that exchange. All exchanges have minimum requirements that must be met before trading can occur in a company's common stock. The NYSE was historically the largest exchange and now generates the most dollar volume in large, well-known companies. Its listing requirements also are the most restrictive. However, while the NASDAQ Stock Market has less restrictive listing requirements than the NYSE, it lists many large technology companies such as Microsoft, Google, Apple, and Cisco Systems that would easily meet the NYSE standards.

Electronic Communication Networks (ECNs)

A competing trading platform to the traditional organized exchanges is the electronic communication networks (ECNs). As previously indicated, ECNs are electronic trading systems that use computers to automatically match buy and sell orders. ECNs are also known as alternative trading systems (ATSs) and have been given SEC approval to be more fully integrated into the national market system by choosing to act either as a broker-dealer or as an exchange. Unlike traditional organized exchanges, ECNs do not have an exchange floor or physical trading posts. An ECN's subscribers can include retail and institutional investors, market makers, and broker-dealers. If a subscriber wants to buy a stock through an ECN, but there are no sell orders to match the buy order, the order cannot be executed. The ECN can wait for a matching sell order to arrive, or if the order is received during normal trading hours, the order can be routed to another market for execution. Some ECNs will let their subscribers see their entire order books, and some will even make their order books available on the web.

Because they offered significant cost advantages, ECNs were a competitive threat for even the most successful floor-based exchange, the New York Stock Exchange. In response, and in keeping with the old adage, "If you can't beat them, buy them," both the New York Stock Exchange and the NASDAQ acquired ECNs. But in the end the ECN model prevailed and the NYSE was bought by the Intercontinental Exchange (ICE).

BATS   The BATS exchange, a relatively young exchange, started as an ECN and attained exchange status in 2008. It now operates four stock exchanges in the United States. Its original BZX and BYX exchanges were combined with the EDGA and EDGX exchanges acquired with their 2014 merger with Direct Edge. According to its website, "The combined BATS Global Markets enterprise is now the largest U.S. equities market operation on any given day." BATS does not list stocks like the NYSE or NASDAQ and is strictly an electronic trading platform that matches orders and offers excellent execution speed and is popular with hedge funds and other professional traders.

The New York Stock Exchange

The New York Stock Exchange (NYSE) is located on Wall Street in New York City. Traditionally, the NYSE had a fixed number of memberships that allowed members to trade on the floor. At its height in 2005, one membership traded for $3.5 million.

In 2006, the NYSE merged with Archipelago, a large ECN, and became a public company. When the NYSE converted to a publicly traded company, NYSE members received stock in the NYSE Group and were given a trading license with an annual fee attached. Now owned by ICE, it operates as a subsidiary of the ECN.

Most trading on the floor of the NYSE occurs around a special group of traders known as **designated market makers (DMMs)**. Technically, DMMs succeeded the "**specialist**" system, but for most purposes DMMs fill the same role as that previously filled by specialists. Specialists were employed by NYSE member firms but were assigned by the exchange to trade specific stocks. Specialists made a market in their assigned stocks by standing ready to buy or sell shares at the current bid and ask prices. In other words, the specialist was required to buy when no one else was buying, and sell when no one else was selling. This obligation was not onerous when securities were actively traded. On a normal trading day for IBM, Coca-Cola, and DuPont, millions of shares are traded. However, smaller companies generally trade far less often. National Presto, a relatively small company traded on the NYSE, had an average daily trading volume of 35,000 shares as of January 2018.

Suppose you placed an order to sell 100 shares of National Presto at the market price. If the broker who executed your order arrives at the National Presto trading post and no buyer is present, the broker can't wait around hoping that a buying broker will appear soon. He has other orders to execute. Instead, the broker could sell the shares to the designated market maker who was always available and obligated to buy. The designated market maker would buy the shares for her own inventory. Later, when another broker showed up at the trading post looking to buy shares in National Presto, the designated market maker would sell the 100 shares that she purchased from the first broker earlier in the day.

As you might imagine, standing ready to buy shares when no one else will do so can be very risky. In a classic case, specialists stabilized the market by absorbing wave after wave of sell orders when President Reagan was shot in 1981. The specialists continued to buy even as stock prices continued to fall. So why were specialists willing to do this? In exchange for helping to maintain orderly markets, the specialist was allowed to "peek" at all the other unfilled orders, and this gave him a profit opportunity in normal trading periods.

While the specialist system had endured since the 1800s, technological changes made the specialist's job less profitable and more risky. The DMM now fills the specialist's position, but the DMM has greater flexibility regarding when he must step in to stabilize market prices. While the DMM no longer can "peek" at the order flow, he can earn small profits on many trades because he enjoys some priority in having his trades filled.

The cost advantage enjoyed by ECNs and electronic exchanges has significantly reduced the floor activity of specialists at the NYSE. As a public company, the NYSE has not been willing to stand pat while trading systems and capital markets evolve around it. In addition to acquiring the large ECN Archipelago, the NYSE also merged with the largest European exchange, Euronext. In December 2012, NYSE Euronext itself agreed to be acquired by Intercontinental Exchange (ICE), a large electronic commodity trading exchange. The merger was completed in 2013, and Euronext was spun off to satisfy regulators in the European Union.

The NASDAQ Market

The NASDAQ Stock Market used to be considered an over-the-counter market even though it had listing requirements for the companies that traded on its market. However, as of August 1, 2006, the NASDAQ became officially recognized as a national securities exchange by the SEC. This designation really doesn't change the way securities trade on the NASDAQ Stock Market, but it does allow the exchange to charge fees for data and market information. All trades on the NASDAQ are done electronically but there is no physical location, and there are no designated market makers as on the NYSE floor. NASDAQ is the largest exchange in the United States by dollar trading volume, and it often trades more shares on a daily basis than the NYSE. Like the NYSE, the NASDAQ Stock Market has gone through a transformation from a not-for-profit company to a for-profit company.

NASDAQ has always been an electronic stock exchange known for its trading technology and its listing of many of the world's largest technology companies such as Google, Cisco, Microsoft, and Apple. NASDAQ created SuperMontage, an electronic trading system that integrates the trading process with limit orders, time stamps for receipt of orders, multiple quotes, and more. The speed with which an exchange can process an order is extremely important to traders, and both the NYSE and NASDAQ claim to have the fastest order processing.

NASDAQ stocks are divided between global market issues and small cap issues. As the name implies, the global market issues represent larger NASDAQ companies that must meet higher listing standards than the small cap market. The standards are not as high as those on the NYSE but cover most of the same areas: net tangible assets, net income, pretax income, public float (shares outstanding in the hands of the public), operating history, market value of the float, a minimum share price, the number of shareholders, and the number of market makers. Because the listing requirements are lower than those on the NYSE, many small public companies choose to begin trading on the NASDAQ Stock Market, but as they get larger, they often decide to stay there long after they have exceeded the listing requirements of the NYSE. In particular, technology companies have shown an inclination to remain listed on NASDAQ, which historically has adopted technological innovations in trading more rapidly than the more traditional NYSE.

NASDAQ prides itself on its corporate governance, efficiency, and surveillance systems that avoid conflicts of interest and market manipulation. With the passage of the Sarbanes–Oxley Act of 2002, corporate governance issues became more important to all publicly traded companies, including NASDAQ. It is incumbent on NASDAQ to be a corporate governance role model for its listed firms and it has set a high standard in that area.

Foreign Exchanges

As the industrialized world has grown, capital markets around the world have increased in size and importance. As a sign of the importance of international capital markets, large U.S. international companies—such as IBM, Intel, and McDonald's—trade on the Tokyo and Frankfurt stock exchanges, and many foreign companies trade on the New York Stock Exchange—such as Sony and TDK of Japan, Royal Dutch Petroleum and Philips G.N.V. of the Netherlands, and BMW and Siemens of Germany.

Table 14-2 breaks down markets by geographic area and shows market capitalization, value of share trading, number of trades, and number of listed companies by

Table 14-2   World markets by geographic region

	Column 1 Ending 30-Jun-16	Column 2 Ending 31-Dec-16	Column 3 Ending 30-Jun-17	Column 1 to Column 3
Domestic market capitalization (in millions of USD)	**67,322,043.0**	**72,640,819.5**	**78,294,272.3**	**16.30%**
Americas	29,143,221.8	31,469,733.9	33,266,176.5	14.15%
Asia-Pacific	23,237,355.0	25,222,244.2	27,439,744.8	18.08%
Europe–Middle East–Africa	14,941,466.2	15,948,841.4	17,588,321.0	17.71%
Value of share trading* (USD millions)	**44,989,113.6**	**41,505,862.9**	**40,877,012.1**	**−9.14%**
Americas	23,052,674.5	20,898,074.7	21,027,170.9	−8.79%
Asia-Pacific	15,551,040.6	15,255,619.6	13,798,784.2	−11.27%
Europe–Middle East–Africa	6,385,398.5	5,352,168.6	6,051,057.0	−5.24%
Number of trades* (thousands of trades)	**10,731,359.1**	**9,882,313.1**	**9,418,633.1**	**−12.23%**
Americas	3,693,973.6	3,108,648.6	2,770,258.7	−25.01%
Asia-Pacific	6,058,308.0	5,892,690.2	5,685,867.1	−6.15%
Europe–Middle East–Africa	979,077.5	880,974.3	962,507.2	−1.69%
Number of listed companies (full number)	**45,409.0**	**45,497.0**	**45,634.0**	**0.50%**
Americas	10,011.0	9,903.0	9,893.0	−1.18%
Asia-Pacific	25,386.0	25,626.0	25,985.0	2.36%
Europe–Middle East–Africa	10,012.0	9,968.0	9,756.0	−2.56%

*Trades registered through electronic order book.

Source: Worldwide Federation of Exchanges (accessed February 9, 2018).

regions. The table also shows the percentage change from June 30, 2016, to June 30, 2017. While the market capitalizations have increased because of rising stock prices, the other categories show declines. In comparing regional capitalization, it is interesting that Asia-Pacific is catching up to the Americas and is far ahead of Europe–Middle East–Africa (EMEA). Asia-Pacific also has more than 2.5 times the number of companies as both the Americas and EMEA. Table 14-2 reinforces the growth of capitalism across the globe.

Other Financial Exchanges

In addition to the stock exchanges shown in Table 14-1, other financial exchanges have grown dramatically over the last decade. In particular, several futures exchanges have grown so large that they rival or exceed the traditional stock exchanges in market value. Corporations use futures markets to hedge various types of risk. Foreign exchange futures are discussed in Chapter 21. Companies can also use interest rate futures to hedge against the risk of rising interest rates. These are two of the more important classes of financial futures contracts traded on futures exchanges, but there are futures available to hedge a wide variety of risks. Companies can use futures to hedge against changing commodity prices, too much hot or cold weather, or inadequate rain.

One of the largest futures exchanges is the CME Group, which was created in 2007 from the merger of the Chicago Mercantile Exchange (CME) and the Chicago Board of Trade. See the Finance in Action box earlier in the chapter for an interesting discussion of the CME Group. Eurex and the London International Financial Futures and Options Exchange (LIFFE) are similar European futures exchanges. Intercontinental Exchange (ICE) is an Atlanta-based futures and options exchange noted for trading in oil, coal, gas, and electricity futures.

Market Efficiency

There are several concepts of **market efficiency** and there are many degrees of efficiency, depending on which market we are talking about. Markets in general are efficient when (1) prices adjust rapidly to new information; (2) there is a continuous market, in which each successive trade is made at a price close to the previous price (the faster the price responds to new information and the smaller the differences in price changes, the more efficient the market); and (3) the market can absorb large dollar amounts of securities without destabilizing the prices.

A key variable affecting efficiency is the certainty of the income stream. The more certain the expected income, the less volatile price movements will be. Fixed income securities, with known maturities, have reasonably efficient markets. The most efficient market is that for U.S. government securities, with the short-term Treasury bill market being exemplary. Corporate bond markets are somewhat efficient, but less so than government bond markets. A question that is still widely debated and researched by academics is the degree of efficiency for common stock. We do know that trading common stock in the United States has become cheaper and more efficient with the advent of decimalization, ECNs, and online brokerages.

The Efficient Market Hypothesis

If stock markets are efficient, it is very difficult for investors to select portfolios of common stocks that can outperform the stock market in general. The efficient market hypothesis is stated in three forms—the weak, semistrong, and strong.

The weak form simply states that past price information is unrelated to future prices, and that trends cannot be predicted and taken advantage of by investors. The semistrong form states that prices currently reflect all *public* information. Most of the research in this area focuses on changes in public information and on the measurement of how rapidly prices converge to a new equilibrium after new information has been released. The strong form states that all information, *both private and public,* is immediately reflected in stock prices.

Generally, researchers have indicated that markets are somewhat efficient in the weak and semistrong sense, but not in the strong sense (private, insider information is valuable—though generally illegal to use for quick profits).

Our objective in bringing up this subject is to make you aware that much current research is focused on the measurement of market efficiency. As communications systems advance, information gets disseminated faster and more accurately. Furthermore, securities laws are forcing fuller disclosure of corporate data. It would appear that our security markets are generally efficient, but far from perfect, in digesting information and adjusting stock prices.

Ethics

Depending on whom you talk to about dark pools, you will get different points of view. We are referring not to swimming pools but to markets where securities are traded and concealed from the public markets. In a dark pool, trading occurs between institutional investors, usually in large blocks of 10,000 to 100,000 shares or more. Sometimes these markets are referred to as "Alternative Trading Systems" that match trades between buyers and sellers. Dark pools work much like ECNs, except that the size of the orders and the prices are not available to the other traders in the pool or to the public. In other words, these trades don't show up on the consolidated tape run by the public markets.

For critics of the dark pool, the concern is that they lack transparency because the size and prices are hidden from participants in the public market. There are also concerns that the trades in this market take liquidity out of the public markets. The end result could be less efficient pricing in the public markets like the NYSE. NASDAQ-OMX and BATS Global Markets asked the SEC to force trades to take place on public exchanges unless the customer could prove that they were getting a much-improved price. Canadian and Australian regulators have already done this to stem the rise in off-exchange trading. There is a fear that dark pool operators will send small unwanted trades to public markets, and that public market liquidity will be eroded causing individual investors to get less efficient pricing.

However, if you are a hedge fund manager, a mutual fund manager, insurance company, or other large institutional investor, you are happy that you can hide your trades from other institutional investors. Dark pools can also restrict participants such as high-frequency traders from entering the pool. Institutional investors feel that they get more efficient executions and lower transaction costs by using dark pools. They accomplish this by crossing orders at the midpoint of a quoted best bid and offer price, thereby reducing the bid–ask spread.

The three largest dark pool operators in the United States are UBS, Credit Suisse, and Deutsche Bank. They are about to be joined by a few more. In 2015 Fidelity Investments and eight other big money managers, including BlackRock, BNY Mellon, JPMorgan, and T. Rowe Price, are creating a dark pool for the benefit of mutual fund shareholders to cut costs and eliminate high-frequency traders. Even NASDAQ has asked the SEC about operating a dark pool and has solicited interest from several existing dark pool operators to take over their pools.

Many investors think dark pools are unfair and even unethical. What do you think? Which side do you take?

Regulation of the Security Markets

Organized securities markets are regulated by the Securities and Exchange Commission (SEC) and by the self-regulation of the exchanges. The OTC market is controlled by the National Association of Securities Dealers. Three major laws govern the sale and subsequent trading of securities. The Securities Act of 1933 pertains to new issues of securities, while the Securities Exchange Act of 1934 deals with trading in the securities markets. Another major piece of legislation is the Securities Acts Amendments of 1975, whose main emphasis is on a national securities market. The primary purpose of these laws is to protect unwary investors from fraud and manipulation and to make the markets more competitive and efficient by forcing corporations to make relevant investment information public. The Sarbanes–Oxley Act of 2002, discussed in more detail on page 471, also provides additional protection for investors.

Before we move on to this traditional legislation, it is important to point out that the most comprehensive financial reform legislation since the Great Depression was passed in 2010 (the **Dodd–Frank Wall Street Reform and Consumer Protection Act**). The legislation was passed in response to the government bailout of huge American companies such as General Motors, Chrysler, AIG, Bank of America, and others with close to a trillion dollars of taxpayer money. The action was taken under the so-called Too Big to Fail doctrine in which large companies were bailed out by the government because their failure would have had a devastating effect on the economy. One of the stated purposes of the Dodd–Frank Act is to never let that happen again. Large banks are now required to submit plans, commonly known as **living wills**, that describe the strategy that the bank will use for a rapid bankruptcy resolution in the event of a crisis. Dodd–Frank also specifies additional regulation of hedge funds, derivatives, credit cards, mortgages, and other financial products. Because the Dodd–Frank Act is very broad and enormously complex, we can expect that regulatory agencies will continue crafting and implementing regulations for several years.

The Securities Act of 1933

The **Securities Act of 1933** was enacted after congressional investigations of the abuses present in the securities markets during the 1929 crash. Its primary purpose was to provide full disclosure of all pertinent investment information whenever a corporation sold a new issue of securities. For this reason, it is sometimes referred to as the truth-in-securities act. The Securities Act of 1933 has several important features:

1. All offerings except government bonds and bank stocks that are to be sold in more than one state must be registered with the SEC.[1]
2. The registration statement must be filed 20 days in advance of the date of sale and must include detailed corporate information.[2] If the SEC finds the information misleading, incomplete, or inaccurate, it will delay the offering until the registration statement is corrected. The SEC in no way certifies that the security is fairly priced, but only that the information seems to be accurate.
3. All new issues of securities must be accompanied by a prospectus containing the same information appearing in the registration statement. Usually included in the prospectus are a list of directors and officers; their salaries, stock options, and shareholdings; financial reports certified by a CPA; a list of the underwriters; the purpose and use of the funds to be provided from the sales of securities; and any other reasonable information that investors

---

[1]Actually, the SEC was not established until 1934. References to the SEC in this section refer to 1934 to the present. The FTC performed these functions in 1933.
[2]Shelf registration, which was initiated by the SEC in 1982, changes this provision somewhat. Shelf registration is discussed in Chapter 15.

may need before they can wisely invest their money. A preliminary prospectus may be distributed to potential buyers before the offering date, but it will not contain the offering price or the underwriting fees. It is called a "red herring" because stamped on the front in red letters are the words *preliminary prospectus.*

4. For the first time, officers of the company and other experts preparing the prospectus or the registration statement could be sued for penalties and recovery of realized losses if any information presented was fraudulent, factually wrong, or omitted.

The Securities Exchange Act of 1934

This act created the **Securities and Exchange Commission** to enforce the securities laws. The SEC was empowered to regulate the securities markets and those companies listed on the exchanges. Specifically, the major points of the **Securities Exchange Act of 1934** are these:

1. Guidelines for insider trading were established. Insiders must hold securities for at least six months before they can sell them. This is to prevent them from taking quick advantage of information that could result in a short-term profit. All short-term profits are payable to the corporation.[3] Insiders were at first generally thought to be officers, directors, employees, or relatives. In the late 1960s, however, the SEC widened its interpretation to include anyone having information that was not public knowledge. This could include security analysts, loan officers, large institutional holders, and many others who had business dealings with the firm.

2. The Federal Reserve's Board of Governors became responsible for setting margin requirements to determine how much credit would be available to purchasers of securities.

3. Manipulation of securities by conspiracies among investors was prohibited.

4. The SEC was given control over the proxy procedures of corporations (a proxy is an absent stockholder's vote).

5. In its regulation of companies traded on the markets, the SEC required that certain reports be filed periodically. Corporations must file quarterly financial statements and annual 10-K reports with the SEC and send annual reports to stockholders. The 10-K report has more financial data than the annual report and can be very useful to an investor or a loan officer. Most companies will now send 10-K reports to stockholders on request.

6. The act required all security exchanges to register with the SEC. In this capacity, the SEC supervises and regulates many pertinent organizational aspects of exchanges, such as the mechanics of listing and trading.

---

[3]In the mid-1980s, Congress and the SEC passed legislation to make the penalty three times the size of the gain.

Chapter 14   Capital Markets   **471**

The Securities Acts Amendments of 1975

The major focus of the **Securities Acts Amendments of 1975** was to direct the SEC to supervise the development of a national securities market. No exact structure was put forth, but the law did assume that any national market would make extensive use of computers and electronic communication devices. In addition the law prohibited fixed commissions on public transactions and also prohibited banks, insurance companies, and other financial institutions from buying stock exchange memberships to save commission costs for their own institutional transactions. This act is a worthwhile addition to the securities laws, since it fosters greater competition and more efficient prices. Much progress has already been made on the national market system as mandated by this act. We are finally seeing the coming together of markets through the Intermarket Trading System, the computerization of markets as demonstrated by the electronic communication networks (ECNs), and a much more competitive market system than we had in 1975.

The Sarbanes–Oxley Act of 2002

The **Sarbanes–Oxley Act of 2002** was previously discussed in Chapters 1 and 2, so only limited coverage will be provided here. Although it is not directly related to security trading as the first three acts are, you should still be familiar with it.

After the debacle related to false financial reporting and the associated negative impact on stock values in the early 2000s, Congress passed the Sarbanes–Oxley Act. Among the major provisions are the authorization of an independent private sector board to oversee the accounting profession, the creation of new penalties and long prison terms for corporate fraud and document destruction, restrictions on accounting firms from providing consulting services to audit clients, and other similar provisions.

Perhaps most important of all, the act holds corporate executives legally accountable for the accuracy of their firm's financial statements. When the CEO must sign off along with the chief financial officer (CFO), the monitoring starts to get serious. The president of the firm can no longer use as an excuse the fact that he or she did not know what was going on.

Sarbanes–Oxley also imposes new internal control requirements on public firms. It is difficult to know whether the cost of these requirements is worth the benefits that are enjoyed by the public. Many small companies have exited the public markets since Sarbanes–Oxley was passed, either by going private or being acquired. Also, foreign companies have shown a preference for listing shares in London in recent years, rather than in the United States. It is yet to be seen whether this is a good or bad development. Fortunately, as markets around the world become more integrated, firms have greater flexibility to choose where they will be listed and regulated, and investors can choose the level of regulation that they prefer by selecting investments monitored by their regulator of choice.

SUMMARY

In the capital markets, corporations compete for funds not only among themselves but also with governmental units of all kinds. The U.S. Treasury raises funds to finance the federal government deficit; federal agencies such as the Student Loan Marketing Association are continually raising long-term funds; and state and local governments raise funds for public works such as sewers, roads, and university dormitories. Corporations account for a significant percentage of all funds raised in the capital market, and most of that is obtained through the sale of corporate debt.

We depicted a three-sector economy consisting of households, corporations, and governmental units, and showed how funds flow through the capital markets from suppliers of funds to the ultimate users. This process is highly dependent on the efficiency of the financial institutions that act as intermediaries in channeling the funds to the most productive users.

Security markets were traditionally divided into organized exchanges and over-the-counter markets, but electronic communication networks have altered the traditional structure of markets. ECNs have taken advantage of the cost efficiencies made available by improved communication and computer technologies. Although the New York Stock Exchange is the largest organized exchange in the world, it has undergone many changes to cope with competitive threats posed by new technologies. In particular, the NYSE converted to a public corporation, merged with the Archipelago ECN, and merged with Europe's largest exchange, Euronext, only to be swallowed up by the Intercontinental Exchange (ICE) in 2013 and forced to spin off Euronext. Similarly, NASDAQ has gone public, acquired two ECNs, and also acquired OMX, a Nordic exchange. As foreign markets become increasingly important, more consolidation of smaller markets will occur.

Throughout this chapter we have tried to present the concept of efficient markets doing an important job in allocating financial capital. The existing markets provide liquidity for both the corporation and the investor, and they are efficient in adjusting to new information. Reducing the trading spread between the bid and asked prices has reduced costs for investors and has most likely helped make the market more efficient in terms of fair pricing.

Because of the laws governing the markets, much information is available for investors, and this in itself creates more competitive prices. In the future, we expect even more efficient markets, with a national market system using the best of both exchanges and ECN systems.

LIST OF TERMS

money markets   452
capital markets   452
federally sponsored credit agencies   456
municipal securities   457
internally generated funds   458
three-sector economy   458
financial intermediaries   460

secondary trading   461
electronic communication networks
   (ECNs)   462
dual trading   462
listing requirements   463
designated market makers
   (DMMs)   464

DISCUSSION QUESTIONS

1. In addition to U.S. corporations, what government groups compete for funds in the U.S. capital markets? *(LO14-2)*

2. In which foreign industry has privatization been most important? *(LO14-1)*

3. How does foreign investment help the U.S. government? *(LO14-1)*

4. What is a key tax characteristic associated with state and local (municipal) securities? *(LO14-2)*

5. What are three forms of corporate securities discussed in the chapter? *(LO14-2)*

6. Do corporations rely more on external or internal funds as sources of financing? *(LO14-2)*

7. Explain the role of financial intermediaries in the flow of funds through the three-sector economy. *(LO14-3)*

8. What are electronic communication networks (ECNs)? Generally speaking, are they currently part of the operations of the New York Stock Exchange and the NASDAQ Stock Market? *(LO14-4)*

9. Why is secondary trading in the security markets important? *(LO14-4)*

10. How would you define efficient security markets? *(LO14-5)*

11. The efficient market hypothesis is interpreted in a weak form, a semistrong form, and a strong form. How can we differentiate its various forms? *(LO14-5)*

12. What was the primary purpose of the Securities Act of 1933? *(LO14-6)*

13. What act of Congress created the Securities and Exchange Commission? *(LO14-6)*

14. What was the purpose of the Sarbanes–Oxley Act of 2002? *(LO14-6)*

WEB EXERCISE

1. This chapter on capital markets focuses on long-term financing and the various stock markets. Each stock market has its own listing requirements, and this exercise will look at the New York Stock Exchange listing requirements and listing fees. Students interested in repeating this exercise for NASDAQ may easily find the same information at www.nasdaq.com.

2. Go to the New York Stock Exchange's website at www.nyse.com. At the top of the page click on "NYSE." Click on "List"; then select "Get Started" and click

"NYSE Domestic Listing Standards." Scroll down to see the necessary information. Answer the following questions about being listed:

a. How many round lot holders (100 shares) are necessary?

b. How many public shares are necessary?

c. What are the Market Value Criteria?

d. What is the Alternative #1 Earnings Test?

Note: Occasionally a topic we have listed may have been deleted, updated, or moved into a different location on a website. If you click on the site map or site index, you will be introduced to a table of contents that should aid you in finding the topic you are looking for.

LEARNING OBJECTIVES

LO 15-1 Investment bankers are intermediaries between corporations in need of funds and the investing public. They also provide important advice.

LO 15-2 Investment bankers, rather than corporations, normally take the risk of successfully distributing corporate securities and for this there are costs involved.

LO 15-3 Distribution of new securities may involve dilution in earnings per share.

LO 15-4 Corporations turn to investment bankers when making the critical decision about whether to go public (distribute their securities in the public markets) or stay private.

LO 15-5 Leveraged buyouts rely heavily on debt in the restructuring of a corporation.

Investment Banking

Public and Private Placement

Initial public offerings (IPOs) are securities sold to the public for the first time. When an IPO is for a new issue of common stock, the equity offering creates a public market for the shares and the stock will end up trading on one of the security markets like the New Stock Exchange, the NASDAQ market, or some international market. Usually the sale of the new shares is a combination of shares sold by the company and shares sold by the owners of the company. When a new issue of bonds is sold, all the proceeds go to the company issuing the bonds. The market for IPOs is somewhat volatile and dependent on the level of the stock market and the health of the economy. So when the stock market is rising and high, more companies try to time their offering to take advantage of the high demand for common stock. Conversely when the market is in the doldrums and undervalued, companies will hold off on the issue of new common stock. This behavior results in a rather uneven flow of deals to the market over time.

Table 15-1 presents examples of IPOs from 2014 through the early part of 2018 and includes a variety of issues ranging from the $25 billion issue from Alibaba to the $287 million offering from Trivago. The Alibaba Group Holding is a Chinese Internet company that competes with Google and other online search companies. It was one of the biggest new issues of all time, while Trivago, the online travel company, is a more normal-size IPO with many smaller than $200 million. Notice the international stock exchanges associated with the Saudi National Commercial Bank, Pirelli & C SpA, ZhongAn Online, General Insurance Corp. of India Ltd., and Loma Negra CIASA. Sometimes a foreign company, like Alibaba, chooses to have its IPO on a U.S. exchange, and this was the case in 2017 with PagSeguro Digital Ltd., a Brazilian company.

While Alibaba was the star of 2014, Facebook was the IPO poster child for 2012 and on its way to over a billion users when it went public. The issue price of $38 per share valued the company at $104 billion, the largest valuation ever for a newly listed

Table 15-1   Examples of equity IPOs 2014–2018

Priced	Type	Issuer	Value ($ millions)	Exchange
September 18, 2014	IPO	Alibaba Group Holding	$25,032.30	New York Stock Exchange-NYSE
November 7, 2014	IPO	Saudi National Commercial Bank	5,996.80	Saudi Arabia
March 1, 2017	IPO	Snap Inc.	3,910.00	New York Stock Exchange-NYSE
September 29, 2017	IPO	Pirelli & C SpA	2,821.50	Borsa Italiana
October 15, 2015	IPO	First Data Corp.	2,560.00	New York Stock Exchange-NYSE
January 24, 2018	IPO	PagSeguro Digital Ltd.	2,265.80	New York Stock Exchange-NYSE
June 21, 2017	IPO	Altice USA Inc.	2,151.70	New York Stock Exchange-NYSE
January 31, 2017	IPO	Invitation Homes Inc.	1,771.00	New York Stock Exchange-NYSE
September 21, 2017	IPO	ZhongAn Online P & C Insurance Co. Ltd.	1,753.50	Hong Kong Exchange-Main Board
October 17, 2017	IPO	General Insurance Corp. of India Ltd.	1,724.60	Bombay Stock Exchange-BSE, National Stock Exchange of India
January 18, 2018	IPO	ADT Inc.	1,470.00	New York Stock Exchange-NYSE
October 31, 2017	IPO	Loma Negra CIASA	1,096.90	Buenos Aires Stock Exchange, New York Stock Exchange-NYSE
March 23, 2017	IPO	Silver Run Acquisition Corp. II	1,035.00	NASDAQ-US
December 16, 2016	IPO	Trivago	287.21	NASDAQ Global Select

Initial public offerings on U.S. exchanges, including non-U.S. issuers.

Sources: www.nasdaq.com/markets/ipos/activity; dealogic.com; www.nyse.com/ipo-center/filings (accessed all February 4, 2018).

public company. The company's share of the proceeds was $16 billion, and the rest went to existing shareholders. Facebook's initial public offering (IPO) was one of 94 that occurred in 2012, but this followed the worst environment in modern times for companies wishing to go public. As a worldwide financial crisis took hold in 2008, companies were forced to shelve plans for raising new capital through IPOs. By one count, only 21 companies went public in 2008. Even the revived IPO market of 2012 looked weak when compared to the hot IPO market of the 1990s. Between 1993 and 1999, on average more than 460 companies went public every year. In particular, during the late 1990s investors seemed to go wild over companies that had anything to do with the Internet. It seemed that if a company ended its name with ".com" or was connected to the Internet because of its business model, it could easily raise capital without having any cash flow or earnings. Investors were willing to pay high prices for stocks based on expectations that one day the companies would make large profits. Sometimes things worked out well.

Amazon.com, became a public company in 1998, as did eBay, the Internet auction company. Actually, eBay was one of those rare Internet companies that made money, and the demand for shares of its initial public offering was 10 times greater than the shares available for sale. Goldman Sachs, its managing investment banker, priced the shares at $18 per share for the 3.5 million shares available for sale on the day of the offering. The opening price for eBay common stock was $53.50 per share. It never traded at its anticipated offering price of $18.

Amazon and eBay are examples of two winners. Amazon's stock price soared to new highs and split (2:1) three times, so an initial investor would have multiple shares for each share purchased. When Amazon peaked out at $113 in late 1999, an original investor had earned a 7,533 percent return in less than two years. Then, as the Internet stock bubble collapsed, the price of Amazon's stock fell by more than 95 percent to $5.50 per share in late 2001. By July 2015, Amazon's stock traded for over $435. It had recovered all of the earlier decline almost four times over.

eBay was another highly successful Internet business, and because of stock splits an original investor would have 24 shares of eBay today for each original share purchased. After accounting for splits, the stock traded as high as $765 per original share ($18) by March 2000. Then the stock's price fell by 79 percent before the end of that year. However, eBay continued to be a successful business, and its price eventually recovered to rise to new highs. Both Amazon and eBay had business strategies that worked. Although they were overpriced in 1999, their business met real market needs, and the companies continued to grow. Eventually their stock prices recovered. In contrast, many other Internet-based "new economy" companies failed or were acquired at low prices by other firms.

Sometimes investors think that all they have to do is buy IPOs and they will get rich. Unfortunately it doesn't always work out that way. Many companies that went public during the Internet bubble of the late 1990s and 2000 crashed and burned, losing investors their total investment. So while we marvel at the success of companies like Alibaba, we never seem to hear about the failures that go bankrupt or lose 80 percent of their issue price within 12 months of their public offerings. So did the investment banker misprice these issues, or did their projections turn out to be wrong? What does an investment banker actually do for a company in an initial public offering? Keep reading.

The Role of Investment Banking

The **investment banker** is the link between the corporation in need of funds and the investor. As a middleman, the investment banker is responsible for designing a security offering and selling the securities to the public. The investment banking fraternity has long been thought of as an elite group—with appropriate memberships in the country club, the yacht club, and other such venerable institutions. However, several changes have occurred in the investment banking industry over the last decade.

Investment Banking Competition   Competition has become the new way of doing business, in which the fittest survive and prosper, while others drop out of the game. Raising capital has become an international proposition, and firms need to be very large to compete. This concentration of capital allows large firms to take additional risks and satisfy the needs of an increasingly hungry capital market. There have been international consolidations under way for some time, with foreign banks buying U.S. firms and U.S. banks buying foreign firms. The high level of global concentration is shown in Table 15-2 with the top 10 global investment bankers listed by revenue generated. The top 10 investment bankers accounted for 49.0 percent of the total revenue generated.

Table 15-2   Global ranking of investment bankers, 2017 vs. 2016

	FY 2017			FY 2016	
Bank	**Revenue ($ millions)**	**% Share**	**Rank**	**Revenue ($ millions)**	**% Share**
JPMorgan	6,645.00	8.1	1	5,974.90	7.9
Goldman Sachs	5,906.00	7.2	2	4,946.40	6.5
BofA Merrill Lynch	5,022.80	6.1	3	4,511.50	6.0
Morgan Stanley	4,772.00	5.8	4	4,296.20	5.7
Citi	4,372.90	5.3	5	3,622.00	4.8
Credit Suisse	3,724.60	4.5	6	3,162.70	4.2
Barclays	3,479.40	4.2	7	3,122.50	4.1
Deutsche Bank	2,655.00	3.2	8	2,729.90	3.6
UBS	1,838.40	2.2	11	1,657.00	2.2
RBC Capital Markets	1,820.70	2.2	10	1,684.40	2.2
Subtotal	40,236.80	49.0		35,707.50	47.1
Total	**82,145.50**	**100**		**75,745.20**	**100**

Source: Dealogic, www.dealogic.com.

Enumeration of Functions

As a middleman in the distribution of securities, the investment banker has a number of key roles. These functions are described next.

Underwriter   In most cases, the investment banker is a risk taker. The investment banker will contract to buy securities from the corporation and resell them to other security dealers and the public. By giving a "firm commitment" to purchase the securities from the corporation, the investment banker is said to **underwrite** any risks that might be associated with a new issue. While the risk may be fairly low in handling a bond offering for ExxonMobil or General Electric in a stable market, such may not be the case in selling the shares of a lesser-known firm in a volatile market environment.

Though most large, well-established investment bankers would not consider managing a public offering without assuming the risk of distribution, smaller investment houses may handle distributions for relatively unknown corporations on a "**best-efforts**," or commission, **basis**. Some issuing companies even choose to sell their own securities directly. Both the "best-efforts" and "direct" methods account for a relatively small portion of total offerings.

Market Maker   During distribution and for a limited time afterward, the investment banker may make a market in a given security—that is, engage in the buying and selling of the security to ensure a liquid market. The investment banker may also provide research on the firm to encourage active investor interest.

Advisor   The investment banker may advise clients on a continuing basis about the types of securities to be sold, the number of shares or units for distribution, and the timing of the sale. A company considering a stock issuance to the public may be persuaded, in counsel with an investment banker, to borrow the funds from an insurance company or, if stock is to be sold, to wait for two more quarters of earnings before going to the market. The investment banker also provides important advisory services in the area of mergers and acquisitions, leveraged buyouts, and corporate restructuring.

Agency Functions   The investment banker may act as an **agent** for a corporation that wishes to place its securities privately with an insurance company, a pension fund, or a wealthy individual. In this instance, the investment banker will shop around among potential investors and negotiate the best possible deal for the corporation.

Table 15-3 illustrates the fees generated for each product serviced by investment bankers. The table is divided into three sections that highlight the fees generated by

Table 15-3 Banking leaders based on fees for the year ended December 26, 2017		
A table of the most dominant investment banks; by products, regions, and industries.		
		January 1, 2017, to December 26, 2017
Category	**Bank**	**Fees ($m)**
Global Investment Banking	JPMorgan	6,731.79
Mergers & Acquisitions	Goldman Sachs & Co.	2,381.45
Bonds	JPMorgan	2,204.68
Equity	Morgan Stanley	1,484.84
Loans	Bank of America Merrill Lynch	1,284.47
Category Regions/Nations	**Bank**	**Fees ($m)**
Americas	JPMorgan	4,615.44
United States of America	JPMorgan	4,175.48
Europe	JPMorgan	1,512.58
Central Asia/Asia-Pacific	Bank of China Ltd.	1,196.17
China	Bank of China Ltd.	1,076.42
Japan	Sumitomo Mitsui Finl. Grp. Inc.	983.32
United Kingdom	JPMorgan	452.53
India	State Bank of India	141.92
Hong Kong	HSBC Holdings plc	134.11
Brazil	Banco Bradesco SA	127.38
Africa/Middle East/Central Asia	Citigroup Inc.	115.29
Singapore	DBS Group Holdings	88.50
Category Industries	**Bank**	**Fees ($m)**
Financials	JPMorgan	1,917.10
Energy and Power	JPMorgan	764.74
Healthcare	JPMorgan	715.13
High Technology	JPMorgan	651.92
Industrials	JPMorgan	555.77
Materials	Goldman Sachs & Co.	400.33
Real Estate	Bank of America Merrill Lynch	388.37
Consumer Products and Services	Goldman Sachs & Co.	322.65
Retail	Bank of America Merrill Lynch	301.86
Media and Entertainment	Goldman Sachs & Co.	261.11
Government and Agencies	JPMorgan	257.57
Telecommunications	Bank of America Merrill Lynch	247.33
Consumer Staples	JPMorgan	241.24

Data as of December 26, 2017.

Regions and Industries table includes fees generated on transactions excluded from Thomson Reuters's standard league tables.

Source: https://markets.ft.com/data/league-tables/tables-and-trends (accessed January 31, 2018).

Table 15-4   Underwriting fees and number of deals by quarter and product

(in billions of dollars)	Mergers & Acquisitions	Equity Offerings	Bond Offerings	Loans
1st Quarter 2017	$ 7.201	$ 5.813	$ 8.234	$ 5.660
2nd Quarter 2017	$ 7.233	$ 5.783	$ 8.143	$ 5.866
3rd Quarter 2017	$ 7.145	$ 5.213	$ 7.952	$ 4.879
4th Quarter 2017	$ 5.720	$ 5.502	$ 6.779	$ 5.433
Total Fees for 2017	$ 27.299	$ 22.311	$ 31.108	$ 21.838
Percentage breakdown	26.62%	21.75%	30.33%	21.29%

	Mergers & Acquisitions	Equity Offerings	Bond Offerings	Loans
1st Quarter 2017	9,058	1,706	5,967	3,560
2nd Quarter 2017	9,302	1,749	7,616	3,076
3rd Quarter 2017	9,031	1,717	6,808	3,299
4th Quarter 2017	7,282	1,994	5,500	2,372
Total Deals for 2017	34,673	7,166	25,891	12,307
Percentage breakdown	43.32%	8.95%	32.35%	15.38%
Average fee per deal	$787,327	$3,113,452	$1,201,499	$1,774,437

Source: https://markets.ft.com/data/league-tables/tables-and-trends (accessed January 31, 2018).

the leading investment bank for each type of banking activity, for each geographic region, and for each industry. One thing to take away from the table is that not only do U.S. investment banks dominate this global industry but JPMorgan leads in more areas than the other banks. Also notice that banks have areas of expertise that attract clients. This is evident both by geographic region and by industry. For example, if you are interested in media and entertainment, you might choose Goldman Sachs but you might prefer Merrill Lynch for telecommunications.

Rather than looking at the leadership of individual investment banks, Table 15-4 presents a quarter-by-quarter look at the industry as a whole. Bond offerings generate the most fees followed by mergers and acquisitions, while equity offerings and syndicated loans are in third and fourth places. However, when you look at the bottom line of the table that shows average fee per deal, you can see that equity offerings have the highest fee because they are also the riskiest. Mergers and acquisitions have the lowest fee per deal because they have the least risk.

The Distribution Process

The actual distribution process requires the active participation of a number of parties. The principal or **managing investment banker**, often referred to as the **bookrunner**, will call on other investment banking houses to share the burden of risk and to aid in the distribution. To this end, they will form an **underwriting syndicate** comprising as few as 2 or as many as 100 investment banking houses. In Figure 15-1 we see a typical case in which a hypothetical firm, the Maxwell Corporation, wishes to issue 250,000 additional shares of stock with Bank of America Merrill Lynch as the managing underwriter and an underwriting syndicate of 15 firms.

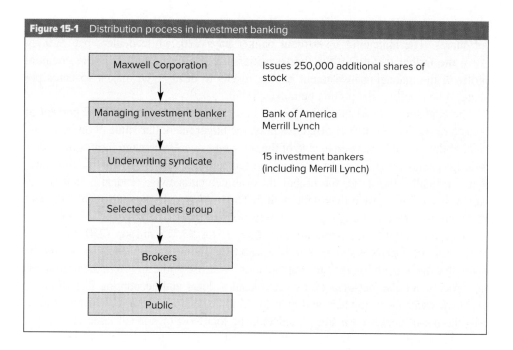

Figure 15-1   Distribution process in investment banking

The underwriting syndicate will purchase shares from the Maxwell Corporation and distribute them through the channels of distribution. Syndicate members will act as wholesalers in distributing the shares to brokers and dealers who will eventually sell the shares to the public. Large investment banking houses may be vertically integrated, acting as underwriter-dealer-brokers and capturing all fees and commissions.

The Spread   The **underwriting spread** represents the total compensation for those who participate in the distribution process. If the public or retail price is $21.50 and the managing investment banker pays a price of $20.00 to the issuing company, we say there is a total spread of $1.50. The $1.50 may be divided among the participants, as indicated in Figure 15-2.

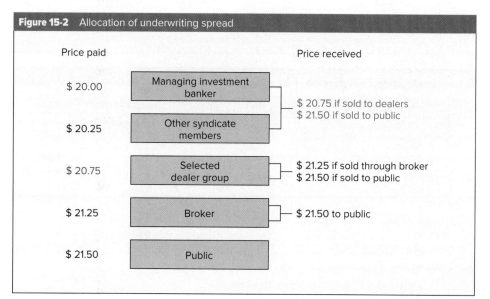

Figure 15-2   Allocation of underwriting spread

Note that the lower a party falls in the distribution process, the higher the price for shares. The managing investment banker pays $20, while dealers pay $20.75. Also, the farther down the line the securities are resold, the higher is the potential profit. If the managing investment banker resells to dealers, he makes 75 cents per share; if he resells to the public, he makes $1.50.

The total spread of $1.50 in the present case represents approximately 7 percent of the offering price ($1.50/$21.50). Generally, the larger the dollar value of an issue, the smaller the spread is as a percentage of the offering price. Percentage figures on underwriting spreads for U.S. corporations are presented in Table 15-4. This table illustrates that the smaller the issue, the higher the fees percentagewise, and also that equity capital is more expensive than debt capital. The higher equity spreads reflect the fact that there is more uncertainty with common stock than for other types of capital.

Since the Maxwell Corporation stock issue is for $5.375 million (250,000 shares × $21.50), the 7 percent spread is in line with SEC figures in Table 15-5. It should be noted that the issuer bears not only the "give-up" expense of the spread in the underwriting process but also out-of-pocket costs related to legal and accounting fees, printing expenses, exchange listing fees, and so forth. As indicated in Table 15-6, when the spread plus the out-of-pocket costs are considered, the total cost of a small issue is high but decreases as the issue size increases. Of course substantial benefits may still be received.

Table 15-5   Underwriting compensation as a percentage of proceeds

Size of Issue ($ millions)	Spread	
	Common Stock	Debt
Under 0.5	11.3%	7.4%
0.5–0.9	9.7	7.2
1.0–1.9	8.6	7.0
2.0–4.9	7.4	4.2
5.0–9.9	6.7	1.5
10.0–19.9	6.2	1.0
20.0–49.9	4.9	1.0
50.0 and over	2.3	0.8

Source: Securities and Exchange Commission data.

Table 15-6   Total costs to issue stock (percentage of total proceeds)

Size of Issue ($ millions)	Common Stock		
	Spread	Out-of-Pocket Cost*	Total Expense
Under 0.5	11.3%	7.3%	18.6%
0.5–0.9	9.7	4.9	14.6
1.0–1.9	8.6	3.0	11.6
2.0–4.9	7.4	1.7	9.1
5.0–9.9	6.7	1.0	7.7
10.0–19.9	6.2	0.6	6.8
20.0–49.9	4.9	0.8	5.7
50.0 and over	2.3	0.3	2.6

*Out-of-pocket cost of debts is approximately the same.

Source: Securities and Exchange Commission data.

Pricing the Security

Because the syndicate members purchase the stock for redistribution in the marketing channels, they must be careful about the pricing of the stock. When a stock is sold to the public for the first time (i.e., the firm is going public), the managing investment banker will do an in-depth analysis of the company to determine its value. The study will include an analysis of the firm's industry, financial characteristics, and anticipated earnings and dividend-paying capability. Based on valuation techniques that the underwriter deems to be appropriate, a price will be tentatively assigned and will be compared to that enjoyed by similar firms in a given industry. If the industry's average price-earnings ratio is 20, the firm is likely to be priced near this norm. Anticipated public demand will also be a major factor in pricing a new issue.

The great majority of the issues handled by investment bankers are, however, additional issues of stocks or bonds for companies already trading publicly. When additional shares are to be issued, the investment bankers will generally set the price at slightly below the current market value. This process, known as **underpricing**, will help ensure a receptive market for the securities.

At times, an investment banker also will underwrite the sale of large blocks of stock for existing stockholders, rather than for the company. When holders of these blocks wish to sell too many shares for normal channels to handle, the investment banker will manage the sale and underprice the stock below current market prices. This process is known as a secondary offering. Secondary offerings occur after an IPO, also known as a primary offering, in which securities are sold to the public for the first time. Secondary offerings often combine shareholder blocks with additional shares being issued directly by the company. Table 15-3 refers to secondary offerings in the category "Follow-on."

A secondary offering can also occur without shareholder blocks being included. Three of the largest equity offerings ever were secondary offerings that occurred in December 2009. Several banking giants (Citigroup, Bank of America, and Wells Fargo) raised over $52 billion in new capital to pay back the U.S. government for bailout funding received the previous year. These banks wished to avoid restrictions on their activities that the government had imposed until repayments were made.

Debt versus Equity Offerings

Students are often surprised that debt offerings outnumber equity offerings in number and dollar amounts. Perhaps it is because we are bombarded with daily Dow Jones updates in the financial press that stock seems to take preference over bonds. Table 15-7, however, shows that for 2017 and 2016, debt offerings were more than eight times equity offerings. In 2017, $6.998 trillion of debt was issued globally, while $872 billion of equity was issued. There were 22,899 debt offerings and 6,442 equity offerings. It is no surprise that debt was the more common offering. Interest rates had started to move up and companies were trying to lock in low-cost debt before rates began their up cycle. Rates moved up in early 2018 and the Fed was expected to raise rates three or four times during the year.

Dilution

A problem a company faces when issuing additional securities is the actual or perceived **dilution of earnings** effect on shares currently outstanding. In the case of the Maxwell Corporation, the 250,000 new shares may represent a 10 percent increment to shares

Warren Buffett's Bailout of Goldman Sachs

Managerial

At the peak of the recent financial crisis, Goldman Sachs turned to Warren Buffett's Berkshire Hathaway Inc. to bail it out of trouble. After Bear Stearns and Lehman Brothers collapsed at the start of the global financial crisis, Goldman Sachs found itself short of capital. Fortunately, Buffett stood ready with billions to invest. Buffett's Berkshire Hathaway bought $5 billion of Goldman Sachs Series G preferred stock yielding a 10 percent guaranteed annual return. Along with the preferred stock came warrants to buy an additional $5 billion of common stock, or more precisely, 43.5 million shares of Goldman Sachs at $115 per share.

Before Buffett closed the deal on September 23, 2008, Goldman Sachs (ticker symbol GS) traded for $113. After the announcement the stock rose to $129.95 and closed on the day at $125.05. Just by investing $5 billion, the value of Buffett's warrants rose by $10 per share, or $435 million. Buffett's investment didn't end Goldman's troubles completely. Over the next two months, financial markets kept getting worse, and Goldman Sachs stock fell as low

as $54.54 per share. As the financial crisis bottomed out and the government stabilized the markets, bank and investment bank stock prices increased. The Goldman Sachs stock price hit a high of $193.60 toward the end of 2009, and by June 2013, it traded at $165 per share.

Berkshire Hathaway had until October 1, 2013, to purchase the 43.5 million shares. By March 2013, it was clear to Goldman Sachs that the company didn't need another $5 billion from Buffett through the exercise of the 43.5 million shares of stock, so instead it agreed to a swap. Goldman would subtract the $115 strike price from the average market price 10 days prior to October 1 and give Buffett the value in shares. This was advantageous for Buffett because he didn't have to come up with $5 billion in cash, and instead he received 13.06 million shares or 2.8 percent ownership in Goldman Sachs. As of February 2, 2018, those shares were worth approximately $3.4 billion, not a bad return on top of a 10 percent annual dividend payment of $500 million over five years.

Table 15-7 Global debt and equity capital markets bookrunner rankings

Global Equity Capital Markets Bookrunner Ranking						Global Debt Capital Markets Bookrunner Ranking					
	FY 2017			FY 2016			FY 2017			FY 2016	
Bookrunner	Value $bn	#	Rank	Value $bn	#	Bookrunner	Value $bn	#	Rank	Value $bn	#
Goldman Sachs	68.24	373	2	48.82	274	Citi	492.37	2,248	2	409.93	1,950
Morgan Stanley	67.07	419	3	48.03	270	JPMorgan	455.19	2,175	1	429.31	2,121
JPMorgan	61.84	406	1	56.44	338	BofA Merrill Lynch	440.27	1,834	3	389.47	1,924
Citi	47.87	369	4	34.53	257	Goldman Sachs	324.50	1,477	5	300.54	1,278
BofA Merrill Lynch	43.13	312	5	34.01	225	Barclays	312.03	1,395	4	339.68	1,347
UBS	37.42	231	8	24.34	194	Morgan Stanley	296.93	1,718	6	281.43	1,787
Credit Suisse	33.58	290	6	31.31	231	HSBC	256.13	1,290	7	273.38	1,233
Deutsche Bank	27.66	202	7	30.14	168	Deutsche Bank	253.56	1,177	8	257.24	1,097
Barclays	25.84	193	9	20.84	146	Wells Fargo Securities	235.19	1,609	9	249.46	1,729
CITIC Securities	17.31	93	10	17.80	76	BNP Paribas	193.53	831	10	172.36	735
Subtotal	**429.96**	**1,524**		**346.24**	**1,240**	*Subtotal*	**3,259.70**	**9,467**		**3,102.80**	**9,490**
Subtotal (percent of total)	**49.28%**	**23.66%**		**47.65%**	**23.02%**	*Subtotal (percent of total)*	**46.58%**	**41.34%**		**45.94%**	**37.23%**
Total	**872.45**	**6,442**		**726.68**	**5,387**	**Total**	**6,998.70**	**22,899**		**6,754.20**	**25,487**

Source: Dealogic, www.dealogic.com (accessed January 31, 2018).

currently in existence. Perhaps the firm had earnings of $5 million on 2,500,000 shares before the offering, indicating earnings per share of $2. With 250,000 new shares to be issued, earnings per share will temporarily slip to $1.82 ($5,000,000 ÷ 2,750,000).

The proceeds from the sale of new shares may well be expected to provide the increased earnings necessary to bring earnings back to at least $2. While financial theory dictates that a new equity issue should not be undertaken if it diminishes the overall wealth of current stockholders, there may be a perceived time lag in the recovery of earnings per share as a result of the increased shares outstanding. For this reason, there may be a temporary weakness in a stock when an issue of additional shares is proposed. In most cases this is overcome with time.

Market Stabilization

Another problem may set in when the actual public distribution begins—namely, unanticipated weakness in the stock or bond market. Since the sales group normally has made a firm commitment to purchase stock at a given price for redistribution, it is essential that the price of the stock remain relatively strong. Syndicate members, committed to purchasing the stock at $20 or better, could be in trouble if the sale price falls to $19 or $18. The managing investment banker is generally responsible for stabilizing the offering during the distribution period and may accomplish this by repurchasing securities as the market price moves below the initial public offering price.

The period of **market stabilization** usually lasts two or three days after the initial offering, but it may extend up to 30 days for difficult-to-distribute securities. In a very poor market environment, stabilization may be virtually impossible to achieve. Consider Facebook's initial public offering on Friday, May 18, 2012. The initial IPO price was set at $38 by the lead underwriter, Morgan Stanley. The offering was a big news event, and many small investors rushed into the stock in the first minutes of trading. The stock was extremely volatile on the first day of trading, but the stock price never fell below the offering price because Morgan Stanley was actively buying shares when the price hit $38.

Figure 15-3 shows that the price fell to $38 during the morning when Morgan Stanley apparently intervened. The price fell back to $38 later in the day as price support activities held the price above $38 at the close.

Facebook's price quotes near the end of the first trading day show the magnitude of the price support. In Figure 15-4, notice that there is a bid for almost 15 million shares of Facebook stock at exactly $38 per share just before 12 p.m., when the stock bottomed at $38 and again for about 7 million shares at the end of the day. These are most likely bids by Morgan Stanley attempting to support the price at that level. To put the size of this support into perspective, it was not unusual for the bid size to be less than 5,000 shares in later transactions.

On Monday, May 21, the price support was removed and the price fell to $34. By September, the price had collapsed to a low of $17.55. Investors who understood that the underwriter was only temporarily supporting the price were probably able to avoid these early losses. Those investors who held their stock for the long term would have been amply rewarded as the stock traded at $190 per share in early 2018.

Manipulation of prices in security markets is normally illegal. Market stabilization or underwriter price support is a rare exception to the general market manipulation prohibition. Temporary market stabilization is accepted by the Securities and Exchange Commission as necessary for smoothly functioning new-issue markets.

Figure 15-3   Facebook share price on the first day of trading

Figure 15-4   Facebook closing quotes on May 18, 2012

Facebook Inc. (FB) - NasdaqGS

38.18 ▲0.18(0.47%)   4:00PM EDT |

Prev Close:	38.00	Day's Range:	38.00–45.00
Open:	42.05	52wk Range:	N/A
Bid:	38.00 × 9999900	Volume:	566,546,504
Ask:	38.01 × 154300	Avg Vol (3m):	N/A
1y Target Est:	40.00	Market Cap:	104.00B
Beta:	N/A	P/E (ttm):	87.76
Next Earnings Date:	N/A	EPS (ttm):	0.43
		Div & Yield:	N/A (N/A)

Aftermarket

The investment banker is also interested in how well the underwritten security behaves after the distribution period because the banker's ultimate reputation rests on bringing strong securities to the market. This is particularly true of initial public offerings.

Exhaustive research shows that initial public offerings tend to perform well in the immediate **aftermarket**. According to Professor Jay Ritter at the University of Florida, between 1980 and 2017 there were more than 8,360 initial public offerings in the United States. The average first-day return for these stocks was 18 percent. In many countries, the initial aftermarket returns are even higher. In fact, IPOs are underpriced in every country where stocks are publicly traded.

After the issuance, initial public offerings appear to lose their luster. Over the first three years of trading, excluding the first-day price jump, IPO returns are approximately 7.5 percent lower than those of similar firms. The typical IPO is a good deal for investors who purchase shares from the underwriter at the offering price, but after the first day of trading most companies underperform the market for several years. There are variations from the average depending on the industry. For example, technology and biotech might have higher returns and IPOs sponsored by venture capital companies might also have higher returns, so don't assume the average is the rule.

Shelf Registration

The Securities and Exchange Commission also allows a filing process called shelf registration under SEC Rule 415. **Shelf registration** permits large companies, such as IBM or Citigroup, to file one comprehensive registration statement that outlines the firm's financing plans for up to the next two years. Then, when market conditions seem appropriate, the firm can issue the securities without further SEC approval. Future issues are thought to be sitting on the shelf, waiting for the appropriate time to appear.

Shelf registration is at variance with the traditional requirement that security issuers file a detailed registration statement for SEC review and approval every time they plan a sale. Whether investors are deprived of important "current" information as a result of shelf registration is difficult to judge. While shelf registration was started on an experimental basis by the SEC in 1982, it has now become a permanent part of the underwriting process. Shelf registration has been most frequently used with debt issues, with relatively less utilization in the equity markets (corporations do not wish to announce equity dilution in advance).

Shelf registration has contributed to the concentrated nature of the investment banking business, previously discussed. The strong firms are acquiring more and more business and, in some cases, are less dependent on large syndications to handle debt issues. Only investment banking firms with a big capital base and substantial expertise are in a position to benefit from this registration process.

The Gramm–Leach–Bliley Act Repeals the Glass–Steagall Act   The Glass–Steagall Act, passed after the great crash of 1929 and bank runs of the early 1930s, required U.S. banks to separate their commercial banking operations and investment banking operations into two different entities. Banks like J.P. Morgan were forced to sell off Morgan Stanley. Congress took this position because they thought the risk of the securities business impaired bank capital and put the banking system at risk of default. As global financial markets grew, it became clear that U.S. commercial and investment banks were at a competitive disadvantage against large European and Japanese banks, who were not hobbled by these restrictions. Foreign banks were universal banks and could offer traditional banking services as well as insurance, securities brokerage, and investment banking.

In 1999 the U.S. Congress passed the Gramm–Leach–Bliley Act, which repealed Depression-era laws that had separated banking, brokerage, insurance, and investment banking. Now banks may engage in all these activities. The Federal Reserve and the Treasury, however, still have the power to impose restrictions on the activities of banks. Recently the Fed and Treasury have been concerned that banks' investments into risky venture capital companies may impair their capital. The Fed has effectively banned some banks from participating in this merchant banking activity unless they set aside reserves equal to 50 percent of their capital. This allows the strong banks to participate in the venture capital market but forces the weak ones to sit on the sidelines.

The Dodd–Frank law enacted in 2010 included the Volcker Rule, named for a former Federal Reserve chairman Paul Volcker. The rule is intended to restrict banks from making certain risky investments that the repeal of Glass–Steagall allowed. The Volcker Rule has been criticized as a watered-down version of the old Glass–Steagall restrictions.

Public versus Private Financing

Our discussion to this point has assumed the firm was distributing stocks or bonds in the public markets (as explained in Chapter 14). However, many companies, by choice or circumstance, prefer to remain private—restricting their financial activities to direct negotiations with bankers, insurance companies, and so forth. Let us evaluate the advantages and the disadvantages of **public placement** versus private financing and then explore the avenues open to a privately financed firm.

Advantages of Being Public

First of all, the corporation may tap the security markets for a greater amount of funds by selling securities to the public. With over 90 million individual stockholders in the country, combined with thousands of institutional investors, the greatest pool of funds is channeled toward publicly traded securities. Furthermore, the attendant prestige of a public security may be helpful in bank negotiations, executive recruitment, and the marketing of products. Some corporations listed on the New York Stock Exchange actually allow stockholders a discount on the purchase of their products.

Stockholders of a heretofore private corporation may also sell part of their holdings if the corporation decides to go public. A million-share offering may contain 500,000 authorized but unissued corporate shares and 500,000 existing stockholder shares. The stockholder is able to achieve a higher degree of liquidity and to diversify his or her portfolio. A publicly traded stock with an established price may also be helpful for estate planning.

Finally, going public allows the firm to play the merger game, using marketable securities for the purchase of other firms. A public company can purchase another firm using its own stock as currency, whereas a private firm might be forced to buy using cash. The high visibility of a public offering may even make the acquiring firm a potential recipient of attractive offers for its own securities. (This may not be viewed as an advantage by firms that do not wish to be acquired.)

Disadvantages of Being Public

The company must make all information available to the public through SEC and state filings. Not only is this tedious, time-consuming, and expensive, but also important corporate information on profit margins and product lines must be divulged. The CEO (chief executive officer) and the CFO (chief financial officer) must adapt to being public relations representatives to all interested members of the securities industry.

Another disadvantage of being public is the tremendous pressure for short-term performance placed on the firm by security analysts and large institutional investors. Quarter-to-quarter earnings reports can become more important to top management than providing a long-run stewardship for the company. A capital budgeting decision calling for the selection of Alternative A—carrying a million dollars higher net present value than Alternative B—may be discarded in favor of the latter because Alternative B adds two cents more to next quarter's earnings per share.

In a number of cases, the blessings of having a publicly quoted security may become quite the opposite. Although a security may have had an enthusiastic reception in a strong "new-issues" market, such as that of 1967–68, 1981–83, or 1998–99, a dramatic erosion in value may later occur, causing embarrassment and anxiety for stockholders and employees.

As was evidenced in Tables 15-5 and 15-6, there can be a high cost to going public. For small firms, the underwriting spread and the out-of-pocket costs can run in the 15–18 percent range. Moreover, after going public the firm faces higher compliance costs because of various public disclosure requirements. In response to the collapse of Enron Corporation and its accounting firm, Arthur Andersen and Co., Congress passed the Sarbanes–Oxley Act of 2002 which created several costly new requirements.

Public Offerings

A Classic Example—Rosetta Stone Goes Public

A classic example of an IPO is that of Rosetta Stone Inc., which went public on April 16, 2009. The company offers self-study language software for over 30 languages. Prior to the offering, the company filed a registration statement with the SEC that included a prospectus that was distributed to potential investors. Every public offering must be preceded by a prospectus that offers details about the company and the offering. The front page of Rosetta Stone's prospectus is shown in Figure 15-5.

As shown in the figure, 6.25 million shares (top of page) were offered to the public at a price of $18 per share (middle of page). Underwriting commissions were $1.26 per share, exactly 7 percent of the offer price. Also, the company received only half of the remaining proceeds. The other half went to shareholders who sold part of their interest in the company. Table 15-8 on page 491 shows the out-of-pocket costs that Rosetta Stone incurred.

Members of the underwriting syndicate are shown along the bottom of Figure 15-5. Morgan Stanley was the lead underwriter with William Blair & Company listed as a co-lead. The other members of the syndicate are listed below these underwriters. On the whole, the features shown in Figure 15-5 are all very standard for primary offerings.

The day of the offering, Rosetta Stone's shares began trading on the NYSE at $23 and closed at $25.12, for a first-day gain of more than 39 percent ($25 − $18)/$18. This is a good example of the first-day underpricing that frequently accompanies IPOs. Over the next several months, the price of Rosetta Stone continued to climb, and

Figure 15-5 Rosetta Stone's prospectus

Filed Pursuant to Rule 424(b)(4)
Registration No. 333-153632

6,250,000 Shares

Rosetta Stone Inc.

COMMON STOCK

Rosetta Stone Inc. is offering 3,125,000 shares of its common stock and the selling stockholders are offering 3,125,000 shares of common stock. We will not receive any proceeds from the sale of shares by the selling stockholders. This is our initial public offering and no public market currently exists for our shares.

Our common stock has been approved for listing on the New York Stock Exchange under the symbol "RST."

Investing in our common stock involves risks. See "Risk Factors" beginning on page 13.

PRICE $18.00 A SHARE

	Price to Public	Underwriting Discounts and Commissions	Proceeds to Company	Proceeds to Selling Stockholders
Per Share	**$18.00**	$1.26	$16.74	$16.74
Total	$112,500,000	$7,875,000	$52,312,500	$52,312,500

The selling stockholders have granted the underwriters the right to purchase up to an additional 937,500 shares of common stock to cover over-allotments.

The Securities and Exchange Commission and state securities regulators have not approved or disapproved these securities, or determined if this prospectus is truthful or complete. Any representation to the contrary is a criminal offense.

Morgan Stanley & Co. Incorporated expects to deliver the shares of common stock to purchasers on April 21, 2009.

MORGAN STANLEY

WILLIAM BLAIR & COMPANY

JEFFERIES & COMPANY

PIPER JAFFRAY

ROBERT W. BAIRD & CO.

April 15, 2009

Table 15-8   Out-of-pocket costs for Rosetta Stone IPO

	Amount Paid
SEC registration fee	$ 6,819
FINRA filing fee	12,719
Initial NYSE listing fee	157,500
Legal fees and expenses	700,000
Accounting fees and expenses	2,000,000
Printing expenses	250,000
Transfer agent and registrar fees and expenses	10,000
Miscellaneous expenses	346,982
Total	$3,484,020

Source: Rosetta Stone prospectus.

the stock traded for almost $31 per share on August 10, 2009. After the stock market closed on that day, Rosetta Stone announced that it had filed another registration statement with the SEC for a secondary offering of its common stock. Most of the stock to be sold in the secondary offering would come from two shareholders who owned large stakes prior to the IPO, not from new stock issued by the company. Because very little of the stock would be newly issued, dilution would not be a problem. Nevertheless, the financial markets interpreted this news negatively. If two large insiders believed the stock should be sold at this price, then perhaps the market price was too high.

Over the next week, Rosetta Stone's price fell to $20 per share, a 35 percent drop in one week. On August 17, the firm announced that the secondary offering was canceled. The stock price immediately stabilized, and the stock rose in value to over $22 per share by the end of the month. Figure 15-6 shows Rosetta Stone's stock price performance and the S&P 500 Index return during all of 2009.

Figure 15-6   2009 stock returns for Rosetta Stone and S&P 500 Index

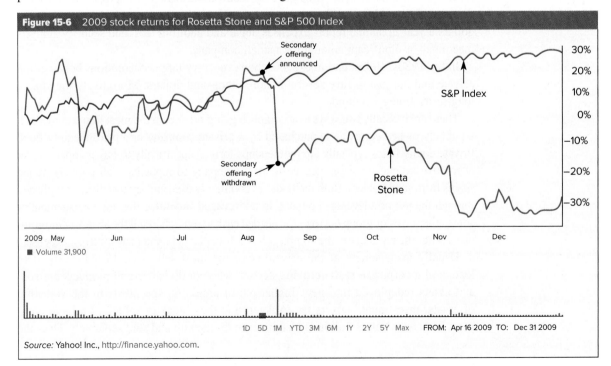

Source: Yahoo! Inc., http://finance.yahoo.com.

This narrative offers several general observations about IPOs and secondary offerings. IPOs are typically underpriced and have high first-day returns. Consistent with Rosetta Stone's original plan, secondary offerings frequently occur after a stock has risen significantly in value. Often the stockholders sell because they want to diversify their portfolio, but the market generally interprets secondary offerings as a sign that company managers or insiders view the stock as overvalued, and the share price declines when the offering is announced. However, Rosetta Stone's decline was larger than most.

Private Placement

Private placement refers to the selling of securities directly to insurance companies, pension funds, and wealthy individuals, rather than through the security markets. This financing device may be employed by a growing firm that wishes to avoid or defer an initial public stock offering or by a publicly traded company that wishes to incorporate private funds into its financing package. Private placements exceed 50 percent of all long-term corporate debt outstanding.

The advantages of private placement are worthy of note. First, there is no lengthy, expensive registration process with the SEC. Second, the firm has greater flexibility in negotiating with one or a handful of insurance companies, pension funds, or bankers than is possible in a public offering. Because there is no SEC registration or underwriting, the initial costs of a private placement may be considerably lower than those of a public issue. However, the interest rate on bonds is usually higher to compensate the investor for holding a less liquid obligation.

Going Private and Leveraged Buyouts

Throughout the years, there have always been some public firms **going private**. In the 1970s, a number of firms gave up their public listings to be private, but these were usually small firms. Management figured it could save several hundred thousand dollars a year in annual report expenses, legal and auditing fees, and security analysts meetings—a significant amount for a small company.

In the 1980s, 1990s, and mid-2000s, however, very large corporations began going private and not just to save several hundred thousand dollars. More likely they had a long-term strategy in mind.

There are basically two ways to accomplish going private. In the most frequent method, a publicly owned company is purchased by a private company or a private equity fund. Private equity funds typically are partnerships formed specifically to buy companies. An alternative avenue for going private is for a company to repurchase all publicly traded shares from stockholders. Both methods are commonly used and are usually accomplished through the use of a leveraged buyout. In a **leveraged buyout,** either the management or some other investor group borrows the needed cash to repurchase all the shares of the company. After the repurchase, the company has substantial debt and heavy interest expense.

Usually management of the private company must sell assets to reduce the debt load, and a corporate **restructuring** occurs, wherein divisions and products are sold and assets redeployed into new, higher-return areas. As specialists in the valuation of assets, investment bankers try to determine the "breakup value" of a large company. This is its value if all its divisions were divided up and sold separately. Over the

Tulip Auctions and the Google IPO

While traditional investment banking relies on institutional relationships, there is a move afoot to do some initial public offerings on the Internet using auctions. Most individual investors (especially those with less than million-dollar accounts) find it very difficult to acquire shares in a traditional IPO. Shares are typically allocated to mutual funds, pension funds, and other institutional investors who have connections with the investment bankers. Often, these institutions are repeat customers who participate in most of an underwriter's offerings. While this is obviously bad for small investors, firms that are going public also have concerns with the traditional distribution system. They wonder whose interest the underwriter is looking out for. Are they looking out for the issuer? Or is the banker looking out for the interests of the institutional investors who are the banker's repeat customers?

In 1998, William Hambrecht founded WR Hambrecht & Co., which helped pioneer U.S. stock auctions. Hambrecht's Open IPO® auctions are based on the method developed to auction Dutch tulip bulbs in the 17th century. In a "Dutch" auction, prices are determined after all prospective buyers have placed bids. Then one price is set for all buyers. That price is the highest price at which all the securities can be sold to the bidders. No investor pays more than his bid price, but many will receive securities at a price that is less than their bid. Dutch auctions are commonly used to sell U.S. Treasury securities, and about 150 auctions of Treasuries are held each year. One of the attractive features of Dutch auctions is that connections don't matter. Mom-and-Pop investors can compete for shares alongside big institutional investors.

In August 2004, Google Inc. went public using a variation on the Dutch auction. Google's IPO was, by far, the largest auction-based offering ever. The auction rules ensured that small investors could participate because orders as small as 5 shares were accepted. In traditional IPOs, allocations of less than 100 shares are rare, although most deals have no official minimum. Google's IPO did not go off without a hitch. The company originally estimated a selling range between $108 and $135 per share, but the eventual issue price was only $85 per share. Noting this fact, many Wall Street bankers and professional investors declared the IPO auction a failure. Of course, there is no evidence that a traditional IPO would have yielded a higher initial selling price, and Google paid underwriting fees of only 2.8 percent, which is less than the norm. On the first day of trading, Google's price rose in the aftermarket to $100.34, an 18 percent gain that is about average for IPOs. By January 2009, Google's price had risen above $600 per share.

In 2005, Chicago investment research firm Morningstar Inc. chose to go public using Hambrecht's Open IPO system. However, traditional Wall Street underwriters strongly discouraged Morningstar from using the auction format. After all, the traditional underwriting method is extremely profitable for underwriters and institutional investors. Institutional investors clearly did not receive preferential treatment in the Morningstar IPO. Investment behemoth Fidelity Investments received no shares in the IPO. Its $17.50 bid for 2.2 million Morningstar shares was too low. The auction clearing price was set at $18.50. Morningstar paid underwriting fees of less than 2 percent of the offering proceeds, much less than would be expected in a traditional offering.

Internet-based auctions may eventually capture a significant share of the underwriting market, but that time is probably still far off.

www.google.com

long run, these strategies can be rewarding, and these companies may again become publicly owned. For example, Beatrice Foods went private in 1986 for $6.2 billion. One year later, it sold various pieces of the company—Avis, Coke Bottling, International Playtex, and other assets worth $6 billion—and still had assets left valued at $4 billion for a public offering.

However, not all leveraged buyouts have worked as planned. Because they are based on the heavy use of debt, any shortfall in a company's performance after the buyout can prove disastrous.

It should be further pointed out that the impetus to going private was once again stimulated in 2002 by the Sarbanes–Oxley Act, which greatly increased the reporting requirements and potential liability for publicly traded companies. This was especially true for smaller companies where the financial burden of reporting was a significant expense. Many of these decided to go private.

International Investment Banking Deals

Privatization

Beginning in the 1980s and continuing to date, governments around the world have privatized companies previously owned by the state. The word "privatization" can be confusing, because in the United States we refer to many companies as "publicly owned" when they are actually owned by private investors. So-called public companies like General Electric, Intel, and Boeing are not owned by the government. They are owned by private individuals, mutual funds, pension funds, and other investors. This has been a common practice in the United States for over 100 years. However, in many countries—especially socialist and communist countries—the auto industry, steel industry, aerospace industry, and virtually all other major industries have been owned by the state. The process of **privatization** involves investment bankers taking companies public, but instead of selling companies formerly owned by individuals, the companies sold had been previously owned by governments.

Although Britain privatized its state-owned steel industry in the 1950s, in many respects, the privatization of British Telecom in 1984 was the first significant effort to turn state-owned businesses into private companies. Subsequently, a wave of privatizations swept Western Europe, Latin America, and the more capitalist countries of Asia. With the collapse of the USSR, many of the former communist countries such as Poland, Hungary, and the Czech Republic began to privatize their industries with public offerings of common stock. In recent years, China and Russia have joined the push toward reducing government ownership of assets.

Around the world, governments continue to own a wealth of assets. Consider the United States, a country with a tradition of private ownership. The federal and state governments still own 88 percent of Alaska's land, over 320 million acres. Almost all of the roads in the United States are owned by state, local, and federal governments. There may be good reasons for state ownership of these assets, but as the public demands more services from the government, a huge source of potential cash could be tapped by the privatization of some of these assets. In 2006 Indiana effectively privatized the Indiana East-West Toll Road by leasing the road to a Spanish-Australian partnership, which now operates it. The road needed to be upgraded, and the Indiana government balked at spending taxpayer money on a toll road when other needs were deemed to be more pressing. In many other countries, the fraction of wealth owned by the state is much higher than in the United States. It can be expected that governments around the world will continue to privatize government businesses and assets.

SUMMARY

The investment banker acts as an intermediary between corporations in need of funds and investors having funds, such as the investing public, pension funds, and mutual funds, to name a few. Of course the investment banker charges a fee to the corporation selling securities, and the fee is based on the size of the offering, the risk associated with the company, and whether the security is equity or debt.

The role of the investment banker is critical to the distribution of securities in the U.S. economy. The investment banker serves as an underwriter or the risk taker by purchasing securities from the issuing corporation and redistributing them to the public; he or she may continue to maintain a market in the distributed securities after they have been sold to the public. The investment banking firm can also help a company sell a new issue on a "best-efforts" basis. As corporations become larger and more global, they need larger investment banks, and this has caused consolidation in the investment banking industry. A few large investment banks that are able to take down large blocks of securities and compete in international markets now dominate the industry.

Investment bankers also serve as important advisors to corporations by providing advice on mergers, acquisitions, foreign capital markets, and leveraged buyouts, and also on resisting hostile takeover attempts. The fees earned for this advice can be substantial.

The advantages of selling securities in the public markets must be weighed against the disadvantages. While going public may give the corporation and major stockholders greater access to funds, as well as additional prestige, these advantages quickly disappear in a down market. Furthermore the corporation must open its books to the public and orient itself to the short-term emphasis of investors.

Companies may decide to go from public to private. This trend was evident in the late 1980s, 1990s, and mid-2000s with many large companies going private through leveraged buyouts. However, a number of these companies again publicly distributed their shares a year or two later, generating large profits for their owners in the process.

LIST OF TERMS

investment banker   477
underwrite   478
"best-efforts" basis   478
agent   479
managing investment banker   480
bookrunner   480
underwriting syndicate   480
underwriting spread   481
underpricing   483
dilution of earnings   483

market stabilization   485
aftermarket   487
shelf registration   487
public placement   488
private placement   492
going private   492
leveraged buyout   492
restructuring   492
privatization   494

DISCUSSION QUESTIONS

1. In what way is an investment banker a risk taker? *(LO15-2)*
2. What is the purpose of market stabilization activities during the distribution process? *(LO15-1)*

3. Discuss how an underwriting syndicate decreases risk for each underwriter and at the same time facilitates the distribution process. *(LO15-2)*

4. Discuss the reason for the differences between underwriting spreads for stocks and bonds. *(LO15-2)*

5. What is shelf registration? How does it differ from the traditional requirements for security offerings? *(LO15-1)*

6. Discuss the benefits accruing to a company that is traded in the public securities markets. *(LO15-4)*

7. What are the disadvantages to being public? *(LO15-4)*

8. If a company were looking for capital by way of a private placement, where would it look for funds? *(LO15-1)*

9. How does a leveraged buyout work? What does the debt structure of the firm normally look like after a leveraged buyout? What might be done to reduce the debt? *(LO15-5)*

10. How might a leveraged buyout eventually lead to high returns for a company? *(LO15-5)*

11. What is privatization? *(LO15-5)*

PRACTICE PROBLEMS AND SOLUTIONS

Dilution effect
of new issue
(LO15-3)

1. Dawson Motor Company has 6 million shares outstanding with total earnings of $12 million. The company is considering issuing 1.5 million new shares.

    a. What will be the immediate dilution in earnings per share?

    b. If the new shares can be sold at $25 per share and the proceeds will earn 12 percent, will there still be dilution? Based on the new EPS, should the new shares be issued?

Underwriting costs
(LO15-2)

2. Gallagher Corp. will issue 300,000 shares at a retail (public) price of $40. The company will receive $37.90 per share and incur $160,000 in out-of-pocket expenses.

    a. What is the percentage spread?

    b. What percentage of the total value of the issue (based on the retail price) are the out-of-pocket costs?

Solutions

1. *a.* Earnings per share before the stock issue:

$$\frac{\$12,000,000}{6,000,000} = \$2.00$$

Earnings per share after the stock issue:

$$\frac{\$12,000,000}{7,500,000} = \$1.60$$

$$
\begin{array}{ll}
\$2.00 & \text{Before} \\
\underline{1.60} & \text{After} \\
\$0.40 & \text{Dilution}
\end{array}
$$

b.   New income = 12% × (1.5 million shares × $25) = 12% × 37,500,000

$$= \$4,500,000$$

Total income = $12,000,000 + $4,500,000 = $16,500,000

Earnings per share based on the additional income included in total income:

$$\text{EPS} = \frac{\$16,500,000}{7,500,000} = \$2.20$$

There is no longer dilution. Earnings per share will grow from the initial amount of $2.00 to $2.20. The new shares should be issued.

2. *a.*   Percentage spread $= \dfrac{\$\,\text{Spread}}{\text{Public price}}$

$ Spread = Public price − Net to corporation

$2.10 = $40 − 37.90

Percentage spread $= \dfrac{\$2.10}{\$40} = 5.25\%$

b.

Retail (public) price	$ 40
Number of new shares	× 300,000
Total retail value	$12,000,000

$$\frac{\text{Out-of-pocket costs}}{\text{Total retail value}} = \frac{\$160,000}{\$12,000,000} = 1.33\%$$

PROBLEMS

▦ connect Selected problems are available with Connect. Please see the preface for more information.

Basic Problems

1. Louisiana Timber Company currently has 5 million shares of stock outstanding and will report earnings of $9 million in the current year. The company is considering the issuance of 1 million additional shares that will net $40 per share to the corporation.

    Dilution effect of stock issue (LO15-3)

    a.   What is the immediate dilution potential for this new stock issue?

    b.   Assume the Louisiana Timber Company can earn 11 percent on the proceeds of the stock issue in time to include it in the current year's results. Should the new issue be undertaken based on earnings per share?

2. The Hamilton Corporation Company has 4 million shares of stock outstanding and will report earnings of $6,910,000 in the current year. The company is considering the issuance of 1 million additional shares that can only be issued at $30 per share.

    Dilution effect of stock issue (LO15-3)

    a.   Assume the Hamilton Corporation Company can earn 7.0 percent on the proceeds. Calculate the earnings per share.

    b.   Should the new issue be undertaken based on earnings per share?

3. American Health Systems currently has 6,400,000 shares of stock outstanding and will report earnings of $10 million in the current year. The company

    Dilution effect of stock issue (LO15-3)

is considering the issuance of 1,700,000 additional shares that will net $30 per share to the corporation.

    a.   What is the immediate dilution potential for this new stock issue?

    b.   Assume that American Health Systems can earn 9 percent on the proceeds of the stock issue in time to include them in the current year's results. Calculate earnings per share. Should the new issue be undertaken based on earnings per share?

Dilution effect of stock issue (LO15-3)

4.   Using the information in Problem 3, assume that American Health Systems 1,700,000 additional shares can only be issued at $18 per share.

    a.   Assume that American Health Systems can earn 6 percent on the proceeds. Calculate earnings per share.

    b.   Should the new issue be undertaken based on earnings per share?

Dilution and pricing effect of stock issue (LO15-3)

5.   Jordan Broadcasting Company is going public at $50 net per share to the company. There also are founding stockholders that are selling part of their shares at the same price. Prior to the offering, the firm had $26 million in earnings divided over 11 million shares. The public offering will be for 5 million shares; 3 million will be new corporate shares and 2 million will be shares currently owned by the founding stockholders.

    a.   What is the immediate dilution based on the new corporate shares that are being offered?

    b.   If the stock has a P/E of 30 immediately after the offering, what will the stock price be?

    c.   Should the founding stockholders be pleased with the $50 they received for their shares?

Underwriting spread (LO15-2)

6.   Solar Energy Corp. has $4 million in earnings with 4 million shares outstanding. Investment bankers think the stock can justify a P/E ratio of 21. Assume the underwriting spread is 5 percent. What should the price to the public be?

Underwriting spread (LO15-2)

7.   Tiger Golf Supplies has $25 million in earnings with 7 million shares outstanding. Its investment banker thinks the stock should trade at a P/E ratio of 31. Assume there is an underwriting spread of 7.8 percent. What should the price to the public be?

Underwriting spread (LO15-2)

8.   Assume Sybase Software is thinking about three different size offerings for issuance of additional shares.

Size of Offer		Public Price	Net to Corporation
a.	1.1 million	$30	$27.50
b.	7.0 million	$30	28.44
c.	28.0 million	$30	29.15

What is the percentage underwriting spread for each size offer?

Underwriting spread (LO15-2)

9.   Walton and Company is the managing investment banker for a major new underwriting. The price of the stock to the investment banker is $23 per share. Other syndicate members may buy the stock for $24.25. The price to the selected dealers group is $24.80, with a price to brokers of $25.20. Finally, the price to the public is $29.50.

    a.   If Walton and Company sells its shares to the dealer group, what will the percentage return be?

    b.   If Walton and Company performs the dealer's function also and sells to brokers, what will the percentage return be?

    c.   If Walton and Company fully integrates its operation and sells directly to the public, what will its percentage return be?

10. The Wrigley Corporation needs to raise $44 million. The investment banking firm of Tinkers, Evers & Chance will handle the transaction.

    a.   If stock is utilized, 2,300,000 shares will be sold to the public at $20.50 per share. The corporation will receive a net price of $19 per share. What is the percentage underwriting spread per share?

    b.   If bonds are utilized, slightly over 43,700 bonds will be sold to the public at $1,009 per bond. The corporation will receive a net price of $994 per bond. What is the percentage of underwriting spread per bond? (Relate the dollar spread to the public price.)

    c.   Which alternative has the larger percentage of spread? Is this the normal relationship between the two types of issues?

Underwriting spread
(LO15-2)

11. Kevin's Bacon Company Inc. has earnings of $9 million with 2,100,000 shares outstanding before a public distribution. Seven hundred thousand shares will be included in the sale, of which 400,000 are new corporate shares, and 300,000 are shares currently owned by Ann Fry, the founder and CEO. The 300,000 shares that Ann is selling are referred to as a secondary offering, and all proceeds will go to her.

    The net price from the offering will be $16.50, and the corporate proceeds are expected to produce $1.8 million in corporate earnings.

    a.   What were the corporation's earnings per share before the offering?

    b.   What are the corporation's earnings per share expected to be after the offering?

Secondary offering
(LO15-2)

12. Becker Brothers is the managing underwriter for a 1.45-million-share issue by Jay's Hamburger Heaven. Becker Brothers is "handling" 10 percent of the issue. Its price is $27 per share, and the price to the public is $28.95.

    Becker also provides the market stabilization function. During the issuance, the market for the stock turns soft, and Becker is forced to purchase 50,000 shares in the open market at an average price of $27.50. It later sells the shares at an average value of $27.20.

    Compute Becker Brothers overall gain or loss from managing the issue.

Market stabilization and risk
(LO15-2)

13. Trump Card Co. will issue stock at a retail (public) price of $32. The company will receive $29.20 per share.

    a.   What is the spread on the issue in percentage terms?

    b.   If the firm demands receiving a new price only $2.20 below the public price suggested in part *a*, what will the spread be in percentage terms?

    c.   To hold the spread down to 2.5 percent based on the public price in part *a*, what net amount should Trump Card Co. receive?

Underwriting costs
(LO15-2)

14. Winston Sporting Goods is considering a public offering of common stock. Its investment banker has informed the company that the retail price will be $16.85

𝕏
Underwriting costs
(LO15-2)

per share for 550,000 shares. The company will receive $15.40 per share and will incur $180,000 in registration, accounting, and printing fees.

a.   What is the spread on this issue in percentage terms? What are the total expenses of the issue as a percentage of total value (at retail)?

b.   If the firm wanted to net $15.99 million from this issue, how many shares must be sold?

Intermediate Problems

P/E ratio for new public issue (LO15-2)

15.   Richmond Rent-A-Car is about to go public. The investment banking firm of Tinkers, Evers & Chance is attempting to price the issue. The car rental industry generally trades at a 20 percent discount below the P/E ratio on the Standard & Poor's 500 Stock Index. Assume that index currently has a P/E ratio of 25. The firm can be compared to the car rental industry as follows:

	Richmond	Car Rental Industry
Growth rate in earnings per share	15%	10%
Consistency of performance	Increased earnings 4 out of 5 years	Increased earnings 3 out of 5 years
Debt to total assets	52%	39%
Turnover of product	Slightly below average	Average
Quality of management	High	Average

Assume, in assessing the initial P/E ratio, the investment banker will first determine the appropriate industry P/E based on the Standard & Poor's 500 Index. Then a half point will be added to the P/E ratio for each case in which Richmond Rent-A-Car is superior to the industry norm, and a half point will be deducted for an inferior comparison. On this basis, what should the initial P/E be for the firm?

Dividend valuation model for new public issue (LO15-1)

16.   The investment banking firm of Einstein & Co. will use a dividend valuation model to appraise the shares of the Modern Physics Corporation. Dividends (D_1) at the end of the current year will be $1.64. The growth rate ($g$) is 8 percent and the discount rate (K_e) is 13 percent.

a.   What should be the price of the stock to the public?

b.   If there is a 7 percent total underwriting spread on the stock, how much will the issuing corporation receive?

c.   If the issuing corporation requires a net price of $31.30 (proceeds to the corporation) and there is a 7 percent underwriting spread, what should be the price of the stock to the public? (Round to two places to the right of the decimal point.)

Comparison of private and public debt offering (LO15-1)

17.   The Landers Corporation needs to raise $1.60 million of debt on a 20-year issue. If it places the bonds privately, the interest rate will be 10 percent. Twenty thousand dollars in out-of-pocket costs will be incurred. For a public issue, the interest rate will be 9 percent, and the underwriting spread will be 2 percent. There will be $120,000 in out-of-pocket costs. Assume interest on the debt is paid semiannually, and the debt will be outstanding for the full 20-year period, at which time it will be repaid.

For each plan, compare the net amount of funds initially available—inflow—to the present value of future payments of interest and principal to determine net present value. Assume the stated discount rate is 12 percent annually. Use 6 percent semiannually throughout the analysis. (Disregard taxes.)

Advanced Problems

18. Midland Corporation has a net income of $19 million and 4 million shares outstanding. Its common stock is currently selling for $48 per share. Midland plans to sell common stock to set up a major new production facility with a net cost of $21,120,000. The production facility will not produce a profit for one year, and then it is expected to earn a 13 percent return on the investment. Stanley Morgan and Co., an investment banking firm, plans to sell the issue to the public for $44 per share with a spread of 4 percent.

Features associated with a stock distribution (LO15-3)

    a. How many shares of stock must be sold to net $21,120,000? (Note: No out-of-pocket costs must be considered in this problem.)

    b. Why is the investment banker selling the stock at less than its current market price?

    c. What are the earnings per share (EPS) and the price-earnings ratio before the issue (based on a stock price of $48)? What will be the price per share immediately after the sale of stock if the P/E stays constant?

    d. Compute the EPS and the price (P/E stays constant) after the new production facility begins to produce a profit.

    e. Are the shareholders better off because of the sale of stock and the resultant investment? What other financing strategy could the company have tried to increase earnings per share?

19. The Presley Corporation is about to go public. It currently has aftertax earnings of $7,200,000, and 2,100,000 shares are owned by the present stockholders (the Presley family). The new public issue will represent 800,000 new shares. The new shares will be priced to the public at $25 per share, with a 5 percent spread on the offering price. There will also be $260,000 in out-of-pocket costs to the corporation.

Dilution and rates of return (LO15-3)

    a. Compute the net proceeds to the Presley Corporation.

    b. Compute the earnings per share immediately before the stock issue.

    c. Compute the earnings per share immediately after the stock issue.

    d. Determine what rate of return must be earned on the net proceeds to the corporation so there will not be a dilution in earnings per share during the year of going public.

    e. Determine what rate of return must be earned on the proceeds to the corporation so there will be a 5 percent increase in earnings per share during the year of going public.

20. Tyson Iron Works is about to go public. It currently has aftertax earnings of $4,400,000, and 4,200,000 shares are owned by the present stockholders. The new public issue will represent 500,000 new shares. The new shares will be priced to the public at $25 per share with a 3 percent spread on the offering price. There will also be $280,000 in out-of-pocket costs to the corporation.

Dilution and rates of return (LO15-3)

    a. Compute the net proceeds to Tyson Iron Works.

    b. Compute the earnings per share immediately before the stock issue.

c. Compute the earnings per share immediately after the stock issue.

d. Determine what rate of return must be earned on the net proceeds to the corporation so there will not be a dilution in earnings per share during the year of going public.

e. Determine what rate of return must be earned on the proceeds to the corporation so there will be a 10 percent increase in earnings per share during the year of going public.

Aftermarket for new public issue (LO15-4)

21. I. B. Michaels has a chance to participate in a new public offering by Hi-Tech Micro Computers. His broker informs him that demand for the 700,000 shares to be issued is very strong. His broker's firm is assigned 25,000 shares in the distribution and will allow Michaels, a relatively good customer, 1.3 percent of its 25,000 share allocation.

The initial offering price is $30 per share. There is a strong aftermarket, and the stock goes to $32 one week after issue. The first full month after issue, Mr. Michaels is pleased to observe his shares are selling for $33.50. He is content to place his shares in a lockbox and eventually use their anticipated increased value to help send his son to college many years in the future. However, one year after the distribution, he looks up the shares in *The Wall Street Journal* and finds they are trading at $28.50.

a. Compute the total dollar profit or loss on Mr. Michaels's shares one week, one month, and one year after the purchase. In each case, compute the profit or loss against the initial purchase price.

b. Also compute this percentage gain or loss from the initial $30 price.

c. Why might a new public issue be expected to have a strong aftermarket?

Leveraged buyout (LO15-5)

22. The management of Mitchell Labs decided to go private in 2002 by buying in all 2.80 million of its outstanding shares at $24.80 per share. By 2006, management had restructured the company by selling off the petroleum research division for $10.75 million, the fiber technology division for $8.45 million, and the synthetic products division for $20 million. Because these divisions had been only marginally profitable, Mitchell Labs is a stronger company after the restructuring. Mitchell is now able to concentrate exclusively on contract research and will generate earnings per share of $1.10 this year. Investment bankers have contacted the firm and indicated that if it reentered the public market, the 2.80 million shares it purchased to go private could now be reissued to the public at a P/E ratio of 15 times earnings per share.

a. What was the initial cost to Mitchell Labs to go private?

b. What is the total value to the company from (1) the proceeds of the divisions that were sold, as well as (2) the current value of the 2.80 million shares (based on current earnings and an anticipated P/E of 15)?

c. What is the percentage return to the management of Mitchell Labs from the restructuring? Use answers from parts *a* and *b* to determine this value.

COMPREHENSIVE PROBLEM

The Bailey Corporation, a manufacturer of medical supplies and equipment, is planning to sell its shares to the general public for the first time. The firm's investment banker, Robert Merrill and Company, is working with Bailey Corporation in determining a number of items. Information on the Bailey Corporation follows:

Bailey Corporation
(Impact of new public offering)

(LO15-4)

BAILEY CORPORATION Income Statement For the Year 20X1	
Sales (all on credit)	$42,680,000
Cost of goods sold	32,240,000
Gross profit	$ 10,440,000
Selling and administrative expenses	4,558,000
Operating profit	$ 5,882,000
Interest expense	600,000
Net income before taxes	5,282,000
Taxes	2,120,000
Net income	$ 3,162,000

BAILEY CORPORATION Balance Sheet As of December 31, 20X1	
Assets	
Current assets:	
Cash	$ 250,000
Marketable securities	130,000
Accounts receivable	6,000,000
Inventory	8,300,000
Total current assets	$ 14,680,000
Net plant and equipment	13,970,000
Total assets	$28,650,000
Liabilities and Stockholders' Equity	
Current liabilities:	
Accounts payable	$ 3,800,000
Notes payable	3,550,000
Total current liabilities	$ 7,350,000
Long-term liabilities	5,620,000
Total liabilities	$ 12,970,000
Stockholders' equity:	
Common stock (1,800,000 shares at $1 par)	$ 1,800,000
Capital in excess of par	6,300,000
Retained earnings	7,580,000
Total stockholders' equity	$ 15,680,000
Total liabilities and stockholders' equity	$28,650,000

a. Assume that 800,000 new corporate shares will be issued to the general public. What will earnings per share be immediately after the public offering? (Round to two places to the right of the decimal point.) Based on the price-earnings ratio of 12, what will the initial price of the stock be? Use earnings per share after the distribution in the calculation.

b. Assuming an underwriting spread of 5 percent and out-of-pocket costs of $300,000, what will net proceeds to the corporation be?

c. What return must the corporation earn on the net proceeds to equal the earnings per share before the offering? How does this compare with current return on the total assets on the balance sheet?

d. Now assume that, of the initial 800,000 share distribution, 400,000 belong to current stockholders and 400,000 are new shares, and the latter will be added to the 1,800,000 shares currently outstanding. What will earnings per share be immediately after the public offering? What will the initial market price of the stock be? Assume a price-earnings ratio of 12, and use earnings per share after the distribution in the calculation.

e. Assuming an underwriting spread of 5 percent and out-of-pocket costs of $300,000, what will net proceeds to the corporation be?

f. What return must the corporation now earn on the net proceeds to equal earnings per share before the offering? How does this compare with current return on the total assets on the balance sheet?

 W E B   E X E R C I S E

1. Initial public offerings (IPOs) were covered in the chapter. Let's take a closer look at two actual issues. Go to www.nasdaq.com/markets/ipos. For the first two issues under "Latest IPOs," do the following steps all the way through, one company at a time. Use the menu in the left margin to navigate the IPO.

2. a. Click on and write down the company name.

   b. Write a short paragraph about what the company does or its products.

   c. Scroll down and record the date the company went public.

   d. Write down the actual offer price.

   e. Write down the offering amount (mil.).

   f. Record the name of the lead underwriter or underwriters and record the total number in the syndicate. You will find this under "Experts."

Note: Occasionally a topic we have listed may have been deleted, updated, or moved into a different location on a website. If you click on the site map or site index, you will be introduced to a table of contents that should aid you in finding the topic you are looking for.

LEARNING OBJECTIVES

LO 16-1 Analyzing long-term debt requires consideration of the collateral pledged, method of repayment, and other key factors.

LO 16-2 Bond yields are important to bond analysis and are influenced by how bonds are rated by major bond rating agencies.

LO 16-3 An important corporate decision is whether to call in and reissue debt (refund the obligation) when interest rates decline.

LO 16-4 Long-term lease obligations have many characteristics similar to debt and are recognized as a form of indirect debt by the accounting profession.

LO 16-5 When a firm fails to meet its financial obligations, it may be subject to bankruptcy.

Long-Term Debt and Lease Financing

For those who invest in the highly rated bonds of firms such as ExxonMobil, Johnson & Johnson, and Microsoft, there is very little to worry about. You get a higher return than you could get on U.S. government securities while still being able to sleep soundly at night.

However, for those who invest in bonds of companies in telecommunications or the homebuilding industry, sleep may not come so easily. In the case of the latter, 16 of the 21 largest homebuilders had negative cash flow during the last recession.

As one example, D.R. Horton Inc. of Fort Worth, Texas, the second largest homebuilder in the United States, saw its earnings per share drop from a peak value of $4.62 in 2005 to a negative $8.34 in 2008 and a continued loss in 2009. It suffered from high inventories of unsold homes, rising foreclosures, tightened lending standards, and declining home values. By 2012 year-end, the housing market started to recover and D.R. Horton reported earnings per share of $2.77. The improving housing market allowed the company to increase prices on the homes it sold. Between 2008 and 2012, Horton brought down its debt-to-equity ratio from 105 percent to 59 percent, and management stated that the company was in the best position of its existence. By early 2015, Standard & Poor's had raised Horton's credit rating to BB, but D.R. Horton did not reach a new stock market high until 2017, a decade later.

The Expanding Role of Debt

The amount of corporate debt has increased over time as corporations grew with the economy. Sometimes the increased use of debt was due to business expansion in capital-intensive industries like airlines and telecommunications. Some companies simply did not generate enough internal funds from operations to fund expansion, so they sold bonds to finance their growth. Other firms decided to recapitalize and repurchased their common stock with funds raised from bond offerings. One thing that hasn't changed is the cyclical nature of financial leverage ratios as the economy expands and contracts and interest rates move up and down.

One ratio you may remember from Chapter 3 is the times-interest-earned ratio. This ratio divides the operating income (EBIT) by the interest expense and indicates how many times the company can cover its interest expense. The higher the number, the more protected are the interest payments and the bondholders. The interesting thing about this ratio is that it indirectly includes the amount of debt on the balance sheet. As the amount of debt goes up, interest payments usually rise also. However, when interest rates fall, companies can refinance their debt at lower interest rates just like homeowners refinance their homes when mortgage rates decline. So the times-interest-earned ratio is also affected by the interest rates (coupon rates) on their bonds. Two companies can have the same amount of debt but different interest rates associated with their debt, and even though they have the same operating income, their interest coverage ratios would be different.

In 1977, the average U.S. manufacturing corporation had its interest payment covered by operating earnings at a rate of eight times. By the time the financial crisis ended in 2007–08, the average times interest earned was down to 2.4 times. Figure 16-1 shows times interest earned for Macy's Inc. since 1999, along with Macy's Earnings before Interest and Taxes. Although interest rates declined dramatically over the last 20 years, Macy's times-interest-earned ratio did not. Like many companies, Macy's took advantage of low interest rates to increase leverage and to borrow using longer-term debt, which carries a higher interest rate. Of course, financial leverage creates risk, which can be seen in the firm's earnings and times interest earned for the year ended January 2009. This earnings collapse coincides with the financial crisis that peaked in the fall of 2008.

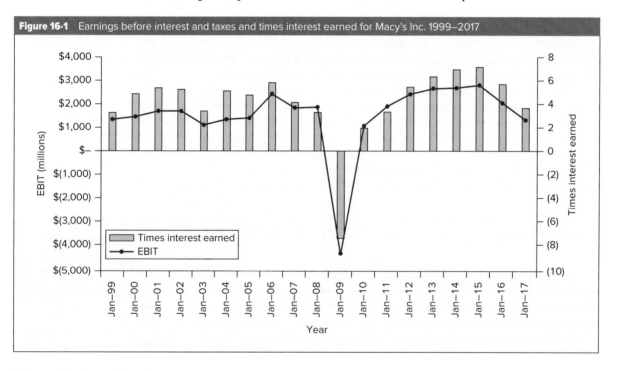

Figure 16-1   Earnings before interest and taxes and times interest earned for Macy's Inc. 1999–2017

The Debt Contract

The corporate bond represents the basic long-term debt instrument for most large U.S. corporations. The bond agreement specifies such basic items as the par value, the coupon rate, and the maturity date.

Par Value   This is the initial value of the bond. The **par value** is sometimes referred to as the principal or face value. Most corporate bonds are initially traded in $1,000 units.

Coupon Rate   This is the actual interest rate on the bond, usually payable in semi-annual installments. To the extent that interest rates in the market go above or below the coupon rate after the bond has been issued, the market price of the bond will change from the par value.

Maturity Date   The **maturity date** is the final date on which repayment of the bond principal is due.

The bond agreement is supplemented by a much longer document termed a bond **indenture**. The indenture, often containing over 100 pages of complicated legal wording, covers every detail surrounding the bond issue—including collateral pledged, methods of repayment, restrictions on the corporation, and procedures for initiating claims against the corporation. The corporation appoints a financially independent trustee to administer the provisions of the bond indenture under the guidelines of the Trust Indenture Act of 1939. Let's examine two items of interest in any bond agreement: the security provisions of the bond and the methods of repayment.

Security Provisions

A **secured debt** is one in which specific assets are pledged to bondholders in the event of default. Only infrequently are pledged assets actually sold and the proceeds distributed to bondholders. Typically the defaulting corporation is reorganized and existing claims are partially satisfied by issuing new securities to the participating parties. The stronger and better secured the initial claim, the higher the quality of the new security to be received in exchange. When a defaulting corporation is reorganized for failure to meet obligations, existing management may be terminated and, in extreme cases, held legally responsible for any imprudent actions.

A number of terms are used to denote collateralized or secured debt. Under a **mortgage agreement**, real property (plant and equipment) is pledged as security for the loan. A mortgage may be senior or junior in nature, with senior requiring satisfaction of claims before payment is given to junior debt. Bondholders may also attach an **after-acquired property clause**, requiring that any new property be placed under the original mortgage.

You should realize not all secured debt will carry every protective feature, but rather represents a carefully negotiated position including some safeguards and rejecting others. Generally, the greater the protection offered a given class of bondholders, the lower is the interest rate on the bond. Bondholders are willing to assume some degree of risk to receive a higher yield.

Unsecured Debt

A number of corporations issue debt that is not secured by a specific claim to assets. In Wall Street jargon, the name **debenture** refers to a long-term, unsecured corporate bond. Among the major participants in debenture offerings are such prestigious firms as ExxonMobil, IBM, Dow Chemical, and Intel. Because of the legal problems associated with "specific" asset claims in a secured bond offering, the trend is to issue unsecured debt—allowing the bondholder a general claim against the corporation—rather than a specific lien against an asset.

Even unsecured debt may be divided between high-ranking and subordinated debt. A **subordinated debenture** is an unsecured bond in which payment to the holder will occur only after designated senior debenture holders are satisfied. The hierarchy of creditor obligations for secured as well as unsecured debt is presented in Figure 16-2, along with consideration of the position of stockholders.

A classic case of the ranking of bondholders (debtholders) and stockholders took place on June 1, 2009, when General Motors went into bankruptcy. The government provided over $50 billion in funds to GM to help it survive and ultimately come out of bankruptcy as a stronger company. The U.S. government owned 60 percent of the common stock of General Motors in early 2010 and was able to sell a $13.6 billion stake when GM came to the market with an IPO in November 2010. By December 2013, the U.S government had sold all of its shares in GM.

When GM went into bankruptcy, the common stockholders (with the lowest priority of claims, as shown at the bottom of Figure 16-2) received nothing for their shares. This was quite a disappointment to the stockholders who only two years earlier held shares that were valued at $40 and paying a $2 annual dividend.

Preferred stockholders also received nothing—the next major class, reading up the scale in Figure 16-2, were the unsecured debtholders. They unhappily received 10 cents on the dollar (in this case, there was no distinction between senior and subordinated unsecured debt).

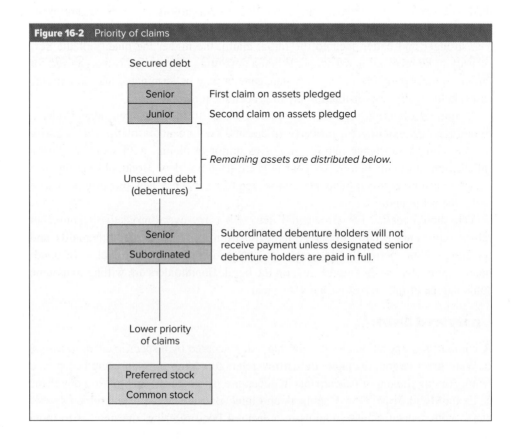

Figure 16-2   Priority of claims

Finally, the secured debtholders (whether senior or junior) were paid off in full with the sell-off of secured assets. The unsecured bondholders were given 10 percent of the new company's common stock with warrants to purchase another 15 percent in the future.

For a further discussion of payment of claims and the hierarchy of obligations, the reader should see Appendix 16A, "Financial Alternatives for Distressed Firms," which also covers other bankruptcy considerations.

Methods of Repayment

The method of repayment for bond issues may not always call for one lump-sum disbursement at the maturity date. Some Canadian and British government bonds are perpetual in nature. In 1951, West Shore Railroad Company issued bonds that were scheduled to mature in 2361 (410 years later). More recently, the Coca-Cola Company and the Walt Disney Company have issued "century" bonds that mature in 100 years. Nevertheless most bonds have some orderly or preplanned system of repayment. In addition to the simplest arrangement—a single-sum payment at maturity—bonds may be retired by serial payments, through sinking-fund provisions, through conversion, or by a call feature.

Serial Payments   Bonds with **serial payment** provisions are paid off in installments over the life of the issue. Each bond has its own predetermined date of maturity and receives interest only to that point. Although the total issue may span over 20 years, 15 or 20 different maturity dates may be assigned specific dollar amounts.

Sinking-Fund Provision   A less structured but more popular method of debt retirement is through the use of a **sinking fund**. Under this arrangement semiannual or annual contributions are made by the corporation into a fund administered by a trustee for purposes of debt retirement. The trustee takes the proceeds and purchases bonds from willing sellers. If no willing sellers are available, a lottery system may be used among outstanding bondholders.

Conversion   A more subtle method of reducing debt outstanding is to provide for debt conversion into common stock. Although this feature is exercised at the option of the bondholder, a number of incentives or penalties may be utilized to encourage conversion. The mechanics of convertible bond trading are discussed at length in Chapter 19, "Convertibles, Warrants, and Derivatives."

Call Feature   A **call provision** allows the corporation to retire or force in the debt issue before maturity. The corporation will pay a premium over par value of 5 to 10 percent—a bargain value to the corporation if bond prices are up. Modern call provisions usually do not take effect until the bond has been outstanding at least 5 to 10 years. Often the call provision declines over time, usually by 0.5 to 1 percent per year after the call period begins. A corporation may decide to call in outstanding debt issues when interest rates on new securities are considerably lower than those on previously issued debt (let's get the high-cost, old debt off the books).

An Example: Eli Lilly's 6.77 Percent Bond

Now that we have covered the key features of the bond indenture, let us examine an existing bond. More specific features of this bond are found in Table 16-1, which provides information about a bond issued by Eli Lilly. In December 2017,

Table 16-1   Eli Lilly's bond offering

Eli Lilly Bonds Due January 1, 2036

Moody's Rating: A2

Indenture Date: January 5, 1996

Authorized: $300,000,000

Outstanding: $194,960,000

Securing of Obligation: A direct unsecured obligation

Interest Payable: January 1, July 1

Grace Period: 30 days

Trustee: Citibank

Call Feature: None

Trading Exchange: OTC

Price Range Year	High	Low
2017	$141.74	$129.58
2016	148.11	132.12
2015	143.64	129.28
2014	135.40	127.46
2013	143.96	123.22
2012	152.54	133.18
2011	138.43	113.50
2010	131.26	110.00
2009	123.18	118.72
2008	122.04	117.36
2007	108.36	102.41
2006	106.26	101.38
2005	105.62	93.84
2004	100.28	89.99

Sources: NASDAQ TRACE, Mergent Online, and https://investor.lilly.com/financial-information/debt-securities

we find that Eli Lilly & Co., one of the largest drug companies in the world, has a 6.77 percent bond due in 2036. The bond carried a Moody's rating of A2.

As we can see in Table 16-1, the 6.77 percent bond had an original authorized offering of $300 million (third line). The trustee is Citibank, and it is the trustee's obligation to make sure that Eli Lilly adheres to the terms of the offering. The information in Table 16-1 also provides other pertinent information found in the indenture, such as the interest payment dates (January 1 and July 1), denomination of each bond, security provisions, call features, and high and low bond prices.

Notice that the bond trades above its face value. Corporate bond prices are quoted as a percentage of par value, which is almost always $1,000. This table shows an important relationship between interest rates and bond prices. As interest rates went down after 2004, the price of this long-term bond went up.

Soccer Bonds Bounce Back

International soccer is big business, and big businesses often issue bonds. Football Club Internazionale Milano SpA, often known simply as "Inter Milan," became one of the most recent sports franchises to issue bonds. However, the bonds carry an interesting twist that encourages the bondholders to cheer on the team. The five-year $354 million bond is secured by the team's broadcasting and sponsorship rights. If Inter Milan plays poorly, the eight-time Italian league champion might see its broadcasting revenues decline. This has happened to a soccer bond in the past.

In the early 2000s Leeds United FC of the English Premier League borrowed heavily when it was on a winning streak. But after several years of winning football, the team incurred injuries and poor play that left the team out of the top tier of the Premier League. As a result, the team did not qualify for the UEFA Champions League for two years in a row. Revenue declined.

Feeling pressure to make debt payments, the team sold off star players, but this caused the team to play even more poorly. By 2003

the team was demoted to a lower league (in soccer terms, the team was "relegated") and lost even more revenue. The team was forced to sell its stadium and its training ground in the autumn of 2004. Eventually, Leeds was relegated to the third-level league and a sale of the team was forced on the club.

Inter Milan may have learned from Leeds's predicament. It has issued bonds that are tied directly to the team's revenue stream. The bond was issued by a special purpose vehicle, rather than by the team's corporate owner itself, potentially insulating the club from disaster if revenues fail to meet the promised bond payouts. This technique is quite common for municipalities in the United States, where the local-government-issued bonds are known as "revenue bonds." Revenue bonds pay off only if there is enough revenue from a particular project (like a toll road). Of course, no one cheers for a toll road, while Inter Milan probably picked up a few fans who have more than a normal rooting interest in the team's success.

Bond Prices, Yields, and Ratings

The financial manager must be sensitive to interest rate changes and price movements in the bond market. For example, the treasurer's interpretation of market conditions will influence the timing of new issues, the coupon rate offered, and the maturity date. In case you may think bonds maintain stable long-term price patterns, you need merely consider bond pricing during the five-year period 1967–72. When the market interest rate on outstanding 30-year, Aaa corporate bonds went from 5.10 percent to 8.10 percent, the average price of existing bonds dropped 36 percent. A conservative investor would be quite disillusioned to see a $1,000, 5.10 percent bond now quoted at $640.[1] Though most bonds are virtually certain to be redeemed at their face value at maturity ($1,000 in this case), this is small consolation to the bondholder who has many decades to wait. At times, bonds also greatly increase in value, such as they did in 1984–85, 1990–92, 1994–95, 2007–08, and 2011–12 when interest rates declined.

As indicated in the paragraph above and in Chapter 10, the price of a bond is directly tied to current interest rates. One exception to this rule was discussed at the beginning of the chapter; that is, when bankruptcy becomes a key factor in pricing and valuation. We will look at the more normal case where interest rates are the key factor in determining price.

A bond paying 5.10 percent ($51 a year) will fare quite poorly when the going market rate is 8.10 percent ($81 a year). To maintain a market in the older issue, the

---

[1]Bond prices are generally quoted as a percentage of original par value. In this case, the quote would read 64.

price is adjusted downward to reflect current market demands. The longer the life of the issue, the greater the influence of interest rate changes on the price of the bond. The same process will work in reverse if interest rates go down. A 30-year, $1,000 bond initially issued to yield 8.10 percent would go up to almost $1,500 if interest rates declined to 5.10 percent (assuming the bond is not callable). A further illustration of interest rate effects on bond prices is presented in Table 16-2 for a bond paying 12 percent interest. Observe that not only interest rates in the market but also years to maturity have a strong influence on bond prices.

Table 16–2	Interest rates and bond prices (face value is $1,000 and annual coupon rate is 12%)						
	A	B	C	D	E	F	G	H
1	Rate in the Market (%)—Annual Yield to Maturity*						
2	Years to Maturity	8%	10%	12%	14%	16%		
3	1	$1,037.72	$1,018.59	$1,000.00	$981.92	$964.33		
4	15	$1,345.84	$1,153.72	$1,000.00	$875.91	$774.84		
5	25	$1,429.64	$1,182.56	$1,000.00	$861.99	$755.33		
6						=+PV(F2/2,A5*2,–120/2,–1000)	
7						+PV(rate,nper,pmt,[fv])	

Prices are based on semiannual payments.
Thus, the annual rate is divided by two and the periods are multiplied by 2.
Cash flow inputs are entered as negative values as required by Excel's PV function.

From 1945 through the early 1980s, the pattern had been for long-term interest rates to move upward (Figure 16-3). However, long-term interest rates have generally been declining since 1982. The figure shows both Moody's Aaa bond yields for the highest quality corporate bonds and Moody's Baa bonds, which are three notches lower than the highest investment-grade bonds. The graph does illustrate the pattern of rates over time but also that the highest-quality bonds always have a lower interest rate than lower quality bonds. See the bond rating section for more details on bond quality.

Bond Yields

Bond yields are quoted three different ways: **coupon rate**, **current yield**, and **yield to maturity**. We will apply each to a $1,000 par value bond paying $100 per year interest for 10 years. The bond is currently priced at $900.

Nominal Yield (Coupon Rate)   Stated interest payment divided by the par value.

$$\frac{\$100}{\$1,000} = 10\%$$

Current Yield   Stated interest payment divided by the current price of the bond.

$$\frac{\$100}{\$900} = 11.11\%$$

Yield to Maturity   The yield to maturity is the interest rate that will equate future interest payments and the payment at maturity (principal payment) to the current market price. This represents the concept of the internal rate of return. In the present case, an interest rate of 11.75 percent will equate interest payments of $100 for

---

FINANCIAL CALCULATOR

Bond Yield

Value	Function
10	N
−900	PV
100	PMT
1000	FV
Function	Solution
CPT	
I/Y	11.75

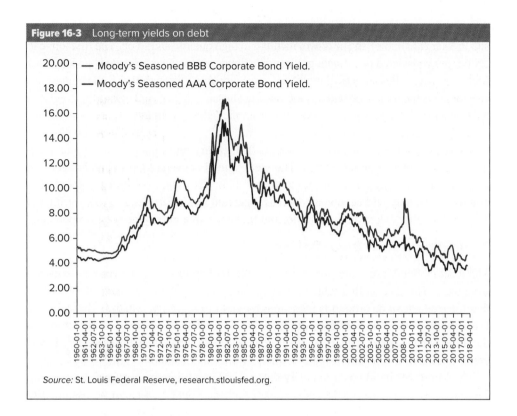

Figure 16-3   Long-term yields on debt

— Moody's Seasoned BBB Corporate Bond Yield.
— Moody's Seasoned AAA Corporate Bond Yield.

Source: St. Louis Federal Reserve, research.stlouisfed.org.

10 years and a final payment of $1,000 to the current price of $900. Calculating yield to maturity is discussed in detail in Chapter 10.[2]

When financial analysts speak of bond yields, the general assumption is that they are speaking of yield to maturity. This is deemed to be the most significant measure of return.

Bond Ratings

Both the issuing corporation and the investor are concerned about the rating their bond is assigned by the two major bond rating agencies—Moody's Investor Service and Standard & Poor's Corporation. The higher the rating assigned a given issue, the lower the required interest payments are to satisfy potential investors. This is because highly rated bonds carry lower risk. A major industrial corporation may be able to issue a 30-year bond at 5.5 to 6 percent yield to maturity because it is rated Aaa, whereas a smaller, regional firm may only qualify for a B rating and be forced to pay 9 or 10 percent.

As an example of **bond rating** systems, Moody's Investor Service provides the following nine categories of ranking:

Aaa   Aa   A   Baa   Ba   B   Caa   Ca   C

---

[2]A formula may be used to approximate yield to maturity.

$$\text{Approximate yield to maturity } (Y') = \frac{\text{Annual interest payment} + \dfrac{\text{Principal payment} - \text{Price of the bond}}{\text{Number of years to maturity}}}{0.6(\text{Price of the bond}) + 0.4(\text{Principal payment})}$$

$$Y' = \frac{\$100 + \dfrac{\$1,000 - 900}{10}}{0.6(\$900) + 0.4(\$1,000)} = 11.70\%$$

The first two categories of bond ratings represent the highest quality (for example, IBM and Procter & Gamble); the next two, medium to high quality; and so on. The first four categories are considered investment grade, while bonds below that are labeled "junk bonds." Moody's also applies numerical modifiers to categories Aa through B: 1 is the highest in a category, 2 is the midrange, and 3 is the lowest. Thus, a rating of Aa2 means the bond is in the midrange of Aa. Standard & Poor's has a similar letter system with + and – modifiers.

Bonds receive ratings based on the corporation's ability to make interest payments, its consistency of performance, its size, its debt-equity ratio, its working capital position, and a number of other factors. The yield spread between higher- and lower-rated corporate bonds changes with the economy. If investors are pessimistic about economic events, they will accept as much as 3 percent less return to go into securities of very high quality, whereas in more normal times the spread may be only 1.5 percent.

Examining Actual Bond Ratings

Three actual bond issues are presented in Table 16-3 to illustrate the various terms we have used. The data in this table reflect market conditions in February 2018. Recall that the true return on a bond is measured by yield to maturity, which is shown in the last column of the table. Microsoft Corp. bonds have the lowest expected return for the three bonds shown. This is primarily due to the fact that Microsoft has the highest credit of AAA, which denotes an extremely strong financial condition.

The Microsoft bond has a maturity date in 2035 and a coupon rate of 3.5 percent. The bond was issued in 2015 (not shown) and the coupon rate can be assumed to reflect the prevailing interest rate environment at that time. However, a 3.5 percent yield does not meet yield requirements for February 2018. Thus, the bond is valued at less than its $1,000 par ($994.79). The bond's yield to maturity is slightly higher than the coupon rate, because the current bond price is slightly lower than the par value.

Apple's bond has an S&P rating of AA+, which is still a very high investment-grade rating. The Apple bond's slightly higher yield to maturity reflects the slightly lower credit rating, and it probably also reflects the nine-years-later maturity date of the bond. As discussed in Chapter 6, longer-termed bonds typically have slightly higher interest rates.

The J.C. Penney bond has a speculative-grade rating of BB-. Despite its shorter maturity and collateral protection, the Penney bond has the highest yield to maturity. Investors appear to be aware that there are some uncertainties about the company's ability to pay off the bond in full in 2023.

The bonds in Table 16-3 can be refunded if the companies desire. The meaning and benefits of refunding will be made clear in the following section.

Table 16-3   Outstanding bond issues

Name	Coupon	Coupon Type	Collateral	Maturity Date	S&P Rating	Price	Yield to Maturity
Microsoft Corp.	3.5	Fixed	SR Unsecured	2/12/2035	AAA	$ 994.79	3.541
Apple Inc.	4.45	Fixed	SR Unsecured	5/6/2044	AA+	1,087.73	3.912
J.C. Penney Corp.	5.875	Fixed	1st lien	7/1/2023	BB–	964.36	6.67

Source: Bloomberg, February 2018.

One of the most memorable tales from *One Thousand and One Nights* is the story of Ali Baba, who opened a door to great riches with the password "Open Sesame." China's richest man, Jack Ma, certainly knew the story when he launched the Chinese e-commerce company Alibaba.com in 1999. In September 2014, Alibaba Group Holding executed the largest initial public offering in history, raising $25 billion. Two months later, it was raising capital again in the bond market.

Alibaba provides services similar to Amazon and eBay, but its market value is greater than either one. The company's biggest market is China, but it has aspirations to expand and compete all over the world. While the company now has other web portals for business-to-consumer and consumer-to-consumer trans-actions, the group began with Alibaba.com, now the world's largest business-to-business e-commerce site. Before Alibaba.com, if you wanted to find a Chinese supplier of 5,000 tiny electric motors, you needed a contact in China who could visit manufacturers to negotiate a price. Now, you go to Alibaba.com where dozens of suppliers post product availability for 500 or 500,000 units.

Alibaba's big bond offering was for $8 billion, but the offering consisted of six "tranches." Each tranche was a specific class of bond within the offering with a different due date and different terms. The five fixed-rate tranches were:

- $1,000 million 1.625% notes due in 3 years
- $2,250 million 2.500% notes due in 5 years
- $1,500 million 3.125% notes due in 7 years
- $2,250 million 3.600% notes due in 10 years
- $700 million 4.500% notes due in 20 years

By spreading out the maturities in the offering, Alibaba locked in its financing costs for several years. The company also issued a sixth tranche of $300 million in floating rate notes denominated in Singapore dollars.

One of the challenges faced by multinational corporations is matching financing decisions with their expected operating activities. Alibaba's use of multiple tranches that mixed fixed rates with floating rates, offered multiple maturities with differing coupon amounts, and promised repayments in a mix of currencies suggests a significant level of financial sophistication, either by the firm or by its investment bank.

The Refunding Decision

Assume you are the financial vice president for a corporation that has issued bonds at 11.75 percent, only to witness a drop in interest rates to 9.5 percent. If you believe interest rates will rise rather than sink further, you may wish to redeem the expensive 11.75 percent bonds and issue new debt at the prevailing 9.5 percent rate. This process is labeled a **refunding** operation. It is made feasible by the call provision that enables a corporation to buy back bonds at close to par, rather than at high market values, when interest rates are declining.

A Capital Budgeting Problem

The refunding decision involves outflows in the form of financing costs related to redeeming and reissuing securities, and inflows represented by savings in annual interest costs and tax savings. In the present case, we shall assume the corporation issued $10 million worth of 11.75 percent debt with a 25-year maturity and the debt has been on the books for 5 years. The corporation now has the opportunity to buy back the

515

old debt at 10 percent above par (the call premium) and to issue new debt at 9.5 percent interest with a 20-year life. The underwriting cost for the old issue was $125,000, and the underwriting cost for the new issue is $200,000. We shall also assume the corporation is in the 35 percent tax bracket and uses a 6 percent discount rate for refunding decisions. Since the savings from a refunding decision are certain—unlike the savings from most other capital budgeting decisions—we use the aftertax cost of new debt as the discount rate, rather than the more generalized cost of capital.[3] Actually, in this case, the aftertax cost of new debt is 9.5 percent (1 − Tax rate), or 9.5% × 0.65 = 6.18%. We round to 6 percent. The facts in this example are restated as follows:

	Old Issue	New Issue
Size	$10,000,000	$10,000,000
Interest rate	11.75%	9.5%
Total life	25 years	20 years
Remaining life	20 years	20 years
Call premium	10%	—
Underwriting costs	$125,000	$200,000
Tax bracket	35%	
Discount rate	6%	

Let's go through the capital budgeting process of defining our outflows and inflows and determining the net present value.

Step A—Outflow Considerations

1.   *Payment of call premium*—The first outflow is the 10 percent call premium on $10 million, or $1 million. This prepayment penalty is necessary to call in the original issue. Being an *out-of-pocket* tax-deductible expense, the $1 million cash expenditure will cost us only $650,000 on an aftertax basis. We multiply the expense by (1 − Tax rate) to get the aftertax cost.

$$\$1,000,000\ (1 - T) = \$1,000,000\ (1 - 0.35) = \$650,000$$

Net cost of call premium = $650,000

2.   *Underwriting cost on new issue*—The second outflow is the $200,000 underwriting cost on the new issue. The actual cost is somewhat less because the payment is tax-deductible, though the write-off must be spread over the life of the bond. While the actual $200,000 is being spent now, equal tax deductions of $10,000 a year will occur over the next 20 years (in a manner similar to depreciation).

The tax savings from a *noncash* write-off are equal to the amount times the tax rate. For a company in the 35 percent tax bracket, $10,000 of annual tax deductions

---

[3]A minority opinion would be that there is sufficient similarity between the bond refunding decision and other capital budgeting decisions to disallow any specialized treatment. Also note that although the bondholders must still bear some risk of default, for which they are compensated, the corporation assumes no risk.

will provide $3,500 of tax savings each year for the next 20 years. The present value of these savings is the present value of a $3,500 annuity for 20 years at 6 percent interest, which is approximately $40,145, as shown in the margin.

The net cost of underwriting the new issue is the actual expenditure now, minus the present value of future tax savings as indicated below.

Actual expenditure	$200,000
− PV of future tax savings	40,145
Net cost of underwriting expense on the new issue	$159,855

Step B—Inflow Considerations

The major inflows in the refunding decision are related to the reduction of annual interest expense and the immediate write-off of the underwriting cost on the old issue.

3. *Cost savings in lower interest rates*—The corporation will enjoy a 2.25 percentage point drop in interest rates, from 11.75 percent to 9.50 percent, on $10 million of bonds.

11.75% × $10,000,000	$1,175,000
9.50% × $10,000,000	950,000
Savings	$ 225,000

Since we are in the 35 percent tax bracket, this is equivalent to $146,250 of aftertax benefits per year for 20 years. We have taken the savings and multiplied by one minus the tax rate to get the annual aftertax benefits.

$$\$225,000 \ (1 - T)$$
$$\$225,000 \ (1 - 0.35)$$
$$\$146,250$$

Applying a 6 percent discount rate for a 20-year annuity yields an approximate present value of $1,677,476, as shown in the margin.

Cost savings in lower interest rates $1,677,476

4. *Underwriting cost on old issue*—There is a further cost savings related to immediately writing off the remaining underwriting costs on the old bonds. Note that the initial amount of $125,000 was spent 5 years ago and was to be written off for tax purposes over 25 years at $5,000 per year. Since 5 years have passed, $100,000 of old underwriting costs have not been amortized as indicated in the following:

Original amount	$125,000
Written off over five years	25,000
Unamortized old underwriting costs	$100,000

A tax benefit is associated with the immediate write-off of old underwriting costs, which we shall consider shortly.

FINANCIAL CALCULATOR

PV of Annuity

Enter	Function
20	N
6	I/Y
0	FV
−3500	PMT

Function	Solution
CPT	
PV	40,144.72

FINANCIAL CALCULATOR

PV of Annuity

Enter	Function
20	N
6	I/Y
0	FV
−146250	PMT

Function	Solution
CPT	
PV	1,677,475.98

Note, however, that this is not a total gain. We would have gotten the $100,000 additional write-off eventually if we had not called in the old bonds. By calling them in now, we simply take the write-off sooner. If we extended the write-off over the remaining life of the bonds, we would have taken $5,000 a year for 20 years. Discounting the 20-year annuity at 6 percent, we get an approximate present value of $57,350, as shown in the margin.

Thus, we are getting a write-off of $100,000 now, rather than a present value of future write-offs of $57,350. The gain in immediate tax write-offs is $42,650. The tax savings from a *noncash* tax write-off equal the amount times the tax rate. Since we are in the 35 percent tax bracket, our savings from this write-off are $14,928. The following calculations, which were discussed earlier, are necessary to arrive at $14,928.

Immediate write-off	$100,000
− PV of future write-off	57,350
Gain from immediate write-off	$ 42,650

$$\$42,650 \ (T)$$

$$\$42,650 \ (0.35) = \$14,928$$

Net gain from the underwriting on the old issue $14,928

Step C—Net Present Value

We now compare our outflows and our inflows from the prior pages.

Outflows		Inflows	
1. Net cost of call premium	$650,000	3. Cost savings in lower interest rates	$1,677,476
2. Net cost of underwriting expense on new issue	159,855	4. Net gain from underwriting cost on old issue	14,928
	$809,855		$1,692,404

Present value of inflows	$1,692,404
Present value of outflows	809,855
Net present value	$ 882,549

The refunding decision has a positive net present value, suggesting that interest rates have dropped to a sufficiently low level to indicate refunding is in order. The only question is: Will interest rates go lower—indicating an even better time for refunding? There is no easy answer. Conditions in the financial markets must be carefully considered.

A number of other factors could be plugged into the problem. For example, there could be overlapping time periods in the refunding procedure when both issues are outstanding and the firm is paying double interest (hopefully for less than a month). The dollar amount in these cases, however, tends to be small and is not included in the analysis.

In working problems, you should have minimum difficulty if you follow the four suggested calculations on the prior pages. In each of the four calculations we had the following tax implications:

1. Payment of call premium—the cost equals the amount times (1 − Tax rate) for this *cash tax-deductible expense.*

2. Underwriting costs on new issue—we pay an amount now and then amortize it over the life of the bond for tax purposes. This subsequent amortization is similar to depreciation and represents a *noncash write-off* of a tax-deductible expense. The tax saving from the amortization is equal to the amount times the tax rate.

3. Cost savings in lower interest rates—cost savings are like any form of income, and we will retain the cost savings times (1 − Tax rate).

4. Underwriting cost on old issue—once again, the writing off of underwriting costs represents a *noncash write-off* of a tax-deductible expense. The tax savings from the amortization are equal to the amount times the tax rate.

Other Forms of Bond Financing

As interest rates continued to show increasing volatility in the 1980s and early 1990s, two innovative forms of bond financing became very popular and remain so today. We shall examine the zero-coupon rate bond and the floating rate bond.

The **zero-coupon rate bond**, or zero-coupon bond, as the name implies, does not pay interest. It is, however, sold at a deep discount from face value. The return to the investor is the difference between the investor's cost and the face value received at the end of the life of the bond. From an investor's point of view, an advantage of the zero coupon bond is that there are no coupons to reinvest and the yield to maturity on the bond is locked in for the life of the bond. A dramatic case of a zero-coupon bond was an issue offered by PepsiCo Inc. in 1982, in which the maturities ranged from 6 to 30 years. The 30-year $1,000 par value issue could be purchased for $26.43, providing a yield of approximately 12.75 percent. The purchase price per bond of $26.43 represented only 2.643 percent of the par value. A million dollars worth of these 30-year bonds could be initially purchased for a mere $26,430.

The advantage to the corporation is that there is immediate cash inflow to the firm, without any outflow until the bonds mature. Furthermore, the difference between the initial bond price and the maturity value may be amortized for tax purposes by the corporation over the life of the bond. This means the corporation will be taking annual deductions without current cash outflow.

From the investor's viewpoint, the zero-coupon bonds allow him or her to lock in a multiplier of the initial investment. For example, investors may know they will get three times their investment after a specified number of years. The major drawback is that the annual increase in the value of bonds is taxable as ordinary income as it accrues, even though the bondholder does not get any cash flow until maturity. For this reason most investors in zero-coupon rate bonds have tax-exempt or tax-deferred status (pension funds, foundations, charitable organizations, individual retirement accounts, and the like).

The prices of the bonds tend to be highly volatile because of changes in interest rates. Even though the bonds provide no annual interest payment, there is still an initial yield to maturity that may prove to be too high or too low with changes in the marketplace.

The bonds listed in Table 16-4 are examples of zero-coupon bonds. The bonds sell at a considerable discount from par value of $1,000 since they all have some time remaining until maturity.

Table 16-4 Zero-coupon bonds					
Name	**S&P Rating**	**Coupon**	**Maturity Date**	**Price**	**Yield to Maturity**
HSBC Bank PLC	AA−	0.00	2/26/2030	$522.31	2.74
Barclays Bank PLC	A	0.00	3/27/2027	$706.65	3.872
NRW.Bank	AA−	0.00	1/29/2035	€790.27	1.396

Source: Bloomberg, February 2018.

Another interesting type of bond issue is the **floating rate bond** (long popular in European capital markets). In this case, instead of a change in the price of the bond, the interest rate paid on the bond changes with market conditions (usually monthly or quarterly). Thus, a bond that was initially issued to pay 9 percent may lower the interest payments to 6 percent during some years and raise them to 12 percent in others. The interest rate is usually tied to some overall market rate, such as the yield on Treasury bonds (perhaps 120 percent of the going yield on long-term Treasury bonds).

The price of a floating rate bond stays close to the $1,000 par value since the coupon adjusts with changes in market rates. The advantage to investors in floating rate bonds is that they have a constant (or almost constant) market value for the security, even though interest rates vary. An exception is that floating rate bonds often have broad limits that interest payments cannot exceed. For example, the interest rate on a 6 percent initial offering may not be allowed to go over 10 percent or below 3 percent. If long-term interest rates dictated an interest payment of 12 percent, the payment would still remain at 10 percent. This could cause some short-term loss in market value. To date, floating rate bonds have been relatively free of this problem. From an investor's point of view, the best time to own floating rate bonds is when interest rates are expected to rise.

Zero-coupon rate bonds and floating rate bonds represent a relatively small percentage of the total market of new debt offerings. Nevertheless, they should be part of a basic understanding of long-term debt instruments.

Advantages and Disadvantages of Debt

The financial manager must consider whether debt will contribute to or detract from the firm's operations. In certain industries, such as airlines, very heavy debt utilization is a way of life, whereas in other industries (drugs, photographic equipment) reliance is placed on other forms of capital.

Benefits of Debt

The advantages of debt may be enumerated as:

1. Interest payments are tax-deductible. Because the maximum corporate tax rate is in the mid-30 percent range, the effective aftertax cost of interest is approximately two-thirds of the dollar amount expended.

2. The financial obligation is clearly specified and of a fixed nature (with the exception of floating rate bonds). Contrast this with selling an ownership interest in which stockholders have open-ended participation in profits; however, the amount of profits is unknown.

3. In an inflationary economy, debt may be paid back with "cheaper dollars." A $1,000 bond obligation may be repaid in 10 or 20 years with dollars that have shrunk in value by 50 or 60 percent. In terms of "real dollars," or purchasing power equivalents, one might argue that the corporation should be asked to repay something in excess of $2,000. Presumably, high interest rates in inflationary periods compensate the lender for loss in purchasing power, but this is not always the case.

4. The use of debt, up to a prudent point, may lower the cost of capital to the firm. To the extent that debt does not strain the risk position of the firm, its low after-tax cost may aid in reducing the weighted overall cost of financing to the firm.

Drawbacks of Debt

Finally, we must consider the disadvantages of debt:

1. Interest and principal payment obligations are set by contract and must be met, regardless of the economic position of the firm.

2. Indenture agreements may place burdensome restrictions on the firm, such as maintenance of working capital at a given level, limits on future debt offerings, and guidelines for dividend policy. Although bondholders generally do not have the right to vote, they may take virtual control of the firm if important indenture provisions are not met.

3. Utilized beyond a given point, debt may depress outstanding common stock values.

Eurobond Market

A market with an increasing presence in world capital markets is that in Eurobonds. A **Eurobond** may be defined as a bond payable in the borrower's currency but sold outside the borrower's country. The Eurobond is usually sold by an international syndicate of investment bankers and includes bonds sold by companies in Switzerland, Japan, the Netherlands, Germany, the United States, and Britain, to name the most popular countries. An example might be a bond of a U.S. company, payable in dollars and sold in London, Paris, Tokyo, or Frankfurt. Disclosure requirements in the Eurobond market are less demanding than those of the Securities and Exchange Commission or other domestic regulatory agencies. Examples of several Eurobonds are presented in Table 16-5.

Table 16-5 Examples of Eurobonds

Name	S&P Rating	Coupon	Maturity Date	Amount Outstanding (in thousands)	Currency Denomination
Coca-Cola European Partners	BBB+	1.875	3/18/2030	$ 500,000	EUR
Apple Inc.	AA+	1.625	11/10/2026	1,400,000	EUR
Royal Bank of Scotland	BBB+	2.91	6/21/2036	15,000,000	JPY
3M Co.	AA−	1.875	11/15/2021	600,000	EUR

Source: Bloomberg, February 2018.

Leasing as a Form of Debt

When a corporation contracts to lease an oil tanker or a computer and signs a noncancelable, long-term agreement, the transaction has similar characteristics to the purchase of an asset on credit. In other words, entering into a lease creates both an asset and a liability that should be recognized on a company's balance sheet. There are two parties to a lease, the lessee and the lessor. The lessee is the party that uses the asset, and the lessor is the party that provides the asset to the lessee. In this section, we will consider leases from the perspective of the lessee, the user of the property.

For the lessee, the lease agreement creates an asset and a liability on the balance sheet. The commitment to making lease payments is recorded on the books as a liability, and the oil tanker or computer is presented on the balance sheet as an asset.

Long-term leasing has not always been recognized as a debt obligation on the balance sheet, but since the mid-1960s there has been a strong movement by the accounting profession to force companies to fully divulge all information about leasing obligations and to indicate the equivalent debt characteristics. This view has been bolstered by the release of *Accounting Standards Update 2016-02*, which requires that all leases, with the exception of short-term leases (less than 12 months), be included as an asset and a liability on the balance sheet. Consider the case of firm ABC, whose balance sheet is shown in Table 16-6.

Table 16-6 Balance sheet ($ millions)			
Current assets	$ 50	Current liabilities	$ 50
Fixed assets	150	Long-term liabilities	50
		Total liabilities	$100
		Stockholders' equity	100
Total assets	$200	Total liabilities and stockholders' equity	$200

Before *ASU 2016-02*, certain types of leases were not required to be presented on the balance sheet, giving the lessee an opportunity to engage in a practice known as "off-balance-sheet financing." In effect, operating leases allowed companies to conceal liabilities that arose from these leases, and some leases were structured in a way that ensured that the lessee would not need to record a liability. Now, however, the lessee must recognize a right-of-use asset and a corresponding lease liability on the balance sheet, as shown in Table 16-7.

We see that a right-of-use asset and a corresponding lease liability have been recognized on the balance sheet. A right-of-use asset and lease liability will be recognized for all leases of more than 12 months. Short-term leases of less than 12 months can be written off as a lease expense without impacting the balance sheet. Comparing the balance sheet before the lease (Table 16-6) to the balance sheet after the signing of the lease (Table 16-7), shows the effect that leasing has on certain financial ratios. Note that the addition of the right-of-use asset and corresponding lease liability has caused the total-debt-to-assets ratio to increase from 50 percent to 66.7 percent. It is important to realize how recognizing leases on the balance sheet impacts key financial ratios of a corporation.

Table 16-7 Revised balance sheet ($ millions)			
Current assets	$ 50	Current liabilities	$ 50
Fixed assets	150	Long-term liabilities	50
Right of-use asset*	100	Lease liability*	100
		Total liabilities	$200
		Stockholders' equity	100
Total assets	$300	Total liabilities and stockholders' equity	$300

*New entries

$$\textit{Original}: \quad \frac{\text{Total debt}}{\text{Total assets}} = \frac{\$100 \text{ million}}{\$200 \text{ million}} = 50\%$$

$$\textit{Revised}: \quad \frac{\text{Total debt}}{\text{Total assets}} = \frac{\$200 \text{ million}}{\$300 \text{ million}} = 66.7\%$$

Finance Lease versus Operating Lease

There are two types of leases: finance leases and operating leases. Both types must be capitalized and placed on the balance sheet. However, their treatment on the income statement differs. A **finance lease** is recognized whenever any of the five following conditions is present:

1. The arrangement transfers ownership of the property to the lessee (the leasing party) by the end of the lease term.
2. The lease grants the lessee an option to purchase the underlying asset that the lessee is reasonably certain to exercise.
3. The lease term is for the major part of the remaining economic life of the underlying asset.
4. The present value of all payments under the lease exceeds substantially all of the fair value of the leased asset.
5. The asset is of such a specialized nature that it probably has no alternative use to the lessor at the end of the lease term.

A lease that meets any of these five criteria is a finance lease. Otherwise, the lease is an **operating lease**. An operating lease is usually short-term and is often cancelable at the option of the lessee (the party using the asset). Often operating leases provide for the lessor to maintain the asset, since the lessor is likely to get the asset back from the lessee. Operating leases are used most frequently with such assets as automobiles and office equipment, while finance leases are used with oil drilling equipment, airplanes and rail equipment, certain forms of real estate, and other long-term assets. Finance leases account for the greatest volume of leasing obligations.

Income Statement Effect

Both operating and finance leases call for presenting a right-of-use asset on the balance sheet. The asset's initial value is equal to the present value of the lease payments. A lease liability equal to the right-of-use asset value is also initially recorded. However, the two lease types differ in their income statement treatments. Operating leases require the lessee to record a series of identical lease expense deductions during each year of the lease. For example, if a lease calls for $100,000 in total over five years, the lease expense is $20,000 per year. This is true even when the actual lease payments vary from year to year.

In contrast, under a finance lease, no lease expense is recorded. Instead, straight-line amortization expense is recorded on the right-of-use asset. Also, the lessee records interest expense based on any remaining outstanding lease liability.

Income Statement Impacts Operating vs. Finance Leases	
Operating Lease	**Finance Lease**
Lease Expense; Calculated Straight-Line on the sum of the scheduled lease payments	**Lease Expense**; None/zero
Amortization Expense; None/zero	**Amortization Expense**; Calculated Straight-Line based on the original present value of the right-of-use asset
Interest Expense; None/zero	**Interest Expense**; Calculated on the outstanding lease liability

In summary, a finance lease involves two expense classifications, interest and amortization, while an operating lease recognizes a single lease expense. Before closing this section, we should note that tax rules for recording leases are different from those established for financial reporting under *ASU 2016-02*. For tax purposes, lease payments for most operating leases will be expensed in the year they are paid.[4]

Advantages of Leasing

Why is leasing so popular? It has emerged as a trillion-dollar industry, with such firms as IBM Global Financing, Wells Fargo Advisors, and Boeing Capital Corp. providing an enormous amount of financing. Major reasons for the popularity of leasing include the following:

1. The lessee may lack sufficient funds or the credit capability to purchase the asset from a manufacturer, who is willing, however, to accept a lease arrangement or to arrange a lease obligation with a third party.

2. The provisions of a lease obligation may be substantially less restrictive than those of a bond indenture.

3. There may be no down payment requirement, as would generally be the case in the purchase of an asset (leasing allows for a larger indirect loan).

4. The lessor may possess greater expertise regarding the leased property—allowing for expert product selection, maintenance, and eventual resale. Through this process, the negative effects of obsolescence may be reduced.

5. Creditor claims on certain types of leases, such as real estate, are restricted in bankruptcy and reorganization proceedings. Leases on chattels (non–real estate items) have no such limitation.

6. Finally, certain retail malls or office complexes are generally available only to be leased, not purchased.

---

[4]Income tax treatment for these operating leases is similar to the way *ASU 2016-02* treats leases of less than 12 months.

There are also some tax factors to be considered. Where one party to a lease is in a higher tax bracket than the other party, certain tax advantages, such as depreciation write-off or research-related tax credits, may be better utilized. For example, a wealthy party may purchase an asset for tax purposes, then lease the asset to another party in a lower tax bracket for actual use.

Leasing land also has tax advantages. Lease payments on the use of land are tax-deductible, whereas land ownership does not allow a similar deduction for depreciation.

Finally, firms occasionally engage in a sale-leaseback arrangement, in which assets owned by the lessee are sold to the lessor and then immediately leased back. This process provides the lessee with an infusion of capital, while allowing the lessee to continue to use the asset. Even though the dollar costs of a leasing arrangement are often higher than the dollar costs of owning an asset, the advantages cited in this section may outweigh the direct cost factors.

SUMMARY

As a first consideration, corporate bonds may be secured by a lien on a specific asset or may carry an unsecured designation, indicating the bondholder possesses a general claim against the corporation. A special discussion of the hierarchy of claims for firms in financial distress is presented in Appendix 16A.

Both the issuing corporation and the investor are concerned about the rating their bond is assigned by the two major bond rating agencies—Moody's Investor Service and Standard & Poor's Corporation. The higher the rating assigned a given issue, the lower the required interest payments needed to satisfy potential investors. This is because highly rated bonds carry lower risk.

Bond refundings may take place when interest rates are going down. The financial manager must consider whether the savings in interest will compensate for the additional cost of calling in the old issue and selling a new one.

The zero-coupon rate bond, as the name implies, does not pay interest. It is, however, sold at a deep discount from face value. The return to the investor is the difference between the investor's cost and the face value received at the end of the life of the bond.

A second type of innovative bond issue is the floating rate bond. In this case, instead of a change in the price of the bond, the interest rate paid on the bond changes with market conditions (usually monthly or quarterly).

When a corporation contracts to lease an oil tanker or a computer and signs a non-cancelable, long-term agreement, the transaction has all the characteristics of a debt obligation, and should be recognized as such on the financial statements of the firm.

Leases create a right-of-use asset and an equal lease liability for the lessee.

LIST OF TERMS

par value   507
maturity date   507
indenture   507
secured debt   507
mortgage agreement   507

after-acquired property clause   507
debenture   507
subordinated debenture   508
serial payment   509
sinking fund   509

DISCUSSION QUESTIONS

1. Corporate debt has been expanding very dramatically in the last three decades. What has been the impact on interest coverage, particularly since 1977? *(LO16-1)*

2. What are some specific features of bond agreements? *(LO16-1)*

3. What is the difference between a bond agreement and a bond indenture? *(LO16-1)*

4. Discuss the relationship between the coupon rate (original interest rate at time of issue) on a bond and its security provisions. *(LO16-1)*

5. Take the following list of securities and arrange them in order of their priority of claims: *(LO16-1)*

Preferred stock   Senior debenture
Subordinated debenture   Senior secured debt
Common stock   Junior secured debt

6. What method of "bond repayment" reduces debt and increases the amount of common stock outstanding? *(LO16-3)*

7. What is the purpose of serial repayments and sinking funds? *(LO16-1)*

8. Under what circumstances would a call on a bond be exercised by a corporation? What is the purpose of a deferred call? *(LO16-3)*

9. Discuss the relationship between bond prices and interest rates. What impact do changing interest rates have on the price of long-term bonds versus short-term bonds? *(LO16-2)*

10. What is the difference between the following yields: coupon rate, current yield, yield to maturity? *(LO16-2)*

11. How does the bond rating affect the interest rate paid by a corporation on its bonds? *(LO16-2)*

12. Bonds of different risk classes will have a spread between their interest rates. Is this spread always the same? Why? *(LO16-2)*

13. Explain how the bond refunding problem is similar to a capital budgeting decision. *(LO16-3)*

14. What cost of capital is generally used in evaluating a bond refunding decision? Why? *(LO16-3)*

15. Explain how the zero-coupon rate bond provides return to the investor. What are the advantages to the corporation? *(LO16-2)*

16. Explain how floating rate bonds can save the investor from potential embarrassments in portfolio valuations. *(LO16-2)*

17. Discuss the advantages and disadvantages of debt. *(LO16-1)*

18. What is a Eurobond? *(LO16-1)*

19. What do we mean by capitalizing lease payments? *(LO16-4)*

20. Explain the close parallel between a finance lease and the borrow–purchase decision from the viewpoint of both the balance sheet and the income statement. *(LO16-4)*

PRACTICE PROBLEMS AND SOLUTIONS

1. The Gorden Corporation has a bond outstanding with $85 annual interest payments, a market price of $860, and a maturity date in seven years.

   Compute the following:

   a. The coupon rate.

   b. The current yield.

   c. The yield to maturity.

   Bond yields
   (LO16-2)

2. The Hudson Corporation has a $15 million bond obligation outstanding which it is considering refunding. Though the bonds were initially issued at 9 percent, the interest rates on similar issues have declined to 7.2 percent. The bonds were originally issued for 15 years and have 10 years remaining. The new issue would be for 10 years. There is a 9 percent call premium on the old issue. The underwriting cost on the new $15,000,000 issue is $200,000, and the underwriting on the old issue was $450,000. The company is in a 30 percent tax bracket, and it will use a 5 percent discount rate (rounded aftertax cost of debt) to analyze the refunding decision.

   Should the old issue be refunded with new debt?

   Refunding decision
   (LO16-3)

Solutions

1. *a.* $85 interest/$1,000 par = 8.5% coupon rate

   b. $85 interest/$860 market price = 9.88% current yield

   c. See the nearby calculator keystrokes. The yield to maturity is 11.52%.

2. **Outflows**

   1. Payment of call premium (cost)

      $$\$15,000,000 \times 9\% = \$1,350,000$$

      $$\$1,350,000 \times (1 - 0.30) = \$945,000$$

   2. Underwriting cost on new issue

      Actual expenditure........... $200,000

      Amortization of cost ($200,000/10) × 0.30

      $20,000 × (0.30) = $6,000 tax savings per year

      PV of future tax savings ($n = 10$, $i = 5\%$)

      $6,000 × 7.722 = $46,332

Actual expenditure	$200,000
− PV of future tax savings	46,332
Net cost of underwriting expense on new issue	$153,668

FINANCIAL CALCULATOR

Bond Yield

Value	Function
7	N
−860	PV
85	PMT
1000	FV

Function	Solution
CPT	
I/Y	11.52

Inflows

3. Cost savings in lower interest rates

9% (interest on old bonds) × $15,000,000 = ...	$1,350,000 per year
7.2% (interest on new bonds) × $15,000,000 = ...	1,080,000 per year
Savings per year	$270,000
Savings per year after tax $270,000 (1 − 0.3)	$189,000
PV of future savings ($n = 10$, $i = 5\%$)	
$189,000 × 7.722 = ...	$1,459,458

4. Underwriting cost on old issue

Original amount	$450,000
Annual write-off $450,000/15 = ...	30,000
Amount written off over initial 5 years at $30,000 per year	$150,000
Unamortized old underwriting cost	$300,000

    PV of future write-off of $30,000 per year:

    $n = 10$ (years remaining $i = 5\%$)

    PV = 30,000 × 7.722 = $231,660

    Take the difference between the unamortized old underwriting costs of $300,000 and the PV of the future write-off of $231,600.

Immediate write-off of unamortized old underwriting costs	$300,000
− PV of future write-off	231,660
Net gain from immediate write-off	$ 68,340
Multiply this figure by the tax rate to get the net tax benefit	$ 68,340
of the immediate write-off	0.30
	$ 20,502

Summarize the inflows and outflows to get the net present value.

Outflows		Inflows	
1. Net cost of call premium	$ 945,000	3. Cost savings in lower interest rates	$1,459,458
2. Net cost of underwriting expense on new issue	153,668	4. Net gain from underwriting expense on old issue	20,502
	$1,098,668		$1,479,960

Present value of inflows	$1,479,960
Present value of outflows	1,098,668
Net present value	$ 381,292

Due to the positive net present value, the old issue should be refunded.

PROBLEMS

■ connect Selected problems are available with Connect. Please see the preface for more information.

Basic Problems

Assume the par value of the bonds in the following problems is $1,000 unless otherwise specified.

1. The Pioneer Petroleum Corporation has a bond outstanding with an $85 annual interest payment, a market price of $800, and a maturity date in five years. Find the following:

    a. The coupon rate.

    b. The current rate.

    c. The yield to maturity.

    Bond yields (LO16-2)

2. Preston Corporation has a bond outstanding with an $80 annual interest payment, a market price of $1,250, and a maturity date in 10 years. Assume the par value of the bonds is $1,000. Find the following:

    a. The coupon rate.

    b. The current rate.

    c. The yield to maturity.

    Bond yields (LO16-2)

3. Harold Reese must choose between two bonds: Bond X pays $95 annual interest and has a market value of $900. It has 10 years to maturity. Bond Z pays $95 annual interest and has a market value of $920. It has 2 years to maturity.

    a. Compute the current yield on both bonds.

    b. Which bond should he select based on your answer to part *a?*

    c. A drawback of current yield is that it does not consider the total life of the bond. For example, the yield to maturity on Bond X is 11.21 percent. What is the yield to maturity on Bond Z?

    d. Has your answer changed between parts *b* and *c* of this question?

    Bond yields (LO16-2)

4. An investor must choose between two bonds: Bond A pays $72 annual interest and has a market value of $925. It has 10 years to maturity. Bond B pays $62 annual interest and has a market value of $910. It has 2 years to maturity. Assume the par value of the bonds is $1,000.

    a. Compute the current yield on both bonds.

    b. Which bond should she select based on your answer to part *a?*

    c. A drawback of current yield is that it does not consider the total life of the bond. For example, the yield to maturity on Bond A is 8.33 percent. What is the yield to maturity on Bond B?

    d. Has your answer changed between parts *b* and *c* of this question in terms of which bond to select?

    Bond yields (LO16-2)

**Secured vs.
unsecured debt
(LO16-1)**

5. Match the yield to maturity in column 2 with the security provisions (or lack thereof) in column 1. Higher returns tend to go with greater risk.

(1) Security Provision	(2) Yield to Maturity
a. Debenture	a. 6.85%
b. Secured debt	b. 8.20%
c. Subordinated debenture	c. 7.76%

**Bond value
(LO16-2)**

6. The Florida Investment Fund buys 58 bonds of the Gator Corporation through a broker. The bonds pay 10 percent annual interest. The yield to maturity (market rate of interest) is 12 percent. The bonds have a 10-year maturity.

    Using an assumption of semiannual interest payments:
    a. Compute the price of a bond (refer to "Semiannual Interest and Bond Prices" in Chapter 10 for review if necessary).
    b. Compute the total value of the 58 bonds.

**Bond value
(LO16-2)**

7. Cox Media Corporation pays an 11 percent coupon rate on debentures that are due in 10 years. The current yield to maturity on bonds of similar risk is 8 percent. The bonds are currently callable at $1,110. The theoretical value of the bonds will be equal to the present value of the expected cash flow from the bonds.
    a. Find the market value of the bonds using semiannual analysis.
    b. Do you think the bonds will sell for the price you arrived at in part *a?* Why?

**Effect of bond rating
change
(LO16-2)**

8. The yield to maturity for 10-year bonds is as follows for four different bond rating categories:

Aaa	9.40%	Aa2	10.00%
Aa1	9.60%	Aa3	10.60%

    The bonds of Falter Corporation were rated as Aaa and issued at par a few weeks ago. The bonds have just been downgraded to Aa2. Determine the new price of the bonds, assuming a 10-year maturity and semiannual interest payments. (Refer to "Semiannual Interest and Bond Prices" in Chapter 10 for a review if necessary.)

**Interest rates and
bond ratings
(LO16-2)**

9. Twenty-five-year B-rated bonds of Parker Optical Company were initially issued at a 12 percent yield. After 10 years the bonds have been upgraded to Aa2. Such bonds are currently yielding 10 percent to maturity. Use Table 16-2 to determine the price of the bonds with 15 years remaining to maturity. (You do not need the bond ratings to enter the table; just use the basic facts of the problem.)

**Interest rates and
bond ratings
(LO16-2)**

10. A previously issued A2, 15-year industrial bond provides a return three-fourths higher than the prime interest rate of 11 percent. Previously issued A2 public utility bonds provide a yield of three-fourths of a percentage point higher than previously issued A2 industrial bonds of equal quality. Finally, new issues of A2 public utility bonds pay three-fourths of a percentage point more than previously issued A2 public utility bonds.

What should be the interest rate on a newly issued A2 public utility bond?

11. A 17-year, $1,000 par value zero-coupon rate bond is to be issued to yield 7 percent.

    a. What should be the initial price of the bond? (Take the present value of $1,000 for 17 years at 7 percent.)

    b. If immediately upon issue, interest rates dropped to 6 percent, what would be the value of the zero-coupon rate bond?

    c. If immediately upon issue, interest rates increased to 9 percent, what would be the value of the zero-coupon rate bond?

Zero-coupon rate bond
(LO16-2)

12. Assume a zero-coupon bond that sells for $403 and will mature in 10 years at $1,250. What is the effective yield to maturity? (Compute PV_{IF} and go to Appendix B for the 10-year figure to find the answer, or compute FV_{IF} and go to Appendix A for the 10-year figure to find the answer. Either approach will work.)

Zero-coupon bond yield
(LO16-2)

13. You buy an 8 percent, 25-year, $1,000 par value floating rate bond in 1999. By the year 2004, rates on bonds of similar risk are up to 11 percent. What is your one best guess as to the value of the bond?

Floating rate bond
(LO16-2)

Intermediate Problems

14. Seventeen years ago, the Archer Corporation borrowed $6,500,000. Since then, cumulative inflation has been 65 percent (a compound rate of approximately 3 percent per year).

    a. When the firm repays the original $6,500,000 loan this year, what will be the effective purchasing power of the $6,500,000? (Hint: Divide the loan amount by one plus cumulative inflation.)

    b. To maintain the original $6,500,000 purchasing power, how much should the lender be repaid? (Hint: Multiply the loan amount by one plus cumulative inflation.)

    c. If the lender knows he will receive only $6,500,000 in payment after 17 years, how might he be compensated for the loss in purchasing power? A descriptive answer is acceptable.

Effect of inflation on purchasing power of bond
(LO16-2)

15. A $1,000 par value bond was issued 25 years ago at a 12 percent coupon rate. It currently has 15 years remaining to maturity. Interest rates on similar obligations are now 8 percent.

    a. What is the current price of the bond? (Look up the answer in Table 16-2.)

    b. Assume Ms. Bright bought the bond three years ago when it had a price of $1,050. What is her dollar profit based on the bond's current price?

    c. Further assume Ms. Bright paid 30 percent of the purchase price in cash and borrowed the rest (known as buying on margin). She used the interest payments from the bond to cover the interest costs on the loan. How much of the purchase price of $1,050 did Ms. Bright pay in cash?

    d. What is Ms. Bright's percentage return on her cash investment? Divide the answer to part *b* by the answer to part *c*.

    e. Explain why her return is so high.

Profit potential associated with margin
(LO16-2)

Loss exposure and
profit potential
(LO16-2)

16.   A $1,000 par value bond was issued 20 years ago at a 9 percent coupon rate. It currently has 5 years remaining to maturity. Interest rates on similar debt obligations are now 10 percent.

    a.   Compute the current price of the bond using an assumption of semiannual payments.

    b.   If Mr. Robinson initially bought the bond at par value, what is his percentage loss (or gain)?

    c.   Now assume Mrs. Pinson buys the bond at its current market value and holds it to maturity, what will her percentage return be?

    d.   Although the same dollar amounts are involved in part *b* and *c,* explain why the percentage gain is larger than the percentage loss.

Advanced Problems

Advanced refunding
decision
(LO16-3)

17.   The Bowman Corporation has a $18 million bond obligation outstanding, which it is considering refunding. Though the bonds were initially issued at 10 percent, the interest rates on similar issues have declined to 8.5 percent. The bonds were originally issued for 20 years and have 10 years remaining. The new issue would be for 10 years. There is a 9 percent call premium on the old issue. The underwriting cost on the new $18,000,000 issue is $530,000, and the underwriting cost on the old issue was $380,000. The company is in a 35 percent tax bracket, and it will use an 8 percent discount rate (rounded aftertax cost of debt) to analyze the refunding decision.

    a.   Calculate the present value of total outflows.

    b.   Calculate the present value of total inflows.

    c.   Calculate the net present value.

    d.   Should the old issue be refunded with new debt?

Refunding decision
(LO16-3)

18.   The Robinson Corporation has $43 million of bonds outstanding that were issued at a coupon rate of 11¾ percent 7 years ago. Interest rates have fallen to 10¾ percent. Mr. Brooks, the vice president of finance, does not expect rates to fall any further. The bonds have 17 years left to maturity, and Mr. Brooks would like to refund the bonds with a new issue of equal amount also having 17 years to maturity. The Robinson Corporation has a tax rate of 30 percent. The underwriting cost on the old issue was 2.4 percent of the total bond value. The underwriting cost on the new issue will be 1.7 percent of the total bond value. The original bond indenture contained a 5-year protection against a call, with a 9 percent call premium starting in the sixth year and scheduled to decline by one-half percent each year thereafter. (Consider the bond to be 7 years old for purposes of computing the premium.) Assume the discount rate is equal to the aftertax cost of new debt rounded up to the nearest whole number.

    a.   Compute the discount rate.

    b.   Calculate the present value of total outflows.

    c.   Calculate the present value of total inflows.

    d.   Calculate the net present value.

Call premium
(LO16-3)

19.   The Sunbelt Corporation has $40 million of bonds outstanding that were issued at a coupon rate of 12⅞ percent 7 years ago. Interest rates have fallen to 12 percent. Mr. Heath, the vice president of finance, does not expect rates to fall any further.

The bonds have 18 years left to maturity, and Mr. Heath would like to refund the bonds with a new issue of equal amount also having 18 years to maturity. The Sunbelt Corporation has a tax rate of 36 percent. The underwriting cost on the old issue was 2.5 percent of the total bond value. The underwriting cost on the new issue will be 1.8 percent of the total bond value. The original bond indenture contained a 5-year protection against a call, with an 8 percent call premium starting in the sixth year and scheduled to decline by one-half percent each year thereafter (consider the bond to be 7 years old for purposes of computing the premium). Assume the discount rate is equal to the aftertax cost of new debt rounded up to the nearest whole number. Should the Sunbelt Corporation refund the old issue?

20. Krawczek Company will enter into a lease agreement with Heavy Equipment Co. where Krawczek will make lease payments over the next 5 years. The lease is noncancelable and requires equal annual payments of $20,000 per year beginning on January 1 of the first year. The last payment will be January 1 of year 5, and Krawczek will continue to use the asset until December 31 of that year. Other important information includes the following:

   •   The fair value of the equipment is $140,000.

   •   The applicable discount rate is an 8 percent annual rate.

   •   The economic life of the asset is 10 years.

   •   Krawczek does not guarantee the residual value of the asset at the end of the lease, and it does not expect to keep the asset at the end of the term.

   •   The asset is a standard piece of equipment.

   a.   Is the lease an operating lease or a finance lease?

   b.   What will be the lease expense shown on the income statement at the end of year 1?

   c.   What will be the interest expense shown on the income statement at the end of year 1?

   d.   What will be the amortization expense shown on the income statement at the end of year 1?

Finance lease or operating lease (LO16-4)

21. The Harris Company is the lessee on a four-year lease with the following payments at the end of each year:

   Year 1: $10,000

   Year 2: $15,000

   Year 3: $20,000

   Year 4: $25,000

An appropriate discount rate is 7 percent, yielding a present value of $48,055.

   a.   If the lease is an operating lease,

      i.   What will be the initial value of the right-of-use asset?

      ii.   What will be the initial value of the lease liability?

      iii.   What will be the lease expense shown on the income statement at the end of year 1?

      iv.   What will be the interest expense shown on the income statement at the end of year 1?

      v.   What will be the amortization expense shown on the income statement at the end of year 1?

Financial statement effects of leases (LO16-4)

b. If the lease is a finance lease,

    i.   What will be the initial value of the right-of-use asset?

    ii. What will be the initial value of the lease liability?

    iii. What will be the lease expense shown on the income statement at the end of year 1?

    iv. What will be the interest expense shown on the income statement at the end of year 1?

    v.   What will be the amortization expense shown on the income statement at the end of year 1?

COMPREHENSIVE PROBLEM

Broadband Inc.
(Bond prices,
refunding)
(LO16-2 & 16-3)

Barton Simpson, the chief financial officer of Broadband Inc. could hardly believe the change in interest rates that had taken place over the last few months. The interest rate on A2 rated bonds was now 6 percent. The $30 million, 15-year bond issue that his firm has outstanding was initially issued at 9 percent 5 years ago.

Because interest rates had gone down so much, he was considering refunding the bond issue. The old issue had a call premium of 8 percent. The underwriting cost on the old issue had been 3 percent of par, and on the new issue it would be 5 percent of par. The tax rate would be 30 percent and a 4 percent discount rate would be applied for the refunding decision. The new bond would have a 10-year life.

Before Barton used the 8 percent call provision to reacquire the old bonds, he wanted to make sure he could not buy them back cheaper in the open market.

a. First compute the price of the old bonds in the open market. Use the valuation procedures for a bond that were discussed in Chapter 10 (use annual analysis). Determine the price of a single $1,000 par value bond.

b. Compare the price in part *a* to the 8 percent call premium over par value. Which appears to be more attractive in terms of reacquiring the old bonds?

c. Now do the standard bond refunding analysis as discussed in this chapter. Is the refunding financially feasible?

d. In terms of the refunding decision, how should Barton be influenced if he thinks interest rates might go down even more?

WEB EXERCISE

1. We will examine the debt ratios for two airlines. First go to finance.yahoo.com. In the "Quote Lookup" box, enter "LUV" for Southwest Airlines. Select Southwest Airlines. Click on "Financials" and scroll down and select "Balance Sheet."

2. Compute the ratio of long-term debt to total stockholders' equity for the three years shown. Do the same thing for total liabilities to total stockholders' equity.

3. Go back to the "Quote Lookup" box and follow the same process for Delta Air Lines (DAL). Write a paragraph summary of the two airlines' debt ratios. Which company is in better condition?

Note: Occasionally a topic we have listed may have been deleted, updated, or moved into a different location on a Web site. If you click on the site map or site index, you will be introduced to a table of contents that should aid you in finding the topic you are looking for.

APPENDIX | 16A

Financial Alternatives for Distressed Firms

A firm may be in financial distress because of **technical insolvency** or bankruptcy. The first term refers to a firm's inability to pay its bills as they come due. Thus, a firm may be technically insolvent, even though it has a positive net worth; there simply may not be sufficient liquid assets to meet current obligations. The second term, **bankruptcy**, indicates the market value of a firm's assets are less than its liabilities and the firm has a negative net worth. Under the law, either technical insolvency or bankruptcy may be adjudged as a financial failure of the business firm.

Many firms do not fall into either category but are still suffering from extreme financial difficulties. Perhaps they are rapidly approaching a situation in which they cannot pay their bills or their net worth will soon be negative.

Firms in the types of financial difficulty discussed in the first two paragraphs may participate in out-of-court settlements or in-court settlements through formal bankruptcy proceedings under the National Bankruptcy Act.

Out-of-court settlements, where possible, allow the firm and its creditors to bypass certain lengthy and expensive legal procedures. If an agreement cannot be reached on a voluntary basis between a firm and its creditors, in-court procedures will be necessary.

Out-of-Court Settlement

Out-of-court settlements may take many forms. Four alternatives will be examined. The first is an **extension**, in which creditors agree to allow the firm more time to meet its financial obligations. A new repayment schedule will be developed, subject to the acceptance of the creditors.

A second alternative is a **composition**, under which creditors agree to accept a fractional settlement of their original claim. They may be willing to do this because they believe the firm is unable to meet its total obligations and they wish to avoid formal bankruptcy procedures. In the case of either a proposed extension or a composition, some creditors may not agree to go along with the arrangements. If their claims are relatively small, major creditors may allow them to be paid off immediately in full to hold the agreement together. If their claims are large, no out-of-court settlement may be possible, and formal bankruptcy proceedings may be necessary.

A third type of out-of-court settlement may take the form of a **creditor committee** established to run the business. Here the parties involved assume management can no longer effectively conduct the affairs of the firm. Once the creditors' claims have been partially or fully settled, a new management team may be brought in to replace the creditor committee. The outgoing management may be willing to accept the imposition of a creditor committee only when formal bankruptcy proceedings appear likely and they wish to avoid that stigma. Sometimes creditors are unwilling to form such a committee because they fear lawsuits from other dissatisfied creditors or from common or preferred stockholders.

A fourth type of out-of-court settlement is an **assignment**, in which assets are liquidated without going through formal court action. To effect an assignment, creditors must agree on liquidation values and the relative priority of claims. This is not an easy task.

In actuality, there may be combinations of two or more of the above-described out-of-court procedures. For example, there may be an extension as well as a composition, or a creditor committee may help to establish one or more of the alternatives.

In-Court Settlements—Formal Bankruptcy

When it is apparent an out-of-court settlement cannot be reached, the next step is formal bankruptcy. Bankruptcy proceedings may be initiated voluntarily by the company or, alternatively, by creditors.

Once the firm falls under formal bankruptcy proceedings, a referee is appointed by the court to oversee the activities. The referee becomes the arbitrator of the proceedings, whose actions and decisions are final, subject only to review by the court. A trustee will also be selected to properly determine the assets and liabilities of the firm and to carry out a plan of reorganization or liquidation for the firm.

Reorganization   If the firm is to be reorganized (under the Bankruptcy Act's Chapter 11 restructuring), the plan must prove to be fair and feasible. An **internal reorganization** calls for an evaluation of current management and operating policies. If current management is shown to be incompetent, it will probably be discharged and replaced by new management. An evaluation and possible redesign of the current capital structure is also necessary. If the firm is top-heavy with debt (as is normally the case), alternate securities, such as preferred or common stock, may replace part of the debt.[1] Any restructuring must be fair to all parties involved.

An **external reorganization**, in which a merger partner is found for the firm, may also be considered. The surviving firm must be deemed strong enough to carry out the financial and management obligations of the joint entities. Old creditors and stockholders may be asked to make concessions to ensure that a feasible arrangement is established. Their motivation is that they hope to come out further ahead than if such a reorganization were not undertaken. Ideally the firm should be merged with a strong firm in its own industry, although this is not always possible. The savings and loan and banking industries have been particularly adept at merging weaker firms with stronger firms within the industry.

Liquidation

A **liquidation** or sale of assets may be recommended when an internal or external reorganization does not appear possible and it is determined that the assets of the firm are worth more in liquidation than through a reorganization. Priority of claims becomes extremely important in a liquidation, because it is unlikely that all parties will be fully satisfied in their demands.

The priority of claims in a bankruptcy liquidation is as follows:

1. Cost of administering the bankruptcy procedures (lawyers get in line first).
2. Wages due workers if earned within three months of filing the bankruptcy petition. The maximum amount is $600 per worker.
3. Taxes due at the federal, state, or local level.
4. Secured creditors to the extent that designated assets are sold to meet their claims. Secured claims that exceed the sales value of the pledged assets are placed in the same category as other general creditor claims.

---

[1]Another possibility is income bonds, in which interest is payable only if earned.

5. General or unsecured creditors are next in line. Examples of claims in this category are those held by debenture (unsecured bond) holders, trade creditors, and bankers who have made unsecured loans.

    There may be senior and subordinated positions within category 5, indicating that subordinated debt holders must turn over their claims to senior debt holders until complete restitution is made to the higher-ranked category. Subordinated debenture holders may keep the balance if anything is left over after that payment.

6. Preferred stockholders.

7. Common stockholders.

The priority of claims 4 through 7 is similar to that presented in Figure 16-2 of the chapter.

    Let us examine a typical situation to determine "who" should receive "what" under a liquidation in bankruptcy. Assume the Mitchell Corporation has a book value and liquidation value as shown in Table 16A-1. Liabilities and stockholders' claims are also presented.

    We see that the liquidation value of the assets is far less than the book value ($700,000 versus $1.3 million). Also, the liquidation value of the assets will not cover the total value of liabilities ($700,000 compared to $1.1 million). Since all liability claims will not be met, it is evident that lower-ranked preferred stockholders and common stockholders will receive nothing.

    Before a specific allocation is made to the creditors (those with liability claims), the three highest priority levels in bankruptcy must first be covered. That would include

Table 16A-1 Financial data for the Mitchell Corporation

Assets	Book Value	Liquidation Value
Accounts receivable	$ 200,000	$160,000
Inventory	410,000	240,000
Machinery and equipment	240,000	100,000
Building and plant	450,000	200,000
	$1,300,000	$700,000

Liabilities and Stockholders' Claims	
Liabilities:	
Accounts payable	$ 300,000
First lien, secured by machinery and equipment*	200,000
Senior unsecured debt	400,000
Subordinated debentures	200,000
Total liabilities	$1,100,000
Stockholders' claims:	
Preferred stock	50,000
Common stock	150,000
Total stockholders' claims	$ 200,000
Total liabilities and stockholders' claims	$1,300,000

*A lien represents a potential claim against property. The lien holder has a secured interest in the property.

Table 16A-2　Asset values and claims

Assets		Creditor Claims	
Asset values in liquidation	$700,000	Accounts payable	$ 300,000
Administrative costs, wages,		First lien, secured by	
and taxes	−100,000	machinery and equipment	200,000
Remaining asset values	$600,000	Senior unsecured debt	400,000
		Subordinated debentures	200,000
		Total liabilities	$1,100,000

the cost of administering the proceedings, allowable past wages due to workers, and overdue taxes. For the Mitchell Corporation, we shall assume these total $100,000. Since the liquidation value of assets was $700,000, that would leave $600,000 to cover creditor demands, as indicated in the left-hand column of Table 16A-2.

Before we attempt to allocate the values in the left-hand column of Table 16A-2 to the right-hand column, we must first identify any creditor claims that are secured by the pledge of a specific asset. In the present case, there is a first lien on the machinery and equipment of $200,000. Referring back to Table 16A-1, we observe that the machinery and equipment has a liquidation value of only $100,000. The secured debt holders will receive $100,000, with the balance of their claim placed in the same category as the unsecured debt holders. In Table 16A-3, we show asset values available for unsatisfied secured claims and unsecured debt (top portion) and the extent of the remaining claims (bottom portion).

In comparing the available asset values and claims in Table 16A-3, it appears that the settlement on the remaining claims should be at a 50 percent rate ($500,000/$1,000,000). The allocation will take place in the manner presented in Table 16A-4.

Each category receives 50 percent as an initial allocation. However, the subordinated debenture holders must transfer their $100,000 initial allocation to the senior debt holders in recognition of their preferential position. The secured debt holders and those having accounts payable claims are not part of the senior-subordinated arrangement and, thus, hold their initial allocation position.

Table 16A-3　Asset values available for unsatisfied secured claims and unsecured debt holders—and their remaining claims

Asset values:	
Asset values in liquidation	$ 700,000
Administrative costs, wages, and taxes	100,000
Remaining asset values	$ 600,000
Payment to secured creditors	−100,000
Amount available to unsatisfied secured claims and unsecured debt	$ 500,000
Remaining claims of unsatisfied secured debt and unsecured debt:	
Secured debt (unsatisfied first lien)	$ 100,000
Accounts payable	300,000
Senior unsecured debt	400,000
Subordinated debentures	200,000
	$1,000,000

Table 16A-4   Allocation procedures for unsatisfied secured claims and unsecured debt

(1) Category	(2) Amount of Claim	(3) Initial Allocation (50%)	(4) Amount Received
Secured debt (unsatisfied 1st lien)	$ 100,000	$ 50,000	$ 50,000
Accounts payable	300,000	150,000	150,000
Senior unsecured debt	400,000	200,000	300,000
Subordinated debentures	200,000	100,000	0
	$1,000,000	$500,000	$500,000

Table 16A-5   Payments and percent of claims

(1) Category	(2) Total Amount of Claim	(3) Amount Received	(4) Percent of Claim
Secured debt (1st lien)	$200,000	$150,000	75%
Accounts payable	300,000	150,000	50
Senior unsecured debt	400,000	300,000	75
Subordinated debentures	200,000	0	0

Finally, in Table 16A-5, we show the total amounts of claims, the amount received, and the percent of the claim that was satisfied.

The $150,000 in column (3) for secured debt represents the $100,000 from the sale of machinery and equipment, and $50,000 from the allocation process in Table 16A-4. The secured debt holders and senior unsecured debt holders come out on top in terms of percent of claim satisfied (it is coincidental that they are equal). Furthermore, the subordinated debt holders and, as previously mentioned, the preferred and common stockholders receive nothing. Naturally, allocations in bankruptcy will vary from circumstance to circumstance. Working problem 16A-1 will help to reinforce many of the liquidation procedure concepts discussed in this section.

List of Terms

technical insolvency 535	**assignment** 535	
bankruptcy 535	**internal reorganization** 536	
extension 535	**external reorganization** 536	
composition 535	**liquidation** 536	
creditor committee 535		

Discussion Questions

16A–1.   What is the difference between technical insolvency and bankruptcy? *(LO16-5)*

16A–2.   What are four types of out-of-court settlements? Briefly describe each. *(LO16-5)*

16A–3.   What is the difference between an internal reorganization and an external reorganization under formal bankruptcy procedures? *(LO16-5)*

16A–4.   What are the first three priority items under liquidation in bankruptcy? *(LO16-5)*

Problem

Settlement
of claims in
bankruptcy
liquidation
(LO16-5)

16A–1.   The trustee in the bankruptcy settlement for Titanic Boat Co. lists the following book values and liquidation values for the assets of the corporation. Liabilities and stockholders' claims are also shown.

a.   Compute the difference between the liquidation value of the assets and the liabilities.

b.   Based on the answer to part *a,* will preferred stock or common stock participate in the distribution?

Assets

	Book Value	Liquidation Value
Accounts receivable	$1,400,000	$1,200,000
Inventory	1,800,000	900,000
Machinery and equipment	1,100,000	600,000
Building and plant	4,200,000	2,500,000
Total assets	$8,500,000	$5,200,000

Liabilities and Stockholders' Claims

Liabilities:	
Accounts payable	$2,800,000
First lien, secured by machinery and equipment	900,000
Senior unsecured debt	2,200,000
Subordinated debenture	1,700,000
Total liabilities	$7,600,000
Stockholders' claims:	
Preferred stock	$ 250,000
Common stock	650,000
Total stockholders' claims	$ 900,000
Total liabilities and stockholders' claims	$8,500,000

c.   Assuming the administrative costs of bankruptcy, workers' allowable wages, and unpaid taxes add up to $400,000, what is the total remaining asset value available to cover secured and unsecured claims?

d.   After the machinery and equipment are sold to partially cover the first lien secured claim, how much will be available from the remaining asset liquidation values to cover unsatisfied secured claims and unsecured debt?

e.   List the remaining asset claims of unsatisfied secured debt holders and unsecured debt holders in a manner similar to that shown at the bottom portion of Table 16A-3.

f.   Compute a ratio of your answers in part *d* and *e.* This will indicate the initial allocation ratio.

g.   List the remaining claims (unsatisfied secured and unsecured) and make an initial allocation and final allocation similar to that shown in Table 16A-4. Subordinated debenture holders may keep the balance after full payment is made to senior debt holders.

h.   Show the relationship of amount received to total amount of claim in a similar fashion to that of Table 16A-5. Remember to use the sales (liquidation) value for machinery and equipment plus the allocation amount in part *g* to arrive at the total received on secured debt.

17

LEARNING OBJECTIVES

LO 17-1 Common stockholders are the owners of the corporation and therefore have a claim to undistributed income, the right to elect the board of directors, and other privileges.

LO 17-2 Cumulative voting provides minority stockholders with the potential for some representation on the board of directors.

LO 17-3 A rights offering gives current stockholders a first option to purchase new shares.

LO 17-4 Poison pills and other similar provisions may make it difficult for outsiders to take over a corporation against management's wishes.

LO 17-5 Preferred stock is an intermediate type of security that falls somewhere between debt and common stock.

Common and Preferred Stock Financing

The ultimate ownership of the firm resides in **common stock**, whether it is in the form of all outstanding shares of a closely held corporation or one share of Facebook. In terms of legal distinctions, it is the common stockholder alone who directly controls the business. While control of the company is legally in the shareholders' hands, it is practically wielded by management on an everyday basis. It is also important to realize that a large creditor may exert tremendous pressure on a firm to meet certain standards of financial performance, even though the creditor has no voting power.

Small, growing companies often operate at a loss until they reach critical mass. Start-up biotech firms frequently fall into this category along with small technology companies competing with the big guys like Intel and Qualcomm. Tower Semiconductor Inc. is one such tech company. Tower Semiconductor Inc. is headquartered in Israel with its subsidiary Jazz Semiconductor Inc. located in the United States and its wholly owned subsidiary, TowerJazz Japan, Ltd., in Japan. TowerJazz operates three fabrication facilities in Japan through a joint venture with Panasonic. These companies operate collectively under the brand name TowerJazz and trade on the NASDAQ stock exchange under the ticker symbol TSEM. The company fabricates integrated circuits for more than 200 customers worldwide in industries such as automotive, defense, medical, and aerospace. Their foundries fabricate semiconductors like radio frequency chips used in cell phones.

According to S&P Capital IQ, TSEM lost money from 2009 (−$10.65 per share) to 2013 (−$2.72 per share) and finally turned an aftertax profit of $0.07 per share in 2014. In fact 2014 was a breakout year for TowerJazz with record revenues of $828 million, a 64 percent increase over 2013.

TowerJazz would not have gotten to this point in its corporate life without the ability to sell common stock in public markets like NASDAQ. It is very expensive to operate and build foundries, and it takes a critical mass and high utilization rate within the foundries to make money. To get to this point TSEM had to continually sell new stock to finance its operations that were losing money. The company sold 35 million shares in 2008, 39 million shares in 2009, and 66.5 million shares in 2010.

By 2012 the stock was trading for less than $1. NASDAQ has a rule that a stock cannot stay listed if it continuously trades under $1. If a company can't get its stock price above $1 within 180 days and keep it there for 30 days, the stock will be delisted; in other words, it can no longer be traded on NASDAQ.

By August 2012, shares of TSEM had ballooned from 125 million in 2008 to over 330 million, and the stock price was trading at $0.52. On August 2 TowerJazz had a 1 for 15 reverse split, reducing the number of shares to about 22 million. The share price closed at $9.01 on August 6, the day the reverse split became effective. We should point out that during 2013, TSEM share count increased by another 25.4 million shares as the company converted some capital notes into stock and warrants and stock options were exercised. Tower reported EPS of $2.90 for the year ended 2017 with sales of $1.39 billion and 98 million shares of common stock outstanding. By May 2018, it had a market capitalization of $2.7 billion and a stock price of $27.50.

Without investors willing to take a risk on companies like Tower Semiconductor, these small companies would not have a chance to mature and become profitable. The ability to sell common stock to balance debt in the capital structure makes the stock markets important to corporations.

In this chapter, we will also look closely at preferred stock. Preferred stock plays a secondary role in financing the corporate enterprise. It represents a hybrid security, combining some of the features of debt and common stock. Though preferred stockholders do not have an ownership interest in the firm, they do have a priority of claims to dividends that is superior to that of common stockholders.

To understand the rights and characteristics of the different means of financing, we shall examine the powers accorded to shareholders under each arrangement. In the case of common stock, everything revolves around three key rights: the residual claim to income, the voting right, and the right to purchase new shares. We shall examine each of these in detail and then consider the rights of preferred stockholders.

Common Stockholders' Claim to Income

All income that is not paid out to creditors or preferred stockholders automatically belongs to common stockholders. Thus we say they have a **residual claim to income**. This is true regardless of whether these residual funds are actually paid out in dividends or retained in the corporation. A firm that earns $10 million before capital costs and pays $1 million in interest to bondholders and an equal amount in dividends to preferred stockholders will have $8 million available for common stockholders.[1] Perhaps half of that will be paid out as common stock dividends. The balance will be reinvested in the business for the benefit of stockholders, with the hope of providing even greater income, dividends, and price appreciation in the future.

Of course, it should be pointed out that the common stockholder does not have a legal or enforceable claim to dividends. Whereas a bondholder may force the corporation into bankruptcy for failure to make interest payments, the common stockholder

---

[1]Tax consequences related to interest payments are ignored for the present.

must accept circumstances as they are or attempt to change management if a new dividend policy is desired.

Occasionally a company will have several classes of common stock outstanding that carry different rights to dividends and income. For example, Google, Facebook, and Ford Motor Company have two separate classes of common stock that differentiate the shares of the founders from other stockholders and grant preferential rights to founders' shares.

Although there are over 90 million common stockholders in the United States, increasingly ownership is being held by large institutional interests, such as pension funds, mutual funds, or bank trust departments, rather than individual investors. As would be expected, management has become more sensitive to these large stockholders who may side with corporate raiders in voting their shares for or against merger offers or takeover attempts (these topics are covered in Chapter 20).

Table 17-1 presents a list of major companies with high percentages of common stock owned by institutional investors at the beginning of 2018. Wal-Mart Stores Inc. is at the bottom of the list with a 31 percent institutional ownership while Motorola Solutions is now 92 percent owned by institutions. Large companies are institutional favorites, perhaps because the sheer size of the shares outstanding allows for large trades and a high level of liquidity.

Table 17-1	Institutional ownership of U.S. companies
Company Name	**Institutional Ownership (%)**
Motorola Solutions Inc.	92%
eBay Inc.	90%
Microsoft Corp.	75%
Kellogg Co.	73%
PepsiCo Inc.	72%
Bristol-Myers Squibb Co.	71%
3M Co.	68%
Johnson & Johnson	68%
Lockheed Martin Corp.	66%
Walt Disney Co.	63%
Amazon.com Inc.	61%
Procter & Gamble Co.	61%
Facebook Inc.	60%
Apple Inc.	59%
Tesla Inc.	58%
Coca-Cola Co.	58%
General Electric Co.	57%
International Business Machines Corp.	55%
ExxonMobil Corp.	53%
Wal-Mart Stores Inc.	31%

Source: CFRA by S&P Global (accessed January 24, 2018).

The Voting Right

Because common stockholders are the owners of a firm, they are accorded the right to vote in the election of the board of directors and on all other major issues. Common stockholders may cast their ballots as they see fit on a given issue, or assign a **proxy**, or "power to cast their ballot," to management or some outside contesting group. As mentioned in the previous section, some corporations have different classes of common stock with unequal voting rights.

There is also the issue of "founders' stock." Perhaps the Ford Motor Company is the biggest and best example of such stock. Class B shares were used to differentiate between the original **founders' shares** and those shares sold to the public. The founders wanted to preserve partial control of the company while at the same time raise new capital for expansion. The regular common stock (no specific class) has one vote per share and is entitled to elect 60 percent of the board of directors, and the Class B shares have one vote per share but are entitled, as a class of shareholders, to elect 40 percent of the board of directors. Class B stock is reserved solely for Ford family members or their descendants, trusts, or appointed interests. The Ford family has a very important position in Henry Ford's company without owning more than about 3½ percent of the current outstanding stock. Both common and Class B stockowners share in dividends equally, and no stock dividends may be given unless to both common and Class B stockholders in proportion to their ownership.

While common stockholders and the different classes of common stock that they own may, at times, have different voting rights, they do have a vote. Bondholders and preferred stockholders may vote only when a violation of their corporate agreement exists and a subsequent acceleration of their rights takes place. This is a very rare occurrence but occasionally it happens, as in the case of Continental Illinois Corporation. The bank was on the edge of bankruptcy in 1984, and failed to pay dividends on one series of preferred stock for five quarters from July 1, 1984, to September 30, 1985. The preferred stockholder agreement stated that failure to pay dividends for six consecutive quarters would result in the preferred stockholders being able to elect two directors to the board to represent their interests. Continental Illinois declared a preferred dividend in November 1985 and paid all current and past dividends on the preferred stock, thus avoiding the special voting privileges for preferred stockholders. Continental was subsequently bought by Bank of America.

Cumulative Voting

The most important voting matter is the election of the board of directors. As indicated in Chapter 1, the board has primary responsibility for the stewardship of the corporation. If illegal or imprudent decisions are made, the board can be held legally accountable. Furthermore, members of the board of directors normally serve on a number of important subcommittees of the corporation, such as the audit committee, the long-range financial planning committee, and the salary and compensation committee. The board may be elected through the familiar majority rule system or by cumulative voting. Under **majority voting**, any group of stockholders owning over 50 percent of the common stock may elect all of the directors. Under **cumulative voting**, it is possible for those who hold less than a 50 percent interest to elect some of the directors. The provision for some minority interests on the board is important to those who, at times, wish to challenge the prerogatives of management.

The type of voting has become more important to stockholders and management with the threat of takeovers, leveraged buyouts, and other challenges to management's control of the firm. In many cases, large minority stockholders, seeking a voice in the operations and direction of the company, desire seats on the board of directors. To further their goals, several have gotten stockholders to vote on the issue of cumulative voting at the annual meeting.

How does this cumulative voting process work? A stockholder gets one vote for each share of stock he or she owns, times one vote for each director to be elected. The stockholder may then accumulate votes in favor of a specified number of directors.

Assume there are 10,000 shares outstanding, you own 1,001, and nine directors are to be elected. Your total votes under a cumulative election system are:

Number of shares owned	1,001
Number of directors to be elected	9
Number of votes	9,009

Let us assume you cast all your votes for the one director of your choice. With nine directors to be elected, there is no way for the owners of the remaining shares to exclude you from electing a person to one of the top nine positions. If you own 1,001 shares, the majority interest could control a maximum of 8,999 shares. This would entitle them to 80,991 votes.

Number of shares owned (majority)	8,999
Number of directors to be elected	9
Number of votes (majority)	80,991

These 80,991 votes cannot be spread thinly enough over nine candidates to stop you from electing your one director. If they are spread evenly, each of the majority's nine choices will receive 8,999 votes (80,991/9). Your choice is assured 9,009 votes as previously indicated. Because the nine top vote-getters win, you will claim one position. Note that candidates do not run head-on against each other (such as Place A or Place B on the ballot), but rather that the top nine candidates are accorded directorships.

To determine the number of shares needed to elect a given number of directors under cumulative voting, the following formula is used:

$$\text{Shares required} = \frac{\text{Number of directors desired} \times \text{Total number of shares outstanding}}{\text{Total number of directors to be elected} + 1} + 1 \qquad (17\text{-}1)$$

Hewlett Packard Corporate Governance, Stewardship and Facebook Inc.

Managerial

"Corporate governance" refers to the way a company is managed by the board of directors. Most experts on corporate governance believe that a separation of the duties of the chairman of the board and the chief executive officer (CEO) gives the board of directors more control over the direction of the company and its management. A board of directors should be independent of the CEO and should include many independent board members who are not employees of the company, because employees are under the control of the CEO. Good governance includes information transparency so that stockholders and employees know the actions taken by the board. In all situations, an independent board member should chair the audit committee. In the case of Apple, Tim Cook, the chairman of the board, is separate from the CEO. Facebook is quite the opposite, with Mark Zuckerberg being chairman of the board, CEO, and controlling stockholder.

Morningstar publishes financial analyst reports that provide valuation metrics such as fair value, price ratios, and dividend yield and income and balance sheet data. It also publishes a stewardship rating of *poor, standard,* or *exemplary* for each company it evaluates. One of the key areas it examines is the allocation of capital. A quote from Morningstar explains its stewardship rating:

> [Our rating] represents our assessment of management's stewardship of shareholder capital, with particular emphasis on capital allocation decisions. Analysts consider companies' investment strategy and valuation, financial leverage, dividend and share buyback policies, execution, compensation, related party transactions, and accounting practices. Corporate governance practices are only considered if they've had a demonstrated impact on shareholder value. . . . Analysts judge stewardship from an equity holder's

perspective. Ratings are determined on an absolute basis. Most companies will receive a Standard rating, and this is the default rating in the absence of evidence that managers have made exceptionally strong or poor capital allocation decisions.[1]

Other organizations also evaluate how a company has performed in the areas of the environment, social responsibility, and governance; MSCI EGS Research is one company that does this and Fidelity Investments provides the information for most companies where it presents a research report. 3M, highlighted in Chapter 1, and Apple and Facebook are compared in the following table using metrics from both Morningstar and MSCI EGS Research:

	3M	Apple Inc.	Facebook
Stewardship[1]	Exemplary	Standard	Standard
Environment[2]	Leader	Average	Leader
Social[2]	Average	Average	Laggard
Governance[2]	Leader	Average	Average

While Morningstar gives Facebook a rating of average for governance because of its focus on long-term returns and good allocation of capital, Morningstar has this to say:

> Our main knock on Facebook's management is its use of multiple class structures that may limit the voice of minority shareholders. The firm is proposing a Class C capital stock offering in the form of stock dividend for current Class A and Class B shareholders, mainly to preserve Zuckerberg's more than 53% voting interest. Class C shares will not have any voting rights. . . .

[1]Morningstar company reports, Facebook, November 2, 2017.

[2]MSCI EGS Research, Fidelity Investments, January 29, 2018.

The formula reaffirms that in the previous instance, 1,001 shares would elect one director.

$$\frac{1 \times 10,000}{9 + 1} + 1 = \frac{10,000}{10} + 1 = 1,001$$

If three director positions out of nine are desired, 3,001 shares are necessary.

$$\frac{3 \times 10,000}{9 + 1} + 1 = \frac{30,000}{10} + 1 = 3,001$$

Note that, with approximately 30 percent of the shares outstanding, a minority interest can control one-third of the board. If instead of cumulative voting a majority rule system were utilized, a minority interest could elect no one. The group that controlled 5,001 or more shares out of 10,000 would elect every director.

As a restatement of the problem: If we know the number of minority shares outstanding under cumulative voting and wish to determine the number of directors that can be elected, we use this formula:

$$\text{Number of directors that can be elected} = \frac{(\text{Shares owned} - 1) \times (\text{Total number of directors to be elected} + 1)}{(\text{Total number of shares outstanding})} \qquad (17\text{-}2)$$

Plugging 3,001 shares into the formula, we show:

$$\frac{(3,001 - 1)(9 + 1)}{10,000} = \frac{3,000(10)}{10,000} = 3$$

If the formula yields an uneven number of directors, such as 3.3 or 3.8, you always round down to the nearest whole number (i.e., 3).

It is not surprising that 22 states require cumulative voting in preference to majority rule, that 18 consider it permissible as part of the corporate charter, and that only 10 make no provision for its use. Such consumer-oriented states as California, Illinois, and Michigan require cumulative voting procedures.

Delaware does not require cumulative voting and is viewed as having a legal system that is lenient on corporations; it should come as no surprise that many companies are legally registered in the State of Delaware.

The Right to Purchase New Shares

In addition to a claim to residual income and the right to vote for directors, the common stockholders may also enjoy a privileged position in the offering of new securities. If the corporate charter contains a **preemptive right** provision, holders of common stock must be given the first option to purchase new shares. While only two states specifically require the use of preemptive rights, most other states allow for the inclusion of a **rights offering** in the corporation charter.

The preemptive right provision ensures that management cannot subvert the position of present stockholders by selling shares to outside interests without first offering them to current shareholders. If such protection were not afforded, a 20 percent stockholder might find his or her interest reduced to 10 percent through the distribution of new shares to outsiders. Not only would voting rights be diluted, but proportionate claims to earnings per share would be reduced.

The Use of Rights in Financing

Many corporations also engage in a preemptive rights offering to tap a built-in market for new securities—the current investors. Rights offerings are not only used by many U.S. companies, but are especially popular as a fund-raising method in Europe. It is quite common in European markets for companies to ask their existing shareholders to help finance expansion.

For example, Telephon A.B. Ericsson, a Swedish company, had a $3 billion rights offering in August 2002 to raise new funds. The collapse of the Internet bubble in 2000 caused a huge decline in sales and earnings, and Ericsson was in need of new capital. What better place to look for equity capital than the existing stockholders. If they already believe in the company and own shares, they might be willing to ante up more money to keep the company alive. This also happened in 2009 in the banking crisis. Many banks were short of their required capital requirements and needed new infusions of equity capital. The American banks relied mostly on secondary offerings available to anyone while the European banks relied on rights offerings. See the Finance in Action Box on HSBC Holdings plc as an example.

Most rights offerings are successful in getting shareholders to exercise their rights to buy new shares. When all the shares are not exercised by shareholders, the investment banker in charge of the offering exercises the rest and sells them in the open market. Additionally, the number of shares a shareholder can buy is conditional on the number of shares he or she owns, and there is a ratio of new shares to shares already owned. This is shown in column 4 of Table 17-2, and you can see that there is no standard ratio. In the HSBC Holding rights offering, for every 12 shares a stockholder owned, he or she could buy 5 new shares, while for Tejon Ranch, a shareholder could buy 1 new share for every 5 shares owned.

Usually the investment banker in charge of the rights offering will price the new shares at a discount to the price of the existing shares. The price of the new shares is stated on the announcement day, and the underpricing is expressed as the offering price of the new shares compared to the market price of the shares traded on the market on the day of the announcement. The more the shares are underpriced, the more likely it is that the rights will be exercised. The underpricing is shown in column 5. All the companies in the table except ITUS, a developmental biotech company, were very close to 100 percent subscribed. In many cases they were oversubscribed and sold more shares than their original announcement indicated. In the case of Tejon Ranch, a 270,000-acre real estate company 60 miles north of Los Angeles, it originally announced a $75 million rights offering but was oversubscribed, and the investment banker was allowed to sell an extra $15 million.

Table 17-2   Rights offerings big and small

	(1) Funds Raised	(2) Country	(3) Shares Exercised	(4) New Shares to Old Shares	(5) Percent Underpriced	(6) Date
HSBC Holding plc	12.85 billion British Pounds	England	97.0	5 new for every 12 existing shares	41	4/4/2009
Olam International Ltd.	249 million SGD	Singapore	97	1 new for every 22 existing shares	92	6/6/2011
PA Resources AB	700 million SEK	Sweden	7,000 million	6 new for every 1 existing share	58	1/9/2013
ITUS Corporation	$4.7 million	United States	39	1 new for every 1 existing share	15–25% depending on the weighted ave. stock price	2/24/2017
Banco Santander SA	7.072 billion EUR	Spain	100	1 new for every 1 existing share	17.75	7/4/2017
Tejon Ranch Co.	$90 million	United States	100	1 new share for every 5 existing shares	14.2	10/4/2017

Sources: Bloomberg, Globe Newswire, PR Newswire, 123Jump.com, and corporate websites.

To illustrate the use of rights, let's take a look at a hypothetical company, Watson Corporation, which has 9 million shares outstanding and a current market price of $40 per share (the total market value is $360 million). Watson needs to raise $30 million for new plant and equipment and will sell 1 million new shares at $30 per share.[2] As part of the process, it will use a rights offering in which each old shareholder receives a first option to participate in the purchase of new shares.

Each old shareholder will receive one right for each share of stock owned and may combine a specified number of rights plus $30 cash to buy a new share of stock. Let us consider these questions:

1.   How many rights should be necessary to purchase one new share of stock?
2.   What is the monetary value of these rights?

Rights Required   Since 9 million shares are currently outstanding and 1 million new shares will be issued, the ratio of old to new shares is 9 to 1. On this basis, the old stockholder may combine nine rights plus $30 cash to purchase one new share of stock.

A stockholder with 90 shares of stock would receive an equivalent number of rights, which could be applied to the purchase of 10 shares of stock at $30 per share. As indicated later in the discussion, stockholders may choose to sell their rights, rather than exercise them in the purchase of new shares.

Monetary Value of a Right   Anything that contributes toward the privilege of purchasing a considerably higher priced stock for $30 per share must have some market value. Consider the following two-step analysis.

---
[2]If this were not a rights offering, the discount from the current market price would be much smaller. The new shares might sell for $38 or $39.

Nine old shares sold at $40 per share, or for $360; now one new share will be introduced for $30. Thus we have a total market value of $390 spread over 10 shares. After the rights offering has been completed, the average value of a share is theoretically equal to $39.[3]

Nine old shares sold at $40 per share	$360
One new share will sell at $30 per share	30
Total value of 10 shares	$390
Average value of one share	$ 39

The rights offering thus entitles the holder to buy a stock that should carry a value of $39 (after the transactions have been completed) for $30. With a differential between the anticipated price and the subscription price of $9 ($39 − $30) and nine rights required to participate in the purchase of one share, the value of a right in this case is $1.

Average value of one share	$39
Subscription price	30
Differential	$ 9
Rights required to buy one share	9
Value of a right	$ 1

Formulas have been developed to determine the value of a right under any circumstance. Before they are presented, let us examine two new terms that will be part of the calculations—*rights-on* and *ex-rights*. When a rights offering is announced, a stock initially trades **rights-on**; that is, if you buy the stock, you will also acquire a right toward a future purchase of the stock. After a certain period (say four weeks), the stock goes **ex-rights**—when you buy the stock, you no longer get a right toward the future purchase of stock. Consider the following:

Date		**Value of Stock**	**Value of Right**
March 1:	Stock trades rights-on	$40	$1 (part of $40)
April 1:	Stock trades ex-rights	39	$1
April 30:	End of subscription period	39	—

Once the ex-rights period is reached, the stock will go down by the theoretical value of the right. The remaining value ($39) is the ex-rights value. Though there is a time period remaining between the ex-rights date (April 1) and the end of the subscription period (April 30), the market assumes the dilution has already occurred. Thus the ex-rights value reflects the same value as can be expected when the new, underpriced $30 stock issue is sold. In effect, it projects the future impact of the cheaper shares on the stock price.

The formula for the value of the right when the stock is trading rights-on is:

$$R = \frac{M_0 - S}{N + 1} \tag{17-3}$$

---

[3]A number of variables may intervene to change the value. This is a "best" approximation.

where

M_0 = Market value—rights-on, $40

S = Subscription price, $30

N = Number of rights required to purchase a new share of stock; in this case, 9

$$\frac{\$40 - \$30}{9 + 1} = \frac{\$10}{10} = \$1$$

Using Formula 17-3 we determined that the value of a right in the Watson Corporation offering was $1. An alternative formula giving precisely the same answer is:

$$R = \frac{M_e - S}{N} \qquad\qquad (17\text{-}4)$$

The only new term is M_e, the market value of the stock when the shares are trading ex-rights. It is $39. We show:

$$R = \frac{\$39 - \$30}{9} = \frac{\$9}{9} = \$1$$

These are all theoretical relationships, which may be altered somewhat in reality. If there is great enthusiasm for the new issue, the market value of the right may exceed the initial theoretical value (perhaps the right will trade for 1.375).

Effect of Rights on Stockholder's Position

At first glance, a rights offering appears to bring great benefits to stockholders. But is this really the case? Does a shareholder really benefit from being able to buy a stock that is initially $40 (and later $39) for $30? Don't answer too quickly!

Think of it this way: Assume 100 people own shares of stock in a corporation and one day decide to sell new shares to themselves at 25 percent below current value. They cannot really enhance their wealth by selling their own stock more cheaply to themselves. What is gained by purchasing inexpensive new shares is lost by diluting existing outstanding shares.

Take the case of stockholder A, who owns nine shares before the rights offering and also has $30 in cash. His holdings would appear as follows:

Nine old shares at $40	$360
Cash	30
Total value	$390

If he receives and exercises nine rights to buy one new share at $30, his portfolio will contain:

Ten shares at $39 (diluted value)	$390
Cash	0
Total value	$390

Clearly he is no better off. A second alternative would be for him to sell his rights in the market and stay with his position of owning only nine shares and holding cash. The outcome is:

Nine shares at $39 (diluted value)	$ 351
Proceeds from sale of nine rights	9
Cash	30
Total value	$390

As indicated previously, whether he chooses to exercise his rights or not, the stock will still go down to a lower value (others are still diluting). Once again, his overall value remains constant. The total value received for the rights ($9) exactly equals the extent of dilution in the value of the original nine shares.

The only foolish action would be for the stockholder to regard the rights as worthless securities. He would then suffer the pains of dilution without the offset from the sale of the rights.

Nine shares at $39 (diluted value)	$351
Cash	30
Total value	$381

Empirical evidence indicates this careless activity occurs 2 to 3 percent of the time.

Desirable Features of Rights Offerings

You may ask, If the stockholder is no better off in terms of total valuation, why undertake a rights offering? There are a number of possible advantages.

As previously indicated, by giving current stockholders a first option to purchase new shares, the firm protects the stockholders' current position in regard to voting rights and claims to earnings. Of equal importance, the use of a rights offering gives the firm a built-in market for new security issues. Because of this built-in base, distribution costs are likely to be lower than under a straight public issue in which investment bankers must underwrite the full risk of distribution.[4]

Also, a rights offering may generate more interest in the market than would a straight public issue. There is a market not only for the stock but also for the rights. Because the subscription price is normally set 15 to 25 percent below current value, there is the "nonreal" appearance of a bargain, creating further interest in the offering.

A last advantage of a rights offering over a straight stock issue is that stock purchased through a rights offering carries lower margin requirements. The **margin requirement** specifies the amount of cash or equity that must be deposited with a brokerage house or a bank, with the balance of funds eligible for borrowing. Though not all investors wish to purchase on margin, those who do so prefer to put down a minimum amount. While normal stock purchases may require a 50 percent margin (half cash, half borrowed), stock purchased under a rights offering may be bought with as little as 25 percent down, depending on the current requirements of the Federal Reserve Board.

---

[4]Though investment bankers generally participate in a rights offering as well, their fees are less because of the smaller risk factor.

HSBC Holdings plc Rights Offering

HSBC Holdings plc is Europe's biggest bank with a worldwide presence. It is also known as Hong Kong Shanghai Banking Corporation, and while it was originally focused in Asia, now Europe accounts for over 50 percent of its assets, Hong Kong and Asia-Pacific about 25 percent, and North America 20 percent, with Latin America about 5 percent. The credit crisis of 2007–2009 put tremendous pressure on HSBC's capital ratios. HSBC had set aside loan-loss reserves of $53 billion during 2007–2009 to cover investments in U.S. subprime debt and direct exposure to loans packaged into securitized financings, but it needed more equity capital. European banks like the U.S. banks found it difficult to sell their high-risk assets, and many like HSBC, Royal Bank of Scotland, UBS of Switzerland, Bank America, Citibank, and others were forced to either write down their assets or sell them at fire-sale prices. This caused their capital ratios to shrink below the required limit of 6 percent.

The solution was to find equity capital in the form of common stock and preferred stock. Common stock was high-risk equity without a guaranteed dividend and was considered tier 1 capital, while preferred stock was considered tier 2 capital. Total capital had to equal a minimum of 6 percent with tier 1 capital (common stock and common shareholder equity) equaling a minimum of 4 percent. Most banks and investors wanted ratios well above 6 percent in the uncertain economy with more potential losses from bank loans and investments looming on the horizon. In the United States, the U.S. government bought several hundred billion dollars of preferred stock in many banks to bolster their capital, and banks like Bank of America, Citigroup, and others also sold common stock through secondary offerings. As Table 17-2 shows, in Europe, banks used rights offerings to raise capital.

HSBC did not want to borrow from the British government, so on March 2, 2009, it announced a rights offering intended to raise approximately $17.7 billion (£12.85 billion) through the sale of 5.06 billion shares of common stock. The rights offering was successful, and 97 percent of the shares were sold to existing stockholders with the investment bankers exercising the 3 percent that was left over. Before the rights offering, HSBC's tier 1 capital ratio was 8.3 percent; after the rights offering, the ratio jumped to 9.8 percent, which was at the upper end of the 7.5 to 10.0 percent target HSBC liked to maintain.

HSBC trades in the United States as an ADR (American Depository Receipt). When the bank announced the offering on March 2, 2009, the price of its ADR in the United States was $28.25. By November 2009 the stock had hit a high of $59.01 and a low of $33.33 on April 1, 2016, and had recovered to $55.12 by January 2018. You might want to check on the stock price to see how HSBC is doing. The ticker symbol is HBC.

Poison Pills

During the last two decades, a new wrinkle was added to the meaning of rights when firms began receiving merger and acquisition proposals from companies interested in acquiring voting control of the firm. The management of many firms did not want to give up control of the company, and so they devised a method of making the firm very unattractive to a potential acquisition-minded company. As you can tell from our discussion of voting provisions, for a company using majority voting, a corporate raider needs to control only slightly over 50 percent of the voting shares to exercise total control. Management of companies considered potential takeover targets began to develop defensive tactics in fending off these unwanted takeovers. One widely used strategy is called the *poison pill*.

A **poison pill** may be a rights offer made to existing shareholders of company X with the sole purpose of making it more difficult for another firm to acquire company X.

Most poison pills have a trigger point. When a potential buyer accumulates a given percentage of the common stock (for example, 25 percent), the other shareholders may receive rights to purchase additional shares from the company, generally at very low prices. If the rights are exercised by shareholders, this increases the total shares outstanding and dilutes the potential buyer's ownership percentage. Poison pill strategies often do not have to be voted on by shareholders to be put into place. At International Paper Company, however, the poison pill issue was put on the proxy ballot and 76 percent of the voting shareholders sided with management to maintain the poison pill defense. This was surprising because many institutional investors are opposed to the pill. They believe it lowers the potential for maximizing shareholder value by discouraging potential high takeover bids.

American Depository Receipts

American Depository Receipts (ADRs) are certificates that have a legal claim on an ownership interest in a foreign company's common stock. The shares of the foreign company are purchased and put in trust in a foreign branch of a major U.S. bank. The bank, in turn, receives and can issue depository receipts to the American shareholders of the foreign firm. These ADRs (depository receipts) allow foreign shares to be traded in the United States much like common stock. ADRs have been around for a long time and are sometimes referred to as American Depository Shares (ADSs).

Since foreign companies want to tap into the world's largest capital market, the United States, they need to offer securities for sale in the United States that can be traded by investors and have the same liquidity features as U.S. securities. ADRs imitate common stock traded on the New York Stock Exchange. Foreign companies such as HSBC Holdings (English), Nestlé (Swiss), Heineken (Dutch), and Sony (Japanese) that have common stock trading on their home exchanges in London, Zurich, Amsterdam, and Tokyo also issue ADRs in the United States.

An American investor (or any foreign investor) can buy American Depository Shares of foreign companies from around the world on the New York Stock Exchange and the NASDAQ Stock Market. Table 17-3 shows the American Depository Shares (Receipts) for nine regions in January 2018. The table includes Global Depository Receipts (GDRs), which are patterned after ADRs but can be issued by international companies and traded globally rather than just on U.S. markets. Table 17-3 also includes the market where the depository receipts trade, and you can see that the vast majority of them trade over-the-counter. Although the bigger multinational companies, like Seimans, Novartis, Total, HSBC, and Banco Santander, are usually traded on the major exchanges.

There are many advantages to American Depository Shares for the U.S. investor. The annual reports and financial statements are presented in English according to generally accepted accounting principles. Dividends are paid in dollars and are more easily collected than if the actual shares of the foreign stock were owned. Although ADRs are considered to be more liquid, less expensive, and easier to trade than buying foreign companies' stock directly on that firm's home exchange, there are some drawbacks.

Even though the ADRs are traded in the U.S. market in dollars, they are still traded in their own countries in their local currencies. This means that the investor in ADRs is subject to a foreign currency risk if the exchange rates between the two countries

Table 17-3	Depository receipts—American and global foreign company listings on U.S. exchanges and over-the-counter		

Region or Country	Total	By Major Market	Total
Australia & New Zealand	230	London Stock Exchange	210
Central and Eastern Europe	256	Luxembourg	139
Continental Europe	704	NASDAQ	125
Latin America	217	NYSE	249
Middle East/N. Africa/the Gulf	145	Over-the-Counter	2,270
North Asia	944	Euronext & Frankfurt	4
South Asia	381	Singapore & Hong Kong	6
Sub-Saharan Africa	98	Singapore	4
United Kingdom & Ireland	331	Unlisted	299
	3,306		3,306

Source: www.adrbnymellon.com/dr_search_by_country.jsp (accessed January 24, 2018).

change. Also, most foreign companies do not report their financial results as often as U.S. companies. Furthermore, there is an information lag as foreign companies need to translate their reports into English. By the time the reports are translated, some of the information has already been absorbed in the local markets and by international traders.

Preferred Stock Financing

Having discussed bonds in Chapter 16 and common stock in this chapter, we are prepared to look at an intermediate or hybrid form of security known as **preferred stock**. You may question the validity of the term *preferred,* for preferred stock does not possess any of the most desirable characteristics of debt or common stock. In the case of debt, bondholders have a contractual claim against the corporation for the payment of interest and may throw the corporation into bankruptcy if payment is not forthcoming. Common stockholders are the owners of the firm and have a residual claim to all income not paid out to others. Preferred stockholders are merely entitled to receive a stipulated dividend and, generally, must receive the dividend before the payment of dividends to common stockholders. However, their right to annual dividends is not mandatory for the corporation, as is true of interest on debt, and the corporation may forgo preferred dividends when this is deemed necessary.

For example, XYZ Corporation might issue 7 percent preferred stock with a $100 par value. Under normal circumstances, the corporation would pay the $7 per share dividend. Let us also assume it has $1,000 bonds carrying 6.8 percent interest and shares of common stock with a market value of $50, normally paying a $1 cash dividend. The 6.8 percent interest must be paid on the bonds. The $7 preferred dividend has to be paid before the $1 dividend on common stock, but both may be waived without threat of bankruptcy. The common stockholder is the last in line to receive payment, but the common stockholder's potential participation is unlimited. Instead of getting a $1 dividend, the investor may someday receive many times that much in dividends and also capital appreciation in stock value.

Justification for Preferred Stock

Because preferred stock has few unique characteristics, why might the corporation issue it and, equally important, why are investors willing to purchase the security?

Most corporations that issue preferred stock do so to achieve a balance in their capital structure. It is a means of expanding the capital base of the firm without diluting the common stock ownership position or incurring contractual debt obligations.

Even here, there may be a drawback. While interest payments on debt are tax-deductible, preferred stock dividends are not. Thus the interest cost on 6.8 percent debt may be only 4.5 to 5 percent on an aftertax cost basis, while the aftertax cost on 7 percent preferred stock would be the stated amount. A firm issuing the preferred stock may be willing to pay the higher aftertax cost to assure investors it has a balanced capital structure, and because preferred stock may have a positive effect on the costs of the other sources of funds in the capital structure.

Investor Interest Primary purchasers of preferred stock are corporate investors, insurance companies, and pension funds. To the corporate investor, preferred stock offers a very attractive advantage over bonds. The 2017 Tax Cuts and Jobs Act reduced the dividend tax exemption for all companies receiving either preferred or common dividends from another corporation. For companies owning between 20 and 80 percent of another company, any dividends received from that company are taxed at the company's regular tax rate. Most companies don't fall into this category. For companies owning less than 20 percent of another company, the tax exclusion was reduced from 70 percent to 50 percent. This reduction makes sense because the corporate tax rate was reduced from 35 percent to 21 percent. Thus the effective tax rate on dividends is 10.5 percent, which maintains the previous effective tax rate under the old tax law. On a preferred stock issue paying a 7 percent dividend, only 50 percent would be taxable. By contrast, all the interest on bonds is taxable to the recipient except for municipal bond interest.

Assume a taxable bond is paying 5.00 percent interest in 2018. Since interest on bonds receives no preferential tax treatment for the corporate investor, the aftertax bond yield must be adjusted by the investing corporation's marginal tax rate.

In this example, we shall use a tax rate of 21 percent, which is the new corporate tax rate under the 2017 act.

$$\text{Aftertax bond yield} = \text{Before-tax bond yield} \times (1 - \text{Tax rate})$$
$$= 5.00\% \, (1 - 0.21)$$
$$= 3.95\%$$

The corporate bondholder will receive 3.95 percent as an aftertax yield.

Now let's look at preferred stock, which is also paying 5.00 percent. For preferred stock, the adjustment includes the advantageous 50 percent tax provision. Also under current tax laws, the tax rate on dividends for the majority of companies is 21 percent. The computation for aftertax return for preferred stock is as follows:

$$\text{Aftertax preferred yield} = \text{Before-tax preferred stock yield} \times [1 - (\text{Tax rate})(0.50)]$$
$$= 5.00\% \times [1 - (0.21)(0.50)]$$
$$= 5.00\% \times (1 - 0.105)$$
$$= 5.00\% \times (0.895)$$
$$= 4.47\%$$

The aftertax yield on preferred stock is clearly higher than the aftertax bond yield (4.47 percent versus 3.95 percent) due to the tax advantage that corporations are allowed. The exception reduces the effect of triple taxation. If you trace the taxes on the income stream, the distributing company (company A) pays a tax on its earnings and the corporate holder of the preferred stock (company B) pays a tax on the dividend received. The stockholders of company B will pay a tax on any dividend they receive, which would include the dividend from company A that is included in company B's income.

Summary of Tax Considerations   Tax considerations for preferred stock work in two opposite directions. First, they make the aftertax cost of debt cheaper than preferred stock to the issuing corporation because interest is deductible to the payer. Second, tax considerations generally make the receipt of preferred dividends more valuable than corporate bond interest to corporate investors because 70 percent of the dividend is exempt from taxation.

Provisions Associated with Preferred Stock

A preferred stock issue contains a number of stipulations and provisions that define the stockholder's claim to income and assets.

1. Cumulative Dividends   Most issues represent **cumulative preferred stock** and have a cumulative claim to dividends. That is, if preferred stock dividends are not paid in any one year, they accumulate and must be paid in total before common stockholders can receive dividends. If preferred stock carries a $10 cash dividend and the company does not pay dividends for three years, preferred stockholders must receive the full $30 before common stockholders can receive anything.

The cumulative dividend feature makes a corporation very aware of its obligation to preferred stockholders. When a financially troubled corporation has missed a number of dividend payments under a cumulative arrangement, there may be a financial recapitalization of the corporation in which preferred stockholders receive new securities in place of the dividend that is in arrears (unpaid). Assume the corporation has now missed five years of dividends under a $10-a-year obligation and the company still remains in a poor cash position. Preferred stockholders may be offered $50 or more in new common stock or bonds as forgiveness of the missed dividend payments. Preferred stockholders may be willing to cooperate in order to receive some potential benefit for the future.

2. Conversion Feature   Like certain forms of debt, preferred stock may be convertible into common shares. Thus $100 in preferred stock may be convertible into a specified number of shares of common stock at the option of the holder. One new wrinkle on convertible preferreds is the use of **convertible exchangeable preferreds** that allow the company to force conversion from convertible preferred stock into convertible debt. This can be used to allow the company to take advantage of falling interest rates or to allow the company to change preferred dividends into tax-deductible interest payments when it is to the company's advantage to do so. The topic of convertibility is discussed at length in Chapter 19, "Convertibles, Warrants, and Derivatives."

3. Call Feature   Also, preferred stock, like debt, may be callable; that is, the corporation may retire the security before maturity at some small premium over par. This, of course, accrues to the advantage of the corporation and to the disadvantage of the preferred stockholder. A preferred issue carrying a call provision will be accorded a slightly higher yield than a similar issue without this feature. The same type of refunding decision applied to debt obligations in Chapter 16 could also be applied to preferred stock.

4. Participation Provision   A small percentage of preferred stock issues are **participating preferreds**; that is, they may participate over and above the quoted yield when the corporation is enjoying a particularly good year. Once the common stock dividend equals the preferred stock dividend, the two classes of securities may share equally in additional payouts.

5. Floating Rate   Beginning in the 1980s, some preferred stock issuers made the dividend adjustable in nature, and this stock is classified as **floating rate preferred stock**. Typically the dividend is changed on a quarterly basis, based on current market conditions. Because the dividend rate changes only quarterly, there is still some possibility of a small price change between dividend adjustment dates. Nevertheless, it is less than the price change for regular preferred stock.

Investors that participate in floating rate preferred stock do so for two reasons: to minimize the risk of price changes and to take advantage of potential tax benefits associated with preferred stock corporate ownership. The price stability actually makes floating rate preferred stock the equivalent of a safe short-term investment even though preferred stock is normally thought of as long term in nature.

6. Auction Rate Preferred Stock   **Auction rate preferred stock** is sometimes referred to as Dutch auction preferred stock, and is similar to floating rate preferred stock. Though it is actually a long-term security, it behaves like a short-term one. The auction rate preferred dividend is reset through a periodic auction that keeps the dividend yield consistent with current market conditions. The auction periods vary for each issue and can be 7, 14, 28, 49, or 91 days with some issues being reset semiannually or annually. The concept of a Dutch auction means the stock is issued to the bidder willing to accept the lowest yield and then to the next lowest bidder, and so on until all the preferred stock is sold. This is much like the Treasury bill auction held by the U.S. Treasury on a regular basis. This auction process at short-term intervals allows investors to keep up with the changing interest rates in the short-term market. Some corporate investors prefer to buy Dutch auction preferred stock because it allows them to invest at short-term rates and take advantage of the tax benefits available to them with preferred stock investments.

This type of security works well as long as there are participants at the auction willing to bid on the securities. If there are no bidders, the rate stays the same, and investors are stuck with the return until another auction can be held. One of the consequences of the financial crisis was that the auction rate securities market dried up on February 7, 2008. The auction rate market froze as large institutional investors such as Citigroup,

Morgan Stanley, and Merrill Lynch failed to bid. These banks couldn't afford to take risks on buying assets that could become illiquid, and by not bidding they created an illiquid market that many short-term investors depended upon for liquidity. This problem continued throughout 2008 and into 2009 as investors were stuck holding assets that could not be sold. Several lawsuits were filed by states, municipalities, pension funds, and by the Securities and Exchange Commission. Eventually many institutions agreed to buy back or redeem the securities at par. For all practical purposes, this market is frozen for now; maybe over time with new protections, it might recover.

7. Par Value   A final important feature associated with preferred stock is par value. Unlike the par value of common stock, which is often only a small percentage of the actual value, the par value of preferred stock is set at the anticipated market value at the time of issue. The par value establishes the amount due to preferred stockholders in the event of liquidation. Also, the par value of preferred stock determines the base against which the percentage or dollar return on preferred stock is computed. Thus 10 percent preferred stock would indicate $10 a year in preferred dividends if the par value were $100, but only $5 annually if the par value were $50.

Comparing Features of Common and Preferred Stock and Debt

In Table 17-4, we compare the characteristics of common stock, preferred stock, and bonds. You should consider the comparative advantages and disadvantages of each.

In terms of the risk-return features of these three classes of securities and also of the other investments discussed earlier in Chapter 7, we might expect the risk-return patterns depicted in Figure 17-1. The lowest return is obtained from savings accounts, and the highest return and risk are generally associated with common stock. In between, we note that short-term instruments generally, though not always, provide lower returns than longer-term instruments. We also observe that government securities pay lower returns than issues originated by corporations because of the lower risk involved. Next on the scale after government issues is preferred stock. This hybrid form of security may pay a lower return than even well-secured corporate debt instruments because of the 70 percent tax-exempt status of preferred stock dividends to corporate purchasers. Thus the focus of preferred stock is not just on risk-return trade-offs but also on aftertax return.[5]

Next we observe increasingly high return requirements on debt, based on the presence or absence of security provisions and the priority of claims on unsecured debt. At the top of the scale is common stock. Because of its lowest priority of claim in the corporation and its volatile price movement, it has the highest demanded return.

Though extensive research has tended to validate these general patterns, short-term or even intermediate-term reversals have occurred, in which investments with lower risk have outperformed investments at the higher end of the risk scale.

---

[5]In a strict sense, preferred stock does not belong on the straight line because of its unique tax characteristics.

Table 17-4   Features of alternative security issues

	Common Stock	Preferred Stock	Bonds
1. Ownership and control of the firm	Belongs to common stockholders through voting rights and residual claim to income	Limited rights when dividends are missed	Limited rights under default in interest payment
2. Obligations to provide return	None	Must receive payment before common stock	Contractual obligation
3. Claim to assets in bankruptcy	Lowest claim of any security holder	Bondholders and creditors must be satisfied first	Highest claim
4. Cost of distribution	Highest	Moderate	Lowest
5. Risk-return trade-off	Highest risk, highest return (at least in theory)	Moderate risk, moderate return	Lowest risk, moderate return
6. Tax status of payment by corporation	Not deductible	Not deductible	Tax-deductible Cost = Interest payment × (1 − Tax rate)
7. Tax status of payment to recipient	70 percent of dividend to another corporation is tax-exempt	Same as common stock	Municipal bond interest is tax-exempt

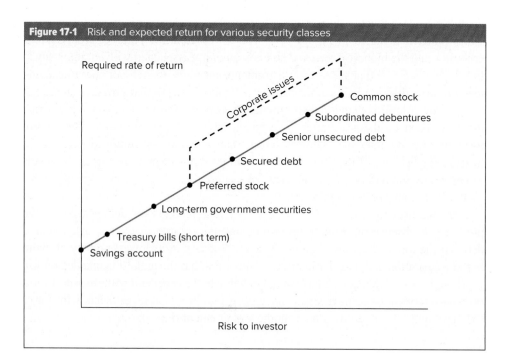

Figure 17-1   Risk and expected return for various security classes

SUMMARY

Common stock ownership carries three primary rights or privileges. First, there is a residual claim to income. All funds not paid out to other classes of securities automatically belong to the common stockholder; the firm may then choose to pay out these residual funds in dividends or to reinvest them for the benefit of common stockholders.

Because common stockholders are the ultimate owners of the firm, they alone have the privilege of voting. To expand the role of minority stockholders, many corporations use a system of cumulative voting, in which each stockholder has voting power equal to the number of shares owned times the number of directors to be elected. By cumulating votes for a small number of selected directors, minority stockholders are able to have representation on the board.

Common stockholders may also enjoy a first option to purchase new shares. This privilege is extended through the procedure known as a rights offering. A shareholder receives one right for each share of stock owned and may combine a certain number of rights, plus cash, to purchase a new share. While the cash or subscription price is usually somewhat below the current market price, the stockholder neither gains nor loses through the process.

A poison pill represents a rights offer made to existing shareholders of a company with the sole purpose of making it more difficult for another firm or outsiders to take over a firm against management's wishes. Most poison pills have a trigger point tied to the percentage ownership in the company that is acquired by the potential suitor. Once the trigger point is reached, the other shareholders (the existing shareholders) have the right to buy many additional shares of company stock at low prices. This automatically increases the total number of shares outstanding and reduces the voting power of the firm wishing to acquire the company.

A hybrid, or intermediate, security, falling between debt and common stock, is preferred stock. Preferred stockholders are entitled to receive a stipulated dividend and must receive this dividend before any payment is made to common stockholders. Preferred dividends usually accumulate if they are not paid in a given year, though preferred stockholders cannot initiate bankruptcy proceedings or seek legal redress if nonpayment occurs.

Finally, common stock, preferred stock, bonds, and other securities tend to receive returns over the long run in accordance with risk, with corporate issues generally paying a higher return than government securities.

REVIEW OF FORMULAS

1. $$\text{Shares required} = \frac{\text{Number of directors desired} \times \text{Total number of shares outstanding}}{\text{Total number of directors to be elected} + 1} + 1 \qquad (17\text{-}1)$$

2. $$\text{Number of directors that can be elected} = \frac{(\text{Shares owned} - 1) \times (\text{Total number of directors to be elected} + 1)}{(\text{Total number of shares outstanding})} \qquad (17\text{-}2)$$

3. $R = \dfrac{M_0 - S}{N + 1}$ (17-3)

R is the value of a right

M_0 is the market value of the stock—rights-on (stock carries a right)

S is the subscription price

N is the number of rights required to purchase a new share of stock

4. $R = \dfrac{M_e - S}{N}$ (17-4)

R is the value of a right

M_e is the market value of stock—ex-rights (stock no longer carries a right)

S is the subscription price

N is the number of rights required to purchase a new share of stock

LIST OF TERMS

DISCUSSION QUESTIONS

1. Why has corporate management become increasingly sensitive to the desires of large institutional investors? *(LO17-1)*

2. Why might a corporation use a special category such as founders' stock in issuing common stock? *(LO17-1)*

3. What is the purpose of cumulative voting? Are there any disadvantages to management? *(LO17-2)*

4. How does the preemptive right protect stockholders from dilution? *(LO17-3)*

5. If common stockholders are the *owners* of the company, why do they have the last claim on assets and a residual claim on income? *(LO17-1)*

6. During a rights offering, the underlying stock is said to sell "rights-on" and "ex-rights." Explain the meaning of these terms and their significance to current stockholders and potential stockholders. *(LO17-3)*

7. Why might management use a poison pill strategy? *(LO17-4)*

8. Preferred stock is often referred to as a hybrid security. What is meant by this term as applied to preferred stock? *(LO17-5)*

9. What is the most likely explanation for the use of preferred stock from a corporate viewpoint? *(LO17-5)*

10. Why is the cumulative feature of preferred stock particularly important to preferred stockholders? *(LO17-2)*

11. A small amount of preferred stock is participating. What would your reaction be if someone said common stock is also participating? *(LO17-4)*

12. What is an advantage of floating rate preferred stock for the risk-averse investor? *(LO17-4)*

13. Put an X by the security that has the feature best related to the following considerations. You may wish to refer to Table 17-4. *(LO17-1 & 17-5)*

	Common Stock	Preferred Stock	Bonds
a. Ownership and control of the firm			
b. Obligation to provide return			
c. Claims to assets in bankruptcy			
d. High cost of distribution			
e. Highest return			
f. Highest risk			
g. Tax-deductible payment			
h. Payment partially tax-exempt to corporate recipient			

PRACTICE PROBLEMS AND SOLUTIONS

1. *a.* George Kelly wishes to elect 5 of the 13 directors on the Data Processing Corp. board. There are 98,000 shares of the company's stock outstanding. How many shares will be required to accomplish this goal?

   Cumulative voting *(LO17-2)*

   b. Jennifer Wallace owns 60,001 shares of stock in the Newcastle Corp. There are 12 directors to be elected with 195,000 shares outstanding. How many directors can Jennifer elect?

2. Dunn Resources has issued rights to its shareholders. The subscription price is $60. Four rights are needed along with the subscription price of $60 to buy one new share. The stock is selling for $72 rights-on.

   Rights offering *(LO17-3)*

   a. What is the value of one right?

   b. After the stock goes ex-rights, what will the new stock price be?

Solutions

1. *a.* Shares required $= \dfrac{\text{(Number of directors desired)} \times \text{(Total number of shares outstanding)}}{\text{Total number of directors to be elected} + 1}$

   $$= \frac{5 \times 98{,}000}{13 + 1} + 1$$

   $$= \frac{490{,}000}{14} + 1$$

   $$= 35{,}000 + 1 = 35{,}001 \text{ shares}$$

b. $\dfrac{\text{Number of directors}}{\text{that can be elected}} = \dfrac{\begin{array}{c}(\text{Shares owned} - 1) \times \\ (\text{Total number of directors to be elected} + 1)\end{array}}{\text{Total number of shares outstanding}}$

$$= \frac{(60{,}001 - 1) \times (12 + 1)}{195{,}000}$$

$$= \frac{60{,}000 \times 13}{195{,}000} = \frac{780{,}000}{195{,}000} = 4 \text{ directors}$$

2. a. $R = \dfrac{M_0 - S}{N + 1}$

$R = $ Value of a right

$M_0 = $ Market value rights-on. This is the value before the effect of the right offering, $72.

$S = $ Subscription price $60.

$N = $ Number of rights necessary to purchase a new share 4.

$$R = \frac{\$72 - 60}{4 + 1} = \frac{\$12}{5} = \$2.40$$

b. The market value of the stock ex-rights (after the effect of the rights offering) is equal to M_0 (the market value before the rights offering) minus the value of a right (R).

$M_e = M_0 - R$

$M_e = $ Market value of the stock ex-rights

$M_0 = \$72$

$R = \$2.40$

$M_e = \$72 - \$2.40 = \$69.60$

PROBLEMS

connect Selected problems are available with Connect. Please see the preface for more information.

Basic Problems

Residual claims to earnings (LO17-1)

1. Folic Acid Inc. has $20 million in earnings, pays $2.75 million in interest to bondholders, and pays $1.80 million in dividends to preferred stockholders.
   a. What are the common stockholders' residual claims to earnings?
   b. What are the common stockholders' legal, enforceable claims to dividends?

Residual claims to earnings (LO17-1)

2. Time Watch Co. has $46 million in earnings and is considering paying $6.45 million in interest to bondholders and $4.35 million to preferred stockholders in dividends.
   a. What are the bondholders' contractual claims to payment? (You may wish to review Table 17-4.)
   b. What are the preferred stockholders' immediate contractual claims to payment? What privilege do they have?

3. Katie Homes and Garden Co. has 10,640,000 shares outstanding. The stock is currently selling at $52 per share. If an unfriendly outside group acquired 25 percent of the shares, existing stockholders will be able to buy new shares at 30 percent below the currently existing stock price.

    Poison pill (LO17-4)

    a. How many shares must the unfriendly outside group acquire for the poison pill to go into effect?

    b. What will be the new purchase price for the existing stockholders?

4. Mr. Meyers wishes to know how many shares are necessary to elect 5 directors out of 14 directors up for election in the Austin Power Company. There are 150,000 shares outstanding. (Use Formula 17-1 to determine the answer.)

    Cumulative voting (LO17-2)

5. Dr. Phil wishes to know how many shares are necessary to elect 6 directors out of 14 directors up for election for the board of the Winfrey Publishing Company. There are 340,000 shares outstanding. (Use Formula 17-1 to determine the answer.)

    Cumulative voting (LO17-2)

6. Carl Hubbell owns 6,001 shares of the Piston Corp. There are 12 seats on the company board of directors, and the company has a total of 78,000 shares of stock outstanding. The Piston Corp. utilizes cumulative voting.

    Cumulative voting (LO17-2)

    Can Mr. Hubbell elect himself to the board when the vote to elect 12 directors is held next week? (Use Formula 17-2 to determine if he can elect one director.)

7. Betsy Ross owns 927 shares in the Hanson Fabrics Company. There are 15 directors to be elected, and 33,500 shares are outstanding. The firm has adopted cumulative voting.

    Cumulative voting (LO17-2)

    a. How many total votes can be cast?

    b. How many votes does Betsy control?

    c. What percentage of the total votes does she control?

8. The Beasley Corporation has been experiencing declining earnings but has just announced a 50 percent salary increase for its top executives. A dissident group of stockholders wants to oust the existing board of directors. There are currently 14 directors and 32,500 shares of stock outstanding. Mr. Wright, the president of the company, has the full support of the existing board. The dissident stockholders control proxies for 15,001 shares. Mr. Wright is worried about losing his job.

    Dissident stockholder group and cumulative voting (LO17-2)

    a. Under cumulative voting procedures, how many directors can the dissident stockholders elect with the proxies they now hold? How many directors could they elect under majority rule with these proxies?

    b. How many shares (or proxies) are needed to elect nine directors under cumulative voting?

9. Midland Petroleum is holding a stockholders' meeting next month. Ms. Ramsey is the president of the company and has the support of the existing board of directors. All 12 members of the board are up for reelection. Mr. Clark is a dissident stockholder. He controls proxies for 34,001 shares. Ms. Ramsey and her friends on the board control 44,001 shares. Other stockholders, whose loyalties are unknown, will be voting the remaining 24,998 shares. The company uses cumulative voting.

    Dissident stockholder group and cumulative voting (LO17-2)

    a. How many directors can Mr. Clark be sure of electing?

b.   How many directors can Ms. Ramsey and her friends be sure of electing?

c.   How many directors could Mr. Clark elect if he obtains all the proxies for the uncommitted votes? (Uneven values must be rounded down to the nearest whole number regardless of the amount.) Will he control the board?

d.   If nine directors were to be elected, and Ms. Ramsey and her friends had 60,001 shares and Mr. Clark had 40,001 shares plus half the uncommitted votes, how many directors could Mr. Clark elect?

Strategies under cumulative voting
(LO17-2)

10.   Mr. Michaels controls proxies for 40,000 of the 75,000 outstanding shares of Northern Airlines. Mr. Baker heads a dissident group that controls the remaining 35,000 shares. There are seven board members to be elected and cumulative voting rules apply. Michaels does not understand cumulative voting and plans to cast 100,000 of his 280,000 (40,000 × 7) votes for his brother-in-law, Scott. His remaining votes will be spread evenly between three other candidates.

How many directors can Baker elect if Michaels acts as described? Use logical numerical analysis rather than a set formula to answer the question. Baker has 245,000 votes (35,000 × 7).

Intermediate Problems

⚡

Different classes of voting stock
(LO17-1)

11.   Rust Pipe Co. was established in 1994. Four years later the company went public. At that time, Robert Rust, the original owner, decided to establish two classes of stock. The first represents Class A founders' stock and is entitled to 9 votes per share. The normally traded common stock, designated as Class B, is entitled to one vote per share. In late 2010, Mr. Stone, an investor, was considering purchasing shares in Rust Pipe Co. While he knew the founders' shares were not often present in other companies, he decided to buy the shares anyway because of a new technology Rust Pipe had developed to improve the flow of liquids through pipes.

Of the 1,450,000 total shares currently outstanding, the original founder's family owns 51,825 shares. What is the percentage of the founder's family votes to Class B votes?

Rights offering
(LO17-3)

12.   Boles Bottling Co. has issued rights to its shareholders. The subscription price is $45 and four rights are needed along with the subscription price to buy one of the new shares. The stock is selling for $55 rights-on.

a.   What would be the value of one right?

b.   If the stock goes ex-rights, what would the new stock price be?

Procedures associated with a rights offering
(LO17-3)

13.   Computer Graphics has announced a rights offering for its shareholders. Carol Stevens owns 1,400 shares of Computer Graphics stock. Four rights plus $54 cash are needed to buy one of the new shares. The stock is currently selling for $66 rights-on.

a.   What is the value of a right?

b.   How many of the new shares could Carol buy if she exercised all her rights? How much cash would this require?

c.   Carol doesn't know if she wants to exercise her rights or sell them. Would either alternative have a more positive effect on her wealth?

14. Todd Winningham IV has $4,800 to invest. He has been looking at Gallagher Tennis Clubs Inc. common stock. Gallagher has issued a rights offering to its common stockholders. Six rights plus $48 cash will buy one new share. Gallagher's stock is selling for $66 ex-rights.

    a. How many rights could Todd buy with his $4,800? Alternatively, how many shares of stock could he buy with the same $4,800 at $66 per share?

    b. If Todd invests his $4,800 in Gallagher rights and the price of Gallagher stock rises to $70 per share ex-rights, what would his dollar profit on the rights be? (First compute profit per right.)

    c. If Todd invests his $4,800 in Gallagher stock and the price of the stock rises to $70 per share ex-rights, what would his total dollar profit be?

    d. What would be the answer to part *b* if the price of Gallagher's stock falls to $40 per share ex-rights instead of rising to $70?

    e. What would be the answer to part *c* if the price of Gallagher's stock falls to $40 per share ex-rights?

Investing in rights (LO17-3)

15. Mr. and Mrs. Anderson own two shares of Magic Tricks Corporation's common stock. The market value of the stock is $58. The Andersons also have $46 in cash. They have just received word of a rights offering. One new share of stock can be purchased at $46 for each two shares currently owned (based on two rights).

    a. What is the value of a right?

    b. What is the value of the Andersons' portfolio before the rights offering? (Portfolio in this question represents stock plus cash.)

    c. If the Andersons participate in the rights offering, what will be the value of their portfolio, based on the diluted value (ex-rights) of the stock?

    d. If they sell their two rights but keep their stock at its diluted value and hold onto their cash, what will be the value of their portfolio?

Effect of rights on stockholder position (LO17-3)

Advanced Problems

16. Walker Machine Tools has 5.5 million shares of common stock outstanding. The current market price of Walker common stock is $52 per share rights-on. The company's net income this year is $17.5 million. A rights offering has been announced in which 550,000 new shares will be sold at $46.50 per share. The subscription price plus 5 rights is needed to buy one of the new shares.

    a. What are the earnings per share and price-earnings ratio before the new shares are sold via the rights offering?

    b. What would the earnings per share be immediately after the rights offering? What would the price-earnings ratio be immediately after the rights offering? (Assume there is no change in the market value of the stock, except for the change when the stock begins trading ex-rights.) Round all answers to two places after the decimal point.

Relation of rights to EPS and the price-earnings ratio (LO17-3)

17. The Omega Corporation has some excess cash that it would like to invest in marketable securities for a long-term hold. Its vice president of finance is considering three investments (Omega Corporation is in a 35 percent tax bracket and the tax rate on dividends is 20 percent). Which one should she select based on aftertax return: (*a*) Treasury bonds at a 10 percent yield; (*b*) corporate bonds at a 13 percent yield; or (*c*) preferred stock at an 11 percent yield?

Aftertax comparison of preferred stock and other investments (LO17-5)

Preferred stock
dividends in arrears
(LO17-5)

18. National Health Corporation (NHC) has a cumulative preferred stock issue outstanding, which has a stated annual dividend of $8 per share. The company has been losing money and has not paid preferred dividends for the last five years. There are 350,000 shares of preferred stock outstanding and 650,000 shares of common stock.

  a.   How much is the company behind in preferred dividends?

  b.   If NHC earns $13,500,000 in the coming year after taxes but before dividends, and this is all paid out to the preferred stockholders, how much will the company be in arrears (behind in payments)? Keep in mind that the coming year would represent the sixth year.

  c.   How much, if any, would be available in common stock dividends in the coming year if $13,500,000 is earned as explained in part *b?*

✗

Preferred stock
dividends in arrears
(LO17-5)

19. Robbins Petroleum Company is four years in arrears on cumulative preferred stock dividends. There are 690,000 preferred shares outstanding, and the annual dividend is $6.50 per share. The vice president of finance sees no real hope of paying the dividends in arrears. She is devising a plan to compensate the preferred stockholders for 80 percent of the dividends in arrears.

  a.   How much should the compensation be?

  b.   Robbins will compensate the preferred stockholders in the form of bonds paying 12 percent interest in a market environment in which the going rate of interest is 8 percent for similar bonds. The bonds will have a 10-year maturity. Using the bond valuation table in Chapter 16 (Table 16-2), indicate the market value of a $1,000 par value bond.

  c.   Based on market value, how many bonds must be issued to provide the compensation determined in part *a?* (Round to the nearest whole number.)

Preferred stock
dividends in arrears
and valuing common
stock
(LO17-5)

20. Enterprise Storage Company has $440,000 shares of cumulative preferred stock outstanding, which has a stated dividend of $7.75. It is six years in arrears in its dividend payments.

  a.   How much in total dollars is the company behind in its payments?

  b.   The firm proposes to offer new common stock to the preferred stockholders to wipe out the deficit. The common stock will pay the following dividends over the next four years:

D_1	$1.15
D_2	1.25
D_3	1.35
D_4	1.45

The company anticipates earnings per share after four years will be $4.09 with a P/E ratio of 10.

The common stock will be valued as the present value of future dividends plus the present value of the future stock price after four years. The discount rate used by the investment banker is 14 percent. Round to two places to the right of the decimal point. What is the calculated value of the common stock?

  c.   How many shares of common stock must be issued at the value computed in part *b* to eliminate the deficit (arrearage) computed in part *a?* Round to the nearest whole number.

21. The treasurer of Kelly Bottling Company (a corporation) currently has $150,000 invested in preferred stock yielding 8 percent. He appreciates the tax advantages of preferred stock and is considering buying $150,000 more with borrowed funds. The cost of the borrowed funds is 13 percent. He suggests this proposal to his board of directors. They are somewhat concerned by the fact that the treasurer will be paying 5 percent more for funds than the company will be earning on the investment. Kelly Bottling is in a 35 percent tax bracket, with dividends taxed at 20 percent.

    Borrowing funds to purchase preferred stock
    (LO17-5)

    a. Compute the amount of the aftertax income from the additional preferred stock if it is purchased.

    b. Compute the aftertax borrowing cost to purchase the additional preferred stock. That is, multiply the interest cost times $(1 - T)$.

    c. Should the treasurer proceed with his proposal?

    d. If interest rates and dividend yields in the market go up six months after a decision to purchase is made, what impact will this have on the outcome?

22. Barnes Air Conditioning Inc. has two classes of preferred stock: floating rate preferred stock and straight (normal) preferred stock. Both issues have a par value of $100. The floating rate preferred stock pays an annual dividend yield of 4 percent, and the straight preferred stock pays 5 percent. Since the issuance of the two securities, interest rates have gone up by 2.50 percent for each issue. Both securities will pay their year-end dividend today.

    Floating rate preferred stock
    (LO17-5)

    a. What is the price of the floating rate preferred stock likely to be?

    b. What is the price of the straight preferred stock likely to be? Refer back to Chapter 10 and use Formula 10-4 to answer this question.

COMPREHENSIVE PROBLEM

The Crandall Corporation currently has 100,000 shares outstanding that are selling at $50 per share. It needs to raise $900,000. Net income after taxes is $500,000. Its vice president of finance and its investment banker have decided on a rights offering but are not sure how much to discount the subscription price from the current market value. Discounts of 10 percent, 20 percent, and 40 percent have been suggested. Common stock is the sole means of financing for the Crandall Corporation.

Crandall Corporation
(Rights offering and the impact on shareholders)
(LO17-3)

    a. For each discount, determine the subscription price, the number of shares to be issued, and the number of rights required to purchase one share. (Round to one place after the decimal point where necessary.)

    b. Determine the value of one right under each of the plans. (Round to two places after the decimal point.)

    c. Compute the earnings per share before and immediately after the rights offering under a 10 percent discount from the market price.

    d. By what percentage has the number of shares outstanding increased?

    e. Stockholder X has 100 shares before the rights offering and participated by buying 20 new shares. Compute his total claim to earnings both before and after the rights offering (that is, multiply shares by the earnings per share figures computed in part *c*).

    f. Should Stockholder X be satisfied with this claim over a longer period of time?

COMPREHENSIVE PROBLEM

**Electro Cardio
Systems Inc.**

(Poison pill strategy)
(LO17-4)

Dr. Robert Grossman founded Electro Cardio Systems Inc. (ECS) in 2001. The principal purpose of the firm was to engage in research and development of heart pump devices. Although the firm did not show a profit until 2006, by 2010 it reported after-tax earnings of $1,200,000. The company had gone public in 2004 at $10 a share. Investors were initially interested in buying the stock because of its future prospects. By year-end 2010, the stock was trading at $42 per share because the firm had made good on its promise to produce lifesaving heart pumps and, in the process, was now making reasonable earnings. With 850,000 shares outstanding, earnings per share were $1.41.

Dr. Grossman and the members of the board of directors were initially pleased when another firm, Parker Medical Products, began buying their stock. John Parker, the chairman and CEO of Parker Medical Products, was thought to be a shrewd investor and his company's purchase of 50,000 shares of ECS was taken as an affirmation of the success of the heart pump research firm.

However, when Parker bought another 50,000 shares, Dr. Grossman and members of the board of directors of ECS became concerned that John Parker and his firm might be trying to take over ECS.

Upon talking to his attorney, Dr. Grossman was reminded that ECS had a poison pill provision that took effect when any outside investor accumulated 25 percent or more of the shares outstanding. Current stockholders, excluding the potential takeover company, were given the privilege of buying up to 500,000 new shares of ECS at 80 percent of current market value. Thus new shares would be restricted to friendly interests.

The attorney also found that Dr. Grossman and "friendly" members of the board of directors currently owned 175,000 shares of ECS.

   a.   How many more shares would Parker Medical Products need to purchase before the poison pill provision would go into effect? Given the current price of ECS stock of $42, what would be the cost to Parker to get up to that level?

   b.   ECS's ultimate fear was that Parker Medical Products would gain over a 50 percent interest in ECS's outstanding shares. What would be the additional cost to Parker to get 50 percent (plus 1 share) of the stock outstanding of ECS at the current market price of ECS stock? In answering this question, assume Parker had previously accumulated the 25 percent position discussed in question *a*.

   c.   Now assume that Parker exceeds the number of shares you computed in part *b* and gets all the way up to accumulating 625,000 shares of ECS. Under the poison pill provision, how many shares must "friendly" shareholders purchase to thwart a takeover attempt by Parker? What will be the total cost? Keep in mind that friendly interests already own 175,000 shares of ECS and to maintain control, they must own one more share than Parker.

   d.   Would you say the poison pill is an effective deterrent in this case? Is the poison pill in the best interest of the general stockholders (those not associated with the company)?

1. 3M (Minnesota Mining & Manufacturing Co.) was listed in Table 17-1 as one of the companies having a large percentage of institutional ownership. Institutional ownership represents stock held by nonindividuals such as pension funds, mutual funds, or bank trust departments. Let's learn more about the company.

    Go to 3M's website, www.3m.com, and follow these steps: Select "United States—English." On the home page click on "About Us" and select "Investor Relations." Click on "Stock Information" and select "Stock Quote and Chart."

2. Scroll down and write down the following:

    a. Recent price

    b. "52-week high"

    c. "52-week low"

    d. "52-week price percent change"

    e. "Volume"

3. Continue scrolling down the page to "Investment Calculator" and click on "Chart $10,000 invested in 3M." How much would your investment be worth if you reinvested dividends? Compare that to how much you would have if you did not reinvest your dividends.

4. Scroll down further and click on "Data Book."

    a. How has 3M's stock performed over the time given?

    b. What has happened to the P/E ratio and can you give a reason it has changed?

    c. How has the dividend grown over time? Would this have an impact on your observation in Question 3?

    d. What has happened to the annual earning per share?

    e. How has the dividend changed, and how might this be impacted by the growth in earnings per share?

Note: Occasionally a topic we have listed may have been deleted, updated, or moved into a different location on a website. If you click on the site map or site index, you will be introduced to a table of contents that should aid you in finding the topic you are looking for.

18

Dividend Policy and Retained Earnings

One of the best-performing companies in the stock market over the last several decades has been a cigarette company. No way, you say! Guess again. It goes by an alias, but don't be confused. Altria Group Inc. is the name for Philip Morris in the U.S. market, the producer of Marlboro, Benson & Hedges, Merit, Virginia Slims, and other tobacco products. Over 50 percent of the cigarettes sold in the United States are Philip Morris products. The name change was made so the company would not be confused with Philip Morris International that was spun off from Altria in March 2008. Owners of Altria received one share of Philip Morris International for every one share of Altria. Altria's ticker symbol remains MO, the old symbol for Philip Morris.

Altria is continually under attack by lawyers and state and federal regulators for selling a product that may cause cancer and heart disease. So separating the companies had the advantage of separating legal claims on only U.S. operations rather than on the whole company. Philip Morris International is expected to take advantage of international cigarette consumption without the liability of U.S. legal claims against it. For example, China, with over a billion people, accounts for over 25 percent of the world's cigarette consumption.

At one time, Altria also owned Kraft Foods and Miller Brewing, but in an attempt to increase its focus, it spun off Kraft as an independent company in March 2007, giving 0.68 shares of Kraft for every 1 share of Altria. Altria sold Miller to SAB Brewing in 2002 but kept a 28.5 percent stake in SAB. In December 2007, Altria acquired John Middleton Inc., a leading manufacturer of machine-made large cigars, for $2.9 billion. In January 2009, it acquired UST Inc. for $11.7 billion. UST is the largest U.S. manufacturer of smokeless tobacco products. To complicate matters, in October 2012 Kraft split into two companies: Kraft Food Group and Mendelez International Inc. To complicate matters even more, in October 2016, Anheuser-Busch InBev SA/NV acquired SABMiller. As a result, Phillip Morris U.S.A. received about 9.6 percent equity interest in the new, combined firm. It also used some of the $5.3 billion it received to buy another $1.6 billion in additional AB InBev shares to boost its stake to 10.2 percent.

If you owned 100 shares of Altria at the beginning of 2008, in addition to the Altria shares you would now have 100 shares of Philip Morris International, 22 shares of Kraft Foods Group, and 68 shares of Mendelez International. No wonder Altria has been such a solid performer in the stock market. Perhaps more important than the spin-offs has been its dividend policy. It is one of the highest dividend–paying stocks on the New York Stock Exchange. Altria's board of directors set a 75 percent payout ratio for the company once all the spin-offs had occurred. You may wonder how it can spend over $14 billion on acquisitions and still pay such high dividends relative to earnings. Altria is a company that would be called a "cash cow." It generates tons of cash with very few opportunities for reinvestment. According to Standard & Poor's, dividends for 2018 are estimated to be $2.64 per share out of estimated earnings per share of $3.97 (a 66 percent payout ratio). The stock price in February 2018 was $66.00 per share and so the dividend yield (dividend per share divided by the stock price) was exactly 4.0 percent. Of equal importance, the company has raised its dividend every year for the last 48 years with one exception. In the year of the international spin-off, the dividend for Altria went down but the dividend for the combined firms was up.

Of course, paying high dividends is not the right strategy for every company, particularly young, growth companies that need to retain funds to create growth. Read on to find out more.

The Marginal Principle of Retained Earnings

In theory, CEOs and board members concerned about dividends should ask, "How can the best use of the funds be made?" The rate of return that the corporation can achieve on retained earnings for the benefit of stockholders must be compared to what stockholders could earn if the funds were paid to them in dividends. This is known as the **marginal principle of retained earnings**. Each potential project to be financed by internally generated funds must provide a higher rate of return than the stockholder could achieve on other investments. We speak of this as the opportunity cost of using stockholder funds.

Life Cycle Growth and Dividends

One of the major influences on dividends is the corporate growth rate in sales and the subsequent return on assets. Figure 18-1 shows a corporate **life cycle** and the corresponding dividend policy that is most likely to be found at each stage. A small firm in the initial stages of development (Stage I) pays no dividends because it needs all its profits (if there are any) for reinvestment in new productive assets. If the firm is successful in the marketplace, the demand for its products will create growth in sales, earnings, and assets, and the firm will move into Stage II. At this stage, sales and returns on assets will be growing at an increasing rate, and earnings will still be reinvested. In the early part of Stage II, stock dividends (distribution of additional shares) may be instituted and, in the latter part of Stage II, low cash dividends may be started to inform investors that the firm is profitable but cash is also needed for internal investments.

After the growth period, the firm enters Stage III. The expansion of sales continues, but at a decreasing rate, and return on investment may decline as more competition enters the market and tries to take away the firm's market share. During this period, the firm is more and more capable of paying cash dividends, as the asset expansion rate slows

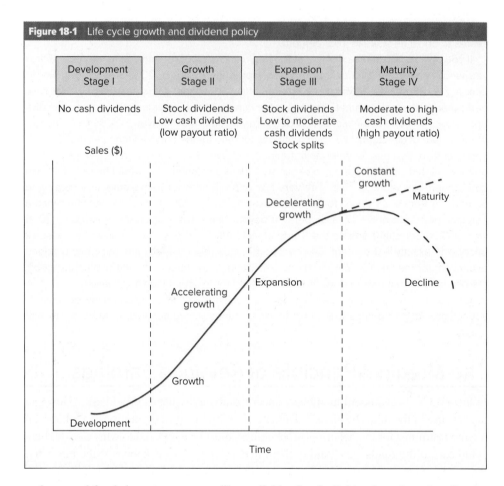

Figure 18-1 Life cycle growth and dividend policy

and external funds become more readily available. Stock dividends and stock splits are still common in the expansion phase, and the dividend payout ratio usually increases from a low level of 5 to 15 percent of earnings to a moderate level of 20 to 30 percent of earnings. Finally, at Stage IV, maturity, the firm maintains a stable growth rate in sales similar to that of the economy as a whole; and, when risk premiums are considered, its return on assets level out to those of the industry and the economy. In unfortunate cases, firms suffer declines in sales if product innovation and diversification have not occurred over the years. In Stage IV, assuming maturity rather than decline, dividends might range from 35 to 40 percent of earnings. These percentages will be different from industry to industry, depending on the individual characteristics of the company, such as operating and financial leverage and the volatility of sales and earnings over the business cycle.

As the chapter continues, more will be said about stock dividends, stock splits, the availability of external funds, and other variables that affect the dividend policy of the firm.

Dividends as a Passive Variable

In the preceding analysis, dividends were used as a passive decision variable: They are to be paid out only if the corporation cannot make better use of the funds for the benefit of stockholders. The active decision variable is retained earnings. Management decides how much retained earnings will be spent for internal corporate needs, and the residual (the amount left after internal expenditures) is paid to the stockholders in cash dividends.

An Incomplete Theory

The only problem with the **residual theory of dividends** is that we have not recognized how stockholders feel about receiving dividends. If the stockholders' only concern is achieving the highest return on their investment, either in the form of *corporate retained earnings remaining in the business or as current dividends paid out,* then there is no issue. But if stockholders have a preference for current funds, for example, over retained earnings, then our theory is incomplete. The issue is not only whether reinvestment of retained earnings or dividends provides the highest return, but also how stockholders react to the two alternatives.

While some researchers maintain that stockholders are indifferent to the division of funds between retained earnings and dividends, others disagree. Though there is no conclusive proof one way or the other, the judgment of most researchers is that investors have some preference between dividends and retained earnings.

Arguments for the Relevance of Dividends

A strong case can be made for the relevance of dividends because they resolve uncertainty in the minds of investors. Though retained earnings reinvested in the business theoretically belong to common stockholders, there is still an air of uncertainty about their eventual translation into dividends. Thus it can be hypothesized that stockholders might apply a higher discount rate (K_e) and assign a lower valuation to funds that are retained in the business as opposed to those that are paid out.

It is also argued that dividends may be viewed more favorably than retained earnings because of the **information content of dividends**. In essence, the corporation is telling the stockholder, "We are having a good year, and we wish to share the benefits with you." If the dividend per share is raised, then the information content of the dividend increase is quite positive while a reduction in the dividend generally has negative information content. Even though the corporation may be able to generate the same or higher returns with the funds than the stockholder and perhaps provide even greater dividends in the future, some researchers find that "in an uncertain world in which verbal statements can be ignored or misinterpreted, dividend action does provide a clear-cut means of making a statement that speaks louder than a thousand words."

The primary contention in arguing for the relevance of dividend policy is that stockholders' needs and preferences go beyond the marginal principle of retained earnings. The issue is not only who can best utilize the funds (the corporation or the stockholder) but also what are the stockholders' preferences. In practice, it appears that most corporations adhere to the following logic. First, investment opportunities relative to a required return (marginal analysis) are determined. This is then tempered by some subjective notion of stockholders' desires. Corporations with unusual growth prospects and high rates of return on internal investments generally pay a relatively low dividend (or no dividend). For the more mature firm, an analysis of both investment opportunities and stockholder preferences may indicate that a higher rate of payout is necessary. Examples of dividend policies of selected major U.S. corporations are presented in Table 18-1. Companies in the table are ranked from the highest expected growth rate to the lowest expected growth rate. Remember, it is future cash flows that determine stock values and not the past growth rates. Several of these companies are expected to grow faster than their previous five-year growth rate, and some are

Table 18-1   Corporate dividend policy

Name	Historical Growth in EPS Past 5 Years (2013–2017)	Estimated Growth in EPS Next 5 Years (2018–2022)	Dividend Payment as a Percentage of Aftertax Earnings (payout ratio) 2018	Dividend Yield 2018
Category 1–Rapid Growth				
Amazon–Online Services	−1.0%	60.0%	0.0%	0.0%
Cree Inc.–Semiconductor (LED)	0.0%	49.0%	0.0%	0.0%
Netflix, Inc.–Technology	−1.0%	44.5%	0.0%	0.0%
Facebook	N/A	31.5%	0.0%	0.0%
Finisar Corp.–Optical Subsystems	9.0%	28.0%	0.0%	0.0%
Alphabet/Google Inc.–Internet	13.5%	15.5%	0.0%	0.0%
VMWARE–Virtualization Software	33.0%	10.0%	0.0%	0.0%
Under Armour, Inc.–Apparel	23.0%	3.5%	0.0%	0.0%
Standard & Poor's 500	**9.4%**	**13.4%**	**43%**	**1.8%**
Category 2–Slow Growth				
Apple Inc.–Consumer Electronics	16.5%	14.5%	24%	1.6%
Pfizer Inc.–Pharmaceutical	2.0%	12.0%	68%	3.8%
American Eagle Outfitters–Apparel	2.5%	9.0%	35%	2.9%
Tiffany & Company–Jewelry	6.5%	8.0%	47%	2.0%
JPMorgan Chase–Banking	10.5%	8.0%	30%	2.0%
Intel Corp.–Technology	7.0%	7.5%	34%	2.3%
Southern Company–Utility	3.0%	3.5%	76%	4.6%
Gilead Sciences–Biotech	43.0%	−0.5%	33%	2.9%

Sources: Company data from various issues of Value Line Investment Survey;
Standard & Poor's data from the S&P website (accessed February 5, 2018).

expected to grow more slowly. Notice that the high-growth firms have a propensity to retain earnings rather than pay dividends, while the slow-growth firms have a rather large payout ratio. The normal payout has been approximately 35–40 percent of aftertax earnings. The Standard & Poor's 500 index is included as a reference point for the average of the 500 large companies in the index. Also notice that, besides the various payout ratios of the slower growth companies, the dividend yields are also included, which relates the stock price to the dividend's cash flow. In general the more slowly a company is expected to grow, the higher the dividend yield. Thinking back on Chapter 12, if a company doesn't have capital budgeting projects that add to the value of the firm, it is better to give the money to your stockholders and let them reinvest it.

Dividend Stability

In considering stockholder desires in dividend policy, a primary factor is the maintenance of stability in dividend payments. Thus corporate management must not only ask, "How many profitable investments do we have this year?" It must also ask, "What has been the pattern of dividend payments in the last few years?" Though earnings

Standard & Poor's identifies companies that have been able to raise their dividends over 25 consecutive years as *Dividend Aristocrats*. Companies qualify for this title on a worldwide basis and on a country basis. As of January 25, 2018, 53 U.S. companies earned the distinctive title. You are probably familiar with some of them. According to dripinvesting.org, at the beginning of 2018 there were 118 companies that met this 25-year dividend criteria. The table contains a list of the superstars.

Standard & Poor's states that "since 1926, dividends have contributed nearly a third of total equity return while capital gains have contributed two-thirds. The S&P 500 Dividend Aristocrats index captures sustainable dividend income and capital gain appreciation potential, which are both key factors in investors' total return expectations." *

From 2007 through 2017, the Dividend Aristocrats outperformed the S&P 500 Index over that period and returned an annualized total rate of return of 12.14 percent versus the S&P 500 total return of 8.50 percent. If you compounded that extra 3.64 percent over that 10-year period, $10,000 invested in the aristocrats would be worth $31,448, while the S&P 500 would be worth only $22,609. Perhaps that extra 3.64 percent is worth quite a bit more than meets the eye.

Companies that can join this elite club give their shareholders some confidence that their dividends won't be cut, will continue to increase, and just might outperform a market index made up of the S&P 500 stocks. If you compare the 54 aristocrats to the remaining 446 companies of the S&P 500, the difference in returns would be even more significant over this time period.

Company Name	Industry	Years
3M Co.	Industrials	60
Coca-Cola Co.	Consumer staples	55
Colgate-Palmolive	Consumer staples	54
Dover Corp.	Industrials	62
Emerson Electric	Industrials	61
Genuine Parts	Consumer discretionary	61
Johnson & Johnson	Health care	55
Lowe's	Consumer discretionary	55
Procter & Gamble	Consumer staples	61

Sources: S&P Dow Jones Indices, "Strategy: The S&P 500 Dividend Aristocrats," www.spdji.com; http://dripinvesting.org/Tools/Tools.htm.

may change from year to year, the dollar amount of cash dividends tends to be much more stable, increasing in value only as new permanent levels of income are achieved. Note in Figure 18-2 the considerably greater volatility of earnings per share compared to dividends per share for the 500 large U.S. corporations represented by the Standard & Poors 500 Index.

During the first 20 years depicted in Figure 18-2, dividends did not have any noticeable downturn until 2008 when the financial crisis began to appear. Starting in the first quarter of 2008, companies began to cut their dividends in response to expected profit declines.

Most of the decline in dividends was caused by financial companies that were caught in an avalanche of bad debts and billions of dollars of losses. Bank of America cut its dividend from $2.58 to $0.04. Citibank, JPMorgan, Wells Fargo, PNC Corp, Fannie Mae, Freddie Mac, and AIG cut their dividends. General Electric cut its dividend for the first time since 1938, and companies like Pfizer, CBS, and others also cut their dividends. In 2009 Standard & Poor's reported that corporations had cut their dividends by 21 percent, and that was down from cuts that were made in 2008.

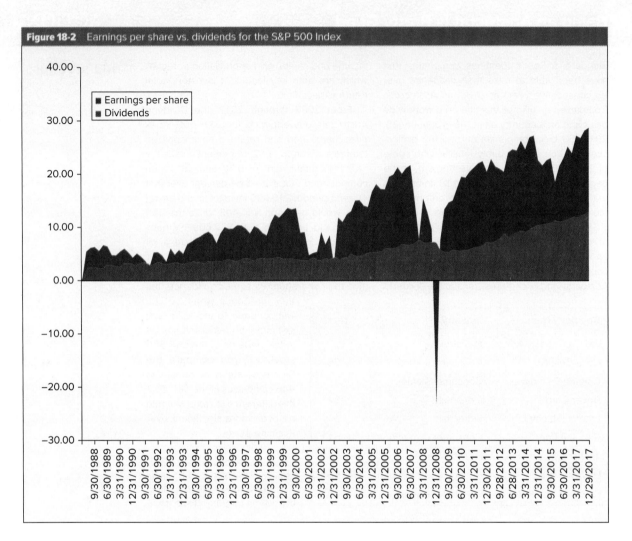

Figure 18-2   Earnings per share vs. dividends for the S&P 500 Index

This was the worst percentage decline in dividends since 1938. Figure 18-2 shows that by the end of 2009, profits started to recover and dividend cuts seemed to have stopped. After reporting improved earnings in 2010, corporations began to increase their dividends, and by 2013 dividends had passed their previous peak.

Dividends continued their upward trend into 2018, which was expected to set new records after the tax cuts of 2017 gave companies smaller taxes and more money to distribute to stockholders. An interesting fact is that even though quarterly earnings fluctuated and dividends had a series of declines, on average the payout ratio during this 30-year time period averaged 44 percent. In the 10 years between 1997 and 2007 the payout ratio averaged 43 percent. The 2007-to-2017 period averaged 38.4 percent due to the effects of the financial crisis, but during the years 2014 to 2017 the average was back to 45 percent.

By maintaining a record of relatively stable dividends, corporate management hopes to lower the discount rate (K_e) applied to future dividends of the firm, thus raising the value of the firm. The operative rule appears to be that a stockholder would much prefer to receive $1 a year for three years, rather than 75 cents for the first year,

$1.50 for the second year, and 75 cents for the third year—for the same total of $3. Once again, we temper our policy of marginal analysis of retained earnings to include a notion of stockholder preference, with the emphasis on stability of dividends.

Other Factors Influencing Dividend Policy

Corporate management must also consider the legal basis of dividends, the cash flow position of the firm, and the corporation's access to capital markets. Other factors that must be considered include management's desire for control and the tax and financial positions of shareholders. Each is briefly discussed.

Legal Rules

Most states forbid firms to pay dividends that would impair the initial capital contributions to the firm. For this reason, dividends may be distributed only from past and current earnings. To pay dividends in excess of this amount would mean the corporation is returning to investors their original capital contribution (raiding the capital). If the ABC Company has the following statement of net worth, the maximum dividend payment would be $20 million.

Common stock (1 million shares at $10 par value)*	$ 10,000,000
Retained earnings	20,000,000
Net worth	$30,000,000

*If there is a "paid-in capital in excess of par" account, some states will allow additional dividend payments while others will not. To simplify the problem for now, paid-in capital in excess of par is not considered.

Why all the concern about impairing permanent capital? Since the firm is going to pay dividends only to those who contributed capital in the first place, what is the problem? Clearly there is no abuse to the stockholders, but what about the creditors? They have extended credit on the assumption that a given capital base would remain intact throughout the life of the loan. While they may not object to the payment of dividends from past and current earnings, they must have the protection of keeping contributed capital in place.[1]

Even the laws against having dividends exceed the total of past and current earnings (retained earnings) may be inadequate to protect creditors. Because retained earnings are merely an accounting concept and in no way certify the current liquidity of the firm, a company paying dividends equal to retained earnings may, in certain cases, jeopardize the operation of the firm. Let us examine Table 18-2.

Theoretically, management could pay up to $15,000,000 in dividends by selling assets even though current earnings are only $1,500,000. In most cases, such frivolous action would not be taken; but the mere possibility encourages creditors to closely watch the balance sheets of corporate debtors and, at times, to impose additional limits on dividend payments as a condition for the granting of credit.

---

[1]Of course, on liquidation of the corporation, the contributed capital to the firm may be returned to common stockholders after creditor obligations are met. Normally stockholders who need to recoup all or part of their contributed capital sell their shares to someone else.

Table 18-2 Dividend policy considerations			
Cash	$ 500,000	Debt	$10,000,000
Accounts receivable	4,500,000	Common stock	10,000,000
Inventory	15,000,000	Retained earnings	15,000,000
Plant and equipment	15,000,000		$35,000,000
	$35,000,000		
		Current earnings	$ 1,500,000
		Potential dividends	$15,000,000

Cash Position of the Firm

Not only do retained earnings fail to portray the liquidity position of the firm, but there are also limitations to the use of current earnings as an indicator of liquidity. As described in Chapter 4, "Financial Forecasting," a growth firm producing the greatest gains in earnings may be in the poorest cash position. As sales and earnings expand rapidly, there is an accompanying buildup in receivables and inventory that may far outstrip cash flow generated through earnings. Note that the cash balance of $500,000 in Table 18-2 represents only one-third of the current earnings of $1,500,000. A firm must do a complete funds flow analysis before establishing a dividend policy.

Access to Capital Markets

The medium-to-large-size firm with a good record of performance may have relatively easy access to the financial markets. A company in such a position may be willing to pay dividends now, knowing it can sell new common stock or bonds in the future if funds are needed. Some corporations may even issue debt or stock now and use part of the proceeds to ensure the maintenance of current dividends. Though this policy seems at variance with the concept of a dividend as a reward, management may justify its action on the basis of maintaining stable dividends. In the era of the late 1990s and 2000s, only a relatively small percentage of firms had sufficient ease of entry to the capital markets to modify their dividend policy in this regard.

Desire for Control

Management must also consider the effect of the dividend policy on its collective ability to maintain control. The directors and officers of a small, closely held firm may be hesitant to pay any dividends for fear of diluting the cash position of the firm.

A larger firm, with a broad base of shareholders, may face a different type of threat in regard to dividend policy. Stockholders, spoiled by a past record of dividend payments, may demand the ouster of management if dividends are withheld.

Tax Position of Shareholders

You might think that a corporation paying a dividend would not worry about the tax consequences of dividends to their stockholders. When taxes on qualified dividends are higher than taxes on capital gains, companies have a higher propensity to repurchase their stock than raise their dividend. A stock repurchase theoretically pushes up the price of the stock and creates gains for stockholders who can then sell enough stock to receive the same amount of money as they would have received as a dividend but at a lower tax rate. This assumes the capital gain is long term. Investors in high tax brackets have a preference for stocks that have the potential to generate capital gains rather than dividends when the tax rate on dividends is higher than the tax rate on long-term capital gains.

Table 18-3 provides the tax rates in effect under the Tax Cuts and Jobs Act of 2017. However, investors do not have all of their income taxed at these rates. A large percentage of common stock in the United States is held in tax-deferred retirement funds by individuals, and dividends are allowed to be reinvested tax-free. Of course, when a person retires and starts taking money out of these accounts, then the taxes are due.

To help fund the Affordable Care Act, Congress created the **net investment income tax,** which taxes investment income above a certain amount at an extra 3.8 percent. This extra tax becomes effective for single taxpayers with modified adjusted gross income of more than $200,000 and for taxpayers filing jointly with

Table 18-3   Tax Cuts and Jobs Act of 2017 (2018 tax rates)

SECTION ONE	TAX ON LONG-TERM CAPITAL GAINS AND QUALIFIED DIVIDENDS	
Single	**Income** **Married/Filing Jointly** **and Qualifying Widow(er)s**	**Tax Rate**
$0–$38,600	$0–$77,200	0%
$38,601–$425,800	$77,201–$479,000	15%
Over $425,800	Over $479,000	20%

Additional 3.8% federal net investment income (NII) tax applies to individuals on the lesser of NII or modified AGI in excess of $200,000 (single) or $250,000 [married/filing jointly and qualifying widow(er)s].

SECTION TWO	2018 INCOME TAX RATES			
	If Taxable **Income Is Over**	**but Not** **Over**	**The Tax Is**	**Of the** **Amount Over**
Married/filing jointly and **qualifying widow(er)s**	$ 0	$ 19,050	$ 0 + 10%	$ 0
	$ 19,050	$ 77,400	$ 1,905 + 12%	$ 19,050
	$ 77,400	$165,000	$ 8,907 + 22%	$ 77,400
	$165,000	$315,000	$ 28,179 + 24%	$165,000
	$315,000	$400,000	$ 64,179 + 32%	$315,000
	$400,000	$600,000	$ 91,379 + 35%	$400,000
	$600,000	–	$ 161379 + 37%	$600,000
Single	$ 0	$ 9,525	$ 0.00 + 10%	$ 0
	$ 9,525	$ 38,700	$ 9,525.50 + 12%	$ 9,525
	$ 38,700	$ 82,500	$ 4,543.50 + 22%	$ 38,700
	$ 82,500	$157,500	$ 14,089.5 + 24%	$ 82,500
	$157,500	$200,000	$32,089.50 + 32%	$157,500
	$200,000	$500,000	$45,689.50 + 35%	$200,000
	$500,000	–	$ 150,689 + 37%	$500,000

Since short-term capital gains and ordinary dividends are considered ordinary income, they are taxed at the rates given in Section Two of Table 18-3.

more than $250,000. Despite President Trump's desire to eliminate the Affordable Care Act, Congress left this provision in the new tax law and it is still in effect unless changed in a subsequent tax law or adjustment. This is yet one more reason why investors should hold dividend-paying stocks in tax-free retirement accounts.

Prior to the Jobs and Growth Tax Relief Act of 2003, dividends were taxed at a maximum rate of 39.6 percent and capital gains at a maximum rate of 20 percent. With the passage of the 2003 Tax Act (Bush tax cuts), dividends and capital gains were taxed at a maximum rate of 15 percent. In a deal between the Republican House of Representatives, the Democratic Senate, and President Obama, the American Taxpayer Relief Act of 2013 was enacted. The new tax rates left most of the Bush era tax cuts in place but raised the rates on very high-income taxpayers to 20 percent. The Tax Cuts and Jobs Act of 2017 left the rates on dividends and long-term capital gains the same but increased the amount of income needed before the tax became effective.

Notice that Table 18-3 distinguishes between **ordinary dividends** and **qualified dividends**. The qualified dividend is a subset of an ordinary dividend and is taxed at a lower rate. The Internal Revenue Service (IRS) assumes all corporate dividends are ordinary income and not capital gains; but given certain conditions, an investor can pay a lower tax rate on qualified dividends. These rates for qualified dividends are given in section one of Table 18-3. While a corporation can't refine its dividend policy to such a micro level, it is interesting to see the benefits of being a long-term investor. In order to benefit from the lower tax rate on dividends, the investor must hold the stock for at least 121 days and for more than 60 days before the stock goes ex-dividend. The dividend must also be paid by a U.S. corporation or qualified foreign corporation. Your brokerage house will report both types of dividends on your annual tax statement. For now, it is important only to notice the difference in the two tax rates and to understand that there is a benefit to being a long-term stockholder rather than a trader.

Table 18-3 also includes the rates for capital gains and dividends so you can compare tax rates between them. It should be pointed out that only long-term capital gains (assets held over a year) are taxed at the maximum rate of 15 to 20 percent depending on your taxable income. Short-term capital gains and ordinary dividends are taxed at the taxpayer's normal rate given in Table 18-3 section two. For our purposes in this discussion and in the problems at the end of the chapter, we shall assume capital gains are long term. Those in the lowest tax brackets are now taxed at zero percent on both types of income.

Dividend Payment Procedures

Given that we have examined the many factors that influence dividend policy, let us track the actual procedures for announcing and paying a dividend. Though dividends are quoted on an annual basis, the payments actually take place over four quarters during the year. For example, in 2015 Intel paid an annual cash dividend of $0.96, $1.04 in 2016, and $1.08 in 2017. Its new dividend rate for 2018 was $0.30 per quarter or $1.20 per year. If we divide the annual dividend per share by the current stock price, the result is called the **dividend yield**, which is the percentage return provided by the cash dividend based on the current market price. Because Intel's stock was selling at $52.78 per share in May 2018, the expected dividend yield at the time was 2.27 percent ($1.20/$52.78). This is a slightly higher dividend yield compared to the

2 percent paid by the S&P 500 Index. Also because Intel had expected earnings per share of $3.85 for 2018, the **dividend payout ratio** was 31.1 percent ($1.20/$3.85). It should be pointed out that the expected cash flow per share is more than $4.00 for 2018, and so Intel has plenty of cash to meet its dividend payment.

Three key dates are associated with the declaration of a quarterly dividend: the ex-dividend date, the holder-of-record date, and the payment date.

We begin with the **holder-of-record date**. On this date, the firm examines its books to determine who is entitled to a cash dividend. To have your name included on the corporate books, you must have bought or owned the stock before the **ex-dividend date**, which is two business days before the holder-of-record date. If you bought the stock on the ex-dividend date or later, your name will eventually be transferred to the corporate books, but you bought the stock without the current quarterly dividend privilege. Thus we say you bought the stock ex-dividend.[2] As an example, a stock with a holder-of-record date of March 4 will go ex-dividend on March 2. You must buy the stock by March 1 (three days before the holder-of-record date and a day before the ex-dividend date) to get the dividend. Investors are very conscious of the date on which the stock goes ex-dividend, and the value of the stock will go down by the value of the quarterly dividend on the ex-dividend date (all other things being equal). Finally, in our example, we might assume the **dividend payment date** is April 1 and checks will go out to entitled stockholders on or about this time.

Stock Dividend

A **stock dividend** represents a distribution of additional shares to common stockholders. The typical size of such dividends is in the 10 percent range, so a stockholder with 10 shares might receive 1 new share in the form of a stock dividend. Larger distributions of 20 to 25 percent or more are usually considered to have the characteristics of a stock split, a topic to be discussed later in the chapter.

Accounting Considerations for a Stock Dividend

Assume that before the declaration of a stock dividend, the XYZ Corporation has the net worth position indicated in Table 18-4.

Table 18-4 XYZ Corporation's financial position before stock dividend		
Capital accounts	Common stock (1,000,000 shares at $10 par)	$10,000,000
	Capital in excess of par	5,000,000
	Retained earnings	15,000,000
	Net worth	$30,000,000

If a 10 percent stock dividend is declared, shares outstanding will increase by 100,000 (10 percent times 1 million shares). An accounting transfer will occur between retained earnings and the two capital stock accounts based on the market value of the

---

[2]In this case, the old stockholder will receive the dividend.

Table 18-5 XYZ Corporation's financial position before stock dividend		
Capital accounts	Common stock (1,100,000 shares at $10 par)	$11,000,000
	Capital in excess of par	5,500,000
	Retained earnings	13,500,000
	Net worth	$30,000,000

stock dividend. If the stock is selling at $15 a share, we will assign $1 million to common stock (100,000 shares times $10 par) and $500,000 to capital in excess of par. The latter value is based on 100,000 new shares times ($15 − $10), or $5. In the calculation in parentheses, we subtracted par value from market value. The net worth position of XYZ after the transfer is shown in Table 18-5.

Value to the Investor

An appropriate question might be: Is a stock dividend of real value to the investor? Suppose your finance class collectively purchased $1,000 worth of assets and issued 10 shares of stock to each class member. Three days later it is announced that each stockholder will receive an extra share. Has anyone benefited from the stock dividend? Of course not! The asset base remains the same ($1,000), and your proportionate ownership in the business is unchanged (everyone got the same new share). You merely have more paper to tell you what you already knew.

The same logic is essentially true in the corporate setting. In the case of the XYZ Corporation, shown in Tables 18-4 and 18-5 above, we assumed 1 million shares were outstanding before the stock dividend and 1.1 million shares afterward. Now let us assume the corporation had aftertax earnings of $6.6 million. Without the stock dividend, earnings per share would be $6.60, and with the stock dividend $6.00.

$$\text{Earnings per share} = \frac{\text{Earnings after taxes}}{\text{Shares outstanding}}$$

Without stock dividend:

$$= \frac{\$6.6 \text{ million}}{1 \text{ million shares}} = \$6.60$$

With stock dividend:

$$= \frac{\$6.6 \text{ million}}{1.1 \text{ million shares}} = \$6.00$$
$$(10\% \text{ decline})$$

Earnings per share have gone down by exactly the same percentage that shares outstanding increased. For further illustration, assuming that stockholder A had 10 shares before the stock dividend and 11 afterward, what are his or her total claims to earnings? As expected, they remain the same, at $66.

$$\text{Claim to earnings} = \text{Shares} \times \text{Earnings per share}$$

Without stock dividend: $10 \times \$6.60 = \$66$

With stock dividend: $11 \times \$6.00 = \$66$

Taking the analogy one step further, assuming the stock sold at 20 times earnings before and after the stock dividend, what is the total market value of the portfolio in each case?

Total market value = Shares × (Price-earnings ratio × Earnings per share)

Without stock dividend:

$$10 \times (20 \times \$6.60)$$
$$10 \times \$132 = \$1,320$$

With stock dividend:

$$11 \times (20 \times \$6.00)$$
$$11 \times \$120 = \$1,320$$

The total market value is unchanged. Note that if the stockholder sells the 11th share to acquire cash, his or her stock portfolio will be worth $120 less than it was before the stock dividend.

Possible Value of Stock Dividends

There are limited circumstances under which a stock dividend may be more than a financial sleight of hand. If, at the time a stock dividend is declared, the cash dividend per share remains constant, the stockholder will receive greater total cash dividends. Assume the annual cash dividend for the XYZ Corporation will remain $1 per share even though earnings per share decline from $6.60 to $6.00. In this instance, a stockholder going from 10 to 11 shares as the result of a stock dividend has a $1 increase in total dividends. The overall value of his total shares may then increase in response to larger dividends.

Use of Stock Dividends

Stock dividends are frequently used by growth companies as a form of "informational content" in explaining the retention of funds for reinvestment purposes. This was indicated in the discussion of the life cycle of the firm earlier in the chapter. A corporation president may state, "Instead of doing more in the way of cash dividends, we are providing a stock dividend. The funds remaining in the corporation will be used for highly profitable investment opportunities." The market reaction to such an approach may be neutral or somewhat positive.

Another use of stock dividends may be to camouflage the inability of the corporation to pay cash dividends and to cover up the ineffectiveness of management in generating cash flow. The president may proclaim, "Though we are unable to pay cash dividends, we wish to reward you with a 15 percent stock dividend." Well-informed investors are likely to react negatively.

Stock Splits

A **stock split** is similar to a stock dividend, only more shares are distributed. For example, a two-for-one stock split would double the number of shares outstanding. In general, the rules of the New York Stock Exchange and the Financial Accounting Standards Board encourage distributions in excess of 20 to 25 percent to be handled as stock splits.

The accounting treatment for a stock split is somewhat different from that for a stock dividend, in that there is no transfer of funds from retained earnings to the capital accounts but merely a reduction in par value and a proportionate increase in the number of shares outstanding. For example, a two-for-one stock split for the XYZ Corporation would necessitate the accounting adjustments shown in Table 18-6.

Table 18-6   XYZ Corporation before and after stock split

Before	
Common stock (1 million shares at $10 par)	$10,000,000
Capital in excess of par	5,000,000
Retained earnings	15,000,000
	$30,000,000
After	
Common stock (2 million shares at $5 par)	$10,000,000
Capital in excess of par	5,000,000
Retained earnings	15,000,000
	$30,000,000

In this case, all adjustments are in the common stock account. Because the number of shares is doubled and the par value halved, the market price of the stock should drop proportionately. There has been much discussion in the financial literature about the impact of a split on overall stock value. While there might be some positive benefit, that benefit is difficult to capture after the split has been announced. Perhaps, after a two-for-one split, a $66 stock will only drop to $34 or $35, instead of $33, if the market perceives the split as good news.

The primary purpose of a stock split is to lower the price of a security into a more popular trading range. A stock selling for over $100 per share may be excluded from consideration by many small investors. Splits are also popular because only stronger companies that have witnessed substantial growth in market price are in a position to participate in them.

Reverse Stock Splits

In the bear market of the early 2000s and again after the market meltdown in 2009 when the Dow Jones closed under 7,000, the **reverse stock split** became popular. In this case, a firm exchanges fewer shares for existing shares with the intent of increasing the stock price. An example might be a one-for-four reverse stock split in which you would get one new share in place of four old shares. A stockholder who held 100 shares would now own 25. With total earnings unaffected by the reverse stock split, earnings per share should increase fourfold because there would be only one-fourth as many shares outstanding.

It is also hoped that the stock price will increase fourfold. Perhaps you originally had 100 shares at $2 per share and now you have 25 shares at $8. The stock price does not always increase by a commensurate amount. Keep in mind that a reverse stock split is normally used by firms whose stock has plummeted in value. The announcement of a reverse stock split may represent further evidence that the firm is having problems.

One useful purpose of a reverse stock split is to attempt to place a stock's value at a level that is acceptable to the New York Stock Exchange or the NASDAQ for trading purposes. Both exchanges will delist a stock if its value remains under $1 for an extended period of time (such as six months).

As an example, Lucent Technologies was in danger of being delisted from the New York Stock Exchange in late 2002 because its stock had been in a $0.40–0.70 range for a number of months. After a 3-for-1 reverse stock split, the stock's price settled in at $1.50. At least for a while, Lucent was out of danger of being delisted. Eventually Lucent merged with the French telecom equipment company, Alcatel. It is now Alcatel-Lucent and is listed on the NYSE under the ticker symbol ALU.

During the financial crisis of 2007–2009, more and more firms were forced to use reverse splits to maintain their share price and listing on the exchanges. For example, AIG enacted a 1-for-20 reverse split July 1, 2009.

Repurchase of Stock as an Alternative to Dividends

A firm with excess cash may choose to make a **corporate stock repurchase** of its own shares in the market, rather than pay a cash dividend. For this reason, the stock repurchase decision may be thought of as an alternative to the payment of cash dividends.

The benefits to the stockholder are equal under either alternative, at least in theory. For purposes of our study, the Morgan Corporation's financial position is described by the data in Table 18-7.

Table 18-7 Financial data of Morgan Corporation	
Earnings after taxes	$3,000,000
Shares	1,000,000
Earnings per share	$3
Price-earnings ratio	10
Market price per share	$30
Excess cash	$2,000,000

Assume the firm is considering a repurchase of its own shares in the market. The firm has $2 million in excess cash, and it wishes to compare the value to stockholders of a $2 cash dividend (on the million shares outstanding) as opposed to spending the funds to repurchase shares in the market. If the cash dividend is paid, the shareholder will have $30 in stock and the $2 cash dividend. On the other hand, the $2 million may be used to repurchase shares at slightly over market value (to induce sale).[3] The overall benefit to stockholders is that earnings per share will go up as the number of shares outstanding is decreased. If the price-earnings ratio of the stock remains constant, then the price of the stock should also go up. If a purchase price of $32 is used to induce sale, then 62,500 shares will be purchased.

$$\frac{\text{Excess funds}}{\text{Purchase price per share}} = \frac{\$2,000,000}{\$32} = 62,500 \text{ shares}$$

---

[3]To derive the desired equality between the two alternatives, the purchase price for the new shares should equal the current market price plus the proposed cash dividend under the first alternative ($30 + $2 = $32).

IBM Repurchases Common Stock Worth Billions of Dollars

Since 1995, IBM has bought back over $100 billion of its own common stock. In May 2007, IBM borrowed $11.5 billion to buy back $12.5 billion of the stock. It used $1 billion cash and borrowed the rest through an international subsidiary. Using this subsidiary allowed IBM to use cash that was generated overseas. If IBM had repatriated the earnings from overseas to the United States, it would have been subject to income taxes on repatriated earnings, but the maneuver allowed the firm to use the money and avoid taxes. In February 2008, the board of directors authorized another $15 billion for the company's stock repurchase program, and again in October 2009, IBM added another $5 billion to the repurchase program. In total, for the years 2007 through 2011, IBM repurchased $50 billion of its common stock. In 2014 it completed $19.5 billion in stock repurchases.

There are many reasons why companies repurchase their own stock. First, they usually have large free cash flows and no earth-shattering new capital budgeting projects or acquisitions to make. If they raise the dividend, stockholders will expect the dividend to remain stable or rise. By repurchasing common stock,

they create no expectation that this process will continue indefinitely. In the case of IBM, an investor might expect this repurchase program to continue from year to year, but it would not be possible to predict a dollar amount. In 1994, IBM had 2.350 billion shares outstanding, but by the end of 2014 the company had only 985 million shares outstanding. There hasn't been a year since 1996 when IBM has not repurchased common stock. As you can imagine, this has helped increase IBM's earnings per share because fewer shares will increase earnings per share.

Between 2004 and 2014, IBM's earnings per share has grown at an annual rate of 13.0 percent. During this time, revenues have grown only 6.5 percent per year. One negative consequence of large stock repurchases like IBM's buybacks is that the book value shrinks as equity is taken off the balance sheet. In the case of IBM, the book value per share grew only 2.5 percent per year over the last 10 years, even as stockholders' equity declined from $29.7 billion to $24.0 billion. In addition, the debt-to-equity ratio rose from 49.8 percent to 137.5 percent. This is a game that will eventually have to end, even for venerable IBM.

Total shares outstanding are reduced to 937,500 (1,000,000 − 62,500). Revised earnings per share for the Morgan Corporation become:

$$\frac{\text{Earnings after taxes}}{\text{Shares}} = \frac{\$3,000,000}{937,500} = \$3.20$$

Since the price-earnings ratio for the stock is 10, the market value of the stock should go to $32. Thus we see that the consequences of the two alternatives are presumed to be the same as shown in the following:

(1) Funds Used for Cash Dividend		(2) Funds Used to Repurchase Stock	
Market value per share	$30		
Cash dividend per share	2		
	$32	Market value per share	$32

In either instance, the total value is $32. Theoretically, the stockholder would be indifferent with respect to the two alternatives as long as the tax rate on dividends and capital gains are equal.[4]

---

[4]Some would argue that the capital gains tax can be completely avoided. If you hold the stock until you die, there is no capital gains tax on your estate. An estate tax will have to be paid on property valued over $2 million, but that is different from a capital gains tax. (The $2 million exemption will increase over time.)

Other Reasons for Repurchase

In addition to using the repurchase decision as an alternative to cash dividends, corporate management may acquire its own shares in the market because it believes they are selling at a low price. A corporation president who sees his firm's stock decline by 25 to 30 percent over a six-month period may determine the stock is undervalued and the best investment available to the corporation. Research shows that firms that repurchase their shares exhibit positive stock price returns. The repurchase announcement is known as the signaling hypothesis for open-market stock repurchases.

By repurchasing shares, the corporation can maintain a constant demand for its own securities and perhaps stave off further decline. Stock repurchases by corporations were partially credited with stabilizing the stock market after the 508-point crash on October 19, 1987.

In Table 18-8, we see some recent stock repurchases announced and completed by major U.S. corporations. In many cases, companies may take years to complete stock repurchases, and they may time the repurchase depending on stock price behavior.

The year 2018 is expected to be a bonus year for stock buybacks. The 2017 tax act reduced the corporate tax rate to 21 percent and instituted a territorial tax system that taxes income in the country where the income is generated. This puts U.S. companies on equal footing with foreign competitors. Companies were sitting on several *trillion* dollars in overseas accounts, not wanting to bring the money home and pay a tax. The new tax law

Table 18-8   Billion-dollar stock repurchases

Companies Announcing Stock Buybacks in December 2017	$ (billions)
Boeing (NYSE:BA)	$ 18.00
Home Depot (NYSE: HD)	15.00
Oracle Corp. (NYSE: ORCL)	12.00
Merck Co. (NYSE: MRK)	10.00
Honeywell International Inc. (NYSE: HON)	8.00
Anthem Inc. (NYSE: ANTM)	7.30
Bank of America (NYSE: BAC)	5.00
MasterCard Inc. (NYSE: MA)	4.00
Baker Hughes (NYSE: BHGE)	3.00
Humana Inc. (NYSE: HUM)	3.00
United Continental Holdings Inc. (NYSE: UAL)	3.00
PPG Industries Inc. (NYSE: PPG)	2.50
American Tower Corp. (NYSE: AMT)	2.00
Kellogg Co. (NYSE: K)	1.50
Prudential Financial Inc. (NYSE: PRU)	1.50
T-Mobile US Inc. (NASDAQ: TMUS)	1.50
Waste Management Inc. (NYSE: WM)	1.25
Dover Corp. (NYSE: DOV)	1.00
Edwards Lifesciences Corp. (NYSE: EW)	1.00
DaVita Inc. (NYSE: DVA)	1.00
Total Buybacks Planned in Billions of $	**$101.55**

Source: www.marketwatch.com/story/20-fresh-stock-buybacks-could-send-100-billion-back-to-shareholders-2017-12-16 (accessed February 9, 2018).

has motivated companies to bring money home at low tax rates, and it is expected that many companies will use this cash hoard to buy back stock. In fact, Table 18-8 shows only companies that announced buybacks once they realized the new tax law would be passed.

For example, the $10 billion announcement by Merck will take place over five years unless the board decides to accelerate the buyback plan. That could happen if profits soar beyond expectations based on new drugs.

Apple Inc. bought back $23 billion of stock in 2013 and another $45 billion in 2014, setting records for one year. Tim Cook and the board of directors started the buyback process in 2012 under pressure from Carl Icahn, an activist investor who complained that Apple was sitting on too much cash and not doing anything productive with it. Cash is a low-return asset and penalizes the return on assets and return on equity. The Apple board agreed to the strategy and since has been an active buyer of its own shares, even selling bonds to finance some of the purchases. With Apple now sitting on $265 billion of cash that it can bring back to the United States it announced at its annual meeting in May that it would repurchase $100 billion of stock and raise its 2018 dividend by 16 percent.

Reacquired shares may also be used for employee stock options or as part of a tender offer in a merger. A firm that has too much cash on its balance sheet may also reacquire part of its shares as a protective device against being taken over as a merger candidate.

One overlooked advantage of stock repurchases is that total dividend payments are reduced as stock is retired. The company can then use this cash savings to increase the dividends on the remaining shares. This allows dividends to grow faster than they would have. For example, IBM's dividends grew at a rate of 17.5 percent from 2002 to 2013 while earnings per share grew at 10.5 percent. Some of the difference can be accounted for by a rising payout ratio, but some of the extra growth can be traced to spreading the total dividends over fewer shares due to the stock repurchases.

Stock buybacks seem to be a strategy that will continue whether supported by financial theory or not.

Dividend Reinvestment Plans

Years ago, many companies started **dividend reinvestment plans** for their shareholders. These plans take various forms, but basically they provide the investor with an opportunity to buy additional shares of stock with the cash dividend paid by the company. Some plans will sell treasury stock or authorized but unissued shares to the stockholders. With this type of plan, the company is the beneficiary of increased cash flow, since dividends paid are returned to the company for reinvestment in common stock. These types of plans have been very popular with cash-short public utilities, and often public utilities will allow shareholders a 5 percent discount from market value at the time of purchase. This is justified because no investment banking or underwriting fees need be paid.

Under a second popular dividend reinvestment plan, the company's transfer agent, usually a bank, buys shares of stock in the market for the stockholder with the dividend. This plan provides no cash flow for the company; but it is a service to the shareholder, who benefits from much lower transaction costs, the right to own fractional shares, and more flexibility in choosing between cash and common stock. Usually a shareholder can also add cash payments of between $500 and $1,000 per month to his or her dividend payments in order to buy stock and receive the same lower transaction costs.

SUMMARY

In choosing either to pay a dividend to stockholders or to reinvest the funds in the company, management's first consideration is whether the firm will be able to earn a higher return for the stockholders. However, we must temper this "highest return theory" with a consideration of stockholder preferences and the firm's need for earnings retention and growth as presented in the life cycle growth curve.

Dividends provide information content to shareholders. An increase in the dividend is generally interpreted as a positive signal while dividend cuts are negative, and shareholders generally prefer dividend stability. The dividend payout ratio (dividends/earnings) often signals where a firm is in its life cycle stage. During the initial stages, dividends will be small or nonexistent, while in the later stages, dividends normally increase.

Other factors influencing dividend policy are legal rules relating to maximum payments, the cash position of the firm, the firm's access to capital markets, and management's desire for control.

An alternative (or a supplement) to cash dividends may be the use of stock dividends and stock splits. While neither of these financing devices directly changes the intrinsic value of the stockholders' position, they may provide communication to stockholders and bring the stock price into a more acceptable trading range. A stock dividend may take on actual value when total cash dividends are allowed to increase. Nevertheless, the alert investor will watch for abuses of stock dividends—situations in which the corporation indicates that something of great value is occurring when, in fact, the new shares that are created merely represent the same proportionate interest for each shareholder.

Repurchase of a firm's own shares increases a firm's earnings per share and may provide a positive signal to shareholders.

LIST OF TERMS

marginal principle of retained
   earnings   573
life cycle   573
residual theory of dividends   575
information content of dividends   575
net investment income tax   581
ordinary dividend   582
qualified dividend   582
dividend yield   582

dividend payout ratio   583
holder-of-record date   583
ex-dividend date   583
dividend payment date   583
stock dividend   583
stock split   585
reverse stock split   586
corporate stock repurchase   587
dividend reinvestment plans   590

DISCUSSION QUESTIONS

1. How does the marginal principle of retained earnings relate to the returns that a stockholder may make in other investments? *(LO18-1)*

2. Discuss the difference between a passive and an active dividend policy. *(LO18-1)*

3. How does the stockholder, in general, feel about the relevance of dividends? *(LO18-1)*

4. Explain the relationship between a company's growth possibilities and its dividend policy. *(LO18-2)*

5. Since initial contributed capital theoretically belongs to the stockholders, why are there legal restrictions on paying out the funds to the stockholders? *(LO18-3)*

6. Discuss how desire for control may influence a firm's willingness to pay dividends. *(LO18-3)*

7. If you buy stock on the ex-dividend date, will you receive the upcoming quarterly dividend? *(LO18-1)*

8. How is a stock split (versus a stock dividend) treated on the financial statements of a corporation? *(LO18-4)*

9. Why might a stock dividend or a stock split be of limited value to an investor? *(LO18-4)*

10. Does it make sense for a corporation to repurchase its own stock? Explain. *(LO18-5)*

11. What advantages to the corporation and the stockholder do dividend reinvestment plans offer? *(LO18-1)*

PRACTICE PROBLEMS AND SOLUTIONS

Stock dividend
(LO18-4)

1. United Equipment Corp. shows the following capital accounts before a 10 percent stock dividend:

Common stock (200,000 shares at $5 par)	$1,000,000
Capital in excess of par	600,000
Retained earnings	2,400,000
Net worth	$4,000,000

The firm's shares have a market price of $20. Show the revised capital accounts after the 10 percent stock dividend.

Effect of stock dividend on the stockholders
(LO18-4)

2. *a.* Assume United Equipment Corp. in the prior problem had total earnings of $400,000 before the stock dividend. It also had a P/E ratio of 10. What were the EPS and stock price before the stock dividend?

   b. After the stock dividend, what will earnings per share and the stock price be? Assume the P/E ratio stays at 10.

   c. Albert Gonzales owned 100 shares before and 110 after the stock dividend. What is the value of his portfolio (total holdings) before and after the stock dividend? Is he any better off as a result of the stock dividend?

Solutions

1. Revised capital accounts after the 10 percent stock dividend:

Common stock (220,000 shares at $5 par)*	$1,100,000
Capital in excess of par†	900,000
Retained earnings‡	2,000,000
Net worth	$4,000,000

*20,000 more shares are added to common stock.

†Added capital in excess of par is equal to the number of new shares times the (market price minus par value).

$$20,000 \times (\$20 - \$5) = 20,000 \times \$15 = \$300,000$$

This value is added to the initial value of capital in excess of par to arrive at total capital in excess of par.

$$\$300,000 + 600,000 = \$900,000$$

‡The retained earnings shown are equal to the initial retained earnings value minus the addition to common stock of $100,000 and the addition to "capital in excess of par" of $300,000.

$$\$2,400,000 - \$100,000 - \$300,000 = \$2,000,000$$

2. *a.* EPS before the stock dividend = Earnings/Shares = $400,000/200,000 = $2
   Stock price before the stock dividend = P/E ratio × EPS = 10 × $2 = $20

   b. EPS after the stock dividend = Earnings/Shares = $400,000/220,000 = $1.82
   Stock price after the stock dividend = 10 × $1.82 = $18.20

   c. Value of portfolio before the stock dividend:

   $$100 \text{ shares} \times \$20 \text{ stock price} = \$2,000$$

   Value of portfolio after the stock dividend:

   $$110 \text{ shares} \times 18.20 \text{ stock price} = \$2,002$$

   The only difference between the before and after stock price is due to rounding ($2,000 versus $2,002). Albert Gonzales is no better off.

PROBLEMS

connect Selected problems are available with Connect. Please see the preface for more information.

Basic Problems

1. Moon and Sons Inc. earned $120 million last year and retained $72 million. What is the payout ratio?

   Payout ratio (LO18-1)

2. Ralston Gourmet Foods Inc. earned $360 million last year and retained $252 million. What is the payout ratio?

   Payout ratio (LO18-1)

3. Swank Clothiers earned $640 million last year and had a 30 percent payout ratio. How much did the firm add to its retained earnings?

   Payout ratio (LO18-1)

4. Polycom Systems earned $553 million last year and paid out 25 percent of earnings in dividends.

    a. By how much did the company's retained earnings increase?

    b. With 100 million shares outstanding and a stock price of $101, what was the dividend yield? (Hint: First compute dividends per share.)

5. The following companies have different financial statistics. What dividend policies would you recommend for them? Explain your reasons.

	Turtle Co.	Hare Corp.
Growth rate in sales and earnings	22%	4%
Cash as a percentage of total assets	5	20

6. Planetary Travel Co. has $240,000,000 in stockholders' equity. Eighty million dollars is listed as common stock and the balance is in retained earnings. The firm has $500,000,000 in total assets and 2 percent of this value is in cash. Earnings for the year are $40,000,000 and are included in retained earnings.

    a. What is the legal limit on current dividends?

    b. What is the practical limit based on liquidity?

    c. If the company pays out the amount in part b, what is the dividend payout ratio? (Compute this based on total dollars rather than on a per share basis because the number of shares is not given.)

    Payout ratio = Dividends/Earnings

7. A financial analyst is attempting to assess the future dividend policy of Environmental Systems by examining its life cycle. She anticipates no payout of earnings in the form of cash dividends during the development stage (I). During the growth stage (II), she anticipates 12 percent of earnings will be distributed as dividends. As the firm progresses to the expansion stage (III), the payout ratio will go up to 35 percent and will eventually reach 58 percent during the maturity stage (IV).

    a. Assuming earnings per share will be as follows during each of the four stages, indicate the cash dividend per share (if any) during each stage.

Stage I	$0.10
Stage II	1.80
Stage III	2.80
Stage IV	3.70

    b. Assume in Stage IV that an investor owns 325 shares and is in a 15 percent tax bracket. What will be the investor's aftertax income from the cash dividend?

    c. In what two stages is the firm most likely to utilize stock dividends or stock splits?

8. Squash Delight Inc. has the following balance sheet:

Stock split and stock dividend
(LO18-4)

Assets	
Cash	$ 100,000
Accounts receivable	300,000
Fixed assets	600,000
Total assets	$1,000,000
Liabilities	
Accounts payable	$ 150,000
Notes payable	50,000
Common stock (50,000 shares @ $2 par)	100,000
Capital in excess of par	200,000
Retained earnings	500,000
	$1,000,000

Capital accounts = { Common stock, Capital in excess of par, Retained earnings }

The firm's stock sells for $10 a share.

a. Show the effect on the capital account(s) of a two-for-one stock split.

b. Show the effect on the capital accounts of a 10 percent stock dividend. Part *b* is separate from part *a*. In part *b*, do not assume the stock split has taken place.

c. Based on the balance in retained earnings, which of the two dividend plans is more restrictive on future cash dividends?

9. In doing a five-year analysis of future dividends, the Dawson Corporation is considering the following two plans. The values represent dividends per share.

Policy on payout ratio
(LO18-1)

Year	Plan A	Plan B
1	$1.70	$0.60
2	1.70	2.50
3	1.70	0.30
4	1.90	5.00
5	1.90	1.30

a. How much in total dividends per share will be paid under each plan over the five years?

b. Mr. Bright, the vice president of finance, suggests that stockholders often prefer a stable dividend policy to a highly variable one. He will assume that stockholders apply a lower discount rate to dividends that are stable. The discount rate to be used for Plan A is 11 percent; the discount rate for Plan B is 14 percent. Compute the present value of future dividends. Which plan will provide the higher present value for the future dividends? (Round to two places to the right of the decimal point.)

10. The stock of Pills Berry Company is currently selling at $60 per share. The firm pays a dividend of $1.80 per share.

𝕏

Dividend yield
(LO18-1)

a. What is the annual dividend yield?

b. If the firm has a payout rate of 50 percent, what is the firm's P/E ratio?

Dividend yield
(LO18-1)

Ex-dividends date
and stock price
(LO18-1)

11. The shares of the Dyer Drilling Co. sell for $60. The firm has a P/E ratio of 15. Forty percent of earnings is paid out in dividends. What is the firm's dividend yield?

12. Peabody Mining Company's common stock is selling for $50 the day before the stock goes ex-dividend. The annual dividend yield is 5.6 percent, and dividends are distributed quarterly. Based solely on the impact of the cash dividend, by how much should the stock go down on the ex-dividend date? What will the new price of the stock be?

Intermediate Problems

Stock dividend
and cash dividend
(LO18-4)

13. The Western Pipe Company has the following capital section in its balance sheet. Its stock is currently selling for $6 per share.

Common stock (50,000 shares at $2 par)	$100,000
Capital in excess of par	100,000
Retained earnings	250,000
	$450,000

The firm intends to first declare a 15 percent stock dividend and then pay a 25-cent cash dividend (which also causes a reduction of retained earnings). Show the capital section of the balance sheet after the first transaction and then after the second transaction.

✕

Cash dividend
policy
(LO18-1)

14. Phillips Rock and Mud is trying to determine the maximum amount of cash dividends it can pay this year. Assume its balance sheet is as follows:

Assets	
Cash	$ 386,000
Accounts receivable	836,000
Fixed assets	1,048,000
Total assets	$2,270,000
Liabilities and Stockholders' Equity	
Accounts payable	$ 459,000
Long term payable	371,000
Common stock (295,000 shares at $1 par)	295,000
Retained earnings	1,145,000
Total liabilities and stockholders' equity	$2,270,000

   a. From a legal perspective, what is the maximum amount of dividends per share the firm could pay?

   b. In terms of cash availability, what is the maximum amount of dividends per share the firm could pay?

   c. Assume the firm earned an 18 percent return on stockholders' equity last year. If the board wishes to pay out 50 percent of earnings in the form of dividends, how much will dividends per share be? (Round to two places to the right of the decimal point.)

15. The Vinson Corporation has earnings of $500,000 with 250,000 shares outstanding. Its P/E ratio is 20. The firm is holding $300,000 of funds to invest

or pay out in dividends. If the funds are retained, the aftertax return on investment will be 15 percent, and this will add to present earnings. The 15 percent is the normal return anticipated for the corporation, and the P/E ratio would remain unchanged. If the funds are paid out in the form of dividends, the P/E ratio will increase by 10 percent because the stockholders in this corporation have a preference for dividends over retained earnings. Which plan will maximize the market value of the stock?

Z
Dividends and
stockholder wealth
maximization
(LO18-2)

Advanced Problems

16. Omni Telecom is trying to decide whether to increase its cash dividend immediately or use the funds to increase its future growth rate. It will use the dividend valuation model originally presented in Chapter 10 for purposes of analysis. The model was shown as Formula 10-9 and is reproduced here (with a slight addition in definition of terms):

Dividend valuation
model and wealth
maximization
(LO18-2)

$$P_0 = \frac{D_1}{K_e - g}$$

P_0 = Price of the stock today

D_1 = Dividend at the end of the first year
     $D_0 \times (1 + g)$

D_0 = Dividend today

K_e = Required rate of return

g = Constant growth rate in dividends

D_0 is currently $2.50, K_e is 10 percent, and g is 5 percent.

   Under Plan A, D_0 would be *immediately* increased to $3.00 and K_e and g will remain unchanged.

   Under Plan B, D_0 will remain at $2.50 but g will go up to 6 percent and K_e will remain unchanged.

   a. Compute P_0 (price of the stock today) under Plan A. Note D_1 will be equal to $D_0 \times (1 + g)$ or $3.00 (1.05). K_e will equal 10 percent, and g will equal 5 percent.

   b. Compute P_0 (price of the stock today) under Plan B. Note D_1 will be equal to $D_0 \times (1 + g)$ or $2.50 (1.06). K_e will be equal to 10 percent, and g will be equal to 6 percent.

   c. Which plan will produce the higher value?

17. Wilson Pharmaceuticals' stock has done very well in the market during the last three years. It has risen from $55 to $80 per share. The firm's current statement of stockholders' equity is as follows:

Stock split and its
effects
(LO18-4)

Common stock (5 million shares issued at par value of $10 per share)	$ 50,000,000
Paid-in capital in excess of par	13,000,000
Retained earnings	57,000,000
Net worth	$120,000,000

    a.   How many shares would be outstanding after a two-for-one stock split? What would be its par value?

    b.   How many shares would be outstanding after a three-for-one stock split? What would be its par value?

    c.   Assume that Wilson earned $11 million. What would its earnings per share be before and after the two-for-one stock split? After the three-for-one stock split?

    d.   What would be the price per share after the two-for-one stock split? After the three-for-one stock split? (Assume that the price-earnings ratio of 36.36 stays the same.)

    e.   Should a stock split change the price-earnings ratio for Wilson?

Stock dividend and its effect
(LO18-4)

18. Ace Products sells marked playing cards to blackjack dealers. It has not paid a dividend in many years, but is currently contemplating some kind of dividend. The capital accounts for the firm are as follows:

Common stock (2,400,000 shares at $5 par)	$12,000,000
Capital in excess of par*	5,000,000
Retained earnings	23,000,000
Net worth	$40,000,000

*The increase in capital in excess of par as a result of a stock dividend is equal to the new shares created times (Market price – Par value).

The company's stock is selling for $20 per share. The company had total earnings of $4,800,000 during the year. With 2,400,000 shares outstanding, earnings per share were $2.00. The firm has a P/E ratio of 10.

    a.   What adjustments would have to be made to the capital accounts for a 10 percent stock dividend? Show the new capital accounts.

    b.   What adjustments would be made to EPS and the stock price? (Assume the P/E ratio remains constant.)

    c.   How many shares would an investor end up with if he or she originally had 70 shares?

    d.   What is the investor's total investment worth before and after the stock dividend if the P/E ratio remains constant? (There may be a $1 to $2 difference due to rounding.)

Stock dividend and cash dividend
(LO18-4)

19. Health Systems Inc. is considering a 15 percent stock dividend. The capital accounts are as follows:

Common stock (6,000,000 shares at $10 par)	$ 60,000,000
Capital in excess of par*	35,000,000
Retained earnings	75,000,000
Net worth	$170,000,000

*The increase in capital in excess of par as a result of a stock dividend is equal to the shares created times (Market price – Par value).

The company's stock is selling for $32 per share. The company had total earnings of $19,200,000 with 6,000,000 shares outstanding and earnings per share were $3.20. The firm has a P/E ratio of 10.

a. What adjustments would have to be made to the capital accounts for a 15 percent stock dividend? Show the new capital accounts.

b. What adjustments would be made to EPS and the stock price? (Assume the P/E ratio remains constant).

c. How many shares would an investor have if he or she originally had 80?

d. What is the investor's total investment worth before and after the stock dividend if the P/E ratio remains constant? (There may be a slight difference due to rounding.)

e. Assume Mr. Heart, the president of Health Systems, wishes to benefit stockholders by keeping the cash dividend at a previous level of $1.25 in spite of the fact that the stockholders now have 15 percent more shares. Because the cash dividend is not reduced, the stock price is assumed to remain at $32.

   What is an investor's total investment worth after the stock dividend if he/she had 80 shares before the stock dividend?

f. Under the scenario described in part *e,* is the investor better off?

g. As a final question, what is the dividend yield on this stock under the scenario described in part *e?*

20. Worst Buy Company has had a lot of complaints from customers of late, and its stock price is now only $2 per share. It is going to employ a one-for-five reverse stock split to increase the stock value. Assume Dean Smith owns 140 shares.

   Reverse stock split (LO18-4)

a. How many shares will he own after the reverse stock split?

b. What is the anticipated price of the stock after the reverse stock split?

c. Because investors often have a negative reaction to a reverse stock split, assume the stock only goes up to 80 percent of the value computed in part *b*. What will the stock's price be?

d. How has the total value of Dean Smith's holdings changed from before the reverse stock split to after the reverse stock split (based on the stock value computed in part *c*)? To get the total value before and after the split, multiply the shares held times the stock price.

21. The Carlton Corporation has $5 million in earnings after taxes and 2 million shares outstanding. The stock trades at a P/E of 20. The firm has $4 million in excess cash.

   Cash dividend versus stock repurchase (LO18-5)

a. Compute the current price of the stock.

b. If the $4 million is used to pay dividends, how much will dividends per share be?

c. If the $4 million is used to repurchase shares in the market at a price of $54 per share, how many shares will be acquired? (Round to the nearest share.)

d. What will the new earnings per share be? (Round to two places to the right of the decimal.)

e. If the P/E ratio remains constant, what will the price of the securities be? By how much, in terms of dollars, did the repurchase increase the stock price?

f. Has the stockholders' total wealth changed as a result of the stock repurchase as opposed to receiving the cash dividend?

g. What are some reasons a corporation may wish to repurchase its own shares in the market?

Retaining funds versus paying them out
(LO18-1)

22. The Hastings Sugar Corporation has the following pattern of net income each year, and associated capital expenditure projects. The firm can earn a higher return on the projects than the stockholders could earn if the funds were paid out in the form of dividends.

Year	Net Income	Profitable Capital Expenditure
1	$14 million	$ 7 million
2	16 million	11 million
3	12 million	6 million
4	16 million	8 million
5	16 million	9 million

The Hastings Corporation has 3 million shares outstanding. (The following questions are separate from each other.)

a. If the marginal principle of retained earnings is applied, how much in total cash dividends will be paid over the five years?

b. If the firm simply uses a payout ratio of 30 percent of net income, how much in total cash dividends will be paid?

c. If the firm pays a 10 percent stock dividend in years 2 through 5, and also pays a cash dividend of $3.40 per share for each of the five years, how much in total dividends will be paid?

d. Assume the payout ratio in each year is to be 20 percent of the net income and the firm will pay a 10 percent stock dividend in years 2 through 5, how much will dividends per share for each year be? (Assume the cash dividend is paid after the stock dividend.)

COMPREHENSIVE PROBLEM

Modern Furniture Company
(Dividend payments versus stock repurchases)
(LO18-5)

Modern Furniture Company had finally arrived at the point where it had a sufficient excess cash flow of $4.8 million to consider paying a dividend. It had 3 million shares of stock outstanding and was considering paying a cash dividend of $1.60 per share. The firm's total earnings were $12 million, providing $4.00 in earnings per share. The stock traded in the market at $88.00 per share.

However, Al Rosen, the chief financial officer, was not sure that paying a cash dividend was the best route to go. He had recently read a number of articles in *The Wall Street Journal* about the advantages of stock repurchases and before he made a recommendation to the CEO and board of directors, he decided to do a number of calculations.

    a.   What is the firm's P/E ratio?

    b.   If the firm paid the cash dividend, what would be its dividend yield and dividend payout ratio per share?

    c.   If a stockholder held 100 shares of stock and received the cash dividend, what would be the total value of his portfolio (stock plus dividends)?

    d.   Assume instead of paying the cash dividend, the firm used the $4.8 million of excess funds to purchase shares at slightly over the current market value of $88 at a price of $89.60. How many shares could be repurchased? (Round to the nearest share.)

    e.   What would the new earnings per share be under the stock repurchase alternative? (Round to three places to the right of the decimal point.)

    f.   If the P/E ratio stayed the same under the stock repurchase alternative, what would be the stock value per share? If a stockholder owned 100 shares, what would now be the total value of his portfolio? (This answer should be approximately the same as the answer to part *c.*)

WEB EXERCISE

1. Facebook is a profitable, rapid-growth media company. This presumably justifies the firm not paying a cash dividend.

2. Go to www.finance.yahoo.com and enter "FB (Facebook)" in the "Quote Lookup" box. Click "Financials" and scroll down to "Income Statement."

3. Compute the following ratios for the most recent full year.

a. Net income/Total revenue (aftertax profit margin) ....   %

b. Cost of revenue/Total revenue ....

c. Growth in earnings per share ....

d. Income tax expense/Net income ....

4. Write a one-paragraph summary about Facebook's ability to beat the analysts' targets in step 1. Do not automatically assume the firm will be able to beat the target numbers because Facebook is in a highly competitive environment. Some years it will beat the target numbers and other years it will not.

Note: Occasionally a topic we have listed may have been deleted, updated, or moved into a different location on a website. If you click on the site map or site index, you will be introduced to a table of contents that should aid you in finding the topic you are looking for.

19

Convertibles, Warrants, and Derivatives

LEARNING OBJECTIVES

LO 19-1 Convertible securities can be converted to common stock at the option of the owner.

LO 19-2 Because these securities can be converted to common stock, they may move with the value of common stock.

LO 19-3 Convertible bonds have a pure bond value based on interest paid and the market-demanded rate of return.

LO 19-4 Warrants are similar to convertibles in that they give the warrant holder the right to acquire common stock.

LO 19-5 Accountants require that the potential effect of convertibles and warrants on earnings per share be reported on the income statement.

LO 19-6 Derivative securities such as options and futures can be used by corporate financial managers for hedging activities.

There are as many types of securities as there are innovative corporate treasurers or forward-looking portfolio managers. As we have discussed in the previous chapters, corporate financial managers usually raise long-term capital by selling common stock, preferred stock, or bonds. Occasionally a company will issue convertible securities, which are a hybrid security combining the features of debt and common equity or preferred stock and common equity. Sometimes to sweeten a straight debt offering, the financial manager may attach warrants to a bond offering. Warrants are a type of derivative security because they derive their value from the underlying common stock price. Other derivative securities introduced in this chapter are options and futures contracts.

Convertible bonds and convertible preferred stock are not used on a regular basis by corporations raising funds, but are used occasionally to diversify a company's capital structure. New issues of convertible bonds run in streaks as chief financial officers (CFOs) and corporate treasurers try to take advantage of interest rate forecasts and lock in low-cost debt. When CFOs expect interest rates to rise, they are more likely to lock in low-cost debt capital before interest rates go up. Convertible securities offer the chief financial officer an alternative source of financing that combines the features of common stock and debt. The following BioMarin Pharmaceutical example of convertible notes is still outstanding and matures in 2024.

On August 7, 2017, BioMarin sold $450 million of subordinated convertible senior notes due in 2024 paying 0.599 percent interest. BioMarin stated that most of the funds would be used for the purpose of repaying some or all of its 0.75 percent senior subordinated convertible notes due October 2018 in the amount of $375 million and the extra $75 million would be used for other corporate purposes. So not only did BioMarin raise funds to pay off debt coming due, but it did so at a lower interest rate.

BioMarin is a biotech company that has grown from $548 million in 2013 to an expected $1.753 billion in 2019, according to Merrill Lynch research. The sales growth rate from 2015 to 2017 ranged between 16.5 percent and 25.4 percent, with a 20 percent growth in sales expected in 2019, accompanied by over a 100 percent growth rate in earnings. All it takes is one blockbuster drug for a company like BioMarin to bust through $2 billion in sales. Investors seem to be willing to take a low interest rate in exchange for a high growth rate that will eventually create value for the common stock. The notes are convertible into 8.0212 shares at a stock price of $124.67. You may want to look up the stock price BMRN (ticker symbol) to see if the stock goes above its conversion price. If the stock isn't converted to common stock by the maturity date, the investors will at least get back their initial investment.

A second example pertains to a financial institution. On January 15, 2008, Citigroup, the banking giant, announced a quarterly loss of over $20 billion, due to an $18 billion write-off in its subprime mortgage division and a $4 billion reserve for loan losses in consumer lending and credit cards. Because banks are required to maintain a minimum level of regulatory capital in order to operate, the bank needed to raise additional capital to offset the losses that had reduced its equity capital.

It turned to convertible preferred stock to the tune of $14.5 billion. Because of Citi's high risk at the time, the dividend yield was set at a high 7 percent, and the price at which the preferred stock could be converted into common stock was set 20 percent above the current market price of the common stock at the time of sale. The convertible preferred was converted to common stock in 2009 to help Citi increase its capital ratios.

Convertible Securities

Specifically, a **convertible security** is a bond or share of preferred stock that can be converted, at the option of the holder, into common stock. Thus the owner has a fixed income security that can be transferred into common stock if and when the affairs of the firm indicate such a conversion is desirable. Even though convertible securities are most often converted into common stock, some convertible preferred stock is exchangeable, in turn, into convertible bonds, which are then convertible into common stock. Additionally, when a company is merged with another company, sometimes the convertible securities of the acquired company may become convertible into common stock of the surviving company. While these departures from the norm are interesting, in this chapter we focus on convertible bonds (debentures) that result in the potential for common stock ownership and recognize that the same principles apply to other forms of convertibles.

When a convertible debenture is initially issued, a **conversion ratio** to common stock is specified. The ratio indicates the number of shares of common stock into which the debentures may be converted. Assume that in 2018 the Williams Company issued $10 million of 25-year, 6 percent convertible debentures, with each $1,000 bond convertible into 20 shares of common stock. The conversion ratio of 20 may also be expressed in terms of a **conversion price**. To arrive at the conversion price, we divide the par value of the bond by the conversion ratio of 20. In the case of the Williams Company, the conversion price is $50. Conversely, the conversion ratio may also be found by dividing the par value by the conversion price ($1,000/$50 = 20).

Value of the Convertible Bond

As a first consideration in evaluating a convertible bond, we must examine the value of the conversion privilege. In the above case, we might assume that the common stock is selling at $45 per share, so the total **conversion value** is $900 ($45 × 20). Nevertheless, the bond may sell for par or face value ($1,000) in anticipation of future developments in the common stock and because interest payments are being received on the bonds. With the bond selling for $1,000 and a $900 conversion value, the bond would have a $100 **conversion premium**, representing the dollar difference between market value and conversion value. The conversion premium generally will be influenced by the expectations of future performance of the common stock. If investors are optimistic about the prospects of the common stock, the premium may be large.

If the price of the common stock really takes off and goes to $60 per share, the conversion privilege becomes quite valuable. The bonds, which are convertible into 20 shares, will go up to at least $1,200 and perhaps more. Note that you do not have to convert to common immediately, but may enjoy the price movement of the convertible in concert with the price of the common.

What happens if the common stock goes in the opposite direction? Assume that instead of going from $45 to $60 the common stock drops from $45 to $25—what will happen to the value of the convertible debentures? We know the value of a convertible bond will go down in response to the drop in the common stock, but will it fall all the way to its conversion value of $500 (20 × $25 per share)? The answer is clearly no because the debenture still has value as an interest-bearing security. If the going market rate of interest in straight debt issues of similar maturity (25 years) and quality is 8 percent, we would say the debenture paying 6 percent has a pure bond value of $785.46.[1] The **pure bond value** equals the value of a bond that has no conversion features but has the same risk as the convertible bond being evaluated. Thus a convertible bond has a **floor value**[2] but no upside limitation. When a convertible bond sells at a premium to the floor value, it has a potential **downside risk** because the stock price could fall. We define downside risk as the difference between the market price and the floor value. To calculate the downside risk in percent, divide the dollar amount by which the market price could fall (before it reaches the floor value) by the market price. The price pattern for the convertible bond is depicted in Figure 19-1.

We see in Figure 19-1 the effect on the convertible bond price as the common stock price, shown along the x-axis, is assumed to change. Note that the floor (pure bond) value for the convertible is well above the conversion value when the common stock price is very low. As the common stock price moves to higher levels, the convertible bond price moves together with the conversion value. Where the pure bond value equals the conversion value, we have the parity point (P).

Representative information on outstanding convertible bonds is presented in Table 19-1. Almost all bonds have a par value of $1,000, and so by comparing the market value of the bond in the second column to the par value of $1,000, you can see that the table is divided into three sections: bonds selling at a premium to par value; bonds selling close to par value; and bonds selling at a discount to par value.

The first group of bonds is selling at a premium to par value and their conversion values are all above the pure bond values. These bonds would be selling to the right of the parity point in the middle of Figure 19-1, and their market price is being supported by their conversion value rather than their pure bond value. When bonds like these sell at premiums to their pure bond value, they have a large downside risk and usually have low conversion premiums. The market price is being supported by a common stock price that is higher than the conversion price. In these cases, as the common stock price falls, the market price will follow the conversion value down. For example, if you look at

---

[1]This price is based on discounting procedures covered in Chapter 10, "Valuation and Rates of Return." Semiannual interest payments are assumed.

[2]The floor value can change if interest rates in the market change. For ease of presentation, we shall assume they are constant for now.

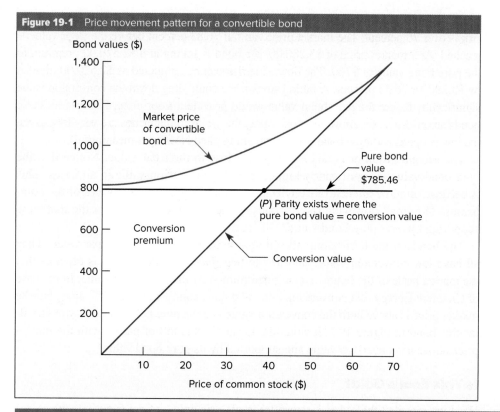

Figure 19-1   Price movement pattern for a convertible bond

Table 19-1   Pricing patterns for convertible bonds outstanding, prices on January 22, 2018

Issue	Coupon	Maturity	Conversion Value	Market Value of Bond	Pure Bond Value	Conversion Premium	Downside Risk*	Yield to Maturity on Bond
Convertibles Selling at a Premium to Par Value								
VeriSign 3.25S2037	$32.50	8/15/2037	$3,265.60	$3,280.00	$760.00	0%	76.83%	NMF
Meritor 7.875s2026	78.75	9/1/2026	2,006.70	2,190.00	910.00	9%	58.45%	NMF
Trinity Industries 3.875s2036	38.75	12/1/2036	1,456.90	1,552.50	990.00	7%	36.23%	0.7%
AmTrust Fin'l 5.5s2021	55.00	12/15/2021	1,024.30	1,309.60	970.00	28%	25.93%	5.8%
Tesla Motors 2.375s2022	12.50	3/1/2021	1,031.80	1,216.30	900.00	18%	26.01%	NMF
Convertibles Selling Close to Par								
Colony Fin'l 5s2023	$50.00	10/15/2023	$ 912.10	$1,025.00	$940.00	12%	8.29%	4.5%
Starwood Pprty Trst 4.375s2023	43.75	10/1/2023	814.40	1,008.80	960.00	24%	4.84%	4.2%
DFC Global 3s2028	30.00	4/1/2028	492.65	1,001.30	990.00	103%	1.13%	3.0%
Jefferies Group 3.875s2029	38.75	11/1/2029	479.50	997.50	980.00	108%	1.75%	3.9%
Nuance Commun 2.75s2031	27.50	11/1/2031	530.40	985.00	920.00	86%	6.60%	2.9%
Convertibles Selling at a Discount to Par Value								
Cheniere Energy 4.25s2045	$42.50	9/15/2045	$ 393.40	$ 723.80	$550.00	84%	24.01%	6.5%
RAIT Financial Trust 4s2033	40.00	10/1/2033	40.20	936.30	970.00	999%	−3.60%	4.7%
Intercept Pharmaceut 3.25s2023	32.50	7/1/2023	276.70	778.80	860.00	181%	−10.43%	8.6%
Theravance 2.125s2023	21.25	1/15/2023	465.30	988.80	740.00	112%	25.16%	2.4%
SunPower Corp 4s2023	40.00	7/1/2023	310.20	835.00	780.00	169%	6.59%	8.3%

*Downside Risk = (Market Value − Pure Bond Value)/Market Value

Source: Data from *The Value Line Convertibles Survey,* January 22, 2018.

VeriSign's bond on the first line, the conversion premium is 0 percent and the downside risk is over 76 percent. The market price can fall 76.83 percent before the floor value is reached. At a market price of $3,280.00, the bond is selling at a $2,520.00 premium to the pure bond value of $760. The downside risk can be computed as $2,520.00 divided by $3,280, or 76.83 percent. A falling stock price could drag down the conversion value significantly before the pure bond value would provide a floor price. Because all these bonds are priced so far above their par value, the yields to maturities are very low, given the low coupons and high bond prices, and are marked NMF (not meaningful).

The second group of bonds is selling at close to their par value. Notice that the pure bond value is significantly higher than the conversion value in all cases. This is because of a low interest rate environment and depressed stock prices of the companies. The small downside risk for these bonds is an indication that the market is supported by their pure bond value.

The bonds in the third group all sell at a discount to their $1,000 par value. They all have low conversion values and low-to-negative downside risk. It is obvious that the market price of the bonds is being determined by the pure bond value. In the case of Cheniere Energy, the conversion value and pure bond value are $157 apart but the market price is above both the conversion value and the pure bond value. If you visualize this bond in Figure 19-1, it would be located to the left of parity, with the market price above its conversion value and supported by its pure bond value.

Is This Fool's Gold?

Have we repealed the old risk-return trade-off principle—to get superior returns, we must take larger than normal risks? With convertible bonds, we appear to limit our risk while maximizing our return potential.

Although there is some truth to this statement, there are many qualifications. For example, once convertible debentures begin going up in value, say to $1,100 or $1,200, the downside protection becomes pretty meaningless. In the case of the Williams Company in our earlier example in Figure 19-1, the floor is at $785.46. If an investor were to buy the convertible bond at $1,200, he or she would be exposed to $414.54 in potential losses (hardly adequate protection for a true risk averter). Also if interest rates in the market rise, the floor value, or pure bond value, could fall, creating more downside risk.

A second drawback with convertible bonds is that the purchaser is invariably asked to accept below-market rates of interest on the debt instrument. The interest rate on convertibles is generally one-third below that for instruments in a similar risk class at time of issue. In the sophisticated environment of the bond and stock markets, one seldom gets an additional benefit without having to suffer a corresponding disadvantage.

You will also recall that the purchaser of a convertible bond normally pays a premium over the conversion value. For example, if a $1,000 bond were convertible into 20 shares of common stock at $45 per share, a $100 conversion premium would be involved initially. If the same $1,000 were invested directly in common stock at $45 per share, 22.2 shares could be purchased. In this case, if the shares go up in value, we have 2.2 more shares on which to garner a profit.

Lastly, convertibles may suffer from the attachment of a call provision giving the corporation the option of redeeming the bonds at a specified price above par ($1,000) in the future. In a subsequent section, we will see how the corporation can use this device to force the conversion of the bonds into common stock.

None of these negatives is meant to detract from the fact that convertibles carry some inherently attractive features if they are purchased with appropriate objectives in mind. If the investor wants downside protection, he or she should search out convertible bonds trading below par, perhaps within 10 to 15 percent of the floor value. Though a fairly large move in the stock may be necessary to generate upside profit, the investor has the desired protection and some hope for capital appreciation.

Advantages and Disadvantages to the Corporation

Having established the fundamental characteristics of the convertible security from the *investor* viewpoint, let us now turn the coin over and examine the factors a corporate financial officer must consider in weighing the advisability of a convertible offer for the firm.

Not only has it been established that the interest rate paid on convertible issues is lower than that paid on a straight debt instrument, but also the convertible feature may be the only device for allowing smaller corporations access to the bond market. For small risky companies, investor acceptance of new debt may be contingent on a special sweetener, such as the ability to convert to common stock.

Convertible debentures are also attractive to a corporation that believes its stock is currently undervalued. You will recall in the case of the Williams Company, $1,000 bonds were convertible into 20 shares of common stock at a conversion price of $50. Since the common stock had a current price of $45 and new shares of stock might be sold at only $44,[3] the corporation effectively received $6 over current market price, assuming future conversion. Of course, one can also argue that if the firm had delayed the issuance of common stock or convertibles for a year or two, the stock might have gone up from $45 to $60 and new common stock might have been sold at this lofty price.

To translate this to overall numbers for the firm, if a corporation needs $10 million in funds and offers straight stock now at a net price of $44, it must issue 227,273 shares ($10 million shares/$44). With convertibles, the number of shares potentially issued is only 200,000 shares ($10 million/$50). Finally if no stock or convertible bonds are issued now and the stock goes up to a level at which new shares can be offered at a net price of $60, only 166,667 shares will be required ($10 million/$60).

Table 19-2 presents a composite picture of convertible bonds outstanding as of January 2018. The typical convertible is priced to have a conversion premium of about 20 percent. However this premium will be affected by the coupon rate and the optimism or pessimism in the stock market or for the particular company selling the new convertible. As Table 19-2 shows, the average conversion premium for the median convertible bond in the *Value Line Convertibles Survey* is 25 percent, which is slightly above its historical average.

The size of the convertible bond market is relatively small compared to the markets for nonconvertible corporate bonds and common stocks, as can be seen from the 187.3 billion size of the market covered by Value Line in Table 19-2. By comparison, the total market value of nonconvertible U.S. corporate bonds and common stock is over $30 trillion.

---

[3]There is always a bit of underpricing to ensure the success of a new offering.

Table 19-2 Characteristics of convertible bonds, January 22, 2018	
Average price of the underlying common stock	$ 48.32
Average price of the convertible bond	$1,260.90
Yield to maturity	5.4%
Dividend yield on underlying common stock	2.1%
Conversion premium	25%
Premium over pure bond value	27%
Total market size ($ billions)	$ 187.3

Source: Data from *The Value Line Convertibles Survey*, January 22, 2018.

One comparison that shows up in the table is the difference between the yield to maturity on convertible bonds of 5.4 percent and the dividend yields of the underlying common stock of 2.1 percent. This is an indication that the companies that sell convertible securities are generally smaller companies that are growing fast and have small dividend payout ratios, which results in low dividend yields. While a few companies that sell convertible bonds may be high-quality companies, most are small companies with low credit ratings and high risk.

Inherent in a convertible issue is the presumed ability of the corporation to force the security holder to convert the present instrument to common stock. We will examine this process.

Forcing Conversion

How does a corporation desirous of shifting outstanding debt to common stock force conversion? The principal device is the call option provision. As previously indicated, when the value of the common stock goes up, the convertible security will move in a similar fashion. Table 19-3 provides additional evidence of this point. Some particularly successful convertibles trade at many times the initial value of $1,000 as shown in the "Market Price" column of Table 19-3.

If companies wanted to call in the bonds (pay off the bonds before maturity) to force conversion to common stock, this is how it would work.

For the bonds with $1,000 call prices, the company is able to call the bond after a certain date specified in the bond indenture. When the bond is called, the bondholder has the option of taking the par value (or call price) or taking the shares of common stock. Given that all these bonds are selling at a premium over par value of $1,000 and the call price, any rational investor would take the shares of stock, and this is how companies create **forced conversion** when they call a bond. In one stroke through forced conversion, the balance sheet changes, the debt becomes equity, and the debt disappears. The result is that the debt-to-equity ratio and the debt-to-assets ratio decline. In most cases, the conversion also helps the company increase cash flow by substituting lower or no dividends for the interest expense. Even though interest is a tax-deductible expense up to a point as set out by the 2017 Tax Cuts and Jobs Act, this increase in cash flow is still usually true.

It should be pointed out that not all bonds are callable at par. Some may be callable at 5 to 10 percent over par, but the same principles apply. Bonds that are not callable may not be able to be redeemed until maturity but the bondholder still may

Table 19-3   Successful convertible bonds and preferred stock not yet called

Pricing Date January 22, 2018

Convertible Securities	Market Price	Convertible Current Yield	Common Stock Dividend Yield	Par Value or Call Price	Call Date**
Convertible Bonds					
Lam Research 2.625s2041	$5,673.80	0.50%	0.00%	$1,000.00	NCB
Micron Tech 2.375s2032	4,536.30	0.40%	NIL	1,000.00	5/4/19
Micron Tech 3.125s2032	4,470.00	0.70%	NIL	1,000.00	5/4/21
Micron Technology 2.125s33 (F)	3,961.30	0.50%	NIL	1,000.00	2/20/20
Microchip Technology 2.125s2037	3,876.30	0.50%	1.50%	1,000.00	NCB
Millennium Chem 4s2023	3,641.30	1.10%	NIL	1,000.00	11/15/2023
Anthem (WellPoint) 2.75s2042	3,257.60	0.80%	1.00%	1,000.00	NC
Intel Corp 3.25s2039	2,073.80	1.60%	2.20%	1,000.00	8/5/19
Bristow Group 4.5s2023	1,273.80	3.50%	0.00%	1,000.00	NC
j2 Global 3.25s2029	1,256.30	2.60%	1.60%	1,000.00	NCB
Convertible Preferred Stocks					
NCR Corporation $5.50A	$1,250.75	0.40%	0.00%	$100.00	NC
Post Holdings $2.50	153.88	1.60%	0.00%	100.00	2/15/19
Virtus Investment Part $7.25D	111.75	6.50%	1.40%	100.00	NC
Huntington Bancshares $85.00A	1,359.25	6.50%	0.30%	1,000.00	NC
Bank of America $72.50 SeriesL	1,277.00	5.70%	0.6	1,000.00	NC

*A call price of 0 indicates the bond is not callable at all. A call price of NCB in most cases means the bond is not callable except under certain conditions and in some cases the bondholder can sell (put) the bond back to the company under certain conditions depending upon the price of the bond.

**Most convertible preferred stocks do not have call dates but they can force conversion if their underlying common stock price hits a certain level and stays there for a period of time.

Source: Data from *The Value Line Convertibles Survey*, January 22, 2018.

have the option to convert to common stock. However, since the cash flow from the bond is usually higher than the dividend yield, there is no advantage in converting to common stock.

Conversion may also be encouraged through a **step-up in the conversion price** over time. When the bond is issued, the contract may specify the conversion provisions:

	Conversion Price	Conversion Ratio
First five years	$40	25.0 shares
Next three years	45	22.2 shares
Next two years	50	20.0 shares
Next five years	55	18.2 shares

At the end of each time period, there is a strong inducement to convert rather than accept an adjustment to a higher conversion price and a lower conversion ratio.

Accounting Considerations with Convertibles

Decades ago, the full impact of the conversion privilege as it applied to convertible securities, warrants (long-term options to buy stock), and other dilutive securities was not adequately reflected in reported earnings per share. Since all of these securities may generate additional common stock in the future, the potential effect of this dilution (the addition of new shares to the capital structures) should be considered. The accounting profession has applied many different measures to earnings per share over the years, most recently replacing the concepts of primary earnings per share and fully diluted earnings per share with **basic earnings per share** and **diluted earnings per share**. In 1997 the Financial Accounting Standards Board issued "Earnings per Share" *Statement of Financial Accounting Standards No. 128,* which covers the adjustments that must be made when reporting earnings per share.

If we examine the financial statements of the XYZ Corporation in Table 19-4, we find that the earnings per share reported is not adjusted for convertible securities and is referred to as basic earnings per share.

Table 19-4   XYZ Corporation

1. Capital section of balance sheet:	
Common stock (1 million shares at $10 par)	$10,000,000
4.5% convertible debentures (10,000 debentures of $1,000; convertible into 40 shares per bond, or a total of 400,000 shares)	10,000,000
Retained earnings	20,000,000
Net worth	$40,000,000
2. Condensed income statement:	
Earnings before interest and taxes	$ 2,950,000
Interest (4.5% of $10 million of convertibles)	450,000
Earnings before taxes	$ 2,500,000
Taxes (40%)	1,000,000
Earnings after taxes	$ 1,500,000
3. Basic earnings per share:	

$$\frac{\text{Earnings after taxes}}{\text{Shares of common stock}} = \frac{\$1,500,000}{1,000,000} = \$1.50 \qquad (19\text{-}1)$$

Diluted earnings per share adjusts for all potential dilution from the issuance of any new shares of common stock arising from convertible bonds, convertible preferred stocks, warrants, or any other options outstanding. The comparison of basic and diluted earnings per share gives the analyst or investor a measure of the potential effects of these securities.

We get diluted earnings per share for the XYZ Corporation by assuming that 400,000 new shares will be created from potential conversion, while at the same time allowing for the reduction in interest payments that would occur as a result of the conversion of the debt to common stock. Since before-tax interest payments on the convertibles are $450,000, the aftertax interest cost ($270,000) will be saved and can be added back to income. Aftertax interest cost is determined by multiplying interest payments by one minus the tax rate, or $450,000 (1 − 0.40) = $270,000. Making the appropriate adjustments to the numerator and denominator, we show adjusted earnings per share:

$$\frac{\text{Diluted earnings}}{\text{per share}} = \frac{\text{Adjusted earnings after taxes}}{\text{Shares outstanding} + \text{All convertible securities}^4} \qquad (19\text{-}2)$$

$$= \frac{\overset{\substack{\text{Reported} \\ \text{earnings}}}{\$1,500,000} + \overset{\substack{\text{Interest} \\ \text{savings}}}{\$270,000}}{1,000,000 + 400,000} = \frac{\$1,770,000}{1,400,000} = \$1.26$$

We see a $0.24 reduction from the basic earnings per share number of $1.50 in Formula 19-1 at the bottom of Table 19-4. The new figure is the value that a sophisticated security analyst would utilize.

Financing through Warrants

A **warrant** is an option to buy a stated number of shares of common stock at a specified price (the exercise price) over a given time period. For example, a warrant of Citigroup shown in Table 19-5 in the "Out-of-the-Money" section at the bottom of the table allows the holder to buy one share of common stock at $106.10 per share from Citigroup until January 1, 2019. The common stock price has to move up more than $29.26 before it will have any actual value. Bank of America (second line from the top) also has warrants maturing in January of 2019. This warrant has a much lower exercise price of $13.30 and is $17.89 in the money. Both warrants allow the warrant holder to purchase one share of common stock for each warrant. This is not always the case. Because of stock splits, stock dividends, or original terms of issue, you can often find that one warrant will buy two or three shares of stock or even fractional shares. In the case of Bank of America, if the stock price moves above the exercise price by expiration, the warrant holder will exercise the option and buy stock from the bank. This would provide more equity capital and achieve the original purpose for both banks.

Warrants are sometimes issued as a **financial sweetener** in a bond offering, and they may enable the firm to issue debt when this would not be otherwise feasible because of a low quality rating or a high interest rate environment. The warrants are usually detachable from the bond issue, have their own market price, and are generally traded on the New York Stock Exchange or over-the-counter. After warrants are detached, the initial debt to which they were attached remains in existence as a stand-alone bond. Often the bond price will fall and the bond yield will rise once the warrants are detached.

Because a warrant is dependent on the market movement of the underlying common stock and has no "security value" as such, it is highly speculative. If the common stock of the firm is volatile, the value of the warrants may change dramatically.

In prior time periods, Tri-Continental Corporation warrants went from $\frac{1}{32}$ to 75¾, while United Airlines warrants moved from 4½ to 126. Of course this is not a one-way street, as holders of LTV warrants will attest as they saw their holdings dip from 83 to 2¼.

Notice that Table 19-5 is divided into two sections. A warrant listed as **out-of-the-money** indicates that the exercise price is above the current stock price. **In-the-money warrants** have stock prices above the exercise price and have an intrinsic value.

---

[4]Other types of securities that create common stock, such as warrants and options, would also be included.

Table 19-5   Relationships determining warrant prices

Firm, Places of Warrant Listing, Stock Listing, and Expiration Date	Warrant Price	Stock Price	Exercise Price	Number of Shares	Intrinsic Value ($)	Speculative Premium ($)
			In-the-Money Warrants			
Amer Int'l Grp 2021 wt NYS, NYS, 1/19/21	$19.00	$60.97	$45.00	1	$15.97	$3.03
Bank of America 2019 wt NYS, NYS, 1/16/19	18.38	31.19	13.30	1	17.89	0.49
Kingsway Financial Services 2023 wt NYS, OTC, 9/15/23	2.25	5.25	5.00	1	0.25	2.00
Gen'l Motors 2019 B wt NYS, NYS, 7/10/19	26.25	44.07	18.33	1	25.74	0.51
Hartford Fin'l Services 2 NYS, NYS, 6/26/19	50.00	55.29	9.77	1	45.52	4.48
Lincoln National 2019 wt NYS, NYS, 7/10/19	80.00	84.37	10.72	1	73.65	6.35
			Out-of-the-Money Warrants			
Ambac Fin'l Group 2023 wt OTC, OTC, 4/30/23	$ 5.75	$16.07	$16.67	1	−$0.60	$6.35
Citigroup 2019 wt NYS, NYS, 1/4/19	0.13	76.84	106.1	1	−29.26	29.39
Solar 3D 2020 wt OTC, OTC, 3/8/20	0.13	2.93	4.15	1	−1.22	1.35
Zions Bancorp 2020 wt OTC, OTC, 5/22/20	3.45	25.67	36.63	1	−10.96	14.41

In reality a warrant cannot have a negative value so in this example of out-of-the-money warrants, the negative value indicates how much the stock price has to rise to reach the exercise price.
OTC = Over-The-Counter; NYS = New York Stock Exchange.
Source: The Value Line Convertibles Survey, January 22, 2018.

Valuation of Warrants

Because the value of a warrant is closely tied to the underlying stock price, we can develop a formula for the **intrinsic value** of a warrant:

$$I = (M - E) \times N \qquad (19\text{-}3)$$

where

I = Intrinsic value of a warrant

M = Market value of common stock (stock price)

E = Exercise price of a warrant

N = Number of shares each warrant entitles the holder to purchase

Using the prior data from Table 19-5, we see that General Motors Co. common stock was trading at $44.07 per share. Each warrant carried with it the option to purchase one share of the General Motors Co. common stock at an **exercise price** of $18.33 per share. Using Formula 19-3, the intrinsic value is $25.74 or ($44.07 − $18.33) × 1.

The warrant was selling at $26.25 per warrant. This was $0.51 per warrant more than its intrinsic value of $25.74. This $0.51 is called the **speculative premium**. In this case GM is so far in the money that the speculative premium is almost nonexistent. If you look at American International Group (top line), you see a different story. AIG's warrant is trading at $19.00 but has an intrinsic value of only $15.97 with a speculative premium of $3.03. Because AIG's warrant doesn't expire until 2021, the premium is heavily affected by time to expiration.

Investors are willing to pay a speculative premium because a small percentage gain in the stock price may generate large percentage increases in the warrant price. Formula 19-4 demonstrates the calculation of the speculative premium:

$$S = W - I \qquad \qquad (19\text{-}4)$$

where

S = Speculative premium

W = Warrant price

I = Intrinsic value

For General Motors Co., we use the formula to show the calculation of the previously stated speculative premium of $0.51:

$$S = W - I$$
$$\$0.51 = \$26.25 - \$25.74$$

613

Some warrants may at times have negative speculative premiums. This simply means that the warrant price is less than the intrinsic value and the warrant is underpriced. It is also possible that the warrants are not traded very often; and while the common stock may trade daily, the warrant doesn't trade at the same time, so the prices of the warrant and the common stock are not synchronized.

We can also see from Table 19-5 that all the out-of-the-money warrants have negative intrinsic value. We show this as a negative to indicate that the stock price is below the exercise price. It would be fair to say that the intrinsic value is zero because in fact you can never really have a negative value. It is still possible in a rising stock market that these companies could see their stock price double or triple in two or three years and thereby reward the owner of the warrant.

It is opportunities like this that entice investors to buy bonds with warrants attached. Bond investors are willing to accept lower interest rates when warrants are attached because they know that the warrants have potential value that could be far in excess of the interest rate on the bond. This expectation of potential profit is what makes warrants financial sweeteners.

The typical relationship between the warrant price and intrinsic value of a warrant is depicted in Figure 19-2. We assume the warrant entitles the holder to purchase one new share of common at $20. Although the intrinsic value of the warrant is theoretically negative at a common stock price between 0 and 20, the warrant still carries some value in the market. Also observe that the difference between the market price of the warrant and its intrinsic value is diminished at the upper ranges of value. Two reasons may be offered for the declining premium.

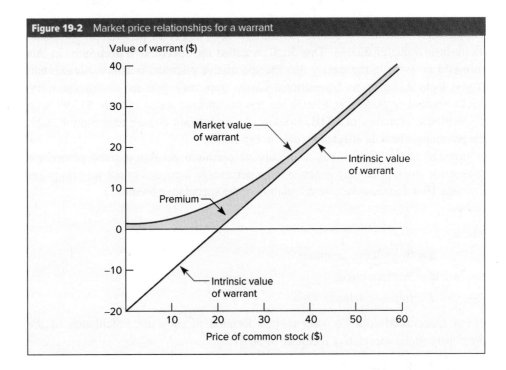

Figure 19-2 Market price relationships for a warrant

First the speculator loses the ability to use leverage to generate high returns as the price of the stock goes up. When the price of the stock is relatively low, say $25, and the warrant is in the $5 range, a 10-point movement in the stock could mean a 200 percent gain in the value of the warrant, as indicated in the left panel of Table 19-6.

Table 19-6 Leverage in valuing warrants	
Low Stock Price	**High Stock Price**
Stock price, $25; warrant price, $5* + 10-point movement in stock price	Stock price, $50; warrant price, $30 + 10-point movement in stock price
New warrant price, $15 (10-point gain)	New warrant price, $40 (10-point gain)
Percentage gain in warrant $= \dfrac{\$10}{\$5} \times 100 = 200\%$	Percentage gain in warrant $= \dfrac{\$10}{\$30} \times 100 = 33\%$

*The warrant price would be greater than $5 because of the speculative premium. Nevertheless, we use $5 for ease of computation.

At the upper levels of stock value, much of this leverage is lost. At a stock value of $50 and a warrant value of $30, a 10-point movement in the stock would produce only a 33 percent gain in the warrant as indicated in the right panel of Table 19-6.

Another reason speculators pay a very low premium at higher stock prices is that there is less downside protection. A warrant selling at $30 when the stock price is $50 is more vulnerable to downside movement than is a $5 to $10 warrant when the stock is in the $20s.

Use of Warrants in Corporate Finance

Let us examine the suitability of warrants for corporate financing purposes. As previously indicated, warrants may allow for the issuance of debt under difficult circumstances. While a straight debt issue may not be acceptable or may be accepted only at extremely high rates, the same security may be well received because detachable warrants are included. Warrants may also be included as an add-on in a merger or acquisition agreement. A firm might offer $20 million in cash plus 10,000 warrants in exchange for all the outstanding shares of the acquisition candidate. Warrants may also be issued in a corporate reorganization or bankruptcy to offer the shareholders a chance to recover some of their investment if the restructuring goes well.

The use of warrants has traditionally been associated with aggressive high-flying firms such as speculative real estate companies, airlines, and conglomerates. However, in the 1970s staid and venerable American Telephone & Telegraph (AT&T) came out with a $1.57 billion debt offering, sweetened by the use of warrants.

As a financing device for creating new common stock, warrants may not be as desirable as convertible securities. A corporation with convertible debentures outstanding may force the conversion of debt to common stock through a call, while no similar device is available to the firm with warrants. The only possible inducement might be a step-up in exercise price—whereby the warrant holder pays a progressively higher option price if he does not exercise by a given date.

Accounting Considerations with Warrants

As with convertible securities, the potential dilutive effect of warrants must be considered.[5] The accountant must compute the number of new shares that could be created by the exercise of all warrants, with the provision that the total can be reduced

---

[5]Under most circumstances, if the market price is below the option price, dilution need not be considered; see *APB Opinion 15*, par. 35.

by the assumed use of the cash proceeds to purchase a partially offsetting amount of shares at the market price. Assume that warrants to purchase 10,000 shares at $20 are outstanding and that the current price of the stock is $50. We show the following:

1. New shares created	10,000
2. Reduction of shares from cash proceeds (computed below)	4,000
Cash proceeds = 10,000 shares at $20 = $200,000	
Current price of stock = $50	
Assumed reduction in shares outstanding from	
cash proceeds = $200,000/$50 = 4,000	
3. Assumed net increase in shares from exercise	
of warrants (10,000 − 4,000)	6,000

In computing diluted earnings per share, we will add 6,000 shares to the denominator, with no adjustment to the numerator. This of course will lead to some dilution in earnings per share. Its importance must be interpreted by the financial manager and security analyst.

Derivative Securities

There are many types of derivative securities, but those that are most important to a basic financial management course are options and futures contracts.[6] **Derivative securities** have value derived from an underlying security. In the case of equity options, the value is derived by the underlying common stock. Futures contracts on government bonds or Treasury bills derive their value from those government securities, and futures contracts on oil or wheat have those commodities as determinants of their basic values. Our intent here is to present basic conceptual material that introduces you to derivative securities.

Options

Options give the owner the right, but not the obligation, to buy or sell an underlying security at a set price for a given period of time. Companies often reward their most valuable employees with stock options as part of their compensation. An employee stock option is very similar to a warrant. An employee may be given an option to buy 10,000 shares of stock from the company at $25 per share. The employee stock option can have a life of 5 to 10 years and is supposed to motivate employees to focus on stockholder value. After all, if the stock goes to $100 per share over the life of the option, the employee could buy 10,000 shares of stock from the company for $250,000, sell the stock for $1 million (10,000 × $100) and pocket a taxable profit of $750,000. This is a phenomenon that has driven employee compensation for many companies.[7] Employee stock options are worth understanding; you never know when you might get offered a bonus package consisting of an employee stock option.

A **call option** is similar to an employee stock option in that it is an option to buy securities at a set price for a specific period of time, but it is usually traded between individual investors and not exercisable from the company. The Chicago Board Options Exchange is the foremost market for trading options. In a standardized call

---

[6]Warrants, which were discussed in the prior section, are also a form of derivatives.
[7]However, when misused, employee stock options have come under heavy criticism.

option, the writer of the call option guarantees that he or she will sell you 100 shares of stock at a set price. For this guarantee, the buyer of the call option pays the call writer a premium, perhaps $1 or $2 per share. If the option allows an investor to buy the stock at $40 per share and the stock closes at $38 on the expiration date, then the call writer keeps the premium and the call buyer loses his or her investment. On the other hand, if the stock closes at $45 per share, the owner of the call has the right to pay the call writer $40 per share for the 100 shares and the writer must deliver the 100 shares. There are also other ways to close out the position at a profit that go beyond the scope of this discussion.

A **put option** is an option to sell securities to the option writer at a set price for a specific period of time. A put works just the opposite of a call. The put writer guarantees to buy the shares from you at a set price. The put buyer generally thinks that there is a good probability that the underlying stock will fall in price, and he or she wants to hedge the risk of loss by giving the put writer a premium for the guarantee of transferring the stock at a set price. For example, if the put owner has an option to "put" (sell) the stock at $80 per share, the option would only be exercised if the stock price was less than $80. If the stock went to $65, the owner of the put could sell 100 shares to the writer of the put for $80 per share ($8,000). A profit of $1,500 would be garnered. Puts are often used as hedges against falling security prices, and the financial manager who is in charge of the corporate pension fund could use this tactic to help insure the pension portfolio from declining in value.

Futures

Unlike options, **futures contracts** impose on both parties the obligation to complete a purchase or sale transaction at a later date. Futures contracts are very common for commodities, currencies, and interest rate securities, especially government bonds. One characteristic of futures contracts is that the contract requires a very small down payment (margin) to control the futures contract. Often the down payment is 5 percent of the value of the underlying value of the securities or commodities. The major futures exchanges are the Chicago Board of Trade (CBOT) and Chicago Mercantile Exchange (CME), and they merged in 2007.

Let us suppose that Southwest Airlines was concerned that the price of oil might rise over the next six months. It could buy futures contracts on oil to be delivered six months from now at a price of $60 per barrel. If the price were $80 per barrel six months from now, it would exercise its right to buy oil at $60 per barrel, or $20 cheaper, than the market price at that time. All this is done on paper, but the $20 profit is real. Airlines such as Southwest, Lufthansa, and others have used this strategy many times to their benefit. The hedge can go against you when prices drop, and you could have bought fuel at lower prices without wasting money on the hedging strategy. With a hedging strategy using futures contracts, the airline does not actually lock in a price of fuel and would lose only the value of the futures contract if prices fell. However, some airlines have locked in pricing contracts with oil companies only to see prices fall. In these cases, they may be worse off than if they had hedged with futures contracts.

A similar strategy could be used by Pillsbury or General Mills to lock in the price of the wheat they buy to make flour. Using futures contracts guarantees the price for both the farmer who might sell the futures contract and the manufacturer who buys the futures contract. Futures contracts have varying time periods, and the participants usually have monthly choices out to one year. With futures contracts you do not take physical possession of the item; the gains or losses are all settled on paper.

Other futures contracts that are commonly used to hedge corporate financial strategies are interest rate futures or foreign currency futures. One common financial futures strategy is to hedge against interest rate movements. Perhaps you are building a new plant and you intend to pay for the plant by borrowing money through a mortgage. In the short term, the treasurer has negotiated a one-year construction loan at a floating rate. When the plant is complete, the treasurer will borrow the full amount from a mortgage banker on a 30-year fixed rate loan and repay the construction loan. If interest rates go up during the next 12 months, the treasurer will pay more money for the loan. To hedge rising interest rates, the treasurer can use a financial futures contract either to lock in a rate or to profit from an increase in rates. If rates go up, the treasurer can take the profit on the financial futures contract and use the profit to offset higher interest costs.

Strategies on using options and futures are usually taught in an advanced finance course. For those of you wanting to accelerate your knowledge, we suggest you continue the learning process.

SUMMARY

A number of security devices related to the debt and common stock of the firm are popular. Each security offers downside protection or upside potential, or a combination of these features.

A convertible security is a bond or share of preferred stock that can be converted into common stock at the option of the holder. Thus the holder has a fixed income security that will not go below a minimum amount because of the interest or dividend payment feature, and, at the same time, he or she has a security that is potentially convertible to common stock. If the common stock goes up in value, the convertible security will appreciate as well. From a corporate viewpoint, the firm may force conversion to common stock through a call feature and thus achieve a balanced capital structure. Interest rates on convertibles are usually lower than those on straight debt issues.

A warrant is an option to buy a stated number of shares of stock at a specified price over a given time period. The warrant has a large potential for appreciation if the stock goes up in value. Warrants are used primarily as sweeteners for debt instruments or as add-ons in merger tender offers or bankruptcy proceedings. When warrants are exercised, the basic debt instrument to which they may be attached is not eliminated, as is the case for a convertible debenture. The potential dilutive effect of warrants and convertible securities must be considered in computing earnings per share.

Derivative securities such as options and futures can be used to hedge risk such as the decline in the value of a pension fund portfolio, an oil price shock, an interest rate change, or a currency fluctuation. An option is the right, but not the obligation, to buy or sell a security at a set price for a fixed period of time. An employee stock option is one type of option contract and so are calls and puts. A call option is an option to buy while a put option is an option to sell. A futures contract is the agreement that provides for sale or purchase of a specific amount of a commodity or financial product at a designated time in the future at a given price.

REVIEW OF FORMULAS

1. Basic earnings per share $= \dfrac{\text{Earnings after taxes}}{\text{Shares of common stock}}$ (19-1)

2. $\dfrac{\text{Diluted earnings}}{\text{per share}} = \dfrac{\text{Adjusted earnings after taxes}}{\text{Shares outstanding} + \text{All convertible securities}^{*}}$ (19-2)

*Other types of securities that create common stock, such as warrants and options, would also be included.

3. Intrinsic value of a warrant

$$I = (M - E) \times N \qquad (19\text{-}3)$$

where

$I = $ Intrinsic value of a warrant
$M = $ Market value of common stock
$E = $ Exercise price of a warrant
$N = $ Number of shares each warrant entitles the holder to purchase

4. Speculative premium of a warrant

$$S = W - I \qquad (19\text{-}4)$$

where

$S = $ Speculative premium
$W = $ Warrant price
$I = $ Intrinsic value

LIST OF TERMS

convertible security   603
conversion ratio   603
conversion price   603
conversion value   603
conversion premium   604
pure bond value   604
floor value   604
downside risk   604
forced conversion   608
step-up in the conversion price   609
basic earnings per share   610
diluted earnings per share   610

warrant   611
financial sweetener   611
out-of-the-money warrant   611
in-the-money warrant   611
intrinsic value   612
exercise price   612
speculative premium   613
derivative securities   616
options   616
call option   616
put option   617
futures contracts   617

DISCUSSION QUESTIONS

1. What are the basic advantages to the corporation of issuing convertible securities? *(LO19-1)*

2. Why are investors willing to pay a premium over the theoretical value (pure bond value or conversion value)? *(LO19-2)*

3. Why is it said that convertible securities have a floor price? *(LO19-3)*

4. The price of Haltom Corporation 5¼ 2019 convertible bonds is $1,380. For the Williams Corporation, the 6⅛ 2018 convertible bonds are selling at $725. *(LO19-3)*

   a. Explain what factors might cause their prices to be different from their par values of $1,000.

   b. What will happen to each bond's value if long-term interest rates decline?

5. How can a company force conversion of a convertible bond? *(LO19-1)*

6. What is meant by a step-up in the conversion price? *(LO19-1)*

7. Explain the difference between basic earnings per share and diluted earnings per share. *(LO19-5)*

8. Explain how convertible bonds and warrants are similar and different. *(LO19-1 & 19-4)*

9. Explain why warrants are issued. (Why are they used in corporate finance?) *(LO19-4)*

10. What are the reasons that warrants often sell above their intrinsic value? *(LO19-4)*

11. What is the difference between a call option and a put option? *(LO19-6)*

12. Suggest two areas where the use of futures contracts is most common. What percentage of the value of the underlying security is typical as a down payment in a futures contract? *(LO19-6)*

13. You buy a stock option with an exercise price of $50. The cost of the option is $4. If the stock ends up at $56, do you have a profit or loss with a call option? With a put option? *(LO19-6)*

PRACTICE PROBLEMS AND SOLUTIONS

Features of a convertible bond
(LO19-1)

1. Scientific Instruments has a $1,000 par value convertible bond outstanding with a conversion ratio of 25. The common stock is selling for $45. The convertible bond is selling for $1,165.70.

   a. What is the conversion value?

   b. What is the conversion premium?

   c. What is the conversion price?

   d. If the common stock price falls to $20, and the pure bond price is $780, will the bond sell for greater than its conversion value?

Value of warrants
(LO19-1)

2. Eaton Hotel Corp. has warrants outstanding that allow the warrant holder to purchase 1.3 shares of stock per warrant at $9 per share (exercise price). The common stock is currently selling for $14.50, and the warrant is selling for $9.75.

   a. What is the intrinsic (minimum value) of the warrant?

   b. What is the speculative premium on this warrant?

   c. If the common stock price goes up to $19 and the speculative premium goes down to $1.50, what will be the price of the warrant?

Solutions

1. a. Conversion value = Stock price × Conversion ratio = $45 × 25 = $1,125

   b. Conversion premium = Convertible bond price − Conversion value

   $$= \$1,165.70 - \$1,125.00 = \$40.70$$

 c. Conversion price = Par value/Conversion ratio = $1,000/25 = $40

 d. First compute the new conversion value:

  Conversion value = Stock price × Conversion ratio = $20 × 25 = $500

The newly computed conversion value ($500) is below the pure bond value ($780), so the bond will definitely sell at a price above the conversion value.

2. *a.* Intrinsic value

$$I = (M - E) \times N$$

 where

  I = Intrinsic value of a warrant

  M = Market value of common stock...................... $14.50

  E = Exercise price of a warrant $9.00

  N = Number of shares each warrant entitles
    the holder to purchase.................................... 1.3

  $I = (\$14.50 - \$9.00) \times 1.3 = \$5.50 \times 1.3 = \$7.15$

 b. Speculative premium

$$S = W - I$$

 where

  S = Speculative premium

  W = Warrant price $9.75

  I = Intrinsic value $7.15

  $S = \$9.75 - \$7.15 = \$2.60$

 c. First compute the new intrinsic value:

$$I = (M - E) \times N$$
$$I = (\$19 - \$9) \times 1.3 = \$10 \times 1.3 = \$13$$

Then add the new speculative premium of $1.50 to the intrinsic value of $13 to get the price of the warrant.

  The warrant price is $13 + $1.50 = $14.50.

PROBLEMS

connect Selected problems are available with Connect. Please see the preface for more information.

Basic Problems

1. Preston Toy Co. has warrants outstanding that allow the holder to purchase a share of stock for $22 (exercise price). The common stock is currently selling for $28, while the warrant is selling for $9.25 per share.

 Value of warrants
 (LO19-4)

 a. What is the intrinsic (minimum) value of this warrant?

 b. What is the speculative premium on this warrant?

Value of warrants
(LO19-4)

2. Quantum Inc. has warrants outstanding that allow the holder to purchase 1.5 shares of stock per warrant at $30 per share (exercise price). Thus each individual share can be purchased at $30 with the warrant. The common stock is currently selling for $36. The warrant is selling for $12.

   a. What is the intrinsic (minimum) value of this warrant?

   b. What is the speculative premium on this warrant?

   c. What should happen to the speculative premium as the expiration date approaches?

Breakeven on
warrants
(LO19-4)

3. The warrants of Integra Life Sciences allow the holder to buy a share of stock at $11.75 and are selling for $2.85. The stock price is currently $8.50. To what price must the stock go for the warrant purchaser to at least be assured of breaking even?

Breakeven on
warrants
(LO19-4)

4. The warrants of Dragon Pet Co. allow the holder to buy a share of stock at $26.20 and are selling for $14.10. The stock price is currently $23.50. To what price must the stock go for the warrant purchaser to at least be assured of breaking even?

Features of
convertible bond
(LO19-1)

5. Plunkett Gym Equipment Inc. has a $1,000 par value convertible bond outstanding that can be converted into 25 shares of common stock. The common stock is currently selling for $34.75 a share, and the convertible bond is selling for $960.

   a. What is the conversion value of the bond?

   b. What is the conversion premium?

   c. What is the conversion price?

Assume all bonds in the following problems have a par value of $1,000.

Features of
convertible bond
(LO19-1)

6. O'Reilly Moving Company has a $1,000 par value convertible bond outstanding that can be converted into 20 shares of common stock. The common stock is currently selling for $43.10 a share, and the convertible bond is selling for $900.00.

   a. What is the conversion value of the bond?

   b. What is the conversion premium?

   c. What is the conversion price?

Price of a
convertible bond
(LO19-2)

7. The bonds of Goniff Bank & Trust have a conversion premium of $90. Their conversion price is $20. The common stock price is $16.50. What is the price of the convertible bonds?

Price of a
convertible bond
(LO19-2)

8. The bonds of Generic Labs Inc. have a conversion premium of $70. Their conversion price is $25. The common stock price is $22.50. What is the price of the convertible bond?

Conversion
premium for bond
(LO19-2)

9. Sherwood Forest Products has a convertible bond quoted on the NYSE bond market at 90. (Bond quotes represent percentage of par value. Thus 70 represents $700, 80 represents $800, and so on.) It matures in 10 years and carries a coupon rate of 5½ percent. The conversion ratio is 25, and the common stock is currently selling for $33 per share on the NYSE.

   a. Compute the conversion premium.

   b. At what price does the common stock need to sell for the conversion value to be equal to the current bond price?

10. Reynolds Technology has a convertible bond outstanding, trading in the marketplace at $835. The par value is $1,000, the coupon rate is 9 percent, and the bond matures in 25 years. The conversion ratio is 20, and the company's common stock is selling for $41 per share. Interest is paid semiannually.

    a. What is the conversion value?

    b. If similar bonds, which are not convertible, are currently yielding 12 percent, what is the pure bond value of this convertible bond? (Use semiannual analysis as described in Chapter 10.)

Conversion value and pure bond value (LO19-1)

11. Pittsburgh Steel Company has a convertible bond outstanding, trading in the marketplace at $960. The par value is $1,000, the coupon rate is 10 percent, and the bond matures in 20 years. The conversion price is $55, and the company's common stock is selling for $48 per share. Interest is paid semiannually. If nonconvertible bonds of similar risk are currently yielding 12 percent, what will be the pure bond value of the Pittsburgh Steel Company bonds? (Use semiannual analysis.)

Pure bond value and change in interest rates (LO19-3)

Intermediate Problems

12. The Olsen Mining Company has been very successful in the last five years. Its $1,000 par value convertible bonds have a conversion ratio of 32. The bonds have a quoted interest rate of 7 percent a year. The firm's common stock is currently selling for $41.30 per share. The current bond price has a conversion premium of $10 over the conversion value.

    a. What is the current price of the bond?

    b. What is the current yield on the bond (annual interest divided by the bond's market price)?

    c. If the common stock price goes down to $23.40 and the conversion premium goes up to $100, what will be the new current yield on the bond?

Current yield on a convertible bond (LO19-1)

13. Standard Olive Company of California has a convertible bond outstanding with a coupon rate of 5 percent and a maturity date of 20 years. It is rated Aa, and competitive, nonconvertible bonds of the same risk class carry a 10 percent return. The conversion ratio is 15. Currently the common stock is selling for $35 per share on the New York Stock Exchange.

    a. What is the conversion price?

    b. What is the conversion value?

    c. Compute the pure bond value. (Use semiannual analysis.)

    d. Draw a graph that includes the pure bond value and the conversion value but not the convertible bond price. For the stock price on the horizontal axis, use 10, 20, 30, 40, 50, and 60.

    e. Calculate the crossover point at which the pure bond value equals conversion value.

✗ *Conversion value versus pure bond value (LO19-1)*

14. Defense Systems Inc. has convertible bonds outstanding that are callable at $1,070. The bonds are convertible into 33 shares of common stock. The stock is currently selling for $39.25 per share.

    a. If the firm announces it is going to call the bonds at $1,070, what action are bondholders likely to take and why?

Call feature with a convertible bond (LO19-1)

b.   Assume that instead of the call feature, the firm has the right to drop the conversion ratio from 33 down to 30 after 5 years and down to 27 after 10 years. If the bonds have been outstanding for 4 years and 11 months, what will the price of the bonds be if the stock price is $40? Assume the bonds carry no conversion premium.

c.   Further assume that you anticipate that the common stock price will be up to $42.50 in two months. Considering the conversion feature, should you convert now or continue to hold the bond for at least two more months?

Convertible bond and rates of return *(LO19-2)*

15. Vernon Glass Company has $15 million in 10 percent convertible bonds outstanding. The conversion ratio is 40, the stock price is $17, and the bond matures in 10 years. The bonds are currently selling at a conversion premium of $45 over their conversion value.

     If the price of the common stock rises to $23 on this date next year, what would your rate of return be if you bought a convertible bond today and sold it in one year? Assume on this date next year, the conversion premium has shrunk from $45 to $20.

Price appreciation with a warrant *(LO19-4)*

16. Assume you can buy a warrant for $6 that gives you the option to buy one share of common stock at $14 per share. The stock is currently selling at $18 per share.

a.   What is the intrinsic value of the warrant?

b.   What is the speculative premium on the warrant?

c.   If the stock rises to $29 per share and the warrant sells at its theoretical value without a premium, what will be the percentage increase in the stock price and the warrant price if you buy the stock and the warrant at the prices stated earlier? Explain this relationship.

Profit potential with a warrant *(LO19-4)*

17. The Redford Investment Company bought 100 Cinema Corp. warrants one year ago and would like to exercise them today. The warrants were purchased at $24 each, and they expire when trading ends today (assume there is no speculative premium left). Cinema Corp. common stock is selling today for $50 per share. The exercise price is $30 and each warrant entitles the holder to purchase two shares of stock, each at the exercise price.

a.   If the warrants are exercised today, what would the Redford Investment Company's dollar profit or loss be?

b.   What is the Redford Investment Company's percentage rate of return?

Comparing returns on warrants and common stock *(LO19-4)*

18. The Gifford Investment Company bought 90 Cable Corporation warrants one year ago and would like to exercise them today. The warrants were purchased at $25 each, and they expire when trading ends today. (Assume there is no speculative premium left.) Cable Corporation common stock was selling for $49 per share when Gifford Investment Company bought the warrants. The exercise price is $41, and each warrant entitles the holder to purchase two shares of stock, each at the exercise price.

a.   What was the intrinsic value of a warrant at that time?

b.   What was the speculative premium per warrant when the warrants were purchased? The purchase price, as indicated earlier, was $25.

c.   What would Gifford's total dollar profit or loss have been had it invested the $2,250 directly in Cable Corporation's common stock one year ago at $49 per share? Cable Corporation common stock is selling today for $59 per share.

    d.   What would the percentage rate of return be on this common stock invest-
ment? Compare this to the rate of return on the warrant computed when
the common stock was selling for $59 per share.

19. Mr. John Hailey has $1,000 to invest in the market. He is considering the
purchase of 50 shares of Comet Airlines at $20 per share. His broker suggests
that he may wish to consider purchasing warrants instead. The warrants are
selling for $10, and each warrant allows him to purchase one share of Comet
Airlines common stock at $18 per share.

**Return calculations
with warrants
(LO19-4)**

    a.   How many warrants can Mr. Hailey purchase for the same $1,000?

    b.   If the price of the stock goes to $40, what would be his total dollar and
percentage return on the stock?

    c.   At the time the stock goes to $40, the speculative premium on the warrant
goes to 0 (though the market value of the warrant goes up). What would be
Mr. Hailey's total dollar and percentage returns on the warrant?

    d.   Assuming that the speculative premium remains $3.50 over the intrinsic
value, how far would the price of the stock have to fall from $40 before the
warrant has no value?

20. Online Network Inc. has net income of $650,000 in the current fiscal year.
There are 100,000 shares of common stock outstanding along with convertible
bonds, which have a total face value of $1.6 million. The $1.6 million is
represented by 1,600 different $1,000 bonds. Each $1,000 bond pays 6 percent
interest. The conversion ratio is 10. The firm is in a 30 percent tax bracket.

Ӿ

**Earnings per share
with warrants
(LO19-5)**

    a.   Compute basic earnings per share.

    b.   Compute diluted earnings per share.

21. Myers Drugs Inc. has 1.20 million shares of stock outstanding. Earnings after
taxes are $9 million. Myers also has warrants outstanding which allow the holder
to buy 100,000 shares of stock at $15 per share. The stock is currently selling for
$50 per share.

**Earnings per share
with convertibles
(LO19-5)**

    a.   Compute basic earnings per share.

    b.   Compute diluted earnings per share considering the possible impact of the
warrants. Use the following formula:

$$\frac{\text{Earnings after taxes}}{\text{Shares outstanding} + \text{Assumed net increase in shares from the warrants}}$$

Advanced Problems

22. Tulsa Drilling Company has $1.3 million in 12 percent convertible bonds
outstanding. Each bond has a $1,000 par value. The conversion ratio is 40,
the stock price is $36, and the bonds mature in 10 years. The bonds are
currently selling at a conversion premium of $60 over the conversion value.

Ӿ

Conversion value and
changing pure bond
value *(LO19-3)*

    a.   Today, one year later, the price of Tulsa Drilling Company common
stock has risen to $46. What would your rate of return be if you had
purchased the convertible bond one year ago and sold it today? Assume
that on the date of sale, the conversion premium has shrunk from $60
to $10. (Hint: Don't forget to include the interest payment for
the first year.)

b. Assume the yield on similar nonconvertible bonds has fallen to 8 percent at the time of sale. What would the pure bond value be at that point? (Use semiannual analysis.) Would the pure bond value have a significant effect on valuation then?

Falling stock prices and pure bond value (LO19-3)

23. Manpower Electric Company has 6 percent convertible bonds outstanding. Each bond has a $1,000 par value. The conversion ratio is 20, the stock price $36, and the bonds mature in 16 years.

a. What is the conversion value of the bond?

b. Assume after one year, the common stock price falls to $30.50. What is the conversion value of the bond?

c. Also, assume after one year, interest rates go up to 10 percent on similar bonds. There are 15 years left to maturity. What is the pure value of the bond? Use semiannual analysis.

d. Will the conversion value of the bond (part b) or the pure value of the bond (part c) have a stronger influence on its price in the market?

e. If the bond trades in the market at its pure bond value, what would be the conversion premium (stated as a percentage of the conversion value)?

COMPREHENSIVE PROBLEM

Fondren Exploration, Ltd.

(Rates of return on convertible bond investments) (LO19-1)

Fondren Exploration, Ltd. has 1,000 convertible bonds ($1,000 par value) outstanding, each of which may be converted to 50 shares of stock. The $1 million worth of bonds has 25 years to maturity. The current price of the stock is $26 per share. The firm's net income in the most recent fiscal year was $270,000. The bonds pay 12 percent interest. The corporation has 150,000 shares of common stock outstanding. Current market rates on long-term nonconvertible bonds of equal quality are 14 percent. A 35 percent tax rate is assumed.

a. Compute diluted earnings per share.

b. Assume the bonds currently sell at a 5 percent conversion premium over conversion value (based on a stock price of $26). However, as the price of the stock increases from $26 to $37 due to new events, there will be an increase in the bond price, and a zero conversion premium. Under these circumstances, determine the rate of return on a convertible bond investment that is part of this price change, based on the appreciation in value.

c. Now assume the stock price is $16 per share because a competitor introduced a new product. Would the conversion value be greater than the pure bond value, based on the interest rates stated above? (See Table 16-2 in Chapter 16 to get the bond value without having to go through the actual computation.)

d. Referring to part c, if the convertible traded at a 15 percent premium over the conversion value, would the convertible be priced above the pure bond value?

e. If long-term interest rates in the market go down to 10 percent while the stock price is at $23, with a 6 percent conversion premium, what would the difference be between the market price of the convertible bond and the pure bond value? Assume 25 years to maturity, and once again use Table 16-2 for part of your answer.

COMPREHENSIVE PROBLEM

United Technology Corporation (UTC) has $40 million of convertible bonds outstanding (40,000 bonds at $1,000 par value) with a coupon rate of 11 percent. Interest rates are currently 8 percent for bonds of equal risk. The bonds have 15 years left to maturity. The bonds may be called at a 9 percent premium over par. They are convertible into 30 shares of common stock. The tax rate for the company is 25 percent.

United Technology Corp.

(A call decision with convertible bonds) *(LO19-1)*

The firm's common stock is currently selling for $41, and it pays a dividend of $3.50 per share. The expected income for the company is $38 million with 6 million shares outstanding.

Thoroughly analyze the bond and determine whether the firm should call the bond at the 9 percent call premium. In your analysis, consider the following:

a. The impact of the call on basic and diluted earnings per share (assume the call forces conversion).

b. The consequences of your decision on financing flexibility.

c. The net change in cash outflows to the company as a result of the call and conversion.

WEB EXERCISE

1. In this web exercise we use the Chicago Board Options Exchange website to cover options. While we will stay with basic coverage of the material, this website is capable of taking you into much more complex areas of derivative securities than the textbook. Go to www.cboe.com and click on "Products," and then on the drop-down menu select "Products Main."

2. What are the first five products offered?

3. Click on "VIX Volatility." What does the title stand for? Why might this be considered a measure of risk?

4. Go back and click on "Products" at the top of the screen. Click on "Options on Single Stocks and Exchange Traded Products" in the drop-down menu. What is the purpose of these derivative products issued on ETPs?

Note: Occasionally a topic we have listed may have been deleted, updated, or moved into a different location on a website. If you click on the site map or site index, you will be introduced to a table of contents that should aid you in finding the topic you are looking for.

Expanding the Perspective of Corporate Finance

CHAPTER 20
External Growth through Mergers

CHAPTER 21
International Financial Management

>>> RELATED WEBSITES

finance.yahoo.com
www.opic.gov

External Growth through Mergers

LEARNING OBJECTIVES

LO 20-1 Firms engage in mergers for financial motives and to increase operating efficiency. Tax benefits and other factors must also be considered.

LO 20-2 Companies may be acquired through cash purchases or by one company exchanging its shares for another company's shares.

LO 20-3 The potential impact of the merger on earnings per share and stock value must be carefully assessed.

LO 20-4 The diversification benefits of a merger should be evaluated.

LO 20-5 Some buyouts are unfriendly and are strongly opposed by the potential candidates.

Berkshire Hathaway is a multinational holding company run by Warren Buffett, who is acclaimed as one of America's most astute investors. Over the years, Berkshire Hathaway has purchased entire companies and acquired large ownership stakes in others. In 2013 Buffet made headlines with the purchase of H. J. Heinz Company. The announcement stated that the total offer was $23 billion in cash plus assumption of debt for a total of $28 billion. Berkshire Hathaway put up $12.1 billion in cash with the rest coming from 3G Capital of New York, which would indicate that Berkshire held the majority interest in Heinz. This was one of the first times that Buffett partnered with another company for a purchase.

Berkshire Hathaway has a habit of buying whole companies and letting them continue as wholly owned subsidiaries. If you go to www.berkshirehathaway.com, you will find links to over 50 subsidiary companies, some with well-known names like Helzberg Diamonds, Johns Manville, Fruit of the Loom, and GEICO Insurance. In 2009 Berkshire Hathaway made the biggest purchase in the company's history. The company already owned 22.6 percent of the Burlington Northern Santa Fe (BNSF) railway and acquired the remaining 77.4 percent for $44 billion, which included $34 billion in cash and the assumption of $10 billion in debt. In 2011 it acquired Lubrizol, a maker of industrial lubricants and molecular chemicals used in pharmaceuticals, for $9 billion. The Berkshire Hathaway portfolio also includes large ownership positions in companies such as American Express, Pepsi, IBM, and Wells Fargo to name a few. In October of 2017 Berkshire bought a 38.6 percent interest in Pilot Flying J, a leading company providing services to trucking companies. You may have seen Pilot gas stations as you traveled down U.S. highways. In 2023 Berkshire will acquire another 41.4 percent bringing its holdings to 80 percent.

Many industries over the last several decades have undergone consolidation through mergers. These have occurred for many reasons such as an attempt to reduce costs through elimination of duplicate services, acquisition of new technology, or simply the desire to become bigger and more globally competitive. Some of these industries include airlines, telecommunications, and banking.

In February 2013 U.S. Airways and American Airlines announced a merger valued at $11 billion. American Airlines was coming out of bankruptcy proceedings, and the debtholders who controlled the destiny of American Airlines supported a plan proposed by the smaller

U.S Airways to acquire American. The new company is called American Airlines, and the former American Airlines debt holders received $8 billion in common stock of the new entity while U.S. Airways received $3 billion. This is a case of the whale being swallowed by the shark. The merger results have proved rewarding to investors. The common stock price on February 25, 2013, was $13.61, and by February 13, 2018, the stock closed at $50.87 for a gain of 373 percent. This acquisition/merger perhaps completes the consolidation of the U.S. airline industry. Earlier in the 2000s, United Airlines merged with Continental and Delta merged with Northwest Airlines. In previous times, other grand old names such as Eastern Airlines, Pan American, Braniff, and TWA were either acquired or went bankrupt.

Another area of increased merger activity has been the pharmaceutical industry. Drug company giant Pfizer acquired Warner-Lambert and Pharmacia, as well as Wyeth, and in February 2015 made a $17 billion offer for Hospira. According to Dealogic, in 2014 health care mergers and acquisitions dominated all industries with 938 U.S. deals worth $310 billion. This set a record and was up 57 percent from 2013. The premium paid over closing market prices the day before the offer was 34 percent and was 5 percent lower than the 39 percent premiums paid in 2010. Premiums can fluctuate over time based on industries, market optimism, and strategic fit between the merged companies. The premiums in 2013 were half of those in 2014. Perhaps the biggest premium paid in this industry was Gilead's 89 percent premium for its $11 billion purchase of Pharmasset in 2011.

The energy sector has also been active in the merger game with combinations between Exxon and Mobil, British Petroleum (BP) and Amoco, and Chevron and Texaco. There are two factors encouraging consolidation in this industry—the hazardous risk of finding new sources of energy and the unsettling presence of volatile oil prices.

Mergers have also had a significant impact in aerospace, entertainment, consumer products, and technology. For a historical perspective, please note the largest completed or announced mergers in the United States (and world) in Table 20-1.

Table 20-1	Largest mergers from 2010 to 2018			
Rank	Year	Purchaser	Purchased	Transaction value (in billions USD)
1	2013	Verizon Communications	Verizon Wireless	$130.0
2	2015	Dow Chemical	DuPont	130.0
3	2015	Anheuser-Busch InBev	SAB Miller	130.0
4	2016	AT&T Inc.	Time Warner	108.7
5	2015	Heinz	Kraft	100.0
6	2016	Linde AG	Praxair	80.0
7	2015	Charter Communications	Time Warner Cable	78.7
8	2015	Actavis	Allergan, Inc	70.5
9	2015	Royal Dutch Shell	BG Group	70.0
10	2017	CVS Health	Aetna	70.0
11	2015	Dell	EMC Corporation	67.0

You can also see from Figure 20-1 that mergers and acquisitions are affected by the economy. Figure 20-1 shows merger and acquisition activity from 1985 to February 2017. The numbers peaked during the Internet bubble of the late nineties and then peaked again before the financial crisis. They declined during 2008 and 2009 (the worst of the financial crisis), and as the stock market reached new highs in 2016 and 2017, merger activity picked up.

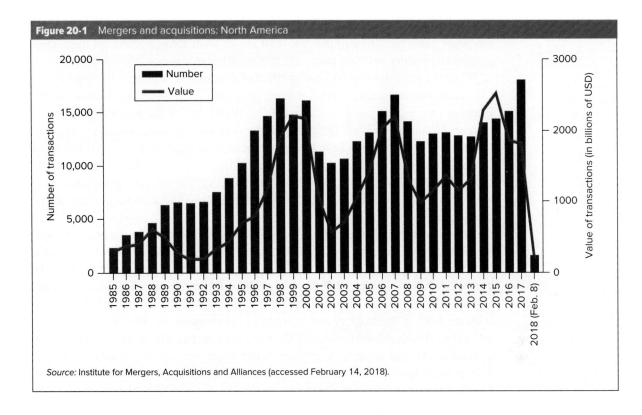

Figure 20-1   Mergers and acquisitions: North America

Source: Institute for Mergers, Acquisitions and Alliances (accessed February 14, 2018).

In the following sections, we more fully examine the motives for business combinations; the establishment of negotiated terms of exchange with the associated accounting implications; and the stock market effect of mergers.

Motives for Business Combinations

A business combination may take the form of either a merger or a consolidation. A **merger** is defined as a combination of two or more companies in which the resulting firm maintains the identity of the acquiring company. In a **consolidation**, two or more companies are combined to form a new entity. A consolidation might be utilized when the firms are of equal size and market power. For our discussion, the primary emphasis will be on mergers, though virtually all of the principles presented could apply to consolidations as well.

Financial Motives

Portfolio Effect   The motives for mergers and consolidations are both financial and nonfinancial. We examine the financial motives first. As discussed in Chapter 13, a merger allows the acquiring firm to enjoy a potentially desirable **portfolio effect** by achieving risk reduction while perhaps maintaining the firm's rate of return. If two firms that benefit from opposite phases of the business cycle combine, their variability in performance may be reduced. Risk-averse investors may then discount the future performance of the merged firm at a lower rate and thus assign it a higher valuation than that assigned to the separate firms. The same point can be made in regard to multinational mergers.

Through merger, a firm that has holdings in diverse economic and political climates can enjoy some reduction in the risks that derive from foreign exchange translation, government politics, military takeovers, and localized recessions.

While the portfolio diversification effect of a merger is intellectually appealing—with each firm becoming a mini–mutual fund unto itself—the practicalities of the situation can become quite complicated. No doubt one of the major forces behind merger movements in prior decades was the desire of the conglomerates for diversification. The lessons we have learned from most conglomerates is that too much diversification can strain the operating capabilities of the firm. In the case of Berkshire Hathaway, because the companies in their portfolio are kept as separate operating companies, Berkshire might be considered a holding company rather than a conglomerate.

As one form of evidence on the lack of success of some of these earlier mergers, the ratio of divestitures[1] to new acquisitions was only 11 percent in 1967, but it rose to over 50 percent generations later. As examples, Sears spent the early 1990s shedding itself of its Allstate insurance division, its Coldwell Banker real estate brokerage, and also Dean Witter, its entry into the stock brokerage business. Unfortunately Sears itself is on the brink of bankruptcy and continues to close stores in 2018. Eastman Kodak sold off its chemical holdings during the same time period. The stock market reaction to divestitures may actually be positive when it can be shown that management is freeing itself from an unwanted or unprofitable division.[2] In the case of Eastman Kodak, the spun-off division Eastman Chemical is doing quite well as of 2018, while the old Kodak declared bankruptcy in January 2012 after failing to see the impact of digital photography on its old-fashioned film business. It emerged from bankruptcy in September 2013, and time will tell how it will do.

Access to Financial Markets   A second financial motive is the improved financing posture that a merger can create as a result of expansion. Larger firms may enjoy greater access to financial markets and thus be in a better position to raise debt and equity capital. Such firms may also be able to attract larger and more prestigious investment bankers to handle future financing. Greater financing capability may also be inherent in the merger itself. This is likely to be the case if the acquired firm has a strong cash position or a low debt-equity ratio that can be used to expand borrowing by the acquiring company.

Tax Inversions   In recent years and peaking in 2014, U.S. companies were acquiring foreign companies in low-tax countries and changing their corporate headquarters overseas, thus being taxed as a foreign company. For example, in 2014 Burger King acquired Tim Hortons and became domiciled in Canada. Medtronics acquired an Irish company and is now taxed as an Irish company even though its operational headquarters is in Minneapolis. Given that the United States had one of the highest tax rates on corporate earnings (35 percent) in the world, at that time companies figured they could save bundles in taxes by moving their headquarters to countries like Ireland, which

---

[1]A divestiture is a spin-off or a sell-off of a subsidiary or a division.
[2]J. Fred Weston, "Divestitures: Mistakes or Learning," *Journal of Applied Corporate Finance* 4 (Summer 1989), pp. 68–76.

has a corporate tax rate of 12.5 percent. In fact, the U.S. Treasury estimated that tax inversions could cost over $33 billion in lost taxes over the next decade. Fortunately the 2017 Tax Cuts and Jobs Act rectified the situation by putting corporations on a territorial tax system and lowering corporate tax rates to 21 percent. A territorial tax system taxes earnings in the country where the income is earned and this puts U.S. companies on the same footing as foreign competitors and eliminates the need for inversions. U.S. companies no longer need to keep foreign earnings abroad to avoid paying U.S. taxes when they bring the cash back to the United States.

It is estimated that U.S. companies have over $2 trillion in corporate accounts overseas, and now with the new tax code, this money can be brought back to the United States without a huge tax bill. It is expected that this influx of capital will result in dividend increases, more stock buybacks, and debt repurchases, but more importantly for this chapter, more mergers and acquisitions.

Tax Loss Carryforward   A final financial motive is the **tax loss carryforward** that might be available in a merger if one of the firms has previously sustained a tax loss.

In the following example, we assume firm A acquires firm B, which has a $220,000 tax loss carryforward. We look at firm A's financial position before and after the merger. The assumption is that the firm has a 20 percent tax rate.

The tax shield value of a carryforward to firm A is equal to the loss involved times the tax rate ($220,000 × 20 percent = $44,000). Based on the carryforward, the company can reduce its total taxes from $60,000 to $16,000 (far right column in blue below), and thus it could pay $44,000 for the carryforward alone (this is on a nondiscounted basis).

	2016	2017	2018	Total Values
Firm A (without merger):				
Before-tax income	$100,000	$100,000	$100,000	$300,000
Taxes (20%)	20,000	20,000	20,000	60,000
Income available to stockholders	$ 80,000	$ 80,000	$ 80,000	$240,000
	2016	**2017**	**2018**	**Total Values**
Firm A (with merger and associated tax benefits):				
Before-tax income	$100,000	$100,000	$100,000	$300,000
Tax loss carryforward	100,000	100,000	20,000	220,000
Net taxable income	$ 0	$ 0	$ 80,000	$ 80,000
Taxes (20%)	0	0	16,000	16,000
Income available to stockholders	$100,000	$100,000	$ 84,000*	$284,000*

*Before-tax income minus taxes ($100,000 − $16,000 = $84,000).

As would be expected, income available to stockholders also has gone up by $44,000 ($284,000 − $240,000 = $44,000). The values in red can be found in the far right column above. Of course firm B's anticipated operating gains and losses for future years must also be considered in analyzing the deal. The 2017 Tax Cuts and Jobs Act states that net operating losses can be carried forward indefinitely. Although with the lower tax rate of 21 percent the benefits of this type of transaction is not as beneficial as it used to be.

A generation ago, the corporate conglomerate was thought to be the ideal business model. Firms such as LTV, Litton, and Textron all owned subsidiaries that were in widely different industries.

The advantages of the conglomerate organization were thought to be many. First of all, to the extent that the firm's subsidiaries are non-correlated or negatively correlated, there is risk reduction. For example, a firm that owns airlines, oil companies, machine tools manufacturers, banks, and hotels is going to be influenced by different factors during the up-and-down phases of a business cycle. To the extent there is risk reduction and investors are risk-averse (do not like risk), there should be a higher valuation for the firm's stock. Furthermore, the firm should have greater capacity to take on debt because there will be less variability in earnings and cash flow.

Also, there are tax advantages. Losses in one division of the firm can be written off against gains in another. While the same goal of lower taxes could be achieved in a single-industry firm through tax loss carrybacks and carryforwards, that is a much more tedious process.

Furthermore, the conglomerate's internal allocation of capital to the most efficient divisions and away from the least efficient divisions may be more effective than the overall stock market in accomplishing the same goal between companies. The managers of a conglomerate are viewing the financial performance of each industry's division on a daily or weekly basis as opposed to the stock market where there is a lag in reporting performance, and not all investors are well informed even when information is available.

But wait a minute! Don't run out and buy stock in a conglomerate just yet. Research has shown that single-line businesses tend to have higher operating profitability than the subsidiary of a conglomerate in the same industry. This is due to greater focus. A conglomerate may represent a "jack of all trades, but a master of none."

Also a failing business cannot have a value below zero if operated on its own, but may have a negative value if it is part of an otherwise profitable conglomerate. Its losses can continue to eat into the profits and value of the nonrelated divisions. Such was the case with Tenneco in the 1990s when the firm's money-losing farm equipment business drained the profits and incentives from its auto parts and chemical divisions.

What about stock market performance? How do conglomerates compare to single-industry firms in terms of providing returns to investors? There are enough studies on this topic to fill up a midsize university's library. The results of hundreds of studies are pretty much a draw.

What is not a draw is the overall value assigned to conglomerates versus single industry firms. There is a diversification discount of 13 to 15 percent on average (Berger and Otek, *Journal of Finance*, 1995). This has also been confirmed by later studies. Furthermore, the more unrelated the divisions, the greater the discount.

Take the example of Fortune Brands. It operated in four major industries: hardware and home improvement; office products; golf and leisure products; and wine and spirits. Some of its better-known labels across the board are Master Lock, Titleist golf balls, and Jim Beam bourbon.

True to form, when the imputed value of each division (based on the value of publicly traded companies in the same industry) is added together on a weighted average basis, the total value is approximately 15 percent greater than the stock market value of Fortune Brands (Kelleher, Working Paper, 2003). Thus we speak of a diversification discount of approximately 15 percent for the conglomerate firm. In this case, the whole (the conglomerate) is less than the sum of the parts.

Fortune listened to its financial advisors and, before splitting into two companies, sold its Acushnet golf business for $1.225 billion and then spun off Fortune Brands Home and Security and Beam into two separate companies in October 2011. Beam was later acquired for $13.6 billion at a 25 percent premium over its closing stock price on January 12, 2014. The downfall of General Electric, another venerable conglomerate, is a story still unfolding. Problems surfaced in 2017 when the new CEO, John Flannery, was given the task of fixing GE. The market had a "show me" attitude and drove the stock price down from the high $20s to a low of $14.29 on February 9, 2018.

Nonfinancial Motives

The nonfinancial motives for mergers and consolidations include the desire to expand management and marketing capabilities as well as the acquisition of new products.

While mergers may be directed toward either **horizontal integration** (that is, the acquisition of competitors) or **vertical integration** (the acquisition of buyers or sellers of goods and services to the company), antitrust policy generally precludes the elimination of competition. For this reason, mergers are often with companies in allied but not directly related fields. The pure conglomerate merger of industries in totally unrelated industries is still undertaken, but less frequently than in the past.

Perhaps the greatest management motive for a merger is the possible synergistic effect. **Synergy** is said to occur when the whole is greater than the sum of the parts. This "2 + 2 = 5" effect may be the result of eliminating overlapping functions in production and marketing as well as meshing together various engineering capabilities. In terms of planning related to mergers, there is often a tendency to overestimate the possible synergistic benefits that might accrue.

Motives of Selling Stockholders

Most of our discussion has revolved around the motives of the acquiring firm that initiates a merger. Likewise, the selling stockholders may be motivated by a desire to receive the acquiring company's stock—which may have greater acceptability or activity in the marketplace than the stock they hold. Also, when cash is offered instead of stock, this gives the selling stockholders an opportunity to diversify their holdings into many new investments. As will be discussed later in the chapter, the selling stockholders generally receive an attractive price for their stock that may well exceed its current market or book value.

In addition, officers of the selling company may receive attractive postmerger management contracts as well as directorships in the acquiring firm. In some circumstances, they may be allowed to operate the company as a highly autonomous subsidiary after the merger (though this is probably the exception).[3]

A final motive of the selling stockholders may simply be the bias against smaller businesses that has developed in this country and around the world. Real clout in the financial markets may dictate being part of a larger organization. These motives should not be taken as evidence that all or even most officers or directors of smaller firms wish to sell out—a matter that we shall examine further when we discuss negotiated offers versus takeover attempts.

Terms of Exchange

In determining the price that will be paid for a potential acquisition, a number of factors are considered, including earnings, cash flow, dividends, and growth potential. We shall divide our analysis between cash purchases and stock-for-stock exchanges, in which the acquiring company trades stock rather than paying cash for the acquired firm.

---

[3]This is most likely to happen when the acquiring firm is a foreign company.

Cash Purchases

The cash purchase of another company can be viewed within the context of a capital budgeting decision. Instead of purchasing new plant or machinery, the purchaser has opted to acquire a *going concern.* For example, assume the Invest Corporation is analyzing the acquisition of the Sell Corporation for $1 million. The Sell Corporation has expected cash flow (aftertax earnings plus depreciation) of $100,000 per year for the next 5 years and $150,000 per year for the 6th through the 20th years. Furthermore, the synergistic benefits of the merger (in this case, combining production facilities) will add $10,000 per year to cash flow. Finally, the Sell Corporation has a $50,000 tax loss carryforward that can be used immediately by the Invest Corporation. Assuming a 20 percent tax rate, the $50,000 loss carryforward will shield $10,000 of profit from taxes immediately. The Invest Corporation has a 10 percent cost of capital, and this is assumed to remain stable with the merger. Our analysis would be as follows:

Cash outflow:			
Purchase price			$1,000,000
Less tax shield benefit from tax loss carryforward ($50,000 × 20%)			10,000
Net cash outflow			$ 990,000
Cash inflows:			
Years 1–5:	$100,000	Cash inflow	
	10,000	Synergistic benefit	
	$110,000	Total cash inflow	
Present value of $110,000 × 3.791			$ 417,010
Years 6–20:	$150,000	Cash inflow	
	10,000	Synergistic benefit	
	$160,000	Total cash inflow	
Present value of $160,000 × 4.723			755,680
Total present value of inflows			$1,172,690

The present value factor for the first five years (3.791) is based on $n = 5$, $i = 10$ percent, and can be found in Appendix D. For the 6th through the 20th years, we take the present value factor in Appendix D for $n = 20$, $i = 10$ percent, and subtract the present value factor for $n = 5$, $i = 10$ percent. This allows us to isolate the 6th through the 20th years with a factor of 4.723 (8.514 − 3.791).

Finally, the net present value of the investment is found by subtracting the outflow from the present value of the inflows:

Total present value of inflows	$1,172,690
Net cash outflow	990,000
Net present value	$ 182,690

The acquisition appears to represent a desirable alternative for the expenditure of cash, with a positive net present value of $182,690.

In the market environment of the last several decades, some firms could be purchased at a value below the replacement costs of their assets and thus represented a potentially desirable capital investment. As an extreme early example, Anaconda Copper had an asset replacement value of $1.3 billion when the firm was purchased by Atlantic Richfield for $684 million in the 1980s. With the stock market gains and losses of the last two decades, such bargain purchases may still be found.

Stock-for-Stock Exchange

On a stock-for-stock exchange, we use a somewhat different analytical approach, emphasizing the earnings per share impact of exchanging securities (and ultimately the market valuation of those earnings). The analysis is made primarily from the viewpoint of the acquiring firm. The shareholders of the acquired firm are concerned mainly about the initial price they are paid for their shares and about the outlook for the acquiring firm.

Assume that Expand Corporation is considering the acquisition of Small Corporation. Significant financial information on the firms before the merger is provided in Table 20-2.

Table 20-2　Financial data on potential merging firms

	Small Corporation	Expand Corporation
Total earnings	$200,000	$500,000
Number of shares of stock outstanding	50,000	200,000
Earnings per share	$4.00	$2.50
Price-earnings ratio (P/E)	7.5×	12×
Market price per share	$30.00	$30.00

We begin our analysis with the assumption that one share of Expand Corporation ($30) will be traded for one share of Small Corporation ($30). In actuality, Small Corporation will probably demand more than $30 per share because the acquired firm usually gets a premium over the current market value. We will later consider the impact of paying such a premium.

If 50,000 new shares of Expand Corporation are traded in exchange for all the old shares of Small Corporation, Expand Corporation will then have 250,000 shares outstanding. At the same time, its claim to earnings will go to $700,000 when the two firms are combined. Postmerger earnings per share will be $2.80 for the Expand Corporation, as indicated in Table 20-3.

Table 20-3　Postmerger earnings per share

Total earnings: Small ($200,000) + Expand ($500,000)	$700,000
Shares outstanding in surviving corporation:	
Old (200,000) + New (50,000)	250,000

$$\text{New earnings per share for Expand Corporation} = \frac{\$700,000}{250,000} = \$2.80$$

A number of observations are worthy of note. First, the earnings per share of Expand Corporation have increased as a result of the merger, rising from $2.50 to $2.80. This has occurred because Expand Corporation's P/E ratio of 12 was higher than the 7.5 P/E ratio of Small Corporation at the time of the merger (as previously presented in Table 20-2). Whenever a firm acquires another entity whose P/E ratio is lower than its own, there is an immediate increase in earnings per share.

Of course, if Expand Corporation pays a price higher than Small Corporation's current market value, which is typically the case, it may be paying equal to or more than its own current P/E ratio for Small Corporation. For example, at a price of $48 per share for Small Corporation, Expand Corporation will be paying 12 times Small Corporation's earnings, which is exactly the current P/E ratio of Expand Corporation. Under these circumstances, there will be no change in postmerger earnings per share for Expand Corporation.

Endless possibilities can occur in mergers based on stock-for-stock exchanges. Even if the acquiring company increases its immediate earnings per share as a result of the merger, it may slow its future growth rate if it is buying a less aggressive company. Conversely, the acquiring company may dilute immediate postmerger earnings per share by paying a high price, but increase its potential growth rate for the future as a result of acquiring a rapidly growing company.

The ultimate test of a merger rests with its ability to maximize the market value of the acquiring firm. This is sometimes a difficult goal to achieve but is the measure of the success of a merger.

Portfolio Effect

Inherent in all of our discussion is the importance of the merger's portfolio effect on the risk-return posture of the firm. The reduction or increase in risk may influence the P/E ratio as much as the change in the growth rate. To the extent that we are diminishing the overall risk of the firm in a merger, the postmerger P/E ratio and market value may increase even if the potential earnings growth is unchanged. Business risk reduction may be achieved through acquiring another firm that is influenced by a set of factors in the business cycle opposite from those that influence the acquiring firm, while financial risk reduction may be achieved by restructuring the postmerger financial arrangements to include less debt.

Perhaps Expand Corporation may be diversifying from a heavy manufacturing industry into the real estate/housing industry. While heavy manufacturing industries move with the business cycle, the real estate/housing industry tends to be counter-cyclical. Even though the expected value of earnings per share may remain relatively constant as a result of the merger, the standard deviation of possible outcomes may decline as a result of risk reduction through diversification, as is indicated in Figure 20-2.

We see that the expected value of the earnings per share has remained constant at $2.50 in this instance but the standard deviation has gone down. Because there is less risk in the corporation, the investor may be willing to assign a higher valuation, thus increasing the price-earnings ratio. Of course, the acquiring company must be capable of managing the acquired company.

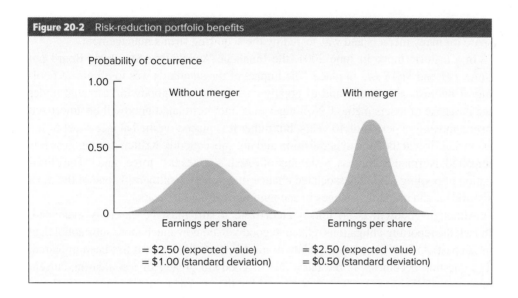

Figure 20-2   Risk-reduction portfolio benefits

Accounting Considerations in Mergers and Acquisitions

The role of financial accounting has significance in the area of mergers and acquisitions. Prior to 2001, there were competing accounting methods for recording mergers and acquisitions. The first method was a **pooling of interests**, under which the financial statements of the firms were combined, subject to minor adjustments, and no goodwill was credited.

To qualify for a pooling of interests, certain criteria had to be met:

1. The acquiring corporation issues only common stock, with rights identical to its old outstanding voting stock, in exchange for substantially all of the other company's voting stock.

2. The acquired firm's stockholders maintain an ownership position in the surviving firm.

3. The combined entity does not intend to dispose of a significant portion of the assets of the combined companies within two years.

4. The combination is effected in a single transaction.

Goodwill may be created when the second type of merger recording—a purchase of assets—is used. Because of the criteria described above (particularly items 1 and 2), a purchase of assets treatment, rather than a pooling of interests treatment, was generally necessary when the tender offer was in cash, bonds, preferred stock, or common stock with restricted rights. Before 2001, under a **purchase of assets** accounting treatment, any excess of purchase price over book value had to be recorded as goodwill and written off over a maximum period of 40 years. If a company purchased a firm with a $4 million book value (net worth) for $6 million, $2 million of goodwill was created on the books of the acquiring company, and it had to be written off over a maximum period of 40 years. This would cause a $50,000-per-year reduction in reported earnings ($2 million/40 years). Under a pooling of interests accounting treatment, you will recall, goodwill is not created.

The writing off of goodwill had a devastating effect on postmerger earnings per share for many mergers and was feared by the acquiring firm's management.

In a historic move in June 2001, the Financial Accounting Standards Board put *SFAS 141* and *SFAS 142* in place. The impact of the standards was to eliminate pooling of interests accounting and to greatly change the way goodwill is treated under the purchase of assets method. No longer must merger-related goodwill be amortized over a maximum period of 40 years, but rather it is placed on the balance sheet of the acquiring firm at the time of acquisition and not subsequently written down unless it is impaired. Norman N. Strauss, a member of FASB's issues task force, said, "The elimination of pooling [and the associated change in goodwill treatment] is one of the most significant and dramatic changes in accounting treatment in years."[4]

Although goodwill is no longer amortized, it still must be carefully evaluated. In fact, the reporting obligations related to goodwill are now much more substantial than in the past. At least once a year goodwill must be tested to see if it has been impaired. The question becomes, "Is the fair value of goodwill greater or less than its current book value?" This can be determined by taking the present value of future cash flows, subtracting out liabilities, and arriving at a value. If goodwill is impaired (less than book value), part of it must be immediately written down against operating income.

In writing the new merger reporting requirements, the FASB was generous in one respect. It allowed reporting companies to take a one-time write-down of all past goodwill impairment at the time of adoption by the firm (the January 1, 2002, calendar year for most companies). This feature not only gave the firm a one-time opportunity to clear the slate, but the impairment was treated as a "change in accounting principles" and not directly charged to operating results. This is significant because impairment charges (after 2002) come directly out of reported income.

Negotiated versus Tendered Offers

Traditionally, mergers have been negotiated in a friendly atmosphere between officers and directors of the participating corporations. Product lines, quality of assets, and future growth prospects are discussed, and eventually an exchange ratio is hammered out and reported to the investment community and the financial press.

A not-so-friendly offer has been developed, the **takeover tender offer**, in which a company attempts to acquire a target firm against its will. One of the most notorious examples was the announced intent of American Express to take over McGraw-Hill. At that time, the stock of McGraw-Hill was selling at $26 per share. The initial American Express offer was for $34, and eventually the offer went up to $40. McGraw-Hill fought off the offer by maintaining that American Express would obstruct the independent character required of a publisher. McGraw-Hill discouraged the unwelcome offer from American Express, but many small McGraw-Hill stockholders sued the publisher, claiming calling off the merger caused them to lose an opportunity to advance the cash value of their holdings. Figure 20-3 indicates that hostile takeovers have declined significantly in recent years.

---

[4]N. B. Strauss, from S. R. Moehrle and J. A. Reynolas-Moehrle, "Say Goodbye to Pooling and Goodwill Amortization," *Journal of Accountancy* (September 2001), pp. 31–38.

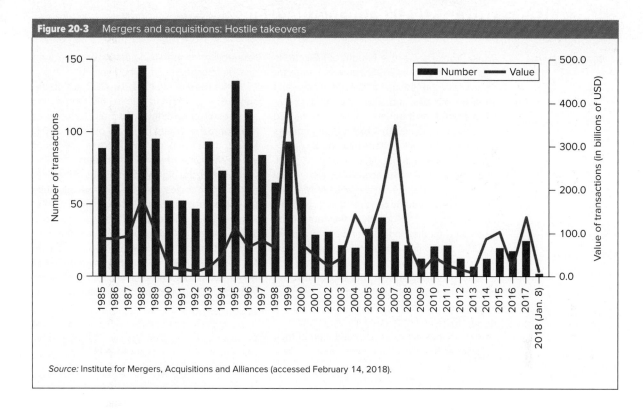

Figure 20-3   Mergers and acquisitions: Hostile takeovers

Source: Institute for Mergers, Acquisitions and Alliances (accessed February 14, 2018).

Not all companies can fend off the unwanted advances of suitors. An entire vocabulary has developed on Wall Street around the concept of the target takeover. For example, the **Saturday night special** refers to a surprise offer made just before the market closes for the weekend and takes the target company's officers by surprise. By the time the officers can react, the impact of the offer has already occurred. Perhaps a stock is trading at $20 and an unfriendly offer comes in at $28. Though the offer may please the company's stockholders, its management faces the dangers of seeing the company going down the wrong path in a merger and perhaps being personally ousted.

To avoid an unfriendly takeover, management may turn to a **white knight** for salvation. A white knight represents a third firm that management calls on to help it avoid the initial unwanted tender offer. One famous white knight was Chevron, which acquired Gulf Oil and saved the firm from an unwanted tender offer from T. Boone Pickens and Mesa Petroleum.[5] A white knight can also save a firm from bankruptcy or failure. This happened many times during the financial crisis of 2008–2009. The Italian company Fiat saved a struggling Chrysler, PNC Bank rescued National City Bank, and JPMorgan Chase bought Bear Stearns before it went under. Several of the bank mergers were arranged with help from the Federal Reserve and U.S. Treasury.

Many firms that wish to avoid takeovers have moved their corporate offices to states that have tough prenotification and protection provisions in regard to takeover offers.

---

[5]The situation was reversed for T. Boone Pickens and Mesa Petroleum in 1995 as they fell victim to unfriendly takeover offers.

Why CEOs Like the Merger Game

When Procter & Gamble bought out Gillette in a $62 billion deal in 2005, some felt sorry for James Kilts, the top man at Gillette, who would soon be out of a job. The tears could have been spared. As it turned out, Mr. Kilts walked away from the deal with $153 million in profits on the Gillette stock options he owned.

Employees did not fare nearly as well. Procter & Gamble announced 6,000 jobs would be eliminated after the merger. Mitchell Marks, a San Francisco strategy consultant and specialist on mergers, said, "People think they are joining a company for the long haul, and boom, the rug is pulled out from under them because the CEO wants a quick payday."*

David Yermack, a New York University business professor, expresses a similar sentiment in describing outgoing CEOs in merger deals by saying, "Many of them really dip in and take an extra bonus, an extra augmentation of their contract at the 11th hour, when there is very little ability for the stockholders or even their own directors to do anything about it."*

In the case of Mr. Kilts, the CEO at Gillette, some thought he had earned his big payday as a result of turning around the fortunes of the company when he took over in 2001. He cut back the firm's debt burden and spent wisely to revitalize key brand names.

However, the big payoff for CEOs in mergers all too often comes after the top executive has misguided the company. Take the case of John Zeglis at AT&T Wireless. The firm went public at $30 a share in 2001, but in 2004 the firm was sold to Cingular Wireless for $15 per share. Mr. Zeglis was CEO during this entire period of falling values, but walked away from the merger with $32 million in added compensation.

*Mark Maremart, "No Razor Here: Gillette Chief Executive to Get a Giant Payday," *The Wall Street Journal*, January 31, 2005, pp. A1, A14.

Other companies have bought portions of their own shares to restrict the amount of stock available for a takeover or have encouraged employees to buy stock under corporate pension plans. Other protective measures include increasing dividends to keep stockholders happy and staggering the election of members of the boards of directors to make outside power plays more difficult to initiate. Possible target companies have also bought up other companies to increase their own size and make themselves more expensive and less vulnerable. One of the key rules for avoiding a targeted takeover is to never get caught with too large a cash position. A firm with large cash balances serves as an ideal target for a leveraged takeover. The acquiring company can negotiate a bank loan based on the target company's assets and then go into the marketplace to make a cash tender offer. For example, CIT Financial left itself wide open when it sold a banking subsidiary for $425 million. At that point, CIT had cash balances equal to $20 per share for shares that had a market value in the $30 to $40 range. RCA bought the company for $65 per share.

Also, the poison pill, discussed at some length in Chapter 17, is an effective device for protection. It may give those in an entrenched position the ability to accumulate new shares at well below the market price in order to increase their percentage of ownership. This privilege is usually triggered when an unwanted outside group accumulates a certain percentage of the shares outstanding (such as 25 percent).

While a takeover bid may not appeal to management, it may be enticing to stockholders, as previously indicated. Herein lies the basic problem. The bidding may get so high that stockholders demand action. The desire of management to maintain the status quo can conflict with the objective of stockholder wealth maximization.

Premium Offers and Stock Price Movements

Few merger candidates are acquired at their current market value. Typically a **merger premium** of 40 to 60 percent (or more) is paid over the premerger price of the acquired company. For example, Johnson & Johnson bought Neutrogena Corp. at $35.25 per share, a price 70 percent above its premerger value.

It is not surprising that a company that is offered a large premium over its current market value has a major upside movement. The only problem for the investor is that much of this movement may occur before the public announcement of the merger offer.[6] If a firm is selling at $25 per share when informal negotiations begin, it may be $36 by the time an announced offer of $40 is made. Still, there are good profits to be made if the merger goes through.

The only problem with this strategy or of any merger-related investment strategy is that the merger may be called off. In that case the merger candidate's stock, which shot up from $25 to $36, may fall back to $25, and the Johnny-come-lately investor would lose $11 per share. In Table 20-4, we consider the case of three canceled mergers. In these three cases, the cause of cancellation was antitrust issues both with the European regulators and the U.S. Justice Department. The major point of the table is that when a price is inflated by a merger premium, that premium evaporates when the merger is canceled. In some cases, the disappointment causes the price to decline below its pre-announcement price. Of course, if a new suitor comes along shortly after cancellation (or causes the original cancellation), the price may quickly rebound.

Table 20-4 Stock movement of potential acquirees					
Acquiring Firm—Target Firm	**Target Firm Preannouncement Price**	**One Day after Announcement**	**Day Merger Cancelled**	**Percentage Decline**	**Reason for Cancelled Merger**
AT&T—T-Mobil 2011					U.S. antitrust issues
$39 billion acquisition	$13.69	$15.37	$11.43	25.63%	
UPS—TNT Express 2012–2013					European Union antitrust issues
$6.8 billion acquisition	$ 8.04	$13.11	$ 6.80	48.13%	
Deutche Boerse—NYSE/Euronext					European Union antitrust issues
$10 billion acquisition	$32.80	$37.96	26.43	30.37%	

Two-Step Buyout

A merger ploy that has been undertaken in recent times is the **two-step buyout**. Under this plan, the acquiring company attempts to gain control by offering a very high cash price for 51 percent of the shares outstanding. At the same time, it announces a second, lower price that will be paid later, either in cash, stock, or bonds. As an example, an acquiring company may offer stockholders of a takeover target company a $70 cash offer that can be executed in the next 20 days (for 51 percent of the shares outstanding). Subsequent to that time period, the selling stockholders will receive $57.50 in preferred stock for each share.

---

[6]This upside movement is often the result of insider trading on nonpublished information. While the SEC tries to control this activity, it is quite difficult to do.

This buyout procedure accomplishes two things. First, it provides a strong inducement to stockholders to quickly react to the offer. Those who delay must accept a lower price. Second, it allows the acquiring company to pay a lower total price than if a single offer is made. In the example here, a single offer may have been made for $68 a share. Assume 1 million shares are outstanding. The single offer has a total price tag of $68,000,000, while the two-step offer would have called for only $63,875,000.

Single offer:

$$1,000,000 \text{ shares at } \$68 = \$68,000,000$$

Two-step offer:

$$510,000 \text{ shares (51\%) at } \$70.00 = \$35,700,000$$
$$490,000 \text{ shares (49\%) at } \$57.50 = \underline{28,175,000}$$
$$\$63,875,000$$

An example of a two-step buyout was the Mobil Oil attempt to acquire 51 percent of Marathon Oil shares at a price of $126 in cash, with a subsequent offer to buy the rest of the shares for $90 face value debentures. In this case, Marathon Oil decided to sell to U.S. Steel, which also made a two-step offer of $125 in cash or $100 in notes to later sellers. Incidentally, before the bidding began, Marathon Oil was selling for $60 a share.[7]

The SEC has continued to keep a close eye on two-step buyouts. Government regulators fear that smaller stockholders may not be sophisticated enough to compete with arbitrageurs or institutional investors in rapidly tendering shares to ensure receipt of the higher price. The SEC has emphasized the need for a pro rata processing of stockholder orders, in which each stockholder receives an equal percentage of shares tendered.

On Thursday, November 29, 2012, 3M issued a press release announcing the successful completion of its merger with Ceradyne at a price of $35 per share. The tender offer to buy the shares expired on November 27, and at that time, 93.4 percent of the fully diluted shares had been tendered or guaranteed for delivery by investment companies holding shares for clients. This left approximately 6.6 percent of shares untendered. According to the press release, the merger agreement calls for Ceradyne to issue an equal amount of shares not tendered at the $35 per share price. This closes out the merger at 100 percent. Those shareholders who had not tendered their shares were given rights to receive $35 in cash without interest and subject to any withholding taxes that may have occurred from the sale. This strategy makes sure that 3M does not have a small percentage of minority owners in the acquired company, which could cause legal and appraisal problems down the road if the shareholders wanted to turn in their stock certificates. This is not necessarily a traditional two-stage offer but does act to force shareholders to sell against their wishes. It also meets the concerns of the SEC about shareholders receiving two different prices for the same shares.[8]

Similar measures to the two-step buyout are likely to develop in the future as companies continue to look for more attractive ways to acquire other companies. Such new activity can be expected in the mergers and acquisitions area where some of the finest minds in the investment banking and legal community are continually at work.

---

[7]U.S. Steel spun off Marathon Oil a number of years later, and it now trades on the NYSE as a separate company.
[8]http://news.3m.com/press-release/company/3m-completes-acquisition-ceradyne.

SUMMARY

Corporations may seek external growth through mergers to reduce risk, to improve access to the financial markets through increased size, or to obtain tax carryforward benefits. A merger may also expand the marketing and management capabilities of the firm and allow for new product development. While some mergers promise synergistic benefits (the $2 + 2 = 5$ effect), this can be an elusive feature, with initial expectations exceeding subsequent realities.

The *cash* purchase of another corporation takes on many of the characteristics of a classical capital budgeting decision. In a *stock-for-stock* exchange, there is often a trade-off between immediate gain or dilution in earnings per share and future growth. If a firm buys another firm with a P/E ratio lower than its own, there is an immediate increase in earnings per share, but the long-term earnings growth prospects must also be considered. The ultimate objective of a merger, as is true of any financial decision, is stockholder wealth maximization, and the immediate and delayed effects of the merger must be evaluated in this context.

To the extent that we are diminishing the overall risk of the firm in a merger, the postmerger P/E ratio and market value may increase even if the potential earnings growth is unchanged. Business risk reduction may be achieved through acquiring another firm that is influenced by a set of factors in the business cycle opposite from those that influence our own firm, while financial risk reduction may be achieved by restructuring the postmerger financial arrangements to include less debt.

In the recent merger movement, the unsolicited tender offer for a target company has gained in popularity. Offers are made at values well in excess of the current market price, and management of the target company becomes trapped in the dilemma of maintaining its current position versus agreeing to the wishes of the acquiring company, and even the target company's own stockholders.

LIST OF TERMS

merger 631
consolidation 631
portfolio effect 631
tax loss carryforward 633
horizontal integration 635
vertical integration 635
synergy 635
pooling of interests 639
goodwill 639
purchase of assets 639
takeover tender offer 640
Saturday night special 641
white knight 641
merger premium 643
two-step buyout 643

DISCUSSION QUESTIONS

1. Name three industries in which mergers have been prominent. *(LO20-1)*
2. What is the difference between a merger and a consolidation? *(LO20-1)*
3. Why might the portfolio effect of a merger provide a higher valuation for the participating firms? *(LO20-4)*
4. What is the difference between horizontal integration and vertical integration? How does antitrust policy affect the nature of mergers? *(LO20-1)*

5. What is synergy? What might cause this result? Is there a tendency for management to *over-* or *underestimate* the potential synergistic benefits of a merger? *(LO20-1)*

6. If a firm wishes to achieve immediate appreciation in earnings per share as a result of a merger, how can this be best accomplished in terms of exchange variables? What is a possible drawback to this approach in terms of long-range considerations? *(LO20-3)*

7. It is possible for the postmerger P/E ratio to move in a direction opposite to that of the immediate postmerger earnings per share. Explain why this could happen. *(LO20-3)*

8. How is goodwill now treated in a merger? *(LO20-2)*

9. Suggest some ways in which firms have tried to avoid being part of a target takeover. *(LO20-5)*

10. What is a typical merger premium paid in a merger or acquisition? What effect does this premium have on the market value of the merger candidate, and when is most of this movement likely to take place? *(LO20-1)*

11. Why do management and stockholders often have divergent viewpoints about the desirability of a takeover? *(LO20-5)*

12. What is (are) the purpose(s) of the two-step buyout from the viewpoint of the acquiring company? *(LO20-2)*

PRACTICE PROBLEMS AND SOLUTIONS

Tax loss
carryforward
(LO20-1)

1. American Century Corp. is considering acquiring Southern Homes Inc. Southern Homes has a tax loss carryforward of $240,000. Projected earnings for American Century Corp. are as follows:

	20X1	20X2	20X3	Total Values
Before-tax income	$80,000	$70,000	$180,000	$330,000
Taxes (30%)	24,000	21,000	54,000	99,000
Income available to stockholders	$56,000	$49,000	$126,000	$231,000

a. How much of American Century's total taxes can be reduced by the tax loss carryforward? Keep in mind its tax rate is 30 percent as shown.

b. How much will the total income to shareholders be for each year if the acquisition occurs? Use the same approach as that shown on page 633 of the chapter.

Impact of merger on
earnings per share
(LO20-3)

2. Assume the following financial data for the Rotan Corp. and the Mosley Corp.

	Rotan	Mosley
Total earnings	$300,000	$600,000
Number of shares of stock outstanding	100,000	300,000
Earnings per share	$3.00	$2.00
Price-earnings ratio (P/E)	16.7×	25×
Market price per share	$50	$50

If all the shares of Rotan Corp. are exchanged for Mosley Corp. on a share-for-share basis, what will the postmerger earnings per share be for Mosley Corp.? Use an approach similar to that in Table 20-3.

Solutions

1. *a.*   Reduction in taxes due to tax loss carryforward = Loss × Tax rate

$$= \$240{,}000 \times 0.30 = \$72{,}000$$

b.   Mosley Corp. (with the merger and the associated benefits).

	20X1	20X2	20X3	Total Values
Before-tax income	$80,000	$70,000	$180,000	$330,000
Taxes loss carryforward	80,000	70,000	90,000	240,000
Net taxable income	0	0	$ 90,000	$ 90,000
Taxes (30%)	0	0	27,000	27,000
Income available to stockholders (Before-tax income − Taxes)	$80,000	$70,000	$153,000*	$303,000†

*Before-tax income minus taxes = $180,000 − $27,000 = $153,000
†Before-tax income minus taxes = $330,000 − $27,000 = $303,000

2.   Total earnings:

Rotan	$300,000
Mosley	600,000
	$900,000

Shares outstanding in surviving corporation:

$$\text{Old } (300{,}000) + \text{New } (100{,}000) = 400{,}000$$

$$\text{New earnings per share for the Mosley Corp.} = \frac{\text{Earnings}}{\text{Shares}} = \frac{\$900{,}000}{400{,}000} = \$2.25$$

PROBLEMS

connect Selected problems are available with Connect. Please see the preface for more information.

Basic Problems

1.   The Clark Corporation desires to expand. It is considering a cash purchase of Kent Enterprises for $3 million. Kent has a $700,000 tax loss carryforward that could be used immediately by the Clark Corporation, which is paying taxes at the rate of 30 percent. Kent will provide $420,000 per year in cash flow (after-tax income plus depreciation) for the next 20 years. If the Clark Corporation has a cost of capital of 13 percent, should the merger be undertaken?

Tax loss carryforward (LO20-1)

Tax loss
carryforward
(LO20-1)

2. Assume that Western Exploration Corp. is considering the acquisition of Ogden Drilling Company. The latter has a $470,000 tax loss carryforward. Projected earnings for the Western Exploration Corp. are as follows:

	20X1	20X2	20X3	Total Values
Before-tax income	$185,000	$250,000	$370,000	$805,000
Taxes (35%)	64,750	87,500	129,500	281,750
Income available to stockholders	$120,250	$162,500	$240,500	$523,250

   a.　How much will the total taxes of Western Exploration Corp. be reduced as a result of the tax loss carryforward?

   b.　How much will the total income available to stockholders be for the three years if the acquisition occurs? Use the same format as that in the text.

Cash acquisition with
deferred benefits
(LO20-2)

3. J & J Enterprises is considering a cash acquisition of Patterson Steel Company for $4,500,000. Patterson will provide the following pattern of cash inflows and synergistic benefits for the next 20 years. There is no tax loss carryforward.

	Years		
	1–5	6–15	16–20
Cash inflow (aftertax)	$490,000	$650,000	$850,000
Synergistic benefits (aftertax)	45,000	65,000	75,000

   The cost of capital for the acquiring firm is 12 percent. Compute the net present value. Should the merger be undertaken? (If you have difficulty with deferred time value of money problems, consult Chapter 9.)

Cash acquisition with
deferred benefits
(LO20-2)

4. Worldwide Scientific Equipment is considering a cash acquisition of Medical Labs for $1.6 million. Medical Labs will provide the following pattern of cash inflows and synergistic benefits for the next 25 years. There is no tax loss carryforward.

	Years		
	1–5	6–15	16–25
Cash inflow (aftertax)	$150,000	$170,000	$210,000
Synergistic benefits (aftertax)	20,000	30,000	50,000

   The cost of capital for the acquiring firm is 11 percent. Compute the net present value. Should the merger be undertaken?

Impact of merger on
earnings per share
(LO20-3)

5. Assume the following financial data for Rembrandt Paint Co. and Picasso Art Supplies:

	Rembrandt Paint Co.	Picasso Art Supplies
Total earnings	$1,200,000	$3,600,000
Number of shares of stock outstanding	600,000	2,400,000
Earnings per share	$2.00	$1.50
Price-earnings ratio (P/E)	24×	32×
Market price per share	$48	$48

a. If all the shares of Rembrandt Paint Co. are exchanged for those of Picasso Art Supplies on a share-for-share basis, what will postmerger earnings per share be for Picasso Art Supplies? Use an approach similar to that in Table 20-3.

b. Explain why the earnings per share of Picasso Art Supplies changed.

c. Can we necessarily assume that Picasso Art Supplies is better off after the merger?

6. Assume the following financial data for the Noble Corporation and Barnes Enterprises:

𝄪

Impact of merger on earnings per share
(LO20-3)

	Noble Corporation	Barnes Enterprises
Total earnings	$1,820,000	$5,620,000
Number of shares of stock outstanding	650,000	2,810,000
Earnings per share	$2.80	$2.00
Price-earnings ratio (P/E)	20×	28×
Market price per share	$56	$56

a. If all the shares of the Noble Corporation are exchanged for those of Barnes Enterprises on a share-for-share basis, what will postmerger earnings per share be for Barnes Enterprises? Use an approach similar to that in Table 20-3.

b. Explain why the earnings per share of Barnes Enterprises changed.

c. Can we necessarily assume that Barnes Enterprises is better off after the merger?

Intermediate Problems

7. The Jeter Corporation is considering acquiring the A-Rod Corporation. The data for the two companies are as follows:

Mergers and dilution
(LO20-3)

	A-Rod Corp.	Jeter Corp.
Total earnings	$1,000,000	$4,000,000
Number of shares of stock outstanding	400,000	2,000,000
Earnings per share	$2.50	$2.00
Price-earnings ratio (P/E)	12	15
Market price per share	$30	$30

a. The Jeter Corp. is going to give A-Rod Corp. a 60 percent premium over A-Rod's current market value. What price will it pay?

b. At the price computed in part *a*, what is the total market value of A-Rod Corp.? (Use the number of A-Rod Corp. shares times price.)

c. At the price computed in part *a*, what is the P/E ratio Jeter Corp. is assigning A-Rod Corp.?

d. How many shares must Jeter Corp. issue to buy the A-Rod Corp. at the total value computed in part *b*? (Keep in mind that Jeter Corp.'s price per share is $30.)

e. Given the answer to part *d,* how many shares will Jeter Corp. have after the merger?

f. Add together the total earnings of both corporations and divide by the total shares computed in part *e.* What are the new postmerger earnings per share?

g. Why has Jeter Corp.'s earnings per share gone down?

h. How can Jeter Corp. hope to overcome this dilution?

Two-step buyout
(LO20-2)

8. The Hollings Corporation is considering a two-step buyout of the Norton Corporation. The latter firm has 2.5 million shares outstanding and its stock price is currently $40 per share. In the two-step buyout, Hollings will offer to buy 51 percent of Norton's shares outstanding for $62 per share in cash and the balance in a second offer of 840,000 convertible preferred stock shares. Each share of preferred stock would be valued at 40 percent over the current value of Norton's common stock. Mr. Green, a newcomer to the management team at Hollings, suggests that only one offer for all Norton's shares be made at $59.25 per share. Compare the total costs of the two alternatives. Which is better in terms of minimizing costs?

Future tax obligation
to selling stockholder
(LO20-1)

9. Al Simpson helped start Excel Systems several years ago. At the time, he purchased 116,000 shares of stock at $1 per share. Now he has the opportunity to sell his interest in the company to Folsom Corp. for $50 a share in cash. His capital gains tax rate would be 15 percent.

a. If he sells his interest, what will be the value for before-tax profit, taxes, and aftertax profit?

b. Assume, instead of cash, he accepts Folsom Corp. stock valued at $50 per share. He pays no tax at that time. He holds the stock for five years and then sells it for $82.50 (the stock pays no cash dividends). What will be the value for before-tax profit, taxes, and aftertax profit five years from now? His capital gains tax is once again 15 percent.

c. Using a 9 percent discount rate, calculate the aftertax profit. That is, discount back the answer in part *b* for five years and compare it to the answer in part *a.*

Advanced Problems

Premium offers and
stock price movement
(LO20-1)

10. Chicago Savings Corp. is planning to make an offer for Ernie's Bank & Trust. The stock of Ernie's Bank & Trust is currently selling for $44 a share.

a. If the tender offer is planned at a premium of 50 percent over market price, what will be the value offered per share for Ernie's Bank & Trust?

b. Suppose before the offer is actually announced, the stock price of Ernie's Bank & Trust goes to $60 because of strong merger rumors. If you buy the stock at that price and the merger goes through (at the price computed in part *a*), what will be your percentage gain?

c. Because there is always the possibility that the merger could be called off after it is announced, you also want to consider your percentage loss if that happens. Assume you buy the stock at $60 and it falls back to its original value after the merger cancellation, what will be your percentage loss?

d. If there is an 80 percent probability that the merger will go through when you buy the stock at $60, and only a 20 percent chance that it will be called off, does this appear to be a good investment? Compute the expected value of the return on the investment.

11. Assume the Knight Corporation is considering the acquisition of Day Inc. The expected earnings per share for the Knight Corporation will be $4.00 with or without the merger. However, the standard deviation of the earnings will go from $2.40 to $1.60 with the merger because the two firms are negatively correlated.

Ⅻ

Portfolio effect of a merger
(LO20-4)

a. Compute the coefficient of variation for the Knight Corporation before and after the merger (consult Chapter 13 to review statistical concepts if necessary).

b. Discuss the possible impact on Knight's postmerger P/E ratio, assuming investors are risk-averse.

12. General Meters is considering two mergers. The first is with firm A in its own volatile industry, the auto speedometer industry, while the second is a merger with firm B in an industry that moves in the opposite direction (and will tend to level out performance due to negative correlation).

Portfolio consideration and risk aversion
(LO20-4)

a. Compute the mean, standard deviation, and coefficient of variation for both investments (refer to Chapter 13 if necessary).

General Meters Merger with Firm A		General Meters Merger with Firm B	
Possible Earnings ($ in millions)	Probability	Possible Earnings ($ in millions)	Probability
$40	0.30	$40	0.25
60	0.40	60	0.50
80	0.30	80	0.25

b. Assuming investors are risk-averse, which alternative can be expected to bring the higher valuation?

WEB EXERCISE

1. Earlier in the chapter we mentioned Berkshire Hathaway's acquisition of Burlington Northern Santa Fe (BNSF). Let's take a closer look at Berkshire's acquisition activity.

    Go to www.berkshirehathaway.com and click on "Annual & Interim Reports." Download the most recent annual report in PDF format.

2. Read Warren Buffett's letter—it is extraordinary for a chairman and CEO to write such a detailed letter. In that letter you will find a list of investments owned by Berkshire Hathaway. How have these investments performed?

Note: Occasionally a topic we have listed may have been deleted, updated, or moved into a different location on a website. If you click on the site map or site index, you will be introduced to a table of contents that should aid you in finding the topic you are looking for.

21

International Financial Management

LEARNING OBJECTIVES

LO 21-1 A multinational corporation is one that crosses international borders to gain expanded markets.

LO 21-2 A company operating in many foreign countries must consider the effect of exchange rates on its profitability and cash flow.

LO 21-3 Foreign exchange risk can be hedged or reduced.

LO 21-4 Political risk must be carefully assessed in making a foreign investment decision.

LO 21-5 The potential ways for financing international operations are much greater than for domestic operations and should be carefully considered.

Today the world economy is more integrated than ever, and nations depend on one another for many valuable and scarce resources. The United States is dependent on China for textiles and Canada, and Saudi Arabia for oil; China is dependent on the United States and other Western countries for technology and heavy machinery. The World Trade Organization has made it easier for many countries to trade their goods and services without tariffs and import duties, and the economic laws of competitive advantage are at work. Countries like the United States, with a well-educated workforce, provide leading technological products while developing economies such as those in India and China, with large populations and low-cost labor, provide much of the world's labor-intensive goods such as textiles, clothing, and assembled technology products. Additionally, the United States, Canada, and Mexico instituted the North American Free Trade Agreement (NAFTA), which has increased trade among those three countries, but has been critcized by President Trump who is trying to renegotiate the agreement.

This growing interdependence necessitates the development of sound international business relations, which will enhance the prospects for future international cooperation and understanding. It is virtually impossible for any country to isolate itself from the impact of international developments in an integrated world economy. Therefore, world politics continue to play a role in economic development. In an ever-more-connected world, international trade will become still more important.

We are reminded by the events of September 11, 2001; the occurrence of the 2011 tsunami in Japan; the Ebola outbreak of 2014; and the devastating hurricane season of 2017. Terrorism, war, infectious disease, and weather can not only cause economic impacts for short periods of time, but can have catastrophic effects on localized economies or specific industries. With financial markets becoming more global, a major impact in one area of the world can affect economies thousands of miles away. The capital markets are so integrated that world events such as a currency crisis, government defaults on sovereign debt, or terrorism can cause stock and bond markets to suffer emotional declines well beyond the expected economic impact of a major event.

Even when stock and bond markets are relatively stable and free of crisis, companies still have to pay attention to the currency markets. These currency markets impact the price of imports and exports between countries and therefore affect sales and earnings of all companies doing business internationally, whether the company is Japan's Honda, Germany's Bayer, or the United States' Apple. These companies do quite a bit of their business in the three largest and most liquid currencies in the world: the U.S. dollar, the euro, and the Japanese yen.

In January 1999, 11 countries from the European Union adopted the **euro** as their currency, which fully replaced their previous domestic currencies in January 2002. With the addition of Croatia in 2013, the European Union has grown to 28 countries, 19 of which use the euro as their official currency. These 19 countries are referred to as the "Eurozone." In the past, it seemed certain that European Union members would continue to discard their national currencies and adopt the euro. However, economic crises in several European countries are leading some to question the practicality of remaining in the Eurozone. Greece, for example, found that one early benefit of participating in the Eurozone was easier access to international bond markets. However, just because it is easy to borrow does not mean that it is prudent to do so. Greece found it impossible to repay all of its euro debt, and it cannot devalue its currency. Other European countries were forced to make loans to Greece to bail the country out of crisis. But Greece defaulted on some of these loans. More defaults remain possible. Over the next few years, we will see whether monetary integration continues in Europe or whether some countries leave the Eurozone.

Figure 21-1 presents the value of the British pound against the dollar and also the value of the euro against the dollar. Even though Great Britain is a member of the European Union, it has not adopted the euro as its domestic currency but continues to use the pound.

Figure 21-1 shows that the British pound and the euro move up and down against the U.S. dollar in unison. Looking at the trend lines for the euro and the pound, understand that when the trend lines are falling, the dollar is rising. In other words, the dollar buys more euros or pounds. When the trend lines are rising, the dollar is falling. We can think about this in a different way. At the peak of the dollar (low for the euro) in 2001, one euro would buy about $0.84 and at the low of the dollar (peak of the euro) in April 2008, one euro would buy $1.60. This $0.76 swing was a 90.4 percent increase in the value of the euro relative to the dollar. From 1999 to 2002, U.S. companies doing business in Europe had to translate their euros into fewer and fewer dollars, so their foreign earnings in dollar terms were negatively affected by the falling euro. But as the euro rose against the dollar, the trend reversed itself.

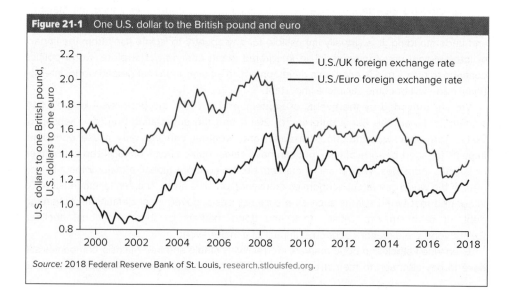

Figure 21-1   One U.S. dollar to the British pound and euro

Source: 2018 Federal Reserve Bank of St. Louis, research.stlouisfed.org.

When financial panics occur, investors usually prefer to hold dollars because the dollar is widely viewed as a stable and safe currency. During the global financial panic that began in late 2008, the dollar rose dramatically in value relative to the British pound and the euro. Notice in Figure 21-1 that between July 2008 and March 2009, the British pound lost over 30 percent of its value relative to the dollar. Thus in early 2009, when U.S. companies began reporting their 2008 year-end earnings, U.S. companies reported a decrease in earnings from European operations because the euro was translated into fewer dollars. While the falling euro and pound (rising dollar) made European vacations more affordable to Americans, it also put U.S. companies who export to Europe at a competitive disadvantage. American-made goods became more expensive to Europeans who pay for their products in pounds or euros.

The significance of international business corporations becomes more apparent if we look at the size of foreign sales relative to domestic sales for major American corporations. Table 21-1 shows companies such as Coca-Cola with foreign sales of 52.5 percent, ExxonMobil with foreign sales of 66.4 percent, and other companies with large percentages of foreign sales.

Table 21-1 International sales of selected U.S. companies		
	Foreign Sales (% of total sales)	**Fiscal Year-End**
Coca-Cola	52.5	31-Dec-17
ExxonMobil	66.4	31-Dec-17
General Electric	56.9	31-Dec-17
IBM	62.2	31-Dec-17
Johnson & Johnson	47.4	31-Dec-17
JPMorgan Chase	22.9	31-Dec-17
McDonald's	66.5	31-Dec-17
Microsoft	49.7	30-Jun-17
Procter & Gamble	58.0	30-Jun-17

Just as foreign operations affect the performance of American businesses, developments in international financial markets also affect our lifestyles. If you took a trip to Europe in April 2011, you would have received about 0.68 euros per dollar. But if you took a second trip four years later, in April 2015, your dollar would get you 0.94 euros, an increase of almost 39 percent. On the other hand, Europeans traveling to the United States would have suffered a 39 percent decline in purchasing power. The value of currencies changes on a daily basis, occasionally by significant amounts, and often reversing directions. For example, after the euro rose against the dollar for several years, it plunged by 17 percent in the first months of 2010 over concerns that Greece and other European countries might default on their sovereign debt.

This chapter deals with the dimensions of doing business worldwide. We believe it provides a basis for understanding the complexities of international financial decisions. Such an understanding is important if you work for a multinational manufacturing firm, a large commercial bank, a major brokerage firm, or any firm involved in international transactions.

The Multinational Corporation: Nature and Environment

The focus of international financial management has been the multinational corporation. One might ask, just what is a **multinational corporation (MNC)**? Some definitions of a multinational corporation require that a minimum percentage (often 30 percent or more) of a firm's business activities be carried on outside its national borders. For our understanding, however, any firm doing business across its national borders is considered a multinational enterprise. Multinational corporations can take several forms. Four are briefly examined.

Exporter An MNC could produce a product domestically and export some of that production to one or more foreign markets. This is perhaps the least risky method—reaping the benefits of foreign demand without committing any long-term investment to that foreign country.

Licensing Agreement A firm with exporting operations may get into trouble when a foreign government imposes or substantially raises an import tariff to a level at which the exporter cannot compete effectively with the local domestic manufacturers. The foreign government may even ban imports at times. When this happens the exporting firm may grant a license to an independent local producer to use the firm's technology in return for a license fee or a royalty. In essence, then, the MNC will be exporting technology, rather than the product, to that foreign country.

Joint Venture As an alternative to licensing, the MNC may establish a joint venture with a local foreign manufacturer. The legal, political, and economic environments around the globe are more conducive to the joint venture arrangement than any of the other modes of operation. Historical evidence also suggests that a joint venture with a local entrepreneur exposes the firm to the least amount of political risk. This position is preferred by most business firms and by foreign governments as well.

Fully Owned Foreign Subsidiary Although the joint venture form is desirable for many reasons, it may be hard to find a willing and cooperative local entrepreneur with sufficient capital to participate. Under these conditions, the MNC may have to go it alone. For political reasons, however, a wholly owned foreign subsidiary is becoming more of a rarity. The reader must keep in mind that whenever we mention a *foreign affiliate* in the ensuing discussion, it could be a joint venture or a fully owned subsidiary.

As the firm crosses its national borders, it faces an environment that is riskier and more complex than its domestic surroundings. Sometimes the social and political environment can be hostile. Despite these difficult challenges, foreign affiliates often are more profitable than domestic businesses. A purely domestic firm faces several basic risks, such as the risk related to maintaining sales and market share, the financial risk of too much leverage, the risk of a poor equity market, and so on. In addition to these types of risks, the foreign affiliate is exposed to foreign exchange risk and political risk. While the foreign affiliate experiences a larger amount of risk than a domestic firm, it actually lowers the portfolio risk of its parent corporation by stabilizing the combined operating cash flows for the MNC. This risk reduction occurs because foreign and domestic economies are less than perfectly correlated.

Foreign business operations are more complex because the host country's economy may be different from the domestic economy. The rate of inflation (or deflation) in a foreign country will almost certainly be different than in the United States. The rules of taxation are different. The structure and operation of financial markets and institutions also vary from country to country, as do financial policies and practices.

The presence of a foreign affiliate benefits the host country's economy. Foreign affiliates have been a decisive factor in shaping the pattern of trade, investment, and the flow of technology between nations. They can have a significant positive impact on a host country's economic growth, employment, trade, and balance of payments. The growth of MNCs has also reduced geopolitical risk and improved world peace. Countries with trade ties are less likely to go to war against one another. These positive contributions, however, are occasionally overshadowed by allegations of wrongdoing. For example, some host countries have charged that foreign affiliates subverted their governments and caused instability of their currencies. The less developed countries (LDCs) have, at times, alleged that foreign businesses exploit their labor with low wages.

The multinational companies are also under constant criticism in their home countries where labor unions charge the MNCs with exporting jobs, capital, and technology to foreign nations while avoiding their fair share of taxes. Despite all these criticisms, multinational companies have managed to survive and prosper. The MNCs are well positioned to take advantage of imperfections in the global markets. Furthermore, since current global resource distribution favors the MNCs' survival and growth, it may be concluded that multinational corporations are here to stay.

Foreign Exchange Rates

Suppose you are planning to spend a semester in London studying the culture of England. To put your plan into operation you will need British currency—that is, British pounds (£)—so you can pay for your expenses during your stay. How many British pounds you can obtain for $1,000 will depend on the exchange rate at that time. The relationship between the values of two currencies is known as the **exchange rate**. The exchange rate between U.S. dollars and British pounds is stated as dollars per pound or pounds per dollar. For example, the quotation of $2.00 per pound is the same as £0.50 per dollar (1/$2.00). At this exchange rate you can purchase 500 British pounds with $1,000. A quick Internet search for "foreign exchange rates" or just "fx rates" will deliver multiple sources of up-to-the minute exchange rate data. Figure 21-2 depicts Canadian dollars, Japanese yen, Swiss francs, and Swedish kronor because they are used by some of the United States' major trading partners. This figure shows the amount of each currency that one can exchange for one U.S. dollar.

There is no guarantee that any currency will stay strong relative to other currencies, and the dollar is no exception. Several factors have combined to strengthen the U.S. dollar relative to the euro and the British pound since 2007. The first factor was a "flight to quality" during the financial crisis that began late in that year. This strengthening may be only temporary. Of particular concern is the unsustainably high U.S. budget deficit. On the other hand, the United States is not the only country that must address unsustainable policies. Many other countries run large budget deficits or have policies in place that may reduce future economic growth. Such policies may lead to a weakening of those countries' currencies, and a relative strengthening of the dollar.

Financial managers should always pay close attention to exchange rates and any changes that might be forecast.

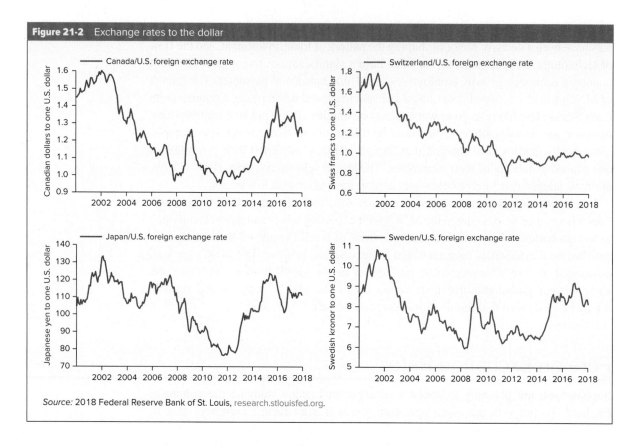

Figure 21-2   Exchange rates to the dollar

Source: 2018 Federal Reserve Bank of St. Louis, research.stlouisfed.org.

Factors Influencing Exchange Rates

The present international monetary system consists of a mixture of "freely" floating exchange rates and fixed rates. The currencies of the major trading partners of the United States are traded in free markets. In such a market, the exchange rate between two currencies is determined by the supply of, and the demand for, those currencies. This activity, however, is subject to intervention by many countries' central banks. Factors that tend to increase the supply or decrease the demand schedule for a given currency will bring down the value of that currency in foreign exchange markets. Similarly, the factors that tend to decrease the supply or increase the demand for a currency will raise the value of that currency. Since fluctuations in currency values result in foreign exchange risk, the financial executive must understand the factors causing these changes in currency values. Although the value of a currency is determined by the aggregate supply and demand for that currency, this alone does not help financial managers understand or predict the changes in exchange rates. Fundamental factors, such as inflation, interest rates, balance of payments, and government policies, are important in explaining both the short-term and long-term fluctuations of a currency value.

Purchasing Power Parity   In theory, a parity between the purchasing powers of two currencies should establish the rate of exchange between the two currencies. Suppose it takes $1.00 to buy one dozen apples in New York and 1.25 euros to buy the same apples in Frankfurt, Germany. Then the rate of exchange between the U.S. dollar and the euro should be €1.25/$1.00 or $0.80/euro. If prices of apples double in New York while the prices in Frankfurt remain the same, the purchasing power of a dollar in New York should drop 50 percent. Consequently, you should be able to exchange $1.00 for only €0.625 in foreign currency markets (or receive $1.60 per euro).

Currency exchange rates tend to vary inversely with their respective purchasing powers to provide the same or similar purchasing power in each country. This is called the **purchasing power parity theory**. When the inflation rate differential between two countries changes, the exchange rate also adjusts to correspond to the relative purchasing powers of the countries.

Interest Rates   Another economic variable that has a significant influence on exchange rates is interest rates. As a student of finance, you should know that investment capital flows in the direction of higher yield for a given level of risk. This flow of short-term capital between money markets occurs because investors seek equilibrium through arbitrage buying and selling. If investors can earn 6 percent interest per year in Country X and 10 percent per year in Country Y, they will prefer to invest in Country Y, provided the inflation rate and risk are the same in both countries. Thus interest rates and exchange rates adjust until the foreign exchange market and the money market reach equilibrium. This interplay between interest rate differentials and exchange rates is called the **interest rate parity theory**.

Balance of Payments   The term **balance of payments** refers to a system of government accounts that catalogs the flow of economic transactions between the residents of one country and the residents of other countries. (The balance of payments statement for the United States is prepared by the U.S. Department of Commerce quarterly and annually.) It resembles the cash flow statement presented in Chapter 2 and tracks the country's exports and imports as well as the flow of capital and gifts. When a country sells (exports) more goods and services to foreign countries than it purchases (imports), it will have a surplus in its balance of trade. Over the last several decades, Japan, through its aggressive competition in world markets, has been exporting more goods than it imports and has been enjoying a trade surplus for quite some time. Since the foreigners who buy Japanese goods are expected to pay their bills in yen, the demand for yen and, consequently, its value, increases in foreign currency markets. On the other hand, continuous deficits in the balance of payments are expected to depress the value of a currency because such deficits would increase the supply of that currency relative to the demand.

Government Policies   A national government may, through its central bank, intervene in the foreign exchange market, buying and selling currencies as it sees fit to support the value of its currency relative to others. Sometimes a given country may deliberately pursue a policy of maintaining an undervalued currency to promote cheap exports. In some countries, the currency values are set by government decree. Even in some free market countries, the central banks fix the exchange rates, subject to periodic review and adjustment. Some nations affect the foreign exchange rate indirectly by restricting the flow of funds into and out of the country. Monetary and fiscal policies also affect the currency value in foreign exchange markets. For example, expansionary monetary policy and excessive government spending are primary causes of inflation, and continual use of such policies eventually reduces the value of the country's currency. Sometimes government policies are at odds with economic reality. In December 2017, the black market rate of exchange for U.S. dollars in Venezuela was 103,000 bolivars per dollar. The official government exchange rate was only 10 bolivars to the U.S. dollar. In truth, only people with political connections could get these rates. On the streets, where most currency transactions in Venezuela actually take place, the black market rate applies.

Other Factors   A pronounced and extended stock market rally in a country attracts investment capital from other countries, thus creating a huge demand by foreigners for that country's currency. This increased demand is expected to increase the value of that currency. Similarly a significant increase in demand for a country's principal exports worldwide is expected to result in a corresponding increase in the value of its currency. In recent years, Australia has enjoyed significantly increased exports to China and other Asian countries. In particular, coal, copper, and natural gas have been exported. While it once required 1.5 AUD to buy a U.S. dollar, in 2013 only 0.97 AUD were required to buy a U.S. dollar. As Asian economies slowed in 2014, Australian exports declined, and so did the AUD. By 2018 it required 1.24 AUD to purchase one U.S. dollar.

Political turmoil in a country often drives capital out of the country into stable countries. A mass exodus of capital, due to the fear of political risk, undermines the value of a country's currency in the foreign exchange market. Venezuela's bolivar lost almost two-thirds of its value against the dollar between 2010 and 2013 due to political turmoil.

Although a wide variety of factors that can influence exchange rates has been discussed, a few words of caution are in order. All of these variables will not necessarily influence all currencies to the same degree. Some factors may have an overriding influence on one currency's value, while their influence on another currency may be negligible at that time.

Spot Rates and Forward Rates

When you look into a major financial newspaper (e.g., *The Wall Street Journal*), you will discover that two exchange rates exist simultaneously for most major currencies—the spot rate and the forward rate. The **spot rate** for a currency is the exchange rate at which the currency is traded for immediate delivery. For example, you walk into a local commercial bank and ask for Swiss francs.[1] The banker will indicate the rate at which the franc is selling, say SF 0.9727/$. If you like the rate, you buy 972.70 francs with $1,000 and walk out the door. This is a spot market transaction at the retail level. The trading of currencies for future delivery is called a forward market transaction. Suppose IBM Corporation expects to receive SF 97,270 from a Swiss customer in 30 days. It is not certain, however, what these francs will be worth in U.S. dollars in 30 days. To eliminate this uncertainty, IBM calls a bank and offers to sell SF 97,270 for U.S. dollars in 30 days. In their negotiation, the two parties may agree on an exchange rate of SF 0.9718/$. This is the same as $1.0290/SF. The 0.9718 quote is in Swiss francs per dollar. The reciprocal or 1.0290 is in dollars per Swiss franc.

---

[1] While Switzerland is a European country, it is not a member of the European Union, and it does not use the euro as its official currency.

Since the exchange rate is established for future delivery, it is a **forward rate**. After 30 days, IBM delivers SF 97,270 to the bank and receives $100,000. The difference between spot and forward exchange rates, expressed in dollars per unit of foreign currency, may be seen in the following typical values:

Rates*	Swiss Franc (SF) ($/SF)	UK Pound ($/£)
Spot	$1.0281	$1.4779
30-day forward	1.0290	1.4776
90-day forward	1.0316	1.4770
180-day forward	1.0358	1.4762
*As of 2015.		

The forward exchange rate of a currency is slightly different from the spot rate prevailing at that time. Since the forward rate deals with a future time, the expectations regarding the future value of that currency are reflected in the forward rate. Forward rates may be greater than the current spot rate (premium) or less than the current spot rate (discount). The preceding table shows the forward rates on the Swiss franc were at a premium in relation to the spot rate, while the forward rates for the British pound were at a discount from the spot rate. This means the participants in the foreign exchange market expected the Swiss franc to appreciate relative to the U.S. dollar in the future and the British pound to depreciate against the dollar. The discount or premium is usually expressed as an annualized percentage deviation from the spot rate. The percentage discount or premium is computed with the following formula:

$$\frac{\text{Forward premium}}{\text{(or discount)}} = \frac{\text{Forward rate} - \text{Spot rate}}{\text{Spot rate}} \times \frac{12}{\substack{\text{Length of} \\ \text{forward contract} \\ \text{(in months)}}} \qquad (21\text{-}1)$$

For example, the 90-day forward contract in Swiss francs, as previously listed, was selling at a 1.362 percent premium:

$$\frac{1.0316 - 1.0281}{1.0281} \times \frac{12}{3} = 1.362\% \text{ (premium)}$$

while the 90-day forward contract in British pounds was trading at a −0.244 percent discount:

$$\frac{1.4770 - 1.4779}{1.4779} \times \frac{12}{3} = -0.244\% \text{ (discount)}$$

Normally the forward premium or discount is between 0.1 percent and 5 percent.

The spot and forward transactions are said to occur in the over-the-counter market. Foreign currency dealers (usually large commercial banks) and their customers (importers, exporters, investors, multinational firms, and so on) negotiate the exchange rate, the length of the forward contract, and the commission in a mutually agreeable fashion. Although the length of a typical forward contract may generally vary between one month and six months, contracts for longer maturities are not uncommon. The dealers, however, may require higher returns for longer contracts.

Cross Rates

Because currencies are quoted against the U.S. dollar in *The Wall Street Journal,* sometimes it may be necessary to work out the **cross rates** for currencies other than the dollar. For example, on April 13, 2015, the Swiss franc was selling for $1.0231 and the British pound was selling for $1.46596. The cross rate between the franc and the pound was 1.43294 (francs/pound). In determining this value, we show that one dollar would buy 0.97747 francs (1/1.0231) and a pound was equal to 1.46596 dollars. Thus 0.97747 Swiss francs per *dollar* times 1.46596 *dollars* per pound equaled 1.43293 Swiss francs per pound.

To determine if your answer is correct, you can check a currency cross rate table such as that shown in Table 21-2. There you will see the cross rate between the Swiss franc and the British pound was, in fact, 1.43294 on April 13, 2015. This very minor difference is normal. GBP along the side stands for British pound and CHF across the top stands for Swiss franc. As in this example, the cross rates for various currencies will not always be perfectly synchronized, but they will be very close because arbitrageurs would quickly buy and sell currencies that had cross rates that deviated from the relationship described. These arbitrageurs would earn risk-free returns while pushing the market back to equilibrium cross rates.

Table 21-2 has currency rates for two dates approximately three years apart (the top and middle of the table). Comparing the rates for the two time periods shows that the U.S. dollar (top line) fell against most major currencies. In particular, the dollar fell against the euro and the Japanese yen. However, the U.S. dollar rose slightly against the British pound. On June 23, 2016, a slight majority of British voters voted for Britain to exit the European Union. The plan for Britain's exit is commonly referred to as "Brexit." In the two days after the Brexit vote, the British pound dropped by over 11 percent against the dollar. It fell against every other major currency as well. Major events, like the Brexit vote, can move currency markets significantly, which is the reason companies seek to manage their foreign exchange risk, as discussed in the next section.

Managing Foreign Exchange Risk

When the parties associated with a commercial transaction are located in the same country, the transaction is denominated in a single currency. International transactions inevitably involve more than one currency (because the parties are residents of different countries). Since most foreign currency values fluctuate from time to time, the monetary value of an international transaction measured in either the seller's currency or the buyer's currency is likely to change when payment is delayed. As a result, the seller may receive less revenue than expected or the buyer may have to pay more than the expected amount for the merchandise. Thus the term **foreign exchange risk** refers to the possibility of a drop in revenue or an increase in cost in an international transaction due to a change in foreign exchange rates. Importers, exporters, investors, and multinational firms are all exposed to this foreign exchange risk.

The international monetary system has undergone a significant change since 1971 when the free trading Western nations basically went from a fixed exchange rate system to a "freely" floating rate system. For the most part, the new system has proved its agility and resilience over the last four decades. Consequently, the exchange rates

Table 21-2   Key currency cross rates

Key currency rates as of April 13, 2015

	USD	EUR	GBP	JPY	CHF	CAD	AUD	NZD	HKD	SGD
USD	1	0.9441	0.68226	120.323	0.97747	1.25934	1.3197	1.3418	7.75009	1.3735
EUR	1.05856	1	0.7221	127.372	1.03475	1.33311	1.39701	1.4205	8.2039	1.4539
GBP	1.46596	1.3849	1	176.388	1.43294	1.84618	1.93469	1.96723	11.362	2.0135
JPY	0.008311	0.78483	0.005669	1	0.8124	1.0463	0.010966	0.011152	0.06441	0.01141
CHF	1.0231	0.9663	0.6979	123.093	1	1.2883	1.3501	1.3728	7.9287	1.4051
CAD	0.7942	0.7502	0.5418	95.542	0.77619	1	1.048	1.0658	6.1538	1.0907
AUD	0.75775	0.7158	0.5169	91.173	0.74065	0.95425	1	1.01682	5.8726	1.0408
NZD	0.7452	0.7039	0.5084	89.664	0.72838	0.93842	0.9835	1	5.775	1.0236
HKD	0.12903	0.12187	0.08801	15.5259	12.6115	0.16245	0.17026	0.17313	1	0.1772
SGD	0.7281	0.68769	0.49664	87.605	0.7117	0.9215	0.96074	0.977	5.6427	1

Key currency cross rates as of February 1, 2018

	USD	EUR	GBP	JPY	CHF	CAD	AUD	NZD	HKD	SGD
USD	1	0.806	0.707	1.088	0.935	1.233	1.240	1.359	7.821	1.313
EUR	1.241	1	0.877	135.052	1.160	1.531	1.539	1.687	9.709	1.629
GBP	1.415	1.140	1	154.019	1.323	1.745	1.755	1.923	11.068	1.857
JPY	0.919	0.007	0.006	1	0.009	0.011	0.011	0.012	0.072	0.012
CHF	1.070	0.862	0.756	116.512	1	1.320	1.327	1.454	8.371	1.404
CAD	0.811	0.653	0.573	88.289	0.758	1	1.006	1.102	6.342	1.064
AUD	0.806	0.650	0.570	87.807	0.754	0.994	1	1.096	6.305	1.058
NZD	0.736	0.593	0.520	80.152	0.688	0.907	0.913	1	5.754	0.965
HKD	0.128	0.103	0.090	13.920	0.119	0.158	0.159	0.174	1	0.168
SGD	0.762	0.614	0.538	82.969	0.712	0.940	0.945	1.036	5.960	1

USD = United States dollar   CHF = Swiss franc   NZD = New Zealand dollar
EUR = European monetary unit   CAD = Canadian dollar   HKD = Hong Kong dollar
GBP = Great Britain pound   AUD = Australian dollar   SGD = Singaporean dollar
JPY = Japanese yen

Source: www.fxstreet.com/rates-charts/exchange-rates/.

have fluctuated over a much wider range than before. The increased volatility of exchange markets has forced multinational firms, importers, and exporters to pay more attention to the function of foreign exchange risk management.

The foreign exchange risk of a multinational company is divided into two types of exposure: accounting or translation exposure and transaction exposure. An MNC's foreign assets and liabilities, which are denominated in foreign currency units, are exposed to losses and gains due to changing exchange rates. This is called accounting or **translation exposure**. The amount of loss or gain resulting from this form of exposure and the treatment of it in the parent company's books depend on the accounting rules established by the parent company's government. In the United States, the rules are spelled out in the *Statement of Financial Accounting Standards (SFAS) No. 52.* Under *SFAS 52* all

The Coca-Cola Company is the world's largest beverage company. Based in Atlanta, Georgia, Coca-Cola had worldwide sales of almost $42 billion in 2016. More than half of these sales were outside the United States. Coke's sales are spread across North America, Latin America, Asia, Europe, and Africa. Although most of its sales and its costs are in foreign countries, Coke reports earnings to its mostly American shareholders in U.S. dollars. It is not surprising that Coke works hard to manage its foreign currency risk. The largest currency positions that it manages include the euro, Japanese yen, Mexican peso, and Brazilian real. Overall, Coke used 73 functional currencies along with the U.S. dollar in 2016. Coke has used derivatives such as forward currency contracts and currency options to buy these currencies in advance and to short them (meaning it has agreed in advance to deliver currency that it does not yet possess).

Sometimes these derivative positions are worth billions of dollars, but it would be an error to think of Coca-Cola as gambling. In the 2016 annual report, Coca-Cola states,

Our Company uses derivative financial instruments primarily to reduce our exposure to adverse fluctuations in foreign currency exchange rates, interest rates, commodity prices and other market risks. We do not enter into derivative financial instruments for trading purposes. As a matter of policy, all of our derivative positions are used to reduce risk by hedging an underlying economic exposure. Because of the high correlation between the hedging instrument and the underlying exposure, fluctuations in the value of the instruments are generally offset by reciprocal changes in the value of the underlying exposure. The Company generally hedges anticipated exposures up to 36 months in advance; however, the majority of our derivative instruments expire within 24 months or less. Virtually all of our derivatives are straightforward over-the-counter instruments with liquid markets.

We monitor our exposure to financial market risks using several objective measurement systems, including a sensitivity analysis to measure our exposure to fluctuations in foreign currency exchange rates, interest rates, and commodity prices.

From this statement, it is clear that a hedge is not meant to be speculative or to make money based on expectations of currency fluctuations. Coca-Cola hedges to protect cash flows that are arising in the ordinary course of its international business. Many other companies are in this same situation. It is important to distinguish between trading for a profit (speculating) and locking in a position (hedging). Derivative contracts often get a bad reputation as risky because a few financial officers have used them to speculate, rather than to hedge. However, large nonfinancial companies, like Coca-Cola, use derivatives mostly to minimize risk.

foreign currency–denominated assets and liabilities are converted at the rate of exchange in effect on the date of balance sheet preparation. An unrealized translation gain or loss is held in an equity reserve account while the realized gain or loss is incorporated in the parent's consolidated income statement for that period. Thus *SFAS 52* partially reduces the impact of accounting exposure resulting from the translation of a foreign subsidiary's balance sheet on reported earnings of multinational firms.

However, foreign exchange gains and losses resulting from international transactions, which reflect **transaction exposure**, are shown in the income statement for the current period. As a consequence of these transactional gains and losses, the volatility of reported earnings per share increases. Three different strategies can be used to minimize this transaction exposure.

1. Hedging in the forward exchange market.
2. Hedging in the money market.
3. Hedging in the currency futures market.

Forward Exchange Market Hedge   To see how transaction exposure can be covered in forward markets, suppose Electricitie de France, an electric company in France, purchases a large generator from the General Electric Company of the United States for 822,400 euros on February 21, 2020, and GE is promised the payment in euros in 90 days. Since GE is now exposed to exchange rate risk by agreeing to receive the payment in euros in the future, it is up to General Electric to find a way to reduce this exposure. One simple method is to hedge the exposure in the forward exchange market with a 90-day forward contract. On February 21, 2020, to establish a forward cover, GE sells a forward contract to deliver the 822,400 euros 90 days from that date in exchange for $1,000,000. On May 22, 2020,[2] GE receives payment from Electricitie de France and delivers the 822,400 euros to the bank that signed the contract. In return, the bank delivers $1,000,000 to GE.

Money Market Hedge   A second way to eliminate transaction exposure in the previous example would have been to borrow money in euros and then convert it to U.S. dollars immediately. When the account receivable from the sale is collected three months later, the loan is cleared with the proceeds. In this case, GE's strategy consists of the following steps.

On February 21, 2020:

1. Borrow 806,275 euros—(822,400 euros/1.02) = 806,274.51 euros—at the rate of 8.0 percent per year for three months. You will borrow less than the full amount of 822,400 euros in recognition of the fact that interest must be paid on the loan. Eight percent interest for 90 days translates into 2.0 percent. Thus 822,400 euros is divided by 1.02 to arrive at the size of the loan before the interest payment.

2. Convert the euros into U.S. dollars in the spot market.

Then on May 22, 2020 (90 days later):

3. Receive the payment of 822,400 euros from Electricitie de France.

4. Clear the loan with the proceeds received from Electricitie de France.

The money market hedge basically calls for matching the exposed asset (account receivable) with a liability (loan payable) in the same currency. Some firms prefer this money market hedge because of the early availability of funds possible with this method.

Currency Futures Market Hedge   Transaction exposure associated with a foreign currency can also be covered in the futures market with a **currency futures contract**. The International Monetary Market (IMM) of the Chicago Mercantile Exchange began trading in futures contracts in foreign currencies on May 16, 1972. Trading in currency futures contracts also made a debut on the London International Financial Futures Exchange (LIFFE) in September 1982. Other markets have also developed

---

[2]February 21, 2020, to May 22, 2020, represents 90 days.

around the world. Just as futures contracts are traded in corn, wheat, hogs, and beans, foreign currency futures contracts are traded in these markets. Although the futures market and forward market are similar in concept, they differ in their operations. To illustrate the hedging process in the currency futures market, suppose that in May Bank of America considers lending 500,000 pesos to a Mexican subsidiary of a U.S. parent company for seven months. The bank purchases the pesos in the spot market, delivers them to the borrower, and simultaneously hedges its transaction exposure by selling December contracts in pesos for the same amount. In December when the loan is cleared, the bank sells the pesos in the spot market and buys back the December peso contracts. The transactions are illustrated for the spot and futures market in Table 21-3:[3]

Table 21-3	Currency futures hedging	
Date	**Spot Market**	**Futures Market**
May 7	Buys 500,000 pesos at $0.0980/peso = $49,000	Sells 500,000 pesos for December delivery at $0.0954/peso = $47,700
December 7	Sells 500,000 pesos at $0.0941/peso = $47,050	Buys 500,000 pesos at $0.0941/peso = $47,050
	Loss $1,950	Gain $650

While the loan was outstanding, the peso declined in value relative to the U.S. dollar. Had the bank remained unhedged, it would have lost $1,950 in the spot market. By hedging in the futures market, the bank was able to reduce the loss to $1,300. A $650 gain in the futures market was used to cancel some of the $1,950 loss in the spot market.

These are not the only means companies have for protecting themselves against foreign exchange risk. Over the years, multinational companies have developed elaborate foreign asset management programs, which involve such strategies as switching cash and other current assets into strong currencies, while piling up debt and other liabilities in depreciating currencies. Companies also encourage the quick collection of bills in weak currencies by offering sizable discounts, while extending liberal credit in strong currencies.

Foreign Investment Decisions

Literally thousands of U.S. firms operate in foreign countries through one or more foreign affiliates. Several explanations are offered for the moves to foreign soil. First, with the emergence of trading blocs in Europe, American firms feared their goods might face import tariffs in those countries. To avoid such trade barriers, U.S. firms started manufacturing in foreign countries. The second factor was that firms were motivated by the significantly lower wage costs prevailing in foreign countries. Firms in labor-intensive industries, such as textiles and electronics, moved some of their operations to countries where labor was cheap. Third, superior American technology gave U.S. firms

---

[3]For purposes of this example, we assumed the peso was trading at a discount in the futures market. Had it been trading at a premium, the hedge would have been even more attractive.

easy access to oil exploration, mining, and manufacturing in many developing nations. A fourth advantage relates to taxes. The U.S.-based multinational firms could postpone payment of U.S. taxes on income earned abroad until such income was actually repatriated (forwarded) to the parent company. This tax deferral provision could be used by an MNC to minimize its tax liability. Some countries, like Israel, Ireland, and South Africa, offer special tax incentives for foreign firms that establish operations there.

Tax law changes taking place in 2018 will replace the deferral of taxes on foreign earnings with a complete exemption from U.S. tax. However, other elements of the new law will encourage MNCs to produce products in the United States.

International diversification also reduces a company's overall risk. The basic premise of portfolio theory in finance is that an investor can reduce the risk level of a portfolio by combining those investments whose returns are less than perfectly positively correlated. In addition to domestic diversification, it is shown in Figure 21-3 that further reduction in investment risk can be achieved by also diversifying across national boundaries. Portfolios with international stocks in Figure 21-3 show a lower standard deviation compared to pure U.S. stock portfolios. It is argued, however, that institutional and political constraints, language barriers, and lack of adequate information on foreign investments prevent investors from diversifying across nations. Multinational firms, on the other hand, through their unique position around the world, derive benefits from international diversification.[4]

While U.S.-based firms took the lead in establishing overseas subsidiaries during the 1950s and 1960s, European and Japanese firms started this activity in the 1970s and

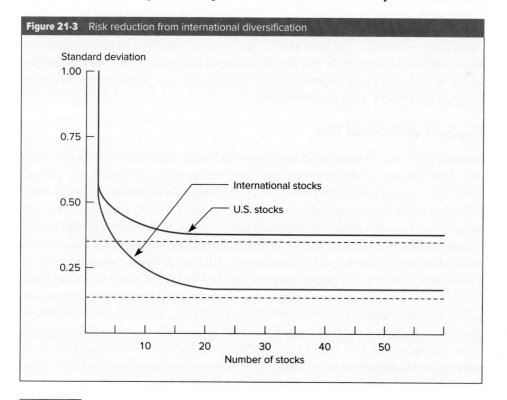

Figure 21-3   Risk reduction from international diversification

---

[4]International mutual funds also have helped investors diversify across national borders.

have continued into the new century. Chinese companies arrived later to the game, but these firms have also expanded into international markets. The flow of foreign direct investment into the United States has proceeded at a rapid rate. These investments employ millions of people. It is evident that the United States is an attractive site for foreign investment. In addition to the international diversification and strategic considerations, many other factors are responsible for this inflow of foreign capital into the United States. Increased foreign labor costs in some countries and saturated overseas markets in others are partly responsible. In Japan, an acute shortage of land suitable for industrial development and a near total dependence on imported oil prompted some Japanese firms to locate in the United States. In Germany, a large number of paid holidays, restrictions limiting labor layoffs, and worker participation in management decision making caused many firms to look favorably at the United States. Political stability, large market size, access to advanced technology, and a highly educated workforce are other primary motivating factors for firms to establish operations in the United States.

Not only do foreign investors make direct investments in U.S. commercial enterprises, foreign investors in the U.S. Treasury bond market have been bankrolling enormous budget deficits that the government has been running up. When the U.S. government began falling $150 to $200 billion into the red on an annual basis in the 1980s, many analysts thought this would surely mean high inflation, high interest rates, and perhaps a recession. They also were sure there would be a "shortage of capital" for investments because of large government borrowing to finance the deficits. For the most part, foreign investors from China, Japan, Western Europe, Canada, and elsewhere have bailed the government out by supplying the necessary capital. Of course, this means the United States is more dependent on flows of foreign capital into the country. We must satisfy our "outside" creditors or face the unpleasant consequences. During the last four decades, we have gone from being the largest lender in the world to the largest borrower. This debt places an enormous burden on future generations of American taxpayers.

Analysis of Political Risk

Business firms tend to make direct investments in foreign countries for a relatively long time. This is because of the time necessary to recover the initial investment. The government may change hands several times during the foreign firm's tenure in that country; and, when a new government takes over, it may not be as friendly or as cooperative as the previous administration. An unfriendly government can interfere with the foreign affiliate in many ways. It may impose foreign exchange restrictions, or the foreign ownership share may be limited to a set percentage of the total. **Repatriation** (transfer) of a subsidiary's profit to the parent company may be blocked, at least temporarily; and, in the extreme case, the government may even **expropriate** (take over) the foreign subsidiary's assets. The multinational company may experience a sizable loss of income or property, or both, as a result of this political interference. Many once well-known U.S. firms, like Anaconda, ITT, and Occidental Petroleum, have lost hundreds of millions of dollars in politically unstable countries. After Venezuelan voters elected socialist revolutionary Hugo Chávez to the office of president in 1999, Venezuela expropriated hundreds of businesses owned both by foreigners and by domestic business owners. Foreign investment almost completely disappeared from the country, and it has not returned.

The best approach to protection against political risk is to thoroughly investigate the country's political stability long before the firm makes any investment in that country. Companies use different methods for assessing political risk. Some firms hire consultants to provide them with a report of political risk analysis. Others form their own advisory committees (little state departments) consisting of top-level managers from headquarters and foreign subsidiaries. After ascertaining the country's political risk level, the multinational firm can use one of the following strategies to guard against such risk:

1.   One strategy is to establish a joint venture with a local entrepreneur. By bringing a local partner into the deal, the MNC not only limits its financial exposure but also minimizes antiforeign feelings. Having a "politically connected" local partner can be very valuable.

2.   Another risk management tactic is to enter a joint venture with larger firms from other countries. For example, an energy company may pursue its oil production operation in Zaire in association with Royal Dutch Petroleum and Nigerian National Petroleum as partners. The foreign government will be more hesitant to antagonize a number of partner firms of many nationalities at the same time.

3.   When the perceived political risk level is high, insurance against such risks can be obtained in advance. **Overseas Private Investment Corporation (OPIC)**, a federal government agency, sells insurance policies to qualified firms. OPIC promotes American investment in Third World countries by insuring against losses due to inconvertibility into dollars of amounts received in a foreign country. Policies are also available from OPIC to insure against expropriation and against losses due to war or revolution. For example, OPIC insures the Rwanda properties of Westport, Connecticut–based Tea Importers Inc. During the five-year Rwandan civil war, the company's tea-processing factory was destroyed, and OPIC paid claims on insurance against political violence. These payments allowed Tea Importers to rebuild and resume production after the war and helped to revive the Rwandan economy. Private insurance companies, such as Lloyds of London, American International Group Inc., CIGNA, and others, issue similar policies to cover political risk.

Political risk umbrella policies do not come cheaply. Coverage for projects in "fairly safe" countries can cost anywhere from 0.3 percent to 12 percent of the insured values per year. Needless to say, the coverage is more expensive or unavailable in troubled countries. OPIC has suspended consideration of new insurance transactions in Venezuela. OPIC's rates are lower than those of private insurers, and its policies extend for up to 20 years, compared to 3 years or less for private insurance policies.

Financing International Business Operations

When the parties to an international transaction are well known to each other and the countries involved are politically stable, sales are generally made on credit, as is customary in domestic business operations. However, if a foreign importer is relatively new or the political environment is volatile, or both, the possibility of nonpayment by the importer is worrisome for the exporter. To reduce the risk of nonpayment, an exporter may request that the importer furnish a letter of credit. The importer's bank normally issues the **letter of credit**, in which the bank promises to subsequently pay the money for the merchandise. For example, assume Archer Daniels Midland (ADM) is negotiating with a South Korean trading company to export soybean meal. The two parties agree on price, method of shipment, timing of shipment, destination point, and the like. Once the basic terms of sale have been agreed to, the South Korean trading company (importer) applies for a letter of credit from its commercial bank in Seoul. The Korean bank, if it so desires, issues such a letter of credit, which specifies in detail all the steps that must be completed by the American exporter before payment is made. If ADM complies with all specifications in the letter of credit and submits to the Korean bank the proper documentation to prove that it has done so, the Korean bank guarantees the payment on the due date. On that date, the American firm is paid by the Korean bank, not by the buyer of the goods. Therefore, all the credit risk to the exporter is absorbed by the importer's bank, which is in a good position to evaluate the creditworthiness of the importing firm.

The exporter who requires cash payment or a letter of credit from foreign buyers of marginal credit standing is likely to lose orders to competitors. Instead of risking the loss of business, American firms can find an alternative way to reduce the risk of nonpayment by foreign customers. This alternative method consists of obtaining export credit insurance. The insurance policy provides assurance to the exporter that should the foreign customer default on payment, the insurance company will pay for the shipment.

Funding of Transactions

Assistance in the funding of foreign transactions may take many forms.

Eximbank (Export-Import Bank)   This agency of the U.S. government facilitates the financing of U.S. exports through its various programs. In its direct loan program, the **Eximbank** lends money to foreign purchasers of U.S. goods such as aircraft, electrical equipment, heavy machinery, computers, and the like. The Eximbank also purchases eligible medium-term obligations of foreign buyers of U.S. goods at a discount from face value. In this discount program, private banks and other lenders are able to rediscount (sell at a lower price) promissory notes and drafts acquired from foreign customers of U.S. firms.

Corporate subsidies are controversial, and congressional authorization for the bank lapsed on July 1, 2015. Several companies like GE and Boeing began to move some production overseas, citing Congress's failure to reauthorize the bank. These actions put pressure on Congress to renew the charter and five months later the bank was reauthorized.

Loans from the Parent Company or a Sister Affiliate   Another source of funds for a foreign affiliate is its parent company or its sister affiliates. In addition to contributing equity capital, the parent company often provides loans of varying maturities to its foreign affiliate. Although the simplest arrangement is a direct loan from the parent to the foreign subsidiary, such a loan is rarely extended because of foreign exchange risk, political risk, and tax treatment. Instead the loans are often channeled through an intermediary to a foreign affiliate. Parallel loans and fronting loans are two examples of such indirect loan arrangements between a parent company and its foreign affiliate. A typical parallel loan arrangement is depicted in Figure 21-4.

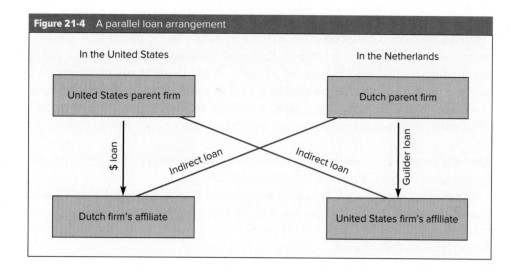

Figure 21-4   A parallel loan arrangement

In the United States

In the Netherlands

United States parent firm

Dutch parent firm

$ loan

Indirect loan

Indirect loan

Guilder loan

Dutch firm's affiliate

United States firm's affiliate

In this illustration of a **parallel loan**, an American firm that wants to lend funds to its Dutch affiliate locates a Dutch parent firm, which needs to transfer funds to its U.S. affiliate. Avoiding the exchange markets, the U.S. parent lends dollars to the Dutch affiliate in the United States, while the Dutch parent lends guilders to the American affiliate in the Netherlands. At maturity, the two loans would each be repaid to the original lender. Notice that neither loan carries any foreign exchange risk in this arrangement. In essence both parent firms are providing indirect loans to their affiliates.

A **fronting loan** is simply a parent's loan to its foreign subsidiary channeled through a financial intermediary, usually a large international bank. A schematic of a fronting loan is shown in Figure 21-5.

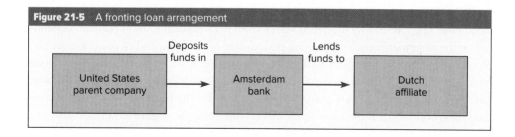

Figure 21-5   A fronting loan arrangement

Deposits
funds in

Lends
funds to

United States
parent company

Amsterdam
bank

Dutch
affiliate

In the example, the U.S. parent company deposits funds in an Amsterdam bank and that bank lends the same amount to the U.S. firm's affiliate in the Netherlands. In this manner, the bank fronts for the parent by extending a risk-free (fully collateralized) loan to the foreign affiliate. In the event of political turmoil, the foreign government is more likely to allow the American subsidiary to repay the loan to a large international bank than to allow the same affiliate to repay the loan to its parent company. Thus the parent company reduces its political risk substantially by using a fronting loan instead of transferring funds directly to its foreign affiliate.

Even though the parent company would prefer that its foreign subsidiary maintain its own financial arrangements, many banks are apprehensive about lending to a foreign affiliate without a parent guarantee. In fact, a large portion of bank lending to foreign affiliates is based on some sort of a guarantee by the parent firm. Usually, because of its multinational reputation, the parent company has a better credit rating than its foreign affiliates. The lender advances funds on the basis of the parent's creditworthiness even though the affiliate is expected to pay back the loan. The terms of a parent guarantee may vary greatly, depending on the closeness of the parent–affiliate ties, parent–lender relations, and the home country's legal jurisdiction.

Eurodollar Loans   The Eurodollar market is an important source of short-term loans for many multinational firms and their foreign affiliates.

Eurodollars are simply U.S. dollars deposited in foreign banks. Although a substantial portion of these deposits are held by European banks or European-based branches of U.S. commercial banks, the prefix "euro" is somewhat misleading because the foreign bank does not need to be located in Europe.

Since the early 1960s, the Eurodollar market has established itself as a significant part of world credit markets. The participants in these markets are diverse in character and geographically widespread. Hundreds of corporations and banks, mostly from the United States, Canada, Western Europe, and Japan, are regular borrowers and depositors in this market.

The Eurodollar system is the biggest source of global funding, in part because of the lower borrowing costs in the Eurodollar market. These lower costs are often attributed to the smaller overhead costs for lending banks and the absence of a compensating balance requirement. Most Eurodollar transactions occur between large banks. Banks with an excess of deposits, relative to profitable lending opportunities, lend their excess funds to other banks who have an excess of opportunities but a shortage of funds. These interbank loans are often priced using the **London Interbank Offered Rate (LIBOR)**. Other Eurodollar borrowers are typically charged a premium above the LIBOR. Interest rates on these loans are calculated by adding a premium to the basic rate. The size of this premium varies from 0.25 percent to 0.50 percent, depending on the customer, length of the loan period, size of the loan, and so on. For example, Northern Indiana Public Service Company obtained a $75 million, three-year loan from Merrill Lynch International Bank. The utility company paid 0.375 points above LIBOR for the first two years and 0.50 points above for the final year of the loan. Over the years, borrowing in the Eurodollar market has been one-eighth to seven-eighths of a percentage point cheaper than borrowing at the U.S. prime interest rate. For information on the LIBOR price fixing scandal, see the Finance in Action box in Chapter 8.

Lending in the Eurodollar market is done almost exclusively by commercial banks. Large Eurocurrency loans are often syndicated by a group of participating banks. The loan agreement is put together by a lead bank, known as the manager, which is usually one of the largest U.S. or European banks. The manager charges the borrower a once-and-for-all fee or commission of 0.25 percent to 1 percent of the loan value. A portion of this fee is kept by the lead bank, and the remainder is shared by all the participating banks. The aim of forming a syndicate is to diversify the risk, which would be too large for any single bank to handle by itself. Multicurrency loans and revolving credit arrangements can also be negotiated in the Eurocurrency market to suit borrowers' needs.

Eurobond Market   When long-term funds are needed, borrowing in the Eurobond market is a viable alternative for leading multinational corporations. The **Eurobond** issues are sold simultaneously in several national capital markets, but denominated in a currency different from that of the nation in which the bonds are issued. The most widely used currency in the Eurobond market is the U.S. dollar. These bonds are dollar-denominated, but they are issued outside the United States. Eurobond issues are underwritten by an international syndicate of banks and securities firms. Eurobonds of longer than seven years in maturity generally have a sinking-fund provision.

Disclosure requirements in the Eurobond market are much less stringent than those required by the Securities and Exchange Commission (SEC) in the United States. Furthermore, the registration costs in the Eurobond market are lower than those charged in the United States. In addition, the Eurobond market offers tax flexibility for borrowers and investors alike. In fact, some Eurobonds are unregistered bearer bonds. Since no record of the bond's ownership is kept by the issuer, these bonds are attractive to foreign owners who wish to evade taxes in their home country. All these advantages of Eurobonds, and particularly bearer bonds, enable the borrowers to raise funds at a lower cost. Nevertheless, a caveat may be in order with respect to the effective cost of borrowing in the Eurobond market. When a multinational firm borrows by issuing a foreign currency–denominated debt issue on a long-term basis, it creates transaction exposure, a kind of foreign exchange risk. If the foreign currency appreciates in value during the bond's life, the cost of servicing the debt could rise. Many U.S. multinational firms borrowed at an approximately 7 percent coupon interest by selling Eurobonds denominated in Deutsche marks and Swiss francs in the late 1980s and early 1990s. Nevertheless, these U.S. firms experienced an average debt service cost of approximately 13 percent, which is almost twice as much as the coupon rate. This increased cost occurred because the U.S. dollar fell with respect to these currencies. Therefore, currency selection for denominating Eurobond issues must be made with extreme care and foresight. To lessen the impact of foreign exchange risk, some Eurobond issues are denominated in multicurrency units.

International Equity Markets   The entire amount of equity capital comes from the parent company for a *wholly owned* foreign subsidiary, but many foreign affiliates are not owned completely by their parent corporations. To avoid nationalistic reactions to wholly owned foreign subsidiaries, such multinational firms as ExxonMobil, General Motors, Ford, and IBM sell shares to worldwide stockholders. It is also believed that widespread foreign ownership of the firm's common stock encourages the loyalty of foreign stockholders and employees toward the firm. Thus selling common stock to residents of foreign countries not only is an important financing strategy but is also a risk-minimizing strategy for many multinational corporations.

As you have learned in Chapter 14, a well-functioning secondary market is essential to entice investors into owning shares. To attract investors from all over the world, reputable multinational firms list their shares on major stock exchanges around the world. Approximately 500 foreign companies are listed on the New York Stock Exchange. Even more foreign firms would sell stock issues in the United States and list on the NYSE and NASDAQ were it not for the tough and costly disclosure

Companies face political as well as business and financial risks when they expand into foreign markets and invest internationally. Political risks include those associated with the policies of a current regime as well as those that may arise due to possible changes in leaders or direction. Investors want to maximize their returns for a given level of risk, so recognizing political risk is an important component of overall risk assessment.

An example of political risk affecting private businesses arose recently in Argentina, where the government decided to expropriate the assets of the country's largest oil company, YPF. YPF was a subsidiary of Spanish multinational oil and gas firm Resol. President Cristina Fernandez de Kirchner, along with influential legislators, led the nationalization efforts. They contended YPF was under-investing in Argentina to keep supplies low and prices artificially high. While this is something that Resol denied, minimizing investment was probably a prudent strategy in light of Argentina's subsequent expropriation of the firm's assets. The expropriation was a result of Argentine attitudes toward the profits and motives of foreign companies.

This came on the heels of the nationalization of Argentine Airlines and also the nationalization of private pensions of Argentine companies and citizens. Furthermore, many in Argentina feel their sovereign debt default in 2001–2002 was a result of free-market policies, thus souring attitudes toward free enterprise.

This example shows that political risks may have major effects on capital flows globally. As one analyst asked regarding Argentina's nationalization policy, "Who wants to invest in a country where the government expropriates private property from one day to the next?" Many multinational companies now avoid investing in Argentina because they are afraid that they may later have their businesses seized by the government. Clearly, political factors are a risk that needs to be assessed when analyzing the total risk-return trade-off that companies face—particularly when investing abroad.

Sources: www.nytimes.com/2012/04/19/world/americas/dismay-over-argentinas-nationalization-plan.html?_r=1; www.reuters.com/article/2012/05/04/us-argentina-ypf-idUSBRE8421GV20120504.

rules in effect in this country and enforced by the Securities and Exchange Commission. Many foreign corporations, such as BP, Unilever, Honda, Hitachi, Sony, Rio Tinto, DeBeers, and the like, accommodate American investors by issuing **American Depository Receipts (ADRs)**. All the American-owned shares of a foreign company are placed in trust in a major U.S. bank. The bank, in turn, will issue its depository receipts to the American stockholders and will maintain a stockholder ledger on these receipts, thus enabling the holders of ADRs to sell or otherwise transfer them as easily as they transfer any American company shares. ADR prices tend to move in a parallel path with the prices of the underlying securities in their home markets.

Looking elsewhere around the world, U.S. firms have listed their shares on the London Stock Exchange, the Toronto Stock Exchange and the Montreal Exchange. To obtain exposure in an international financial community, listing securities on world stock exchanges is a step in the right direction for a multinational firm. This international exposure also brings an additional responsibility for the MNC to understand the preferences and needs of heterogeneous groups of investors of various nationalities. The MNC may have to print and circulate its annual financial statements in many languages. Some foreign investors are more risk-averse than their counterparts in the United States and prefer dividend income over less certain capital gains. Common stock ownership among individuals in countries like Japan and Norway is relatively insignificant, with financial institutions holding substantial amounts of common stock issues. Institutional practices around the globe also vary significantly when it comes to issuing new securities. Unlike in the United States, European commercial banks play a dominant role in the securities business. They underwrite stock issues, manage portfolios, vote the stock they hold in trust accounts, and hold directorships on company boards. In Germany, the banks also run an over-the-counter market in many stocks.

The International Finance Corporation   Whenever a multinational company has difficulty raising equity capital due to lack of adequate private risk capital in a foreign country, the firm may explore the possibility of selling partial ownership to the **International Finance Corporation (IFC)**. This is a unit of the World Bank Group. The International Finance Corporation was established in 1956 and is owned by 189 member countries of the World Bank. Its objective is to further economic development by promoting private enterprises in developing countries. The profitability of a project and its potential benefit to the host country's economy are the two criteria the IFC uses to decide whether to assist a venture. The IFC participates in private enterprise through buying equity shares of a business, providing long-term loans, or a combination of the two for up to 25 percent of the total capital. The IFC expects the other partners to assume managerial responsibility, and it does not exercise its voting rights as a stockholder. The IFC helps finance new ventures as well as the expansion of existing ones in a variety of industries. Once the venture is well established, the IFC sells its investment position to private investors to free up its capital.

Some Unsettled Issues in International Finance

As firms become multinational in scope, the nature of their financial decisions also becomes more complex. A multinational firm has access to more sources of funds than a purely domestic corporation. Interest rates and market conditions vary between the alternative sources of funds, and corporate financial practices may differ significantly between countries. For example, the debt ratios in many foreign countries are higher than those used by U.S. firms. A foreign affiliate of an American firm faces a dilemma in its financing decision: Should it follow the parent firm's norm or that of the host country? Who must decide this? Will it be decided at the corporate headquarters in the United States or by the foreign affiliate? This is a matter of control over financial decisions. Dividend policy is another area of debate. Should the parent company dictate the dividends the foreign affiliate must distribute, or should it be left primarily to the discretion of the foreign affiliate? Foreign government regulations may also influence the decision. Questions like these do not have clear-cut answers. The complex environment in which the MNCs operate does not permit simple solutions. Obviously each situation has to be evaluated individually, and specific guidelines for decision making must be established. Such coordination, it is to be hoped, will result in cohesive policies in the areas of working capital management, capital structure, and dividend decisions throughout the MNC network.

SUMMARY

A significant proportion of earnings for many American companies comes from overseas markets. International business operations have often been more profitable than domestic operations, and this higher profitability is one factor that motivates business firms to go overseas to expand their markets. U.S. multinational firms have played a major role in promoting economic development and international trade for several decades, and foreign firms have invested huge amounts of capital in the United States. Brand-name companies such as Sony, Coca-Cola, Heineken, McDonald's, Nestlé, and BMW are famous the world over.

When a domestic business crosses its national borders to do business in other countries, it enters a riskier and more complex environment. A multinational firm is exposed to foreign exchange risk in addition to the usual business and financial risks. International business transactions are denominated in foreign currencies, and the rate at which one currency unit is converted into another is called the exchange rate. In today's global monetary system, exchange rates of major currencies fluctuate freely and on occasion are volatile. For example on October 7, 1998, the Japanese yen fell over 6 percent versus the U.S. dollar due to adverse economic circumstances; this was a record one-day movement against the U.S. dollar. These floating exchange rates expose multinational business firms to foreign exchange risk.

To deal with this foreign currency exposure effectively, the financial executive of a MNC must understand foreign exchange rates and how they are determined. Foreign exchange rates are influenced by differences in inflation rates among countries, differences in interest rates, governmental policies, and the expectations of the participants in the foreign exchange markets. The international financial manager can reduce the firm's foreign currency exposure by hedging in the forward exchange markets, in the money markets, and in the currency futures market.

Foreign direct investments are usually quite large, and many of them are exposed to enormous political risk. Although discounted cash flow analysis is applied to screen the projects in the initial stages, strategic considerations and political risk are often the overriding factors in reaching the final decisions about foreign investments. Political risk could involve negative policy decisions by a foreign government that discriminate against foreign firms. Political risk could also be the possibility of a country defaulting on sovereign debt—such as Russia did in 1998—or it could be a country's economic policies that have negative impacts on the economy such as inducing high inflation or a recession, high unemployment, and social unrest. Political events are hard to forecast, and this makes analyzing a foreign investment proposal more difficult than analyzing a domestic investment project.

Financing international trade and investments is another important area of international finance that one must understand to raise funds at the lowest cost possible. The multinational firm has access to both the domestic and foreign capital markets. The Export-Import Bank finances American exports to foreign countries. Borrowing in the Eurobond market may appear less expensive at times, but the effect of foreign exchange risk on debt servicing costs must be weighed carefully before borrowing in these markets. Floating common stock in foreign capital markets is also a viable financing alternative for many multinational companies. The International Finance Corporation, which is a subsidiary of the World Bank, also provides debt capital and equity capital to qualified firms. These alternative sources of financing may significantly differ with respect to cost, terms, and conditions. Therefore, the financial executive must carefully locate and use the proper means to finance international business operations.

LIST OF TERMS

euro 654
multinational corporation (MNC) 655
exchange rate 657
purchasing power parity
   theory 659
interest rate parity theory 659
balance of payments 659
spot rate 660
forward rate 661
cross rates 662
foreign exchange risk 662
translation exposure 663
transaction exposure 664
currency futures contract 665
repatriation 668

expropriate 668
Overseas Private Investment
   Corporation (OPIC) 669
letter of credit 669
Eximbank 670
parallel loan 671
fronting loan 671
Eurodollars 672
London Interbank Offered Rate
   (LIBOR) 672
Eurobond 673
American Depository Receipts
   (ADRs) 674
International Finance Corporation
   (IFC) 675

DISCUSSION QUESTIONS

1. What risks does a foreign affiliate of a multinational firm face in today's business world? *(LO21-3 & 21-4)*

2. What allegations are sometimes made against foreign affiliates of multinational firms and against the multinational firms themselves? *(LO21-1)*

3. List the factors that affect the value of a currency in foreign exchange markets. *(LO21-2)*

4. Explain how exports and imports tend to influence the value of a currency. *(LO21-2)*

5. Differentiate between the spot exchange rate and the forward exchange rate. *(LO21-2)*

6. What is meant by translation exposure in terms of foreign exchange risk? *(LO21-2)*

7. What factors would influence a U.S. business firm to go overseas? *(LO21-1)*

8. What procedure(s) would you recommend for a multinational company in studying exposure to political risk? What actual strategies can be used to guard against such risk? *(LO21-4)*

9.   What factors beyond the normal domestic analysis go into a financial feasibility study for a multinational firm? *(LO21-4)*

10. What is a letter of credit? *(LO21-5)*

11. Explain the functions of the following agencies: *(LO21-5)*

Overseas Private Investment Corporation (OPIC)

Export-Import Bank (Eximbank)

International Finance Corporation (IFC)

12. What are the differences between a parallel loan and a fronting loan? *(LO21-5)*

13. What is LIBOR? How does it compare to the U.S. prime rate? *(LO21-5)*

14. What is the danger or concern in floating a Eurobond issue? *(LO21-5)*

15. What are ADRs? *(LO21-5)*

16. Comment on any dilemmas that multinational firms and their foreign affiliates may face in regard to debt ratio limits and dividend payouts. *(LO21-5)*

PRACTICE PROBLEMS AND SOLUTIONS

Cross rates
(LO21-2)

1.   Suppose a Swedish krona is selling for $0.1286 and a Maltan lira is selling for $2.8148. What is the exchange rate (cross rate) of the Swedish krona to the Maltan lira?

Adjusting returns
for exchange rates
(LO21-2)

2.   An investor in the United States bought a one-year New Zealand security valued at 200,000 New Zealand dollars. The U.S. dollar equivalent was $100,000. The New Zealand security earned 15 percent during the year, but the New Zealand dollar depreciated 5 cents against the U.S. dollar during the time period ($0.50/NZD to $0.45/NZD). After transferring the funds back to the United States, what was the investor's return on his $100,000? Determine the total ending value of the New Zealand investment in New Zealand dollars and then translate this value to U.S. dollars by multiplying by $0.45. Then compute the return on the $100,000.

Solutions

1.   One dollar is worth 7.776 Swedish kronor (1/0.1286), and one Maltan lira is worth 2.8148 dollars. Thus 7.776 Swedish kronor per *dollar* times 2.8148 *dollars* per Maltan lira equals 21.89 Swedish kronor per Maltan lira.

2.   Initial value × (1 + earnings)

$$200{,}000 \times 1.15 = 230{,}000 \text{ New Zealand dollars}$$

$$\text{New Zealand dollars} \times 0.45 = \text{U.S. dollars equivalent}$$

$$230{,}000 \times 0.45 = 103{,}500 \text{ U.S. dollars equivalent}$$

$$\frac{\$103{,}500}{\$100{,}000} \times 100 = 103.50 = 3.50\%$$

PROBLEMS

connect Selected problems are available with Connect. Please see the preface for more information.

Basic Problems

1. *The Wall Street Journal* reported the following spot and forward rates for the Swiss franc ($/SF):

Spot	$0.8202
30-day forward	$0.8244
90-day forward	$0.8295
180-day forward	$0.8343

Spot and forward rates *(LO21-2)*

   a. Was the Swiss franc selling at a discount or premium in the forward market?
   b. What was the 30-day forward premium (or discount)?
   c. What was the 90-day forward premium (or discount)?
   d. Suppose you executed a 90-day forward contract to exchange 100,000 Swiss francs into U.S. dollars. How many dollars would you get 90 days hence?
   e. Assume a Swiss bank entered into a 180-day forward contract with Bankers Trust to buy $100,000. How many francs will the Swiss bank deliver in six months to get the U.S. dollars?

2. Suppose a Polish zloty is selling for $0.3414 and a British pound is selling for 1.4973. What is the exchange rate (cross rate) of the Polish zloty to the British pound? That is, how many Polish zlotys are equal to a British pound?

Cross rates *(LO21-2)*

3. From the base price level of 100 in 1979, Saudi Arabian and U.S. price levels in 2008 stood at 200 and 410, respectively. If the 1979 $/riyal exchange rate was $0.26/riyal, what should the exchange rate be in 2008? Suggestion: Using purchasing power parity, adjust the exchange rate to compensate for inflation. That is, determine the relative rate of inflation between the United States and Saudi Arabia and multiply this times $/riyal of 0.26.

Purchasing power theory *(LO21-2)*

4. From the base price level of 100 in 1981, Saudi Arabian and U.S. price levels in 2010 stood at 250 and 100, respectively. Assume the 1981 $/riyal exchange rate was $0.46/riyal. Suggestion: Using the purchasing power parity, adjust the exchange rate to compensate for inflation. That is, determine the relative rate of inflation between the United States and Saudi Arabia and multiply this times $/riyal of 0.46. What would the exchange rate be in 2010?

Continuation of purchasing power theory *(LO21-2)*

Intermediate Problems

5. An investor in the United States bought a one-year Brazilian security valued at 195,000 Brazilian reals. The U.S. dollar equivalent was 100,000. The Brazilian security earned 16 percent during the year, but the Brazilian real depreciated 5 cents against the U.S. dollar during the time period ($0.51 to $0.46). After transferring the funds back to the United States, what was the investor's return on her $100,000? Determine the total ending value of the Brazilian investment in Brazilian reals and then translate this Brazilian value to U.S. dollars. Then compute the return on the $100,000.

Adjusting returns for exchange rates *(LO21-2)*

Adjusting returns
for exchange rates
(LO21-2)

6. A Peruvian investor buys 150 shares of a U.S. stock for $7,500 ($50 per share). Over the course of a year, the stock goes up by $4 per share.

    a. If there is a 10 percent gain in the value of the dollar versus the Peruvian nuevo sol, what will be the total percentage return to the Peruvian investor? First determine the new dollar value of the investment and multiply this figure by 1.10. Divide this answer by $7,500 and get a percentage value, and then subtract 100 percent to get the percentage return.

    b. Instead assume that the stock increases by $7, but that the dollar decreases by 10 percent versus the nuevo sol. What will be the total percentage return to the Peruvian investor? Use 0.90 in place of 1.10 in this case.

Advanced Problem

Hedging exchange
rate risk
(LO21-3)

7. You are the vice president of finance for Exploratory Resources, headquartered in Houston, Texas. In January 20X1, your firm's Canadian subsidiary obtained a six-month loan of 150,000 Canadian dollars from a bank in Houston to finance the acquisition of a titanium mine in Quebec province. The loan will also be repaid in Canadian dollars. At the time of the loan, the spot exchange rate was U.S. $0.8995/Canadian dollar and the Canadian currency was selling at a discount in the forward market. The June 20X1 contract (face value = C$150,000 per contract) was quoted at U.S. $0.8930/Canadian dollar.

    a. Explain how the Houston bank could lose on this transaction assuming no hedging.

    b. If the bank does hedge with the forward contract, what is the maximum amount it can lose?

WEB EXERCISE

Chapter 21 deals with international finance and the decisions that companies have to make when operating in a foreign country. The Overseas Private Investment Corporation (OPIC) is a U.S. agency that helps U.S. companies that operate in developing economies. Its website has a great deal of information about doing business in a foreign country and excellent links to the 140 countries in which it has relationships.

1. Go to www.opic.gov. Go to "Who We Are" and click on "Overview." Describe OPIC's mission.

2. Go to "What We Offer" and click on "Political Risk Insurance." Describe the types of political risks that can be covered.

3. Go back to "What We Offer" and click on "Debt Financing." Describe the business size that qualifies for "Small and Medium-Enterprise Financing" and then describe the types of projects that can be funded. May other co-lenders be involved?

4. Click on "Support for Private Equity." Are equity funds targeted to firms in developing countries?

Note: Occasionally a topic we have listed may have been deleted, updated, or moved into a different location on a website. If you click on the site map or site index, you will be introduced to a table of contents that should aid you in finding the topic you are looking for.

APPENDIX | 21A

Cash Flow Analysis and the Foreign Investment Decision

Direct foreign investments are often relatively large. As we mentioned in the chapter, these investments are exposed to some extraordinary risks, such as foreign exchange fluctuations and political interference, which are nonexistent for domestic investments. Therefore, the final decision is often made at the board of directors level after considering the financial feasibility and the strategic importance of the proposed investment. Financial feasibility analysis for foreign investments is basically conducted in the same manner as it is for domestic capital budgets. Certain important differences exist, however, in the treatment of foreign tax credits, foreign exchange risk, and remittance of cash flows. To see how these are handled in foreign investment analysis, let us consider a hypothetical illustration.

Tex Systems Inc., a Texas-based manufacturer of computer equipment, is considering the establishment of a manufacturing plant in Salaysia, a country in Southeast Asia. The Salaysian plant will be a wholly owned subsidiary of Tex Systems, and its estimated cost is 90 million ringgits (2 ringgits = $1). Based on the exchange rate between ringgits and dollars, the cost in dollars is $45 million. In addition to selling in the local Salaysian market, the proposed subsidiary is expected to export its computers to the neighboring markets in Singapore, Hong Kong, and Thailand. Expected revenues and operating costs are as shown in Table 21A-1. The country's investment climate, which reflects the foreign exchange and political risks, is rated BBB (considered fairly safe) by a leading Asian business journal. After considering the investment climate and the nature of the industry, Tex Systems has set a target rate of return of 20 percent for this foreign investment.

Salaysia has a 25 percent corporate income tax rate and has waived the withholding tax on dividends repatriated (forwarded) to the parent company. A dividend payout ratio of 100 percent is assumed for the foreign subsidiary. Tex Systems's marginal tax rate is 30 percent. It was agreed by Tex Systems and the Salaysian government that the subsidiary will be sold to a Salaysian entrepreneur after six years for an estimated 30 million ringgits. The plant will be depreciated over a period of six years using the straight-line method. The cash flows generated through depreciation cannot be remitted to the parent company until the subsidiary is sold to the local private entrepreneur six years from now. The Salaysian government requires the subsidiary to invest the depreciation-generated cash flows in local government bonds yielding an aftertax rate of 15 percent. The depreciation cash flows thus compounded and accumulated can be returned to Tex Systems when the project is terminated. Although the value of ringgits in the foreign exchange market has remained fairly stable for the past three years, the projected budget deficits and trade deficits of Salaysia may result in a gradual devaluation of ringgits against the U.S. dollar at the rate of 2 percent per year for the next six years.

Note that the analysis in Table 21A-1 is primarily done in terms of ringgits. Expenses (operating, depreciation, and Salaysian income taxes) are subtracted from revenues to arrive at earnings after foreign income taxes. These earnings are then repatriated (forwarded) to Tex Systems in the form of dividends. Dividends repatriated thus begin at 5.25 ringgits (in millions) in year 1 and increase to 18.75 ringgits in year 6. The next item, gross U.S. taxes, refers to the unadjusted U.S. tax obligation.

Table 21A-1   Cash flow analysis of a foreign investment

	Projected Cash Flows (million ringgits unless otherwise stated)					
	Year 1	Year 2	Year 3	Year 4	Year 5	Year 6
Revenues	45.00	50.00	55.00	60.00	65.00	70.00
− Operating expenses	28.00	30.00	30.00	32.00	35.00	35.00
− Depreciation	10.00	10.00	10.00	10.00	10.00	10.00
Earnings before Salaysian taxes	7.00	10.00	15.00	18.00	20.00	25.00
− Salaysian income tax (25%)	1.75	2.50	3.75	4.50	5.00	6.25
Earnings after foreign income taxes	5.25	7.50	11.25	13.50	15.00	18.75
= Dividends repatriated	5.25	7.50	11.25	13.50	15.00	18.75
Gross U.S. taxes (30% of foreign earnings before taxes)	2.10	3.00	4.50	5.40	6.00	7.50
− Foreign tax credit	1.75	2.50	3.75	4.50	5.00	6.25
Net U.S. taxes payable	0.35	0.50	0.75	0.90	1.00	1.25
Aftertax dividend received by Tex Systems	4.90	7.00	10.50	12.60	14.00	17.50
Exchange rate (ringgits/$)	2.00	2.04	2.08	2.12	2.16	2.21
Aftertax dividend (U.S. $)	2.45	3.43	5.05	5.94	6.48	7.92
PV_{IF} (at 20%)	0.833	0.694	0.579	0.482	0.402	0.335
PV of dividends ($)	2.04 +	2.38 +	2.92 +	2.86 +	2.60 +	2.65 = $15.45

As specified, this is equal to 30 percent of foreign earnings before taxes (earnings before Salaysian taxes).[1] For example, gross U.S. taxes in the first year are equal to:

Earnings before Salaysian taxes	7.00
30% of foreign earnings before taxes.............................	30%
Gross U.S. taxes	2.10

From gross U.S. taxes, Tex Systems may take a foreign tax credit equal to the amount of Salaysian income tax paid. Gross U.S. taxes minus this foreign tax credit are equal to net U.S. taxes payable. Aftertax dividends received by Tex Systems are equal to dividends repatriated minus U.S. taxes payable. In the first year, the values are:

Dividends repatriated...	5.25
Net U.S. taxes payable	−0.35
Aftertax dividends received by Tex Systems	4.90

The figures for aftertax dividends received by Tex Systems are all stated in ringgits (the analysis up to this point has been in ringgits). These ringgits will now be converted into dollars. The initial exchange rate is 2.00 ringgits per dollar, and this will go up by 2 percent per year.[2] For the first year, 4.90 ringgits will be translated into 2.45 dollars. Since values are stated in millions, this will represent $2.45 million. Aftertax

---

[1] If foreign earnings had not been repatriated, this tax obligation would not be due.

[2] The 2 percent appreciation means the dollar is equal to an increasing amount of ringgits each year. The dollar is appreciating relative to ringgits, and ringgits are depreciating relative to the dollar. Since Tex Systems's earnings are in ringgits, they are being converted at a less desirable rate each year. Big Tex may eventually decide to hedge its foreign exchange risk exposure.

dividends in U.S. dollars grow from $2.45 million in year 1 to $7.92 million in year 6. The last two rows of Table 21A-1 show the present value of these dividends at a 20 percent discount rate. The *total* present value of aftertax dividends received by Tex Systems adds up to $15.45 million. Repatriated dividends will be just one part of the cash flow. The second part consists of depreciation-generated cash flow accumulated and reinvested in Salaysian government bonds at a 15 percent rate per year. The compound value of reinvested depreciation cash flows (10 million ringgits per year) is:

$$10 \text{ million ringgits } 8.754^* = 87.54 \text{ million ringgits after six years}$$

*Future value at 15 percent for six years (from Appendix C at the end of the book).

These 87.54 million ringgits must now be translated into dollars and then discounted back to the present. Since the exchange rate is 2.21 ringgits per dollar in the 6th year (fourth line from the bottom in Table 21A-1), the dollar equivalent of 87.54 million ringgits is:

$$87.54 \text{ million ringgits } \div 2.21 = \$39.61 \text{ million}$$

The $39.61 million can now be discounted back to the present by using the present value factor for six years at 20 percent (Appendix B).

$$
\begin{array}{l}
\$39.61 \quad \text{million} \\
\underline{\times\, 0.335} \quad \text{PV}_{IF} \\
\$13.27 \quad \text{million}
\end{array}
$$

The final benefit to be received is the 30 million ringgits when the plant is sold six years from now.[3] We first convert this to dollars and then take the present value.

$$30 \text{ million ringgits } \div 2.21 = \$13.57 \text{ million}$$

The present value of $13.57 million after six years at 20 percent is:

$$
\begin{array}{l}
\$13.57 \quad \text{million} \\
\underline{\times\, 0.335} \quad \text{PV}_{IF} \\
\$\ 4.55 \quad \text{million}
\end{array}
$$

The present value of all cash inflows in dollars is equal to:

Present value of dividends	$15.45 million
Present value of repatriated accumulated depreciation	13.27
Present value of sales price for plant	4.55
Total present value of inflows	$33.27 million

The cost of the project was initially specified as 90 million ringgits, or $45 million. In the following calculation, we see the total present value of inflows in dollars is less than the cost, and the project has a negative net present value.

Total present value of inflows	$33.27 million
Cost	45.00
Net present value	($11.73 million)

[3]Capital gains taxes are not a necessary consideration in foreign transactions of this nature.

Problem

Cash flow analysis
with a foreign
investment
(LO21-2)

21A–1. The Office Automation Corporation is considering a foreign investment. The initial cash outlay will be $10 million. The current foreign exchange rate is 2 ugans = $1. Thus the investment in foreign currency will be 20 million ugans. The assets have a useful life of five years and no expected salvage value. The firm uses a straight-line method of depreciation. Sales are expected to be 20 million ugans and operating cash expenses 10 million ugans every year for five years. The foreign income tax rate is 25 percent. The foreign subsidiary will repatriate all aftertax profits to Office Automation in the form of dividends. Furthermore, the depreciation cash flows (equal to each year's depreciation) will be repatriated during the same year they accrue to the foreign subsidiary. The applicable cost of capital that reflects the riskiness of the cash flows is 16 percent. The U.S. tax rate is 40 percent of foreign earnings before taxes.

a.   Should the Office Automation Corporation undertake the investment if the foreign exchange rate is expected to remain constant during the five-year period?

b.   Should Office Automation undertake the investment if the foreign exchange rate is expected to be as follows?

Year 0	$1 = 2.0 ugans
Year 1	$1 = 2.2 ugans
Year 2	$1 = 2.4 ugans
Year 3	$1 = 2.7 ugans
Year 4	$1 = 2.9 ugans
Year 5	$1 = 3.2 ugans

APPENDIXES

Appendix A Future value of $1, FV_{IF} $FV = PV(1 + i)^n$

Period	1%	2%	3%	4%	5%	6%	7%	8%	9%	10%	11%
1	1.010	1.020	1.030	1.040	1.050	1.060	1.070	1.080	1.090	1.100	1.110
2	1.020	1.040	1.061	1.082	1.103	1.124	1.145	1.166	1.188	1.210	1.232
3	1.030	1.061	1.093	1.125	1.158	1.191	1.225	1.260	1.295	1.331	1.368
4	1.041	1.082	1.126	1.170	1.216	1.262	1.311	1.360	1.412	1.464	1.518
5	1.051	1.104	1.159	1.217	1.276	1.338	1.403	1.469	1.539	1.611	1.685
6	1.062	1.126	1.194	1.265	1.340	1.419	1.501	1.587	1.677	1.772	1.870
7	1.072	1.149	1.230	1.316	1.407	1.504	1.606	1.714	1.828	1.949	2.076
8	1.083	1.172	1.267	1.369	1.477	1.594	1.718	1.851	1.993	2.144	2.305
9	1.094	1.195	1.305	1.423	1.551	1.689	1.838	1.999	2.172	2.358	2.558
10	1.105	1.219	1.344	1.480	1.629	1.791	1.967	2.159	2.367	2.594	2.839
11	1.116	1.243	1.384	1.539	1.710	1.898	2.105	2.332	2.580	2.853	3.152
12	1.127	1.268	1.426	1.601	1.796	2.012	2.252	2.518	2.813	3.138	3.498
13	1.138	1.294	1.469	1.665	1.886	2.133	2.410	2.720	3.066	3.452	3.883
14	1.149	1.319	1.513	1.732	1.980	2.261	2.579	2.937	3.342	3.797	4.310
15	1.161	1.346	1.558	1.801	2.079	2.397	2.759	3.172	3.642	4.177	4.785
16	1.173	1.373	1.605	1.873	2.183	2.540	2.952	3.426	3.970	4.595	5.311
17	1.184	1.400	1.653	1.948	2.292	2.693	3.159	3.700	4.328	5.054	5.895
18	1.196	1.428	1.702	2.026	2.407	2.854	3.380	3.996	4.717	5.560	6.544
19	1.208	1.457	1.754	2.107	2.527	3.026	3.617	4.316	5.142	6.116	7.263
20	1.220	1.486	1.806	2.191	2.653	3.207	3.870	4.661	5.604	6.727	8.062
25	1.282	1.641	2.094	2.666	3.386	4.292	5.427	6.848	8.623	10.835	13.585
30	1.348	1.811	2.427	3.243	4.322	5.743	7.612	10.063	13.268	17.449	22.892
40	1.489	2.208	3.262	4.801	7.040	10.286	14.974	21.725	31.409	45.259	65.001
50	1.645	2.692	4.384	7.107	11.467	18.420	29.457	46.902	74.358	117.39	184.57

Appendix A (concluded) Future value of $1

Period	12%	13%	14%	15%	16%	17%	18%	19%	20%	25%	30%
1	1.120	1.130	1.140	1.150	1.160	1.170	1.180	1.190	1.200	1.250	1.300
2	1.254	1.277	1.300	1.323	1.346	1.369	1.392	1.416	1.440	1.563	1.690
3	1.405	1.443	1.482	1.521	1.561	1.602	1.643	1.685	1.728	1.953	2.197
4	1.574	1.630	1.689	1.749	1.811	1.874	1.939	2.005	2.074	2.441	2.856
5	1.762	1.842	1.925	2.011	2.100	2.192	2.288	2.386	2.488	3.052	3.713
6	1.974	2.082	2.195	2.313	2.436	2.565	2.700	2.840	2.986	3.815	4.827
7	2.211	2.353	2.502	2.660	2.826	3.001	3.185	3.379	3.583	4.768	6.276
8	2.476	2.658	2.853	3.059	3.278	3.511	3.759	4.021	4.300	5.960	8.157
9	2.773	3.004	3.252	3.518	3.803	4.108	4.435	4.785	5.160	7.451	10.604
10	3.106	3.395	3.707	4.046	4.411	4.807	5.234	5.696	6.192	9.313	13.786
11	3.479	3.836	4.226	4.652	5.117	5.624	6.176	6.777	7.430	11.642	17.922
12	3.896	4.335	4.818	5.350	5.936	6.580	7.288	8.064	8.916	14.552	23.298
13	4.363	4.898	5.492	6.153	6.886	7.699	8.599	9.596	10.699	18.190	30.288
14	4.887	5.535	6.261	7.076	7.988	9.007	10.147	11.420	12.839	22.737	39.374
15	5.474	6.254	7.138	8.137	9.266	10.539	11.974	13.590	15.407	28.422	51.186
16	6.130	7.067	8.137	9.358	10.748	12.330	14.129	16.172	18.488	35.527	66.542
17	6.866	7.986	9.276	10.761	12.468	14.426	16.672	19.244	22.186	44.409	86.504
18	7.690	9.024	10.575	12.375	14.463	16.879	19.673	22.091	26.623	55.511	112.46
19	8.613	10.197	12.056	14.232	16.777	19.748	23.214	27.252	31.948	69.389	146.19
20	9.646	11.523	13.743	16.367	19.461	23.106	27.393	32.429	38.338	86.736	190.05
25	17.000	21.231	26.462	32.919	40.874	50.658	62.669	77.388	95.396	264.70	705.64
30	29.960	39.116	50.950	66.212	85.850	111.07	143.37	184.68	237.38	807.79	2,620.0
40	93.051	132.78	188.88	267.86	378.72	533.87	750.38	1,051.7	1,469.8	7,523.2	36,119.0
50	289.00	450.74	700.23	1,083.7	1,670.7	2,566.2	3,927.4	5,988.9	9,100.4	70,065.0	497,929.0

Percent

Appendix B Present value of $1, PV_{IF} $PV = FV\left[\dfrac{1}{(1+i)^n}\right]$

Period	1%	2%	3%	4%	5%	6%	7%	8%	9%	10%	11%	12%
						Percent						
1	0.990	0.980	0.971	0.962	0.952	0.943	0.935	0.926	0.917	0.909	0.901	0.893
2	0.980	0.961	0.943	0.925	0.907	0.890	0.873	0.857	0.842	0.826	0.812	0.797
3	0.971	0.942	0.915	0.889	0.864	0.840	0.816	0.794	0.772	0.751	0.731	0.712
4	0.961	0.924	0.888	0.855	0.823	0.792	0.763	0.735	0.708	0.683	0.659	0.636
5	0.951	0.906	0.863	0.822	0.784	0.747	0.713	0.681	0.650	0.621	0.593	0.567
6	0.942	0.888	0.837	0.790	0.746	0.705	0.666	0.630	0.596	0.564	0.535	0.507
7	0.933	0.871	0.813	0.760	0.711	0.665	0.623	0.583	0.547	0.513	0.482	0.452
8	0.923	0.853	0.789	0.731	0.677	0.627	0.582	0.540	0.502	0.467	0.434	0.404
9	0.914	0.837	0.766	0.703	0.645	0.592	0.544	0.500	0.460	0.424	0.391	0.361
10	0.905	0.820	0.744	0.676	0.614	0.558	0.508	0.463	0.422	0.386	0.352	0.322
11	0.896	0.804	0.722	0.650	0.585	0.527	0.475	0.429	0.388	0.350	0.317	0.287
12	0.887	0.788	0.701	0.625	0.557	0.497	0.444	0.397	0.356	0.319	0.286	0.257
13	0.879	0.773	0.681	0.601	0.530	0.469	0.415	0.368	0.326	0.290	0.258	0.229
14	0.870	0.758	0.661	0.577	0.505	0.442	0.388	0.340	0.299	0.263	0.232	0.205
15	0.861	0.743	0.642	0.555	0.481	0.417	0.362	0.315	0.275	0.239	0.209	0.183
16	0.853	0.728	0.623	0.534	0.458	0.394	0.339	0.292	0.252	0.218	0.188	0.163
17	0.844	0.714	0.605	0.513	0.436	0.371	0.317	0.270	0.231	0.198	0.170	0.146
18	0.836	0.700	0.587	0.494	0.416	0.350	0.296	0.250	0.212	0.180	0.153	0.130
19	0.828	0.686	0.570	0.475	0.396	0.331	0.277	0.232	0.194	0.164	0.138	0.116
20	0.820	0.673	0.554	0.456	0.377	0.312	0.258	0.215	0.178	0.149	0.124	0.104
25	0.780	0.610	0.478	0.375	0.295	0.233	0.184	0.146	0.116	0.092	0.074	0.059
30	0.742	0.552	0.412	0.308	0.231	0.174	0.131	0.099	0.075	0.057	0.044	0.033
40	0.672	0.453	0.307	0.208	0.142	0.097	0.067	0.046	0.032	0.022	0.015	0.011
50	0.608	0.372	0.228	0.141	0.087	0.054	0.034	0.021	0.013	0.009	0.005	0.003

								Percent						
Period	13%	14%	15%	16%	17%	18%	19%	20%	25%	30%	35%	40%	50%
1	0.885	0.877	0.870	0.862	0.855	0.847	0.840	0.833	0.800	0.769	0.741	0.714	0.667
2	0.783	0.769	0.756	0.743	0.731	0.718	0.706	0.694	0.640	0.592	0.549	0.510	0.444
3	0.693	0.675	0.658	0.641	0.624	0.609	0.593	0.579	0.512	0.455	0.406	0.364	0.296
4	0.613	0.592	0.572	0.552	0.534	0.515	0.499	0.482	0.410	0.350	0.301	0.260	0.198
5	0.543	0.519	0.497	0.476	0.456	0.437	0.419	0.402	0.328	0.269	0.223	0.186	0.132
6	0.480	0.456	0.432	0.410	0.390	0.370	0.352	0.335	0.262	0.207	0.165	0.133	0.088
7	0.425	0.400	0.376	0.354	0.333	0.314	0.296	0.279	0.210	0.159	0.122	0.095	0.059
8	0.376	0.351	0.327	0.305	0.285	0.266	0.249	0.233	0.168	0.123	0.091	0.068	0.039
9	0.333	0.308	0.284	0.263	0.243	0.225	0.209	0.194	0.134	0.094	0.067	0.048	0.026
10	0.295	0.270	0.247	0.227	0.208	0.191	0.176	0.162	0.107	0.073	0.050	0.035	0.017
11	0.261	0.237	0.215	0.195	0.178	0.162	0.148	0.135	0.086	0.056	0.037	0.025	0.012
12	0.231	0.208	0.187	0.168	0.152	0.137	0.124	0.112	0.069	0.043	0.027	0.018	0.008
13	0.204	0.182	0.163	0.145	0.130	0.116	0.104	0.093	0.055	0.033	0.020	0.013	0.005
14	0.181	0.160	0.141	0.125	0.111	0.099	0.088	0.078	0.044	0.025	0.015	0.009	0.003
15	0.160	0.140	0.123	0.108	0.095	0.084	0.074	0.065	0.035	0.020	0.011	0.006	0.002
16	0.141	0.123	0.107	0.093	0.081	0.071	0.062	0.054	0.028	0.015	0.008	0.005	0.002
17	0.125	0.108	0.093	0.080	0.069	0.060	0.052	0.045	0.023	0.012	0.006	0.003	0.001
18	0.111	0.095	0.081	0.069	0.059	0.051	0.044	0.038	0.018	0.009	0.005	0.002	0.001
19	0.098	0.083	0.070	0.060	0.051	0.043	0.037	0.031	0.014	0.007	0.003	0.002	0
20	0.087	0.073	0.061	0.051	0.043	0.037	0.031	0.026	0.012	0.005	0.002	0.001	0
25	0.047	0.038	0.030	0.024	0.020	0.016	0.013	0.010	0.004	0.001	0.001	0	0
30	0.026	0.020	0.015	0.012	0.009	0.007	0.005	0.004	0.001	0	0	0	0
40	0.008	0.005	0.004	0.003	0.002	0.001	0.001	0.001	0	0	0	0	0
50	0.002	0.001	0.001	0.001	0	0	0	0	0	0	0	0	0

Appendix C Future value of an annuity of $1, FV_{IFA} $$FV_A = A\left[\frac{(1+i)^n - 1}{i}\right]$$

						Percent					
Period	**1%**	**2%**	**3%**	**4%**	**5%**	**6%**	**7%**	**8%**	**9%**	**10%**	**11%**
1	1.000	1.000	1.000	1.000	1.000	1.000	1.000	1.000	1.000	1.000	1.000
2	2.010	2.020	2.030	2.040	2.050	2.060	2.070	2.080	2.090	2.100	2.110
3	3.030	3.060	3.091	3.122	3.153	3.184	3.215	3.246	3.278	3.310	3.342
4	4.060	4.122	4.184	4.246	4.310	4.375	4.440	4.506	4.573	4.641	4.710
5	5.101	5.204	5.309	5.416	5.526	5.637	5.751	5.867	5.985	6.105	6.228
6	6.152	6.308	6.468	6.633	6.802	6.975	7.153	7.336	7.523	7.716	7.913
7	7.214	7.434	7.662	7.898	8.142	8.394	8.654	8.923	9.200	9.487	9.783
8	8.286	8.583	8.892	9.214	9.549	9.897	10.260	10.637	11.028	11.436	11.859
9	9.369	9.755	10.159	10.583	11.027	11.491	11.978	12.488	13.021	13.579	14.164
10	10.462	10.950	11.464	12.006	12.578	13.181	13.816	14.487	15.193	15.937	16.722
11	11.567	12.169	12.808	13.486	14.207	14.972	15.784	16.645	17.560	18.531	19.561
12	12.683	13.412	14.192	15.026	15.917	16.870	17.888	18.977	20.141	21.384	22.713
13	13.809	14.680	15.618	16.627	17.713	18.882	20.141	21.495	22.953	24.523	26.212
14	14.947	15.974	17.086	18.292	19.599	21.015	22.550	24.215	26.019	27.975	30.095
15	16.097	17.293	18.599	20.024	21.579	23.276	25.129	27.152	29.361	31.772	34.405
16	17.258	18.639	20.157	21.825	23.657	25.673	27.888	30.324	33.003	35.950	39.190
17	18.430	20.012	21.762	23.698	25.840	28.213	30.840	33.750	36.974	40.545	44.501
18	19.615	21.412	23.414	25.645	28.132	30.906	33.999	37.450	41.301	45.599	50.396
19	20.811	22.841	25.117	27.671	30.539	33.760	37.379	41.446	46.018	51.159	56.939
20	22.019	24.297	26.870	29.778	33.066	36.786	40.995	45.762	51.160	57.275	64.203
25	28.243	32.030	36.459	41.646	47.727	54.865	63.249	73.106	84.701	98.347	114.41
30	34.785	40.588	47.575	56.085	66.439	79.058	94.461	113.28	136.31	164.49	199.02
40	48.886	60.402	75.401	95.026	120.80	154.76	199.64	259.06	337.89	442.59	581.83
50	64.463	84.579	112.80	152.67	209.35	290.34	406.53	573.77	815.08	1,163.9	1,668.8

Appendix C (concluded) Future value of an annuity of $1

Period	12%	13%	14%	15%	16%	17%	18%	19%	20%	25%	30%
1	1.000	1.000	1.000	1.000	1.000	1.000	1.000	1.000	1.000	1.000	1.000
2	2.120	2.130	2.140	2.150	2.160	2.170	2.180	2.190	2.200	2.250	2.300
3	3.374	3.407	3.440	3.473	3.506	3.539	3.572	3.606	3.640	3.813	3.990
4	4.779	4.850	4.921	4.993	5.066	5.141	5.215	5.291	5.368	5.766	6.187
5	6.353	6.480	6.610	6.742	6.877	7.014	7.154	7.297	7.442	8.207	9.043
6	8.115	8.323	8.536	8.754	8.977	9.207	9.442	9.683	9.930	11.259	12.756
7	10.089	10.405	10.730	11.067	11.414	11.772	12.142	12.523	12.916	15.073	17.583
8	12.300	12.757	13.233	13.727	14.240	14.773	15.327	15.902	16.499	19.842	23.858
9	14.776	15.416	16.085	16.786	17.519	18.285	19.086	19.923	20.799	25.802	32.015
10	17.549	18.420	19.337	20.304	21.321	22.393	23.521	24.701	25.959	33.253	42.619
11	20.655	21.814	23.045	24.349	25.733	27.200	28.755	30.404	32.150	42.566	56.405
12	24.133	25.650	27.271	29.002	30.850	32.824	34.931	37.180	39.581	54.208	74.327
13	28.029	29.985	32.089	34.352	36.786	39.404	42.219	45.244	48.497	68.760	97.625
14	32.393	34.883	37.581	40.505	43.672	47.103	50.818	54.841	59.196	86.949	127.91
15	37.280	40.417	43.842	47.580	51.660	56.110	60.965	66.261	72.035	109.69	167.29
16	42.753	46.672	50.980	55.717	60.925	66.649	72.939	79.850	87.442	138.11	218.47
17	48.884	53.739	59.118	65.075	71.673	78.979	87.068	96.022	105.93	173.64	285.01
18	55.750	61.725	68.394	75.836	84.141	93.406	103.74	115.27	128.12	218.05	371.52
19	63.440	70.749	78.969	88.212	98.603	110.29	123.41	138.17	154.74	273.56	483.97
20	72.052	80.947	91.025	102.44	115.38	130.03	146.63	165.42	186.69	342.95	630.17
25	133.33	155.62	181.87	212.79	249.21	292.11	342.60	402.04	471.98	1,054.8	2,348.80
30	241.33	293.20	356.79	434.75	530.31	647.44	790.95	966.7	1,181.9	3,227.2	8,730.0
40	767.09	1,013.7	1,342.0	1,779.1	2,360.8	3,134.5	4,163.21	5,529.8	7,343.9	30,089.0	120,393.0
50	2,400.0	3,459.5	4,994.5	7,217.7	10,436.0	15,090.0	21,813.0	31,515.0	45,497.0	280,256.0	1,659,76.0

Appendix D Present value of an annuity of \$1, PV_{IFA} $PV_A = A\left[\dfrac{1 - \dfrac{1}{(1+i)^n}}{i}\right]$

Period	1%	2%	3%	4%	5%	6%	7%	8%	9%	10%	11%	12%
1	0.990	0.980	0.971	0.962	0.952	0.943	0.935	0.926	0.917	0.909	0.901	0.893
2	1.970	1.942	1.913	1.886	1.859	1.833	1.808	1.783	1.759	1.736	1.713	1.690
3	2.941	2.884	2.829	2.775	2.723	2.673	2.624	2.577	2.531	2.487	2.444	2.402
4	3.902	3.808	3.717	3.630	3.546	3.465	3.387	3.312	3.240	3.170	3.102	3.037
5	4.853	4.713	4.580	4.452	4.329	4.212	4.100	3.993	3.890	3.791	3.696	3.605
6	5.795	5.601	5.417	5.242	5.076	4.917	4.767	4.623	4.486	4.355	4.231	4.111
7	6.728	6.472	6.230	6.002	5.786	5.582	5.389	5.206	5.033	4.868	4.712	4.564
8	7.652	7.325	7.020	6.733	6.463	6.210	5.971	5.747	5.535	5.335	5.146	4.968
9	8.566	8.162	7.786	7.435	7.108	6.802	6.515	6.247	5.995	5.759	5.537	5.328
10	9.471	8.983	8.530	8.111	7.722	7.360	7.024	6.710	6.418	6.145	5.889	5.650
11	10.368	9.787	9.253	8.760	8.306	7.887	7.499	7.139	6.805	6.495	6.207	5.938
12	11.255	10.575	9.954	9.385	8.863	8.384	7.943	7.536	7.161	6.814	6.492	6.194
13	12.134	11.348	10.635	9.986	9.394	8.853	8.358	7.904	7.487	7.103	6.750	6.424
14	13.004	12.106	11.296	10.563	9.899	9.295	8.745	8.244	7.786	7.367	6.982	6.628
15	13.865	12.849	11.938	11.118	10.380	9.712	9.108	8.559	8.061	7.606	7.191	6.811
16	14.718	13.578	12.561	11.652	10.838	10.106	9.447	8.851	8.313	7.824	7.379	6.974
17	15.562	14.292	13.166	12.166	11.274	10.477	9.763	9.122	8.544	8.022	7.549	7.120
18	16.398	14.992	13.754	12.659	11.690	10.828	10.059	9.372	8.756	8.201	7.702	7.250
19	17.226	15.678	14.324	13.134	12.085	11.158	10.336	9.604	8.950	8.365	7.839	7.366
20	18.046	16.351	14.877	13.590	12.462	11.470	10.594	9.818	9.129	8.514	7.963	7.469
25	22.023	19.523	17.413	15.622	14.094	12.783	11.654	10.675	9.823	9.077	8.422	7.843
30	25.808	22.396	19.600	17.292	15.372	13.765	12.409	11.258	10.274	9.427	8.694	8.055
40	32.835	27.355	23.115	19.793	17.159	15.046	13.332	11.925	10.757	9.779	8.951	8.244
50	39.196	31.424	25.730	21.482	18.256	15.762	13.801	12.233	10.962	9.915	9.042	8.304

Percent

Appendix D (concluded) Present value of an annuity of $1

Period	13%	14%	15%	16%	17%	18%	19%	20%	25%	30%	35%	40%	50%
1	0.885	0.877	0.870	0.862	0.855	0.847	0.840	0.833	0.800	0.769	0.741	0.714	0.667
2	1.668	1.647	1.626	1.605	1.585	1.566	1.547	1.528	1.440	1.361	1.289	1.224	1.111
3	2.361	2.322	2.283	2.246	2.210	2.174	2.140	2.106	1.952	1.816	1.696	1.589	1.407
4	2.974	2.914	2.855	2.798	2.743	2.690	2.639	2.589	2.362	2.166	1.997	1.849	1.605
5	3.517	3.433	3.352	3.274	3.199	3.127	3.058	2.991	2.689	2.436	2.220	2.035	1.737
6	3.998	3.889	3.784	3.685	3.589	3.498	3.410	3.326	2.951	2.643	2.385	2.168	1.824
7	4.423	4.288	4.160	4.039	3.922	3.812	3.706	3.605	3.161	2.802	2.508	2.263	1.883
8	4.799	4.639	4.487	4.344	4.207	4.078	3.954	3.837	3.329	2.925	2.598	2.331	1.922
9	5.132	4.946	4.772	4.607	4.451	4.303	4.163	4.031	3.463	3.019	2.665	2.379	1.948
10	5.426	5.216	5.019	4.833	4.659	4.494	4.339	4.192	3.571	3.092	2.715	2.414	1.965
11	5.687	5.453	5.234	5.029	4.836	4.656	4.486	4.327	3.656	3.147	2.752	2.438	1.977
12	5.918	5.660	5.421	5.197	4.988	4.793	4.611	4.439	3.725	3.190	2.779	2.456	1.985
13	6.122	5.842	5.583	5.342	5.118	4.910	4.715	4.533	3.780	3.223	2.799	2.469	1.990
14	6.302	6.002	5.724	5.468	5.229	5.008	4.802	4.611	3.824	3.249	2.814	2.478	1.993
15	6.462	6.142	5.847	5.575	5.324	5.092	4.876	4.675	3.859	3.268	2.825	2.484	1.995
16	6.604	6.265	5.954	5.668	5.405	5.162	4.938	4.730	3.887	3.283	2.834	2.489	1.997
17	6.729	6.373	6.047	5.749	5.475	5.222	4.988	4.775	3.910	3.295	2.840	2.492	1.998
18	6.840	6.467	6.128	5.818	5.534	5.273	5.033	4.812	3.928	3.304	2.844	2.494	1.999
19	6.938	6.550	6.198	5.877	5.584	5.316	5.070	4.843	3.942	3.311	2.848	2.496	1.999
20	7.025	6.623	6.259	5.929	5.628	5.353	5.101	4.870	3.954	3.316	2.850	2.497	1.999
25	7.330	6.873	6.464	6.097	5.766	5.467	5.195	4.948	3.985	3.329	2.856	2.499	2.000
30	7.496	7.003	6.566	6.177	5.829	5.517	5.235	4.979	3.995	3.332	2.857	2.500	2.000
40	7.634	7.105	6.642	6.233	5.871	5.548	5.258	4.997	3.999	3.333	2.857	2.500	2.000
50	7.675	7.133	6.661	6.246	5.880	5.554	5.262	4.999	4.000	3.333	2.857	2.500	2.000

Percent

This appendix shows the keystrokes for the **HP 12C**. The keystrokes for the **HP 10bii** are almost identical. Here are two small differences:

1. There is no CF₀ key on the **HP 10bii**. Use the CFⱼ key on the 10bii instead.
2. The I key on the **HP 12C** is the I/YR key on the **HP 10bii**.

Chapter 9

Page 259

HP FINANCIAL CALCULATOR

Future Value

Enter	Function
4	N
10	i
−1000	PV
0	PMT

Function	Solution
FV	1,464.10

Page 261

HP FINANCIAL CALCULATOR

Present Value

Enter	Function
4	N
10	i
−1464.1	FV
0	PMT

Function	Solution
PV	1,000.00

Page 262

HP FINANCIAL CALCULATOR

Interest Value

Enter	Function
4	N
1000	PV
−1464.1	FV
0	PMT

Function	Solution
i	10

Page 263

HP FINANCIAL CALCULATOR

Number of Periods

Enter	Function
10	i
1000	PV
−1464.1	FV
0	PMT

Function	Solution
N	4

Page 265

HP FINANCIAL CALCULATOR

FV of Annuity

Enter	Function
4	N
10	i
−1000	PMT
0	PV

Function	Solution
FV	4,641.00

Page 267

HP FINANCIAL CALCULATOR

PV of Annuity

Enter	Function
4	N
10	i
0	FV
−1000	PMT

Function	Solution
PV	3,169.87

Page 273

HP FINANCIAL CALCULATOR

Annuity Payment

Enter	Function
4	N
10	i
−3169.87	PV
0	FV

Function	Solution
PMT	1,000.00

Page 274

HP FINANCIAL CALCULATOR

Interest Rate

Enter	Function
4	N
−3169.87	PV
1000	PMT
0	FV

Function	Solution
i	10.00

Page 275 TOP

HP FINANCIAL CALCULATOR

Number of Payments

Enter	Function
10	i
−3169.87	PV
1000	PMT
0	FV

Function	Solution
N	4.00

Page 275 BOTTOM

HP FINANCIAL CALCULATOR

Future Value

Enter	Function
10	N
4	i
−1000	PV
0	PMT

Function	Solution
FV	1,480.24

Page 276

HP FINANCIAL CALCULATOR

PV of Annuity

Enter	Function
20	N
2	i
0	FV
−2000	PMT

Function	Solution
PV	32,702.87

Page 280 TOP

HP FINANCIAL CALCULATOR

Enter	Function
15	N
9	i
−12,000	PV
0	PMT

Function	Solution
FV	43,709.79

Page 280 MIDDLE

HP FINANCIAL CALCULATOR

Enter	Function
10	N
12	i
−100,000	FV
0	PMT

Function	Solution
PV	32,197.32

Page 280 BOTTOM

HP FINANCIAL CALCULATOR

Enter	Function
20	N
11	i
0	PV
−2,000	PMT

Function	Solution
FV	128,405.66

Page 281 TOP

HP FINANCIAL CALCULATOR

Enter	Function
15	N
10	i
−80,000	PV
0	FV

Function	Solution
PMT	2,517.90

Page 281 MIDDLE

HP FINANCIAL CALCULATOR

Enter	Function
5	N
8	i
0	PV
−20,000	FV

Function	Solution
PMT	5,009.13

Chapter 10

Page 307 TOP

HP FINANCIAL CALCULATOR

PV of Interest Payments

Value	Function
20	N
10	i
0	FV
−100	PMT

Function	Solution
PV	851.36

Page 307 MIDDLE

HP FINANCIAL CALCULATOR

PV of Principal

Value	Function
20	N
10	i
−1000	FV
0	PMT

Function	Solution
PV	148.64

Page 307 BOTTOM

HP FINANCIAL CALCULATOR

Bond Price

Value	Function
20	N
10	i
−1000	FV
−100	PMT

Function	Solution
PV	1000.00

Page 309

HP FINANCIAL CALCULATOR

Bond Price

Value	Function
20	N
12	i
1000	FV
100	PMT

Function	Solution
PV	−850.61

Page 310

HP FINANCIAL CALCULATOR

Bond Price

Value	Function
20	N
8	i
1000	FV
100	PMT

Function	Solution
PV	−1196.36

Page 314

HP FINANCIAL CALCULATOR

Bond Yield

Value	Function
15	N
−931.89	PV
110	PMT
1000	FV

Function	Solution
i	12.00

Page 315

HP FINANCIAL CALCULATOR

Bond Price

Value	Function
40	N
6	i
50	PMT
1000	FV

Function	Solution
PV	−849.54

Page 328

HP FINANCIAL CALCULATOR

Bond Price

Value	Function
15	N
10	i
1000	FV
80	PMT

Function	Solution
PV	−847.88

Chapter 11

Page 343

HP FINANCIAL CALCULATOR

Bond YTM

Value	Function
15	N
−968.50	PV
90	PMT
1000	FV

Function	Solution
i	9.40

Page 361

HP FINANCIAL CALCULATOR

Bond YTM

Value	Function
16	N
−884	PV
78	PMT
1000	FV

Function	Solution
i	9.21

Chapter 12

Page 387

HP FINANCIAL CALCULATOR

IRR (Uneven Inflows)

Value	Function
−10000	CF_0
5000	CF_j
5000	CF_j
2000	CF_j

Function	Solution
IRR/YR	11.1635

Page 388

HP FINANCIAL CALCULATOR

IRR (Uneven Inflows)

Value	Function
−10000	CF_j
1500	CF_j
2000	CF_j
2500	CF_j
5000	CF_j
5000	CF_j

Function	Solution
IRR/YR	14.3329

Chapter 16

Page 512

HP FINANCIAL CALCULATOR

Bond Yield

Value	Function
10	N
−900	PV
100	PMT
1000	FV

Function	Solution
i	11.75

Page 517 TOP

HP FINANCIAL CALCULATOR

PV of Annuity

Enter	Function
20	N
6	i
0	FV
−3500	PMT

Function	Solution
PV	40,144.72

Page 517 BOTTOM

HP FINANCIAL CALCULATOR

PV of Annuity

Enter	Function
20	N
6	i
0	FV
−146250	PMT

Function	Solution
PV	1,677,475.98

Page 518

HP FINANCIAL CALCULATOR

PV of Annuity

Enter	Function
20	N
6	i
0	FV
−5000	PMT

Function	Solution
PV	57,349.61

Page 527

HP FINANCIAL CALCULATOR

Bond Yield

Value	Function
7	N
−860	PV
85	PMT
1000	FV

Function	Solution
i	11.52

Glossary

A

after-acquired property clause   A requirement in a bond issue stipulating that any new equipment purchased after the issue be placed under the original mortgage.

aftermarket   The market for a new security offering immediately after it is sold to the public.

agency theory   This theory examines the relationship between the owners of the firm and the managers of the firm. While management has the responsibility for acting as the agent for the stockholders in pursuing their best interests, the key question considered is: How well does management perform this role?

agent   One who sells, or "places," an asset for another party. An agent works on a commission or fee basis. Investment bankers sometimes act as agents for their clients in private placements.

aging of accounts receivable   Analyzing accounts by the amount of time they have been on the books.

American Depository Receipts (ADRs)   These receipts represent the ownership interest in a foreign company's common stock. The shares of the foreign company are put in trust in a major U.S. bank. The bank, in turn, issues its depository receipts to the American stockholders of the foreign firm. Many ADRs are listed on the NYSE and many more are traded in the over-the-counter market.

American Taxpayer Relief Act of 2013   Legislation that increased taxes on income and dividends for "high income" taxpayers while preserving lower taxes for the middle class wage earners.

annual percentage rate (APR)   A measure of the *effective rate* on a loan. One uses the actuarial method of compound interest when calculating the APR.

annuity   A series of consecutive payments or receipts of equal amounts.

articles of incorporation   A document that establishes a corporation and specifies the rights and limitations of the business entity.

articles of partnership   An agreement between the partners in a business that specifies the ownership interest of each, the methods of distributing profits, and the means for withdrawing from the partnership.

asset-backed commercial paper   Commercial paper that is backed by a specific pledge of assets. This is an exception to the normal case in which commercial paper is unsecured.

asset-backed securities   Public offerings backed by receivables as collateral. Essentially, a firm factors (sells) its receivables in the securities markets.

asset depreciation range   This represents the expected physical life of an asset. Generally, the midpoint of the ADR is utilized to determine what class an asset falls into for depreciation purposes.

asset utilization ratios   A group of ratios that measure the speed at which the firm is turning over or utilizing its assets. They measure inventory turnover, fixed asset turnover, total asset turnover, and the average time it takes to collect accounts receivable.

assignment   The liquidation of assets without going through formal court procedures. In order to effect an assignment, creditors must agree on liquidation values and the relative priority of claims.

auction rate preferred stock   A preferred stock security that matures every seven weeks and is sold (reauctioned) at a subsequent bidding. The concept of Dutch auction means the stock is issued to the bidder willing to accept the lowest yield and then to the next lowest bidder and so on until all the preferred stock is sold.

automated clearinghouse (ACH)   An ACH transfers information between one financial institution and another and from account to account via computer tape. There are approximately 31 regional clearinghouses throughout the United States that claim the membership of over 11,000 financial institutions.

average collection period   Accounts receivable divided by average daily credit sales; calculates how many days it takes to collect the company's accounts receivable.

B

balance of payments The term refers to a system of government accounts that catalogs the flow of economic transactions between countries.

balance sheet A financial statement that indicates what assets the firm owns and how those assets are financed in the form of liabilities or ownership interest.

bankers' acceptances Short-term securities that frequently arise from foreign trade. The acceptance is a draft that is drawn on a bank for approval for future payment and is subsequently presented to the payer.

bank holding company A legal entity in which one key bank owns a number of affiliate banks as well as other nonbanking subsidiaries engaged in closely related activities.

bankruptcy The market value of a firm's assets are less than its liabilities, and the firm has a negative net worth. The term is also used to describe in-court procedures associated with the reorganization or liquidation of a firm.

basic earnings per share Earnings per share unadjusted for dilution. It represents net income divided by shares outstanding.

basis point One basis point equals 1/100 of 1 percent.

bear market A falling stock market in a downward trend. The opposite of a bull market.

best efforts A distribution in which the investment banker agrees to work for a commission rather than actually underwriting (buying) the issue for resale. It is a procedure that is used by smaller investment bankers with relatively unknown companies. The investment banker is not directly taking the risk for distribution.

beta A measure of the volatility of returns on an individual stock relative to the market. Stocks with a beta of 1.0 are said to have risk equal to that of the market (equal volatility). Stocks with betas greater than 1.0 have more risk than the market, while those with betas of less than 1.0 have less risk than the market.

blanket inventory lien A secured borrowing arrangement in which the lender has a general claim against the inventory of the borrower.

bond ratings Bonds are rated according to risk by Standard & Poor's and Moody's Investor Service. A bond that is rated Aaa by Moody's has the lowest risk, while a bond with a C rating has the highest risk. Coupon rates are greatly influenced by a corporation's bond rating.

book-entry transactions A transaction in which no actual paper or certificate is created. All transactions simply take place on the books via computer entries.

bookrunner The principal or managing investment banker who is responsible for the pricing, prospectus development, and legal work involved in the sale of a new issue of securities.

book value Assets minus liabilities. Also see *net worth*.

brokers Members of organized stock exchanges who have the ability to buy and sell securities on the floor of their respective exchanges. Brokers act as agents between buyers and sellers.

bull market A rising stock market. There are many complicated interpretations of this term, usually centering on the length of time that the market should be rising in order to meet the criteria for classification as a bull market. For our purposes, a bull market exists when stock prices are strong and rising over time and investors are optimistic about future market performance.

business risk The risk related to the inability of the firm to hold its competitive position and maintain stability and growth in earnings.

C

call option An option to buy securities at a set price over a specified period of time.

call premium The premium paid by a corporation to call in a bond issue before the maturity date.

call provision Used for bonds and some preferred stock. A call allows the corporation to retire securities before maturity by forcing the bondholders to sell bonds back to it at a set price. The call provisions are included in the bond indenture.

capital Sources of long-term financing that are available to the business firm.

capital asset pricing model A model that relates the risk-return trade-offs of individual assets to market returns. A security is presumed to receive a risk-free rate of return plus a premium for risk.

capital markets Competitive markets for equity securities or debt securities with maturities of more than one year. The best examples of capital market securities are common stock, bonds, and preferred stock.

capital rationing Occurs when a corporation has more dollars of capital budgeting projects with positive net present values than it has money to invest in them. Therefore, some projects that should be accepted are excluded because financial capital is rationed.

capital structure theory A theory that addresses the relative importance of debt and equity in the overall financing of the firm.

carrying costs The cost to hold an asset, usually inventory. For inventory, carrying costs include such items as interest, warehousing costs, insurance, and material-handling expenses.

cash budget A series of monthly or quarterly budgets that indicate cash receipts, cash payments, and the borrowing requirements for meeting financial requirements. It is constructed from the pro forma income statement and other supportive schedules.

cash discount A reduction in the invoice price if payment is made within a specified time period. An example would be 2/10, net 30.

cash flow A value equal to income after taxes plus noncash expenses. In capital budgeting decisions, the usual noncash expense is depreciation.

cash flow cycle The pattern in which cash moves in and out of the firm. The primary consideration in managing the cash flow cycle is to ensure that inflows and outflows of cash are properly synchronized for transaction purposes.

cash flows from financing activities Cash flow that is generated (or reduced) from the sale or repurchase of securities or the payment of cash dividends. It is the third section presented in the statement of cash flows.

cash flows from investing activities Cash flow that is generated (or reduced) from the sale or purchase of long-term securities or plant and equipment. It is the second section presented in the statement of cash flows.

cash flows from operating activities Cash flow information that is determined by adjusting net income for such items as depreciation expense, changes in current assets and liabilities, and other items. It is the first section presented in the statement of cash flows.

certificate of deposit A certificate offered by banks, savings and loans, and other financial institutions for the deposit of funds at a given interest rate over a specified time period.

Check Clearing for the 21st Century Act (Check 21 Act) A 2003 law that allows banks and others to electronically process checks.

coefficient of correlation The degree of associated movement between two or more variables. Variables that move in the same direction are said to be positively correlated, while negatively correlated variables move in opposite directions.

coefficient of variation A measure of risk determination that is computed by dividing the standard deviation for a series of numbers by the expected value. Generally, the larger the coefficient of variation, the greater the risk.

combined leverage The total or combined impact of operating and financial leverage.

commercial paper An unsecured promissory note that large corporations issue to investors. The minimum amount is usually $25,000.

common equity The common stock or ownership capital of the firm. Common equity may be supplied through retained earnings or the sale of new common stock.

common stock Represents the ownership interest of the firm. Common stockholders have the ultimate right to control the business.

common stock equity The ownership interest in the firm. It may be represented by new shares or retained earnings. The same as net worth.

common stock equivalent Warrants, options, and any convertible securities.

compensating balances A bank requirement that business customers maintain a minimum average balance. The required amount is usually computed as a percentage of customer loans outstanding or as a percentage of the future loans to which the bank has committed itself.

composition An out-of-court settlement in which creditors agree to accept a fractional settlement on their original claim.

compounded semiannually A compounding period of every six months. For example, a five-year investment in which interest is compounded semiannually would indicate an n value equal to 10 and an i value at one-half the annual rate.

conglomerate A corporation that is made up of many diverse, often unrelated divisions. This form of organization is thought to reduce risk, but may create problems of coordination.

consolidation The combination of two or more firms, generally of equal size and market power, to form an entirely new entity.

contribution margin The contribution to fixed costs from each unit of sales. The margin may be computed as price minus variable cost per unit.

conversion premium The market price of a convertible bond or preferred stock minus the security's conversion value.

conversion price The conversion ratio divided into the par value. The price of the common stock at which the security is convertible. An investor would usually not convert the security into common stock unless the market price were greater than the conversion price.

conversion ratio The number of shares of common stock an investor will receive if he or she exchanges a convertible bond or convertible preferred stock for common stock.

conversion value The conversion ratio multiplied by the market price per share of common stock.

convertible Eurobonds Convertible Eurobonds are dollar-denominated and sold primarily in Western European countries. They have the safety of a bond but the chance to grow with U.S. stock prices since they are convertible into a U.S. firm's stock.

convertible exchangeable preferred A form of preferred stock that allows the company to force conversion from convertible preferred stock into convertible debt. This can be used to allow the company to take advantage of falling interest rates or to allow the company to change aftertax preferred dividends into tax-deductible interest payments.

convertible security   A security that may be traded into the company for a different form or type of security. Convertible securities are usually bonds or preferred stock that may be exchanged for common stock.

corporate financial markets   Markets in which corporations, in contrast to governmental units, raise funds.

corporate stock repurchase   A corporation may repurchase its shares in the market as an alternative to paying a cash dividend. Earnings per share will go up, and, if the price-earnings ratio remains the same, the stockholder will receive the same dollar benefit as through a cash dividend. A corporation may also justify the repurchase of its stock because it is at a very low price or to maintain constant demand for the shares. Reacquired shares may be used for employee options or as part of a tender offer in a merger or acquisition. Firms may also reacquire part of their shares as a protective device against being taken over as a merger candidate.

corporation   A form of ownership in which a separate legal entity is created. A corporation may sue or be sued, engage in contracts, and acquire property. It has a continual life and is not dependent on any one stockholder for maintaining its legal existence. A corporation is owned by stockholders who enjoy the privilege of limited liability. There is, however, the potential for double taxation in the corporate form of organization: the first time at the corporate level in the form of profits, and again at the stockholder level in the form of dividends.

cost-benefit analysis   A study of the incremental costs and benefits that can be derived from a given course of action.

cost of capital   The cost of alternative sources of financing to the firm. (Also see *weighted average cost of capital.*)

cost of goods sold   The cost specifically associated with units sold during the time period under study.

cost of ordering   The cost component in the inventory decision model that represents the expenditure for acquiring new inventory.

coupon rate   The actual interest rate on the bond, usually payable in semiannual installments. The coupon rate normally stays constant during the life of the bond and indicates what the bondholder's annual dollar income will be.

creditor committee   A committee set up to run the business while an out-of-court settlement is reached.

credit default swaps (CDSs)   Securities that were created by financial institutions as insurance against borrowers defaulting on their loans.

credit terms   The repayment provisions that are part of a credit arrangement. An example would be a 2/10, net 30 arrangement in which the customer may deduct 2 percent from the invoice price if payment takes place in the first 10 days. Otherwise, the full amount is due.

cross rates   The relationship between two foreign currencies expressed in terms of a third currency (the dollar).

cumulative preferred stock   If dividends from one period are not paid to the preferred stockholders, they are said to be in arrears and are then added to the next period's dividends. When dividends on preferred stock are in arrears, no dividends can legally be paid to the common stockholders. The cumulative dividend feature is very beneficial to preferred stockholders since it assures them that they will receive all dividends due before common stockholders can get any.

cumulative voting   Allows shareholders more than one vote per share. They are allowed to multiply their total shares by the number of directors being elected to determine their total number of votes. This system enables minority shareholders to elect directors even though they do not have 51 percent of the vote.

currency futures contract   A futures contract that may be used for hedging or speculation in foreign exchange.

current cost accounting   One of two methods of inflation-adjusted accounting approved by the Financial Accounting Standards Board in 1979. Financial statements are adjusted to the present, using current cost data, rather than an index. This optional information may be shown in the firm's annual report.

current ratio   Current assets divided by current liabilities; a measure of the firm's ability to pay off its current assets.

current yield   The yearly dollar interest or dividend payment divided by the current market price.

D

Data Universal Number System (D-U-N-S)   A system in which a unique nine-digit code is assigned by Dun & Bradstreet to each business in its information base.

dealer paper   A form of commercial paper that is distributed to lenders through an intermediate dealer network. It is normally sold by industrial companies, utility firms, or financial companies too small to have their own selling network.

dealers   Participants in the market who transact security trades over the counter from their own inventory of stocks and bonds. They are often referred to as market makers, since they stand ready to buy and sell their securities at quoted prices.

debenture   A long-term unsecured corporate bond. Debentures are usually issued by large firms having excellent credit ratings in the financial community.

debt-to-total-assets ratio   Total debt divided by total assets; indicates how much of the firm is financed by debt and how much by owners' equity.

debt utilization ratios   A group of ratios that indicates to what extent debt is being used and the prudence with

which it is being managed. Calculations include debt to total assets, times interest earned, and fixed charge coverage.

decision tree   A tabular or graphical analysis that lays out the sequence of decisions that are to be made and highlights the differences between choices. The presentation resembles branches on a tree.

deferred annuity   An annuity that will not begin until some time period in the future.

deflation   Actual declining prices.

degree of combined leverage (DCL)   A measure of the total combined effect of operating and financial leverage on earnings per share. The percentage change in earnings per share is divided by the percentage change in sales at a given level of operation. Other algebraic statements are also used, such as Formula 5-7 and that in footnote 3 in Chapter 5.

degree of financial leverage (DFL)   A measure of the impact of debt on the earnings capability of the firm. The percentage change in earnings per share is divided by the percentage change in earnings before interest and taxes at a given level of operation. Other algebraic statements are also used, such as Formula 5-5.

degree of operating leverage (DOL)   A measure of the impact of fixed costs on the operating earnings of the firm. The percentage change in operating income is divided by the percentage change in volume at a given level of operation. Other algebraic statements are also used, such as Formula 5-3 and that in footnote 2 in Chapter 5.

depreciation   The allocation of the initial cost of an asset over its useful life. The annual expense of plant and equipment is matched against the revenues that are being produced.

depreciation base   The initial cost of an asset that is multiplied by the appropriate annual depreciation percentage in Table 12-13 to determine the dollar depreciation.

derivative securities   These have a value derived from an underlying security such as common stock or a government bond.

designated market makers   A special group of traders on the NYSE floor.

diluted earnings per share   EPS adjusted for all potential dilution from the issuance of any new shares of common stock arising from convertible bonds, convertible preferred stock, warrants, or any other options outstanding.

dilution of earnings   This occurs when additional shares of stock are sold without creating an immediate increase in income. The result is a decline in earnings per share until earnings can be generated from the funds raised.

direct paper   A form of commercial paper that is sold directly by the borrower to the finance company. It is also referred to as finance paper.

discounted loan   A loan in which the calculated interest payment is subtracted, or discounted, in advance. Because this lowers the amount of available funds, the effective interest rate is increased.

discount rate   The rate at which future sums or annuities are discounted back to the present.

disinflation   A leveling off or slowdown of price increases.

dividend payment date   The day on which a stockholder of record will receive his or her dividend.

dividend payout ratio   The percentage of dividends to earnings after taxes. It can be computed by dividing dividends per share by earnings per share.

dividend reinvestment plans   Plans that provide the investor with an opportunity to buy additional shares of stock with the cash dividends paid by the company.

dividend valuation model   A model for determining the value of a share of stock by taking the present value of an expected stream of future dividends.

dividend yield   Dividends per share divided by market price per share. Dividend yield indicates the percentage return that a stockholder will receive on dividends alone.

Dodd–Frank Act   The Wall Street Reform and Consumer Protection Act of 2010, passed by Congress in response to the financial crisis of 2007–2009.

downside risk   The difference between the market price and the floor value.

dual trading   Exists when one security, such as General Motors common stock, is traded on more than one stock exchange. This practice is quite common between NYSE-listed companies and regional exchanges.

Dun & Bradstreet Information Services (DBIS)   A division of Dun & Bradstreet. DBIS is an information company that publishes many different reports that help businesses make credit decisions. Its publications include the reference books *Business Information Report, Financial Stress Report, Payment Analysis Report, Small Business Credit Scoring Report, Commercial Credit Scoring Report, Supplier Evaluation,* and various *Industry Credit Score Reports.*

Du Pont system of analysis   An analysis of profitability that breaks down return on assets between the profit margin and asset turnover. The second, or modified, version shows how return on assets is translated into return on equity through the amount of debt that the firm has. Actually, return on assets is divided by $(1 - \text{Debt/Assets})$ to arrive at return on equity.

E

earnings per share (EPS)   The earnings available to common stockholders divided by the number of common stock shares outstanding.

economic ordering quantity (EOQ)   The most efficient ordering quantity for the firm. The EOQ will allow the firm to minimize the total ordering and carrying costs associated with inventory.

efficient frontier   A line drawn through the optimum point selections in a risk-return trade-off diagram.

efficient market hypothesis   Hypothesis that suggests markets adjust very quickly to new information and that it is very difficult for investors to select portfolios of securities that outperform the market. The efficient market hypothesis may be stated in many different forms, as indicated in Chapter 14.

elective expensing   Writing off an asset in the year of purchase for tax purposes rather than depreciating it over the life of the asset. The maximum annual deduction is $250,000. This procedure is primarily beneficial to small businesses because its availability is phased out when asset purchases become large.

electronic communication networks (ECNs)   Electronic trading systems that automatically match buy and sell orders at specific prices.

electronic funds transfer   A system in which funds are moved between financial institutions using computers.

euro   The common currency shared by the members of the European Monetary Union.

Eurobonds   Bonds payable or denominated in the borrower's currency, but sold outside the country of the borrower, usually by an international syndicate.

Eurodollar certificate of deposit   A certificate of deposit based on U.S. dollars held on deposit by foreign banks.

Eurodollar loans   Loans made by foreign banks denominated in U.S. dollars.

Eurodollars   U.S. dollars held on deposit by European banks and loaned out by those banks to anyone seeking dollars.

exchange rate   The relationship between the value of two or more currencies. For example, the exchange rate between U.S. dollars and British pounds is stated as dollars per British pounds or British pounds per dollar.

ex-dividend date   Two business days before the holder-of-record date. On the ex-dividend date the purchase of the stock no longer carries with it the right to receive the dividend previously declared.

exercise price   The price at which a warrant (or other similar security) allows the investor to purchase common stock.

Eximbank (Export-Import Bank)   An agency of the U.S. government that facilitates the financing of U.S. exports through its miscellaneous programs. In its direct loan program, the Eximbank lends money to foreign purchasers of U.S. products, such as aircraft, electrical equipment, heavy machinery, computers, and the like. The Eximbank also purchases eligible medium-term obligations of foreign buyers of U.S. goods at a discount from face value. In this discount program, private banks and other lenders are able to rediscount (sell at a lower price) promissory notes and drafts acquired from foreign customers of U.S. firms.

expectations hypothesis   The hypothesis maintains that the yields on long-term securities are a function of short-term rates. The result of the hypothesis is that, when long-term rates are much higher than short-term rates, the market is saying that it expects short-term rates to rise. Conversely, when long-term rates are lower than short-term rates, the market is expecting short-term rates to fall.

expected value   A representative value from a probability distribution arrived at by multiplying each outcome by the associated probability and summing up the values.

expropriate   The action of a country in taking away or modifying the property rights of a corporation or individual.

ex-rights   The situation in which the purchase of common stock during a rights offering no longer includes rights to purchase additional shares of common stock.

extension   An out-of-court settlement in which creditors agree to allow the firm more time to meet its financial obligations. A new repayment schedule will be developed, subject to the acceptance of creditors.

external corporate funds   Corporate financing raised through sources outside of the firm. Bonds, common stock, and preferred stock fall in this category.

external reorganization   A reorganization under the formal bankruptcy laws, in which a merger partner is found for the distressed firm. Ideally, the distressed firm should be merged with a strong firm in its own industry, although this is not always possible.

F

factoring   Selling accounts receivable to a finance company or a bank.

federal agency securities   Securities issued by agencies such as the Federal Home Loan Banks and the Federal Land Bank.

federal deficit   Government expenditures are greater than government tax revenues, and the government must borrow to balance revenues and expenditures. These deficits act as an economic stimulus.

federally sponsored credit agencies   Federal agencies, such as the Federal Home Loan Banks and the Federal Land Bank, that issue securities.

Federal National Mortgage Association (Fannie Mae)   A former government agency that is now a government-sponsored enterprise. It is currently a private company trading on the NYSE but maintains its original purpose to provide a secondary market in mortgages.

Federal Reserve discount rate   The rate of interest that the Fed charges on loans to the banking system. A monetary tool for management of the money supply.

federal surplus   This occurs when government tax receipts are greater than government expenditures. Surpluses may have a dampening effect on the economy.

field warehousing   An inventory financing arrangement in which collateralized inventory is stored on the premises of the borrower but is controlled by an independent warehousing company.

FIFO   A system of writing off inventory into cost of goods sold, in which the items purchased first are written off first. Referred to as first-in, first-out inventory method.

finance paper   A form of commercial paper that is sold directly to the lender by the finance company. It is also referred to as direct paper.

Financial Accounting Standards Board (FASB)   A privately supported rule-making body for the accounting profession.

financial capital   Common stock, preferred stock, bonds, and retained earnings. Financial capital appears on the corporate balance sheet under long-term liabilities and equity.

financial disclosure   Presentation of financial information to the investment community.

financial futures market   A market that allows the trading of financial instruments related to a future point in time. A purchase or sale occurs in the present, with a reversal necessitated in the future to close out the position. If a purchase (sale) occurs initially, then a sale (purchase) will be necessary in the future. The market provides for futures contracts in Treasury bonds, Treasury bills, certificates of deposits, GNMA certificates, and many other instruments. Financial futures contracts may be executed on the Chicago Board of Trade, the Chicago Mercantile Exchange, the New York Futures Exchange, and other exchanges.

financial intermediary   A financial institution, such as a bank or a life insurance company, that directs other people's money into such investments as government and corporate securities.

finance lease   A long-term, noncancelable lease. The financial lease has all the characteristics of long-term debt. Under a finance lease, no lease expense is recorded on the income statement. Instead, amortization expense and interest expense are recorded.

financial leverage   A measure of the amount of debt used in the capital structure of the firm.

financial markets   The place of interaction for people, corporations, and institutions that either need money or have money to lend or invest.

financial risk   The risk related to the inability of the firm to meet its debt obligations as they come due.

financial sweetener   Usually refers to equity options, such as warrants or conversion privileges, attached to a debt security. The sweetener lowers the interest cost to the corporation.

fiscal policy   The tax policies of the federal government and the spending associated with its tax revenues.

five Cs of credit   These are used by bankers and others to determine whether a loan will be repaid on time. The five Cs are character, capital, capacity, conditions, and collateral.

fixed asset turnover ratio   Sales divided by fixed assets; indicates how efficiently the company is using its fixed assets to generate one dollar of sales.

fixed charge coverage ratio   Income before fixed charges and taxes divided by fixed charges. A common fixed charge in addition to interest expense is a lease expense. This ratio is considered more rigorous than the times-interest-earned ratio.

fixed costs   Costs that remain relatively constant regardless of the volume of operations. Examples are rent, depreciation, property taxes, and executive salaries.

float   The difference between the corporation's recorded cash balance on its books and the amount credited to the corporation by the bank.

floating rate bond   A bond in which the interest payment changes with market conditions.

floating rate preferred stock   The quarterly dividend on the preferred stock changes with market rates. The market price is considerably less volatile than it is with regular preferred stock.

floor value   Usually equal to the pure bond value. A convertible bond will not sell at less than its floor value even when its conversion value is below the pure bond value.

flotation cost   The distribution cost of selling securities to the public. The cost includes the underwriter's spread and any associated fees.

forced conversion   Occurs when a company calls a convertible security that has a conversion value greater than the call price. Investors will take the higher of the two values and convert the security to common stock, rather than take a lower cash call price.

Foreign Credit Insurance Association (FCIA)   An agency established by a group of 60 U.S. insurance companies.

It sells credit export insurance to interested exporters. The FCIA promises to pay for the exported merchandise if the foreign importer defaults on payment.

foreign exchange risk   A form of risk that refers to the possibility of experiencing a drop in revenue or an increase in cost in an international transaction due to a change in foreign exchange rates. Importers, exporters, investors, and multinational firms alike are exposed to this risk.

foreign trade deficit   A deficit that occurs because Americans buy (import) more foreign goods than American companies sell (export) to foreigners.

forward rate   A rate that reflects the future value of a currency based on expectations. Forward rates may be greater than the current spot rate (premium) or less than the current spot rate (discount).

founders' shares   Stock owned by the original founders of a company. It often carries special voting rights that allow the founders to maintain voting privileges in excess of their proportionate ownership.

free cash flow   Cash flow from operating activities, minus expenditures required to maintain the productive capacity of the firm, minus dividend payouts.

fronting loan   A parent company's loan to a foreign subsidiary is channeled through a financial intermediary, usually a large international bank. The bank fronts for the parent in extending the loan to the foreign affiliate.

fully diluted earnings per share   Equals adjusted earnings after taxes divided by shares outstanding, plus common stock equivalents, plus all convertible securities.

futures contract   A contract to buy or sell a commodity at some specified price in the future.

future value   The value that a current amount grows to at a given interest rate over a given time period.

future value of an annuity   The sum of the future value of a series of consecutive equal payments.

G

going private   The process by which all publicly owned shares of common stock are repurchased or retired, thereby eliminating listing fees, annual reports, and other expenses involved with publicly owned companies.

golden parachute   Highly attractive termination payments made to current management in the event of a takeover of the company.

goodwill   An intangible asset that reflects value above that generally recognized in the tangible assets of the firm.

H

hedging   To engage in a transaction that partially or fully reduces a prior risk exposure by taking a position that is the opposite of your initial position. As an example, you own some copper now but also engage in a contract to sell copper in the future at a set price.

historical cost accounting   The traditional method of accounting, in which financial statements are developed based on original cost.

holder-of-record date   Stockholders owning the stock on the holder-of-record date are entitled to receive a dividend. In order to be listed as an owner on the corporate books, the investor must have bought the stock before it went ex-dividend.

horizontal integration   The acquisition of a competitor.

humped yield curve   A yield curve in which intermediate rates are higher than both short- and long-term rates.

hurdle rate   The minimum acceptable rate of return in a capital budgeting decision.

I

income statement   A financial statement that measures the profitability of the firm over a time period. All expenses are subtracted from sales to arrive at net income.

incremental depreciation   The depreciation on a new asset minus the depreciation on an old asset. Incremental depreciation is multiplied times the tax rate to determine its tax shield benefit.

indenture   A legal contract between the borrower and the lender that covers every detail regarding a bond issue.

indexing   An adjustment for inflation incorporated into the operation of an economy. Indexing may be used to revalue assets on the balance sheet and to automatically adjust wages, tax deductions, interest payments, and a wide variety of other categories to account for inflation.

inflation   The phenomenon of prices increasing with the passage of time.

inflation premium   A premium to compensate the investor for the eroding effect of inflation on the value of the dollar.

information content of dividends   This theory of dividends assumes that dividends provide information about the financial health and economic expectations of the company. If this is true, corporations must actively manage their dividends to provide the market with information.

insider trading   This occurs when someone has information that is not available to the public and then uses this information to profit from trading in a company's common stock.

installment loan   A borrowing arrangement in which a series of equal payments are used to pay off a loan.

institutional investors   Large investors such as pension funds or mutual funds.

interest factor   The tabular value to insert into the various present value and future value formulas. It is based on the number of periods (n) and the interest rate (i).

interest rate parity theory   A theory based on the interplay between interest rate differentials and exchange rates. If one country has a higher interest rate than another country after adjustments for inflation, interest rates and foreign exchange rates will adjust until the foreign exchange rates and money market rates reach equilibrium (are properly balanced between the two countries).

Intermarket Trading System (ITS)   An electronic communications system that links nine markets—NYSE, AMEX, Boston, Chicago, Cincinnati, Pacific, and Philadelphia stock exchanges, the Chicago Board Options Exchange, and the NASDAQ.

internally generated funds   Funds generated through the operations of the firm. The principal sources are retained earnings and cash flow added back from depreciation and other noncash deductions.

internal rate of return (IRR)   A discounted cash flow method for evaluating capital budgeting projects. The IRR is a discount rate that makes the present value of the cash inflows equal to the present value of the cash outflows.

internal reorganization   A reorganization under the formal bankruptcy laws. New management may be brought in and a redesign of the capital structure may be implemented.

international diversification   Achieving diversification through many different foreign investments that are influenced by a variety of factors.

international electronic funds transfer   The movement of funds across international boundaries. It is mainly carried out through SWIFT (Society for Worldwide Interbank Financial Telecommunications).

International Finance Corporation (IFC)   An affiliate of the World Bank established with the sole purpose of providing partial seed capital for private ventures around the world. Whenever a multinational company has difficulty raising equity capital due to lack of adequate private risk capital, the firm may explore the possibility of selling equity or debt (totaling up to 25 percent of total capital) to the International Finance Corporation.

in-the-money warrant   A warrant that has a stock price above the current exercise price.

intrinsic value   As applied to a warrant, this represents the market value of common stock minus the exercise price. The difference is then multiplied by the number of shares each warrant entitles the holder to purchase.

inventory profits   Profits generated as a result of an inflationary economy, in which old inventory is sold at large profits because of increasing prices. This is particularly prevalent under FIFO accounting.

inventory turnover ratio   Sales divided by total inventory; indicates how many times a firm sells and replaces its inventory over the course of a year.

inverted yield curve   A downward-sloping yield curve. Short-term rates are higher than long-term rates.

investment banker   A financial organization that specializes in selling primary offerings of securities. Investment bankers can also perform other financial functions, such as advising clients, negotiating mergers and takeovers, and selling secondary offerings.

J

just-in-time inventory management (JIT)   A system of inventory management that stresses taking possession of inventory just before the time it is needed for production or sale. It greatly reduces the cost of carrying inventory.

L

lease   A contractual arrangement between the owner of equipment (lessor) and the user of equipment (lessee) that calls for the lessee to pay the lessor an established lease payment. There are two kinds of leases: financial leases and operating leases.

letter of credit   A credit letter normally issued by the importer's bank, in which the bank promises to pay out the money for the merchandise when delivered.

level production   Equal monthly production used to smooth out production schedules and employ manpower and equipment more efficiently and at a lower cost.

leverage   The use of fixed-charge items with the intent of magnifying the potential returns to the firm.

leveraged buyout   Existing management or an outsider makes an offer to "go private" by retiring all the shares of the company. The buying group borrows the necessary money, using the assets of the acquired firm as collateral. The buying group then repurchases all the shares and expects to retire the debt over time with the cash flow from operations or the sale of corporate assets. The firm may ultimately go public again.

LIBOR   (See *London Interbank Offered Rate*.)

life cycle   A curve illustrating the growth phases of a firm. The dividend policy most likely to be employed during each phase is often illustrated.

LIFO   A system of writing off inventory into cost of goods sold in which the items purchased last are written off first. Referred to as last-in, first-out inventory method.

limited liability partnership   A special form of partnership to limit liability for most of the partners. Under this arrangement, one or more partners are designated as general partners and have unlimited liability for the debts of the firm, while the other partners are designated as limited partners and are liable only for their initial contribution.

liquidation   A procedure that may be carried out under the formal bankruptcy laws when an internal or external reorganization does not appear to be feasible, and it appears that the assets are worth more in liquidation than through a reorganization. Priority of claims becomes extremely important in a liquidation because it is unlikely that all parties will be fully satisfied in their demands.

liquidity   The relative convertibility of short-term assets to cash. Thus, marketable securities are highly liquid assets, while inventory may not be.

liquidity premium theory   This theory indicates that long-term rates should be higher than short-term rates. The premium of long-term rates over short-term rates exists because short-term securities have greater liquidity, and, therefore, higher rates have to be offered to potential long-term bond buyers to entice them to hold these less liquid and more price-sensitive securities.

liquidity ratios   A group of ratios that allows one to measure the firm's ability to pay off short-term obligations as they come due. Primary attention is directed to the current ratio and the quick ratio.

listing requirements   Financial standards that corporations must meet before their common stock can be traded on a stock exchange. Listing requirements are not standard, but are set by each exchange. The requirements for the NYSE are the most stringent.

living wills   Plans that describe the strategy a bank will use for a rapid bankruptcy resolution in the event of a crisis. The Dodd–Frank Act requires that large banks submit these plans.

lockbox system   A procedure used to expedite cash inflows to a business. Customers are requested to forward their checks to a post office box in their geographical region, and a local bank picks up the checks and processes them for rapid collection. Funds are then wired to the corporate home office for immediate use.

London Interbank Offered Rate (LIBOR)   An interbank rate applicable for large deposits in the London market. It is a benchmark rate, just like the prime interest rate in the United States. Interest rates on Eurodollar loans are determined by adding premiums to this basic rate. Most often, LIBOR is lower than the U.S. prime rate.

M

majority voting   All directors must be elected by a vote of more than 50 percent. Minority shareholders are unable to achieve any representation on the board of directors.

managing investment banker   An investment banker who is responsible for the pricing, prospectus development, and legal work involved in the sale of a new issue of securities. Also known as the bookrunner.

marginal corporate tax rate   The rate that applies to each new dollar of taxable income. For a corporation, the maximum rate is 35 percent. The marginal rate is lower for smaller corporations.

marginal cost of capital   The cost of the last dollar of funds raised. It is assumed that each dollar is financed in proportion to the firm's optimum capital structure.

marginal principle of retained earnings   The corporation must be able to earn a higher return on its retained earnings than a stockholder would receive after paying taxes on the distributed dividends.

margin requirement   A rule that specifies the amount of cash or equity that must be deposited with a brokerage firm or bank, with the balance of funds eligible for borrowing. Margin is set by the Board of Governors of the Federal Reserve Board.

market efficiency   Markets are considered to be efficient when (1) prices adjust rapidly to new information; (2) there is a continuous market, in which each successive trade is made at a price close to the previous price (the faster the price responds to new information and the smaller the differences in price changes, the more efficient the market); and (3) the market can absorb large dollar amounts of securities without destabilizing the prices.

market risk premium   A premium over and above the risk-free rate. It is represented by the difference between the market return (K_m) and the risk-free rate (R_f), and it may be multiplied by the beta coefficient to determine the additional risk-adjusted return on a security.

market segmentation theory   A theory that Treasury securities are divided into market segments by various financial institutions investing in the market. The changing needs, desires, and strategies of these investors tend to strongly influence the nature and relationship of short-term and long-term interest rates.

market stabilization   Intervention in the secondary markets by an investment banker to stabilize the price of a new security offering during the offering period. The purpose of market stabilization is to provide an orderly market for the distribution of the new issue.

market value maximization   The concept of maximizing the wealth of shareholders. This calls for a recognition not only of earnings per share but also how they will be valued in the marketplace.

maturity date   The date on which the bond is retired and the principal (par value) is repaid to the lender.

merger   The combination of two or more companies, in which the resulting firm maintains the identity of the acquiring company.

merger premium   The part of a buyout or exchange offer that represents a value over and above the market value of the acquired firm.

modified accelerated cost recovery system (MACRS)   A system that specifies the allowable depreciation recovery period for different types of assets. The normal recovery period is generally shorter than the physical life of the asset.

modified internal rate of return (MIRR)   A method of evaluation combining the reinvestment rate assumption of the net present value method (cost of capital) with the internal rate of return method.

monetary policy   Management by the Federal Reserve Board of the money supply and the resultant interest rates.

money market accounts   Accounts at banks, savings and loans, and credit unions in which the depositor receives competitive money market rates on a typical minimum deposit of $1,000. These accounts may generally have three deposits and three withdrawals per month and are not meant to be transaction accounts, but a place to keep minimum and excess cash balances. These accounts are insured by various appropriate governmental agencies up to $250,000.

money market fund   A fund in which investors may purchase shares for as little as $500 or $1,000. The fund then reinvests the proceeds in high-yielding $100,000 bank CDs, $25,000–$100,000 commercial paper, and other large-denomination, high-yielding securities. Investors receive their pro rata portion of the interest proceeds daily as a credit to their shares.

money markets   Competitive markets for securities with maturities of one year or less. The best examples of money market instruments would be Treasury bills, commercial paper, and negotiable certificates of deposit.

mortgage agreement   A loan that requires real property (plant and equipment) as collateral.

multinational corporation   A firm doing business across its national borders is considered a multinational enterprise. Some definitions require a minimum percentage (often 30 percent or more) of a firm's business activities to be carried on outside its national borders.

municipal securities   Securities issued by state and local government units. The income from these securities is exempt from federal income taxes.

mutually exclusive   The selection of one choice precludes the selection of any other competitive choice. For example, several machines can do an identical job in capital budgeting. If one machine is selected, the other machines will not be used.

N

National Association of Security Dealers (NASD)   An industry association that supervises the over-the-counter market.

National Market List   The list of the best-known and most widely traded securities on the NASDAQ Stock Market.

net investment income tax   An extra 3.8 percent tax on investment income above a certain amount, created by Congress to help fund the Affordable Care Act.

net present value (NPV)   The NPV equals the present value of the cash inflows minus the present value of the cash outflows with the cost of capital used as a discount rate. This method is used to evaluate capital budgeting projects. If the NPV is positive, a project should be accepted.

net present value profile   A graphic presentation of the potential net present values of a project at different discount rates. It is very helpful in comparing the characteristics of two or more investments.

net trade credit   A measure of the relationship between the firm's accounts receivable and accounts payable. If accounts receivable exceed accounts payable, the firm is a net provider of trade credit; otherwise, it is a net user.

net worth, or book value   Stockholders' equity minus preferred stock ownership. Basically, net worth is the common stockholders' interest as represented by common stock par value, capital paid in excess of par, and retained earnings. If you take all the assets of the firm and subtract its liabilities and preferred stock, you arrive at net worth.

nominal GDP   GDP (gross domestic product) in current dollars without any adjustments for inflation.

nominal yield   A return equal to the coupon rate on a bond.

nonfinancial corporation   A firm not in the banking or financial services industry. The term would primarily apply to manufacturing, wholesaling, and retail firms.

nonlinear break-even analysis   Break-even analysis based on the assumption that cost and revenue relationships to quantity may vary at different levels of operation. Most of our analyses are based on *linear* break-even analysis.

normal yield curve   An upward-sloping yield curve. Long-term interest rates are higher than short-term rates.

O

open-market operations   The purchase and sale of government securities in the open market by the Federal Reserve Board for its own account. The most common method for managing the money supply.

operating lease   A short-term, nonbinding obligation that is easily cancelable.

operating leverage   A reflection of the extent to which fixed assets and fixed costs are utilized in the business firm.

optimum capital structure   A capital structure that has the best possible mix of debt, preferred stock, and common equity. The optimum mix should provide the lowest possible cost of capital to the firm.

options   These give the owner the right but not the obligation to buy or sell an underlying security at a set price for a given time period.

ordinary annuity   A payment stream with payments that occur at the end of each year.

ordinary dividend   A share of a company's profits passed on to the shareholders on a periodic basis.

out-of-the-money warrant   A warrant that has an exercise price above the current stock price.

Overseas Private Investment Corporation (OPIC)   A government agency that sells insurance policies to qualified firms. This agency insures against losses due to inconvertibility into dollars of amounts invested in a foreign country. Policies are also available from OPIC to insure against expropriation and against losses due to war or revolution.

P

parallel loan   A U.S. firm that wishes to lend funds to a foreign affiliate (such as a Dutch affiliate) locates a foreign parent firm (such as a Dutch parent firm) that wishes to loan money to a U.S. affiliate. Avoiding the foreign exchange markets entirely, the U.S. parent lends dollars to the Dutch affiliate in the United States, while the Dutch parent lends guilders to the American affiliate in the Netherlands. At maturity, the two loans would each be repaid to the original lender. Notice that neither loan carries any foreign exchange risk in this arrangement.

participating preferred stock   A small number of preferred stock issues are participating with regard to corporate earnings. For such issues, once the common stock dividend equals the preferred stock dividend, the two classes of securities may share equally in additional dividend payments.

partnership   A form of ownership in which two or more partners are involved. Like the sole proprietorship, a partnership arrangement carries unlimited liability for the owners. However, there is only single taxation for the partners, an advantage over the corporate form of ownership.

par value   Sometimes referred to as the face value or the principal value of the bond. Most bond issues have a par value of $1,000 per bond. Common and preferred stock may also have assigned par values.

passbook savings account   A savings account in which a passbook is used to record transactions. It is normally the lowest yielding investment at a financial institution.

payback   A value that indicates the time period required to recoup an initial investment. The payback does not include the time-value-of-money concept.

percent-of-sales method   A method of determining future financial needs that is an alternative to the development of pro forma financial statements. We first determine the percentage relationship of various asset and liability accounts to sales, and then we show how that relationship changes as our volume of sales changes.

permanent current assets   Current assets that will not be reduced or converted to cash within the normal operating cycle of the firm. Though from a strict accounting standpoint the assets should be removed from the current assets category, they generally are not.

perpetuity   An investment without a maturity date.

planning horizon   The length of time it takes to conceive, develop, and complete a project and to recover the cost of the project on a discounted cash flow basis.

pledging accounts receivables   Using accounts receivable as collateral for a loan. The firm usually may borrow 60 to 80 percent of the value of acceptable collateral.

point-of-sales terminals   Computer terminals in retail stores that either allow digital input or use optical scanners. The terminals may be used for inventory control or other purposes.

poison pill   A strategy that makes a firm unattractive as a potential takeover candidate. For example, when a potential unwanted buyer accumulates a given percentage of a firm's common stock, such as 25 percent, the other shareholders receive rights to purchase additional shares at very low prices. This makes the firm more difficult to acquire. Poison pills may take many different forms.

pooling of interests   A method of financial recording for mergers, in which the financial statements of the firms are combined, subject to minor adjustments, and goodwill is *not* created. The method has been phased out by the Financial Accounting Standards Board (FASB).

portfolio effect   The impact of a given investment on the overall risk-return composition of the firm. A firm must consider not only the individual investment characteristics of a project but also how the project relates to the entire portfolio of undertakings.

precautionary balances   Cash balances held for emergency purposes. Precautionary cash balances are more likely to be important in seasonal or cyclical industries where cash inflows are more uncertain.

preemptive right   The right of current common stockholders to maintain their ownership percentage on new issues of common stock.

preferred stock   A hybrid security combining some of the characteristics of common stock and debt. The dividends paid are not tax-deductible expenses of the corporation, as is true of the interest paid on debt.

present value   The current or discounted value of a future sum or annuity. The value is discounted back at a given interest rate for a specified time period.

present value of an annuity   The sum of the present value of a series of consecutive equal payments.

price-earnings ratio   The multiplier applied to earnings per share to determine current value. The P/E ratio is influenced by the earnings and sales growth of the firm, the risk or volatility of its performance, the debt-equity structure, and other factors.

primary market   The market for the raising of new funds as opposed to the trading of securities already in existence.

prime rate   The rate that a bank charges its most creditworthy customers.

private placement   The sale of securities directly to a financial institution by a corporation. This eliminates the middleman and reduces the cost of issue to the corporation.

privatization   A process in which investment bankers take companies that were previously owned by the government to the public markets.

profitability ratios   A group of ratios that indicates the return on sales, total assets, and invested capital. Specifically, we compute the profit margin (net income to sales), return on assets, and return on equity.

profit margin ratio   Net income divided by sales; shows the overall percentage profit by the company on $1 of sales.

pro forma balance sheet   A projection of future asset, liability, and stockholders' equity levels. Notes payable or cash is used as a plug or balancing figure for the statement.

pro forma financial statements   A series of projected financial statements. Of major importance are the pro forma income statement, the pro forma balance sheet, and the cash budget.

pro forma income statement   A projection of anticipated sales, expenses, and income.

program trading   Computer-based trigger points in the market are established for unusually big orders to buy or sell securities by institutional investors.

prospectus   A document that includes the corporation's important information that has been filed with the Securities and Exchange Commission through the registration statement. It contains the list of officers and directors, financial reports, potential uses of funds, and the like.

proxy   This represents the assignment of the voting right to management or a group of outsiders.

public finance markets   Markets in which national, state, and local governments raise money for highways, education, welfare, and other public activities.

public placement   The sale of securities to the public through the investment banker–underwriter process. Public placements must be registered with the Securities and Exchange Commission.

public warehousing   An inventory financing arrangement in which inventory, used as collateral, is stored with and controlled by an independent warehousing company.

purchase of assets   A method of financial recording for mergers, in which the difference between the purchase price and the adjusted book value is recognized as goodwill. Under new rulings by the FASB, goodwill does not need to be written off under normal circumstances.

purchasing power parity theory   A theory based on the interplay between inflation and exchange rates. A parity between the purchasing powers of two countries establishes the rate of exchange between the two currencies. Currency exchange rates therefore tend to vary inversely with their respective purchasing powers in order to provide the same or similar purchasing power.

pure bond value   The value of the convertible bond if its present value is computed at a discount rate equal to interest rates on straight bonds of equal risk, without conversion privileges.

put option   An option to sell securities at a set price over a specified period of time.

Q

qualified dividend   A subset of an ordinary dividend that is taxed at a lower rate.

quick ratio   Current assets minus inventory divided by current liabilities. This ratio is sometimes called the acid test ratio and is a more stringent measure of liquidity because it eliminates inventory (the least liquid asset) from current assets.

R

real capital   Long-term productive assets (plant and equipment).

real GDP (gross domestic product)   GDP stated in current dollars adjusted for inflation.

real rate of return   The rate of return that an investor demands for giving up the current use of his or her funds on a noninflation-adjusted basis. It is payment for forgoing current consumption. Historically, the real rate of return demanded by investors has been of the magnitude of 2 to 3 percent.

receivable turnover ratio   Sales divided by accounts receivable; indicates how many times a firm collects its accounts receivable in one year. It also indicates how quickly a firm is able to collect payments on its credit sales.

refunding   The process of retiring an old bond issue before maturity and replacing it with a new issue. Refunding will occur when interest rates have fallen and new bonds may be sold at lower interest rates.

regional stock exchanges   Organized exchanges outside of New York that list securities.

reinvestment assumption   An assumption made concerning the rate of return that can be earned on the cash flows generated by capital budgeting projects. The NPV method assumes the rate of reinvestment to be the cost of capital, while the IRR method assumes the rate to be the actual internal rate of return.

repatriation of earnings   Earnings returned to the multinational parent company in the form of dividends.

replacement cost   The cost of replacing the existing asset base at current prices as opposed to original cost.

replacement cost accounting   Financial statements based on the present cost of replacing assets.

replacement decision   The capital budgeting decision on whether to replace an old asset with a new one. An advance in technology is often involved.

required rate of return   That rate of return that investors demand from an investment to compensate them for the amount of risk involved.

reserve requirements   The amount of funds that commercial banks must hold in reserve for each dollar of deposits. Reserve requirements are set by the Federal Reserve Board and are different for savings and checking accounts. Low reserve requirements are stimulating; high reserve requirements are restrictive.

residual claim to income   The basic claim that common stockholders have to income that is not paid out to creditors or preferred stockholders. This is true regardless of whether these residual funds are paid out in dividends or retained in the corporation.

residual theory of dividends   A theory of dividend payout stating that a corporation will retain as much of its earnings as it may profitably invest. If any income is left after investments, the firm will pay dividends. This theory assumes that dividends are a passive decision variable.

restructuring   Process that can take many forms in a corporation, such as changes in the capital structure (liability and equity on the balance sheet). It can also result in the selling of low-profit-margin divisions with

the proceeds reinvested in better investment opportunities. Sometimes restructuring results in the removal of the current management team or large reductions in the workforce. Restructuring has also included mergers and acquisitions.

return on assets (ROA)   Net income divided by assets; shows how much income the firm produces for every dollar invested in assets.

return on equity (ROE)   Net income divided by owners' equity; also called return on investment (ROI). ROE shows how much income is generated by each dollar the owners have invested in the firm.

reverse stock split   A firm exchanging with stockholders fewer shares for existing shares with the intent of increasing the stock price.

rights offering   A sale of new common stock through a preemptive rights offering. Usually one right will be issued for every share held. A certain number of rights may be used to buy shares of common stock from the company at a set price that is lower than the market price.

rights-on   The situation in which the purchase of a share of common stock includes a right attached to the stock.

risk   A measure of uncertainty about the outcome from a given event. The greater the variability of possible outcomes, on both the high side and the low side, the greater the risk.

risk-adjusted discount rate   A discount rate used in the capital budgeting process that has been adjusted upward or downward from the basic cost of capital to reflect the risk dimension of a given project.

risk-averse   An aversion or dislike for risk. In order to induce most people to take larger risks, there must be increased potential for return.

risk-free rate of return   Rate of return on an asset that carries no risk. U.S. Treasury bills are often used to represent this measure, although longer-term government securities have also proved appropriate in some studies.

risk premium   A premium associated with the special risks of an investment. Of primary interest are two types of risk, business risk and financial risk. Business risk relates to the inability of the firm to maintain its competitive position and sustain stability and growth in earnings. Financial risk relates to the inability of the firm to meet its debt obligations as they come due. The risk premium will also differ (be greater or less) for different types of investments (bonds, stocks, and the like).

S

S corporation   A special corporate form of ownership, in which profit is taxed as direct income to the stockholders and thus is taxed only once, as would be true of a partnership. The stockholders still receive all the organizational benefits of a corporation, including limited liability. The Subchapter S designation can apply only to corporations with up to 75 stockholders.

safety stock of inventory   Inventory that is held in addition to regular needs to protect against being out of an item.

Sarbanes–Oxley Act of 2002   An act that was intended to restore confidence in the financial markets by demanding accuracy in financial reporting.

Saturday night special   A merger tender offer that is made just before the market closes for the weekend and takes the target company's officers by surprise.

secondary market   The market for securities that have already been issued. It is a market in which investors trade back and forth with each other.

secondary offering   The sale of a large block of stock in a publicly traded company, usually by estates, foundations, or large individual stockholders. Secondary offerings must be registered with the SEC and will usually be distributed by investment bankers.

secondary trading   The buying and selling of publicly owned securities in secondary markets, such as the New York Stock Exchange and the over-the-counter markets.

secured debt   A general category of debt that indicates the loan was obtained by pledging assets as collateral. Secured debt has many forms and usually offers some protective features to a given class of bondholders.

Securities Act of 1933   An act that is sometimes referred to as the truth in securities act, because it requires detailed financial disclosures before securities may be sold to the public.

Securities Acts Amendments of 1975   The major feature of this act was to mandate a national securities market.

Securities and Exchange Commission (SEC)   The primary regulatory body for security offerings in the United States.

Securities Exchange Act of 1934   Legislation that established the Securities and Exchange Commission (SEC) to supervise and regulate the securities markets.

securitization of assets   The issuance of a security that is specifically backed by the pledge of an asset.

security market line   A line or equation that depicts the risk-related return of a security based on a risk-free rate plus a market premium related to the beta coefficient of the security.

self-liquidating assets   Assets that are converted to cash within the normal operating cycle of the firm. An example is the purchase and sale of seasonal inventory.

self-liquidating loan   A loan in which the use of funds will ensure a built-in or automatic repayment scheme.

semivariable costs   Costs that are partially fixed but still change somewhat as volume changes. Examples are utilities and "repairs and maintenance."

serial payment   Bonds with serial payment provisions are paid off in installments over the life of the issue. Each bond has its own predetermined date of maturity and receives interest only to that point.

shareholder wealth maximization   Maximizing the wealth of the firm's shareholders through achieving the highest possible value for the firm in the marketplace. It is the overriding objective of the firm and should influence all decisions.

shelf registration   A process that permits large companies to file one comprehensive registration statement (under SEC Rule 415) that outlines the firm's financing plans for up to the next two years. Then, when market conditions appear to be appropriate, the firm can issue the securities without further SEC approval.

simulation   A method of dealing with uncertainty, in which future outcomes are anticipated. The model may use random variables for inputs. By programming the computer to randomly select inputs from probability distributions, the outcomes generated by a simulation are distributed about a mean, and, instead of generating one return or net present value, a range of outcomes with standard deviations is provided.

sinking fund   A method for retiring bonds in an orderly process over the life of a bond. Each year or semiannually, a corporation sets aside a sum of money equal to a certain percentage of the total issue. These funds are then used by a trustee to purchase the bonds in the open market and retire them. This method will prevent the corporation from being forced to raise a large amount of capital at maturity to retire the total bond issue.

sole proprietorship   A form of organization that represents single-person ownership and offers the advantages of simplicity of decision making and low organizational and operating costs.

specialists   Ones who make a market in their assigned stocks by standing ready to buy or sell shares at the current bid and ask price.

speculative premium   The market price of the warrant minus the warrant's intrinsic value is an example of a speculative premium.

spontaneous sources of funds   Funds arising through the normal course of business, such as accounts payable generated from the purchase of goods for resale.

spot rate   The rate at which the currency is traded for immediate delivery. It is the existing cash price.

standard deviation   A measure of the spread or dispersion of a series of numbers around the expected value. The standard deviation tells us how well the expected value represents a series of values.

statement of cash flows   Formally established by the Financial Accounting Standards Board in 1987, the purpose of the statement of cash flows is to emphasize the critical nature of cash flow to the operations of the firm. The statement translates accrual-based net income into actual cash dollars.

step-up in the conversion price   A feature that is sometimes written into the contract that allows the conversion ratio to decline in steps over time. This feature encourages early conversion when the conversion value is greater than the call price.

stock dividend   A dividend paid in stock, rather than cash. A book transfer equal to the market value of the stock dividend is made from retained earnings to the capital stock and paid-in-capital accounts. The stock dividend may be symbolic of corporate growth, but it does not increase the total value of the stockholders' wealth.

stock split   A division of shares by a ratio set by the board of directors—two for one, three for one, three for two, and so on. Stock splits usually indicate the company's stock has risen in price to a level that the directors feel limits the trading appeal of the stock. The par value is divided by the ratio set, and the new shares are issued to the current stockholders of record to increase their shares to the stated level. For example, a two-for-one split would increase holdings from one share to two shares.

stockholders' equity   The total ownership position of preferred and common stockholders.

stockholder wealth maximization   The primary goal of financial managers. They maximize the wealth of the firm's shareholders through achieving the highest possible value for the firm.

straight-line depreciation   A method of depreciation that takes the depreciable cost of an asset and divides it by the asset's useful life to determine the annual depreciation expense. Straight-line depreciation creates uniform depreciation expenses for each of the years in which an asset is depreciated.

subordinated debenture   An unsecured bond, in which payment to the holder will occur only after designated senior debenture holders are satisfied.

supernormal growth   Superior growth a firm may achieve during its early years, before leveling off to more normal growth. Supernormal growth is often achieved by firms in emerging industries.

sweep account   An account that allows companies to maintain zero balances with all excess cash swept into an interest-earning account.

synergy   The recognition that the whole may be equal to more than the sum of the parts. The "2 + 2 = 5" effect.

T

takeover tender offer   An unfriendly offer that is not initially negotiated with the management of the target firm. The offer is usually made directly to the stockholders of the target firm.

tax loss carryforward   A loss that can be carried forward for a number of years to offset future taxable income and perhaps be utilized by another firm in a merger or an acquisition.

Tax Reform Act of 1986   Tax legislation that eliminated many of the abuses in the tax code and, at the same time, lowered the overall tax rates.

technical insolvency   When a firm is unable to pay its bills as they come due.

temporary current assets   Current assets that will be reduced or converted to cash within the normal operating cycle of the firm.

term loan   An intermediate-length loan, in which credit is generally extended from one to seven years. The loan is usually repaid in monthly or quarterly installments over its life, rather than with one single payment.

terms of exchange   The buyout ratio or terms of trade in a merger or an acquisition.

term structure of interest rates   The term structure shows the relative level of short-term and long-term interest rates at a point in time.

three-sector economy   The economy consists of three sectors—business, government, and households. Typically, households have been major suppliers of funds, while business and government have been users of funds.

tight money   A term to indicate time periods in which financing may be difficult to find and interest rates may be quite high by normal standards.

times-interest-earned ratio   Operating income dividend by interest expense; a measure of the safety margin a company has with respect to the interest payments it must make to creditors. A high number indicates that there is less risk of default.

total asset turnover ratio   Sales divided by total assets; measures how efficiently an organization utilizes all of its assets to create one dollar of sales. It indicates whether a company is using its assets productively.

trade credit   Credit provided by sellers or suppliers in the normal course of business.

traditional approach to cost of capital   Under the traditional approach, the cost of capital initially declines with the increased use of low-cost debt, but it eventually goes up due to the greater risk associated with increasing debt.

transaction exposure   Foreign exchange gains and losses resulting from *actual* international transactions. These may be hedged through the foreign exchange market, the money market, or the currency futures market.

transactions balances   Cash balances held to pay for planned corporate expenditures such as supplies, payrolls, and taxes, as well as the infrequent acquisitions of long-term fixed assets.

translation exposure   The foreign-located assets and liabilities of a multinational corporation, which are denominated in foreign currency units, and are exposed to losses and gains due to changing exchange rates. This is called accounting or translation exposure.

Treasury bills   Short-term obligations of the federal government.

Treasury Inflation Protection Securities (TIPS)   This security pays interest semiannually that equals a real rate of return specified by the U.S. Treasury plus principal at maturity that is adjusted annually to reflect inflation's impact on purchasing power.

treasury stock   Corporate stock that has been reacquired by the corporation.

trend analysis   An analysis of performance that is made over a number of years in order to ascertain significant patterns.

trust receipt   An instrument acknowledging that the borrower holds the inventory and proceeds for sale in trust for the lender.

two-step buyout   An acquisition plan in which the acquiring company attempts to gain control by offering a very high cash price for 51 percent of the shares of the target company. At the same time, the acquiring company announces a second lower price that will be paid, either in cash, stocks, or bonds, at a subsequent point in time.

U

underpricing   When new or additional shares of stock are to be sold, investment bankers will generally set the price at slightly below the current market value to ensure a receptive market for the securities.

underwriting   The process of selling securities and, at the same time, assuring the seller a specified price. Underwriting is done by investment bankers and represents a form of risk taking.

underwriting spread   The difference between the price that a selling corporation receives for an issue of securities and the price at which the issue is sold to the public. The spread is the fee that investment bankers and others receive for selling securities.

underwriting syndicate   A group of investment bankers that is formed to share the risk of a security offering and also to facilitate the distribution of the securities.

V

variable costs   Costs that move directly with a change in volume. Examples are raw materials, factory labor, and sales commissions.

vertical integration   The acquisition of customers or suppliers by the company.

W

warrant   An option to buy securities at a set price for a given time period. Warrants commonly have a life of one to five years or longer and a few are perpetual.

weighted average cost of capital   The computed cost of capital determined by multiplying the cost of each item in the optimal capital structure by its weighted representation in the overall capital structure and summing up the results.

white knight   A firm that management calls on to help it avoid an unwanted takeover offer. It is an invited suitor.

working capital management   The financing and management of the current assets of the firm. The financial manager determines the mix between temporary and permanent "current assets" and the nature of the financing arrangement.

Y

yield   The interest rate that equates a future value or an annuity to a given present value.

yield curve   A curve that shows interest rates at a specific point in time for all securities having equal risk but different maturity dates. Usually, government securities are used to construct such curves. The yield curve is also referred to as the term structure of interest rates.

yield to maturity   The required rate of return on a bond issue. It is the discount rate used in present-valuing future interest payments and the principal payment at maturity. The term is used interchangeably with market rate of interest.

Z

zero-coupon rate bond   A bond that is initially sold at a deep discount from face value. The return to the investor is the difference between the investor's cost and the face value received at the end of the life of the bond.

Company Index

Subject Index

Key terms and the page numbers where they are defined are in **bold**. Page numbers followed by n refer to footnotes.